DATE DUE

AP 5 '96			
JE 25 '97			
OC 1 9'00			
AG 6 01			

THE AMERICAN EXPLORATION AND TRAVEL SERIES

The *Diario* of Christopher Columbus's First Voyage to America

Cristoforo Colombo (color intaglio, 68.8 × 60.2 cm), by Leonardo Lasansky. Commissioned by the Associates of the James Ford Bell Library, University of Minnesota. Reproduced with permission.

The *Diario* of Christopher Columbus's First Voyage to America 1492–1493

Abstracted by
Fray Bartolomé de las Casas

Transcribed and Translated into English,
with Notes and a Concordance of the Spanish,

BY

Oliver Dunn and James E. Kelley, Jr.

UNIVERSITY OF OKLAHOMA PRESS: NORMAN AND LONDON

To Jane and Peggy

Library of Congress Cataloging-in-Publication Data

Columbus, Christopher.
  The Diario of Christopher Columbus's first voyage to America,
1492–1493.

  (The American exploration and travel series)
  Bibliography: p. 405.
  Includes index.
  1. Columbus, Christopher—Diaries. 2. America—Discovery and
exploration—Spanish. 3. Explorers—America—Di-
aries. 4. Explorers—Spain—Diaries.
I. Casas, Bartolomé de las, 1474–1566. II. Dunn, O. C. (Oliver
Charles), 1909–   . III. Kelley, James E. (James Edward),
1929–   . IV. Title. V. Series.
E118.C725 1988 970.01'5 [B] 87-40551
ISBN: 0–8061–2101–7 (cloth)
ISBN: 0–8061–2384–2 (pbk.)

This book was published with the support of the Program for Cultural
Cooperation Between Spain's Ministry of Culture and United States
Universities.

The paper in this book meets the guidelines for permanence and du-
rability of the Committee on Production Guidelines for Book Longevity
of the Council on Library Resources, Inc. ∞

3 4 5 6 7 8 9 10 11 12

CONTENTS

ILLUSTRATIONS

ACKNOWLEDGMENTS

WE ACKNOWLEDGE with thanks the help that we received in transcribing and translating Columbus's *Diario* from previous editions of the Spanish text and from its previous translations into English. Special thanks are due to Dr. Manuel Alvar for permission to quote, in the footnotes, the canceled passages of the *Diario* in which his reading (*Diario del descubrimiento*, 1976) differs from ours.

Appreciation is also extended to Doubleday & Company for permission to quote, again in the footnotes, from Samuel E. Morison's *Journals and Other Documents on the Life and Voyages of Christopher Columbus* (1963), to the Crown Publishing Group for permission to quote in the footnotes from the Jane-Vigneras edition of *The Journal of Christopher Columbus* (©Copyright 1960 by Clarkson N. Potter, Inc.–New York), and to the Wayne State University Press for permission to reprint the portion of the *Diario* main text (covering the entries for 10 October through 6 December) published previously in *Terrae Incognitae* (vol. 15, 1983) and its book counterpart, *In the Wake of Columbus: Islands & Controversy* (ed. Louis De Vorsey, Jr., and John Parker, 1985).

Particular thanks are due to John Parker, of the James Ford Bell Library of the University of Minnesota, and to the Associates of that library for permission to use the portrait of Columbus by Leonardo Lasansky, commissioned by the Associates. The Director of the National Library, Madrid, has graciously authorized us to reproduce two pages of the mansucript *Diario* as illustrations in the present volume.

We are especially indebted to the Society for the History of Discoveries for providing the opportunity that led to this project and for giving us a sympathetic platform at its annual meetings both to report our progress and to seek the interest, support, and criticism of the membership.

During the long time that this work was in preparation, we engaged in an extensive and helpful correspondence with Robert Fuson, John Parker, Arne Molander, and Robert Power (all of the Society for the History of Discoveries), with Joseph Judge (of the National Geographic Society), and with Eugene Lyon (of the Saint Augustine Restoration Project). We express our warm appreciation for the help and encouragement received from all of these students of Columbus's first voyage to the New World.

West Lafayette, Indiana   OLIVER DUNN
Melrose Park, Pennsylvania   JAMES E. KELLEY, JR.

The *Diario* of Christopher Columbus's First Voyage to America

EDITORS' INTRODUCTION

THIS VOLUME has been prepared to fulfill the need for a more easily available, accurate, and complete transcription of Bartolomé de las Casas's manuscript version of the *Diario* of Christopher Columbus's first voyage to America. Barring the unlikely discovery of the long-lost original *Diario* or of the single complete copy ordered for Columbus by Queen Isabella, Las Casas's partly summarized, partly quoted version of Columbus's copy is as close to the original as it is possible to come. Thus it remains our principal source of information about the historic voyage.

The need for this new edition of the *Diario* emerged in 1981 at a conference on Columbus's first landfall in America, sponsored by the Society for the History of Discoveries (SHD). It became apparent to the conferees, all of whom were scholars of the voyage, that the resolution of a number of important questions depended, at least in part, on an accurate transcription of the *Diario*. Their studies indicated that all of the editions of the *Diario* published since the first, by Navarrete, in 1825 differ, in varying degrees, from the Las Casas manuscript, which has been available since 1962 in a facsimile edition published by Carlos Sanz. This considered opinion led one of the present editors, with critical assistance from the other conference participants, to prepare a partial transcription of the *Diario* for inclusion in the conference proceedings, published in the Society's own journal, *Terrae Incognitae* (vol. 15, 1983). In 1982 the two editors of the present volume agreed to collaborate on a complete transcription and a new translation of the entire journal.

The differences of concern among editions of the *Diario* include expansion of contractions and abbreviations, addition of punctuation and accents, alteration of punctuation, alteration or correction of spelling, omission of Las Casas's canceled text, failure to indicate inserted text, and omission of Las Casas's notes. Manuel Alvar's version, published in 1976, comes close to the ideal but is now out of print. Robert Fuson's 1983 study, "The *Diario de Colón*," discusses the differences among editions, the ways in which they can affect interpretations of the *Diario*, and the impact they have had on the translations that have been made from them into English.

Among the issues on which we hope this new edition of the *Diario* will shed light are the "double accounting" of distances traversed during the outward voyage; the modern equivalents of Columbus's "mile" and "league"; the effects of ocean currents on course bearings and distances made good; compass variation and its effect on course bearings; whether Columbus's navigational methods were based on dead reckoning, latitude sailing, or the bearing of the setting sun; the location of San Salvador, the first landing place; the identity of the "many islands" sighted soon after the fleet's departure from San Salvador; the identity of the second, possibly "unnamed," island sighted; Columbus's route through the islands of the West Indies; and the meaning of the terms *camino de* and *cargar*, the first of which bears on interpretations of Columbus's direction of travel.

Our Transcription of the *Diario* derives principally from the Sanz facsimile (1962), and we have attempted to duplicate, to the extent practicable, the details and peculiarities of the *Diario* manuscript, including original spellings, some of the special characters, canceled words and phrases, and Las Casas's own punctuation and marginal notes. To ensure accuracy, we prepared special computer programs that permitted a standard word processor to handle the many special characters in the manuscript. Additionally, we proofread and corrected the entire computer-printed draft at least three times using the manuscript facsimile as the model.

To complement the new Transcription, we have prepared a new English Translation and a Concordance of the significant words of the Transcription. The Translation was made from the final computer-printed version of the Transcription and then revised twice. We have added notes to explain differences between our Translation and those of earlier translators. While no translation can fully capture the sense and nuances of its model, it is our hope that this work represents an improvement over previous efforts.

THE MANUSCRIPT

It is well known that Columbus kept a running journal of his first voyage to America and that he presented the document to Ferdinand and Isabella on his return to Spain. A copy of the original was made for the Admiral before he departed on his second voyage a few months later, but both the original and the copy eventually disappeared. The manuscript journal that survives is a partly quoted and partly summarized version of Columbus's copy. It was made by Bartolomé de las Casas in the 1530s. The Las Casas manuscript also disappeared for about 250 years but was found around 1790 by Martín Fernández de Navarrete in the library of the Duke of Infantado. It is now in the National Library, Madrid (*sig. vitrina* 6, n. 7). As far as is known, the manuscript is unique. There are no other "original" versions.

The manuscript consists of seventy-six large-sized paper folios written on both sides in a small, cursive hand, forty to fifty lines to the page. According to Navarrete (1825–29, 1:2 n. 1), the handwriting throughout is that of Las Casas. Folios 1 through 67 recto cover the first voyage. Folios 67 verso through 76 verso cover Columbus's third voyage. The manuscript is obviously a working draft, for it includes many passages of canceled text (both single words and phrases) and insertions, sometimes interlinear, sometimes marginal. There is but one figure, a crudely drawn pointing hand labeled *Hallan ya tierra*, marking the start of the paragraph on folio 8 that tells of Rodrigo de Triana's first sighting of San Salvador.

THE TRANSCRIPTION

To the extent possible the printed Transcription follows the basic structure of Las Casas's manuscript. Folio numbers in the manuscript appear only on the recto side of each leaf. To facilitate reference to the manuscript and the preparation of the Concordance, we have retained the folio numbers but have added recto (r) and verso (v) designations. Folio numbers are shown at the top of each Transcription page and in the text where page breaks occur.

In addition, we have assigned each line a number corresponding to its position in the manuscript, so that every line can be identified by a combination of folio and line numbers: for example, "folio 12 recto, line 10," or, in abbreviated form, "12r10." Generally, to reduce clutter, only every fifth line in the Transcription has a printed line number. In other editions with line numbers the numbers have designated lines of the printed page instead of lines of the *Diario* manuscript.

Letter Forms

Most of the letter forms used in the *Diario* are recognizable cursive forms. Comments on particular letters and letter combinations follow.

Sometimes the typical, cursive lowercase *a* is replaced by one that looks like a small Greek omega. If such a letter begins a sentence or a proper noun, it is printed as a capital *A*; if it does not begin a sentence or a proper noun, it is printed as a lowercase *a*.

Lowercase *b* and *v* are often difficult to distinguish, thus accounting for some of the differences among published transcriptions. If the ascender slants left, we have interpreted the letter as a *v*. If it is more vertical and straight, or if it forms a loop to the right, we have interpreted it as a *b*. The letter *v* is also often represented by a lowercase *u*.

The letter *c* appears in several forms. A capital-like form is often used as the first letter of words pronounced with a hard *c*. We have interpreted these as capital *C*'s even where there seems to be no reason for capitalization. Words beginning with a soft *c* are usually written in the manuscript with a large C-shaped letter enclosing a second, smaller *c*. In the Transcription such letters are written as *ç* (with cedilla) and are not distinguished from the small *ç*'s (with cedilla) of the manuscript. Interior *c*'s with a dot below are also printed as *ç*.

The letter combination *ch*, especially in the words *dicho* and *dicha*, is usually written as an elongated figure 8. In the Transcription this is expanded to *ch*. In such words as *Christo* the letter combination *chr* is written Xρ, i.e., as the Greek letters *chi* and *rho*.

The letters *e* and *o*, particularly in the words *les* and *los*, are sometimes impossible to distinguish on the basis of appearance. In such cases, we have made our decision on the basis of grammar or the opinions of other editors.

I's, *Y*'s, and *J*'s in the manuscript are difficult to distinguish, and we cannot be certain that our interpretations always represent Las Casas's intention. Other transcribers have not always agreed in their readings of these letters either.

In many instances letter forms may be read as either lowercase *i*, with a descender, or lowercase *j*. We resolved this difficulty by considering current spelling. Thus the words that might be read as *camjno* and *almjrante* are transcribed as *camino* and *almirante*, but the word that might be read as *iudio* is transcribed as *judio*. Lowercase *i* and *y* are a special problem in the word *muy*, because the last letter, which may have been intended to be an *i*, has a descender making it look like a *y*. In these instances we have transcribed the letter as *y*.

Capital *I*'s, *Y*'s, and *J*'s are so nearly identical in appearance that, again, we have devised special "rules" to deal with them. If a word such as *Jueves* is now spelled with a *J*, the word is so printed, even though the manuscript letter looks more like a capital *I* than a *J*. Initial letters that may be intended as either capital *I* or *Y* are transcribed as *I* unless the same word is found elsewhere beginning with a lowercase *y*. Thus *Yndias*, the usual spelling, is spelled that way even when, in a particular case, the word begins with a letter that might be interpreted as *I*, *Y*, or even *J*. There does not appear to be a clear and unambiguous capital *Y* in the entire manuscript, unless 10v18 contains one.

The letter combinations *par* and *per* are usually written in the manuscript as *p*'s with fancy flourishes beneath. To prevent confusion, they are printed in the Transcription as *p*[*ar*] and *p*[*er*].

The syllable *que* is normally represented by a special letter, starting as a cursive *q* but ending with the tail looping clockwise around the initial part. This syllable is printed as *q̃*.

The syllable *qua* is written rarely as *q̃*. It is printed here as *q̄*.

The syllable *ver* is often shortened to a character that looks like a modern capital *V* with a small loop added on the right side. This appears in the Transcription as *Vr*.

Capitalization

Capitalization in the manuscript is not consistent. Names of weekdays in the date of each entry vary in this respect, all but *martes* and *miércoles* ordinarily, but not always, beginning with capital letters. The opening word of each day's record sometimes begins with a capital, but in general the first words of other sentences are not so distinguished. *Reina* seems to be capitalized more frequently than *rey*, and *gran Can* is almost always so written. Personal and place names rarely begin with capitals. Words beginning with *I* or *J* often start with what look like capital letters, but it is difficult to know whether capitals were really intended.

Word Separation and Compression

Word separation in the manuscript does not always conform to dictionary usage. Words have been separated and combined in the Transcription to produce words of normal Spanish. For example, in line 31r16 *de to dalatormēta dl mūdo* is printed *de toda la tormēta dl mūdo*.

Las Casas frequently compressed adjacent words to form a single word, leaving out the last letter of the first word or the first letter of the second. This produces such words as *q̃stava* (for *que estava*) and *dllas* (for *de ellas*). He also compressed single words by omitting intermediate vowels, such as *dl* for *del* and *dsde* for *desde*.

Other indications of compression are the bars or tildes over letters, particularly over vowels preceding an omitted *n*. Examples are *mūdo* for *mundo* and *vierō* for *vieron*.

Still another compression is the shortening of the letters *miento* when they appear at the end of a word to the letters *mi⁰*, with the superscript *o* signaling the omission.

Some words are abbreviated in a variety of ways. *Almirante*, for example, appears as *almi*, *almirāte*, and *almiᵉ*.

A few words are written in such compressed form that they are nearly unrecognizable: *mrd* for *merced*, *dg* for *Diego*, *suiᵒ* for *servicio*. We have expanded these three words to their complete forms by enclosing the added letters in brackets. The tildes or bars of about twenty frequently used words have been assigned uniform (instead of varying) positions for this edition. Most of the other compressed words are printed as they appear in the manuscript, with exceptions indicated by enclosing added letters in brackets.

The words *como*, *mucho*, and *muy* present a special problem, because even when written out in full, they are usually written with bars over the *m* of *como* and the *u*'s of *mucho* and *muy*. This practice is explained in Juan de Valdés's *Dialogo*, written about 1535. One of the participants in the dialogue asks why such marks are used. The answer given is that they are no more than ornaments of the handwriting. The same answer is given to a question about the slash (*rasguillo*) that appears regularly before the word *o* (i.e., *or*) in the manuscript.

Manuscript Errors

Manuscript errors have been allowed to stand in the Transcription, but significant errors are cited in the footnotes. These include auditive errors, such as *parecian navios* for *para cien navios* (13v43), *un nombre* for *un hombre* (12r43), *para y* for *para ay* (i.e., *para ahi*) (15v24), and *aver comigo* for *aver comido* (15v38).

Punctuation

The manuscript contains a variety of punctuation marks. These have been reproduced in the Transcription just where, and just as, they appear in the manuscript. It should be noted that sentences terminating at a line-ending frequently have no ending punctuation. It is also interesting that one of the two paragraph marks, §, is used only with "significant" paragraphs: for example, on 6 September, the day of the fleet's departure from Gomera; on 10 and 11 October, the days just before and during the first landfall; and on 10 February, 1493, just before the *Niña* reached the Azores on the homeward voyage and Columbus recorded his and the pilots' estimates of their position.

The typical punctuation marks are:

§ or *l*   start of paragraph
l.   full stop

/ or // or : intermediate stop
used after some abbreviations and, in pairs, to set off
numbers in the text

( ) parenthetical remarks

Also note the sections below, on Inserted and Omitted Text and
on Canceled Text. We have tried to maintain as much similarity as
possible between our Transcription and Las Casas's manuscript.
Any differences that do exist are described.

Inserted and Omitted Text

Throughout the manuscript Las Casas inserted text between lines.
Often he inserted a quotation mark (") just below the line of text
where the insertion was to be made. The insertion itself is then
preceded by a second quotation mark, intended to pair with the
first. There is no punctuation at the close of the inserted text.
Occasionally Las Casas used small crosses in place of quotation
marks to note insertions. In the Transcription such interlinear text
is printed between lines, just where Las Casas wrote it, and its point
of insertion is marked by a caret.

Sometimes Las Casas inserted text, usually just above canceled
text, without using either quotation marks or crosses to mark the
insertions. Such insertions are printed in the Transcription just
above the canceled text they were intended to replace.

Las Casas often wrote insertions of extended length in the right
margin of the manuscript, sometimes with a line running to the
insertion from the place in the text to which it applied. These insertions are reproduced here in the right margin opposite the line of
text to which they apply. Their point of insertion in the text is
marked with a small subscript cross (+). Line breaks in the marginal
insertions occur where they did in the manuscript. To facilitate reference to these inserts in the notes and Concordance, individual
lines of each insert are labeled *a*, *b*, *c*, etc.

Blank spaces in the manuscript text have been reproduced in the
Transcription, the length of the blank indicating the approximate
length of the lacuna.

Letters at the ends of some marginally inserted lines are not visible in the manuscript facsimile. From an examination of photo-
graphs of the manuscript in the Library of Congress, it appears that
the omissions are caused by the extension of the handwriting into
the crease between folios, where it does not reproduce in the photo-
copying process. Letters so omitted are supplied in the Transcription from the *Raccolta* (Lollis 1892–94) or other Spanish editions

of the *Diario*. These letters always appear in brackets in the Transcription.

Canceled Text

Las Casas's canceled text has been reproduced in the Transcription. It is indicated by lines through the words or letters. Where the canceled text in the manuscript was not legible, a space with a line through it appears, followed by a question mark in brackets, the length of the line indicating the approximate length of the illegible cancellation.

Alvar's (1976) edition of the *Diario* appears to be the only other one to include canceled text and to identify insertions. We have included both in this edition because they may provide insight into the way Las Casas prepared his manuscript, or they may reveal new information about Columbus's voyage. For example, Las Casas canceled the word *leguas* and substituted *millas* a total of twelve times; there are no instances in which he corrected *millas* to *leguas*. These facts suggest that Las Casas, or the scribe who prepared the copy from which Las Casas worked, was biased for some reason toward writing the word *leguas* when a distance was involved. They also suggest the possibility that some of the "league" distances recorded in the *Diario* are errors for "miles," errors never noticed and corrected by Las Casas.

The possibility of such errors may bear on the identification of the island of Santa María, which the manuscript states is 5 by 10 leagues in size (11r35–38). If "leagues" is the correct unit of measure, then the identification of Santa María as Rum Cay cannot be correct. But measured in mile units of 4,060 English feet each (the probable length of Columbus's mile), Rum Cay *is* about 5 by 10 miles in size.

A similar case may be made regarding Columbus's claim that he could see 28 "leagues" of Fernandina's shoreline. Twenty-eight "miles" is the more likely extent of coastline that he could have seen, corresponding to the English "kenning" and the French *veue*.

In addition to cancellations and insertions, Las Casas's manuscript also includes his own marginal notes. These notes are reproduced here in the left margin opposite the line of text at which they begin. The line breaks in these notes also occur where they did in the manuscript.

Uncertain Readings

Where the correct reading of the manuscript (whether main text, interpolation, canceled text, or notes) is uncertain, the doubtful letters or words are enclosed by brackets and a question mark.

Layout and Style

To make the Transcription and Translation function together, they are printed on facing pages, although parallel line-by-line sequence was not feasible, because of changes in word order. However, page and folio breaks are closely coordinated. Also, for ease in reference, dates of journal entries and folio numbers appear in the running heads, and folio breaks are shown in the left margin about where they appear in the manuscript. With these guideposts it is really quite easy to follow the Transcription and Translation together.

Earlier Spanish Editions

Many previous Spanish editions of the *Diario* have been published. Navarrete's, the first, appeared in 1825. The *Raccolta* edition, edited by Cesare de Lollis, was printed in 1893 as part of the commemorative collection of Columbus material published by the Italian government; Guillén Tato's appeared in 1943; and Carlos Sanz's, in 1962. Sanz's edition includes both the manuscript facsimile on which the present edition is based and a transcription into modern Spanish. More recent editions include one by Joaquín Arce and Gil Esteve, 1971, and one by Manuel Alvar, 1976, the latter a two-volume work that presents both a paleographic and a modernized version of the *Diario*. Alvar's is the most detailed edition, showing the insertions and cancellations in the form of notes.

THE TRANSLATION

Our translation of the *Diario* is a fairly literal one, although not so literal that it makes the English sound awkward. Spanish construction is more flexible than English, and we have not hesitated to rearrange the elements of sentences, when necessary, to make them read like standard English. In some instances pronouns have been replaced by nouns, and ellipses have been expanded to clarify meanings. Genuine additions to the wording of the manuscript are enclosed in brackets.

Las Casas's notes and his canceled text are not included in the Translation. His insertions are included, although they are not distinguished from other text. They can, however, be easily identified by comparison with the Transcription.

Capitalization in the Translation follows modern practice: proper nouns, personal names, names of languages, and religions are capitalized, even though in the Transcription they often are not. On the other hand, where capitals are used in the Transcription without apparent reason, the Translation uses lowercase letters.

Proper names were not always spelled consistently in the Transcription. In the Translation we have usually chosen the most frequent spelling and used it consistently. Exceptions are "Vicente" instead of "Viçeynte," and "Pinzón" in place of "Pinçon." "Hispaniola," instead of "Española," is used to avoid referring to "the Spanish Island," a literal translation of *la isla española*.

Numbers, regardless of the form they take in the Transcription, are written out from one to ten and printed as Arabic numerals above ten. A number beginning a sentence, or one involving a fraction, is written out regardless of its size. We have made certain exceptions to these rules in the interest of coordinating the English Translation with the Spanish Transcription.

The grammatical structure of the Translation closely parallels that of the Transcription. In general, sentences in the Translation end where those in the Transcription end. Internal divisions of sentences in the two texts, Spanish and English, also occur at relatively the same places, although punctuation marks in the Transcription do not correspond exactly with punctuation marks in the Translation. The slashes (/, //) and colons (:) of the former are usually rendered in the Translation as either commas, semicolons, or colons, depending on the requirements of the particular context; however, a punctuation mark does not always appear in the Translation where one appears in the Transcription. We have added internal punctuation sparingly to the Translation where it was required to clarify meaning.

Occasionally it was necessary to alter punctuation more radically. The opening section of the Prologue, for example, seems, grammatically, to be a complex sentence more than a full page in length, and we have treated it as such in the Translation. The actual Spanish text, however, was broken by three full stops by Columbus, by Las Casas, or by the scribe who produced the copy of the original log from which Las Casas copied. We have held such changes to a minimum.

We have tried to use parentheses, brackets, and dashes consistently in the Translation. Passages in which Las Casas seems to be commenting on or explaining something that he has found in the *Diario* are enclosed in parentheses. Brackets are used for editorial additions, and dashes (which appear in only two or three places), for remarks which Columbus himself inserts parenthetically. We have set Las Casas's frequently used parenthetical phrase *diz que,* "he says," off from the rest of the text by commas.

Earlier English Translations

Several other English translations of the *Diario* have been published. The first was Kettell's, which appeared in 1827, only two years after Navarrete's first Spanish edition. Kettell's translation was reissued by Charles Boni in 1924 and by Jonathan Cape in 1931, each under a different title. Markham's edition, published by the Hakluyt Society in 1893, and Thacher's edition, published in 1903, were both based on the Navarrete transcription. Markham's translation was reprinted by Bourne in 1906. Jane's 1930 translation (revised by Vigneras in 1960) was the first English translation based on the Cesare de Lollis *Raccolta* transcription. The most recent English translation is Morison's, 1963, also based on De Lollis but checked against a photographic copy of the original manuscript.

FOOTNOTES

We have added footnotes to serve a number of purposes. Some document peculiarities of the *Diario* manuscript not apparent in the Transcription. Others identify significant differences between Alvar's reading of Las Casas's canceled text and our reading of the same. Some notes illustrate problems of translation by noting significant differences between our version and those of Morison, Jane-Vigneras, and, to a lesser degree, Thacher. Where helpful, we have also added notes to provide background information and interpretation.

Although all the footnote numbers appear in the Translation, the notes are keyed to the folio and line numbers of the Transcription, and key phrases in Spanish are usually supplied. This should make comparison of the Spanish and English easy. Notes pertaining to a particular term appear only with the first occurrence of the term. Other occurrences of the terms can be located by using the Concordance.

Full bibliographic information on the sources cited in the notes is given in the Bibliography.

THE CONCORDANCE

Having the Transcription text in computer-readable form made it relatively easy to prepare a Concordance. Individual words, tagged with their folio and line numbers, were separated from the Transcription, sorted into alphabetical sequence, and tabulated in folio and line-number order. Punctuation marks, Arabic and Roman numerals, and other signs were excluded.

For the most part we retained the orthography of the Transcription. However, certain technical problems involved in grouping like terms made it advisable to print some words differently than the way they appear in the Transcription. The following are the exceptions: all capitalized letters in the *Diario* are shown as lower-case in the Concordance; and abbreviated or incomplete words that we resolved by means of letters within square brackets ([...]) appear under their resolved spellings (e.g., *p[ar]a* appears under *para*, and the abbreviation *Vr* is replaced by *ver* in the Concordance. Compressed word combinations appear under their compressed form; for example, *desta, q̃stava*.

The words were sorted according to the English alphabet. The letter *ç* (with cedilla) is placed between *c* and *d*. Similarly, *ñ* is placed between *n* and *o*. There are no words in the *Diario* that begin with *k* or *w*.

The citations, shown to the right of each word, are listed in ascending order. A typical citation shows the folio number, its recto (r) or verso (v) side, and the line number in which the word appears. If a word appears in more than one line on the same folio, the folio number is shown only once (e.g., 10v8 12 21). This reduces the clutter of the citation lists.

Citations of canceled text are noted by a superscript *c*. Citations of Las Casas's notes are signaled by a superscript *n*. The latter citations specify the folio and line number next to which Las Casas's notes are printed.

The total number of citations of a word is printed just to the left of a word only if the count is relatively high—i.e., cannot be immediately perceived without counting. Citations are not listed for high-frequency words (e.g. *a, de, el, en, la, y*, etc., some thirty in all) that occur over two hundred times in the *Diario*.

Additional entries in the Concordance show variant spellings of certain words. In these entries, made on a line separate from the citations, the first word listed typically shows the most frequent spelling. A standard spelling is used when all the other variants are abbreviations. Each variant-spelling list is prefaced by the total number of occurrences of all the spellings. The printing of variants in preliminary versions of the Concordance was useful in bringing to our attention transcription errors that might otherwise have gone unnoticed.

Words spelled identically but different in meaning are not provided with separate entries in the Concordance, nor have we included multiple-word idioms (e.g., *a la corda*) as elements in the Concordance.

The *Diario* of Christopher Columbus's First Voyage to America

TRANSCRIPTION AND TRANSLATION

Folio 1r

/ Este es el primer viaje y las
derrotas y camino q̃ hizo el
almirãte don xp̄oũal Colon
quãdo dscubrio las yndias
5   puesto sumariamẽte sin el
prologo q̃ hizo a los reyes q̃ va
a la letra y comiẽça desta mar̃a /

In nōīe dñi nr̃i īhu xp̄ī

Porque xp̄ıanissimos y mỹ altos y mũy excelentes
10 y mũy poderosos prinçipes Rey e reyna dlas
españas y dlas Islas dla mar nr̄os .Sr̥s este
presente año de .1492. despues de vr̄as alte
zas aver dado fin a la guerra dlos moros
~~en la mũy grãde çiudad de granada : adõde~~
15 q̃ reynavã en Europa y aver acabado la guer
ra en la mỹ grãde çiudad de granada : adõde
este presente año a dos dias del mes de ene
ro por fuerça de armas vide poner las
vanderas reales de .v.al. en las torres dla
20 alfambra : q̃ es la fortaleza dla d̃ha çiudad : y
vide salir al rey moro a las puertas dla
çiudad y besar las reales manos de vr̄as al
tezas y dl principe mi señor ./. y luego en
aq̃l presente mes por la informaçion q̃ yo
25 avia dado a .v.al. dlas tr̃ras de yndia y de
vn prinçipe q̃ es llamado grã Can q̃ quiere de
zir en nr̄o romãçe rey dlos Reyes (cõmo
mũchas vezes el y sus anteçessores aviã enbia
do a roma a pedir doctores en nr̄a Sancta fe
30 porq̃ le enseñasen en ella y q̃ nũca el san
cto padre le avia proveydo /. y se perdiã tan
tos pueblos cayẽdo en Idolatrias e resçibiẽ
do en si sectas de p[er]diçion /. y .v.al. cõmo ca

1r   This is the first voyage and the
       courses and way that the Admiral
       Don Christóbal Colón took when he
       discovered the Indies, summarized
       except for the prologue that he
       composed for the king and queen,
       which is given in full and begins
       this way:[1]

In the Name of Our Lord Jesus Christ

Whereas,[2] Most Christian and Very Noble and
Very Excellent and Very Powerful Princes, King
and Queen of the Spains and of the Islands of
the Sea, our Lords: This present year of 1492,
after Your Highnesses had brought to an end
the war with the Moors who ruled in Europe and
had concluded the war in the very great city
of Granada, where this present year on the
second day of the month of January I saw the
Royal Standards of Your Highnesses placed by
force of arms on the towers of the Alhambra,
which is the fortress of the said city; and I
saw the Moorish King come out to the gates of
the city and kiss the Royal Hands of Your
Highnesses and of the Prince my Lord; and
later in that same month, because of the report that I had given to Your Highnesses about
the lands of India and about a prince who is
called "Grand Khan," which means in our Spanish language "King of Kings"; how, many times,
he and his predecessors had sent to Rome to
ask for men learned in our Holy Faith in order
that they might instruct him in it and how the
Holy Father had never provided them; and thus
so many peoples were lost, falling into idola-
try and accepting false and harmful religions;
and Your Highnesses, as Catholic Christians

---

1. (1r1–7) These preliminary lines, written in the third person, were undoubt-
edly added by Las Casas.
2. (1r9) This line starts well to the left of the balance of the text of folio 1r.

tholicos xp̄īaños y prinçipes amadores dla S̄acta fe
35 xp̄īaña y acreçẽtadores dlla : y enemigos dla
secta de mahoma y de todas Idolatrias y he
regias : pensar̄o de embiarme a mi xp̄oūal
Colon a las d̄has p[ar]tidas de yndia p[ar]a ver los
d̄hos prinçipes y los pueblos y las t̄r̄r̄as y la

Folio 1v

disposiçion dllas y de todo y la mar̄a q̃ se pu
diera tener p[ar]a la conVrsion dllas a nr̄a S̄ata fe :
y ordenar̄o q̃ yo no fuese por t̄r̄ra al oriente
por donde se costūbra de andar : salvo por el
5   camino de occidente : por donde hasta oy no
sabemos por çierta fe q̃ aya passado nadie /.
asi q̃ despues de aver echado fuera todos los
judios de todos vr̄os Reynos y señorios : en el
mismo mes de enero : mādar̄o vr̄as altezas
10 a mi q̃ con armada suffiçiente me fuese a las d̄has
partidas de yndia /. y p[ar]a ello me hizier̄o
grādes m[erce]des y me anobleçier̄o q̃ dēde
en adelante yo me llamase Don y fuesse
almirāte mayor dla mar occeana y visorey
15 e goVrnador p[er]petuo de todas las Islas y t̄r̄ra firme
q̃ yo descubriese y ganasse : y de aqui adlāte
se dscubriesen y ganasen en la mar occeano
y asi sucediese mi hijo mayor y el asi de
grado en grado p[ar]a siemp^r jamas /. y parti

quādo salio des pachado de la çiudad de grana da el almirāte Colon p[ar]a yr a descubrir las yndias .

yo dla çiudad de granada a doze dias del
mes de mayo dl mesmo año de .1492.
en sabado y vine a la villa de palos que es
puerto de mar a donde yo arme tres navios
mȳ aptos p[ar]a semejāte fecho : y p[ar]ti dl d̄ho puer
25 to mȳ abasteçido de mȳ muchos mātinimientos :

quādo partio el almi^ç dl puerto de palos p[ar]a su descubrimi^o .

y de mūcha gente dla mar a tres dias del
mes de agosto dl d̄ho año en vn viernes
antes dla salida del Sol c̄o media ora : y
lleve el camino dlas Islas de Canaria de vr̄as
30 altezas q̃ son en la d̄ha mar ocçeana p[ar]a de
alli tomar mi derrota y navegar tanto q̃ yo
llegase a las yndias y dar la Embaxada de
vr̄as altezas a aq̃llos prinçipes y cūplir lo q̃
asi me aviā mādado /. y p[ar]a esto pense de

and Princes, lovers and promoters of the Holy
Christian Faith, and enemies of the false doc-
trine of Mahomet and of all idolatries and
heresies, you thought of sending me, Christóbal Colón, to the said regions of India to see
the said princes and the peoples and the lands,
1v   and the characteristics of the lands and of
everything, and to see how their conversion to
our Holy Faith might be undertaken. And you
commanded that I should not go to the East by
land, by which way it is customary to go, but
by the route to the West, by which route we do
not know for certain that anyone previously
has passed. So, after having expelled all the
Jews from all of your Kingdoms and Dominions,
in the same month of January Your Highnesses
commanded me to go, with a suitable fleet, to
the said regions of India. And for that you
granted me great favors and ennobled me so
that from then on I might call myself "Don"
and would be Grand Admiral of the Ocean Sea
and Viceroy and perpetual Governor of all the
islands and lands that I might discover and
gain and [that] from now on might be discovered
and gained in the Ocean Sea; and likewise my
eldest son would succeed me and his son him,
from generation to generation forever. And I
left the city of Granada on the twelfth day of
May in the same year of 1492 on Saturday, and
I came to the town of Palos, which is a sea-
port, where I fitted out three vessels very
well suited for such exploits; and I left the
said port, very well provided with supplies
and with many seamen, on the third day of
August of the said year, on a Friday, half an
hour before sunrise; and I took the route to
Your Highnesses' Canary Islands, which are in
the said Ocean Sea, in order from there to
take my course and sail so far that I would
reach the Indies and give Your Highnesses'
message to those princes and thus carry out
that which you had commanded me to do. And
for this purpose I thought of writing on this

35 escrevir todo este viaje mȳ puntualmēte de
    dia en dia todo lo q̃ yo hiziese y viese y pas
    sasse com̄o adelante se veyra /. tābien Señores
    prinçipes allende de escrevir cada noche lo
    q̃l dia passare : y el dia lo q̃ la noche nave
40 gare : tēgo proposito de hazer carta nueva de
    navegar /. En la qual situare toda la mar e

Folio 2r

    trras del mar ocçeano en sus p[ro]prios lugares
    debaxo su viento y mas componer vn libro
    y poner todo por el semejāte por pintura por
    latitud del equinocial y longitud del occiden
5   te y sobre todo cumple mūcho q̃ yo olvide
    el sueño y tiente mucho el navegar porq̃
    asi cumple las quales serā grā trabajo /.

                                                    viernes .3. de agosto

    Partimos viernes .3. dias de agosto de .1492.
10 años dla barra de Saltes a las ocho oras
    anduvimos con fuerte virazō hasta el poner
    dl Sol hazia el sur sesenta millas q̃ son .15.
                              al sur
    leguas . despues al sudueste y ∧quarta dl
                                        las
    sudueste q̃ era el camino p[ar]a ∧ Canarias .

whole voyage, very diligently, all that I would do and see and experience, as will be seen further along.[1] Also, my Lord Princes, besides writing down each night whatever I experience during the day and each day what I sail during the night, I intend to make a new sailing chart.[2] In it I will locate all of the

2r   sea and the lands of the Ocean Sea in their proper places under their compass bearings and, moreover, compose a book and similarly record all of the same in a drawing, by latitude from the equinoctial line and by longitude from the west;[3] and above all it is very important that I forget sleep and pay much attention to navigation in order thus to carry out these purposes, which will be great labor.

Friday 3 August

We departed Friday the third day of August of the year 1492 from the bar of Saltés at the eighth hour. We went south with a strong sea breeze[4] 60 miles,[5] which is 15 leagues, until sunset; afterward to the southwest and south by west, which was the route for the Canaries.

1. (1v34–37) *Pense . . . veyra.* Events before and including the departure from Palos are referred to as past, while recording the voyage is a plan for the future. This suggests that the Prologue was written while the fleet was sailing to the Canary Islands.

2. (1v37–41) The syntax of this sentence (*Tambien Señores . . . navegar*) is not clear. Is "Columbus" the subject of two verbs in the future indicative tense (*passaré* and *navegaré*), or are *dia* and *noche* the subjects of verbs in the future subjunctive tense (*passare* and *navegare*) Because "Columbus" is the subject of the verbs in the two preceding lines (35 and 36) and because lines 38–40 appear intended to restate those lines, the first alternative is probably correct. With *el dia* and *la noche* read as adverbial phrases ("by day" and "by night"), the grammar would be correct.

3. (2r4–5) *Longitud del occidente.* *Occidente* is used here in the sense of an imaginary fixed line, probably *l'occidente di Tolomeo*, as the prime meridian on Ptolemaic maps was labeled.

4. (2r11) A *virazon* is a wind that regularly blows from the sea toward land during the day and from land toward sea at night. (See Guillén Tato 1951, 128.)

5. (2r12) *Millas.* The length of Columbus's mile is debated among scholars. Morison was so sure it was the Roman mile, of 4,850 feet, that he translated *millas* as "Roman miles" throughout his version of the *Diario*. Others assert that Columbus's mile is a shorter unit, of 5,000 palms, equivalent to about 4,060 English feet, or five-sixths of a Roman mile. All Iberian sailors of Columbus's time recognized 4 Roman miles as the equivalent of 1 Portuguese maritime league (see Kelley 1983, 91).

15
/ anduvierō al Sudueste quarta del sur

El Sabado .4º. de agosto

Domingo .5. de agosto .

/ anduvierō su via entre dia y noche mas
de quarēta leguas .

20
/ ~~Se le quebro~~ Salto /o desencasose el goVrnario
a la Caravela pinta donde yva martin alō
so pinçon a lo q̃ se creyo /o sospecho por in
dustria de vn gomez [R?]ascon y xp̄oūal quin
25 tero cuya era la Caravela porq̃ le pesava
yr aq̃l viaje /. y dize el almiᵉ q̃ antes q̃
partiesen avian hallado en çiertos reveses
y grisquetas como dizē a los d̄hos /. vidose alli
el almiᵉ en grā turbaçion por no poder
30 ayudar a la d̄ha caravela sin su peligro
y dize q̃ alguᵃ pena p[er]dia con saber q̃ mar
tin alōso pinçon era p[er]sona esforçada y de buē
ingenio /. en fin anduvierō entre dia y noche
veynte
~~diez~~ y nueve leguas

lunes .6. de agosto

35
/ tornose a saltar el goVrnalle a la pinta y a
dobarōlo y anduvieron en demāda dla

Martes .7. de agosto .

Folio 2v

Isla de lançarote q̃s vna dlas islas de canaria
y anduvierō entre dia y noche .xxv. leguas .

Saturday 4 August

They went southwest by south.

Sunday 5 August

They went on their way and between day and
night[1] made more than 40 leagues.

Monday 6 August

The rudder of the caravel *Pinta*, in which Martín Alonso Pinzón was traveling, jumped or
came loose from its fastenings, which was believed or suspected to be by design of one Gó-
mez Rascón and [one] Christóbal Quintero,
whose caravel it was, because he disliked going on that voyage. And the Admiral says that
before they departed the said men had been
found making certain objections and quarrel-
some arguments, *reveses y grisquetas*,[2] as they
say. The Admiral was greatly perturbed because he could not help the said caravel without danger to himself and says that his
anguish lessened knowing that Martín Alonso
Pinzón was a valiant person and very ingenious.[3] Finally they made, between day and
night, 29 leagues.

Tuesday 7 August

Again the rudder of the *Pinta* jumped [its
fastenings] and they fixed it and proceeded
2v   looking for the island of Lanzarote, which is
one of the Canary Islands. And they traveled
between day and night 25 leagues.

1. (2r18) *Entre dia y noche* (between day and night) means the 24-hour period
that includes both day and night, not the time between sunrise and sunset (also see
p. 29, n. 3).
2. (2r28) Alvar (1976, 2:19 n. 10) derives the meaning of *grisquetas* (quarrel-
some arguments) from older terms for "Greek." The meaning is a reference to the
Greeks' reputation for being argumentative.
3. (2r32–33) Jane-Vigneras (1960) translates *persona esforçada y de buen ingenio*)
as "a man of courage and of good understanding"; Morison (1963) translates it as "a
man of real power, very ingenious."

/ ovo entre los pilotos dlas tres caravelas
5   opiniones diuersas donde estavā y el almiᵉ
salio mas Vrdadero / y quisiera yr a grā
canaria por dexar la caravela pinta porq̃
yva mal acondiçionada ̶y̶ dl governario y
hazia agua / y quisiera tomar alli otra
10   si la hallara : no pudierō tomarla aq̃l
dia /.

/ Hasta el domīgo en la noche no pudo
el almiᵉ tomar la gomera y m[art]in alō
15   so quedose en aq̃lla Costa de grā canaria
por mādado dl almiᵉ porq̃ no podia na
vegar / despues torno el almiᵉ a canaria o a tenerife
y adobarō mȳ bien la pinta cō mūcho tra
bajo y diligēçia dl almiᵉ de m[art]in alōso
20   y dlos demas y al cabo vinierō a la gome
ra /. vierō salir grā huego de la sierra de
la Isla de tenerife q̃s mȳ alta en gran
                              redōda por
mařa /. hizierō la pinta ∧q̃ era latina /.
torno
̶l̶l̶e̶g̶o̶ a la gomera domingo a dos de se
25   tiēbre cō la pinta adobada /.
dize el almiᵉ q̃ juravā mūchos ̶d̶l̶o̶s̶-[?] hō
bres hōrrados españoles q̃ en la gomera
estavā cō doña Ines peraça madre de guillē
peraça q̃ dspues fue el primer cōde de la
30   gomera q̃ erā vezinos de la Isla del hier
ro : q̃ cada año vian tierra al vveste dlas
Canarias q̃ es al poniente : y otros dla
gomera afirmavā otro ———[?] tanto cō juramēto /.

There were among the pilots of the three caravels diverse opinions about where they were,
and the Admiral came out nearest the truth.
And he would have liked to go to Gran Canaria
to leave the caravel *Pinta*, because she leaked
and sailed badly served by the rudder. And he
would have liked to get another caravel there
if he were to find one. They were not able to
reach it that day.

Up until Sunday night the Admiral could not
reach Gomera, and Martín Alonso remained off
that coast of Gran Canaria by order of the Admiral because he could not steer. Later the
Admiral returned to Gran Canaria or to Tenerife[1] and repaired the *Pinta* very well with
great labor and diligence of the Admiral, of
Martín Alonso, and of the rest, and finally
they came to Gomera. They saw a great fire
come out of the mountains on the island of
Tenerife, which is exceedingly high. They
made the *Pinta* square-rigged because she was
formerly a lateener.[2] He returned to Gomera
Sunday the second of September with the *Pinta*
repaired. The Admiral says that many honorable Spaniards, residents of the island of
Hierro, who were on Gomera with Doña Inés
Peraza, mother of the Guillén Peraza[3] who
later was the first count of Gomera, swore
that every year they saw land to the west of
the Canaries, which is toward the setting
sun;[4] and others of Gomera affirm as much on

1. (2v17) The words *o a tenerife* are boxed in the right margin at the end of
the line.
2. (2v23) The *Niña*, not the *Pinta*, was rerigged square in the Canaries. "Lateeners" carried large triangular sails on yards slung at a 45 to 60° angle to the deck.
"Square-riggers" carried square or rectangular sails on yards parallel to the deck. Square-
rigged vessels were easier to maneuver, although lateeners could sail closer to the wind.
3. (2v28) Inés Peraza was Guillén's sister, not his mother.
4. (2v32) *Poniente* means "toward the setting sun." *Levante* is the corresponding
word relating to the rising sun.

Dize aqui el almiͤ q̃ se acuerda q̃stando
en portugal
35   ~~en la Isla dla madera~~ el año de 1484.
vino vno dla isla dla madera al rey a le
pedir vna caravela p[ar]a yr a esta tr̄ra q̃ via
el qual jurava q̃ cada año la via y siempre
de vna mañ̃a : y t̄abien dize q̃ se acuerda
40   q̃ lo mismo deziā en las Islas dlos açores
y todos estos en vna derrota y en vna mañ̃a
de señal y en vna grādeza /. tomada pues

Folio 3r

agua y leña y Carnes y lo demas que
en la gomera
tenian los hōbres q̃ dexo ∧el almi quā
do fue a la Isla de canaria a adobar la
a la vela
caravela pinta : finalmēte se hizo ∧ dla d̄ha
5   Isla dla gomera con sus tres caravelas
jueves a seys dias de setiembre

Jueves .6. de setiembre

§ partio aq̃l dia por la mañana dl puer
to dla gomera y tomo la buelta p[ar]a yr
10   su viaje : y supo el almiͤ dvna caravela
q̃ venia dla Isla dl hierro q̃ andavā por
alli tres caravelas de portugal p[ar]a lo tomar
devia de ser de enbidia q̃l rey tenia por
averse ydo a castilla /. y anduvo todo aq̃l dia
15   y noche en calma y a la mañana se hallo
entre la gomera y tenerife /.

Viernes .7. de setiembre

/ todo el viernes y el sabado hasta tres oras
de noche estuvo en calmas /.

20   Sabado .8. de setiēbre
/ tres oras de noche sabado comēço a ventar nordes[te?]

oath. The Admiral says here that he remembers
when he was in Portugal in the year 1484 a man
came from the island of Madeira to the king to
ask for a caravel in order to go to this land
that he saw. He swore that each year he saw
it and always in the same way. And also the
Admiral says he remembers that in the islands
of the Azores they say the same thing and that
all Azoreans [agree] on its direction and its
appearance and its size. Then, having taken
3r   water and firewood and meat and the rest
that the men whom the Admiral left at Gomera
obtained while he went to the island of Gran
Canaria to repair the caravel *Pinta*, finally
he set sail from the said island of Gomera
with his three caravels on Thursday the sixth
day of September.

Thursday 6 September

He departed that day in the morning from the
harbor of Gomera and he took the course for
his voyage. And the Admiral learned from a
caravel that was coming from the island of
Hierro that three Portuguese caravels were
sailing in that vicinity in order to capture
him. It must have been from envy that the
king felt because of the Admiral's having gone
away to Castile. And he proceeded all that
day and night in very light winds and in the
morning he found himself between Gomera and
Tenerife.

Friday 7 September

All of Friday and on Saturday until the third
hour of night he was in very light winds.

Saturday 8 September

At the third hour of night on Saturday it com-

y tomo su via y camino al gueste : tu
vo mūcha mar por proa q̃ le estorvava
el camino y andariā aq̃l dia nueve
25   leguas con su noche /.

Domīgo .9. de setiēbre

⅄ anduvo aq̃l dia .15. leguas y acordo con
tar menos dlas q̃ andava porq̃ si el via
je fuese luēgo no se espantase y desmaya
30   se la gente / en la noche anduvo çiento y
        millas
veynte ~~leguas~~ a diez millas por ora q̃ son
[3?]0 leguas /. los marineros goVrnavā mal
decayendo sobre la quarta del norueste y
avn a la media p[ar]tida : sobre lo qual les
35   riño el almi͡c muchas vezes /.

lunes .10º. de setiēbre .

⅄ en aq̃l dia con su noche anduvo sesenta le

Folio 3v

guas a diez millas por ora̶s̶ q̃ son ~~leguas~~
dos leguas y media / p[er]o no contava
sino quarēta y ocho leguas porq̃ no se
asombrase la gente si el viaje fuese lar
5   go /.

martes .11º. de setiēbre

⅄ aq̃l dia navegarō a su via q̃ era el gueste
        .20.
y anduvierō ~~.30.~~ leguas y mas y vie
rō vn grā troço de mastel de nao de

menced to blow from the northeast[1] and he
took his course and route to the west. He
took much water over the bow, which hindered
his way, and he made that day and night nine leagues.

Sunday 9 September

He made 15 leagues that day and he decided to
report less than those actually traveled so
in case the voyage were long the men would not
be frightened and lose courage.[2] In the night
they made 120 miles at ten miles per hour,
which is 30 leagues. The sailors steered
badly, straying to the west by north and even
to the half division [i.e., west-northwest],
because of which the Admiral rebuked them many times.

Monday 10 September

3v   On that day and night[3] they made 60 leagues at
ten miles (which is two leagues and a half)
per hour, but he reported only 48 leagues so
that the men would not be frightened if the
voyage were long.

Tuesday 11 September

That day they sailed on their course, which
was west, and they made 20 leagues and more;
and they saw a big piece of mast from a ship

---

   1.   (3r21)   The word *nordeste* extends well into the right margin, suggesting that it was inserted at a later date.

   2.   (3r27–30)   *Acordo . . . la gente.* A recent study by Kelley (1983, 91) maintains that Las Casas may have misunderstood what Columbus was doing when he gave his crew numerically smaller values of leagues made good than those he recorded privately. Instead of lying to the crew, the Admiral was converting his 5,000-palm (4,060-English foot) miles to the equivalent Portuguese maritime league of 4 Roman miles (of 4,850 English feet each), a unit with which he and all his crew were familiar. The Admiral first divided his estimate of miles made good by four to obtain an intermediate, league-like figure. This quotient was then multiplied by five-sixths to produce the equivalent, but numerically smaller, distance in units of Portuguese maritime leagues, the figure given to the crew. Las Casas thought the larger figure of the intermediate calculation was the Admiral's "true" reckoning and the smaller one a "false" figure provided to allay the fears of the crew (also see p. 21, n. 5).

   3.   (3r37)   *En aquel dia con su noche* is another way of denoting the 24-hour period from sunrise to sunrise (also see p. 23, n. 1).

10 çiento y veynte toneles y no lo pudierō
tomar /. la noche anduvierō cerca de
veynte leguas y conto no mas de
diez y seys por la causa d̄ha /.

15 / aq̄l dia yendo su via anduvierō en
noche y dia .33. leguas contādo me
nos por la d̄ha causa /.

/ aq̄l dia cō su noche yendo a su via q̄ era
20 el gueste anduvierō .xxxiii. leguas y
contava tres o quatro menos /. las cor
rientes lo erā contrarias /. en este dia
al comiēço dla noche las agujas norue
steavā y a la mañana nordesteavā algū
25 tanto /.

/ navegarō aq̄l dia su camino al gueste
cō su noche y anduvierō .xx. leguas : cō
alguna
to ——[?] menos /. aqui ~~vierō~~ dixerō los
caravela niña
30 dla ~~pinta~~ q̄ avian visto vn garxao y vn
rabo de junco [/?] y estas aves nūca se apar
tā de tr̄ra quādo mas .xxv. leguas /. ~~de~~-[?]
~~tierra~~ /.

cō su noche
35 / Navego aq̄l dia∧ .xxvii. leguas su camino
al gueste y algunas mas /. y en esta noche
al principio dlla vierō caer dl çielo vn ma

of 120 *toneles*[1] and they could not salvage it.
In the night they went nearly 20 leagues and
he reported only 16 for the reason stated.

Wednesday 12 September

That day, going on their course, they made 33
leagues night and day, reporting less for the
said reason.

Thursday 13 September

That day and night, going on their course,
which was west, they made 33 leagues and he
reported three or four less. The currents
were against him. On this day at the beginning of night the compasses northwested and
in the morning they northeasted somewhat.[2]

Friday 14 September

They steered on their route west that day and
night and made 20 leagues. He reported a few
less. Here the men of the caravel *Niña* said
that they had seen a tern and a tropic bird,[3]
and these birds never depart from land more
than 25 leagues.

Saturday 15 September

They sailed that day and night 27 leagues and
a few more on their route west. And on this
night, at the beginning of it, they saw a

---

1.   (3v10)   A *tonel* was a volume unit used to measure a ship's capacity, or burthen,
in wine barrels ("tuns") of two pipes each. Quirino da Fonseca estimates that the
Seville tun of two pipes, the one favored by Columbus, was 1.405 cubic meters. The
Biscay tun, or *macho tonel*, the other tun measure used in Spain at the time, was about
1.683 cubic meters. (See Martinez-Hidalgo 1966, 40.)
2.   (3v23–25)   *Las agujas . . . tanto.* What Columbus observed was not magnetic
variation but rather the circular movement of Polaris around the celestial pole. In the
late fifteenth century the radius of this circle was almost 3.5°. See the *Diario* entry for
17 September (4r24–32) for a similar observation and Las Casas's explanation.
3.   (3v30–31)   *Garxao (garajao)* is a word for "any large tern with a bright red
bill." *Rabo de junco* is a tropic bird. See Morison (1963, 53, 14 Sept., nn. 1, 2) for a
discussion of these birds' identities.

ravilloso ramo de huego en la mar le
xos dllos quātro o çinco leguas /.

Folio 4r

navego aq̃l dia y la noche a su camino el
gueste andarian xxxviiii leguas p[er]o no con
to sino -35- 36 tuvo aq̃l dia algunos nū
5   blados llovizno   dize aqui el almi꞉ q̃ oy
y siempre de alli adelante hallarō aygres tem
peratissimos q̃ era plazer grāde el gusto d[e?]
las mañanas q̃ no faltava sino oyr ruyse
ñores dize el : y era el tp̄o como por abril
10 en el andaluzia /. Aqui comēçarō a ver
mūchas manadas de yerva mūy verde q̃
poco avia (segū le pareçia) q̃ se avia desa
pegado de tr̄r̄a [/?] por la qual todos juzgavā
q̃ estavā çerca de alguna Isla p[er]o no de
15 tr̄r̄a firme segūd el almi꞉ q̃ dize porq̃
la tr̄r̄a firme hago mas adelante /

/ Navego a su camino el gueste y andariā en
                              y mas
dia y noche çinquēta leguas ∧ no asento
20 sino -42-[?] .47. ayudavales la corriēte
vierō mūchas yerva y mȳ a menudo y era
yerva de peñas / ~~juzgavā estar çerca de tr̄r̄a /.~~
y venian las yerva de hazia poniente : juzga
vā estar çerca de tr̄r̄a . tomarō los pilotos
25 ~~el Sol y~~ el norte marcādolo y hallarō q̃ las
agujas noruesteavā vna grā quarta : y temi
an los marineros y estavā penados y no deziā
de que . cognosciolo el almi꞉ mādo q̃ torna
sen a marcar el norte -y-[?] en amaneçiēdo y
30 hallarō q̃stavā buenas las agujas /. la causa

marvelous branch of fire fall from the sky
into the sea, distant from them four or five leagues.

4r   Sunday 16 September

He sailed that day and night on his route
west. They made about 39 leagues but he reported only 36. That day he had some storm
clouds and it drizzled. Here the Admiral says
that today and from then on they found such
extremely temperate breezes that the savor of
the mornings was a great delight, for nothing
was lacking except to hear nightingales, he
says; and the weather was like that in April
in Andalusia. Here they began to see many
bunches of very green vegetation which a short
time before (so it appeared) had torn loose
from land, because of which everyone judged
that they were near some island but not near
a large landmass, according to the Admiral, who
says: Because I think the mainland is farther ahead.

Monday 17 September

He sailed on his route west and made, day and
night, somewhat more than 50 leagues. He put
down but 47. The current was helping them.
They saw much weed and very often and it was
vegetation from rocks and it came from a
westerly direction; they judged themselves to
be near land. The pilots took the north,
marking it,[1] and found that the compasses
northwested a full point [i.e., eleven and
one-quarter degrees]; and the sailors were
fearful and depressed and did not say why.
The Admiral was aware of this and he ordered
that the north again be marked when dawn came,
and they found that the compasses were correct. The cause was that the North Star ap-

---

1. (4r24–25) *Tomaron . . . marcandolo*. That is, the pilots took a sight on the
North Star and compared it with its compass bearing. See the *Diario* entry for 13
September (3v23–25) for a similar observation.

fue porꝗ la estrella ꝗ pareçe haze movimiᵒ

aꝗl lunes
y no las agujas [/.?] en amaneçiendo ———[?]
vierō muchas mas yervas y ꝗ pareçian yer
vas de rios en las quales hallarō vn can
35 grejo bivo el qual guardo el almiᶜ y dize ꝗ aꝗllas
fuerō señales çiertas de trra . porꝗ no se hallan
~~sino~~-[?] ochenta leguas de t̄r̄r̄a /. el agua dla mar
hallavā menos salada desde ꝗ salierō dlas Ca
narias /. los ayres siempʳ mas suaves /. yvan
40 mȳ alegres todos y los navios quiē mas podia
andar andava por ver p[ri]mero t̄r̄r̄a viero mū
chas toninas y los dla niña mataro vna / dize

Folio 4v

aqui el almiᶜ ꝗ aꝗllas señales erā del poniē
te donde espero en aꝗl alto dios en cuyas
manos estan todas las victorias ꝗ mȳ presto
nos dara t̄r̄r̄a /. en aꝗlla mañana dize ꝗ vido
5 vna ave blanca ꝗ se llama rabo de Junco
ꝗ no suele dormir en la mar /.

martes .18. de setiēbre
⸗ Navego aꝗl dia con su noche y andarian
y cinco
mas de çincuēta ∧leguas : p[er]o no asento
10 sino .48. llevava en todos estos dias mar
mȳ bonāca comō en el rio de sevilla /. Este
dia martin alōso cō la pinta ———[?] ꝗ era
al ~~almiᶜ~~ almiᶜ dsde su caravela
grā velera no esp[er]o porꝗ dixo ∧ ꝗ avia visto
grā multitud de aves yr hazia el poniē
15 te y ꝗ aꝗlla noche esp[er]ava ver t̄r̄r̄a y por eso
andava tanto /. apareçio a la p[ar]te del norte vna
grā çerrazon ꝗs señal de estar sobre la t̄r̄r̄a /.

pears to move and not the compasses. When
dawn came that Monday they saw much more vegetation and what seemed to be river weed, in
which they found a live crab that the Admiral
kept; and he says that those were sure signs
of land because they are not found [even] 80
leagues[1] from land. They found the seawater
less salty since leaving the Canaries and the
breezes always softer. Everyone went along
very happily and each ship sailed as fast as
it could so as to see land first. They saw
many dolphins[2] and the men of the *Niña* killed one.

4v The Admiral says here that those signs were
from the west where I hope in that mighty God
in Whose hands are all victories that very
soon He will give us land. On that morning he
says that he saw a white bird which is called
a tropic bird and which does not usually sleep
at sea.

Tuesday 18 September

He sailed that day and night and made more
than 55 leagues but set down only 48. On all
these days they had very calm seas, as in the
river at Seville. This day Martín Alonso,
with the *Pinta*, which was a great sailer, did
not wait, because he said to the Admiral from
his caravel[3] that he had seen a great multitude of birds going toward the west and that
that night he was hoping to see land, and for
that reason he was going so fast. There appeared in the north a large cloud mass, which
is a sign of being near land.

1. (4r37) Alvar (1976) reads the canceled text as *fuero*.
2. (4r42) *Tonina* (dolphin). See Morison (1963, 97, 16 Nov., n. 5) for this
identification. Columbus used the word *atún* for "tuna."
3. (4v13) *Al almirante desde su caravela* is an interlinear insert extending well into
the right margin.

miercoles .19. de setiembre

/ navego su camino y entre dia y noche anda

20   ria .xxv. leguas ~~escrivio~~ porq̃ tuviero calma
escrivio .xxii. Este dia a las diez oras vino a la
nao vn alcatraz y a la tarde vierō otro q̃ no suelen
apartarse .xx. leguas de tr̄ra /. ~~creyo~~ [?] ~~el almiᵉ~~
~~vierō~~ vinierō vnos llovizneros sin viento

25   lo q̃ es señal çierta de tierra /. no quiso dete
nerse ~~bal~~ [?] barloventeādo el almiᵉ p[ar]a averiguar
si avia tr̄ra mas de q̃ tuvo por çierto q̃ a la van
da dl norte y dl sur avia algunas Islas co
mo en la Vrdad lo estavā y el yva por me

30   dio dllas : porq̃ su volūtad era de seguir adlā
te hasta las yndias y el tp̄o es bueno porq̃
plaziēdo a dios a la buelta todo se veria . estas son
sus palabras /.   Aqui descubrierō sus
puntos los pilotos : el dla niña se hallava de

35   las canaria .440. leguas : el dla pinta .420.
el dla donde yva el almiᵉ .400. justas /.

Jueves .20. de setiēbre

/ navego este dia al gueste quarta del norue
ste y a la media p[ar]tida : porq̃ se mudarō mū

40   chos vientos cō la calma q̃ avia /. andarian
hasta siete /o ocho leguas /. vinierō a la nao
dos alcatraçes y dspues otro : q̃ fue señal destar
çerca de tr̄ra y vierō mūcha yerva avnq̃l dia pas
sado no avian visto della /. tomarō vn paxaro

Folio 5r

con la mano q̃ era comō garjao era paxaro
de rio y no de mar las pies tenia como
gaviota : vinierō al navio en amaneçiendo
————[?] ~~tres~~ dos /o tres paxaritos de tr̄ra Cantā

Wednesday 19 September

He sailed on his route and between day and
night made about 25 leagues because they
had light winds. He wrote down 22. On this
day at the tenth hour a booby[1] came to the
ship and in the afternoon they saw another;
they do not usually depart more than 20
leagues from land. Some drizzles of rain came
without wind, which is a sure sign of land.
The Admiral did not want to delay by beating
into the wind[2] to find out if there was land,
but he considered it certain that on the north
side and the south there were some islands (as
in truth there were and he was going in between them), because his purpose was to continue forward as far as the Indies, and the
weather was good. And, pleasing God, on the
way back all would be seen. These are his
words. Here the pilots revealed their estimates of position: the pilot of the *Niña* found
himself 440 leagues from the Canaries, the pilot of the *Pinta*, 420, and the pilot of the
ship in which the Admiral sailed, an even 400.

Thursday 20 September

This day he steered west by north and west-
northwest, because the winds shifted a lot in
the calm weather. They probably made no more
than seven or eight leagues. Two boobies came
to the ship and later another, which was a
sign of being near land, and they saw much
weed, although the day before they had not
5r   seen any. They caught a bird by hand
which was like a tern. It was a river bird,
not a seabird; it had feet like a gull's. At
dawn two or three[3] land birds[4] came to the

1. (4v22) *Alcatraz* can mean either a booby or a gannet. See Morison (1963, 55,
19 Sept., n. 1).
2. (4v26) *Barloventeando*, or "beating into the wind," is the word for the series of
zigzag courses (tacks) by which a sailing vessel advances against a wind.
3. (5r4) Alvar (1976) reads the canceled text as *vno o tres*.
4. (5r4) *Paxaritos de tierra*. Morison (1963, 56, 20 Sept., n. 2) omits "land"

5   do y despues antes dl Sol salido desapare
    çierō / dspues vino vn alcatraz venia del gues
    norueste yva al sueste q̃ era señal q̃
                                              q̃
    dexava la tr̄r̄a al guesnorueste por ∧ estas
    aves duermē en tr̄r̄a y por la mañana
10 vā a la mar a buscar su vida y ~~se-~~[?] no se
    alexā .xx. leguas /.

                                        Viernes .21. de setiēbre

    ⚹ aq̃l dia fue todo lo mas calma y dspues
    algun viento andarian entre dia y noche
15 dllo a la via y dello no hasta .13. leguas [/?]
    en amaneçiendo hallaro tanta yerva q̃
    pareçia ser la mar quajada dlla y venia del
    gueste . vierō vn alcatraz / la mar mȳ
    llana coōo vn rio y los ayres los me
20 jores dl mūdo /. vierō vna vallena q̃s
    señal q̃ estavan çerca de tr̄r̄a porq̃ siemp^r ——[?]
    andā çerca /.

                                        Sabado 22. de setiembre

    ⚹ Navego al guesnorueste mas o menos
25 acostandose a vna y a otra p[ar]te : andarian
    .xxx.
    ~~quatorze~~ leguas /. no vian quasi yerva
    vierō vnas pardelas y otra ave /. dize a
    qui el almiᵉ mucho me fue neçessario este
    viento contrario : porq̃ mi gente andavā mȳ
30 estimulados q̃ pensavā q̃ no ventavā en estos
    mares vientos p[ar]a bolver a españa /. ~~despues~~
    ~~vino pareçio mūcha yerva /~~ por vn peda
    daço de dia no ovo yerva : dspues mūy
    espessa /.

aqui comiença
a murmurar
la gēte del largo
viaje etc̄

35
                                        Domīgo .23. de setiembre

    ⚹ Navego al norueste y a las vezes a la quar
    ta del norte y ~~dello~~ a las vezes a su camino
    q̃ era el gueste y andaria hasta .xxvii. le

ship singing, and later, before sunrise,[1]
they disappeared. Later a booby came from the
west-northwest and went southeast, which was a
sign that it left land to the west-northwest,
because these birds sleep on land and in the
morning go out to sea to hunt for food and do
not go farther than 20 leagues from land.

Friday 21 September

That day was mostly calm and later some wind.
They made between day and night no more than
13 leagues, some of it on course and some not.
At dawn they found so much weed that the sea
appeared to be solid with it and it came from
the west. They saw a booby. The sea was very
smooth like a river, and the breezes the best
in the world. They saw a whale, which is a
sign that they were near land, because they
always go close.

Saturday 22 September

He steered west-northwest more or less, in-
clining to one side and the other; they made
about 30 leagues. They saw scarcely any weed.
They saw a few petrels and other birds. The
Admiral says here: this contrary wind was very
necessary for me, because my people were very
worked up thinking that in these seas winds
for returning to Spain did not blow. For a
portion of the day there was no weed; later it
was very thick.

Sunday 23 September

He steered northwest and at times northwest by
north and at times on his route, which was
west, and they made no more than 27 leagues.

---

from his translation, reasoning that it would be impossible to encounter land birds 900
miles from shore.
1. (5r5) Jane-Vigneras (1960) translates *antes dl Sol salido* as "before sunset."

guas /. vierō vna tortola : y vn alcatraz

40   y otro paxarito de rio y otras aves blancas

las yervas erā mūchas y hallavā cangrejos

~~mȳ~~

en ellas /. ~~la mar andava~~ ∧ ~~alta y sin viento /.~~

murmurava la   comō la mar estuviese māsa y llana : mur
[g]ente

Folio 5v

murava la gente diziēdo q̃ pues por

alli no avia mar grāde q̃ nūca ~~avria~~

~~viento~~ ventaria p[ar]a bolver a españa /.

p[er]o dspues alçose mūcho la mar y sin

5   viento q̃ los asombrava / por lo qual dize

aqui el almiᵉ asi que mȳ neçessario

me fue la mar alta q̃ no pareçio

nõ   salvo el tp̄o dlos judios quādo salieron

de egipto contra moysen q̃ los sacava de

10   captiverio /.

lunes .24. de setiēbre

ʎ Navego a su camino al gueste dia y noche

y andarian quatorze leguas y media : Con

to doze /. vino al navio ~~y~~-[?] vn alcatraz y vie

15   rō mūchas pardelas /.

martes .25. de setiēbre

ʎ Esta dia ovo mūcha calma y dspues vēto

y fuerō su camino al gueste hasta la no

che /. yva hablādo el almiᵉ cō martin alō

——[?]

20   so pinçon capitan dla otra caravela pinta sobre

tres dias avia

vna C[ar]ta q̃ le avia enbiado ∧a la caravela don

nota sobre   de segud pareçe tenia pintadas el almiᵉ cier
esta carta

tas yslas por aq̃lla mar : y dezia el mar

tin alonso q̃ estavā en aq̃lla comarca y res

25   pōdia el almiᵉ q̃ asi le pareçia a el : ——[?]

pero puesto q̃ no [Vr?] oviesen dado con ellas

lo devia de aVr causado las corrientes q̃

They saw a dove and a booby and another small
river bird and other white birds. The weed
was plentiful and they found crabs in it.
Since the sea had been calm and smooth the men

5v   complained, saying that since in that region
there were no rough seas, it would never blow
for a return to Spain. But later the sea rose
high and without wind, which astonished them,
because of which the Admiral says here that
the high sea was very necessary for me, [a
sign] which had not appeared except in the
time of the Jews when they left Egypt [and
complained] [1] against Moses, who took them out
of captivity.

Monday 24 September

He steered on his route west day and night and
they made about fourteen leagues and a half; he reported 12. A booby came to the ship and they
saw many petrels.

Tuesday 25 September

This day there was much calm and later it blew
and they went on their way west until night.
The Admiral began talking to Martín Alonso
Pinzón, captain of the other caravel, *Pinta*,
about a chart that he had sent to him on the
caravel three days before, on which the Admiral had apparently drawn certain islands in
that sea; and Martín Alonso said that they
were in that region and the Admiral answered
that so it seemed to him, but since they had
not encountered them it must have been caused
by the currents which always had driven the
vessels northeast and that they had not traveled as far as the pilots said. And at this

1. (5v7–9) The bracketed words in the translation of these lines were supplied
from Las Casas's *Historia* (1951, 1:189).

siemp^r [a?]vian echado los navios al nor
deste y q̃ no avian andado tanto cõmo los
30   pilotos deziã /. y estando en esto dixole el al
mirãte q̃ le enbiase la carta d̃ha /. y enbia
da cõ alguna cuerda comẽço el almi^e a
cartear en ella cõ su piloto y marineros /

al[onso]

al Sol puesto / subio el m[art]in ∧ en la popa
35   de su navio y con mũcha alegria llamo al
almi^e pidiendole albriçias q̃ via tr̄r̄a /. y

con afirmacion

alegro de tr̄r̄a   quãdo se lo oyo dezir ∧el almi. dize q̃ se echo
por m[art]in   a dar grãs a nr̄o señor de rodillas y el
al[ons]o p[er]o m[art]in aloṡo dezia gloria in excelsis deo con
no lo era
40   su gente /. lo mismo hizo la gẽte del almi^e

todos

y los de la niña /. subierõse ∧sobre el mastel
y en la xarçia y todos affirmarõ q̃ era tr̄r̄a y
al almi^e asi pareçio y q̃ avria a ella .25. leguas /.
estuvierõ hasta la noche affirmãdo todos ser tr̄r̄a :

Folio 6r

mãdo el almi^e dexar su camino q̃ era el gues
te y q̃ fuesen todos al sudueste adonde avia
pareçido la tr̄r̄a / avrian andado aq̃l dia al

en

gueste 4º. leguas y media y ∧ la noche al su
5   deste .17. leguas q̃ son .xxi. puesto q̃ de[z]ia

finxia

a la gente .13. leguas /. porq̃ siemp^r ∧ ~~dezia~~ [?] a la
gente q̃ hazia poco camino : porq̃ no les pare
çiese largo /. por mařa q̃ ~~dezia~~ [?] escrivio
por dos caminos aq̃l viaje : el menor fue
10   el fingido : y el mayor el Vrdadero /.
anduvo la mar mȳ llana por lo qual se echa
rõ a nadar mũchos marineros /. vierõn
mũchos dorados y otros peçes /.

point the Admiral said to send the said chart
to him.   And it having been sent over by means
of some cord, the Admiral began to plot their
position on it with his pilot and sailors.   At
sunset Martín Alonso went up on the poop of
his vessel and with much joy called to the
Admiral asking him for a reward:[1] that he saw
land.   And when he heard this said and affirmed,[2] the Admiral says that he threw himself on his knees to give thanks to Our Lord,
and Martín Alonso and his men said *Gloria in
excelsis deo*.   The Admiral's men and those of
the *Niña* did the same.   They all climbed the
masts and into the rigging and all affirmed
that it was land, and so it appeared to the
Admiral, and that it was about 25 leagues off.
Until night everybody continued to affirm it
to be land.   The Admiral ordered the ships

6r   to leave their course, which was west,
and for all of them to go southwest where
the land had appeared.   They had gone that
day about four leagues and a half and during
the night 17 leagues southeast,[3] which makes
21, although he told the men 13 leagues, because he always pretended to the men that
they were making little way so the voyage
would not appear long to them.   So he wrote
that voyage in two ways: the shorter was the
pretended; and the longer, the true.   The sea
became very calm, because of which many sailors went swimming.   They saw many *dorados*[4] and
other fish.

1.   (5v36)   *Albriçias* are a reward to the person who first brings good news.
2.   (5v37)   *Con afirmacion*.   Alvar (1976) is the only editor who disagrees with
this reading of the manusript, writing *al dicho martin* instead of *con afirmacion* and
adding an elaborate note of justification. Either reading of this difficult passage requires
the inclusion of the loop of the *l* in *el* (line 5v38), in our reading as part of the *f* of
afirmacion, and in Alvar's reading as part of the *h* in *dho*. We do not see the *al* or the
d of *dho* that Alvar sees at the beginning of the interlineation.
3.   (6r4–5)   *Sudeste* (southeast) is an error for *sudueste* (southwest), as is shown
by the addition of four and a half leagues "west" and 17 leagues "southeast" to compute
the total distance made good.
4.   (6r13)   *Dorados*.   See Morison (1963, 57 n. 4) for identification of this fish.
In the West Indies and Florida, the *dorado* was known also as "dolphin."   To avoid
confusion, we have left the word untranslated.

15   ⁒ Navego a su camino al gueste ~~çinco millas por~~

dia

~~ora~~-[?] hasta dspues de medio ∧: de alli fuerō

al sudueste hasta cognosçer q̃ lo q̃ dezian

q̃ avia sido tr̄r̄a no lo era sino çielo / andu

vierō dia y noche .31. leguas / y conto a la gē

20   te .24º. la mar era comō vn rio los ayres

dulçes y suauissimos /.

⁒ Navego a su via al gueste anduvo entre dia y

noche .24. leguas : conto a la gēte .20. leguas /.

25   vinierō muchos dorados / matarō vno / vie

rō vn rabo de junco /.

⁒ navego a su camino al gueste : anduvierō dia

y noche cō calmas .14. leguas cōto treze /.

30   hallarō poca yerva : tomarō dos peçes dora

dos / y en los otros navios mas /.

⁒ navego a su camino al gueste anduvierō .24.

leguas Conto a la gente .xxi. por calmas que

35   tuvierō anduvierō entre dia y noche poco /.

rabi

vierō vn ave q̃ se llama ∧ forçado q̃ haze gomitar

a los alcatraçes lo q̃ comen ~~por~~-[?] p[ar]a comerlo

ella y no se mātiene de otra cosa /. es ave dla

mar p[er]o no posa en la mar ni se ap[ar]ta de

40   de tr̄r̄a .20. leguas /. ay destas muchas en las

islas de cabo verde /. despues vierō dos alcatra

ces /. los aygres erā mȳ dulçes y sabrosos

q̃ diz q̃ no faltava sino oyr el ruyseñor

Wednesday 26 September

He steered on his route west until after midday. From there they went southwest until
they recognized that what they had been saying
was land was not land but sky. Day and night
they made 31 leagues, and he told the men 24.
The sea was like a river; the breezes sweet
and very soft.

Thursday 27 September

He steered on his way to the west. He made
between day and night 24 leagues; he told the
men 20 leagues. Many *dorados* came. They
killed one. They saw a tropic bird.

Friday 28 September

He steered on his route to the west. With
light winds, they made day and night 14
leagues; he reported 13. They found little
weed. They caught two *dorados*, and on the
other vessels more.

Saturday 29 September

He steered on his route west. They made 24
leagues. He told the men 21. Because of
calms that they had, they made little way day
and night. They saw a bird that is called a
frigate bird,[1] which makes the boobies throw
up what they eat in order[2] to eat it herself,
and she does not sustain herself on anything
else. It is a seabird, but it does not alight
on the sea nor depart from land 20 leagues.
There are many of these in the islands of Cape
Verde. Later they saw two boobies. The
breezes were very sweet and good smelling and
he says that nothing was missing but to hear
the nightingale; and the sea was smooth as a

1. (6r36) *Rabiforçado* (frigate bird). See Morison (1963, 58, 29 Sept., n. 1).
2. (6r37) Alvar (1976) reads the canceled text as *para*.

Folio 6v

y la mar llana como vn rio / pareçierō dspues
en tres vezes tres alcatraçes /. ~~vierō mūcha yerva~~
y vn forçado : vierō mucha yerva /.

Domingo .30. de setiembre

5   Λ Navego su camino al gueste anduvo entre dia
y noche por las calmas .14. leguas conto on
ze /. vinierō al ~~a nao~~ [?] navio quatro rabos de
Junco q̃s grā señal de tr̄r̄a /. porq̃ tantas aves
de vna naturaleza juntas es señal q̃ no ~~se~~
10   andan desmādadas ni p[er]didas /. vierōse qua
tro alcatraçes en dos vezes : yerva mūcha /.
Nota q̃ las estrellas q̃ se llaman las guardias
quādo anocheçe estan junto al braço de la p[ar]te del
poniente : y quādo amaneçe estan en la linea
15   debaxo dl braço al nordeste : q̃ pareçe q̃ en toda
la noche no andā saluo tres lineas q̃ son ——[?] .9.
oras / y esto cada noche /. esto dize aqui el almiͤ

6v   river. Later three boobies appeared three
        times, and a frigate bird.[1] They saw much weed.

Sunday 30 September

He steered on his route west. He made between
day and night, because of calms, 14 leagues.
He reported 11. There came to the vessel[2]
four tropic birds, which is a great sign of
land because so many birds of one kind together is a sign that they have not wandered
from the flock and are not lost. They sighted
four boobies two different times. There was
much weed. He notes that the stars called
the Guards, when night falls, are next to the
arm on the west side, and when it dawns are on
the line under the arm to the northeast; for
it appears that in the whole night they move
but three lines, which is nine hours; and this
every night.[3] Also the Admiral says here

---

1. (6v3) *Forçado* is an error for *forcado*, which has the same meaning as *rabifor-cado*. See p. 45, n. 1.

2. (6v7) Alvar (1976) misreads the cancellation as *navio*. Las Casas first wrote *ala nao*, then crossed out everything but *al*.

3. (6v12–17) *Nota que las estrellas . . . y esto cada noche*. The word "northeast" (*nordeste*) in this sentence (6v15) should probably read "east" (*este*). The phrases "three lines" (*tres lineas*) and "nine hours" (*.9. oras*) also seem to be in error. The text is referring to the "regiment of the North Star," i.e., to the way in which the positions of the Guard Stars of the Little Dipper (the leading edge of the bowl) were used as a 24-hour clock and to provide a correction for estimating the position of the pole relative to the elevation of the North Star. During each 24-hour day the Guards move counter-clockwise around the pole, gaining about 1°, or four minutes of time, each day, making it necessary to use a table or an instrument called the "nocturnal" to compensate for the changing position of the Guards at midnight when estimating the hour. Garcia de Palacio's revision of the regiment of the North Star to the Gregorian calendar (Palacio 1944, 41) gives a convenient reference point, placing the Guard Stars straight above Polaris (in the head of an imaginary man, with arms stretching east and west, centered at Polaris) at midnight at the end of April. On 30 September (10 October, Gregorian), 163 days later, the midnight position of the Guards would have moved about 163° from this reference position to approximately S by W on a superimposed compass card. This same day (10 October, Gregorian), at Columbus's latitude, of 27°15′N (estimated by McElroy 1941, 223), sunrise and sunset were at about 6:11 A.M. and 5:43 P.M. local solar time, respectively. Adding 45 minutes to both ends of the day to account for dusk puts the minimum duration of night (when the Guards, which are not very bright, can just be seen) at about 11 hours. Thus, at the fall of darkness on this same date, the Guards were almost 40 minutes of time above west, not quite to W by N, but in "the arm on the west side." Eleven hours later, at about dawn, the Guards were located about 1 hour and 40 minutes below east (the man's right arm), just below the ESE rhumb. Clearly, the text is confused. With reference to the regiment of the North Star, a line represents three hours. Thus, if one were to read "east" for the "northeast" of the text, then "the line under the arm to the east" would be "southeast." In this

nō   tābien en anocheçiendo las agujas norueste
            an vna quarta : y en amaneçiēdo estā con la estre
20   lla justo /. por lo qual pareçe q̃ la estrella haze
            movimiº / como las otras estrellas : y las agu
            jas piden siempr la Vrdad /.

                                                        Lunes .1º. de otubre

            ⫽ Navego su camino al gueste anduviērō .25.
25   leguas conto a la gente .20. leguas /. tuviērō
            grāde aguaçero /. el piloto dl almiᶜ tenia oy
            en amaneçiendo q̃ avian andado dsde la isla
            dl hierro hasta aqui .578. leguas al gueste /.
            la cuēta menor q̃ el almiᶜ mostrava a la gē
30   te erā .584. p[er]o la Vrdadera q̃l almiᶜ juz
            gava y guardava erā .707.

                                                        Martes .2. de otubre

            ⫽ Navego a su camino al gueste noche y dia
            .39. leguas : conto a la gēte obra de .30. leguas
                              na
35   la mar llana y bue∧ siempr a dios mūchas gra
            çias sean dadas dixo aqui el almiᶜ yerva
            venia de leste a gueste por el contrario dlo q̃
            solia /. pareçierō mūchos peçes : matose vno
            vierō vn ave blanca q̃ pareçia gaviota /.

[that] when night comes the compasses northwest one-quarter [i.e., one compass point, or
eleven and one-quarter degrees],[1] and when dawn
comes they coincide with the North Star exactly. Because of this it seems that the Star
moves like the other stars, and the compasses
always seek the truth [i.e., true north].

Monday 1 October

He steered on his route west. They made 25
leagues. He told the men 20 leagues. They
had a big rain squall. The Admiral's pilot
held at dawn today that they had made up to
this point 578 leagues west from the island of
Hierro. The smaller account that the Admiral
showed to the men was 584. But the true
account that the Admiral figured and kept to
himself was 707.

Tuesday 2 October

He steered on his route west 39 leagues night
and day; he told the men about 30 leagues.
The sea was always smooth and good, many
thanks be given to God always, the Admiral
said here. Weed was coming from east to west,
contrary to its usual direction. Many fish
appeared; one was killed. They saw a white
bird that appeared to be a gull.

---

event there would be "three lines," or "nine hours," between the western arm and one
line below the eastern arm (i.e., SE). Whatever the correct explanation, it seems absurd
to believe that the Admiral would have thought the 11-hour night lasted only 9 hours.
See Morison (1963, 59 n. 2).

    1. (6v18–22) *Las agujas . . . la Vrdad.* This and earlier discussions (see p. 31,
n. 2) of the difference in compass readings at night and at dawn cannot be explained by
compass variation as it is known today. One would not expect the magnetic variation
to change by more than 11° this far from the magnetic pole in the course of a half day's
sail—say, 60 miles. If the explanation is not the apparent revolution of Polaris around
the celestial pole, it seems likely that the compass was accidently moved too close to a
keg of nails or some other large ferrous mass (e.g., a lombard, gun, sword, knife, belt
buckle, etc.) when it was moved from the protection of the binnacle (a chest or cabinet)
to the open deck for a clear view of the sky.

40   miercoles .3. de otubre

/ Navego su via ordinaria anduvierō .47. leguas

Folio 7r

conto a la gente .40. leguas   aparecierō par
delas : yerva mūcha alguna mȳ vieja y
otra mȳ fresca y traya comō fruta [/.?] no vie
rō aves algunas y creya el almiᵉ que

nõ   5   le quedavā atras las islas q̃ traya pinta
das en su C[ar]ta /.

                                         se
/ dize aqui el almiᵉ que no∧quiso detener barlovēteā
do la semana passada y estos dias q̃ via tantas señales
de tr̄r̄a avnq̃ tenia notiçia de çiertas islas en a

10   q̃lla comarca : por no se detener : pues su fin era
                                si
passar a las yndias y ∧ se detuviera dize el q̃ no
fuera buē seso /.

                                                   Jueves .4º. de otubre

/ Navego a su camino al gueste anduvierō

15   entre dia y noche .63. leguas conto a la
gente .46. leguas   vinierō al navio mas
de quarēta pardales juntos y dos alcatraçes
y al vno dio vna pedrada vn moço dla cara
vela /. vino a la nao vn rabiforçado y vna

20   blanca como gaviota /.

                                                   viernes .5º. de otubre

/ Navego a su camino andarian onze millas
por ora / por noche y dia andarian .57. le
guas porq̃ afloxo la noche algo el viento /.

25   conto a su gente 45. la mar bonāço y llana
a dios   dize muchas grās sean dadas : el ayre
mȳ dulçe y tēprado yerva ninguᵃ aves
pardelas mūchas peces golōdrinos volarō
en la nao mūchos /.

Wednesday 3 October

7r   He steered his usual course. They made 47
leagues. He told the men 40. Petrels appeared. There was much weed, some very old
and other very fresh, and it bore something
like fruit. They did not see any birds and
the Admiral believed that the islands drawn on
his chart lay behind him.

The[1] Admiral says here that he did not want
to delay by beating into the wind the past
week and on these days when he was seeing so
many signs of land, even though he had information about certain islands in that region.
[This was] in order not to delay, since his
objective was to pass to the Indies; and if he
were to delay, he says, it would not make good sense.

Thursday 4 October

He steered on his route to the west. They
made 63 leagues between day and night. He
told the men 46 leagues. There came to the
vessel more than 40 petrels together, and two
boobies, and a ship's boy of the caravel hit
one with a stone. A frigate bird came to the
ship, and a white bird like a gull.

Friday 5 October

He steered on his route. They made about 11
miles per hour. Through day and night they
made about 57 leagues because at night the
wind weakened[2] somewhat. He told his men 45.
The sea was tranquil and smooth, many thanks
be given to God, he says. The breeze [was]
very sweet and temperate. No weed. Many petrels. Many flying fish flew into the ship.

---

1. (7r7) The left margin of this paragraph is placed farther to the left than the
rest of those in the manuscript.

2. (7r24) Jane-Vigneras (1960) mistranslates the word *afloxo* (weakened) as
"freshened." See *Diccionario* (1956), *aflojar*.

30

⎰ Navego su camino al vueste /o gueste q̃s lo
mismo : anduvierō .40. leguas entre dia
y noche   conto a la gēte .33. leguas /.
Esta noche dixo m[art]īn alonso q̃ seria bien na

35 vegar a la ~~4ª~~ [?] quarta del gueste a la parte dl
sudueste : y al almi͠e pareçio q̃ ~~mart~~ dezia esto
m[art]īn alonso por la Isla de çipango : y el
     via
almi͠e ~~dezia~~ q̃ si la erravā q̃ no pudieran
tan presto tomar tr̄r̄a : y q̃ era mejor vna

40 vez yr a la tr̄r̄a firme y despues a las Islas /.

⎰ Navego a su camino el gueste : anduvierō
    millas
.12º ~~leguas~~ por ora [dos?] oras y despues .8º.

Folio 7v

              ora
millas por ora y andaria hasta vna ∧ de Sol
23 leguas conto a la gete .18. en este dia
~~en la mañana~~ [?] al levantar d[l?] Sol la caravela
niña q̃ yva delante por ser velera y anda

5 vā quiē mas podia por ver primero tr̄r̄a
por gozar dla m[erce]d [q̃?] l[os?] reyes a quiē prime
ro la viese avia prometido : levanto vna
vād[e]ra en el topo del mastel y tyro vna
lōbarda por señal q̃ vian tr̄r̄a (porq̃ asi lo

10 avia ordenado el almi͠e   tenia tābien orde
nado que al salir dl sol y al ponerse se jun
tasen todos los navios con el / porq̃ estos
dos tp̄os son mas proprios p[ar]a q̃ los humo
res den mas lugar a ver mas lexos /.

15 Com̄o en la tarde no viesen tr̄r̄a la q̃ pensa
van los dla caravela niña q̃ avian visto :
y porq̃ passavā grā multitud de aves dla

Saturday 6 October

He steered on his route to the *vueste* [west]
or *gueste*, which is the same thing. They made
40 leagues between day and night. He told the
men 33 leagues. Tonight Martín Alonso said
that it would be well to steer southwest by
west; and to the Admiral it seemed that Martín Alonso said this because of the island of
Cipango;[1] and the Admiral saw that if they
missed it they would not be able to strike
land so quickly and that it was better to go
at once to the mainland and afterward to the islands.

Sunday 7 October

He steered on his route west; they made 12
miles per hour [for] two hours and later eight
7v   miles per hour, and they made about 23
leagues up until one hour of sun. He told the
men 18. On this day at sunrise the caravel
Niña, which was going on ahead because she was
a fast sailer (and all of them were going as
fast as they could to see land first and to
enjoy the reward that the sovereigns had promised to the one who first might see it) raised
a flag to the top of the mast and fired a lombard[2] as a signal that they saw land, because
so had ordered the Admiral. He had also ordered that at sunrise and sunset the vessels
should join him, because these two times are
when the atmosphere provides the opportunity
to see farthest. Since in the afternoon they
had not seen the land that the men of the caravel *Niña* thought they had seen; and because
great multitudes of birds were passing from

1. (7r36–37) *Y al almirante . . . çipango.* Jane-Vigneras (1960) translates this
clause as "and the Admiral thought that Martin Alonso did not say this on account of
the island of Cipangu." Alvar (1976) reads the manuscript as *y el almirante pareçio que
no. Dezia esto Martin Alonso por . . . .* We believe that the word preceding *dezia* was
intended to be *Martin*, not *no*, but was crossed out before being completed. Çipango"
is Japan.
2. (7v9) *Lombarda.* A lombard was a small cannon with a range at that time of
some 300 yards (Martinez-Hidalgo 1966, 67). Morison (1963, 61, 7 Oct., n. 2)
thought that its range was 800 to 1,000 yards.

p[ar]te del norte al sudueste por lo qual era
de creer q̃ se yvā a dormir a tr̄ra /o huyan
20 quiça dl invierno q̃ en las tr̄ras de donde
venian devia de querer venir /. + por esto
el almi͛ acordo dexar el camino del gue
este : y pone la proa hazia guesueste con
determinaçion de andar dos dias por aq̃lla
~~antes v[n?]~~
25 via /. esto comēço∧ ~~sol puesto~~ antes vna
ora del sol puesto /. ~~moviale tābien las~~
~~porq̃ las aves~~ andaria en toda la noche
obra de çinco leguas : y .xxiii. del dia : fuerō
por todas veynte y ocho leguas noche y dia /.

a. porq̃ sabia el al
b. mirāte q̃ las
c. mas dlas islas
d. q̃ tienē los por[tu]
e. gueses : por la[s]
f. aves las descu
g. brierō

30   Lunes .8. de otubre

⫽ Navego al guesudueste y andariā entre
dia y noche onze leguas y media /o doze
y a [ratos?] pareçe q̃ anduvierō en la noche quin
millas
ze ~~leguas~~ por ora sino esta mētirosa la
35 letra /. ——[?] tuvierō la mar cōmo el rio de sevi
lla ~~los ayres~~ [?] grās a dios dize el almi͛ los
ayres mȳ dulces cōmo en abril en sevilla q̃s
plazer estar a ellos tā olorosos son /. parecio
de campo y tomarō vno :
la yerva mȳ fresca : muchos paxaritos ∧ q̃ yvā
40 huyēdo al sudueste grajaos y anades /
y vn alcatraz /.

north to southwest, which made it seem likely
that they were flying off to sleep on land,
or perhaps were fleeing from the winter,
which, in the land from which they were
coming, must be about to arrive; and [also]
because the Admiral knew that most of the
islands that the Portuguese hold they discovered through birds,[1] the Admiral agreed
to leave the route west and head west-southeast[2] with the intent to go two days on that
course. This he began[3] one hour before sunset. He made during the whole night about
five leagues, and 23 by day; overall they
went 28 leagues night and day.

Monday 8 October

He steered west-southwest and they made between day and night eleven and a half or 12
leagues, and at times it seems that during the
night they traveled 15 miles per hour if the
writing is not in error. They had a sea like
the river of Seville, thanks to God, the Admiral says, and the breezes as sweet as in
April in Seville, so that it is a pleasure to
be in them they are so fragrant. The weed
seemed very fresh. [There were] many small
land birds, and they caught one.[4] Crows and
ducks[5] were flying off to the southwest, and
one booby.

1. (7v21a–g) *Porque sabia . . . las descubrieron.* This insert appears in the right
margin of the manuscript with a line drawn to a plus sign above the full stop after *venir*
(7v21).

2. (7v23) *Guesueste* (west-southeast). West-southwest is probably the intended
bearing. A note in Jane-Vigneras (1960) indicates that Navarrete (1825–29) was the
first to correct this error.

3. (7v25) Alvar (1976) reads the second cancellation in this line as *con el sol puesto*.

4. (7v39) The insert *de campo y tomaron vno* extends well into the right margin of
the manuscript.

5. (7v40) *Grajaos y anades.* Morison (1963, 8 Oct., n. 2) believes it possible
that *garxao* (*garajao*), a "tern," was intended instead of *grajaos,* "crows." *Anades* is a
generic word for "ducks."

⁄ Navego al sudueste anduvo .5. leguas : mudose
el viento y ~~fue~~-[?] corrio al gueste quarta al norueste
45   ~~deste~~ y anduvo [4?]. leguas : despues cō todas .xi.

Folio 8r

leguas de dia   y a la noche .xx. legua[s]
y media /. conto a la gente .17. legu[a][s?] /
toda la noche oyerō passar paxaros /.

5   § Navego al ~~guesueste~~ guesudueste : anduvie
ro a diez ~~le~~-[?] millas por ora y a ratos
.12. y algu rato a .7. y entre dia y noche
5[9?] leguas : conto a la gēte .44. leguas no
nō   mas /. Aqui la gente ya no lo podia
10   çufrir : quexavase del largo viaje : p[er]o el
almi͠e los esforço lo mejor q̃ pudo dādoles
buena esperāça de los provechos q̃ podrian
aver /. y añidia q̃ por demas era quexar
                    el
se ~~cōmo~~-[?] pues q̃ ∧avia venido a las yndias
15   y q̃ asi lo avia de proseguir hasta hallar
las / con el ayuda de nr̄o Señor /.

§ Navego al guesudueste tuvierō mucha
mar
~~mas~~ mas q̃ en todo el viaje avian te
20   nido /. vierō pardelas y vn junco verde
junto a la nao /. vierō los dla Caravela pin
ta vña Caña y vn palo : y tomaro otro
palillo labrado a lo q̃ pareçia con hyerro
y vn pedaço de Caña : y otra yerva q̃ nace
25   en tierra : y vna tab[l?]illa /. los dla Carave
la niña tābien vierō otras señales de
tr̄ra y vn palillo cargado descaramojos : cō
estas señales respirarō y alegrarōse todos /.

Tuesday 9 October

He steered southwest [and] made five leagues.
The wind changed and he ran west by north[1] and
made four leagues: afterward, in all, 11

8r   by day and at night twenty leagues and a
half. He told the men 17 leagues. All night
they heard birds pass.

Wednesday 10 October

He steered west-southwest; they traveled ten
miles per hour and at times 12 and for a time
seven and between day and night made 59[2]
leagues; he told the men only 44 leagues.
Here the men could no longer stand it; they
complained of the long voyage. But the Admiral encouraged them as best he could, giving
them good hope of the benefits that they would
be able to secure. And he added that it was
useless to complain since he had come to find
the Indies and thus had to continue the voyage
until he found them, with the help of Our Lord.

Thursday 11 October[3]

He steered west-southwest. They took much
water aboard, more than they had taken in the
whole voyage. They saw petrels and a green
bulrush near the ship. The men of the caravel
Pinta saw a cane and a stick, and took on
board another small stick that appeared to
have been worked with iron, and a piece of
cane, and other vegetation originating on
land, and a small plank. The men of the caravel *Niña* also saw other signs of land and a
small stick loaded with barnacles.[4] With these
signs everyone breathed more easily and

1. (7v45) Alvar (1976) reads the canceled text in this line as *de to*.
2. (8r8) The numerals 5 and 9 in the manuscript are both incomplete, the 9 very
much so. However, all Spanish editions consulted report the same figure.
3. (8r17) The entry under the date 11 October includes the events of 12 October,
when land was first sighted.
4. (8r27) The word *escaramojos* (barnacles) also may designate a wild rose, as
Morison (1963) translates, but that meaning seems unlikely in this context.

Anduvierō en este dia hasta puesto el sol
30   .27. leguas /.
§ despues dl Sol puesto navego a su primer
camino al gueste : andarian doze ~~leguas~~ millas

hallan ya   cada ora y hasta dos oras despues de media
tierra   noche andariā .90. millas q̃ son .22. leguas
35   y media /. y porq̃ la Caravela pinta era
mas velera e yva delante dl almirāte
hallo tierra y hizo las señas q̃l almiᶜ avia
mādado /. esta tr̄r̄a vido primero vn mari
nero q̃ se dezia Rodrigo de triana : puesto q̃
40   el almiᶜ a las diez dla noche   Estando enl
castillo de popa vido lūbre avnq̃ fue cosa
tan çerrada q̃ no quiso affirmar q fuese
tr̄r̄a /. pero llamo a pero gutierrez repostero

Folio 8v

destrados dl Rey e dixole q̃ parecia lūbre : q̃
mirasse el y asi lo hizo y vidola : dixolo tābiē
a Rodrigo sanches de segovia q̃l Rey y la Rey
na enviavā en el armada por veedor el qual
5   no vido nada porq̃ no estava en lugar do la
pudiese ver /. desp[ues?] q̃l almiᶜ lo dixo se
vido vna vez /o dos : y era comō vna candeli
lla de Cera q̃ se alçava y levātava [/?] lo qual
a pocos pareçiera ser indiçio de tr̄r̄a /. pero el al
10   mirāte tuvo por çierto estar ~~muy~~ junto a la
tierra /. por lo qual quādo dixerō la salue

cheered up. On this day, up to sunset, they
made 27 leagues.

After sunset he steered on his former course
to the west. They made about 12 miles[1] each
hour and, until two hours after midnight,[2]
made about 90 miles, which is twenty-two
leagues and a half. And because the caravel
Pinta was a better sailer and went ahead
of the Admiral it found land[3] and made the
signals that the Admiral had ordered. A
sailor named Rodrigo de Triana saw this
land first, although the Admiral, at the
tenth hour of the night, while he was on the
sterncastle, saw a light, although it was
something so faint that he did not wish to
affirm that it was land. But he called

8v Pero Gutiérrez, the steward of the king's
dais, and told him that there seemed to be
a light, and for him to look: and thus he
did and saw it. He also told Rodrigo Sánchez
de Segovia, whom the king and queen were sending as *veedor*[4] of the fleet, who saw nothing
because he was not in a place where he could
see it. After the Admiral said it, it was
seen once or twice; and it was like a small
wax candle that rose and lifted up, which to
few seemed to be an indication of land. But
the Admiral was certain that they were near
land, because of which when they recited the

1. (8r32) The word *millas* extends the line into the right margin. It was probably added after the next line was written and the need for the correction from *leguas*
to *millas* was noted. Las Casas substitutes *millas* for *leguas* 12 times in the *Diario* (at
3r31, 7r43, 7v34, 8r6, 8r32, 17v42, 32v33, 54v44, 57v25, 59v7, 60r25, and 60r45),
but never makes the opposite substitution.

2. (8r33–34) Jane-Vigneras (1960) mistranslates the passage *hasta dos oras despues de media noche* (until two hours after midnight) as "up to two hours before
midnight."   After sunset the fleet made 90 miles at 12 miles per hour. Elapsed time
was seven and a half (90/12) hours. Sunset was at 5:40 P.M. local solar time on 11
October (Julian calendar). Adding 45 minutes for dusk, night began at about 6:30
P.M. Seven and a half hours later the time would have been 2:00 A.M. So the physics
and the language are consistent.

3. (8r37) *Hallo tierra.* The importance of this passage is signaled by the figure
of a hand drawn in the left margin, with the index finger pointing to line 31, and by
Las Casas's marginal note: *hallan ya tierra.* Also see pp. 60–61.

4. (8v4) Morison (1963, 63) translates *veedor* as "comptroller." A note in Jane-
Vigneras (1960) indicates that the *veedor* was appointed by the sovereigns to record all
gold, gems, and spices found, to ensure against cheating.

Las Casas Manuscript, folio 8r. Reproduced by permission of the National Library, Madrid, Spain. Also see p. 59, n. 3.

Margin note:

Salio el almyrate
y los de mas en
la primera ysla d[e]
las yndias tier-
nes de mañana
a 12. de otubre
de 1492.

q̃ la acostūbrā dezir e cantar a su mařa

                            rogo y

todos los marineros y se hallan todos : ˄a

monestolos el almiᵉ q̃ hiziesen buena guar

15 da al castillo de proa y mirasen bien por la

tr̄r̄a : y q̃ al q̃ le dixese primero q̃ via tr̄r̄a

le daria luego vn Jubon de ——[?] seda : sin

las otras m[erce]d[e]s que los reyes avian prome

tido que erā diez mill m[araved]īs de juro a quien

20 primero la viese /. a las dos oras despues

de media noche pareçio la tr̄r̄a dla qual esta

rian dos leguas /. amaynarō todas las velas

y quedarō con el treo que es la vela grade

sin bonetas y pusierōse a la Corda tempo

                viernes

25 rizādo hasta el dia ˄q̃ llegarō a vna Isleta

dlos lucayos q̃ se llamava en lengua de

yndios guanahani /. luego vierō gente ds

nuda : y el almiᵉ salio a tr̄r̄a en la barca arma

da : y martin alonso pincon y viçeynte anes

su hrᵒ q̃ era capitan dla niña /. Saco el almiᵉ

la vandera real : y los capitanes con dos

vanderas dla cruz verde : q̃ llevava el al

mirāte en todos los navios por seña : co

vna .f. y vna .y. ençima s̶u̶ de cada letra

35 su corona vna de vn cabo dla .✝. y otra

      [asi?]   vieron

de otro /. puestos en tr̄r̄a l̶l̶e̶g̶a̶r̶ō̶ ̶a̶ ̶v̶n̶o̶s̶

arboles mȳ verdes : y aguas mūchas

y frutas de diversas mařas /. El almiᵉ

llamo a los dos capitanes y a los demas

40 q̃ saltarō en tr̄r̄a y a Rodrigo descobedo

escrivano de toda el armada y a Rodrigo

Salio el almirate
y los demas [e?]n
la primera tr̄r̄a de
las yndias vier
nes de mañana
a .12. de otubre
de 1492

Salve, which sailors in their own way are
accustomed to recite and sing, all being present, the Admiral entreated and admonished
them to keep a good lookout on the forecastle
and to watch carefully for land; and that to
the man who first told him that he saw land he
would later give a silk jacket in addition to
the other rewards that the sovereigns had
promised, which were ten thousand *maravedís*[1]
as an annuity to whoever should see it first.
At two hours after midnight the land appeared,
from which they were about two leagues distant. They hauled down[2] all the sails and
kept only the *treo*, which is the mainsail
without bonnets, and jogged on and off,[3] passing time until daylight Friday, when they
reached an islet of the Lucayas, which was
called Guanahani in the language of the Indians. Soon they saw naked people; and the
Admiral went ashore in the armed launch, and
Martín Alonso Pinzón and his brother Vicente
Anes,[4] who was captain of the *Niña*. The Admiral brought out the royal banner and the
captains two flags with the green cross, which
the Admiral carried on all the ships as a
standard, with an F and a Y, and over each
letter a crown, one on one side of the ✝ and
the other on the other. Thus put ashore they
saw very green trees and many ponds and
fruits of various kinds. The Admiral called
to the two captains and to the others who had
jumped ashore and to Rodrigo Descobedo, the
escrivano[5] of the whole fleet, and to Rodrigo

1. (8v19) A *maravedí* was a copper coin valued at two *blancas*, or 375 to the gold
ducat.
2. (8v22) The Elizabethan English mariners' equivalent to *amaynaron* (hauled
down) was *amaine*, which expressed a sense of urgency: "Lower as fast as you can."
(Smith 1970, 50).
3. (8v24) *Pusieronse a la Corda* (jogging on and off) means tacking back and
forth, intentionally making no headway. See Las Casas's definition at 23v23–25.
4. (8v29) *Anes*. Columbus uses the form "Anes" in every mention of Vicente
except one, when the name is spelled "Yanes." Morison spells the name "Yáñez" and
"Yáñes."
5. (8v41) Jane-Vigneras (1960) and Morison (1963) translate *escrivano* as
"secretary." Jados (1975, 33ff.) translates the Italian equivalent term, *scrivano*, as

sanches de segovia : y dixo q̃ le diesen [p?]or
fe y testimonio : como el por ante todos toma
va como de hecho tomo possession dla d̄ha

Folio 9r

Isla por el rey e por la Reyna sus señores
haziēdo las protestaciones q̃ se requirian co
m̄o mas largo se contiene en los testimo
nios q̃ alli se hizierō por escripto / luego
5   se ayunto alli mūcha gente dla Isla
esto q̃ se sigue son palabras formales de[l?]
almiᶜ en su libro dsu primera navega
çion y dscubrimiᵒ destas yndias /. yo di
ze el porq̃ nos tuviesen mūcha amistad
10   porq̃ cognosci q̃ era gente q̃ mejor se
libraria y conVrteria a nr̄a Sāacta fe con a
mor q̃ no por fuerça : les di a algu
nos dllos vnos bonetes colorados y vnas
cuentas de vidro q̃ se ponian al pescueç[o]
15   y otras cosas mūchas de poco valor cō que
ovierō mucho plazer y quedarō tanto nro[s?]
q̃ era maravilla /. los quales despues
venian a las barcas dlos navios adonde
nos estavamos nadād̄o : y nos trayan papa
20   gayos y hylo de algodon en ovillos y
azagayas y otras cosas mūchas y nos las
trocavan por otras cosas q̃ nos les dava
mos como cuentezillas de vidro y casca
veles /. en fin todo tomavā y davā de aq̃llo
25   q̃ tenian de buena volūtad ./. mas me
pareçio q̃ era gente mȳ pobre de todo /. ellos
andan todos desnudos como su madre los pa
rio : y tābien las mugeres : avnq̃ no vide
mas de vna farto moça /. y todos los que

Sánchez de Segovia; and he said that they
should be witnesses that, in the presence of
all, he would take, as in fact he did take,
possession of the said island for the king
9r and for the queen his lords, making the
declarations that were required, and which at
more length are contained in the testimonials
made there in writing. Soon many people of
the island gathered there. What follows are
the very words of the Admiral in his book
about his first voyage to, and discovery of,
these Indies. I, he says, in order that they
would be friendly to us—because I recognized that they were people who would be better freed [from error] and converted to our
Holy Faith by love than by force—to some of
them I gave red caps, and glass beads which
they put on their chests, and many other
things of small value, in which they took so
much pleasure and became so much our friends
that it was a marvel. Later they came swimming to the ships' launches where we were and
brought us parrots and cotton thread in balls
and javelins and many other things, and they
traded them to us for other things which we
gave them, such as small glass beads and
bells. In sum, they took everything and gave
of what they had very willingly. But it
seemed to me that they were a people very poor
in everything. All of them go around as naked
as their mothers bore them; and the women
also, although I did not see more than one
quite young girl. And all those that I saw

"ship's clerk." Mallett (1967, 202) translates it as "purser." The *escrivano* seems to
have had many responsibilities. His duties (described in articles 55–58 and elsewhere
in Jados, 1975) included maintaining and protecting the ship's register (*cartolario*), the
records of goods and persons carried, financial transactions, and agreements between
those on board ship. If he or anyone else made a false entry in the register, he could
lose his right hand, be branded, and have his possessions confiscated. The *escrivano*
was also the purchasing agent, materials manager, payroll clerk, and executor of practi-
cally every other business management function. But he was also a kind of "officer of
the court." His testimony was equal to that of three other witnesses (Jados 1975,
article 330). Little wonder that he had to be present to record the landing on Guanahani and the formal claim to the lands discovered!

30   yo vi eran todos manc[e]bos q̃ ningu⁰ vide
de edad de mas de .xxx. años /. mȳ biē
hechos de mūy fermosos cuerpos y mūy
buenas caras : los cabellos gruessos quasi
comõ sedas de cola de Cavallos e cortos /.
35   los cabellos traen por encima dlas çejas sal
uo vnos pocos detras q̃ traen largos q̃
jamas cortan . dllos se pintan de prieto : y
ellos son dla color dlos Canarios ni negros
ni blancos : y dellos se pintan de blanco : y dellos
40   de colorado : y dllos dlo q̃ fallan /. y dllos se pin
tan las caras : y dllos todo el cuerpo : y dllos
solos los ojos : y dllos solo el nariz /. ellos
no traen armas ni las cognosçen : porq̃ les
amostre espadas y las tomavan por el filo : y

Folio 9v

se cortavā con ignorãçia /. no tienē algun
~~fierro /o~~ fierro : sus azagayas son vnas varas
sin fierro y algunas dellas tienen al cabo
vn diente de peçe y otras de otras cosas /. ellos
5   todos a vna mano son de buena estatura de
grandeza y buenos gestos biēn hechos /. yo vide
algunos q̃ tenian señales de feridas en sus
cuerpos y les hize señas q̃ era aq̃llos : y ellos
me amostrarō comõ alli venian gente de
10   otras Islas q̃ estavā açerca y les querian tomar
y se defendian y yo crey e creo q̃ aqui vienē
de tr̄ra firme a tomarlos por captivos /. ellos

were young people,[1] for none did I see of more
than 30 years of age. They are very well
formed, with handsome bodies and good faces.
Their hair [is] coarse—almost like the tail
of a horse—and short. They wear their hair
down over their eyebrows except for a little
in the back which they wear long and never
cut. Some of them paint themselves with
black, and they are of the color of the
Canarians, neither black nor white; and some
of them paint themselves with white, and some
of them with red, and some of them with whatever they find. And some of them paint their
faces, and some of them the whole body, and
some of them only the eyes, and some of them
only the nose. They do not carry arms nor are
they acquainted with them, because I showed
them swords and they took them by the edge and
9v   through ignorance cut themselves. They have
no iron. Their javelins are shafts without
iron and some of them have at the end a fish
tooth and others of other things. All of them
alike are of good-sized stature and carry
themselves well. I saw some who had marks of
wounds on their bodies and I made signs to
them asking what they were; and they showed me
how people from other islands nearby came
there and tried to take them, and how they
defended themselves; and I believed and
believe that they come here from *tierra firme*
to take them captive. They should be good and

1. (9r29–30) *Y todos los . . . todos mancebos.* This statement has been used to
support the view that the inhabitants of Guanahani who greeted Columbus on 12 October were all young men except for "one [woman] who was just a girl" (Power 1983,
156). The word *mancebos*, "youths," is masculine, but in Spanish such masculine plural nouns as *hombres*, *jovenes*, and *hijos* can refer to groups made up of individuals of
both sexes. Whether there is, in fact, such a reference depends on context (see Keniston 1937, 37). In Columbus's description of the island of San Salvador and its people
there are several clear references to women. He writes that the natives "all go as naked
as their mothers bore them; and also the women" (9r27–28). Later, going along the
coast on the way to the eastern part of the island, he writes that "many men and
many women came," each bringing something for the Spaniards to eat or drink
(10v22–23). The statement in 9r29 that "I did not see more than one very young
girl" may not mean that he saw just one woman: it may mean that he saw only one
who was very young. No inferences about the relative numbers of men and women
on the island can be drawn from the information provided in the *Diario*.

nõ   dever ser buenos s[er]uidores y de buē ingenio
            q̃ veo q̃ mūy presto dizē todo lo q̃ les dezia :
      15   y creo q̃ ligeramēte se harian xp̄iāños q̃ me
            pareçio q̃ ninguᵃ secta tenian /. yo plaziendo
            a nr̄o señor levare de aqui al tp̄o de mi parti
            da seys a .v.al. p[ar]a q̃ deprendā fablar /. nin
            guna bestia de ninguᵃ mar̃a vide Saluo papa
      20   gayos en esta Isla /. todas son palabras del
            almirāte /.

                                                    Sabado .13. de otubre

            ⸎ luego q̃ amaneçio vinierō a la playa mūchos
            destos hōbres / todos māçebos como dicho tēgo :
      25   y todos de buena estatura / gente m̄ȳ fermosa :
            los cabellos no crespos Saluo corredios y grues
            sos como seda[s?] de Cavallo : y todos dla frēte
            y cabeça mūy ancha mas q̃ otra generaçion
            q̃ fasta aqui aya visto /. y los ̶o̶j̶o̶s̶-[?] ojos m̄ȳ
      30   fermosos y no pequeños : y ellos ninguᵒ
            prieto saluo dla color dlos canarios /. ni se
            deve esperar otra cosa pues esta leste gueste cō
la Isleta de gua   la Isla dl fierro en canaria so vna linea /.
nahani esta en el
altura q̃ la Isla   las piernas mūy derechas todos a vna mano :
dl hierro /. 35   y no barriga saluo mūy bien hecha /. Ellos
Canoas   vinierō a la nao con almadias q̃ son hechas
            del pie de vn arbol como vn barco luēgo
            y todo de vn pedaço y labrado mūy a maravilla
            segū la tr̄r̄a y grādes en q̃ en alguᵒ venian
      40   40. y .45. hōbres /. y otras mas pequeñas
            fasta aver dllas en que venia vn solo hōbre /.
            Remavā con vna pala como de fornero y

Folio 10r

            anda a maravilla / y si se le trastorna luego
            se echan todos a nadar y la enderecan y va
            zian con calabaças q̃ traen ellos . trayan ovi

intelligent servants, for I see that they say
very quickly everything that is said to them;
and I believe that they would become Christians very easily, for it seemed to me that
they had no religion. Our Lord pleasing, at
the time of my departure I will take six of
them from here to Your Highnesses in order
that they may learn to speak. No animal of
any kind did I see on this island except
parrots. All are the Admiral's words.

Saturday 13 October

As soon as it dawned, many of these people
came to the beach—all young as I have said,
and all of good stature—very handsome people,
with hair not curly but straight[1] and coarse,
like horsehair; and all of them very wide in
the forehead and head, more so than any other
race that I have seen so far. And their eyes
are very handsome and not small; and none of
them are black, but of the color of the Canary
Islanders. Nor should anything else be expected since this island is on an east-west
line with the island of Hierro in the Canaries. All alike have very straight legs and no
belly but are very well formed. They came to
the ship with dugouts[2] that are made from the
trunk of one tree, like a long boat, and all
of one piece, and worked marvelously in the
fashion of the land, and so big that in some
of them 40 and 45 men came. And others smaller, down to some in which came one man alone.
They row with a paddle like that of a baker
10r   and go marvelously. And if it capsizes on
them they then throw themselves in the water,
and they right and empty it with calabashes[3]

1.   (9v26) *Corredios* is a Portuguese word for "sliding" or "slipping." Applied to
hair it probably means "smooth" or "sleek." Jane-Vigneras (1960) mistranslates it as
"loose."
2.   (9v36) The Portuguese used the term *almadías* for West African dugouts.
Columbus did not use the West Indian term *canoa* until 26 October (17v32).
3.   (10r3) *Calabazas* (calabashes) are bowls and containers made from the dried,
hollow shells of gourds. The word can also apply to the edible or decorative fruit itself.

llos de algodon filado y papagayos [y?] azaga
5   yas y otras cositas q̃ seria tedio de escrevir
y todo davā por qualquiera cosa q̃ se los diese
y yo estava atento y trabajava de saber si avia
oro : y vide q̃ algunos dellos trayan vn
pedaçuelo colgado en vn agujero q̃ tienen
10 a la nariz /. y por señas pude entender
q̃ yendo al sur /o bolviendo la Isla por el
sur q̃ estava alli vn rey q̃ tenia grādes vaso[s]
dllo y tenia mūy mūcho /. trabaje q̃ fuesen
alla : y despues vide q̃ no entendian en la yda /.

na
15 determine de aguardar fasta maña∧ en la
tarde y despues partir p[ar]a el subdueste q̃
segū muchos dllos me enseñarō dezian
q̃ avia tr̄r̄a al sur y al sudueste y al norue
ste : y q̃stas dl norueste les venian a cō
20 batir mūchas vezes /. y asi yr[e?] al sudueste
a buscar el oro y piedras preciosas /. Esta isla
es bien grāde y mȳ llana y de arboles mȳ
la disposicion   verdes y mūchas aguas y vna laguna en
de guanahani   medio mūy grāde sin ninguᵃ montaña y toda
25 ella verde q̃s plazer de mirarla /. y esta gēte
farto māsa y por la gana de aver de nr̄as̄
Cosas y teniendo q̃ no se les a de dar sin que
den algo y no lo tienen : tomā lo q̃ pueden
y se echan luego a nadar /. mas todo lo q̃ tiene
30 lo dan por qualquiera cosa q̃ les den / que fasta
los pedaços dlas escudillas y dlas taças de
vidro rotas rescatavan fasta q̃ vi dar 16
ovillos de algodon por tres çeotis de portu
gal q̃ es vna blanca de Castilla / y en ellos

that they carry. They brought balls of spun
cotton and parrots and javelins and other
little things that it would be tiresome to
write down, and they gave everything for
anything that was given to them. I was
attentive and labored to find out if there was
any gold; and I saw that some of them wore a
little piece hung in a hole that they have in
their noses. And by signs I was able to
understand that, going to the south or
rounding the island to the south, there was
there a king who had large vessels of it and
had very much gold. I strove to get them to
go there and later saw that they had no
intention of going. I decided to wait until
the afternoon of the morrow and then depart
for the southwest, for, as many of them showed
me, they said there was land to the south and
to the southwest and to the northwest and
that these people from the northwest came to
fight them many times. And so I will go to
the southwest to seek gold and precious
stones. This island is quite big and very
flat and with very green trees and much water
and a very large lake in the middle and
without any mountains; and all of it so green
that it is a pleasure to look at it. And
these people are very gentle, and because of
their desire to have some of our things, and
believing that nothing will be given to them
without their giving something, and not having
anything, they take what they can and then
throw themselves into the water to swim. But
everything they have they give for anything
given to them, for they traded even for pieces
of bowls and broken glass cups, and I even saw
16 balls of cotton given for three Portuguese
çeotis,[1] which is a Castilian *blanca*.[2] And in

---

1. (10r33) The *ceutí* was a copper coin commemorating Portugal's capture of
Ceuta in 1415.
2. (10r34) A *blanca* was a copper coin valued at half a *maravedí*.

35   avria mas de vn arrova de algodon filado /.
esto defendiera y no dexara tomar a nadie
saluo q̃ yo lo mãdara tomar todo p[ar]a v.al
si oviera en Cantidad /. aqui nace en esta isla [/?]
mas por el poco tp̄o no pude dar asi del todo
40   fe /. y tambien aqui nace el oro q̃ traen Colga

Folio 10v

do a la nariz mas por no perder tp̄o quiero
yr a ver si puedo topar a la Isla de çipan
go /. agora com̄o fue noche : todos se fue
rō a tierra / con sus almadias /

5   Domĩgo .14 de otubre

/ En amaneçiendo mãde adereçar el batel
dla nao y las barcas dlas caravelas
y fue al luēgo dla Isla en el camino del
nornordeste p[ar]a ver la otra p[ar]te que era de
10   la p[ar]te del leste q̃ avia /. y tãbien p[ar]a ver
las poblaçiones y vide luego dos /o tres :
y la gente q̃ veniā todos a la playa llamā
donos y dando grãs a dios /. los vnos nos
trayan agua : otros otras cosas de comer :

them there was probably more than an *arroba*[1]
of spun cotton. This I had forbidden and I
did not let anyone take any of it, except that
I had ordered it all taken for Your Highnesses
if it were in quantity. It grows here on this
island, but because of the short time I could
not declare this for sure. And also the gold

10v   that they wear hung in their noses originates
here; but in order not to lose time I want to
go to see if I can find the island of Cipango.
Now, since night had come, all the Indians
went ashore in their dugouts.

Sunday 14 October

As soon as it dawned I ordered the ship's boat
and the launches of the caravels made ready
and went north-northeast[2] along the island in
order to see what there was in the other part,
which was the eastern part. And also to see
the villages, and I soon saw two or three, as
well as people, who all came to the beach
calling to us and giving thanks to God. Some
of them brought us water; others, other things

1. (10r35) An *arroba* (*arrova*) was a commercial weight of one-quarter of a *quintal* (see p. 107, n. 3), equivalent to 11–12 kilograms (*Diccionario* 1956). Seville also had a second *arroba* unit, equal to one-tenth of a *quintal*, used for buying and selling oil.

2. (10v8) *Camino del nornordeste*. "The way to," or "in the direction of" is expressed in the *Diario* by four phrases that include the word *camino*: *camino de* (16 times); *camino a* (25 times); *camino para* (1 time); and *camino* (4 times). Each phrase is followed by a compass direction or by a place name.

Fuson (1983, 63) maintains that the *de* in *camino de* means "from," not "to," and interprets two critical episodes of the voyage on that basis (*Diario* 10r8–9 and 15v22–23). It is not clear whether he thinks that in all, or only in some, cases *camino de* must be read as "the way from." Power (1983, 153 n. 12) admits that the phrase usually means "the road toward," but it can also (he says) be translated as "the road from." He offers no guidance about when it is to be interpreted in one way and when in the other.

The *Diccionario* (1956) gives two examples of *camino de* meaning "the road to": *Camino de Roma, ni mula coja ni bolsa floja* (On the road to Rome, don't take a lame mule or an empty purse) and *Camino de Santiago, tanto anda el cojo como el sano* (On the road to Santiago [since groups travel together] the lame go as fast as the healthy.) A line by Francisco de Quevedo (1580–1645), from the poem *Todo tras si lo lleva el año breve*, provides another: *Antes que sepa andar el pie, se mueve camino de la muerte* (Before the foot knows how to walk, it moves toward death).

Among the 16 appearances of *camino de* in the *Diario* only one requires translation as "the way from." See p. 123, n. 1. The other occurrences can, and should, be translated as "the way to."

15 otros quādo veyan q̃ yo no curava de yr
a tr̄r̄a se echavā a la mar nadādo y venian
y entēdiamos q̃ nos pregūtavan si eramos
venido dl çielo /. Y vino vno viejo en el
batel dentro y otros a bozes grādes llamavā

20 todos hōbres y mugeres : veni[d?] a ver los
hobres que vinierō del çielo traedles de
comer y de bever /. vinierō mūchos y
mūchas mugeres cada vno con algo dādo
grās a dios / echandose al suelo / y levātavā

25 las manos al çielo y despues a bozes
nos llamavā q̃ fuesemos a tierra mas
yo temia de ver vna grāde restinga de pie

çerca

dras q̃ ~~çierra~~-[?] toda aq̃lla Isla al rededor /.
y entremedias queda hondo y puerto

30 p[ar]a quātas naos ay en toda la xp̄iādad
y la entrada dello mūy angosta /. Es verdad
q̃ dentro desta çintha ay algunas baxas :
mas la mar no se mueve mas que dētro
en vn pozo /. y p[ar]a ver todo esto me movi

35 esta mañana porq̃ supiese dar de todo rela
cion a vr̄as aletezas /. y tambien a donde
~~a donde~~ pudiera hazer fortaleza y vide

peninsula

vn pedaço de tr̄r̄a q̃ se haze comō Isla avnq̃
no lo es en q̃ avia seys casas /. el qual se

40 pudiera atajar en dos dias por Isla avnq
yo no veo ser neçessario / porq̃ esta gente
es mūy simplice en armas comō veran v.al

nō

Folio 11r

siete p[er]sonas de siete q̃ yo hize tomar p[ar]a l[e?] llevar y
tomo el al
mirāte de gua deprender nr̄a fabla y bolvellos /. Saluo
nahani que .v. al quādo mādarē pueden los
todos llevar a castilla /o tenellos en la misma

5 Isla captivos /. porq̃ con çinqūeta hobres los
terna todos sojuzgados : y les hara hazer todo
lo q̃ quisiere /. y despues junto cō la d̄ha Isle

to eat; others, when they saw that I did not
care to go ashore, threw themselves into the
sea swimming and came to us, and we understood
that they were asking us if we had come from
the heavens. And one old man got into the
ship's boat, and others in loud voices called
to all the men and women: Come see the men who
came from the heavens. Bring them something
to eat and drink. Many men came, and many
women, each one with something, giving thanks
to God, throwing themselves on the ground; and
they raised their hands to heaven, and afterward they called to us in loud voices to come
ashore. But I was afraid, seeing a big stone
reef that encircled[1] that island all around.
And in between the reef and shore there was
depth and harbor for as many ships as there
are in the whole of Christendom, and the entrance to it is very narrow. It is true that
inside of this belt of stone there are some
shallows, but the sea is no more disturbed
than inside a well. And I bestirred myself
this morning to see all of this, so that I
could give an account of everything to Your
Highnesses, and also to see where a fort could
be made. And I saw a piece of land formed
like an island, although it was not one, on
which there were six houses. This piece of
land might in two days be cut off to make an
island, although I do not see this to be necessary since these people are very naive about
weapons, as Your Highnesses will see from

11r   seven that I caused to be taken in order to carry
them away to you and to learn our language and
to return them. Except that, whenever Your
Highnesses may command, all of them can be taken
to Castile or held captive in this same island;
because with 50 men all of them could be held
in subjection and can be made to do whatever
one might wish. And later [I noticed], near the

---

1. (10v28) Alvar (1976) reads the canceled text as *tierra*.

ta estan guertas de arboles las mas her
mosas q̃ yo vi e tan verdes y con sus hojas
10   como las de castilla en el mes de abril y
de mayo // y mūcha agua /. yo mire todo
aq̃l puerto y despues me bolvi a la nao y
di la vela y vide tantas Islas que yo no
sabia determinarme a qual yria primero /.
15   y aq̃llos hōbres q̃ yo tenia tomādo me dezian
por señas q̃ erā tantas y tantas q̃ no avia
numero /. y anōbrarō -mas-[?] por su nombre
mas de çiento /. por ende yo mire por
la mas grāde y aq̃lla determine andar
20   y asi hago y sera lexos desta de Sant saluador
çinco leguas y las otras dellas mas dellas
menos /. todas son mūy llanas sin mon
-talla-[?] tañas y mūy fertiles y todas pobladas
y se hazē guerra la vna a la otra / avnq̃stos
25   son mūy simplices y mūy lindos cuerpos de hōbres /.

                                                    Lunes .15. de otubre

 ⅄ avia temporejado esta noche con temor
de no llegar a tr̄r̄a a sorgir antes dla
mañana por no saber si la costa era limpia
30   de baxas : y en amaneçiendo cargar velas /
y como la Isla fuese mas lexos de çinco
leguas antes sera siete y la marea me
detuvo seria medio dia quādo llegue a la d̄ha
Isla y falle q̃ aq̃lla haz que es dla parte
35   dla Isla de San saluador se corre norte sur
y an en ella .5. leguas : y la otra que yo
segui se corria leste gueste : y an en ella mas de

said islet, groves of trees, the most beautiful
that I saw and with their leaves as green as
those of Castile in the months of April and May,
and lots of water. I looked over the whole of
that harbor and afterward returned to the ship
and set sail, and I saw so many islands that I
did not know how to decide which one I would go
to first. And those men whom I had taken told
me by signs that they were so very many that
they were numberless. And they named by their
names more than a hundred. Finally I looked for
the largest and to that one I decided to go and
so I am doing. It is about five leagues distant
from this island of San Salvador, and the others
of them some more, some less. All are very flat
without mountains and very fertile and all
populated and they make war on one another, even
though these men are very simple and very handsome in body.

Monday 15 October

I had killed time this night for fear of reaching[1] land to anchor before morning, because of
not knowing whether the coast was clear of
shoals, and as soon as it dawned I spread sail;[2]
and as the island was farther than five leagues,
rather about seven, and the tide detained me, it
was around noon when I reached the said island
and I found that the face which is in the
direction of San Salvador runs north-south and
that there are in it five leagues; and the
other, which I followed, runs east-west, and

1. (11r27–28) *Temor de no llegar.* "A redundant *no* is occasionally found in
clauses dependent upon verbs which imply a negative thought" (Ramsey 1956, 216).
As this example shows, the "negative thought" can also be expressed by nouns, in this
case *temor* (fear).
2. (11r30) Guillén Tato (1951) defines the phrase *cargar velas* as "to lower [*ar-
riar, bajar*] sails." We maintain, on the contrary, that in the present context the phrase
means "to spread or put on sail." Alvar (1976, 59 n.115) expresses the same
opinion. See also *Glosario* (1950, 2:101). The same meaning is required in *Diario*
11r40: *cargue las velas.* The usage may be derived from the meaning of *cargar*, "to
loosen." Here the sails are "loosened" by unfurling or spreading. In this second example, Columbus writes that even with all sail spread, he might not have been able to
reach the western end of Santa María before nightfall.

diez leguas /. y como desta isla vide otra mayor al
gueste : cargue las velas por andar todo aq̃l dia
40   fasta la noche : porq̃ avn no pudiera aver anda
do al cabo del gueste : a la qual puse nōbre la
Isla de Sancta maria dla concepçion y quasi al
poner del Sol sorgi acerca del dho Cabo por saber

Folio 11v

               alli
si avia ~~en ella~~ oro porq̃ estos que yo avia hecho
tomar en la Isla de San salvador me dezian
q̃ ay trayan manillas de oro mūy grandes
a las piernas y a los braços /. yo bien crey q̃
5   todo lo que dezian era burla p[ar]a se fugir /
Con todo mi volūtad era de no passar por
              ~~de~~
ninguᵃ Isla ~~q̃~~ de que no tomase possessiō /.
puesto que tomado de vna : se puede dezir
de todas /. y sorgi e estuve hasta oy mar
10   tes q̃ en amaneçiendo fue a tr̄r̄a con las bar
cas armadas : y sali y ellos que erā mūchos
asi desnudos y dla misma condiçion dla otra isla
de San salvador nos dexarō yr por la Isla y
nos davan lo q̃ les pedia /. y porq̃ el viento
15   cargava a la traviesa ~~sus~~[?] sueste : no me quise
detener y parti p[ar]a la nao : y vna almadia
grande estava abordo dla caravela niña /. y vno

there are in it more than ten leagues. And
since from this island I saw another larger one
to the west, I spread sail to go forward all
that day until night because [otherwise] I
would not yet have been able to reach the western
cape of the island, to which island I gave the
name Santa María de la Concepción. And close to
sundown I anchored near the said cape in order to

11v   find out if there was gold there,[1] because these men
that I have had taken on the island of San Salvador
kept telling me that there they wear very large
bracelets of gold on their legs and on their arms.
I well believe that all they were saying was a ruse
in order to flee. Nevertheless, my intention was
not to pass by any island of which I did not take
possession, although if it is taken of one, it may
be said that it is taken of all. And I anchored
and[2] remained here until today, Tuesday, and at
dawn went ashore with the armed launches. I got
out, and the natives, who were numerous and naked
and of the same character as those of the other
island of San Salvador, let us go around on the
island and gave us what was asked of them. And
because the wind increased and blew toward shore
from the southeast,[3] I did not wish to stay and
departed for the ship; and a large dugout was
alongside the caravel *Niña*. And one of the men

1. (11r38–44) *Y como . . . Santa María de la Concepción*. These lines have been
used to support the view that Columbus bypassed the second island that he saw and
that it was at the western end or cape of a third island, "a larger one to the west," that
he anchored at sunset on 15 October. This view ignores the fact that when Columbus
left his anchorage on the following day, it was with the express purpose of "going to
the other big island that I was seeing to the west" (*para yr a la otra isla grande que yo via
al gueste*) (11v38–39). The idea that Columbus would not land on the second island
that he saw also runs counter to his statement that he did not want to pass any island
without taking possession of it (11v7–9), although he does qualify this plan by saying
that "taken of one, it may be said that it is taken of all." It seems unlikely, however, that
he would have relaxed his efforts at such an early point in the inter-island voyage.
2. (11v9) The word *e* appears to be overwritten on a *y*.
3. (11v14–15) *El viento . . . sueste*. Guillén Tato (1951, 123) defines *traviesa* as
"perpendicular to the side of a ship." Here, however, it must have been a wind blowing
toward shore, *su travesía*, that made Columbus cut short his exploration of Santa María
and return to the fleet. The direction of the wind from the southeast is evidence that
Columbus's anchorage was on the south shore of the island. According to the *Diccionario* (1956), *traviesa* was formerly used in the sense of *travesía*, which seems to be true
here. Woodbridge (1950, 205) omits *traviesa* from his list of old Spanish nautical terms
and is in error about the meaning of *travesía* in *Diario* 27r6.

dlos hōbres dla Isla de Sant salvador que en ella
era : se echo a la mar y se fue en ella /. y la
20   noche de antes a medio echado el otro
y fue atras la almadia : la qual fugio q̃ jamas
fue barca que le pudiese alcançar puesto q̃ le
teniamos grāde avante /. Con todo dio en tr̄r̄a
y dexarō la almadia y algunos dlos de mi
25   compañia salierō en tr̄r̄a tras ellos : y todos
fugerō com̄o gallinas /. y la almadia q̃ avian
dexado la llevamos abordo dla Caravela ni
ña adonde ya de otro cabo venia otra almadia
pequeña con vn hōbre q̃ venia a rescatar vn
30   ovillo de algodon : y se echaro algunos marine
ros a la mar porq̃ el no queria entrar en la
Caravela y le tomarō y yo q̃stava a la popa
dla Nao q̃ vide todo enbie por el y le di vn
bonete Colorado y vnas Cuētas de vidro
35   verdes pequeñas q̃ le puse al braço y dos casca
veles q̃ le puse a las orejas y le māde bol
ver su almadia que tambien tenia en la barca
y le enbie a tr̄r̄a /. y di luego la vela p[ar]a yr a
la otra Isla grāde ———[?] q̃ yo via al gueste /. y māde
40   largar ~~la otra~~ tābien la otra almadia q̃ traya
la ~~otra~~[?] caravela niña por popa /. y vide des
pues en tr̄r̄a al tp̄o de la llegada del otro a quien yo
avia dado las cosas susodichas y no le avia que
rido tomar el ovillo dl algodon // puesto q̃l me
45   lo queria dar /. y todos los otros se llegarō a el
y tenia a grā maravilla e bien le parecio que

Folio 12r

eramos buena gente /. y q̃ el otro [q̃?] se avia
fugido nos avia hecho algun daño y q̃

from the island of San Salvador who was in the *Niña*
threw himself into the sea and went away in the
dugout. And the night before at mid- . . . .[1] thrown
the other and went after the dugout, which fled [so
speedily] that there was never ship's launch that
could overtake it even if we had a big head start.
However, the dugout made land, the natives left the
dugout, and some of the men of my company went
ashore after them; and they all fled like chickens.
And the dugout that they had left we brought alongside the *Niña*, to which now from another cape came
another small dugout with one man who came to
trade a ball of cotton; and some sailors jumped into
the sea because the man did not want to enter the
caravel and they laid hold of him. And I, who was
on the poop of the ship and saw all this, sent for him
and gave him a red bonnet, and some small green
glass beads which I put on his arm, and two bells
which I put on his ears, and I ordered his dugout,
which I also had in the ship's launch, returned to
him and sent him to land. And then I set sail to go
to the other large island that I had in view to the
west. And I also ordered the other dugout, which
the caravel *Niña* was bringing along at her stern,
let loose. And later I saw, on land, at the time of
arrival of the other man—[the man] to whom I
had given the things aforesaid and whose ball of
cotton I had not wanted to take from him, although
he wanted to give it to me—that all the others
went up to him. He considered it a great marvel,
12r   and indeed it seemed to him that we were
good people and that the other man who had fled

---

1. (11v19–20) *La noche de antes a medio.* Something must have been omitted
after *medio* at this point in copying the document that Las Casas used. In his *Historia
de las Indias* (1951, 1:210) it is clear that there were two escapes, not one, and that
only one involved natives of Santa María and a canoe. As a conjectural reconstruction
of the *Diario* text we suggest the following: *Y la noche de antes a medi[a noche se había]
echado [a la mar] el otro y había huido. [Gente de mi compañía] fue atras la almadia . . . .*
In translation the whole passage would read: "And one of the men from the island of
San Salvador who was in the *Niña* threw himself into the sea and went away in the
dugout. And the night before, at midnight, the other man had thrown himself into the
sea and fled. Men of my company went after the dugout . . . ." Las Casas's text does
not make entirely clear that it was the second escape that prompted the chase of the
dugout. The first man presumably swam ashore.

por esto lo llevabamos /. y a esta razon use esto
con el de le mādar alargar y le di las d̄has
5   cosas // porꝗ ~~no estuviese~~ nos tuviese en esta esti
ma /. porꝗ otra vez ~~vr̄as altezas quādo~~ quā
do vr̄as altezas aqui tornē a enbiar no hagā
mala compañia /. y todo lo ꝗ yo le di no valia
quatro m[araved]īs /. y asi parti ꝗ serian las diez
10   oras con el viento sueste y tocava de sur p[ar]a
passar a estotra Isla /. la qual es grandissima y
adonde todos estos hōbres ꝗ yo traygo dla
de San saluador hazen señas ꝗ ay mȳ mū
cho oro / y ꝗ lo traen en los braços en ma
15   nillas y a las piernas y a las orejas y al na
riz y al pescueço /. y avia desta isla de Sancta
maria a esta otra nueve leguas leste gueste /
y se corre toda esta parte dla Isla norueste
sueste /. y se pareçe ꝗ bien avria en esta costa
20   mas de veynte ocho leguas en esta faz /. y
[es?] mȳ llana sin mōtaña ninguᵃ : asi comō a
ꝗlla de Sant saluador y de Sancta maria /. y
todas playas sin roquedos : Saluo ꝗ a todas
ay algunas peñas açerca de tr̄r̄a debaxo del
25   agua por donde es menester abrir el ojo
quādo se quiere surgir e no surgir mūcho a
çerca de tr̄r̄a avnꝗ las aguas son siempre
mȳ claras y se vee el fondo ~~y~~[?] /. desviado
de tr̄r̄a dos tyros de lōbarda : ay en todas estas
30   Islas tanto fondo ꝗ no se puede llegar
a el /. son estas Islas mȳ Vrdes y fertiles y
de ayres mȳ dulçes : y puede aver muchas
cosas ꝗ yo no se porꝗ no me quiero dete
ner por Calar y andar mūchas Islas p[ar]a
35   fallar oro /. y pues estas dan asi estas senas
ꝗ lo traen a los braços y a las piernas y es
oro porꝗ les amostre algunos pedaços del ꝗ
yo tengo : no puedo ————[?] errar con el ayu
da de nro señor ꝗ yo no le falle adonde
40   naçe /. y estando a medio golpho destas dos
Islas es de saber de aꝗlla de Sancta maria

had done us some harm and that for this we were
taking him with us. And the reason that I be-
haved in this way toward him, ordering him set
free and giving him the things mentioned, was in
order that they would hold us in this esteem so
that, when Your Highnesses some other time again
send people here, the natives will receive them
well. And everything that I gave him was not
worth four *maravedís*. And so I departed when it
was about the tenth hour, with the wind southeast
and shifting to the south, in order to pass to
this other island, which is exceedingly large and
where all these men that I am bringing from San
Salvador make signs that there is very much gold
and that they wear rings of it on their arms and
on their legs and in their ears and on their
noses and on their chests. And from this island
of Santa María to this other island it is nine
leagues east-west, and all this part of the island runs northwest-southeast. And it appears
that there may well be on this coast more than
28 leagues on this side. And it is very flat
without any mountains, just like San Salvador
and Santa María. And all the beaches are without rocks, except that at all of them there are
some big rocks near land under the water, where
it is necessary to keep your eyes open when
you wish to anchor and not to anchor close to
land, although the waters are always very clear
and one sees the bottom. And two lombard shots
[away] from land in all of these islands the
bottom is so deep that you cannot reach it.
These islands are very green and fertile and with
sweet-smelling breezes; and there may be many
things that I do not know about because I do not
want to stop, so I can investigate and go to many
islands in order to find gold. And since these
people make signs that they wear it on their arms
and on their legs—and it is gold because I
showed them some pieces that I have of it—I cannot fail with the help of Our Lord to find out
where it originates. And when we were mid-sea
between these two islands, that is, Santa María

y desta grāde a la qual pongo nōbre la ferna

fernādina ———[?] dina : falle vn nōbre solo en vna almadia q̃ se

passava dla Isla de Sancta maria a la fernādina

45   y traya vn poco de su pan q̃ seria tanto como ~~n~~-[?]

Folio 12v

el puño y vna calabaça de agua y vn peda

ço de tierra bermeja hecha en polvo y des

pues amassada : y vnas hojas secas : q̃

deve ser cosa mūy apreçiada entrellos : porq

5   ya me truxerō en sā salvador dellas en

presente /. y traya vn çestillo a su guisa

en q̃ tenia vn ramalejo de cuentezillas de

vidro y dos blancas : por las quales cogno

sci q̃l venia dla Isla de Sant saluador

10   y avi passado a aq̃lla de Sācta maria y se

passava a la fernādina /.   El qual se llego

a la nao   yo le hize entrar q̃ asi lo demā

dava el y le hize poner su almādia en la

nao y guardar todo lo q̃ el traya y le mā

15   de dar de comer pan y miel y de bever

y asi le passare a la fernādina y le dare todo

lo suyo : porq̃ de buenas nuevas de nos

por a nr̄o señor aplaziendo quādo vr̄as alte

zas enbien aca ~~quien~~-[?] que aq̃llos q̃ vinierē

20   resçiban honrra y nos den de todo lo q̃ oviere /.

                                    martes y miercoles .16. de otubre

/ Parti dlas Isla de Sc̄ta maria de Concepçiō

q̃ seria ya çerca de medio dia p[ar]a la Isla

fernādina : la qual amuestra ser grādissima

25   al gueste y navegue todo aq̃l dia con cal

meria no pude llegar a tp̄o de poder ver

el fondo p[ar]a surgir en limpio porq̃ es

en esto mūcho de aver grā diligençia por

and this big one to which I gave the name Fernandina, I found a man who was passing alone in a
dugout from the island of Santa María to Fernandina and who was bringing a small amount of their
bread, which was about the size of a fist, and

12v a calabash of water and a piece of red earth made
into dust and then kneaded and some dry leaves,
which must be something highly esteemed among
them, because earlier, in San Salvador, they
brought some of them to me as a present. And he
was bringing a little native basket in which he
had a string of small glass beads and two *blan-*
cas; because of which I recognized that he was
coming from the island of San Salvador and had
passed to that of Santa María and was passing to
Fernandina. He came up to the ship and I had him
enter, which was what he asked, and I had his
dugout put in the ship and all that he brought
watched over, and I ordered him given bread and
honey and something to drink, and so I will
transport him to Fernandina and I will give him
all of his belongings in order that, through
good reports of us—Our Lord pleasing—when Your
Highnesses send [others] here, those who come
will receive courteous treatment and the natives
will give us of all that they may have.

                                 Tuesday and Wednesday 16 October
I departed from the island of Santa María[1] de la
Concepción, when it was already about noon, for
the island of Fernandina, which showed up very
large to the west, and I sailed all that day in a
very light wind. I could not arrive in time to be
able to see the bottom in order to anchor in the
clear, because in doing this it is important
to have great diligence so as not to lose the

1. (12v22) *Las Isla de Sancta maria.* Some students of the voyage have taken
this ungrammatical construction (plural article with singular noun) to mean that Santa
María consisted of more than one island. For the ways in which other editors of both
Spanish and English versions of the *Diario* have dealt with this matter, see Dunn
(1983a, 44). See also Fuson (1983, 60).

no perder las anclas y asi temporize toda
30 esta noche hasta el dia q̃ vine a vna pobla
çion a donde yo surgi e adonde avia veni
do aq̃l hõbre q̃ yo halle ayer en aq̃lla alma
dia a medio golfo /. El qual avia dado tãtas
nõ   buenas nuevas de nos : q̃ toda esta noche
35 no falto almadias abordo dla nao q̃ nos
trayan agua y dlo q̃ tenian /.   yo a cada
vno le mãdava dar algo es a saber algu
nas cuentezillas diez /o doze dllas de vidro
en vn filo y algunas sonajas de laton
40 destas q̃ valen en castilla vn maravedi
cada vna : y algunas agujetas : de que todo
tenian en grãdissima exçelençia . y tãbiē
los mãdava dar p[ar]a q̃ comiesen quãdo ve

Folio 13r

niᴀn en la nao y miel de acucar /. y despues
a oras de tercia embie el batel de la nao en
tr̄r̄a por agua : y ellos de mũy buena gana
le enseñavã a mi gente adonde estava el agua
5   y ellos mesmos trayan los barriles llenos
al batel y se folgavã mũcho de nos hazer
plazer /. Esta Isla es grãdissima y tengo deter
minado dla rodear : porq̃ segũ puedo entēder
en ella /o açerca della ay mina de oro /.
10 esta Isla esta desviada dla de Sãcta maria 8º
leguas quasi leste gueste y este cabo adonde
yo vine y toda esta costa se corre nornorueste
y sursudueste : y vide bien veynte leguas dlla
mas ay no acabava /. agora escriviendo esto di la
15 vela cõ el viento sur p[ar]a pujar a rodear toda la
Isla / y trabajar hasta q̃ halle samoet q̃ es la
Isla /o ciudad adonde es el oro q̃ asi lo dizen

anchors. And so I lay to all this night until
day, when I came to a village where I anchored
and to which had come that man whom I found
mid-sea yesterday in that dugout. He had given
so many good reports about us that during the
whole night there was no lack of dugouts alongside the ship, to which they brought us water
and of what they had. I ordered something given
to each one, that is to say ten or twelve little
glass beads on a thread, and some brass jingles
of the sort that in Castile are worth a
maravedí each, and some metal lace-ends, all
of which they considered of the greatest
excellence. And also I ordered them given food,
in order that they might eat when they came to

13r   the ship, and molasses. And later, at the
hours of tierce,[1] I sent the ship's boat to
shore for water. And the natives very willingly
showed my people where the water was, and they
themselves brought the filled barrels to the boat
and delighted in pleasing us. This island is
exceedingly large and I have decided to sail
around it, because according to my understanding, on or near it there is a gold mine. This
island is distant from that of Santa María eight
leagues almost east-west, and this cape to which
I came and all this coast runs north-northwest
and south-southwest,[2] and I saw quite 20 leagues
of it but it did not end there. Now, writing
this, I set sail with a south wind to strive to
go around the whole island and to keep trying
until I find Samoet, which is the island or city
where the gold is; for so say all these men who

1. (13r2) *Tercia* (tierce) is one of the liturgical hours, when the pious performed prescribed prayers and other religious duties. Since the exact time of these hours varied with the seasons and the locale, it is difficult to define exactly when they were observed on Columbus's voyage. However, the following schedule, observed on some Italian galleys of the fifteenth century, may be indicative: tierce—three hours after sunrise; sext—noon; nones—the ninth hour, midafternoon; vespers—one hour before sunset, the twenty-third hour, counting from sunset of the previous day (see Mallett 1967, 209 n. 5). Add to this list compline—after sunset, completing the day.
2. (13r12–13) *Nornorueste y sursudueste*. 'South-southwest" (*sursudueste*) is probably a copy error for *sursueste*, "south-southeast," although some students of the *Diario* have thought otherwise. See Fuson (1983, 65).

todos estos q̃ aqui vienē en la nao y nos lo
dezian los dla Isla de San salvador y de Sancta
20   maria /. Esta gente es semejãte a aq̃lla
dlas dhas Islas y vna fabla y vnas costūbres
Saluo q̃stos ya me pareçen algū tanto mas

                                    y
domestica gente y de tracto ∧mas sotiles /.
porq̃ veo q̃ an traydo algodon aqui a la nao
25   y otras cositas q̃ saben mejor refetar el
pagamēto q̃ no hazian los otros /. y a
vn en esta Isla vide paños de algodon
fechos coͦmo mãtillos : y la gente mas dis
puesta y las mugeres traen por delante
30   su cuerpo vna cosita de algodon q̃ escassa
mēte les cobija su natura /. ella es Isla
mūy verde y llana y fertilissima y no pon
go duda q̃ todo el año siembrā panizo
y cogen y asi todas otras cosas /. y vide
35   mūchos arboles mūy diformes dlos nr̄os /.
y dllos mūchos q̃ tenian los ramos de mū
chas maneras : y todo en vn pie /. y vn
ramito es de vna mar̃a y otro de otra : y
tan disforme : q̃ es la mayor maravilla
40   dl mūdo quāta es la diuersidad dla vna
mar̃a a la otra // verbigracia : vn ramo
tenia las fojas de mar̃a de Cañas : y otro

Folio 13v

de mar̃a de lantisco /. y asi en vn solo arbol de
cinco /o seys destas mar̃as : y todos tan diuersos /.
ni estos son enxeridos porq̃ se pueda dezir que el ~~enfor~~-[?]
enxerto lo haze : antes son por los mōtes ni cura
5   dellos esta gente /. no le cognozco secta ninguᵃ
nõ   y creo q̃ mūy presto se tornarian xp̄ianos : porque
ellos son de mūy buen entender /. aqui son los
peçes tan disformes de los nr̄os q̃s maravilla /.
ay algunos hechos coͦmo gallos dlas mas finas colo
10   res del mūdo / azules amarillos Colorados y de
todas colores y otros pintados de mill mar̃as /. y las
Colores son tan finas q̃ no ay hōbre q̃ no se ma

come here in the ship, and so told us the men of
the island of San Salvador and of Santa María.
These people are like those of the said islands
in speech and customs except that these now appear somewhat more civilized and given to commerce and more astute. Because I see that they
have brought cotton here to the ship and other
little things for which they know better how to
bargain payment than the others did. And in this
island I even saw cotton cloths made like small
cloaks, and the people are more intelligent, and
the women wear in front of their bodies a little
thing of cotton that scarcely covers their genitals. It is a very green and flat and exceedingly fertile island and I have no doubt that all
year they sow millet[1] and harvest it and likewise
all other things. And I saw many trees very
different from ours, and among them many which
had branches of many kinds, and all on one trunk.
And one little branch is of one kind, and another
of another, and so different that it is the
greatest wonder in the world how much diversity
there is between one kind and another; that is to
say, one branch has leaves like those of cane,

13v   and another like those of mastic, and thus on a single
tree [there are] five or six of these kinds, and all very
different. Nor are they grafted, because one might
say that grafting does it.[2] Rather, these trees are wild,
nor do these people take care of them. I do not
detect in them any religion and I believe that they
would become Christians very quickly because they
are of very good understanding. Here the fish are so
different from ours that it is a marvel. There are some
shaped like dories,[3] of the finest colors in the world:
blues, yellows, reds, and of all colors; and others
colored in a thousand ways. And the colors are so
fine that there is no man who would not marvel and

1. (13r33) *Panizo* literally means "millet," but the crop referred to is possibly
"maize," which Europeans had not seen before. See Morison (1963, 73 n. 5).
2. (13v3–4) *Se pueda . . . lo haze.* Morison (1963, 72) translates this passage as
"one can say that the grafting is spontaneous."
3. (13v9) *Gallos* (dories) are a small, edible saltwater fish with a golden color.

raville y no tome grā descanso a verlos /. tam
bien ay vallenas   bestias en tr̄r̄a no vide ninguᵃ
15 de ninguna mar̃a / Saluo papagayos y lagartos
vn moço me dixo q̃ vido vna grāde Culebra :
ovejas ni cabras ni otra ninguᵃ bestia —[?] vide
avnq̃ yo e estado aqui mūy poco q̃ es medio dia
mas si las oviese no pudiera errar de ver alguᵃ /.
20 El çerco desta Isla escrivire despues q̃ yo la oviere
arrodeada /.

                                        miercoles .17. de otubre
╱ A medio dia parti dla poblaçion adonde yo estava
                        yr
surgido y adonde tome agua p[ar]a ∧rodear esta isla
25 fernādina y el viento era sudueste y sur : y co[mo]
mi volūtad fuese de seguir esta costa desta isla adonde
yo estava al sueste porq̃ asi se corre toda norno
rueste y sursueste : y queria llevar el d̄ho Camino
dl sur y sueste : porq̃ aq̃lla p[ar]te todos estos yn
30 dios que traygo y otro de quien ove señas en esta
parte del sur a la Isla aq̃llos llamā Samoet a
donde es el oro : y martin alonso pinçon capitan
dla Caravela pinta / en la qual yo māde a tres destos
yndios vino a mi y me dixo q̃ vno dellos mūy
35 çertificadamēte le avia dado a entender q̃ por la
p[ar]te dl nornorueste mūy mas presto arrodearia
la Isla : yo vide q̃ el viento no me ayudava por
el camino q̃ yo queria llevar y era bueno por
el otro : di la vela al nornorueste y quādo fue a
40 çerca dl cabo dla Isla a dos leguas : halle vn mūy ma
ravilloso puerto con vna boca avnq̃ dos bocas se le
puede dezir porq̃ tiene vn Isleo en medio y son
ambas mūy angostas y dentro mūy ancho pareçian
navios si fuera fondo y limpio y fondo al entrada :

take great delight in seeing them.   There are also whales.
On land I saw no animals of any kind except parrots
and lizards. A boy told me that he saw a large snake.
I saw neither sheep nor goats nor any other beast,
although I have been here very little time, for it is
now midday, but if there were any of them I would
not fail to see some.   The circuit of this island I will
write about after I have gone around it.

Wednesday 17 October

At midday I departed from the village where I was
anchored and where I took on water in order to go
around this island of Fernandina, and the wind was
southwest and south. And since my intention had
been to follow this coast of this island where I was to
the southeast, because it all ran north-northwest and
south-southeast, and I wanted to follow the said
course to the south and southeast because in that
region, according to all these Indians that I am
bringing and another from whom I had information,
in this southern region is the island those men call
Samoet, where the gold is. And Martín Alonso
Pinzón, captain of the caravel *Pinta*, in which I had
sent three of these Indians, came to me and told me
that one of them very positively had given him to
understand that by way of the north-northwest I
would go around the island much more quickly. I saw
that the wind was not helping me on the course I
wanted to follow and that it was good for the other;
so I set sail to the north-northwest and when I was
two leagues distant from the end of the island, I
found a very wonderful harbor with one entrance,
although one might say with two, because it has an
isleo[1] in the middle and the entrances are both very
narrow; and inside it would be wide enough for a
hundred ships[2] if it were deep and clean-bottomed

1. (13v42)   An *isleo* is a small island near a coast or another, larger island (Guillén
Tato 1951, 76). The *Diccionario* (1956) defines it as *Isla pequeña situada a la inmediación*
[next to] *a otra mayor*.   The word does not mean simply "small island," as Fuson
(1983, 61) defines it.
2. (13v43–44)   *Pareçian navios* is an auditive error for *para cien navios*, "for a
hundred ships."

45 pareciome razō del ver bien y sondear y asi sur
gi fuera del y fuy en el con todas las barcas de los
navios y vimos q̃ no avia fondo /. y porq̃ pense
quādo yo le vi q̃ era boca de algū rio : avia mādado
llevar barriles p[ar]a tomar agua y en tr̄r̄a halle vnos
50 ocho /o diez hōbres q̃ luego vinierō a nos y nos

Folio 14r

amostrarō [muy?] çerca la poblaçion adonde yo enbie
la gente por agua / vna parte con armas / otros
con barriles y asi la tomarō /. y porq̃ era lexuelos
me detuve por espaçio de dos oras en este t̄p̄o andu
5   ve asi por aq̃llos arboles q̃ erā la cosa mas fer
mosa de ver q̃ otra q̃ se aya visto / veyendo tanta
verdura en tanto grado comō en el mes de mayo
en el andaluzia /. y los arboles todos estan tan disfor
mes dlos nr̄o̅s comō el dia dla noche : y asi las
10 frutas y asi las yervas y las piedras y todas las
cosas /. verdad es q̃ algunos arboles erā dla na
turaleza de otros q̃ ay en castilla : por ende avia
mȳ grā diferēçia /. y los otros arboles de otras ma
neras erā tantos q̃ ay no ay p[er]sona q̃ lo pueda dezir
15 ni asemejar a otros de castilla /. la gente toda
era vna cō los otros ya d̄hos dlas mismas condi
çiones y asi desnudos y dla misma estatura y
davā dlo q̃ tenian por qualquiera cosa q̃ les diesen /.
y aqui vide q̃ vnos moços dlos navios les
20 trocarō azagayas vnos pedaçuelos de escudillas
rotas y de vidro /. y los otros q̃ fuerō por el agua
me dixerō comō aviā estado en sus casas / y q̃
erā de dentro mȳ barridas y limpias : y sus
camas y paramētos de cosas q̃ son comō redes
                          sc. las casas
hamacas   25 de aldogon /. ellas ∧son todas a mar̃a de alfane
estas chimeneas no   ques y mūy altas y buenas chimeneas / mas
son p[ar]a humeros
sino vnas coroni
llas q̃ tienē enci
ma las casas de
paja los [y?]ndios
por esto lo dize /.
puesto q̃ dexan
abierto por arriba
algo p[ar]a q̃ salga
el humo /

and deep at the entrance. There seemed to me good
reason to look at it well and to take soundings, and so
I anchored outside and went into it with all the ships'
launches and we saw that it had no depth. And
because I thought when I saw it that it was the
mouth of some river, I had ordered barrels taken in
order to get water, and on land I found some eight
or ten men who soon came to us and showed us
nearby the village where I sent the men for

14r   water: one group with arms and others with
barrels; and so they got it. And because
it was a bit far I stopped for a period of two
hours and in this time I also walked among those
trees, which were more beautiful to see than any
other thing that has ever been seen, seeing as much
verdure and in such degree as in the month of
May in Andalusia. And all the trees are as different from ours as day from night; and also the
fruits and grasses and stones and everything. It
is true that some trees are of the same character
as others in Castile; nevertheless, there was a
very great difference. And the other trees of
other kinds were so many that there is no one who
can tell it or compare them with others of Castile.
All the people are the same as the others already
mentioned—of the same qualities and likewise naked
and of the same stature—and they gave what they
had for anything the men gave them. And here I saw
that some ships' boys traded a few small pieces of
broken pottery and glass for javelins. And the
others who went for the water told me how they had
been in their houses and that inside they were
well swept and clean and that their beds and furnishings were made of things like cotton nets. The
houses are all made like Moorish campaign tents,
very high and with good smoke holes,[1] but I did not

---

1. (14r26) Jane-Vigneras (1960) translates *chimeneas* as "chimneys." Las Casas's
marginal note indicates that the *chimeneas* are not smoke holes but *coronillas* (little
crowns) on the roof, and that smoke exits from an opening in the roof.

no vide entre mūchas poblaçiones q̃ yo vide [que?]
ninguᵃ q̃ passasse de doze hasta quinze casas /. aqui
fallarō q̃ las mugeres casadas trayan bragas de

30 algodon : las moças no sino saluo algunas que erā
ya de edad de diez y ocho años /. y ay avia
perros mastines y branchetes : y ay fallarō vno
q̃ avia al nariz vn pedaço de oro q̃ seria comō
la mitad de vn castellano : en el qual vierō letras /.

35 reñi yo cō ellos porq̃ no se lo resgatarō y die
rō quāto pedia por ver q̃ era y cuya esta mone
da era : y ellos me respōdierō q̃ nūca se lo oso
resgatar /. dspues de tomada la agua bolvi
a la nao y di la vela y sali al norueste tanto q̃

40 yo descubri toda aq̃lla p[ar]te dla Isla hasta la
costa q̃ se corre leste gueste /. y despues todos
estos yndios tornarō a dezir q̃sta Isla era

                          no
mas pequeña q̃ ∧ la Isla Samoet : y q̃ seria biē
nō   bolver atras por ser en ella mas presto /.   El
          45 viento alli luego nos Calmo y comēço a vētar
buelvēse a la espa   guesnorueste /.   El qual era contrario p[ar]a donde
ñola   aviamos venido /. y asi tome la buelta y navegue

Folio 14v

                              sueste
toda esta noche passada al leste ~~gueste~~ y quādo
al leste ~~solo~~ todo [y?] quādo al sueste / y esto p[ar]a
apartarme dla tr̄ra porq̃ hazia mȳ grā çerra
zon y el tp̄o mȳ cargado /. el era poco y no

5   me dexo llegar a tr̄ra a surgir /. asi que esta
noche llovio mūy fuerte despues de media
noche hasta quasi el dia y avn esta nūblado
p[ar]a llover y nos al cabo dla Isla dla p[ar]te

see among the many villages that I saw any that
surpassed 12 to 15 houses. Here they found that
the married women wore cotton shorts; the young
girls did not, except some who were already 18
years of age. And there there were dogs, mastiffs [1]
and terriers. And there they found a man who had
in his nose a piece of gold which was something
like half of a *castellano*,[2] on which they saw letters. I rebuked them because they did not trade
for it and give as much as he asked in order to see
what it was and whose money it was; and they answered that they never dared to trade with him for
it. After getting the water I returned to the ship
and set sail and went northwest so far that I
viewed all that part of the island as far as the
coast that runs east-west. And later all these Indians said again that this island was smaller than [3]
the island of Samoet and that it would be well to
turn back so as to be there more quickly. The
wind there soon died on us and commenced to blow
west-northwest, which was contrary to the direction
in which we had been coming. And so I turned

14v   about and steered all this past night to the east-
southeast and sometimes due east and sometimes
southeast; and this was so as to keep away from
land because it was heavily overcast and the weather very dirty. There was little [time] [4] and it did
not let me reach land to anchor. Also tonight it
rained very hard after midnight until almost day
and it still is cloudy and looks like rain. And we
[will head] [5] for the southeast cape of the island

---

1. (14r32) *Mastines* (mastiffs). A breed of dog used for hunting and as
watchdogs.

2. (14r34) A *castellano* was a gold coin valued at 480 *maravedís* in the late fifteenth century.

3. (14r43) *Mas pequeña* que no. The occasional use of a redundant *no* after *que*
in the second term of comparisons is a peculiar feature of Spanish. See Ramsey (1956,
215) and Keniston (1937, 605).

4. (14v4) *El era poco*. The noun that *poco* (little) modifies is missing from the
manuscript. Jane-Vigneras (1960) and Morison (1963) interpret the phrase as "little
wind." It is more likely that "time" was the factor that prevented the Admiral from
making an anchorage before nightfall, since he had sailed northwest as far as the east-
west–running north coast of Fernandina before coming about in response to a contrary
wind and deteriorating weather conditions.

5. (14v8) *Nos al cabo de la isla*. The manuscript text lacks a verb. "Sail" or
"head" is a conjecture.

-dla Isla- dl sueste adonde esp[er]o surgir fasta
10 q̃ aclaresca p[ar]a ver las otras Islas / adonde
tengo de yr /. y asi todos -estas-[?] estos dias
despues q̃ en estas yndias estoy a llovido
poco /o mucho ./.   creā .v.al.   que es esta
tr̄r̄a la mejor e mas fertil y temperada y llana
15 y buena q̃ aya en el mūdo /.

                                                    Jueves .18. de otubre

/ dspues q̃ aclarescio segui el viento y fui en
derredor dla Isla quāto pude y surgi al
tp̄o q̃ ya no era de navegar : mas nō fui
20 en tr̄r̄a y en amaneçiendo di la vela /.

                                                    viernes .19. de otubre

/ En amaneçiendo levante las anclas y enbie
la caravela pinta al leste y sueste : y la caravela
niña al -sueste susu- sursueste : y yo con la
25 nao fui al sueste y dado orden q̃ llevasen a
q̃lla buelta fasta medio dia y despues q̃ am
bas se mudasen las derrotas y se recogierō
p[ar]a mi /. y luego antes q̃ andassemos tres oras
vimos vna Isla al leste sobre la qual descar
30 gamos y llegamos a ella todos tres los navios
antes de medio dia a la punta dl norte adonde
haze vn isleo y vn restinga de piedra fuera del
al norte : y otro entre el y la Isla grāde : la
qual anōbrarō estos hōbres de Sā saluador q̃ yo
35 traygo la Isla Saomete : a la qual puse nōbre

where I hope to anchor until the weather clears in
order to see the other islands where I have to go.
And so it has rained a lot, or a little, every day
since I have been in these Indies. May Your Highnesses believe that this land is the best and most
fertile and temperate and level and good that there
is in the world.

Thursday 18 October

After the weather cleared I followed the wind and
went around the island as much as I could[1] and
anchored when the time was not good for navigation;
but I did not go ashore, and when dawn came I set sail.

Friday 19 October

As soon as it dawned I raised the anchors and sent
the caravel *Pinta* to the east and southeast, and the
caravel *Niña* to the south-southeast,[2] and I with
the ship went to the southeast; and I had given orders that they should follow those courses until
noon and then that both should change course and
rejoin me. And soon, before we had traveled three
hours, we saw an island to the east which we bore
down upon, and we all three ships reached it before
noon at the north point where it forms an *isleo*
and a reef of stone outside of it to the north and
another[3] between the *isleo* and the big island,
which these men from San Salvador that I bring with
me call the island of Samoet; to which I gave the

---

1. (14v18) Jane-Vigneras (1960) translates *quanto pude* (as much as I could) as
"when I could do so," as if the Spanish read *quando pude*.

2. (14v24) *Sursueste*. Las Casas first wrote *sueste* (southeast), then realized he
should have written *sursueste* (south-southeast). But in beginning the latter, he mistakenly wrote *susu*. Seeing that this was wrong, he canceled both *sueste* and *susu* with
a single line and wrote *sursueste* following.

3. (14v33) *Otro* (another). The masculine gender of *otro* requires a masculine
antecedent, which would be *isleo*. This implies that there were two *isleos* off the north
point of Samoet (Isabela), not just one. However, in the three additional references to
the *isleo* which follow, the word is always in the singular. Furthermore, the word *restinga* (reef) has been mistakenly given a masculine indefinite article, *un*, which may
have misled Las Casas, or a previous copyist, into a second error by making *otro* and *un*
agree in gender. It is our suggestion that the intended antecedent of *otro* is *restinga*.

la Islabela /. El viento era norte y quedava
el d̄ho Isleo -der-[?] en derrota dla Isla fernā
dina de adonde yo avia p[ar]tido leste gueste
y se corria -al gueste- despues la costa desde
40   el Isleo al gueste y avia en ella doze leguas
fasta vn cabo /. y aqui yo -ha- llame el cabo
hermoso que es dla parte dl gueste /. y asi
es fermoso redondo y mūy fondo sin baxas
fuera del y al comiēço es de piedra y baxo
45   y mas adentro es playa de arena com̄o quasi

Folio 15r

la dha Costa es y ay surgi esta noche viernes
hasta la mañana /. Esta costa toda y la parte
dla Isla q̃ yo vi : es toda quasi playa y la isla
la mas fermosa cosa q̃ yo vi /. q̃ si las otras
5   son mȳ hermosas esta es mas /. es de mu
chos arboles y mūy Vrdes y mūy grādes /. y esta
tr̄r̄a es mas alta q̃ las otras islas falladas /
y en ella alguno altillo no q̃ se le pueda llama[r]

name Islabela.[1] The wind was north and the said
isleo lay on an east-west course from the island of
Fernandina, from which[2] I had departed, and then
the coast ran west[3] from the *isleo* and there were
12 leagues of it as far as a cape. And here I called[4]
the cape Cabo Hermoso,[5] which is in the western
part. And it is indeed beautiful, round and very deep,
without shoals outside of it, and at its beginning it is
of stone and low, and more inland it is sandy beach, as
15r   almost all of the said coast is; and there I anchored
tonight, Friday, until morning. All of this coast and
the part of the island that I saw is almost all beach,
and the island the most beautiful thing that I have
seen. For if the others are very beautiful this one is
more so. It is an island of many very green and very
large trees. And this land is higher than the other
islands found, and there are on it some small heights;[6]
not that they can be called mountains, but they are

1. (14v29–36) *Vimos vna Isla . . . Islabela.* As is made evident in Parker (1983) and other papers in *Terrae Incognitae*, vol. 15, and in Judge (1986), several of the theories about Columbus's first voyage through the West Indies include the view that the islands called Samoet (also spelled Saomete or Saometo in the manuscript) by the Indians and named Isabela by Columbus are what are now known as Crooked and Fortune islands (the latter also known as Long Cay) and that the island on which Columbus hoped to find a town and native king was either the eastern part of Crooked Island or the northern part of Acklins, the third major member of this three-island group. Columbus never gave Acklins a name, and although he knew that Crooked and Fortune were separate islands, the name Isabela appears to denote both and possibly Acklins as well.
    Among those who agree that Columbus did visit Crooked and Fortune, there is still disagreement over his route to and through this island group. Possible copying errors, uncertainty about the meaning of a few terms, and puzzling statements about distances and the bearing of coastlines combine to make the *Diario* account of this part of the voyage one of particular difficulty.
2. (14v38) *De adonde* (from which, or the place from which). Lines 14v36–39 may be read to say either that the island of Fernandina lay on an east-west course from the *isleo* or that Columbus's point of departure from Fernandina was on such a course. The Jane-Vigneras (1960) translation reads: "The said islet lay on the course from the island of Fernandina, from which I had navigated from east to west." Note the spelling "Islabela" in 14v36.
3. (14v40) *Gueste* (west). Almost certainly a copying error for *sueste*, "southeast." The west coast of Crooked Island runs about north-northwest–south-southeast.
4. (14v41) *Llame* (I called, or I named). The manuscript looks as if Las Casas began to write the word *halle* (I found), then crossed out the first two letters, *ha*, and modified and added to the *lle* to make the word read *llame*. Alvar reads the two canceled letters as *he*.
5. (14v41–42) *Cabo hermoso.* Jane-Vigneras puts a period (not in the manuscript) after the word *hermoso* and eliminates a period (in the manuscript) after *parte del gueste*.
6. (15r8) The words *alguno altillo* (some small heights), although singular in form, are taken to be plural in intent, a not uncommon construction in Spanish.

mōtaña mas cosa q̃ afermosea lo otro y parece
10 de mūchas aguas /. alla al medio dla Isla desta
parte al nordeste haze vna grāde angla y
a mūchos arboledos y mūy espessos y muy grā
des /. yo quise yr a surgir en ella p[ar]a Salir
a tr̄r̄a y ver tanta fermosura : mas era el
15 fondo baxo y no podia surgir saluo largo de
tr̄r̄a y el viento era mȳ bueno p[ar]a venir a
este Cabo adonde yo surgi agora : al qual pu
se nōbre cabo fermoso porq̃ asi lo es /. y asi
no surgi en aq̃lla angla y avn porq̃ vide
20 este cabo de alla tan verde y tā fermoso : asi
com̄o todas las otras cosas y tr̄r̄as destas islas
q̃ yo no se adonde me vaya primero / ni
me se cansar los ojos de Vr tan fermosas
verduras y tan diuersas dlas nr̄as /. y avn
25 creo q̃ a en ellas mūchas yervas y mūchos ar
boles q̃ valen mūcho en españa p[ar]a tinturas
y p[ar]a medicinas de espeçeria mas yo no
los cognozco de q̃ llevo grāde pena /. y llegā
do yo aqui a este cabo vino el olor tan bueno
30 y suaue de flores /o arboles dla tierra q̃ era la
cosa mas dulçe dl mūdo /. de mañana antes
q̃ yo de aqui vaya yre en tr̄r̄a a ver q̃ es aqui
en el cabo /. No es la poblaçion saluo alla
mas dentro adonde dizē estos hōbres q̃ yo
35 traygo q̃sta el rey y q̃ trae mucho oro /. y yo
de mañana quiero yr tanto avante q̃ halle la po
blaçion y vea /o aya lengua con este rey q̃ se
gū estos dan las señas : el señorea todas estas
Islas comarcanas : y va vestido y trae sobre si
40 mucho oro /. avnq̃ no doy mūcha fe a sus dezi
res : asi por no los entender yo bien : como

things that beautify the rest; and it seems to have much water. There in the middle of the island,[1] from this part northeast, it forms a great bight[2] and there are many wooded places, very thick and of very large extent. I tried to go there to anchor in it so as to go ashore and see so much beauty; but the bottom was shoal and I could not anchor except far from land and the wind was very good for going to this cape where I am anchored now, to which I gave the name Cabo Hermoso, because such it is. And so I did not anchor in that bight and also because I saw this cape from there, so green and so beautiful; and likewise are all the other things and lands of these islands, so that I do not know where to go first; nor do my eyes grow tired of seeing such beautiful verdure and so different from ours. And I even believe that there are among them many plants and many trees which in Spain are valued for dyes and for medicinal spices; but I am not acquainted with them, which gives me much sorrow. And when I arrived here at this cape the smell of the flowers or trees that came from land was so good and soft that it was the sweetest thing in the world. In the morning, before I leave this place I will go ashore to see what is here on the cape. The town is not here but further inland where these men that I bring say the king is and that he wears much gold. And in the morning I want to go forward so far that I find the town and see or talk with this king of whom these men give the following details: he is the lord of all these nearby islands and he goes about dressed and wearing much gold on his person. Although I do not give much credit to what they say, from not understanding them well and also

1. (15r10–11) In the manuscript the phrase *alla al medio de la Isla* is the beginning of a sentence, not an ending, as Jane-Vigneras (1960, 38) has it. The change in punctuation, coupled with the translation of *desta parte* as "on this part" instead of "from this part," alters the sense of the statements.

2. (15r11) The word *angla* has two meanings: (1) a cape or promontory and (2) a cove, bay, or bight. Guillén Tato (1951, 29) defines it as *cabo* (cape), but in a note he writes that when used by Columbus for "bay," *angla* is an error for *angra*, a concavity in a shoreline or the water in such a concavity. The word *angla* appears eight times in the *Diario*, four times with the meaning "cape" (33r39, 34r11, 34r22, and 40v26) and four times with the meaning "bay" (15r11, 15r19, 34r44, and 54v27). The specific meaning is dependent on the context in which the word appears.

en cognoscer q̃llos son tan pobres de oro
que qualquiera poco q̃ste rey trayga les pare
çe a ellos mucho /. Este aqui yo digo cabo fer

Folio 15v

moso creo q̃ es Isla apartada de Saometo y avn
ay ya otra entremedias pequeña /. ~~yo no~~ yo no
curo asi de ver tanto por menudo porq̃ no
lo podria fazer en çinquenta años : porq̃ quiero
5   ver y descubrir lo mas q̃ yo pudiere p[ar]a bolver
a v̄ras altezas a nr̄o señor aplaziendo en abril
verdad es que fallando adonde aya oro o espeçeria
en cantidad me deterne fasta q̃ yo aya dello quā
to pudiere /. y por esto no fago sino andar p[ar]a
10   ver de topar en ello /.

                                            Sabado .20. de otubre

Ⅹ Oy al sol salido levante las anclas de donde
yo estava con la nao surgido en esta Isla de
saometo al cabo del sudueste adonde yo puse
15   nōbre el cabo dla laguna y a la Isla la Isabe
la p[ar]a navegar al nordeste y al leste de la p[ar]te
dl sueste y sur : adonde entendi destos hōbres
q̃ yo traygo q̃ era la poblaçion y el rey della y
falle todo tan baxo el fondo q̃ no pude entrar
20   ni navegar a ella y vide q̃ siguiendo el camino del
sudueste era mūy grā rodeo /. y por esto determi
ne de me bolver por el camino q̃ yo avia traydo
dl ~~norde~~[?] nornordeste dla p[ar]te del gueste y rode
ar esta isla p[ar]a y /. y el viento me fue tan

from recognizing that they are so poor in gold
that any little bit that the king may wear seems
much to them. This cape here that I call Cabo

15v　Hermoso I believe is on an island separate from
Samoet and also that there is still another small one
in between. I am not taking pains to see much in
detail because I could not do it in 50 years and
because I want to see and explore as much as I can so
I can return to Your Highnesses in April, Our Lord
pleasing. It is true that, finding where there is
gold or spices in quantity, I will stay until I get
as much of it as I can. And for this reason I do
nothing but go forward to see if I come across it.

Saturday 20 October

Today when the sun rose I raised anchor from the
place where I was with the ship anchored at this
island of Samoet at the southwest end, where I gave
to the cape the name Cabo de la Laguna,[1] and to the
island, Isabela, in order to sail northeast and east
from the southeastern and southern part, where I understood from these men I bring that the settlement
and the king of it are; and I found all of the bottom
so shallow that I could not enter or steer for the
settlement; and I saw that following the route to the
southwest was very roundabout. And for this reason
I decided to return by the route that I had taken, to
the north-northeast from the western part, and to go
around this island that way.[2] And the wind was so

1. (15v12–15) *Oy al sol ... laguna.* Columbus's fleet spent the night of 19
October at Cabo Hermoso at the south end of Fortune Island. Yet at dawn the ships
raised anchor at a Cabo de la Laguna. This is possible only if the two capes are in very
close proximity. It seems likely that Cabo de la Laguna was so named because of the
long, narrow lake, or lagoon, that parallels the east coast of Fortune Island at its southern end. Morison (1963) locates Cabo de la Laguna at the passage between Fortune
and Crooked islands, ten miles more or less to the north of Cabo Hermoso. How the
fleet could move this distance in a very brief time is never explained. Morison also
thinks that "Laguna" in the name of the cape refers to the body of water now called the
Bight of Acklins.
2. (15v21–24) *Determiné ... p[ar]a y.* This is a difficult passage. Our understanding of it is that Columbus plans to return by the way he had come (*volver por el
camino que yo avia traído*), i.e., to the Cabo del Isleo, and from there (*la parte del gueste*)
to sail north-northeast (*camino del nornordeste*) around the north side of Crooked
Island. Morison (1963) translates the critical phrases as "*from* the NNE *to* the west"
(italics added). Also see p. 73, n. 2, on Columbus's use of the phrase *camino de.*

25 escasso q̃ yo no nũca pude aver la tr̃ra al lon
    go dla costa saluo en la noche /. y porq̃s peligro
    surgir en estas islas saluo en el dia q̃ se vea
    con el ojo adonde se echa el ancla porq̃ es to
    do mãchas : vna de limpio y otra de non : yo
30 me puse a temporejar a la vela toda esta noche
    dl domĩgo /. las caravelas surgierõ porque
    hallarõ en tr̃ra temprano y pensarõ q̃ a sus
    señas q̃ erã acostũbradas de hazer / yria a sur
    gir mas no quise /.

35   Domĩngo .21. de otubre
    / A las diez oras llegue aqui a este cabo del
    Isleo y surgi y asi mismo las caravelas :
    y despues de aver comigo fui en tr̃ra : adõde
    aqui no avia otra poblacion q̃ vna casa /.
40 En la qual nõ falle a nadie q̃ creo q̃ con te
    mor se aviã fugido / porq̃ en ella estavã to
    dos sus adereços de casa /. yo no le de
    xe tocar nada Saluo q̃ me sali cõ estos
    capitanes y gente a ver la Isla : que si las
45 otras ya vistas son mũy fermosas y verdes

Folio 16r

    y fertibles : esta es mucho mas y de grãdes
    arboledos y mỹ verdes /. aqui es vnas gra
    des lagunas y sobre ellas y a la rueda es el
    arboledo en maravilla /. y aqui y en toda la isla
5   son todos Vrdes y las yervas comõ en el abril
    en el andaluzia /. y el Cantar dlos paxaritos
    q̃ pareçe q̃l hõbre nũca se querria partir de
    aqui /. y las manadas dlos papagayos q̃ ascu
    reçen el sol : y aves y paxaritos de tantas
10 mar̃as y tan diuersas dlas nr̃as : q̃ es ma
    ravilla /. y despues ha arboles de mill mar̃as
    y todos de su mar̃a fruto y todos guelen q̃s
    maravilla /. que yo estoy el mas penado dl mu
    do ~dlo~ de no los cognosçer /. porq̃ ~stoy çierto~

contrary that I was never able to keep to the land
along the coast except at night. And because it is
dangerous to anchor in these islands except during
the day, when one can see with one's own eyes where
the anchor is dropped, because the bottom is all
varied, one part clear and the next not so, I stood
off and on at the alert all this Sunday night. The
caravels anchored because they found themselves near
land early and thought with the signals they were
accustomed to make that I would go to anchor, but I
did not try.

Sunday 21 October

At the tenth hour I arrived here at this Cabo del
Isleo and anchored, and the caravels [did] likewise;
and after having eaten I went ashore, where here
there was no other settlement than one house. In it
I found no one, for I believe that they had fled with
fear, because in it was all their household gear. I
did not let any of it be touched, but went away with
these captains and men to see the island; for if the
others already seen are very beautiful and green and
16r   fertile, this one is much more so and with
large and very green groves of trees. Here there
are some big lakes and over and around them the
groves are marvelous. And here and in all of
the island the groves are all green and the
verdure like that in April in Andalusia. And the
singing of the small birds [is so marvelous]
that it seems that a man would never want to
leave this place. And [there are] flocks of
parrots that obscure the sun; and birds of so
many kinds and sizes, and so different from ours,
that it is a marvel. And also there are trees of
a thousand kinds and all [with] their own kinds
of fruit and all smell so that it is a marvel. I
am the most sorrowful man in the world,[1] not
being acquainted with them. Because I am quite

---

1. (16r14) Alvar (1976) reads the first canceled word in this line as *dllo* and the
second as *seyendo*.

15 soy bien çierto q̃ todos son cosa de valia y de
    llos traygo la demuestra / y asimismo dlas
    yervas /. andãdo asi en çerco de vna destas
    lagunas : vide vna sierpe : la qual matamos
    y traygo el cuero a v̄ras altezas /. Ella co
20 mo nos vido se echo en la laguna y nos le
    seguimos dentro : porq̃ no era m̄y fonda fasta

Juana devio   q̃ con lanças la matamos /. es de siete pal
de ser esta   mos en largo /. creo q̃ destas semejantes ay
    aqui en estas lagunas / mūchas /. aqui cognos
                                    e
25 çi dl lignaloe y mañana ∧determinado de ha
    zer traer a la nao diez quintales porq̃ me di
    zen q̃ vale mūcho /. tambien andãdo en
    busca de m̄y buena agua : fuimos a vna pobla
    çion aqui çerca adonde estoy surto media
30 legua : y la gente della com̄o nos sintierō
    dierō todos a fugir y dexarō las casas y es
    condierō su ropa y lo q̃ tenian por el mōte /.
    yo no dexe tomar nada ni la valia de vn
    alfilel /. despues se llegarō a nos ———[?] vnos
35 hōbres dellos y vno se llego ~~del todo~~ [?] aqui /.
    yo di vnos cascaveles y vnas cuentezillas
    de vidro y quedo mūy contento y mūy alegre /.
    y porq̃ la amistad creciese mas y los requirie
    se algo le hize pedir agua /. y ellos des
40 pues q̃ fui en la nao vinierō luego a la pla
    ya con sus calabaças llenas y folgarō mūcho de

Folio 16v

    darnosla y yo les mãde dar otro ramalejo
    de cuentezillas de vidro y dixerō q̃ de mañana
    vernian aca /. yo queria henchir aqui toda la
    vasija dlos navios de agua : por ende si el
5   t̄po me da lugar luego me p[ar]tire a rodear
    esta isla fasta q̃ yo aya lengua con este rey y
    ver si puedo aver dl el oro q̃ oyo q̃ trae /. y des

certain that all of them are things of value;
and I am bringing samples of them, and likewise
of the plants. Thus walking around one of these
lakes, I saw a serpent,[1] which we killed; and I
am bringing the skin to Your Highnesses. When it
saw us it threw itself into the lake and we
followed it in, because it was not very deep,
until with lances we killed it. It is seven
palmos[2] in length. I believe that there are many
similar ones here in these lakes. Here I recognized aloes, and tomorrow I have decided to have
ten *quintales*[3] [of it] brought to the ship
because I am told that it is very valuable.
Also, walking in search of very good water, we
went to a nearby village, half a league from the
place where I am anchored; and the people of it,
when they heard us, took to flight and left the
houses and hid their clothes and what they had in
the bush. I did not allow anything to be taken,
not even of the value of a pin. Later some of
the men approached us, and one came up to us
here. I gave him some bells and some small glass
beads and he was very pleased and happy. And so
that our friendship would increase and that
something would be asked of them, I ordered that
he be asked for water. And after I went on
shipboard they soon came to the beach with their
calabashes full and were delighted to give it to
16v   us; and I ordered that they be given other trifling
little strings of glass beads and they said that in
the morning they would come around. I wanted to
fill here all the water jars of the ship. Then, if
weather permits, I will soon depart to go around
this island until I have speech with this king and
see if I can get from him the gold that I hear that

---

1. (16r18) *Sierpe*. Ferdinand Columbus (1945, 67) says that the Indians called
the *sierpe* an *iguana*, and that it was their choicest food.
2. (16r22–23) *Palmos*. This (long) palm is one-eighth of the common commercial *cana* (a cloth measure) of southern Europe and is about 24.75 centimeters
long. Thus, the seven-palm *sierpe* was about 5.7 present-day English feet long.
3. (16r26) *Quintales*. The *quintal* (or *cantar*), from the Arabic *qintar*, was a
commercial hundredweight unit.

pues partir p[ar]a otra isla grāde mūcho q̃ creo
q̃ deve ser cipango segū las señas q̃ me dan
10   estos yndios q̃ yo traygo a la qual ellos llamā
Colba /. en la qual dizen q̃ a naos y marcā
tes mūchos y mūy grādes /. y desta isla otra q̃
llamā bofio q̃ tanbien dizen q̃s mūy grāde /.
y a las otras q̃ son entremedio vere asi de pas
15   sada : y segū yo fallare recaudo de oro /o espe
çeria determinare lo q̃ e de fazer /. mas toda
via tengo determinado de yr a la tr̄r̄a firme

                                              dar
nõ   y a la çiudad de quisay y ~~las~~-[?] ∧ las c[ar]tas de vr̄as
altezas al grā Can y pedir respuesta y venir
20   con ella /.

                                              lunes .22. de otubre
/ toda esta noche y oy estuve aqui ~~esp[er]ando~~-[?] aguar
dando si el rey de aqui /o otras p[er]sonas
traherian oro /o otra cosa de sustançia y vinie
25   rō mūchos desta gente semejantes a los otros
dlas otras Islas asi desnudos y asi pintados
dellos de blanco / dellos de colorado / dellos de
prieto / y asi de mūchas mar̃as /. trayan aza
gayas y algunos ovillos de algodon a res
30   gatar /. el qual trocavā aqui cõ algunos ma
rineros por pedaços de vidro de taças quebra
das : y por pedaços descudillas de barro /. al
gunos dllos trayan algunos pedaços de oro
colgado al nariz /. el qual de buena gana
35   davan por vn Cascavel destos de pie de gavi
lano / y por cuētezillas de vidro // mas es
tan poco q̃ nõ es nada /. Que es Vrdad q̃ qual
quiera ~~cosa~~-[?] poca cosa q̃ se les de : ellos tabiē
teniā a grā maravilla nr̄a venida y creyan
40   q̃ eramos venidos dl çielo /. tomamos
agua p[ar]a los navios en vna laguna q̃ aqui
esta çerca dl cabo dl Isleo q̃ asi anõbre / y en

he wears. And afterwards I will leave for another very large island that I believe must be Cipango according to the indications that these Indians that I have give me, and which they call Colba. In it they say there are many and very large ships and many traders.[1] And from this island [I will go to] another which they call Bohío, which also they say is very big. And the others which are in between I will also see on the way; and, depending on whether I find a quantity of gold or spices, I will decide what I am to do. But I have already decided to go to the mainland and to the city of Quinsay and to give Your Highnesses' letters to the Grand Khan and to ask for, and to come with, a reply.

Monday 22 October

All this night and today I stayed waiting [to see] if the king of this place or other persons would bring gold or something else of substance; and there came many of these people, like the others of the other islands, naked and painted, some of them with white, some with red, some with black, and so on in many fashions. They brought javelins and balls of cotton to barter, which they traded here with some sailors for pieces of broken glass cups and for pieces of clay bowls. Some of them were wearing pieces of gold hanging from their noses, and they willingly gave it for a bell of the sort [put] on the foot of a sparrow hawk and for small glass beads; but it is so little that it is no-thing. For it is true that any little thing given to them, as well as our coming, they considered great marvels; and they believed that we had come from the heavens. We took water for the ships from a lake which is here near the Cabo del Isleo, which

---

1. (16v11–12) The word *marcantes* is not in the *Diccionario* (1956). Perhaps it is an error for either *mareantes* or *marchantes*. We have translated the word as "traders," not "sailors," our reason being that Columbus was looking for places of extensive commerce, not primarily places where there were many sailors. Both Morison (1963) and Jane-Vigneras (1960) translate the word as "sailors"; Thacher (1903–1904) has "seamen." The *muchos*, we believe, applies both to "ships" and "traders," whereas *muy grandes* applies to ships alone.

Yuana es esta   la d̄ha laguna martin aloso pinçon capitan dla pin
                 ta mato otra sierpe tal com̄o la otra de ayer de siete
          45   palmos y fize tomar aqui del liñaloe quāto se fallo /

Folio 17r

                                                              martes 23. de otubre

          ⫽ Quisiera oy p[ar]tir p[ar]a la Isla de cuba q creo q̄ deve ser
          çipango segun las señas q̄ dan esta gente dla grād̄e
          za della y riqueza y no me detorne mas aqui ni
     5   esta Isla al rededor p[ar]a yr a la poblacion
                                                          con e
          com̄o tenia determinado p[ar]a aver lengua -de-[?] ste rey
          o señor /. q̄ es por no me detener mūcho pues veo
          q̄ aqui no ay mina de oro y al rodear destas Islas
          a menester mūchas ma-ñas-[?]neras de viento y no
     10   vienta asi com̄o los hōbres querrian /. y pues es
          de andar adonde aya trato grād̄e : digo q̄ no es
          razō de se detener saluo yr a camino y calar
          mūcha tr̄r̄a fasta topar en tr̄r̄a mūy provechosa avnq̄
          mi entender es q̄sta sea mūy provechosa de espeçe
     15   ria mas q̄ yo no la cognozco q̄ llevo la mayor pena
          dl mūd̄o q̄ veo mill -mrs- mařas de arboles que
          tienē cada vno su mařa de fruta y verde agora
          com̄o en españa en el mes de mayo y junio y mill
          mařas de yervas : eso mesmo con flores y de todo
     20   [no se?] cognoscio saluo este liñaloe de q̄ oy mād̄e tā
          biēn traer a la nao mūcho p[ar]a levar a .v.al. /. y no
          e dado ni doy la vela p[ar]a cuba porq̄ no ay viento
          saluo calma muerta y llueve mūcho y llovio ayer
          mūcho sin hazer ningū frio antes el dia haze calor
     25   y las noches temperadas com̄o en mayo en españa
          en el andaluzia /.

                                                              miercoles 24. de otubre

          ⫽ esta noche a media noche levante las anclas dla
          Isla Isabela dl cabo del Isleo q̄s dla p[ar]te del norte

thus I named. And in the said lake Martín Alonso
Pinzón, captain of the *Pinta*, killed another ser-
pent just like yesterday's, seven *palmos* long; and
I ordered as much aloe taken as was found here.

17r   Tuesday 23 October
I should like to leave today for the island of Cuba, which
I believe must be Cipango according to the indications
that these people give of its size and wealth, and I
will not delay here any longer nor   around
this island in order to go to the town, as I had
decided [to do], in order to talk to this king or lord.
[This] is so as not to delay much, since I see that here
there is no gold mine, and that to go around these
islands there is need of many kinds of wind, and the
wind does not blow just as men would wish. And
since one should go where there is large-scale
commerce, I say that there is no reason to delay but
[reason] to go forward and investigate much territory
until we encounter a very profitable land; although
my understanding is that this land may be very
profitable in spices. But that I do not recognize them
burdens me with the greatest sorrow in the world;
for I see a thousand kinds of trees, each of which has
its own kind of fruit, and they are green now as in
Spain in the months of May and June; and there are a
thousand kinds of plants, and the same with flowers
and of everything. Nothing was recognized except
this aloe, of which today I also ordered a lot brought
to the ship to take to Your Highnesses. And I have
not set and am not setting sail for Cuba because there
is no wind, but dead calm. And it is raining a lot and
yesterday it rained a lot without being cold; rather,
the day is hot and the nights temperate, as in May in
Spain in Andalusia.

                                              Wednesday 24 October
Tonight at midnight I weighed anchors from the
island of Isabela, from the Cabo del Isleo, which is in
the northern part, where I was staying, to go to the

30 adonde y estava posado p[ar]a yr a la Isla de Cuba a
    donde oy desta gente q̃ era mūy grāde y de gran
    trato : y avia en ella oro y especerias y naos
    grādes y mercaderos y me amostro q̃ al gues
    -sueste- sudueste yria a ella /. y yo asi lo tēgo
35 porq̃ creo q̃ si es asi como por señas q̃ me
    hiziero todos los yndios destas Islas y aqllos
    q̃ llevo yo en los navios porq̃ por lengua
    no los entiendo : es la Isla de cipango de q̃
    se cuētan cosas maravillosas /. y en las esperas
40 q̃ yo vi y en las pinturas de mapamūdos es
    ella en esta comarca /. y asi navegue fasta el dia
    al guesudueste y amaneçiendo ———[?] calmo el viē
    to y llovio y asi casse toda la noche y estuve asi
    cō poco viento fasta q̃ passava de medio dia y
45 estonçes torno a ventar mūy amoroso y llevava
    todas mis velas dla nao maestra y dos bone
    tas y triquete y çevadera y mezana y vela de
    gavia y el batel por popa /. Asi anduve al ca
    mino fasta q̃ anocheçio : y estonçes me quedava

Folio 17v

    el cabo verde dla Isla fernādina el qual es dla p[ar]te
    de sur a la p[ar]te de gueste me quedava al norueste
    y hazia de mi a el siete leguas /. y porq̃ venta
    va ya rezio y no sabia yo cuāto camino ovie
5   se fasta la d̃ha Isla de Cuba y por no la yr a
    demādar de noche : porq̃ todas estas -estas-[?] islas
    son mȳ fondas a no hallar fondo todo ende
    rredor saluo a tyro de dos lōbardos y esto es todo
    māchado vn pedaço de rrquedo y otro de arena
10 y por esto no se puede seguramēte surgir saluo
    a vista de ojo /. y por tanto acorde de amaynar
    las velas todas saluo el triquete y andar cō
    el y de a vn rato creçia mūcho el viento y hazia
    mūcho camino de q̃ dudava y hera mūy gran
15 çerrazō y llovia : māde amaynar el trinquete
    y no anduvimos esta noche dos leguas etē /.

island of Cuba, which I heard from these people was
very large and of great commerce and that there were
there gold and spices and great ships and merchants;
and they showed me that [sailing] to the west-
southwest I would go to it. And I believe so, because
I believe that it is so according to the signs that all the
Indians of these islands and those that I have with me
make (because I do not understand them through
speech) [and] that it is the island of Cipango of which
marvelous things are told. And in the spheres that I
saw and in world maps it is in this region. And so I
sailed until day to the west-southwest; and at dawn
the wind died down and it rained, and it continued in
this way almost all night, and I was with little wind
until noon passed, and then the wind again blew
gently and I carried all my ship's sails: mainsail and
two bonnets, foresail, spritsail, mizzen, and main
topsail; and the ship's boat at the stern. Thus I
proceeded on my way until night fell; and then Cape Verde,
17v   which is the western part of the southern part of the
island of Fernandina, lay to the northwest at a
distance from me to it of seven leagues. And because
now the wind was blowing strongly and I did not
know how far it might be to the said island of Cuba,
and in order not to go looking for it at night (because
the shores of all these islands are very steep and one
does not find bottom anywhere around them except
at a distance of two lombard shots, and this bottom is
all spotty, one part rocky and another sandy, because
of which one cannot anchor safely except by sight);
therefore I decided to lower all the sails except the
foresail and to proceed with it [only]. And after a
time the wind increased greatly and the ship went fast
but on a doubtful course and the weather was very
thick and it was raining; so I ordered the foresail
lowered and we did not make two leagues this night, etc.

Jueves ~~28~~ [?] .25. de otubre

⟋ Navego dspues dl Sol salido al gueste ~~sudsueste~~
sudueste hasta las nueve oras andarian .5.

20   leguas / despues mudo el camino al gueste
andavā .8. millas por ora hasta la vna dspues
de medio dia y de alli hasta las tres y andariā
.44. millas / entōçes vierō tr̄ra y erā siete /o ocho
Islas en luēgo todas de norte a sur distavan

25   dllas .5. leguas etc̃ .

viernes .26. de otubre

⟋ estuvo dlas d̄has Islas dla p[ar]te dl sur era todo
baxo çinco /o seys leguas surgio por alli /. dixe
r̄o los yndios q̃ llevava q̃ avia dllas a cuba

30   andadura de dia y medio con sus almadias
q̃ son navetas de vn madero adonde no
llevā vela /. estas son las Canoas /. p[ar]tio de alli
p[ar]a cuba . porq̃ ~~por se~~ [?] por las señas q̃ los yndios
le davā dla grādeza y dl oro y p[er]las dlla

35   pensava q̃ era ella conviene a saber çipango /.

Sabado .27. de otubre

salido el Sol
⟋ levāto las anclas∧de aq̃llas Islas q̃ llamo las
Islas de arena por el poco fondo q̃ tenian dla p[ar]te
dl sur hasta seys leguas / anduvo ocho millas

40   por ora hasta la vna del dia al sursudueste y
avrian andado .40. millas / y hasta la noche an
darian 28 ∴ ~~leguas~~ millas al mesmo camino
y antes de noche vierō tr̄ra / estuvierō la noche

Thursday 25 October

After the sun rose he steered west-southwest until the
ninth hour. They made about five leagues. Then he
changed course to the west. They went eight miles an
hour until one hour after noon and from then until
three, and they made about 44 miles. Then they saw
land, and it was seven or eight islands, all extending
from north to south. They were distant from them
five leagues, etc.

Friday 26 October

He went from the southern part of the said islands five
or six leagues. It was all shoal. He anchored there.
The Indians that he brought said that from the islands
to Cuba was a journey of a day and a half in their
dugouts, which are small vessels made of a single
timber which do not carry sails. These are canoes.
He left from there for Cuba, because[1] from the
signs that the Indians gave him of its size and of its
gold and pearls he thought it must be it, that is, Cipango.

Saturday 27 October

At sunrise he weighed anchor from those islands, which
he called the Islas de Arena because of the shallow
bottom that they found to the south for six leagues.
He made eight miles per hour south-southwest until
one hour of the day[2] and probably traveled 40
miles. And up until night they traveled about 28
miles[3] on the same course and before night they saw

1. (17v33) Alvar (1976) reads the canceled text in this line as *porsu*. It looks as
if Las Casas started to write *por senas*, got as far as *por se*, then decided to cancel what
he had written in favor of *por las senas*.
2. (17v40) The phrase *hasta la vna del dia* seems to require the meaning "one
o'clock in the afternoon," not "the first hour of day." Time must be provided to travel
the 40 miles made good since sunrise. If Columbus's ship really sailed eight miles per
hour for the entire period, he would have gone farther. It seems likely that in the shoal
area he was passing through for some 24 miles, he would have proceeded more
cautiously.
3. (17v42) The cancellation of *leguas* and its replacement by *millas* is one of 12
similar changes in the *Diario*. It is worth noting again that there are no changes from
millas to *leguas*.

al rep[ar]aro cō mūcha lluvia q̃ llovio　　anduvierō
45　el sabado fasta el poner dl sol .17. leguas al sur
　　sudueste /

　　　　　　　　　　　　　　　　　　Domīgo 28 dias de otubre

Folio 18r

　　　　　　　　　　　　　　　　　　du
/ fue de alli en demāda de la Isla de cuba al sursu∧ este
a la tr̄r̄a dlla mas çercana y entro en vn rio
mȳ hermoso y mȳ sin peligro de baxas ni
de otros inconvenientes y toda la costa q̃ anduvo por
5　alli era mȳ hōdo y mȳ limpio fasta tr̄r̄a / te
nia la boca del rio doze braças y es bien ancha
p[ar]a barloventear / surgio dentro diz q̃ a tyro de lo
barda /. dize el almiͤ q̃ nūca tan hermosa
　　　　　　　　　　　　　　çercado el rio
cosa vido / lleno de arboles todo ∧fermosos y ver
10　des y diuersos de los nr̄os cō flores y con su
fruto cada vno dsu mar̃a /. aves mūchas y pa
xaritos q̃ cantavā mūy dulçemēte /. avia grā
cantidad de palmas de otra mar̃a q̃ las de guinea
y dlas nr̄as : de vna estatura mediana y los
15　————[?] pies sin aq̃lla camisa y las hojas mȳ
grādes / cō las quales cobijan las casas y la
tierra mȳ llana /. salto el almiͤ en la barca y
fue a tierra y llego a dos casas q̃ creyo ser de
pescadores y q̃ cō temor se huyerō en ————[?]
20　vna dla q̄les hallo vn perro q̃ nūca ladro. y en
ambas casas hallo redes de hilo de palma y cordeles
y anzuelo de cuerno y fisgas de guesso y otros
aparejos de pescar y muchos huegos dentro
y creyo q̃ en cada vna casa se axuntan muchas p[er]sonas /.
25　mādo q̃ no se tocase en cosa de todo ello y asi se
hizo /. la yerva era grāde com̄o enl andaluzia por

land. They spent the night jogging off and on[1]
with much rain. On Saturday up until sunset they
made 17 leagues to the south-southwest.

Sunday 28 October

18r   He went from there to the south-southwest looking
for the nearest land of the island of Cuba and he
entered a very beautiful river free of dangerous shoals
or other obstacles. And the whole coast that he went
along there was very deep and clear [of shallows] all
the way to land. The mouth of the river had a depth
of 12 *brazas*[2] and was quite wide enough for tacking.
He anchored a lombard shot, he says, inside. The
Admiral says that he never saw such a beautiful thing,
full of trees all surrounding the river, beautiful and
green and different from ours, each one with its own
kind of flowers and fruit. [There were] many birds,
and some little birds that sang very sweetly. There
were great numbers of palms, differing from those of
Guinea and from ours: of medium height and the
trunks without covering and the leaves very large.
With them they cover their houses. And the land [is]
very level. The Admiral got into the launch and went
ashore and reached two houses which he thought
belonged to fishermen who had fled in fear. In
one[3] of them he found a dog that never barked, and
in both houses he found nets of palm thread and
cords and a fishhook of horn and fish spears of bone
and other fishing equipment and, inside, many fires;
and he thought that each house was occupied by
many persons jointly. He ordered that not a thing of
all this was to be touched, and thus it was done. The
grass was as tall as in Andalusia in April and May; he

1. (17v44) *Al rep[ar]aro* (jogging off and on). Las Casas inadvertently added
an extra syllable to *al reparo* by writing the fancy *p* that stands for *par*.
2. (18r6) *Braças*. This measure for soundings is probably equivalent to the *aune*
of Provins, a measure of 2.5 feet of 18 digits (the Roman foot), or a total of 45 digits
long. Since the 18-digit foot is about 33 centimeters long, one *braza* (the modern
spelling) is about 2.7 English feet. The sounding lines were probably marked in *varas*
(also 45 digits long), the equivalent measure of Castile, just 11 millimeters longer.
Also see p. 339, n. 1.
3. (18r19) Alvar (1976) reads the cancellation as *vna*.

abril y mayo : hallo verdolagas mūchas y bledos /.
tornose a la barca y anduvo por el rio arriba vn buē
rato y era : diz q̃ grā plazer ver aq̃llas Vrduras
30 y arboledas y dlas aves q̃ no podia dexallas
p[ar]a se bolver /. dize q̃ es aq̃lla Isla la mas hermo
sa q̃ ~~nūca se vido~~ oyos ayā visto : llena de mȳ
buenos puertos y rios hondos y la mar q̃ pa
reçia q̃ nūca se devia de alçar : porq̃ la yerva
35 dla playa llegava hasta quasi el agua . la qual
no suele llegar donde la mar es brava /.
hasta entonçes no avia experimentado en todas aq̃llas
Islas q̃ la mar fuese brava /. la isla dize q̃s
llena de mōtañas mȳ ~~hermosas~~ avnq̃ no son mȳ
40 ~~altas~~ grādes en lōgura saluo altas y toda la
otra tr̄r̄a es alta de la mar̃a de çeçilia /. llena es de
m̄chas aguas segū —————[?] pudo entēder dlos
yndios q̃ cosigo lleva q̃ tomo en la Isla de gua
nahani /. los quales le dizē por señas q̃ ay diez rios
45 grādes : y q̃ cō sus canoas no la pueden çercar en
.xx. dias /. quādo yva a tr̄r̄a ~~salierō al~~ [?] cō los navios
salierō dos almadias /o canoas / y comō vierō q̃ los
marineros entravā en la barca y remavan p[ar]a yr

Folio 18v

a ver el fondo del rio p[ar]a saber donde avian de
surgir : huyero las canoas /. dezian los yndios
nō   q̃ en aq̃lla Isla avia minas de oro y perlas
y vido el almiᵉ lugar apto p[ar]a ellas y almejas
5 q̃s señal dellas / y entendia el almiᵉ q̃ alli ve
nian naos del grā Can y grādes /. y q̃ de alli a
tr̄r̄a firme avia jornada de diez dias   lla
mo el almiᵉ aq̃l rio y puerto de San saluador /.

lunes .29. de otubre

10 / alço las anclas de aq̃l puerto y navego al poniente
p[ar]a yr diz q̃ a la çiudad donde le pareçia q̃ le
dezian los yndios q̃stava aq̃l rey /. vna punta
dla Isla le salia al norueste seys leguas de
alli /. otra punta le salia al leste diez leguas /.

found much purslane and pigweed. He returned to
the launch and went up the river for some time and it
was, he says, a great pleasure to see those green plants
and groves and the birds, for he could not leave to go
back. He says that that island is the most beautiful
that eyes have ever seen: full of good harbors and
deep rivers, and the sea appears as if it must never
rise, because the growth on the beach reaches almost
to the water, which it usually does not where the sea
is rough. Up until then they had not experienced
rough seas in any of those islands. He says that the
island is full of very beautiful mountains, although
they are not great in length, but high, and all the
other land is high after the manner of Sicily. It is full
of streams of water according to what he could[1]
understand from the Indians whom he took in the
island of Guanahani and has with him. They tell
him by signs that there are ten big rivers; and that
with their canoes they cannot circle it in 20 days.
While he was going toward land with the ships,
two dugouts or canoes came out. And when they
saw that the sailors were getting into the launch

18v   and were rowing to go look at the depth of the river
in order to know where they should anchor, the canoes
fled. The Indians said that in that island there were gold
mines and pearls, and the Admiral saw a likely place for
pearls and clams, which are a sign of them. And the
Admiral understood that large ships from the Grand
Khan came there and that from there to *tierra firme*
was a journey of ten days. The Admiral named that
river and harbor San Salvador.

Monday 29 October

He raised anchors from that harbor and headed west in
order, he says, to go to the city where it seemed to him
that the Indians said the king was. From there, six
leagues to the northwest, a point projected from the
island. Ten leagues to the east another point

---

1. (18r42) Alvar (1976) reads the cancellation as *puddo*, which seems unlikely
because of the doubled *d*.

15 andada otra legua vido vn rio no tā grāde entrada
al qual puso nōbre el rio dla luna /. anduvo
hasta ora de bisperas : vido otro rio mȳ mas
grāde q̃ los otros y asi se lo dixerō por señas
los yndios y açerca del vido buenas poblaçio

                                                                          mares
20 nes de casas : llamo al rio el rio de ∧ ~~martes~~ [?] /.
enbio dos barcas a vna poblaçion por aver len
gua y a vna dllas vn yndio dlos q̃ traya porq̃
ya los entēdian algo y mostravā estar contentos
co los xp̄īaños /. dlas quales todos los hōbres
25 y mugeres y criaturas huyerō desmāparādo
las casas cō todo lo q̃ tenian / y mādo el almi͜e q̃
no se tocase en cosa /. las casas diz q̃ erā ya mas
hermosas q̃ las q̃ aviā visto y creya q̃ cuāto mas
se allegase a la tr̄ra firme serian mejores /. erā
30 hecha a mar̄a de alfaneques mȳ grādes y pare
çian tiendas en real sin cōcierto de ~~casas~~ [?] calles
sino vna aca y otra aculla y de dentro mȳ
barridas y linpias y sus adereços mȳ compuestos

                                                         hermosas
todas son de ramos de palma mȳ ∧ ~~compuestas~~ [?] /.
35 hallarō mūchas estatuas en figura de mugeres
y mūchas cabeças en mar̄a de caratona mȳ

nõ   biē labradas /. no se si esto tienē por hermo
sura /o adorā en ellas /. avia perros q̃ jamas
ladrarō : avia avezitas saluajes māsas por sus
40 casas : avia maravillosos adereços de redes
y anzuelos y artifiçios de pescar /. no le tocarō
en cosa dello /. creyo q̃ todos los dla costa deviā
de ser pescadores ∴ q̃ llevā el pescado la tr̄ra dētro :
porq̃ aq̃lla isla es mȳ grāde y tan hermosa
45 q̃ no se hartava dezir bien dlla /. dize q̃ hallo
arboles y frutas de mȳ maravilloso sabor ∴
y dize q̃ deve aver vacas en [e]lla y otros gana

devia de ser de dos : porq̃ vido cabeças en guesso q̃ le pareciero
manati   de vaca /. Aves y paxaritos y el cantar dlos gri

projected from it. Going another league he saw a
river with not so large an entrance,[1] to which he
gave the name Rio de la Luna. He sailed on until
the hour of vespers. He saw another river very much
bigger than the others, and also the Indians told him
this by signs; and nearby he saw good settlements of
houses. He called the river Rio de Mares. He sent
two launches to one settlement to parley, and in one
of them sent one of the Indians that he brought
with him because now the Indians understood the
Spaniards somewhat and appeared to be content
with the Christians. All the men and women and
children fled from them, abandoning the houses with
everything that they had. And the Admiral ordered
that not a thing be touched. The houses, he says,
were now more beautiful than those which they had
seen, and he believed that the more they approached
tierra firme the better they would be. They were
made in the fashion of very large Moorish campaign
tents and they looked like tents in a camp without
any regularity of streets, but one here and another
there; and inside they were very neat and clean and
their furnishings very orderly. All are made of palm
branches [and are] very pretty. They found many
statues in the shape of women and many masklike
heads very well made. I do not know whether this is
because they consider them beautiful or whether they
worship them. There were dogs that never barked;
there were small tame wild birds around their houses;
there was wonderful equipment of nets and hooks
and contrivances for fishing. They did not touch a
thing of it. He believed that all the people of the
coast must have been fishermen who carried the
fish inland, because that island is very large and so
beautiful that he never tired of speaking well of it. He
says that he found trees and fruits of wonderful flavor
and he says that there must be cows on it and other
livestock because he saw skulls that appeared to him
those of cows. [There were] birds of different
sizes, and the singing of the grasshoppers all

---

1. (18v15) The word *entrada*, partially boxed in the right margin, is probably an afterthought.

Folio 19r

llos en toda la noche cō q̃ se holgava todos / los
aryes sabrosos y dulçes de toda la noche ni
frio ni callente /. mas por el camino dlas otras
yslas aq̃lla diz q̃ haziā grā calor y alli
5 no / saluo tēplado como en mayo / atrivuye
el calor dlas otras Islas : por ser mȳ llanas
y por el viento q̃ trayan hasta alli ser levate
y por eso calido / el agua de aq̃llos rios
era salada —[?] a la boca : no supierō de donde
10 bevian los yndios avnq̃ teniā en sus casas
agua dulçe /. en este rio podia los navios bolte
jar p[ar]a entrar y p[ar]a salir y tienē mȳ buenas
señas (o marcas : tienē siete o ocho braças de
fondo a la boca y dentro çinco /. toda aq̃lla mar
15 dize q̃ le p[ar]eçe q̃ deve ser siempᵣ māsa como el rio
de sevilla : y el agua aparejada p[ar]a criar per
las /. hallo caracoles grādes sin sabor   no como
los despaña /. señala la disposiçion dl rio y dl
puerto q[ue] arriba dixo y nōbro san saluador : q̃
20 tiene sus mōtañas hermosas y altas como
la peña dlos enamorados y vna dllas tiene
en çima otro mōtezillo a mařa de vna hermosa
mezquita /. estotro rio y puerto en q̃ agora estava
tiene dla p[ar]te del sueste dos mōtañas : asi redōdas
25 y dla p[ar]te del gueste norueste vn hermoso cabo lla
no q̃ sale fuera /.

esta [?] q̃ el puer
to de barocoa

o es este el de
barocoa por lo q̃
[dize?] dl cabo
llano

martes .30. de otubre

∥ salio dl rio de martes /o de [?] mares al norue
ste y vido cabo lleno de palmas y pusole cabo
30 cabo de palmas dspues de avia andado quinze le
guas /. los yndios q̃ yvā en la caravela pin
ta dixerō q̃ detras de aq̃l cabo avia vn rio y dl

19r   night delighted everyone. The breezes [were] pleas-
      ant and sweet all night long, neither cold nor hot.
      But on the way from[1] the other islands to that one
      he says that it was very hot, and there [where he
      was] it was not, but temperate as in May. He attrib-
      utes the heat of the other islands to their being
      very flat and to the fact that the winds that car-
      ried them there were from the east and for that rea-
      son hot. The water of those rivers was salty at the
      mouth; he did not find out where the Indians drank,
      although they had fresh water in their houses. In
      this river the ships were able to tack to enter and to
      depart, and it has very good [sailing] signs or marks;
      it is seven or eight *brazas* deep at the mouth
      and five within. It appears to him, he says, that
      all of that sea must always be as gentle as the river
      of Seville, and the water suitable for the raising of
      pearls. He found big snails without flavor, not like
      those of Spain. He indicates the character of the
      river and harbor as he tells above, and he named it
      San Salvador. It has beautiful and high mountains
      like the Peña de los Enamorados, and one of them has
      on top another little mountain like a pretty mosque.
      This other river and harbor, in which he now was, has
      two mountains, both round, to the southeast; and to
      the west-northwest [there is] a pretty and flat cape
      that projects out.

Tuesday 30 October

      He went out of the Rio de Mares to the northwest
      and, after he had gone 15 leagues, saw a cape full of
      palms and named it Cabo de Palmas. The Indians in
      the caravel *Pinta* said that behind that cape there
      was a river and that from the river to Cuba was a
      four-day journey. And the captain of the *Pinta* said

1. (19r3–4) *Por el camino . . . aquella.* This is the single place in the *Diario* in
which the phrase *camino de* means "from": "on the way *from* the other islands *to* that
one."

muy as[eg]ura[do]s? an
davā todos por no
enteder a los yn
dios yo creo q̃ la
cuba q̃ los yndios
les dezian era la
provincia de cuba
nacan ———[?] de aq̃lla
Isla de cuba q̃ tiene
minas de oro etc̃
toda esta tr̄r̄a es
la Isla de cuba
y no trra firme .

rio a cuba avia quatro jornadas . y dixo el capi
tā dla pinta q̃ entendia q̃ esta cuba era çiudad
35   y q̃ aq̃lla tr̄r̄a era tr̄r̄a firme mȳ grāde q̃ va
m̄cho al norte . y q̃l rey de aq̃lla tr̄r̄a tenia
guerra cō el gra can al qual ellos llamavā cami
y a su tr̄r̄a /o çiudad faba y otros mūchos nōbres
determino el almi͡e de llegar a aq̃l rio y en
40   biar vn presente al rey dla tr̄r̄a y enbiarle la c[ar]ta
dlos reyes /. y p[ar]a ella tenia vn marinero q̃ a
via andado en guinea en lo mismo : y çiertos
yndios de gua[ha?]nahani q̃ querian yr con el con
q̃ dspues los tornasen a su tr̄r̄a /. al pareçer
45   dl almi͡e distava dla linea equinocial .42 gra
dos hazia la vāda dl norte . sino esta corrupta
la letra de donde treslade esto / y dize q̃ avia
de trabajar de yr al grā Can q̃ pensava q̃stava
por alli /o a la çiudad de Cathay q̃s del gra
                                                        dicho
50   Can / q̃ diz q̃ es mȳ grāde segū le fue ∧ ———[?]
antes q̃ p[ar]tiese despaña /. toda aq̃sta tr̄r̄a dize ser baxa
[y?] hermosa y fonda la mar

Folio 19v

                                                    miercoles 31.º de noviēbre
/ ~~alço las velas~~ toda la noche martes anduvo
barloventeando y vido vn rio donde no pudo
entrar por ser baxa la entrada y pēsarō los
5   Indios q̃ pudierā entrar los navios comō entrava
sus canoas : y navegādo adlante hallo vn cabo q̃
salia mȳ fuera y çercado de baxos y ~~hallo~~ vido
vna Concha /o baya donde podian estar navio peque
ños y no lo pudo encabalgar porq̃l viento se
10   avia tyrado dl todo al norte y toda la costa se cor

por esto q̃ dice aqui
del viento q̃ lle
vaba es çierto q̃
era cuba por la
costa q̃ andava

ria al nornorueste y sueste y otro cabo q̃ vido
adelante ~~se~~[?] le salia mas afuera /. ~~y~~[?] por esto y
por q̃l çielo mostrava de ventar rezio : se ovo de
tornar al rio de mares /.

                                                        .1º.
                                                Jueves ~~ii~~[?] de noviēbre
15
/ En saliendo el sol enbio el almi͡e las barcas
a tr̄r̄a a las casas q̃ alli estavan y hallarō q̃ erā

that he understood that this Cuba was a city and that
that land was a very big landmass that went far to
the north, and that the king of that land was at war
with the Grand Khan, who they call *cami*, and his
land or city, Faba, and many other names. The
Admiral decided to go to that river and to send a
present to the king of the land and to send him the letter
of the sovereigns. And for this purpose he had a sailor
who had gone on the same kind of mission in
Guinea, and certain Indians from Guanahani wished
to go with him so that afterward they would be
returned to their own land. In the opinion of the
Admiral he was distant from the equinoctial line 42
degrees toward the northern side (if the text from
which I took this is not corrupt). And he says that
he must strive to go to the Grand Khan, who he
thought was somewhere around there, or to the city
of Cathay, which belongs to the Grand Khan. For he
says that it is very large, according to what he was
told before he left Spain. All this land, he says, is low
and beautiful, and the sea deep.

19v   Wednesday 31 November [sic]

All Tuesday night he sailed tacking, and he saw a
river where he could not enter because the entrance
was shallow, and the Indians thought that the ships
might be able to enter as their canoes did. And
sailing on he found a cape that jutted very far out
and was surrounded by shoals; and he saw a cove or
bay where small ships could be harbored. And he was
unable to double the cape because the wind had
shifted completely to the north; and the whole coast
ran to the north-northwest and southeast; and another
cape that he saw ahead projected out from the island
even farther. Because of this, and because the sky
looked as if the wind would blow hard, it was necessary to return to the Rio de Mares.

Thursday 1 November

When the sun rose the Admiral sent the launches to
land, to the houses that were there, and they found

toda la gente huida [/?]. y desde a buē rato pa
reçio vn hōbre / y mādo el almi꞉ q̃ lo dexasen
20 asegurar y bolvierōse las barcas /. y despues
de comer torno a enbiar a tr̄r̄a vno de ~~stos~~-[?]
los yndios q̃ llevava : el qual dsde lexos le dio

nõ   bozes diziēdo q̃ no oviesen miedo porq̃ erā bue
na gēte y no haziā mal a nadie + antes dava
25 dlo suyo en mūchas islas q̃ aviā estado /. ~~y echo~~-[?]

a. ni erā del g[ran]
b. Can /

nõ   y echose a nadar el yndio y fue a tr̄r̄a : y dos
dlos de alli lo tomarō de braços y llevarō
lo a vna casa donde se informarō del /. y co
m̄o fuerō çiertos q̃ no se les avia de hazer
30 mal : se aseguarō y vinierō luego a los
navios mas de diez y seys almadias /o cano
as cō algodon hylado y otras cosillas suyas
dlas quales mādo el almi꞉ q̃ no se tomasse
nada : porq̃ supiesen q̃ no buscava el almi꞉

nõ   35 saluo oro a que ellos llamā nucay /.
y asi en todo el dia anduvierō y vinieron de
tr̄r̄a a los navios : y fuerō dlos xp̄ianos a tr̄r̄a
m̄y seguramēte /. el almi꞉ no vido a
alguno dllos oro / p[er]o ~~vido~~-[?] dize el almi꞉ q̃
40 vido a vno dllos vn pedaço de plata labra
do colgado a la nariz : q̃ tuvo por señal q̃ en

nõ   por señas
la tr̄r̄a avia plata /. Dixerō ∧q̃ antes de
tres dias vernian mūchos mercaderes dla
tr̄r̄a dentro a cōprar dlas cosas q̃ alli llevan
45 los xpianos : y darian nuevas del rey de aq̃lla
tr̄r̄a : el qual segū se pudo entender por las
señas q̃ davā q̃stava de alli quatro jornadas
porq̃ ellos avian enbiado mūchos por toda la

Folio 20r

tr̄r̄a a le hazer saber dl almi꞉ /.   Esta gēte dize
el almi꞉ es dla misma Calidad y costūbre dlos
otros hallados : sin ninguᵃ secta q̃ yo cognozca
q̃ fasta oy aquestos q̃ traygo no e visto hazer

nõ   5   ninguᵃ ~~cosa~~-[?] oraçion /. [A?]ntes dizē la salue y
el ave maria cō las manos al çielo com̄o le
amuestran // y hazē la señal dla cruz /.

that all the people had fled. And after quite a time
a man appeared, and the Admiral ordered that they
leave him reassured, and the boats returned. And
after eating, he again sent to land one of the Indians that he had with him, who from afar shouted,
saying that they should have no fear because the
Spaniards were good people and did harm to no one
and were not the Grand Khan's people but rather
gave of their own possessions on many islands where
they had been. And the Indian threw himself into the
water and swam to land, and two of the men of that
place took him by the arms and led him to a house
where they questioned him. And when they were
certain that no harm would be done to them, they
were reassured, and soon more than 16 dugouts or
canoes came to the ships with cotton thread and
other little things of theirs, of which the Admiral
ordered that nothing be taken in order that they
might know that the Admiral was seeking nothing
but gold, which they call *nucay*. And so all day they
came and went between land and the ships, and some
of the Christians went ashore very confidently. The
Admiral did not see gold on any of the Indians. But
the Admiral says that he saw on one of them a piece
of worked silver hung from his nose, which he took
for an indication that there was silver in the land.
The Indians said by signs that in less than three days
many merchants from inland would come to buy
some of the things that the Christians brought,
because they had sent many men throughout the land
to let people know about the Admiral, and [that]
they would give information about the king of that
land, who, according to what could be understood

20r   from the signs that they made, was four days'
journey from there. These people, the Admiral
says, are of the same quality and customs as the
others encountered; they are without any religion that
I know of, for up to the present I have not seen those
whom I have with me do any praying; rather, they say
the *Salve* and the *Ave Maria* with their hands to heaven
as the Spaniards show them; and they make the sign

toda la lengua tābien es vna y todos ami
gos y creo q̃ sean todas estas Islas : y q̃ tengā
10 guerra con el grā chan a q̃ ellos llamā Cavi
la y a la provinçia ba[s?]an /. y asi andā tābiē
desnudos comō los otros /. Esto dize el almiᵉ
El rio dize q̃s mūy hōdo : y en la boca pueden
llegar los navio cō el bordo hasta tr̄r̄a : no llega
15 el agua dulçe a la boca con vna legua / y es
mȳ dulçe /. y es çierto dize el almiᵉ q̃sta es
la tr̄r̄a firme /. y q̃stoy dize el ante zayto y

esta alga
ravia no
entiēdo yo

~~quisay~~ [?] ~~quisay~~ [?] quīsay ciē leguas poco mas
/o poco menos lexos dlo vno y de lo otro y
20 bien se amuestra por la mar q̃ viene de otra
suerte q̃ fasta aqui no a venido y ayer que
yva al norueste falle q̃ hazia frio /.

Viernes 2. de noviēbre

⸗ Acordo el almiᵉ enbiar dos hōbres españoles
25 el vno se llamava Rodrigo de xerez q̃ bivia
en ayamōte : y el otro era vn luys de
torres y avia bivido con el adelātado de mur
çia y avia sido judio y sabia diz q̃ ebrayco y
caldeo y avn algo aravigo /. y con estos enbio
30 dos yndios : vno dlos q̃ cōsigo traya de gua
nahani : y el otro ~~de aq̃lla~~ de aq̃llas casas
q̃ en el rio ~~avia~~ [?] estavā poblados /. dioles
~~fartas~~ [?] sartas de cuētas p[ar]a cōprar de comer
si les faltase : y seys dias de termino p[ar]a q̃
35 bolviesen /. Dioles muestras de espeçeria
p[ar]a ver si alguna della topasen /. dioles
Instruçion / de comō aviā de pregūtar por
el rey de aq̃lla tr̄r̄a y lo q̃ le aviā de hablar
de p[ar]tes dlos reyes de castilla / comō enbiavan
40 al almiᵉ p[ar]a q̃ les diese dsu p[ar]te sus c[ar]tas y
vn presente / y p[ar]a saber dsu estado y cobrar
amistad con el : y favoreçelle en lo q̃ oviese
dllos menester etc̃. y q̃ supiesen de çier

Folio 20v

tas provinçias y pueʳtos y rios de q̃ el almiᵉ
tenia noticia y quāto distavā de alli etc̃.

of the cross. They all speak the same language and all
are friends and I believe that all of these islanders
are friends and that they wage war with the Grand
Khan, whom they call *cavila* and the province, Basan.
And they also go naked like the others. The Admiral
says this. The river, he says, is very deep; and in
the mouth, ships can be laid alongside the shore.
Fresh water is short a league of reaching the mouth,
and it is very fresh. And it is certain, the Admiral
says, that this is *tierra firme* and that I am, he says,
off Zayto and Quinsay a hundred leagues more or
less from the one and from the other; and well this is
shown by the sea, which comes in a way other than
the way it has until now. And yesterday when I was
going to the northwest I found that it was cold.

Friday 2 November

The Admiral decided to send two Spanish men: the one
was called Rodrigo de Xerez, who lived in Ayamonte;
the other was one Luís de Torres, and he had lived
with the *adelantado* of Murcia and had been a Jew and
knew, he says, Hebrew and Chaldean and even a bit of
Arabic. And with these men he sent two Indians:
one from among those he brought with him from
Guanahani and the other from those inhabited houses
on the river. He gave them strings of beads to buy food
if they needed to and six days limit in which to return.
He gave them samples of spicery to see if they came
across any of it. He gave them instructions as to
how they were to inquire about the king of that land
and what they should say to him on behalf of the
sovereigns of Castile: how they had sent the Admiral
in order that he might, on their behalf, give him
their letters and a present, and in order to learn of
his circumstances and to obtain his friendship, and to
favor him in whatever he might need from them, etc.,
and that they might learn about certain provinces and
20v   harbors and rivers of which the Admiral had information, and how far they were distant from there, etc.

Aqui tomo el almi^e el altura cō vn quadrā

esto es falso
porq̃ no
esta cuba
sino en
grados .

te esta noche y hallo q̃stava .42. grados dla

5   linea equinoçial /. y dize q̃ por su cuēta ha

llo q̃ avia andado dsde la Isla del hierro

mill y çiento y quarēta y dos leguas /. y to

davia afirma q̃ aq̃lla es tr̄r̄a firme /.

Sabado .3. de noviēbre

10   ⁄ en la mañana ~~salio en tr̄r̄a el~~ entro en la barca

el almi^e y porq̃ haze el rio en la boca vn

grā lago el qual haze vn singularissimo puer

to mȳ hōdo y limpio de piedras mȳ buena

playa p[ar]a poner ~~los~~ [?] navios a mōte y mūcha le

15   ña : entro por el rio arriba hasta llegar al agua

dulce q̃ seria çerca de dos leguas : y subio en vn

mōtezillo ~~p[ar]a dscubrir~~ por dscubrir algo dla tr̄r̄a

y no pudo ver nada por las grādes arboledas

las quales mȳ frescas / odoriferas /. por lo qual

20   dize no tener duda q̃ no aya yervas aromati

cas /. dize q̃ todo era tan he^rmoso lo q̃ via : q̃

no podia cansar los ojos de ver tanta lindeza /

y los cantos dlas aves y paxaritos /. vinie

rō en aq̃l dia mūchas almadias /o canoas a los

25   navios a resgatar cosas de algodon filado y redes

en q̃ dormian q̃ son hamacas

Domīgo .4. de noviēbre

⁄ luego en amaneçiendo entro el almi^e en la

barca y salio a tr̄r̄a a caçar dlas aves q̃l dia

30   antes avia visto /. despues de buelto vino

a el martin alōso pinçon cō dos pedaços

de canela : y dixo q̃ vn portugues q̃ tenia

en su navio avia visto a vn yndio q̃ traya

dos manojos della grādes : p[er]o q̃ no se la oso

35   resgatar por la pena q̃l almi^e tenia puesta

Here this night the Admiral took the altitude [of the
Pole Star] with a quadrant and he found that he was
42 degrees from the equinoctial line. And he says
that by his account he found that he had gone 1,142
leagues from the island of Hierro. And he still
affirms that that island [of Cuba] is *tierra firme*.

Saturday 3 November

In the morning the Admiral got into the ship's launch,
and since the river mouth forms a large lake making a
most excellent harbor, very deep and free of rocks and
with a very good beach for careening ships and much
firewood, he went up the river until he reached fresh
water, which would be close to two leagues; and he
climbed up a small hill in order to learn something
about the land, and he could not see anything because
of the big groves of trees, which were very fresh and
fragrant. Because of this he says he has no doubt
that there are aromatic plants. He says that everything he saw was so beautiful that his eyes could not
tire looking at such beauty; and [hearing] the songs
of fowl and small birds. That day many dugouts or
canoes came to the ships to trade things of cotton
thread and the nets in which they slept, which are
hammocks.

Sunday 4 November

As soon as it dawned the Admiral embarked in the
launch and went ashore to hunt some of the birds
he had seen the day before. After returning,
Martín Alonso Pinzón came to him with two pieces
of cinnamon and said that a Portuguese[1] he had
in his ship had seen an Indian who was carrying
two big handfuls of it, but that he did not dare
to trade with him for it because of the penalty
that the Admiral had imposed so that no one

---

1. (20v32) The *portugues* was probably Juan Arias de Tavira. See Martinez-
Hidalgo (1966, 72–73, 90–93) for lists of the crew members of Columbus's fleet,
assembled from the researches of Alice Bache Gould. Morison (1942, 1:190–92)
shows somewhat different lists.

[q̃?] nadie resgatase /. dezia mas q̃ aq̃l yndio
traya vnas cosas bermejas como nuezes /.
el contramaestre dla pinta dixo q̃ avia halla
do arboles de Canela : fue el almiᶜ luego alla
40   y hallo q̃ no erā /. mostro el almiᶜ a vnos
yndios de alli canela y pimienta parez que
dla q̃ llevava de castilla p[ar]a muestra : y co

devian me[n]tir   gnosciērōla diz q̃ : y dixerō ~~q̃ çerca~~ por señas
los yndios   q̃ çerca de alli avia mucho de aq̃llo al camino

                        y perlas
45   dl sueste /. mostroles oro ∧y respōdieron çier

Folio 21r

bohio llamavā los   tos viejos q̃ en vn lugar q̃ llamarō bohio
yndios de aq̃llas   avia infinito y q̃ lo trayan al cuello y a las
Islas a las casas   orejas y a los braços y a las piernas : y tābiē
y por eso creo q̃ no perlas /. Entendio mas q̃ dezian q̃ avia
entēdia bien el al naos grādes y mercaderias y todo esto era
mirāte / ante de   al sueste /. entēdio tābien q̃ lexos de alli avia
via de dezir por la hōbres de vn ojo / y otros cōn hoçicos de perros
isla española q̃ lla q̃ comian los hōbres : y q̃ en tomādo vno
mavan haiti /.   lo degollavā y le bevian la sangre : y le corta

todo esto devian de van su natura /. Determino de bolver a la nao
dezir dlos caribes el almiᶜ a esperar los dos hōbres q̃ avia en
                    biado : p[ar]a determinar de partirse a buscar a
10   q̃llas tr̄r̄as : sino truxesen aq̃llos alguna
                    buena nueva dlo q̃ dseavan /. dize mas el
~~aje~~-[?] nō   15   almiᶜ   Esta gente es mȳ māsa y mūy teme
                    rosa desnuda como d̄ho tengo / sin armas y sin
                    ley /. Estas tr̄r̄as son mȳ fertiles : ellos las
                    tienē llenas de mames q̃ son como çanahorias
los ajes /o   q̃ tienē sabor de castañas : y tienē faxones y fa
batatas sō estos 20 vas mȳ diuersas dlas nr̄as y mucho algodon
                    el qual no siembrā y nace por los mōtes arbo

would trade. He also said that that Indian was
carrying some vermilion things like nuts. The
contramaestre[1] of the *Pinta* said he had found
cinnamon trees; the Admiral went there later and
found that they were not. The Admiral showed
cinnamon and pepper to a few of the Indians of
that place (it seems from the samples that he
was bringing from Castile) and he says that they
recognized it; and they said by signs that
nearby to the southeast there was a lot of it.
He showed them gold and pearls, and certain old
21r   men answered that in a place that they called
Bohío there was a vast amount and that they wore
it on neck and in ears and on arms and legs; and
also pearls. Moreover, he understood that they
said that there were big ships and much trade
and that all of this was to the southeast. He
understood also that, far from there, there were
one-eyed men, and others, with snouts of dogs,
who ate men, and that as soon as one was taken
they cut his throat and drank his blood and cut
off his genitals. The Admiral decided to return
to the ship to wait for the two men whom he had
sent and to decide whether to leave and seek
those lands, unless the two men brought good
news of that which they desired. The Admiral
says further: These people are very gentle and very
timid, naked, as has been said before, without
weapons and without law. These lands are very
fertile; the Indians have them full of *mames*,[2]
which are like carrots and have the taste of chestnuts; and they have varieties of bean[3] very different from ours and much cotton, which they do not
plant; and there grow in the mountains very large

1. (20v38) The *contramaestre* was the boatswain, probably Juan Quintero de Algruta, from Huelva. See p. 131, n. 1.
2. (21r18) *Mames* are probably cassava. The words *mames* and *mañes* (22r4)
appear to be copying errors for *niames* (36r36 and 42r4), the *n* and the *i* having been
read mistakenly as *m*. *Mames* is an African word. Columbus says that the West Indians called *niames* "*ajes*" (42r4). For discussion see Morison (1963, 89 n. 6).
3. (21r19–20) Morison (1963) and Jane-Vigneras (1960) both translate *faxones
y favas* as "beans and kidney beans," although Morison (1963, 89 n. 7) notes that there
are so many varieties of beans in Cuba that attempts to be specific are useless.

les grādes : y creo q̃ en todo tp̄o lo aya p[ar]a coger
porq̃ vi lo cogujos abiertos y otros q̃ se abrian y
flores todo en vn arbol y otras mill mañas de

            me
25 frutas q̃ ∧ no es possible escrevir y todo deve ser
cosa provechosa /. todo esto dize el almiᵉ

                                           lunes .5. de noviēbre

⅃ en amaneziendo mādo poner la nao a'mōte
y los otros navios p[er]o no todos juntos sino q̃
30 quedasen siempʳ dos en el lugar donde estavan
por la seguridad / avnq̃ dize q̃ aq̃lla gente era mūy
segura y sin temor se pudieran poner todos los na
vios junto en mōte /. Estando asi vino el contra
maestre dl niña a pedir albriçias al almiᵉ

                              no
35 porq̃ avia hallado almaçiga mas ∧ traya la mue
stra porq̃ se le avia caido /. prometioselas el almiᵉ
y enbio a Rodrigo sanches y a maestre d[ie]g[o] a los
arboles y truxerō vn poco dlla : la qual guar
do p[ar]a llevar a los reyes y tambiē del arbol y dize
40 q̃ se cognoscio q̃ [era?] almaçiga avnq̃ se a de coger
a sus tp̄os : y q̃ avia en aq̃lla comarca p[ar]a sacar
mill quintales cada año /. hallo diz q̃ alli mucho

este deve ser   de aq̃l palo q̃ le pareçio lignaloe /.   Dize mas
barocoa   q̃ aq̃l pueʳto de mares es dlos mejores dl mūdo +   a. y mejores ayres
45 y porq̃ tiene vn cabo de peña altillo / se puede hazer   b. y mas māsa gē
vna fortaleza : p[ar]a q̃ si aq̃llo saliese rico y cosa   c. te /.
grāde : estaria alli los mercaderes seguros + y dize   a. + de qualquiera
nr̄o señor en cuyas manos estan todas las victorias   b. otras naçiones :
aderezca todo lo q̃ fuere su s[er]vi[ci]º /   diz q̃ dixo vn yndio
50 por señas q̃ el almaciga era buena p[ar]a quādo les
dolia el esto[mago]

trees of it; and I believe that they have cotton to
pick in all seasons because I saw open pods, and
others opening, and flowers, all on one tree, and a
thousand other kinds of fruit which it is not
possible for me to describe; and all of these
things should be profitable. All this the Admiral
says.

                                          Monday 5 November

When dawn came, he ordered the ship and the other
vessels pulled out on shore, but not all together,
so that two should always remain in the place where
they were for security; although he says that the
Indians were very trustworthy, and the Spaniards
without fear could have careened all the ships together. At this point the *contramaestre* of the
Niña came to ask for a reward from the Admiral
because he had found mastic; but he did not bring a
sample because he had dropped it. The Admiral
promised it to him and sent Rodrigo Sánchez and
Master Diego to the trees and they brought a little of
it, which he kept to take to the sovereigns, and also
some of the tree; and he says that he recognized
that it was mastic, although it has to be collected
at the right seasons, and that there was in that
region enough to take out a thousand *quintales* each
year. He found there, he says, a lot of that wood
that seemed to him to be aloe. He says further
that that harbor of Mares is among the best in the
world and has the best breezes and the most
gentle people.[1] And because it has a cape of rather
low cliff, a fortress can be made there, in order
that, if that trade should turn out to be a rich
and big thing, merchants would be safe there from
all other nations;[2] and he says that Our Lord, in
Whose hands are all victories, leads the way to all
that will be in His service. He says an Indian
told him by signs that the mastic was good for
stomachache.

1. (21r44a–c) These lines are written in the right margin of the manuscript.
2. (21r47a–b) These lines were added in the right margin of the manuscript.

Folio 21v

ƛ ayer en la noche dize el almiᵉ vinierō los dos
hōbres q̃ avia embiado a ver la tr̄r̄a dentro y le
dixerō como avian andado doze leguas q̃ avia
5 hasta vna poblaçion de çinquēta casas : donde diz q̃

señal de ser pa   avria mill vezinos porq̃ biven mūchos en vna casa /.
cificos   estas casas son de mar̃a de alfaneques grādissimos /
dixerō q̃ los avian resçibido cō grā solenidad segū
su costūbre /. y todos asi hōbres como mugeres los
10 venian a ver / y aposentarōlos en las mejores casas /.
los quales los tocavā y les besavā las manos y
los pies maravillandose y creyēdo q̃ venian del
çielo y asi los[?] se lo davā a entender /. davāles de
comer dlo q̃ tenian /. dixerō q̃ en llegādo los
15 llevarō de bracos los mas hōrrados del pueblo a la
casa principal : y dierōles dos sillas en q̃ assenta

no   rō : y ellos todos se assentarō en el suelo en derre
dor dellos /. el yndio q̃ con ellos yva les notifi
co la mar̃a de bivir dlos xp̄ıāños y como erā bue
20 na gente /. despues salierōse los hōbres : y entra
rō las mugeres y sentarōse dla misma mar̃a
en derredor dellos besandoles las manos y los pies palpādol[os]
atentandolos si erā de carne y de guesso como ellos /.
Rogavāles q̃ se estuviesen alli con ellos al menos
25 por çinco dias /. mostrarō la canela y pimienta -q̃-[?]
-avian llevado-[?] y otras espeçias q̃l almiᵉ les avia dado : y
dixerōles por señas q̃ mucha dlla avia çerca de alli
al sueste : p[er]o q̃ en [alli?] no -la avia- sabian si la avia /.
visto como no tenian recaudo de çiudad se bolvierō :
30 y q̃ si quisierā dar lugar -q̃- a los q̃ con ellos se queriā
venir q̃ mas de quinientos hōbres y mugeres vinie
rā cō ellos : porq̃ pensavā q̃ se bolvian al çielo /.vino
enp[er]o cō ellos vn principal dl pueblo y vn su hijo y
vn hōbre suyo /. hablo co ellos el almiᵉ hizoles

Yesterday during the night, the Admiral says, the two
men came whom he had sent to see the interior and
they told him how they had gone 12 leagues, which
was as far as a settlement of 50 houses, where he says
that there must have been a thousand inhabitants because many live in one house. These houses are like
very large Moorish campaign tents. They said that the
Indians received them with great solemnity, according
to their custom. And everyone came to see them, men
as well as women; and they quartered them in the best
houses. The Indians touched them and kissed their
hands and feet, marveling and believing that the
Spaniards came from the heavens, and so they gave
them to understand. They gave them something to eat
of what they had. The Spaniards said that upon their
arrival the most honorable men of the town led them
by the arm to the principal house and gave them two
chairs, in which they sat; and all of them sat down on
the ground around them. The Indian who went with
them informed the others of the way the Christians
lived and that they were good people. Later the men
left, and the women came in and seated themselves in
the same way around them, kissing their hands and
feet and feeling them,[1] attempting to see if they
were, like themselves, of flesh and bone. They begged
them to stay there with them for at least five days.
The Spaniards showed them the cinnamon and
pepper and other spices that the Admiral had given
them; and the Indians told them by signs that there
was a lot of it near there to the southeast, but that
right there they did not know if there was any. Seeing
that the Indians had no information about a city,
the Spaniards returned; and if they had wanted to
accommodate all who wished to come, more than
500 men and women would have come with them,
because they thought that the Spaniards would return
to the heavens. But an important man of the town
came with them, and [also] a son of his and one of
his men. The Admiral spoke with them and treated

---

1. (21v22) *Palpandolos* (feeling them) is written in the right margin, as if added
later.

35 mūcha hōrra : señalole mūchas tr̄r̄as e Islas q̃ avia
en aq̃llas p[ar]tes /. penso de traerlo a los reyes :
y diz q̃ no supo q̃ se le antojo parez q̃ de miedo : y
de noche escuro quisose yr a tr̄r̄a : y el almiͤ diz q̃
porq̃ tenia la nao en ~~tr̄r̄a~~ seco en tr̄r̄a : no le ~~quiso~~ queriēdo

40 enojar le dexo yr / diziendo q̃ en amaneçiendo

[qual?] necio   tornaria el qual nūca torno /.   hallarō los dos
xpianos por el camino mūcha gente q̃ atravesava a sus
pueblos mugeres y hōbres con vn tizon en la mano
yervas p[ar]a tomar sus sahumerios q̃ acostūbravan /.

45 no hallarō poblaçion por el camino de mas de çinco
casas : y todos les hazian el mismo acatamiͦ /. viero
muchas mar̃as de arboles e yervas y flores odoriferas /
viero aves de muchas mar̃as diuersas dlas despaña saluo

Folio 22r

perdizes y ruysenores q̃ cantava y ansares
q̃ destos ay alli hartos /. bestias de quatro pies
no vierō : saluo perros q̃ no ladravā /. la tr̄r̄a
mȳ fertil y mȳ labrada de aq̃llos mañes

5 y fexoes y havas mȳ diuersas dlas nr̄as /. eso
mismo panizo : y mūcha cantidad de algodon cogi
do y filado y obrado : y q̃ en vna sola casa avian
visto mas de quinientas arrovas : y q̃ se pudiera

y avn diez mil .   aver alli cada año quatro mill quintales /. dize el

10 almiͤ q̃ le p[ar]eçia q̃ no lo sembravā y q̃ da fruto
todo el año : es mȳ fino tiene el capillo grāde /. to
do lo q̃ aq̃lla gente tenia : diz q̃ dava por mȳ vil
preçio : y q̃ vna grā espuerta de algodon : dava por
cabo de agujeta /o otra cosa q̃ se le de /. Son gente

nõ   15 dize el almiͤ mȳ sin mal ni de guerra : dsnudos
todos hōbres y mugeres com̃o sus madres los pa

them with much courtesy. The Indian informed him by signs about many lands and islands that were in those regions. The Admiral thought of taking him to the sovereigns, and he says that he did not know what impulse struck the man (it seems from fear), and in the dark of night he wanted to go ashore; and the Admiral says that because he had the ship hauled out of the water on land, and not wishing[1] to anger him, he let him go, the Indian saying that when dawn came he would return. He never did. The two Christians found along the way many people going back and forth between their villages, men and women with a firebrand of weeds in their hands to take in the fragrant smoke to which they are accustomed. They did not find on their route settlements of more than five houses; and all of them paid them the same respect. They saw many kinds of trees and plants and fragrant flowers; they saw birds of many kinds, different from those of Spain, except par-

22r   tridges and nightingales, which sang, and geese, for of these there are a great many there. Four-footed beasts they did not see, except dogs that did not bark. The earth was very fertile and planted with those *mañes*[2] and bean varieties[3] very different from ours, and with that same millet. And they saw a large quantity of cotton collected and spun and worked; and in a single house they had seen more than five hundred *arrobas*; and that one might get there each year four thousand *quintales* [of it]. The Admiral says that it seemed to him that they did not sow it and that it produces fruit [i.e., cotton] all year. It is very fine and has a large boll. Everything that those people have, he says, they would give for a very paltry price, and that they would give a large basket of cotton for the tip of a lacing or anything else given to them. They are people, says the Admiral, quite lacking in evil and not warlike; [and] all of them, men and women [are] naked as their mothers bore them.

1. (21v39) *Queriendo* (wishing) is written at the end of the line in the right margin, replacing the canceled word *quiso*.
2. (22r4) *Mañes*. Probably *niames*. See p. 133, n. 2.
3. (22r5) *Fexoes y havas*. See p. 133, n. 3.

rio /. Vrdad es q̃ las mugeres traen vna cosa de
algodon solamēte tan grāde q̃ le cobija su natura
y no mas /. y son ellas de mȳ buē acatamiēto

20   ni mȳ negros saluo menos q̃ canarias /. tengo
por d̃ho serenissimos prinçipes (dize aqui el almi^e)
q̃ sabiendo la lengua dispuesta suya personas devo
tas religiosas q̃ luego todos se tornarian xp̄ianos /.

nõ   y asi esp[er]o en nr̄o señor q̃ vr̄as altezas se determi

25   narā a ello con mūcha diligençia p[ar]a tornar a la igle
sia tan grādes pueblos y las conVrtirā : asi comō
an destruydo aq̃llos q̃ no quisierō confessar el
padre y el hijo y el esp[irit]u Sancto : y dspues de sus
dias (q̃ todos somos mortales dexarā sus reynos

30   en mȳ tranquilo estado : y limpios de heregia y
maldad : y serā bien resçibidos dlante el eterno
criador al qual plega de les dar larga vida y

———[?]

acreçentami^o grāde de mayores ~~señorios~~ reynos
y señorios : y volūtad y disposiçion p[ar]a acreçētar

35   la Sancta religiō xp̄iana asi comō hasta aqui tienē
fecho amen /. oy tire la nao de mōte y me

en

despacho p[ar]a partir el jueves ~~el~~ nōbre de dios e
yr al sueste a buscar del oro y espeçerias y des
cubrir tr̄ra /. estas todas son palabras del almirāte /.

.12.[?]

~~lunes de noviēbre~~

40

El qual penso partir el jueves : p[er]o porq̃ le hizo
el viento contrario : no pudo partir hasta doze
dias de noviembre /.

lunes .12. de noviēbre

45   ∤ Partio del pue^rto ~~de mares~~ y rio de mares
al rēdir del quarto de alva : p[ar]a yr a vna Isla
q̃ mucho affirmavā los yndios q̃ traya q̃ se lla
mava baveque : adonde ~~dize~~ segū dizen por
señas q̃ la gente della coge el oro cō candelas de noche

It is true that the women wear a thing of cotton only
so big as to cover their genitals and no more. And
they are very respectful and not very black, less so
than Canarians. I truly believe, most Serene Princes
(the Admiral says here), that, given devout religious
persons knowing thoroughly the language that they
use, soon all of them would become Christian.[1] And
so I hope in Our Lord that Your Highnesses, with
much diligence, will decide to send such persons in
order to bring to the Church such great nations and
to convert them, just as you have destroyed those that
did not want to confess the Father and the Son and
the Holy Spirit, and that after your days (for all of us
are mortal) you will leave your kingdoms in a tranquil
state, free of heresy and evil, and will be well received
before the Eternal Creator, may it please Whom to
give you long life and great increase of your kingdoms
and dominions and the will and disposition to
increase the Holy Christian Religion, as up to now
you have done, amen. Today I pulled the ship off the
beach and made ready to leave on Thursday, in the
name of God, and to go to the southeast to seek gold
and spices and to explore land. All these are the
Admiral's words. He intended to leave on Thursday,
but because a contrary wind came up he could not
leave until the twelfth of November.[2]

Monday 12 November

He left the Puerto and Rio de Mares at the end
of the dawn watch[3] to go to an island that the
Indians he had with him strongly affirmed was
called Baneque, where, as they said by means of
signs, the people of it collected gold at night on

1. (22r22–23) *Que sabiendo . . . tornarian christianos*. The syntax of the Spanish
text is difficult. *Dispuesta* and *suya* both appear to be adjectives modifying *lengua*, although in English it seems more natural to consider *dispuesta* an adverb modifying
sabiendo with the meaning "in an orderly way," "thoroughly," or "properly." But one
might say "knowing the suitable words of their language."
2. (22r41–43) *El qual . . . noviembre*. These lines appear to have been added by
Las Casas to explain why there are no *Diario* entries for 7–11 November.
3. (22r46) *Quarto de alva* (the dawn watch). The successive night watches,
which consisted of four-hour periods starting at about 7:00 P.M., were named *quarto
de prima* (or *primer quarto*), *quarto de la modorra*, and *quarto del alba* (or *terçero quarto*).
See Alvar (1976, 2:103 n. 232).

Folio 22v

en la playa // y despues con martillo diz q̃
hazian vergas dllo /. y p[ar]a yr a ella era me
$\qquad$ poner
nestr ∧ la proa al leste quarta del sueste /. des
pues de aver andado ocho leguas por la costa delā

5   te hallo vn rio : y dende andadas otras quatro
hallo otro rio q̃ pareçia mȳ caudaloso y mayor
q̃ ninguᵒ dlos otros q̃ avia hallado /. no se qui
so detener ni entrar en alguᵒ dllos por dos respe
ctos : el vno y principal porq̃l tp̄o y viento era

10   bueno p[ar]a yr en demāda dla d̄ha Isla de babeque
$\qquad\qquad\qquad\qquad\qquad$ o famosa
lo otro porq̃ si en el oviera alguᵃ pplosa ∧ çiudad
çerca dla mar se pareçiera / y p[ar]a yr por el rio
arriba erā menestr navios pequeños : lo q̃ no erā
los q̃ llevava / y asi se p[er]diera tābiē mūcho tp̄o / y los

15   semejātes rios son cosa p[ar]a descobrirse por si /.
toda aq̃lla costa era poblada / mayormēte çerca dl
rio a quiē puso por nōbre el rio del Sol /. dixo
q̃l domīgo antes onze de noviēbre le avia pare
çido q̃ fuera biē tomar algunas p[er]sonas dlas de aq̃l

20   rio p[ar]a llevar a los reyes : porq̃ aprendierā nr̄a
legua : p[ar]a saber lo q̃ ay en la tr̄r̄a : y porq̃ bolvien
nõ   do sean lenguas dlos xp̄ıanos : y tomē nr̄as costū
bres : y las cosas dla fe /. porq̃ yo vi e cognozco (
(dize el almiᶜ) q̃sta gente no tiene secta ninguᵃ ni son
nõ   25   Idolatras : saluo mȳ māsos y sin saber q̃ sea mal
ni matar a otros ni prender y sin armas / y tan
temerosos q̃ a vna p[er]sona dlos nr̄os fuyen
çiento dllos avnq̃ burlen cō ellos /. y credulos
y cognosçedores q̃ ay dios en el çielo : e firmes

30   q̃ nosotros avemos venido dl çielo : y mȳ p[re]sto a
qualquiera oraçion q̃ nos les digamos q̃ digan
~~y hazē~~ y hazē el señal dla cruz ✝ /. Asi q̃ devē
vr̄as altezas determinarse a los hazeʳ xp̄ıanos :
q̃ creo q̃ si comiēçan en poco tp̄o acabara de los

22v   the beach with lanterns, and afterward, with a
hammer, they said that they would make bars of it.
And in order to go to it, it was necessary to head
east by south. After having made eight leagues
along the coast ahead, he found a river; and after
they had gone another four he found another river
that appeared to carry much water and to be larger
than any of the others that he had found. He did
not wish to stop or go into any of them for two
reasons: the first and principal because the
weather and wind were favorable for going in
search of the said island of Baneque; the other
because if there were some populous or important
city on the river near the sea, it would be seen.
And in order to go up the river it would be necessary to have small vessels, which those he brought
were not. And thus also much time would be lost,
and such rivers are things to be explored by themselves. All of that coast was inhabited, and more
heavily so near the river, to which he gave the
name Rio del Sol. He said that the Sunday before,
the eleventh of November, it had seemed to him
that it might be well to capture some people of
that river in order to take them to the king and
queen so that they might learn our language and
in order to know what there is in that land, and
so that, returning, they might be interpreters for
the Christians, and so that they would take on our
customs and faith. Because I saw and recognize
(says the Admiral) that these people have no religious beliefs, nor are they idolaters. They are
very gentle and do not know what evil is; nor do
they kill others, nor steal; and they are without
weapons and so timid that a hundred of them flee
from one of our men even if our men are teasing
them. And they are credulous and aware that
there is a God in heaven and convinced that we
come from the heavens; and they say very quickly
any prayer that we tell them to say, and they make the
sign of the cross, ✝. So that Your Highnesses ought
to resolve to make them Christians: for I believe that

35   aver convertido a nr̄a Sācta fe multidūbre de
     pueblos : y cobr̄ado gr̄ades señorios y riquezas
     y todos sus pueblos dla españa /. porq̄ sin duda
     es en estas tr̄r̄as gr̄adissima sum̄a de oro q̄ no sin
     causa dizen estos yndios q̄ yo traygo q̄ ha en e
40   stas Islas lugares adonde cavan el oro y lo
     traen al pescueço / a las orejas / y a los braços / e
     a las piernas / y son manillas mȳ gruessas /. y
     tābien ha piedras y ha perlas preciosas y in
     finita espeçeria /. y en este rio de mares de a
45   donde parti esta noche sin duda ha gr̄adissima
     Cantidad de almaçiga / y mayor si mayor se quisie

[no?]   re hazer /. porq̄ los mismos arboles plantandolos
        prenden de ligero : y ha mūchos y mūy gr̄ades y

Folio 23r

     tienē la hoja como lentisco y el fructo : saluo
     q̄ es mayor asi los arboles com̄o la hoja como
     dize plinio e yo e visto en la Isla de xio en el
     ~~ancipla~~-[?] arcipielago y māde sangrar ~~destos~~
5   mūchos destos arboles p[ar]a ver si echaria resina
     p[ar]a la traer y com̄o aya siemp[r] llovido el tp̄o
     q̄ yo e estado en el d̄ho rio no e podido aver dlla //
     saluo mȳ poquita q̄ traygo a .v. al. y tābiē puede
     ser q̄ no es el tp̄o p[ar]a los sangrar q̄ esto creo q̄
10   conviene al tp̄o q̄ los arboles comiēçan a salir
     dl invierno y quierē echar la flor : y aca ya
     tienē el fruto quasi maduro agora /. y tanbiē

nõ   aqui se avria gr̄ade sum̄a de algodon : y creo q̄S
     se venderia mūy bien aca sin le llevar a espa
15   ña : saluo a las gr̄ades çiudades del gr̄a Can q
     se descubrir̄a sin duda : y otras mūchas de otros
     señores q̄ avran en dicha servir a vr̄as altezas
     y adonde se les dar̄a de otras cosas de españa

nõ   y dlas tr̄r̄as de oriente : pues estas son a nos
20   en poniente /. y aqui ha tābien infinito lignaloe
     avnq̄ no es cosa p[ar]a haze[r] gr̄a caudal mas del
     almaçiga es de entēder bien : porq̄ no la ha sal
     vo en la d̄ha Isla de xio : y creo q̄ sacan dello

if you begin, in a short time you will end up having
converted to our Holy Faith a multitude of peoples
and acquiring large dominions and great riches and all
of their peoples for Spain.   Because without doubt
there is in these lands a very great quantity of gold;
for not without cause do these Indians that I bring
with me say that there are in these islands places
where they dig gold and wear it on their chests, on
their ears, and on their arms, and on their legs; and
they are very thick bracelets.   And also there are
stones, and there are precious pearls and infinite
spicery.   And in this Rio de Mares from which I departed tonight there is without doubt an exceedingly
great quantity of mastic and even greater if a
greater production is wanted, because the trees themselves, when planted, bear quickly.   And there are
many and very large ones, and they have a leaf and
23r   fruit like the mastic tree, except that the trees, as
well as the leaf, are larger, as Pliny says, and as I
have seen, [than] on the island of Chios in the Archipelago. And I ordered many of these trees tapped to
see if they would produce resin in order to bring it;
and since it has rained during the whole time that I
have been in the said river I have not been able to
get any of it, except a very little bit which I am
bringing to Your Highnesses. And also it may be that
it is not the season to tap them; for this I believe
is proper to the season when the trees begin to come
out of winter and are almost ready to flower.   And
here they already have nearly ripe fruit.   And also
here there is probably a great quantity of cotton; and
I think that it would sell very well here without taking it to Spain but to the big cities belonging to the
Grand Khan, which doubtless will be discovered, and
to many other cities belonging to other lords who
will be happy to serve Your Majesties and where other
things from Spain and from the lands of the East
will be given to them (since these to us are in the
West). And here also there is infinite aloe, although it
is not a thing to produce a lot of; but with mastic
it would be well to be concerned, because there is
none of it except in the said island of Chios; and I

bien çinquēta mill du[ca]^{dos} si mal no me acuerdo /

    ha

25 y ∧aqui en la boca dl d̄ho rio el mejor pue^rto q̃
fasta oy vi / limpio e ancho e fondo y buē
lugar y asiento p[ar]a haze^r vna villa e fuerte e
que qualesquier navios se puedan llegar
el bordo a los muros : e tr̄r̄a mūy temperada y

30 alta y mūy buenas aguas /. Asi que ayer vino
abordo dla nao vna almadia con seys man
cebos y los çinco entrarō en la nao : estos mād̄e

no fue lo me detener e los traygo /. y despues enbie a
jor dl mūdo esto vna casa q̃ es de la p[ar]te del rio dl poniente y tru

                                chicas

35 xerō siete cabeças de mugeres entre ∧ ~~niñas~~-[?]
e grād̄es y tres niños /. Esto hize porq̃ mejor
se cōportan los hōbres en españa aviendo mu
geres de su tr̄r̄a q̃ sin ellas /. porq̃ ya otras mu
chas vezes se acaeçio traer hōbres de guinea

40 p[ar]a q̃ deprendiesen la lengua en portugal
y despues q̃ bolvian y pensavā de se aprove
char dllos en su tr̄r̄a por la buena copañia

mira q̃ mara q̃ le aviā hecho y dadibas q̃ se les aviā dado :
villa en llegād̄o en tr̄r̄a Jamas parecia /. otros no

45 lo haziā asi /. asi que teniēdo sus mugeres

Folio 23v

ternā gana de negociar lo q̃ se les encargare
y tābien estas mugeres mūcho enseñarā a los
nr̄os su lengua /. la qual es toda vna en
todas estas Islas de yndia / y todos se entien

5 den y todas las andan cō sus almadias : lo
q̃ no han en guinea adonde es mill mar̃as
de lenguas q̃ la vna no entiende la otra /

believe that they derive from it quite fifty thousand
ducados,[1] if I do not remember badly. And there is
here in the mouth of the said river the best harbor
that I have seen up until today, clean and wide and
deep and a good place and site to make a town
and fort where any ships whatever can tie up
alongside the walls; and it is a very temperate
land, and high, and with good water. Yesterday
there came alongside the ship a canoe with
six young men in it, and when five of them
entered the ship, I ordered them detained and
I am bringing them. And later I sent men to
a house which is west of the river, and they
brought seven head of women, counting young
ones and adults, and three small children.[2]
I did this so that the men would behave better in Spain, having women from their country, than without them. Because many other
times it has happened that when men have been
brought from Guinea to Portugal to learn the
language, later, when they returned and the
Portuguese thought that they could make good
use of them in their own country, because of
the good treatment and the gifts that they
gave them, when they got to land they never
appeared. Others did not do it this way.
Having their women, they have a desire to

23v   carry out the business they are charged with.
And also these women will teach our men[3] much
of their language, which is identical in all
of these islands of India, and they all understand one another and go to all the islands in their canoes. This is not so in
Guinea, where there are a thousand kinds of
language and one does not understand the

---

1. (23r24) *Ducados*. Probably the Venetian *ducat*, a 24-carat gold coin weigh-
ing about 3.5111 grams and used in international commerce. See Lane (1985, 321).

2. (23r35–36) *Chicas e grandes y tres niños*. The words *chicas e grandes* here
mean "young and adult," rather than "small and large"; *niños* means "small children,"
not necessarily all "boys." (Cf. Morison 1963, 93.)

3. (23v2–3) Las Casas changes *los nuestros* (our men) to *las nuestras* in his *Historia* (1951); i.e., the Indian women will teach "our women" their language, not "our
men."

Esta noche vino abordo en vna almadia el
marido de vna destas mugeres y padre de

10   tres fijos vn macho y dos fenbras : y dixo

porq̃ no le
distes sus
hijos

q̃ yo le dexase venir cõ ellos y a mi me aplo
go mūcho : y quedā agora todos consolados
con el q̃ deven todos ser pariētes y el es ya
hõbre de .45. años /. todas estas palabras

15   son formales dl almirāte /. dize tambien
arriba q̃ hazia algun frio : y por esto q̃ no le

desto q̃ aqui dize
pareçe q̃ si nave
gara hazia el nor
te en dos dias
sin duda dscubrie
ra la florida /.

fuera buē consejo en invierno navegar al
norte p[ar]a dscubrir /.   Navego este lu
nes hasta el sol puesto .18. leguas al leste

                                              a

20   quarta dl sueste hasta vn cabo ∧q̃ puso
por nõbre el cabo de cuba /.

                                              martes .13. de noviēbre

/ Esta noche toda estuvo a la Corda coṁo dizen
los marineros que es andar barlovente

25   ando y no andar nada : por ver vn abra
q̃ es vn abertura de sierras coṁo entre sier
ra y sierra q̃ le ~~apareçio~~ comēço a ver al
~~sol puesto~~ poner del sol : a donde se mostra
van dos grandissimas mõtañas : y parecia

estas mõtañas
eran la vna
el cabo de cuba
q̃ se llama la pū
ta de mahiçi ~~/o de~~
————[?] ~~: y la~~
~~otra~~ ————[?]
————[?]
————[?] lla
ma a la isla espa
ñola

30   q̃ se ap[ar]tavā la trr̄a de cuba con aq̃lla de
bofio y esto dezian los yndios q̃ consigo lle
vavan / por señas /. venido el dia claro dio
las velas sobre la trr̄a y passo vna punta q̃
le pareçio anoche obra de dos leguas : y entro

                                              leguas

35   en vn grāde golpho çinco ∧al sursudueste y le
quedavā otras çinco p[ar]a llegar al cabo a donde
en medio de dos grādes mōtes hazia vn degolla
do el qual no pudo determinar si era entrada
de mar /. y porq̃ deseava yr a la Isla q̃ llama

40   vā veneque : adonde tenia nueva segū el entēdia

other. Tonight there came alongside in a
canoe the husband of one of these women and
the father of three children, one male and
two female; and he asked me to let him go
with them and he implored me greatly: and all
of them were consoled by him, for they all
must be related, and he is now a man of 45
years. All these are the Admiral's exact
words. He also says above that the weather
was somewhat cold, and for this reason he
might not be well advised to sail north in
winter to explore. He sailed this Monday
before sunset 18 leagues east by south, as
far as a cape to which he gave the name Cabo
de Cuba.

Tuesday 13 November

This whole night he spent *a la corda*, as sailors
say, (which is to tack back and forth and to make no
headway) because of seeing an *abra*,[1] which is an
opening in the mountains like one between mountain
ranges, which he began to see at sunset, at a place
where two extremely large mountains appeared, which
opening seemed to separate the land of Cuba from
that of Bohío; and, by signs, so said the Indians that
he had with him. When daylight came he set sail
toward land and he passed a point that last night
looked to him to be about two leagues off; and he
entered a large expanse of water five leagues to the
south-southwest. Another five leagues remained in
order for him to reach the cape where, in between two
large mountains, a narrow opening was formed. He
could not determine whether this was an inlet from the
sea. And because he wanted to go to the island that
they called Baneque, which, to the east, projected

1. (23v25) Guillén Tato (1951, 21) defines the word *abra* as a harbor somewhat
landlocked (*un tanto cerrado*) or running inland (*profundo*). In Columbus's use it always seems to mean an opening to the sea between mountains, and in this particular
case he thought it was a passage between mountainous islands. For this reason Morison (1963) and Jane-Vigneras (1960) translate *abra* as "pass." Thacher (1903–1904)
has "gap."

 q̃ avia mucho oro la qual isla le salia al leste : co

        alguna

mo no vido ∧grãdes poblaçiones p[ar]a ponerse al ri

gor del viento q̃ le creçia mas q̃ nũca hasta alli :

acordo de hazerse a la mar y andar al leste con el

45 viēto q̃ era norte y andava .8. millas cada ora

y desde las diez dl dia q̃ tomo aq̃lla derrota hasta

el poner dl sol anduvo .56. seys millas q̃ son .14.

leguas al leste dsde el cabo de Cuba . y dla otra t̄r̄r̄a

del bohio q̃ le quedava a sotaviento començando dl cabo

Folio 24r

dl sobredicho golpho descubrio a su pareçer .80.

millas q̃ son .xx leguas : y corriase toda aq̃lla

costa lesueste y guesnorueste /.

                                                miercoles .14. de noviēbre

5 / toda la noche de ayer anduvo al reparo y

barloventeādo (porq̃ dezia q̃ no era razō de

           aq̃llas

navegar entre ∧Islas de noche hasta q̃ las ovie

se descubierto) porq̃ los yndios q̃ traya le

dixerō ayer martes q̃ avria tres jornadas

10 desde el rio de mares / hasta la Isla de vaneq̃ :

q̃ se deve entēder jornadas dsus almadias q̃

pueden andar .7. leguas : y el viento tābiē

le escaseava y aviendo de yr al leste : no podia

sino a la quarta dl sueste y por otros inconvi

15 nientes q̃ alli refiere : se ovo detener ~~a la ma~~-[?]

hasta la mañana /. al salir dl sol determino

de yr a buscar puerto : porq̃ de norte se avia

mudado el viento al nordeste : y si puerto

no ~~hallara f~~ hallara : fuera le neçessario bolver

toward him, and where he had news, according to his understanding, that there was much gold, and since he did not see any big settlement where he could shelter himself from the force of the wind,[1] which increased more than ever before, he decided to make for the sea and go east with the wind, which was north; and he made eight miles each hour and, from the tenth hour of the day, when he took that course, until sunset, he traveled 56 miles[2] to the east, which is 14 leagues, from the Cabo de Cuba. And of the other land, of Bohío, which lay downwind from him,

24r   beginning with the cape of the aforementioned gulf, he surveyed in his opinion 80 miles, which is 20 leagues: and all of that coast ran east-southeast and west-northwest.

Wednesday 14 November

All last night he proceeded under little sail, jogging off and on (because he said that it was not a good idea to sail among those islands at night until they have been explored); because the Indians that he brought told him yesterday, Tuesday, that it was a journey of about three days from the Rio de Mares to the island of Baneque (and this should be understood as days' journeys of their canoes, which can make seven leagues); and the wind also was against them;[3] and having to go east, they could not, except east by south; and because of other obstacles that he tells there, he had to delay until morning. At sunrise he decided to hunt for a harbor, because, from north, the wind had changed to northeast; and if a harbor were not found it would be necessary for him to turn back to the harbors

1. (23v42–43) Guillén Tato (1951, 112) notes that Columbus uses the phrase *para ponerse al rigor del viento* to mean "take shelter from the force of the wind," whereas its dictionary meaning is "to expose oneself to the force of the wind," i.e., exactly the opposite.

2. (23v47) *Anduvo .56. seys millas.* A curious copying error, repeating the last digit of the mileage.

3. (24r12–13) *El viento . . . escaseava* (the wind . . . against them). *Escaseava,* referring to wind, means to change directions toward the bow of a ship, i.e., they were "bucking" the wind (Guillén Tato 1951, 66). Morison (1963), Jane-Vigneras (1960), and Thacher (1903–1904) have the wind "falling off."

20 atras a los pue^rtos q̃ dexava en la Isla de
    cuba /. llego a t̅r̅r̅a aviendo andado aq̃lla
    noche —[?] .24. millas al leste quarta dl sueste
    anduvo al sur . .   millas hasta t̅r̅r̅a : a d̅o̅de
    vio m̅u̅chas entradas y muchas Isletas y
25 pue^rtos : y porq̃l viento era m̅u̅cho y la mar
    m̅y̅ alterada : no oso acometer a entrar : an
    tes corrio por la costa al norueste quarta dl
    gueste mir̅a̅do si avia puerto y vido q̃ avia
    muchos p[er]o no m̅y̅ claros /. despues de
30 aver andado asi .64. ~~y~~ millas : hallo vna en
    trada m̅y̅ h̅o̅da ~~h̅o̅~~[?] ancha vn quarto de mi
    lla y bu̅e̅ pue^rto y rio : donde entro y puso
    la proa al sursudueste y dspues al sur hasta
    llegar al sueste / todo de buena anchura y
35 m̅y̅ fondo /. donde vido tantas Islas q̃ no las
        ——[?]
    pudo contar todas de buena gradeza y ~~altas~~[?]
    m̅y̅ altas ~~tod~~ tierras llenas de diuersos ar
    boles de mill mar̃as e infinitas palmas /.
    maravillose en gr̅a̅ mar̃a ver tantas Islas
40 y tan altas y çertifica a los reyes q̃ ~~desde~~
    las m̅o̅tañas q̃ dsde antier a visto por estas
    costas y las dstas Islas : q̃ le pareçe q̃ no
    las ay mas altas en el m̅u̅do / ni tan her
    mosas y claras sin niebla ni nieve : y
45 al pie dllas gr̅a̅dissimo fondo /. y dize q̃
    cree q̃ estas Islas son aq̃llas Innumera

Folio 24v

        mapam̅u̅dos
    bles q̃ en los ~~mapamumuñdos~~[?] en fin de ori̅e̅te
    se ponen /. y dixo q̃ creia q̃ avia gr̅a̅dissimas
    riquezas y piedras preçiosas y espeçeria en e
    llas : y q̃ dur̅a̅ m̅y̅ mucho al sur y se ensanchan

that he left on the island of Cuba. He reached
land having traveled that night 24 miles east by
south. He traveled south   miles to land,
where he saw many inlets and many islets and
harbors; and because there was much wind and the
sea very rough, he did not dare to try to enter;
instead, he ran along the coast northwest by
west looking to see if there was a harbor, and
he saw that there were many but that he could
not see them very clearly. After having thus
gone 64 miles he found an entrance, very deep
and a quarter of a mile wide, and a good harbor
and river, where he entered and headed south-
southwest and later south until he reached the
southeast; all [of it was] of good width and
very deep. There he saw so many islands that he
could not count them, all of good size and very
high lands, full of trees of a thousand kinds,
and a vast number of palms. He marveled greatly
to see so many and such high islands, and he
assures the sovereigns that it seems to him that
there are no higher mountains in the world than
those he has seen since day before yesterday
along these coasts and on these islands, nor so
beautiful and clear, without mist or snow; and
at their feet very great depth. And he says
that he believes that these islands are those
24v   innumerable ones that in the maps of the
world are put at the eastern end. And he said
that he believed that there were great riches
and precious stones and spices in them, and that
they extend very far south and spread out in all

5   a toda parte /. puso les nōbre la mar de nr̄a
    Señora /. + dize tantas y tales cosas -dsu-[?] d[e] la fer
    tilidad y hermosura y altura destas Islas q̃
    hallo en este puerto : q̃ dize a los reyes q̃ no se
    maravillen de encareçellas tanto : porq̃ los
10 çertifica : q̃ cree q̃ no dize la çentissima parte
    algunas dellas q̃ pareçia q̃ llegā al çielo y he
    chas comō puntas de diamātes : otras -altissima-
    -y-——[?] q̃ sobre su grā altura tienē ençima
    comō vna mesa : y al pie dllas fondo gran
15 dissimo q̃ podra llegar a ellas vna grādissima
    carraca : todas llenas de arboledas y sin peñas /.

a. + y al puerto -puer-
b. -to dl principe- que
c. esta çerca dla boca
d. dla entrada de las dhas
e. Islas : puso puerto
f. del prinçipe / en el
g. qual no entro mas
h. de velle dsde fuera ha
i. sta otra buelta q̃ dio
j. el sabado -des- dla
k. semana venidera
l. como alli parecera /.

                                          Jueves .15. de noviembre

    ⅄ Acordo de andallas estas yslas con las barcas
    dlos navios y dize maravillas dllas : y q̃
20 hallo almaçiga e infinito lignaloe : y algunas
    dllas erā labradas dlas rayzes de q̃ hazen su
    pan los yndios / y hallo aver encēdido huego
    en algunos lugares /. + -hallaron la-[?] gente avia
    alguna y huyerō : en todo lo q̃ anduvo ha
25 llo hōdo de quinze y diez seys braças y todo
    basa q̃ quiere dezir q̃l suelo de abaxo es are
    na y no peñas : lo q̃ q̃ mucho dsean los ma
    rineros / porq̃ las peñas cortan los cables
    dlas anclas dlas naos /.

a. + agua dulce [no]
b. vido /.

directions. He gave them the name of the Mar de
Nuestra Señora; and to the harbor near the
mouth of the entrance to the said islands he
gave the name Puerto del Príncipe, into which he
did not enter but saw it only from outside until
he took another course on Saturday of the coming
week, as will then appear.[1] He says so many and
such things about the fertility and beauty
and height of these islands that he found in this
harbor that he says to the sovereigns that they
should not marvel that he praises them so much,
because he assures them that he believes he does
not tell a hundredth part. Some of them appear
to reach the heavens and are formed like points
of diamonds; others,[2] on their great height, have on
top a flat place, like a table, and at their feet
such exceedingly great depth that a very large carrack
will be able to get close up to them. All of them are
tree covered and without rocks.

Thursday 15 November

He decided to travel about these islands with the
ships' launches and he tells marvelous things about
them; and that he found mastic and a vast quantity of
aloe; and some of the islands were cultivated [and
sown] with the roots of which the Indians make bread;
and he found fires to have been burned in some places.
He saw no fresh water. There were a few people and
they fled. In all the places that he traversed he
found a depth of 15 and 16 *brazas* and all *basa*,
which means that the bottom is sand and not rocks:
which is something sailors desire greatly because the
rocks cut the ships' anchor cables.

1. (24v6a–l) *Y al puerto . . . parecera.* This insert is written in the left margin
of the manuscript with a plus sign in the text marking where the insertion should be
made.
2. (24v12–13) Alvar (1976) reads the canceled text ending line 12 and beginning line 13 as *altissima y antes.*

30   viernes .16. de noviẽbre
∕ porq̃ en todas las p[ar]tes Islas y trras donde entra
va dexava siempre puesta vna cruz : ~~fue~~ [?]
entro en la barca y fue a la boca de aq̃llos pue^rtos
y en vna punta dla tierra hallo dos maderos
35 mȳ grãdes vno mas largo q̃ el otro ~~hechos cruz~~
~~q̃~~ y el vno sobre el otro hechos cruz q̃ diz que
vn carpintero no los pudiera poner mas
                                              mãdo hazer
proporcionados /. y adorada aq̃lla cruz ~~hizo~~
~~poner en aq̃l mismo lugar~~ dlos mismos
40 maderos / vna mūy grãde y alta cruz /. hallo
cañas por aq̃lla playa q̃ no sabia donde na
çian : y creya q̃ las traeria algun rio y las
echava a la playa y tenia en esto razō /. fue
a vna cala —[?] dentro dla entrada dl pue^rto dla p[ar]te
45 [dl?] sueste : (cala es vna entrada angosta q̃ entra el

Folio 25r

agua dl mar en la tierra) alli hazia vn alto
de piedra y peña coṁo cabo : y al pie dl era
mȳ fondo q̃ la may[or]   carraca dl mūdo pu
diera poner el bordo en tr̃ra y avia vn lugar
5 ∕ o rincon donde podian estar seys navios sin
anclas coṁo en vna sala /. pareçiole q̃ se podia
hazer alli vna fortaleza a poca costa : si en algun
tp̄o en aq̃lla mar de Islas resultase algu resga
te famoso /.   bolviendose a la nao hallo los
10 yndios q̃ cōsigo traya q̃ pescavan caracoles
mȳ grãdes q̃ en aq̃llas ~~trra~~ mares ay : y
hizo entrar la gente alli e buscar si avia na
caras q̃ son las hostras donde crian las per
las : y hallarō mūchas / p[er]o no perlas ~~y echo~~
15 ~~lo a q̃~~ y atribuyolo a q̃ no devia de ser el
tp̄o dllas q̃ creya el q̃ era por mayo y junio
hallarō los marineros vn animal q̃ parecia taso
∕o taxo : pescarō tãbien con redes y hallaro
vn pece entre otros muchos q̃ pareçia proprio
20 puerco no coṁo tonina /. el qual diz q̃ era todo

Friday 16 November

Because in all the places, islands, and lands that he
entered he always left a cross set up, he got into the
ship's launch and went to the mouth of those harbors,
and on a point of land he found two very large timbers, one longer than the other, and one [put] upon
the other made a cross. And he says that a carpenter
could not have put them together more suitably.
And having venerated that cross, he ordered made
from the same timbers a very large and high cross.
He found canes along that beach and he did not know
where they originated; he believed that some river
brought them and cast them on the beach. (And in
this he was right.) He went to a *cala* inside the
entrance to the harbor toward the southeast (*cala* is a
25r   narrow entrance where the water of the sea penetrates
the land); there a height of stone and cliff forms
something like a cape, and at its foot it was so very
deep that the biggest carrack in the world could lie
right next to land, and there was a place or corner
where six vessels could lie without anchors, as if
in a hall.[1] It appeared to him that a fortress
could be built there at little cost if at some time
in that sea of islands a notable trade should
develop. Returning to the ship, he found that the
Indians he brought with him were fishing for the
big snails that exist in those seas; and he made
the men get into the water to see if there were
nácaras, which are the oysters where pearls grow.
They found many oysters but no pearls, and he
attributed this to its not being the season for
them, which he believed was in May and June. The
sailors found an animal that appeared to be a
taso, or *taxo*.[2] They also fished with nets and
they found one fish among many others that looked
just like a pig, not like a porpoise, which he says

1. (25r6) Morison (1963) translates the word *sala* (hall) as "drydock," but perhaps Columbus's idea is that the ships would be sheltered, as if inside a building with
walls and a roof. The word *sala* means, among other things, "a large room" (*Diccionario* 1956).

2. (25r17–18) *Tasso* is Italian for "badger." The animal was probably a *hutía*, a
large native rodent. See Las Casas's associated note (at 25r38) and Morison (1963, 97,
16 Nov., n. 4).

concha mȳ tiesta : y no tenia cosa blanda sino la
della
cola y los ojos y vn agujero debaxo ∧ dexa p[ar]a expe
ler sus sup[er]fluydades mandolo salar p[ar]a llevar q̃
lo viesen los reyes /.

Sabado .17. de noviẽbre

25 ⁄ partio Entro en la barca por la maña y fue
a ver las yslas q̃ no avia visto por la vanda
del sudueste vido mūchas otras y my fertiles
y mȳ graçiosas y entre medio dellas mȳ
30 grā fondo /. algunas dellas diuidian arroyos
de agua dulçe : y creya q̃ aq̃lla agua salia
y arroyos salian de algunas fuentes q̃ des
çendia manavā en los altos dlas sierras de
las islas /. de aqui yendo adelante hallo vna
35 ribera dagua mȳ hermosa y dulçe y salia my
fria por lo enxuto della avia vn prado my
lindo y ——[?] palmas muchas y altissimas mas

hutias devian de   q̃ las q̃ avia visto /. hallo nuezes grandes dlas
ser   grādes [?] de yndia creo q̃ dize / y ratones grādes
40 dlos de yndia tabien / aves y cangrejos gradissi
mos /. aves vido mūchas y olor vehemete de
almizque y creyo q̃ lo devia de aver alli   Este
dia de seys mācebos q̃ tomo en el rio de mares q̃
mādo q̃ fuesen en la caravela niña : se huyero los
45 dos mas viejos /

Folio 25v

domingo Sabado .18. de noviẽbre

⁄ Salio en las barcas otra vez con mūcha gente de los navios
la   dla [?] entrada
y fue a poner vna grā cruz a la boca ∧ del dho puer
to dl principe q̃ avia mādado hazer dlos dchos
5 dos maderos en la entrada a la boca dla entra
da dl dho puerto dl prinçipe en vn lugar visto
so y descubierto de arboles : ella mȳ alta y mȳ
hermosa vista /. dize q̃ la mar creçe y descreçe
alli mucho mas q̃ en otro puerto dlo q̃ por aq̃lla
10 tr̄ra aya visto y q̃ no es mas maravilla por las

was all hard shell and had nothing soft except the
tail and the eyes and a hole underneath for
expelling its superfluities. He ordered it salted
to take to Spain so the sovereigns could see it.

Saturday 17 November

In the morning[1] he got into the launch and went to
see the islands that he had not seen. On the southwest side he saw many others and many fertile
and delightful ones, and in between them great
depth. Gorges with fresh water cut through some of
them; and he believed that that water and those
gorges came from some springs that flowed on the
heights of the mountains of the islands. From
here, going forward, he found a stream of beautiful
and fresh water which ran very cold. Along the dry
part of it there was a very pretty meadow and many
extremely high palms, more so than those he had
seen. He found large nuts, the kind from India (I
think that he says), and big rats, also of the
Indian kind, and extremely large crabs. He saw
many birds and [smelled] a strong smell of musk and
he thought that there must be some there. On this
day, of the six youths that he took captive at the
Rio de Mares and ordered to go in the caravel *Niña*,
the two eldest fled.

25v   ### Sunday[2] 18 November

He again left in the launches with many men from the
ships and went to put up the great cross, which he
had ordered made from the aforementioned two
timbers, at the mouth of the entrance to the said
Puerto del Príncipe in a conspicuous place bare of
trees. The cross [was] very tall and a beautiful sight.
He says that the sea rises and falls there much more
than in any other harbor that he has seen in that land
and that it is no wonder, because of the many islands,

1. (25r26) *Maña* is short for *mañana* (morning).
2. (25v1) In correcting the day of the week, Las Casas inadvertently crossed out
the day of the month and forgot to replace it.

mūchas Islas : y q̃ la marea es al reves dlas
nr̄as / porq̃ alli la luna al sudueste quarta del
sur es baxa mar en aq̃l puerto / no partio d[e]
aqui por ser domīgo /

lunes .19. de noviēbre

15

/ Partio antes q̃l sol saliese y cō calma : y despues al medio dia
vento algo al leste   y navego al nornordeste
al poner dl sol le quedava el pue^rto dl prinçipe
al sursudueste y estaria dl siete leguas /. vido
20 la Isla de baneque al leste justo dla qual estaria
60 millas /. navego toda esta noche al nordeste ,
escasso andaria .60. millas y hasta las diez
dl dia martes otras doze q̃ son por todas .18.
leguas / y ~~al cabo~~ [?] al nordeste q̃rta dl norte /

martes .20. de noviēbre

25

/ Quedavāle el baneque o las Islas dl baneque
al lesueste de donde salia ~~avn~~ [?] el viēto q̃ lle
vava contrario : y viendo q̃ no se mudava y la
mar se alterava : determino de dar la buel
30 ta al pue^rto dl p^rncipe de donde avia salido q̃ le
quedava .xxv. leguas /. no quiso yr a la Isleta
q̃ llamo Isabela q̃ le estava .12. lueguas q̃ pudie
ra yr a surgir aq̃l dia : por dos razones /. la
vna porq̃ vido dos Islas al sur las queria ver /.
35 la otra porq̃ los yndios q̃ traya q̃ avia tomado
en guanahani q̃ llamo san salvador q̃ estava ocho

and that the tide is the reverse of ours, because there
when the moon is southwest by south[1] it is low tide
in that harbor.   He did not leave from here because it
was Sunday.

Monday 19 November

He left before the sun came up in very light winds. Later,
at midday,[2] it blew a bit to the east and he sailed
to the north-northeast.   At sunset the Puerto del
Príncipe lay to the south-southwest and about seven
leagues distant.   He saw the island of Baneque due
east, from which he was distant about 60 miles.   He
steered all of this night to the northeast.   He went a
scant 60 miles and up until the tenth hour of day on
Tuesday another 12, which make 18 leagues in all to
the northeast by north.

Tuesday 20 November

Baneque, or the islands of Baneque, lay to the east-
southeast, whence came the wind, which was contrary; and seeing that it was not changing and the sea
rising, he decided to turn back to the Puerto del
Príncipe, from which he had departed and which was
25 leagues distant. He did not want to go to the islet
that he called Isabela, which was 12 leagues from him,
and to which he could have gone to anchor that day,
for two reasons: one, because he saw two islands to
the south that he wanted to see; the other, so that the
Indians that he had with him whom he had taken on
Guanahani (which he called San Salvador), which was

1.   (25v12–13) *La luna . . . del sur*. This peculiar turn of phrase was used for
specifying the time of high or low tide on the first day on which the new moon was
visible each month: the tidal "establishment of the port." On the compass card, viewed
as a 24-hour clock face with north at midnight and east at 6:00 A.M., SW by S makes
1415 hours (2:15 P.M.). If this is a low-water time, then another low is assumed to
occur 12 hours later at NE by N (2:15 A.M.). High tides are assumed to occur six hours
after the lows, at NW by W and SE by E, respectively.   The fifteenth century portolanos by Versi and Rizo put the low-tide establishment around the Huelva-Palos coastal
area at SE by E (Kretschmer 1909, 260, 421).   This implies a high-water establishment there of SW by S, just the reverse of the Admiral's stated low-water establishment
of Puerto Principe.
2.   (25v16) *Al medio dia* was added in the right margin after line 25v17 was
written.

leguas de aq̃lla Isabela : no se le fuesen / dlos qua
les diz q̃ tiene necessidad y por traellos a castilla
etc̃.   tenian diz que entẽdido q̃ en ~~viendo~~-[?] hallãdo
40 oro los avia el almi͞e de dexar tornar a su
t͞r͞r͞a / ~~yendo al~~-[?] llego en paraje dl puerto dl p͏ʳn
cipe / p[er]o no lo pudo tomar porq̃ era de noche y porq̃
lo decayer͞o las corrientes al norueste /. torno a
dar la buelta y puso la proa al nordeste con
45 viento rezio : amãso y mudose el viento al terçero
quarto dla noche puso la proa en el leste quarta
dl nordeste : el viento era susueste : y mudose al
alva de todo en sur y tocava enl sueste /. salido a
marco el puerto dl principe y quedavale al sudueste
50 y quasi a la quarta dl gueste y estaria dl .48. millas
que son .12. leguas /.

Folio 26r

~~q̃ son 12~~-[?] ~~leguas~~ /

miercoles 21. de noviẽbre

/ al sol salido navego al leste con viento sur
anduvo poco por la mar contraria hasta oras de
5 bisperas ovo andado .24. millas /. dspues se ~~mudo~~
mudo el viento al leste y anduvo al sur q̄rta del su
ste y al poner dl sol avia andado .12. millas /
Aqui se hallo el almi͞e en .42. grados dla linea
equinoçial a la p[ar]te del norte com͞o en el pue͏ʳto de
10 mares /. p[er]o aqui dize q̃ tiene suspenso el quadra
te hasta llegar a t͞r͞r͞a q̃ lo adobe / por mar̃a q̃
le pareçia q̃ no devia distar tanto y tenia ra
zon porq̃ no era possible ~~por~~-[?] com͞o no esten
estas yslas sino en   grados /. p[ar]a creer q̄uel
15 quadrante andava bueno le movia ver diz q̃ el
norte tan alto com͞o en castilla / y si esto es ver
dad mũcho allegado y alto andava c͞o la florida /.
p[er]o donde estan luego agora estas Islas q̃ entre
manos traya ? ayudava a esto q̃ hazia diz que

eight leagues from that island of Isabela, would not
flee from him, because, he says, he has need of them
and wants to take them to Castile, etc. They, he says,
had understood that, finding gold, the Admiral would
let them return to their own land. He reached the
neighborhood of the Puerto del Príncipe but could not
make port because it was night and because currents
set him to the northwest. He again changed course
and headed northeast with a strong wind. It calmed
down and changed at the third watch of the night
and he headed east by north. The wind was south-
southeast; and it changed at dawn to due south
veering southeast. When [the sun] came up, he
figured[1] that the Puerto del Príncipe lay to the
southwest, almost southwest by west, and was
about 48 miles, which is 12 leagues, from him.

26r   Wednesday 21 November

When the sun rose he steered east with a south wind.
He made little way because of the contrary sea. Up
to the hour of vespers he had gone 24 miles. Later
the wind changed to east and he went south by east,
and at sunset he had gone 12 miles. Here the Admiral
found that he was 42 degrees north of the equinoctial
line, as at the Puerto de Mares. But here he says that
he is postponing[2] using the quadrant until they
reach land, where it can be fixed. It seemed to him
that the line ought not to be so distant (and he was
right because it was not possible, since these islands
are but in   degrees).[3] To see the North Star as
high as in Castile would persuade him, he says, that
the quadrant was working well. (And if this is true
he would have been near and traveling in the same
latitude as Florida. But where are then these islands
that he had at hand?) It helped him to this con-

---

1. (25v48–49) [*Sol*] *salido amarco*. The word *sol* is not, but should be, in the
manuscript. Also, Jane-Vigneras (1960) omits translating *amarco*.
2. (26r10) *Suspenso* is the irregular past participle of *suspender*. The primary
meaning is to raise or hang something in the air, but the word can also mean to delay
or defer an action or activity. The latter meaning is probably intended here.
3. (26r14) *En   grados*. Las Casas perhaps intended to obtain a correct figure and fill in the blank but then never did so.

20   grā calor : p[er]o claro es q̃ si estuviera en la costa
     dla florida q̃ no oviera calor sino frio : y es
     tābien manifiesto q̃ en quarēta y dos grados en
     ninguᵃ p[ar]te dla tr̄r̄a se cree hazer Calor /. sino fue
     se por alguᵃ causa de per acçidens : lo q̃ hasta oy
25   no ~~se~~ creo yo q̃ se sabe /. por este calor q̃ alli el
     almiᵉ dize q̃ padecia / arguye q̃ en estas yndias
     y por alli donde andava devia de aver mucho oro /
nõ Este dia se aparto martin aloso pincon cō la carave
     la pinta : ~~pero~~ sin obediençia y volutad dl almiᵉ
30   por cudiçia ~~dis~~[?] diz q̃ pensando q̃ vn yndio q̃ el
     almiᵉ avia mādado poner en aq̃lla caravela le

                                    sin esperar
     avia de dar mucho oro /. y asi se fue ∧~~y desaparecio~~[?]
     sin causa de mal tp̄o sino porq̃ quiso /. y dize a
                                tiene
     qui el almiᵉ otras mūchas me —[?] hecho y dicho /.

35   Jueves .22.
     ⅄ miercoles en la noche navego al sur quarta del
     sueste cō el viento leste y era quasi calma /. al ter
     çero quarto vēto nornordeste todavia yva al sur por
     ver aq̃lla tr̄r̄a q̃ por alli le quedava / y quādo salio
40   el sol se hallo tā lexos como el dia passado por las
     corriētes contrarias y quedavale la tr̄r̄a quarēta millas
     esta noche martin alonso siguio el camino dl leste p[ar]a
     yr a la Isla de vaneque donde dizē los yndios q̃ ay
     mūcho oro /. el qual ~~estava siempʳ en yva~~ yva a
45   vista dl almiᵉ y avria hasta el .16. millas / andu
     vo el almiᵉ toda la noche la buelta de tr̄r̄a y hizo tomar

clusion, he says, that it was very hot. (But it is clear
that if he were on the coast of Florida it would not be
hot, but cold; and it is also manifest that in 42
degrees latitude nowhere on earth is it thought to be
hot, if it were not for some accidental cause,
which up to now I do not believe is known.)
Because of the heat that the Admiral says he suffered
there, he argues that in these Indies and there where
he was going there should be much gold. This day,
he says, Martín Alonso Pinzón, because of greed and
without the permission and will of the Admiral, departed with the caravel *Pinta*,[1] thinking that an
Indian whom the Admiral had ordered put on that
caravel was going to give him much gold. And so he
went away without waiting and not by reason of bad
weather, but because he wanted to. And the Admiral
says here that he has done and said to me many other things.

Thursday 22[2]

In the night on Wednesday he steered south by east
with an east wind and it was almost calm. At the
third watch[3] it blew north-northeast.[4] He still went
south to see the land that lay in that direction from
him. And when the sun rose he found himself as far
away as the day before because of the contrary currents; and the land lay 40 miles off. During this
night Martín Alonso continued on his course to the
east in order to go to the island of Baneque where the
Indians say there is much gold. He was in sight of the
Admiral and about 16 miles distant. The Admiral
went all night on a course parallel to the land[5] and

1. (26r29) Alvar (1976) reads the canceled word following *pinta* as *para*, not
pero.
2. (26r35) The name of the month is omitted in the manuscript.
3. (26r37–38) Regarding *al tercero quarto*, "at the third watch," Jane-Vigneras
(1960) always translates *quarto* as "quarter" instead of "watch" (see, e.g., Jane-Vigneras
1960, 68). Also see p. 141, n. 3, and Guillén Tato (1951, 60).
4. (26r38) *Nornordeste*. Morison (1963) incorrectly writes "NNW."
5. (26r46) *Buelta de tierra*. Guillén Tato (1951, 128–29) provides an illustra-
tion of the meaning of *buelta de tierra* ("parallel to the land"). The course is more or
less parallel to a shoreline, whereas its opposite, *vuelta de la mar o de fuera*, is away from
shore.

Folio 26v

algunas dlas velas y tener farol toda la noche
porq̃ le pareçio q̃ venia hazia el / y la noche hizo mȳ
clara y el ventizillo bueno p[ar]a venir a el si qui
siera /.

5   viernes .23. de noviẽbre

⫻ navego el almiᵉ todo el dia hazia la tr̄r̄a al sur
siempʳ con poco viento y la corriente + nūca le dexo   a. ~~devia dejado~~
llegar a ella antes estava oy tā lexos dllas ~~como~~-[?]   b. ~~lugar para~~-[?]
al poner dl sol : com̄o en la maña /. El viento era   c. ~~venir adonde~~-[?]

10   lesnordeste y razona[b?]le p[ar]a yr al sur sino q̃ era
poco /. ~~aq̃lla tr̄r̄a devia ser alguᵃ punta~~ y sobre este
cabo encavalga otra tr̄r̄a /o cabo q̃ va tābiẽ al
leste a quiẽ aq̃llos yndios q̃ llevava llamava
~~en las~~ por aqui   bohio /. la qual dezian q̃ era mȳ grande y q̃ avia
pareçe quā poco los   en ella gente q̃ tenia vn ojo en la frente : y otros
entendia /.   q̃ se llamavā canibales : a quien mostravā tener grā
miedo /. y desq̃ vierō q̃ lleva este camino diz que no
podian hablar : porq̃ los comian : y q̃ son gente
mȳ armada /. el almiᵉ dize q̃ bien cree q̃ ~~ay~~-[?]

20   ~~algo~~ avia algo dllo : mas q̃ pues erā armados se
ria gente de razō : y creya q̃ avrian captivado al
gunos y q̃ porq̃ no bolvian a ————[?] sus tr̄r̄as : di
rian q̃ los comian /. lo mismo creyan dlos xp̄īa
ños y dl almiᵉ al prinçipio q̃ algunos los vieron /.

25   Sabado .24. de noviembre

⫻ Navego aq̃lla noche toda y a la ora de terçia del dia
tomo la tr̄r̄a sobre la Isla llana en aq̃l mismo
lugar : donde avia arribado la semana passada quā

26v   had some of the sails taken in and a lantern set all
night because it appeared to him that Martín Alonso
was coming toward him; and the night was very clear
and the light wind good for coming to him if he were
so to wish.

Friday 23 November

The Admiral steered all day toward the land to the
south, always with little wind, and the current[1]
never let him reach it. Rather, today he was as far
from it at sunset as in the morning. The wind was
east-northeast and right for going south, although it
was light. Beyond this cape [of the land to the
south] appeared another higher land[2] or cape which
also runs to the east, which those Indians that he was
bringing called Bohío, which they said was very large
and that there were people on it who had one eye in
their foreheads, and others whom they called cannibals, of whom they showed great fear. And when they
saw that he was taking this route, he says that they
could not talk, because the cannibals eat them, and
that they are people very well armed. The Admiral
says that well he believes there is something in what
they say, but that since they were armed they must be
people of intelligence; and he believed that they must
have captured some of them and because they did not
return to their own lands they would say that they ate
them. They believed the same thing about the Christians and about the Admiral when some Indians first
saw them.

Saturday 24 November

He sailed all that night and at the hour of tierce
of the [next] day they sighted land near the flat island
in that same place where they had arrived the week be-

1. (26v7a–c) Alvar (1976) reads the canceled text in these lines as *devia desde
dicha parte no venir a veni.*
2. (26v12) *Encabalgar* means, among other things, to rest or lean upon something else. Here, *encabalgar* suggests that the more distant cape seemed to "rest
upon," i.e., to be higher than, the nearer one.

yva
do ∧a la Isla de baneque /. al principio no oso llegar
30   a la tr̄r̄a porq̄ le pareçio q̄ aq̄lla abra de sierras rom
pia la mar mucho en ella /. y en fin llego a la mar
de nr̄a Señora donde avia las mūchas Islas : y entro
en el puerto que dixo arriba pusole nōbre del puerto dl prinçipe ya [?] q̄sta junto a la boca dla entrada dlas
35   Islas /. y dize q̄ si el antes supiera este ——— [?] puerto :
y no no se ocupara en ver las Islas dla mar de nr̄a
señora : no le fuera neçessario bolver atras /. avnq̄
dize q̄ lo da por bien empleado por aver visto las
dchas Islas /. asi q̄ lle——— [?] llegādo a tr̄r̄a en
40   bio la barca y tēto el puerto y hallo mūy buena bar
ra hōda de seys braças y hasta veynte y limpio
todo basa : entro en el poniendo la proa al sudueste
y dspues bolviendo al gueste / quedādo la Isla llana dla

[e?]ste deve ser el
puerto q̄ llamo
Sancta cathalina
porq̄ llego a el su
[bispera?]

p[ar]te dl norte : la qual con otra su vezina hazē vna
laguna de mar en q̄ cabrian todas las naos dspaña
por [?] y podrian estar seguras sin amarras de todos los

Folio 27r

vientos / y esta entrada dla parte dl sueste
q̄ se entra poniendo la proa al sudu- susudueste :
tiene la salida al gueste mūy hōda y muy an
cha /. asi q̄ se puede passar entremedio dlas
5   dchas Islas ∴ y por cognoscimiº dllas : a quien vinie
se dla mar dla p[ar]te dl norte q̄s su travesia dsta
costa /. estan las dchas Islas al pie de vna grāde
mōtaña q̄s su lōgura de leste gueste y es
harto luēga y mas alta y luēga q̄ ninguna
10   de [t]odas las otras que estan en esta costa adonde ay
infinitas /. y haze fuera vna restinga -q̄s- [?]
al luēgo dla dcha mōtaña como vn banco
q̄ llega hasta la entrada /. todo esto dla p[ar]te del
sueste : y tambien dla p[ar]te dla Isla llana : ha
15   ze otra restinga avnq̄sta es pequeña /. y asi en

fore, when he was going to the island of Baneque.
At first he did not dare approach the land because it
seemed to him that the sea broke heavily in that
opening into the mountains, and finally he reached the
Mar de Nuestra Señora where the many islands were.
And he entered the harbor[1] which is near the mouth
of the entrance to the islands. And he says that if
previously he had known of this harbor, and if he
had not been busy seeing the islands of the Mar de
Nuestra Señora, it would not have been necessary
for him to turn back; although he says he considers
that seeing the said islands was time well spent.
So,[2] reaching land, he sent the launch to
examine the harbor and he found a good bar
with a depth of six *brazas* and [inside] up to 20,
and clean-bottomed, all sand. He entered,
pointing the prow southwest and later turning
west, leaving the flat island to the north, which
with another island, its neighbor, formed
a lagoon which would hold all the ships of
Spain, and where they might be secure, without

27r   cables, from all winds. And it is entered
from the southeast and one enters heading
south-southwest.[3] And it has a way out to the
west, very deep and very wide. So one may pass
in between the said islands; and in order that
anyone coming from the north, which is perpendicular to this coast, may recognize them, the
said islands are at the foot of a great mountain whose length runs east-west and is very
long and higher and longer than any of the others that are on this coast, where there are an
infinite number. And outside there is a reef
the length of the said mountain, like a bar
which reaches to the entrance. All of this is
to the southeast. And also, in the direction
of the flat island, there is another reef, al-

1. (26v33–34) Alvar (1976) reads the canceled text that follows *puerto* as *que digo es la que le nombran del puerto dl principe ya*.
2. (26v39) Alvar (1976) reads the canceled text following *asi que* as *lle voy hailo (?)* (Alvar's question mark).
3. (27r2) *Susudueste* (south-southwest). Morison (1963, 101) translates *susu-dueste* as "SSE."

tremedias de ambas ay grāde anchura y fondo
grande comō dho es /. ~~En tomādo agua salien-~~
~~do de~~-[?]   luego a la entrada ~~vido vn rio~~ a la par
te dl sueste ~~vierō vn rio~~ dentro enl mismo
20 puerto vierō vn rio grāde y mūy hermoso
y de mas agua q̃ hasta entōçes avian visto y q̃
bevia el agua dulçe hasta la mar / a la entrada
tiene vn banco : mas despues de entro es my
hōdo de ocho y nueve braças /. esta todo lle
25 no de palmas y de mūchas arboledas comō
los otros /.

Domingo .25. de noviēbre

⁒ Antes dl sol salido entro en la barca y fue a ver
vn cabo /o punta de tr̄ra al sueste dla Isleta llana
30 obra de vna legua y media : porq̃ le parecia
q̃ devia de aVr algū rio bueno /. luego a la entra
da dl cabo dla p[ar]te dl sueste andādo dos tiros
de ballesta : vio venir vn grāde arroyo de my
linda agua q̃ deçendia de vna mōtaña abaxo
35 y hazia grā ruydo /. fue al rio y vio ~~vn~~ en el

estas devia pie   vnas piedras reluzir con vnas māchas en e
dras de [manga?]   llas de color de oro : y acordose q̃ en el rio
sita   tejo q̃ al pie del junto a la mar se halla oro y

no ay duda   pareçiōle q̃ çierto devia de tener oro /. y mādo co
sino q̃ alli lo 40 ger çiertas de aq̃llas piedras . p[ar]a llevar a los re
avia   yes /. estando asi dan bozes los moços grume
                   tes diziendo q̃ vian pinales [/.?] miro por la sierra

ay los pinos al   y vidolos tan grādes y tan maravillosos : q̃ ~~no le~~-[?] po
mirables   dia encareçer su altura y derechura como husos
45 gordos y delgado / donde cognoscio q̃ se podian
hazer navios e infinita tablazon y masteles p[ar]a las

Folio 27v

mayores naos dspaña . vido robles y ma
vn buē rio y
droños y ∧aparejo p[ar]a hazer sierras de

though this one is small. And also, in between
the two reefs, there is great width and depth,
as is said. Close to the entrance, to the
southeast, within the harbor itself, they saw a
large and very beautiful river and with more
water than they had seen up to that time; and
one drank fresh water all the way to the sea.
At the entrance there is a bar, but after entering it is very deep, of eight and nine
brazas. It is all full of palms and many
groves of trees, like the others.

Sunday 25 November

Before sunrise he got into the launch and went
to see a cape or point of land to the southeast
of the flat islet, about one and a half leagues
off, because it seemed to him that some good
river should be there. Soon, at the beginning
of the cape toward the southeast, going two
crossbow shots' distance, he saw coming toward
him a great stream of very pretty water that
descended a mountain and made a great noise.
He went to the river and saw shining in it
some stones with gold-colored spots on them,
and he remembered that in the Tagus River, in
its lower part, near the sea, gold is found;
and it seemed certain to him that this one
should have gold. And he ordered certain of
those stones collected to take to the
sovereigns. While he was thus occupied, the
ships' boys shouted that they saw pine groves.
He looked up toward the mountains and saw
them, so large and admirable that he could not
praise [sufficiently] their height and
straightness, like spindles, thick and thin,
where he recognized that ships could be made,
and vast quantities of planking and masts for
27v   the greatest ships of Spain. He saw
oaks and arbutus[1] and a good river and mate-

---

1. (27v1–2) Jane-Vigneras (1960) and Thacher (1903–1904) translate *madroños* as "strawberry tree," an alternative name for *arbutus*. See Morison (1963, 102,n.5)
for a discussion.

agua /. la tr̄r̄a —[?] y los ayres mas templa

dos q̃ hasta alli : por la altura y hermosura

5   dlas sierras /. vido por la playa mūchas otras

piedras de color de hierro : y otras que dezian

algunos q̃ erā de minas de plata todas las

quales trae el rio . alli cojo vna entena y mastel

p[ar]a la mezana dla caravela niña /. llego a la

10   boca dl rio y entro en vna cala al pie de aq̃l cabo

dla p[ar]te dl sueste mūy hōda y grande en q̃ cabri

an çient naos sin alguna amarra ni anclas /.

y el puerto ~~tal~~ q̃ los ojos otro tal nūca vieron /.

lasierras altissimas de las quales descendian

15   mūchas aguas lindissimas : todas las sierras

llenas de pinos y por todo aq̃llo diuersissi

mas y hermosissimas florestas de arboles /.

otros dos /o tres rios le quedavā atras /. enca

reçe todo esto en grā maña a los reyes : y mue

20   stra aver resçibido de verlo y mayormēte

los pinos inextimable alegria y gozo /. + y

afirma no encareçello la çentissima p[ar]te dlo

q̃ es : y q̃ plugo a nr̄o Señor de le mostrar

siempre vna cosa mejor q̃ otra : y siemp^r

25   en lo q̃ hasta alli avia descubierto yva de biē

en mejor /. ansi en las tr̄r̄as y arboledas

Margin notes (left):

————[?]

~~llamolo el pue[rto]~~
~~de sāta cath[ali]~~
~~na porq̃ ll[ego]~~
~~alli dia de s[ta]~~
~~cathalina~~ [?]

todo çierto cō
gra razon

Margin notes (right):

a. porq̃ se pod[ia]
b. hazer alli q[ua]
c. tos navios ds[ea]
d. ren / traye[ndo]
e. los adereço[s]
f. si no fuer[a]
g. madera y [pez]
h. q̃ alli se ha[ria]
i. harta /

rial to make water-powered sawmills. The
land and breezes [were] more temperate than
[they had experienced] elsewhere because of
the height and beauty of the mountains. He
saw along the beach many other stones the
color of iron and others that some said were
from silver mines, all of which the river
brought. There they took a yard and a mast
for the mizzen of the caravel *Niña*. He
reached the mouth of the river and went into
an opening at the foot of that cape, toward
the southeast, which was very deep and large,
and in which there would be room[1] for a
hundred ships without any cables or anchors.
And the harbor was such that eyes never saw
another like it. The mountains were extremely
high, and many beautiful streams descended
from them. All the mountains were full of
pines and everywhere the most diverse and
beautiful groups of trees. Two or three other
rivers lay behind him. He praises all of this
very highly to the sovereigns. And he indicates that he had received from seeing it,
and even more so from the pine trees, inesti-
mable joy and pleasure; because as many ships
as might be wanted could be made there, bringing out their equipment except for wood and
pitch, of which a great plenty would be made
there. He affirms that he is not praising[2] it
a hundredth part of what it is, and that it
pleased Our Lord always to show him one thing
better than the other, and that always, in
what he had discovered up to this point, he
had gone from good to better, as well in lands

1. (27v11–12) Las Casas's canceled notes at lines 27v11 and 27v12 are actually
written in the right margin of the manuscript. Alvar (1976) reads the note at 27v11
as *en sueste*.

2. (27v22) *No encareçello* (not praising it). *Encarecer* means to raise the price of
something, or to praise. Morison (1963, 102) translates the passage in 27v22–23 as
"he had not described the hundredth part of what is there," whereas the meaning seems
to be that Columbus could have praised it a hundred times more than he actually has
without exaggerating. In 27v25, Morison (1963) translates *descubierto* (discovered or
found) as "described."

y yervas y frutos y flores : como en las
gentes : y siemp[r] de diuersa maña : y asi en
vn lugar como en otro /. los mismo en los
30   puertos y en las aguas /. y finalmēte dize
q̃ quãdo el q̃ lo vee le es tan grãde admiraçion : qua
to mas sera a quie[n] lo oyere : y q̃ nadie lo podra creer
si no lo viere /.

lunes .26. de noviembre

35   / Al salir dl Sol levãto las ————[?] anclas dl puerto
de Sancta cathalina adonde estava dentro dla isla
llana : y navego de luengo dla costa con poco
                    sudueste
viento ∧al camino dl cabo dl pico q̃ era ~~subdueste~~
al sueste /. llego al cabo tarde porq̃ le calmo el
40   viento : y llegado vido al sueste q̄rta dl leste otro
cabo q̃staria del .60. millas : y de alli vido otro
cabo q̃ estaria hazia el navio al sueste q̄rta del
sur ∴ y pareciole q̃staria del .20. millas al
qual puso nōbre el cabo de Campana al qual
45   no pudo llegar de dia porq̃ le torno a calmar
dl todo el viento / andaria en todo aq̃l dia .32.

Folio 28r

millas q̃ son .8. leguas /. dentro dlas
quales noto y marco nueve ~~puestas~~-[?]
puertos mȳ señalados los quales todos
los marineros hazian maravillas / y cin
5   co rios grãdes porq̃ ~~andava~~-[?] yva siempre jū
to cō tr̄r̄a / p[ar]a ver lo bien todo /. toda aq̃lla
tr̄r̄a es mōtañas altissimas mȳ hermosas
y no secas ni de peñas : sino todas andables
y valles hermosissimos /. y asi los valles como las
10   mōtañas erā llenos de arboles altos y frescos
q̃ era gloria mirarlos y pareçia q̃ erā mūchos
pinales /. y tabien detras dl dho cabo dl pico dla

and groves and plants and fruits and flowers
as in people, and always of different sorts,
and likewise in one place as in another, and
the same in harbors and waters.   And finally
he says that, when to him who sees it it is so
greatly admirable, how much more so will it be
to him who hears about it, and that no one
will be able to believe it if he does not see it.

Monday 26 November

At sunrise he raised anchor[1] from the Puerto
de Santa Cathalina, where he was behind the
flat island, and sailed along the coast with a
light southwest wind in the direction of the
Cabo del Pico, which was to the southeast.   He
arrived late at the cape because the wind died
down, and having arrived he saw to the southeast by east another cape which was about 60
miles off; and he saw another cape that lay
toward the southeast by south from the ship;
and it appeared to him to be about 20 miles
away.   He gave it the name of Cabo de Campana.
He could not reach it during the day because
the wind again died completely.   He made in
that entire day about 32 miles, which is

28r   eight leagues, within which he noted and marked [on
his chart?] nine outstanding harbors,[2] which all the
sailors thought were admirable, and five big rivers,
since he always went close to the land in order to see
everything well. All of that land is [made up of] extremely high and beautiful mountains, neither dry
nor rocky, but all traversable and with most beautiful
valleys.   The valleys, as well as the mountains, were
full of tall refreshing trees so that it was delightful to see them; and it appeared that many of
them were pine groves.   And also, behind the said

1.   (27v35)   Alvar (1976) reads the canceled text preceding *anclas* as *ancl.*
2.   (28r2–3) *Noto . . . señalados* (He noted . . . outstanding harbors). *Marcar* is a
technical term used in various contexts: "marking the north," "marking directions"
(probably on a chart), "figuring." See Guillén Tato (1951, 87). Jane-Vigneras (1960)
translates *señalados* as "well-outlined," Morison (1963) as "remarkable."

parte dl sueste : estan dos Isletas q̃ terna cada vna
en çerco dos leguas : y dentro dllas tres mara

15 villosos puertos y dos grā̃des rios /. en toda
esta costa no vido poblado ninguᵒ dsde la mar
podria ser averlo y ay señales dllo /. porq̃ don
de quiera q̃ saltavā̃ ~~ombres~~-[?] en tr̄ra hallavā̃ señales
de aver gente y huegos mū̃chos /. estimava q̃

20 la tr̄ra q̃ oy vido dla p[ar]te dl sueste del cabo de can
pana : era la Isla q̃ llamavā̃ los yndios bohio

                        y   lo
~~porq̃ lo~~-[?] ∧pareçe∧: porq̃l d̄ho cabo esta apartado de aq̃lla
tr̄ra /. toda la gē̃te q̃ ~~q̃~~ hasta oy a hallado diz que
tiene grā̃dissimo temor dlos de caniba /o canima

25 y dizē̃ q̃ biven en esta Isla de bohio : la qual deve
este bohio devia ser   de ser mȳ grā̃de segū̃ —[?] le pareçe /. y cree
la Isla española : po   q̃ van a tomar a q̃llos a sus ~~casas~~ tr̄ras y casas
~~para~~-[?] comō sean mȳ cobardes : y no saben de ar
                          le parece q̃
mas /. y a esta causa ∧aq̃llos yndios q̃ traya : no

30 suelen poblarse a la costa dla mar por ser vezi
nos a esta tr̄ra /. los quales diz q̃ dspues q̃ le vierō̃
tomar la ———[?] buelta desta tr̄ra no podian hablar
~~ni les podia quitar el miedo~~/ temiendo q̃ los —[?] avian de
comer / y no les podia quitar el temor /. y deziā̃
no los entendian 35 q̃ no tenian sino vn ojo y la cara de perro : y cre
ya el almiᵉ q̃ mē̃tian : y sentia el almiᵉ q̃ deviā̃
de ser dl señorio del gran Can que los captiva
[van?] /.

                                                      Martes 27. de noviembre

40 ℓ ayer al poner dl Sol llego çerca de vn cabo
~~Sto Campana~~-[?] q̃ llamo campana y porq̃l çielo
claro y el viento poco : no quiso yr a tr̄ra a
surgir avnq̃ tenia de sotaviento çinco /o seys
puertos maravillosos : porq̃ se detenia mas dlo q̃

Folio 28v

queria por el ———[?] apetito y delectaçion q̃
tenia y resçebia de ver y mirar la hermosu
ra y frescura de aq̃llas tr̄ras donde quiera

Cabo del Pico to the southeast, there are two islets,
each of which has a circuit of two leagues, and behind
them three admirable harbors and two big rivers. On
all of this coast he saw no populated places from the
sea, [although] it may be that there were some and
there were signs of them because, wherever they went
ashore,[1] they found indications of people and many
fires. He judged that the land that he saw today
southeast of the Cabo de Campana was the island that
the Indians called Bohío, and it seemed so because the
said cape is separated from that land. All the people
that he has found up to today, he says, have extreme
fear of the men of Caniba, or Canima, and they say
that they live on this island of Bohío, which must be
very large, as it seems to him; and they believe that
they are going to take them to their lands and houses
since they are very cowardly and know nothing about
weapons. And because of this it appears to him that
those Indians he has with him do not usually settle on
the seacoast because of being neighbors to this land.
He says that after they saw him take the route to this
land they could not speak, fearing that they would
have them to eat;[2] and he could not take away their
fear. And they say that they have but one eye and the
face of a dog; and the Admiral thought they were
lying and felt that those who captured them must
have been under the rule of the Grand Khan.

Tuesday 27 November

Yesterday at sunset he arrived near a cape that he called
Campana and because the sky [was] clear and the wind
faint he did not want to go [close] to land to anchor,
although downwind he had five or six admirable
harbors; he was delaying more than he wished be-
28v   cause of the desire[3] and delight that he had and received from seeing and looking at the beauty and
freshness of those lands wherever he entered. And

1. (28r18) Alvar (1976) reads the canceled text preceding *en tierra* as *ombre* (?)
(Alvar's question mark).
2. (28r33–34) *Los avian de comer. Avian de* has been added in the right margin of
line 33 to replace the canceled word that precedes it.
3. (28v1) Alvar (1976) reads the canceled text preceding *apetito* as *t cadicion.*

 q̃ entrava : y por no se tardar en proseguir lo
5   q̃ pretendia /. por estas razones se tuvo aq̃lla
noche a la corda ~~q̃ es q̃ aver q̃ tienē las~~[?] y tem
porejar hasta el dia /. y porq̃ los aguajes y cor
rientes lo avian echado aq̃lla noche mas de
çinco /o seys leguas al sueste adelante de donde
10   avia anocheçido : y le avia pareçido la tr̄r̄a de
Campana : ~~acordo bolver atras~~ y allende aq̃l
cabo pareçia vna grāde entrada q̃ mostrava
diuidir vna tr̄r̄a de otra y hazia comō Isla en
medio : acordo bolver atras con viento su
15   dueste y vino adonde le avia pareçido el aber
tura : y hallo q̃ no era sino vna grāde baya
y al cabo dlla dla p[ar]te del ~~sudueste~~ sueste vn cabo
en el qual ay vna mōtaña alta y quadrada q̃
pareçia Isla /. Salto el viento en el norte y
20   torno a tomar la buelta del sueste por correr
la costa y dscubrir todo lo q̃ por alli oviese /. y
                         de aq̃l
vido luego al pie ∧ ~~del~~[?] cabo de campana vn
puerto maravilloso y vn grā rio : y de a vn
quarto de legua otro rio : y de alli a media legua
25   otro rio : y dēde a otra media legua otro rio : y
dende a vna legua otro rio : y dende a otra
otro rio : y dende a otro quarto otro rio : y ——[?]
dende a otra legua otro rio grāde / dsde el qual
~~avria~~ hasta el cabo de campana avria .20. millas
30   y le quedā al sueste /. y los mas destos rios
tenian ~~muy~~ grādes entradas y anchas y limpias
con sus puertos maravillosos p[ar]a naos grā
dissimas : sin bancos de arena ni de pedras ni
restringas /. viniendo asi por la costa a la parte
35   dl sueste dl d̄ho postrero rio : hallo vna grāde
poblaçion la mayor q̃ hasta oy aya hallado : y
vido venir infinita gente a la ribera dla mar dā
do grādes bozes todos dsnudos con sus azagayas
en la mano /. deseo de hablar cō ellos y amay
40   no las velas y surgio : y enbio las barcas
dla nao y dla caravela por mañ̄a ordenados

so as not to delay in furthering his purpose, for
these reasons that night was spent jogging on and
off[1] and killing time until day. And because the
tidal flows and currents that night had set him
five or six leagues southeast,[2] beyond the place
where he had been at nightfall, and where the land
of Campana had appeared to him, and where beyond
that cape there appeared a large opening that indicated a division of one land from another, and
where something like an island was formed in between, he decided to turn back with a southwest
wind and go where the opening had appeared. He
found that it was but a large bay and at the southeast end of it [there was] a cape on which there
was a high square mountain that appeared to be an
island. The wind shifted quickly to north and he
again took a course to the southeast to run along
the coast and to survey everything that might be
there. And he soon saw at the foot of that Cabo de
Campana an admirable harbor and a big river; and a
quarter of a league away, another river; and from
there a half league, another river; and beyond, at
another half league, another river; and beyond, a
league further, another river; and another league
beyond that, another river; and after another quarter league, another river; and another league beyond that, another big river, from which to the
Cabo de Campana was about 20 miles to the southeast. And most of these rivers had big and wide
and clear entrances with admirable harbors for the
very largest ships, without sandbanks or stony
shallows or reefs. Coming thus along the coast to
the southeast of the last river mentioned, he found
a great settlement, the largest that he had found up
until now; and he saw a great number of men come
to the seashore shouting, all naked, with their
javelins in their hands. He desired to speak with
them, and hauled down the sails and anchored; and
he sent the launches of the ship and of the caravel

1.   (28v6) Alvar (1976) reads the canceled text following *a la corda* as *qu'es que
avnque'l . . . nen las.*
2. (28v9) *Sueste* (southeast). This bearing may be in error. The context and prevail-
ing currents seem to imply that they drifted to the northwest.

 q̃ no hiziesen daño alguno a los yndios ni lo

resçibiesen : mãdando q̃ les diesen algunas

cosillas de aq̃llos resgates : los yndios hizie

45   rō adamanes de no los dexar salitar en tr̄ra y ~~resi~~ [?]

Folio 29r

resistillos / y viendo q̃ las barcas se allegava

mas a tr̄ra y q̃ no les avian miedo : se aparta

rō dla mar /. y creyēdo q̃ saliendo dos /o tres

hobres dlas barcas no temierā : salierō tres

5   xp̄ıanos diziēdo q̃ no oviesen miedo en su lengua

porq̃ sabian algo dlla por la conversaçion dlos

q̃ traen consigo : en fin dierō todos a huyr [q?]

ni grāde ni chico quedo /. fuerō los tres xp̄ıa

ños a las casas q̃ son de paja y dla hechura de

10   las otras q̃ avian visto : y no hallarō a nadie

ni cosa en alguª dllas /. bolvierōse a los na

a medio dia

vios y alcarō velas ∧p[ar]a yr a vn cabo hermo

so q̃ quedava al leste q̃ avia hasta el ocho leguas .

aviendo andado media legua por la misma baya

15   vido el almiᶜ a la p[ar]te dl sur vn singularissimo

puerto y dla p[ar]te dl sueste vnas tr̄rās hermosas

a maravilla asi comõ vna vega mōtuosa dentro

en estas mōtañas : y parecian grādes humos y gra

mūy

des poblaçiones en ellas y las tr̄ras ∧labradas : por

20   lo qual determino de se baxar a este puerto y

provar si podia aver lengua o pratica cō ellos /.

el qual era tal q̃ si a los otros pueʳtos avia alabado

este dize q̃ alabava mas cō las tr̄rās y tēplança

y comarca dellas y poblaçion / dize maravi

25   llas dla lindeza dla tr̄ra y dlos arboles don

siempʳ donde ay pal   de ay pinos y palmas y dla grāde vega q̃ avn

mas dlas mȳ

altas es fertilis

sima tr̄rā -   de llano

dize q̃ no es llana de   q̃ no es llana ∧q̃ va al sursueste ~~-q̃-~~ : p[er]o es llana

llano quiere

dezir q̃ no es rasa   de mōtes llanos y baxos la mas hermosa cosa

del mūdo y salen por ella mūchas riberas de

30   aguas q̃ desçienden destas mōtañas /. despues

de surgida la nao salto el almiᶜ en la barca p[ar]a

so[l?]dar el pueʳto q̃s comõ vna escodilla y quā

do fue frōtero dla boca al sur hallo vnª entrada

with orders that they should do no harm to the Indians, but not receive any either, and commanding
that they give them some little things from the
trade goods. The Indians made gestures threaten-
ing to resist them and not to let them land, but
29r   seeing that the launches were approaching land more
closely and that the Spaniards were not afraid of
them, they withdrew from the sea. Believing that if
only two or three men got out of the launches the
Indians would not be afraid, three Christians got
out, saying in their language not to be afraid,
because they knew a bit of it through association
with those they brought with them; but finally all
took to flight and neither grown-ups nor little ones
remained. The three Christians went to the houses,
which are of straw, made the same way as the others
they had seen; and they did not find anyone or
anything in any of them. They returned to the ships
and raised sail at noon to go to a beautiful cape that
lay to the east eight leagues distant. Having gone
half a league along the same bay, the Admiral saw
to the south a most singular harbor and to the
southeast some marvelously beautiful fields like a
fertile rolling plain within the mountains; and
there appeared much smoke and large settlements in
them and the fields were very well tended. Because
of this he decided to go down to this harbor and to
see if he could talk or deal with them. The harbor
was such that, if he had praised the other harbors,
this one, he says, he praised more, with its fields
and temperate climate and surrounding region and
settlement. He says marvelous things of the beauty
of the land and of the trees, where there are pines
and palms, and of the great plain, which, although
it is not entirely flat where it goes to the south-
southeast but is rolling with gentle and low hills,
is the most beautiful thing in the world. And there
run through it many streams of water that descend
from these mountains. After the ship anchored, the
Admiral got into the launch in order to sound the
harbor, which is shaped like a soup bowl, and when
he was opposite the mouth he found to the south an

de vn rio q̃ tenia de anchura q̃ podia entrar vna

35 galera por ella y de tal mar̃a q̃ no se via hasta

q̃ se llegase a ella . y entrãdo por ella tanto como

[dl?] longura dla barca tenia çinco braças ~~de fõdo~~

y de ocho de hõdo / andãdo por ella fue cosa

maravillosa y las arboledas y frescuras y el agua

40 clarissima y las aves ~~q̃~~ y amenidad : q̃ dize q

le parecia q̃ no quisiera salir de alli / yva diziē

en su cõpañia

do a los hobres q̃ llevava ∧q̃ p[ar]a haze^r relacion a los

reyes dlas cosas q̃ vian : no bastarã mill lēguas

a referillo / ni su mano p[ar]a lo escrevir q̃ le parecia

45 q̃stava encantado / deseava q̃ aq̃llo vierã mūchas

Folio 29v

otras p[er]rsonas prudētes y de credito dlas quales

dize ser çierto q̃ no encareçierã estas cosas

menos q̃ el /. Dize mas el almi^e aqui estas palabra[s]

sera

quato ~~es~~ el benefiçio q̃ de aqui se puede aver

nõ   5 yo no lo escrivo /. es cierto ~~q̃~~-[?] señores prinçipes

q̃ donde ay tales tr̃r̃as q̃ deve de aver infini

tas cosas de provecho : mas yo no me detē

go / En ningud puerto porq̃ querria ver to

das las mas tr̃r̃as q̃ yo pudiese p[ar]a hazer re

10 lacion dellas a vr̃as altezas : y tãbien no se

la lengua y la gente destas tr̃r̃as no me en

tienden ni yo ni otro q̃ yo tēga a ellos / y

estos yndios q̃ yo traygo muchas vezes le

nõ.   entiendo vna cosa por otra al contrario : ni

15 fio mūcho dllos / porq̃ mūchas vezes an pro

a nr̄o

vado a fugir /. mas agora plaziēdo ∧ ~~a dios~~

señor vere lo mas q̃ yo pudiere y —[?] poco a

poco andare entendiendo y cognosçiendo y fa

re enseñar esta lēgua a p[er]sonas de mi casa

20 porq̃ veo q̃s toda la lengua vna fasta a

qui /. y dspues se sabrã los benefiçios y se

estos

trabajara de hazer todos ∧pueblos xp̄īanos /

porq̃ de ligero se hara : porq̃ ellos no tie

entrance to a river which was wide enough for a
galley to enter through it and of such a sort
that it could not be seen until one reached it. And
having gone into it as far as the length of the
launch, it had a depth of five to eight *brazas*.
Going through it was a wonderful thing [because of]
the groves of trees, the freshness, and the extremely clear water, and the birds, and its attractive-
ness. He says that it seemed to him that one might
not wish to leave that place. He kept telling the
men who were in his company that, in order to report
to the sovereigns the things they were seeing, a
thousand tongues would not suffice to tell it or his
hand to write it; for it seemed to him that it was
enchanted. He wished that many other prudent and

29v   creditable persons would see it, of whom he says
he is certain that they would praise these things no
less than he. Moreover, the Admiral says here these
words:[1] How great the benefit will be that can be
obtained from this place I do not write. It is certain, Lord Princes, that where there are such lands
there should be a vast number of profitable things.
But I am not delaying in any harbor because I would
like to see all the lands that I can in order to report
on them to Your Highnesses. Also I do not know
the language, and the people of these lands do not
understand me nor do I, nor anyone else that I have
with me, them. And many times I understand one
thing said by these Indians that I bring for another, its contrary; nor do I trust them much,
because many times they have tried to flee. But
now, pleasing Our Lord, I will see the most that I
can and little by little I will progress in understanding and acquaintance, and I will have this
tongue taught to persons of my household because I
see that up to this point it is a single language.
And later the benefits will be known and efforts
will be made to make all these peoples Christian;
because it will be done easily, since they have no

1.   (29v3) *Palabras* is written in the right margin of the manuscript. It is probably
a later insertion. The preceding word, *estas*, may also be an insertion.

 nē secta ninguᵃ ni son Idolatras / y vr̄as

25　altezas mādarā hazeʳ en estas p[ar]tes çiudad
e fortaleza : y se convertirā estas tr̄r̄as /. y
çertifico a .v.al. q̃ debaxo dl sol no me
pareçe q̃ las puede aver mejores : en fer
tilidad en temperāçia de frio y calor /. en

30　abūdançia de aguas buenas y sanas y no co
m̄o los rios de guinea q̃ ~~s pestilençia~~ son
todos pestilençia /. porq̃ loado nr̄o Señor
hasta oy de toda mi gente no a avido p[er]rsona
q̃ le aya mal la cabeça ni estado en cama

35　por dolençia : saluo vn viejo de dolor de
piedra de q̃ el estava toda su vida apassio
nado / y luego sano al cabo de dos dias /.

　　　　　　　　　　　　　los
Esto q̃ digo es en todos tres ∧navios /.
asi que plazera a dios q̃ vr̄as altezas enbia

40　ran aca /o vernā hōbres doctos y veran des
pues la Vrdad de todo /. y porq̃ atras ten
go hablado dl sitio de villa e fortaleza en
el ~~puerto~~ rio de mares por el buē pueʳto

Folio 30r

y por la comarca es çierto q̃ todo es Vrdad lo q̃
yo dixe mas no a ninguᵃ comp[ar]acion de alla
aqui ni dla mar de nr̄a Señora /. porq aqui
deve aver infra la tierra / grādes poblacio

5　nes y gente Inumerable y cosas de grāde
provecho /. porq̃ aqui y en todo lo otro dscubier
to y tengo esperāça ~~des~~ de descubrir antes q̃
yo vaya a castilla : digo q̃ terna toda la xpian
dad negociaçion en ellas /. quāto mas la espa

10　ña a quien deve estar subjecto todo /. y digo
q̃ .v. altezas no deven consentir q̃ aqui trate
ni faga pie ningund estrāgero / saluo catholi

nõ.　cos xp̄ianos : pues esto fue el fin y el comien
ço dl proposito que fuese por acreçēntamiº

15　y gloria dla religion xpiana : ni venir a
estas p[ar]tes ninguº q̃ no sea buē xp̄iaño /. ~~des~~
~~pues~~ todas son sus palabras /. Subio alli
por el rio arriba y hallo vnos braços del rio

false religion nor are they idolaters. And Your
Highnesses will order made in these regions a city
and fortress; and these lands will be converted.
And I assure Your Highnesses that it seems to me
that under the sun there can be no better lands: in
fertility and mildness of cold and heat, in abundance of good and healthful water, not like the
rivers of Guinea, which are all pestilential, because, praise be to Our Lord, up until now of all my
people there has been no one who has had a headache
or been in bed with illness except one old man, from
the pain of the stone which he has suffered all his
life; and then he recovered after two days. This
that I tell is [true] of all three ships. So that
it will please God that Your Highnesses will send,
or that there will come, learned men and then they
will see the truth of everything. And although,
further back, I have spoken of the site of a town
and fortress in the harbor of the Rio de Mares, because of the good harbor and the region—and cer-
30r   tainly all that I said is true—there is no
comparing that place with this nor [the Puerto de
Mares] with the Mar de Nuestra Señora: here, inland, there should be great settlements and innumerable people and things of great profit, since
here, and in all else discovered and that I have
hope of discovering before I go to Castile, I say
that the whole of Christendom will do business in
these lands; and how much more so Spain, to which
everything should be subject. And I say that
Your Highnesses ought not to consent that any
foreigner set foot or trade here except Catholic
Christians, since the beginning and end of the
enterprise was the increase and glory of the
Christian Religion, nor [consent that] anyone
come to these regions who is not a good Christian. All these are his words. He went up the
river and found some of its branches, and going

y rodeãdo el puerto hallo a la boca dl rio estava
20   vnas -ab- arboledas my graçiosas como vna my
deleytable gue^rta y alli hallo vna almadia
/o canoa hecha de vn madero tan grãde como
vna fusta de doze bãcos mũy hermosa varada
ataraçana /o
debaxo de vna ∧ramada hecha de madera [y?]
25   cubierta de grãdes hojas de palma / por mara
q̃ ni el sol ni el agua le podian hazer daño /
y dize q̃ alli era el proprio lugar p[ar]a hazer vna
villa /o çiudad y fortaleza por el bue puerto
buenas aguas / buenas t̃r̃as / buenas co
30   marcas y mucha leña /.

miercoles .28. de noviebre

/ Estuvose en aq̃l pue^rto aq̃l dia porq̃ llovia
y hazia grã çerrazõ avnq̃ podia correr toda
la costa c̃o el viento q̃ era sudueste y fuera a
35   popa [/?] p[er]o porq̃ no pudiera ver bien la t̃r̃a y no
sabiendola es peligroso a los navios no se p[ar]tio /
saliẽrõ a t̃r̃a la gente dlos navios a lavar su
ropa / -fuerõ a-[?] entrarõ algunos dllos vn rato
por la t̃r̃a adentro hallarõ grãdes poblaciones
40   y las casas vazias porq̃ se avian huydo to
dos : tornarose por otro rio abaxo mayor q̃ aq̃l
donde estavan en el pue^rto /

Jueves .29. de noviebre

/ porq̃ llovia y el çielo estava de la mañ̃a çerrado

Folio 30v

que ayer no se partio / llegarõ algunos
çerca
dlos xp̃ianos a otra poblaçion ∧dla p[ar]te de
norueste y no hallarõ en las casas a
nadie ni nada : y en el camino toparo c̃o
5   vn viejo q̃ no les pudo huyr : tomarole
y dixerõle q̃ no le querian haze^r mal : y di

around the harbor he found at the mouth of the
river some attractive groves of trees like a delightful garden; and there he found a handsome
dugout, or canoe, made of one timber, as big as a
fusta[1] of 12 rowing benches, drawn up under a
shelter or shed made of wood and covered with big
palm leaves, so that neither sun nor water could
damage it. And he says that there was the very
place to make a town or city and fortress because
of the good harbor, the good water, good lands,
the good region, and much firewood.

Wednesday 28 November

He stayed in that harbor that day because it was
raining and the clouds were very heavy, although
he could have run along the whole coast with the
wind, which was southwest and would have been at
his stern. But because he would not have been
able to see the land well, and not knowing it is
dangerous to ships, he did not leave. The men of
the ships went ashore to wash their clothes.
Some of them went inland for a while; they found
large settlements and the houses empty because
everyone had fled. They returned down another
river larger than that one where they were in the
harbor.

Thursday 29 November

Because it was raining and the sky cloudy,
30v   like yesterday, he did not depart. Some of the
Christians went as far as another nearby settlement to
the northwest and found nothing and no one in the
houses. On the way they chanced to encounter an old
man who could not flee from them. They caught
him and told him that they did not want to harm

---

1. (30r23) A *fusta* was a small, galleylike longship, usually propelled by oars, although some carried sail on a single mast. Guillén Tato (1951, 69).

erōle algunas cosillas dl resgate y dexarōlo

vestillo y

el almiᶜ quisiera vello p[ar]a ∧tomar lengua dl /.
porq̃ le cōtentava mucho la felicidad de aq̃lla

10   tr̄r̄a y disposicion q̃ p[ar]a poblar en ella avia y juzgava q
devia de aver grādes poblaçiones /. hallaron
en vna casa vn pan de çera q̃ truxo a los re
yes / y dize q̃ donde çera ay tābiē deve aver

esta çera vino alli   otras mil cosas buenas /. hallarō tābien los
de yucatan y por
esto creo q̃sta tr̄r̄a
es cuba   15   marineros -vna-[?] en casa : vna cabeça de hōbre
dentro en vn çestillo cubierto con otro cestillo
y colgado de vn poste dla casa : y dla misma
maña hallarō otra en otra -casa- poblaçion /.
creyo el almiᶜ q̃ -seria-[?] devia ser de algunos

20   prinçipales dl linaje : porq̃ aq̃llas casas era
de maña q̃ se acojen en ellas mūcha gente en

parientes

vna sola : y deven ser desçendiētes ——[?] de vno solo /.

viernes .30. de noviēbre

25   ⫽ No se pudo partir porq̃l viento era levāte mȳ
cōtrario a su camino : enbio ocho hōbres bien

con ellos

armados y ∧dos yndios dlos q̃ traya p[ar]a q̃
viesen aq̃llos pueblos dla tr̄r̄a dentro y
por aver lengua /. llegarō a mūchas casas

30   y no hallarō a nadie ni nada q̃ todos se aviā
huydo /. vierō quatro māçebos q̃stavā cavā
do en su heredades   asi como vierō los xpianos
dierō a huyr / no los pudierō alcançar /. an
duvierō diz q̃ mūcho camino / vierō muchas po

35   blaçiones y tierra fertilissima y toda labrada
y grādes riberas de agua / y çerca de vna vie
rō vna almadia /o canoa de noventa y çinco
palmos de lōgura de vn solo madero mȳ her
mosa : y q̃ en ella cabrian y navegarian çien

40   to y çinquēta p[er]rsonas /

him, and they gave him some small things from the
trade goods and let him go. The Admiral would have
liked to see him to give him some clothes and talk
with him because he was very pleased with the felicity
of that land and its suitability for settlement, and he
judged that[1] there ought to be big towns [in it].
They found in one house a loaf of wax that he took
to the sovereigns, and he says that where there is
wax there also should be a thousand other good
things. The sailors also found in a house a man's
head inside a basket covered with another small
basket and hung on a post of the house; and in the
same way they found another in another settlement.
The Admiral thought that they must be those of
important persons of the family, because those
houses were such that many people were sheltered in
a single one, and they probably are relatives, de-
scendants of one man only.

Friday 30 November

He could not depart because the wind was east, very
contrary to his route. He sent eight well-armed men
and with them two Indians of those he brought in
order that they might see those inland towns and to
parley. They reached many houses and found nothing
and nobody, for all had fled. They saw four youths
who were digging in their plots of land. As soon as
they saw the Christians they took to flight, and the
Christians could not catch them. The Spaniards, he
says, went a long way. They saw many settlements
and extremely fertile land, all well cultivated, and
large streams of water. Near one stream they saw a
handsome dugout or canoe 95 *palmos* in length, made
of a single timber; and in it a hundred and fifty
persons would fit and navigate.

---

1. (30v10) *Juzgava que* is written in the right margin of the manuscript and is
probably an insertion.

Sabado .1º. dia de diziēbre

⚓ no se p[ar]tio por la misma causa dl viento contra
rio y porq̃ llovia mūcho : asento vna cruz gra
de a la entrada de aq̃l pueᵗto q̃ creo llamo el
45   puerto Sancto sobre vnas peñas bivas /. la punta
es aq̃lla q̃sta dla parte dl sueste a la entrada dl

Folio 31r

puerto /. y quien oviere de entrar en este puerto
se deve llegar mas sobre la p[ar]te dl norueste
de aq̃lla ——[?]-punta- punta : q̃ sobre la otra dl sueste /. puesto
q̃ al pie de ambas junto cō la peña ay doze bracas de
5   hōdo y mȳ limpio /. mas a la entrada dl pueᵗto
sobre la punta dl sueste ay vna baxa q̃ sobreagua
la qual ——[?] dista -tanto-[?] dla punta tanto q̃ -po-[?] se podria
passar entremedias aviendo neçessidad porq̃ al
pie de la baxa y dl cabo todo es fondo de doze y de
10   quinze braças y a la entrada se a de poner la proa
al sudueste /.

Domingo .2. de diziēbre

⚓ todavia fue contrario el viento y no pudo partir
dize q̃ todas las noches dl mūdo vienta terral : y
15   q̃ todas las naos q̃ alli estuvierē no ayā miedo
de toda la tormēta dl mūdo porq̃ no puede reca
lar dentro por vna baxa q̃ esta al principio dl
puerto etc̃. En la boca de aq̃l rio diz q̃ hallo vn
grumete çiertas piedras q̃ pareçen tener oro tru
20   xolas p[ar]a mostrar a los reyes /. dize q̃ ay por alli
a tyro de lōbarda grādes rios /.

lunes .3. de diziēbre

⚓ por causa de q̃ hazia siempʳ tpō contrario no
partia de aq̃l pueᵗto / y acordo de yr a ver
25   vn cabo mȳ hermoso -q̃-[?] vn quarto de legua
del pueᵗto dla p[ar]te dl sueste / fue cō las barcas
y alguna gente armada. al pie del cabo avia
vna boca de vn buē rio puesta la proa al sue

Saturday 1 December

He did not depart for the same reason of contrary
wind and because it was raining a lot. He set up a
large cross at the entrance to that harbor (which I
believe he named the Puerto Santo) on top of some
living rocks. This point is the one to the southeast at the entrance to the harbor. He who may have
31r   to enter this harbor should get nearer to the northwest part of that point[1] than to the other part, the
southeast, although at the foot of both parts next to
the rock there is 12 *brazas* depth and very clean. But
at the entrance to the harbor, off the southeast point,
there is a shoal that sticks out above the water,
distant from the point far enough to let one pass
between, in case of necessity, because at the foot of
the shoal and of the cape there is depth of 12 to 15
brazas and at the entrance one should head to the
southwest.

Sunday 2 December

The wind was still contrary and he could not depart.
He says that every blessed night it blew from land, and
that all the ships that might in future be there should
have no fear of all the storms in the world, because
they cannot reach ships inside because of a shoal that
lies at the beginning of the harbor, etc. In the mouth
of that river he says that a ship's boy found certain
stones that appeared to contain gold. He took them
to show to the sovereigns. He says there are large
rivers around there at the distance of a lombard shot.

Monday 3 December

Because the weather was always contrary he did not
leave that harbor, and he decided to go to see a very
beautiful cape a quarter of a league from the harbor
to the southeast. He went with the launches and
some armed men. At the foot of the cape there
was a mouth of a good river and the launch headed

1.   (31r3) Alvar (1976) reads the canceled text preceding *punta* as *misma*.

ste p[ar]a entrar y tenia çiento passos de anchura

fondo

30 tenia vna braça de ∧ ~~en la~~ a la entrada /o en

la boca : p[er]o dentro avia doze braças ~~y diz q̃~~ y

çinco y quatro y dos : y cabrian en el quātos

navios ay en españa /. dexādo vn braço de

aq̃l rio fue al sueste y hallo vna caleta en

35 q̃ vido çinco mȳ grādes almadias q̃ los yndios

llamā Canoas como fustas mȳ hermosas

y labradas q̃ era diz q̃ era plazer vellas y al

pie dl mōte vido todo labrado /. estavā deba

xo de arboles mȳ espessos /. y yendo por vn

40 camino q̃ salia a ellas fuerō a dar a vna atara

çana mȳ biē ordenada y cubierta q̃ ni sol ni

agua no les podia hazeʳ daño / y debaxo dlla

avia otra canoa ~~como vna fusta~~ hecha de vn

madero como las otras como vna fusta de diez

45 y siete bancos q̃ era plazer ver las labores q̃ tenia

y su hermosura /. Subio vna mōtaña arriba

y despues hallola toda llana y senbrada de mū

chas cosas dla tr̄r̄a y calabaças q̃ era gloria vella :

y en medio della estava vna grā poblacion /.

Folio 31v

dio de subito ~~cō la~~ sobre la gente dl pueblo

y como los vierō hobres y mugeres dan

de huyr /. asegurolos el yndio q̃ llevava

cōsigo dlos q̃ traya diziēdo q̃ no oviesen

5 miedo q̃ gente buena era : hizolos dar el

almiᶜ cascaveles y sortijas de laton : y ~~con~~

contezuelas de vidro verdes y amarillas : con [q̃?]

fuerō mȳ contētos /. visto q̃ no tenian oro

ni otra cosa preçiosa y q̃ bastava dexallos segu

era

10 ros : y q̃ toda la comarca ~~es~~ poblada y huydos

nō ——[?]   los demas de miedo y certifica el almiᶜ a los

reyes q̃ diez hōbres hagā huyr a diez mill .

southeast to enter. The mouth or entrance was a
hundred *passos*[1] in width and a *braza* in depth,[2] but
inside it was 12 [*brazas*] and [down to] five and
four and two; and it would hold as many ships as
there are in Spain. Leaving an arm of that river he
went to the southeast and found an inlet in which he
saw five very large dugouts, which the Indians call
canoes, like very handsome *fustas*, fashioned in such
a way that it was, he says, a pleasure to see them;
and at the foot of the mountain he saw everything
well cultivated. The [canoes] were under very thick
trees. And going along a path that went out to
them they came upon a very well arranged boat
shed, covered in such a way that neither sun nor
water could do harm to the canoes; and under
it there was another canoe made of one timber
like the others, like a *fusta* of 17 benches, and
it was a pleasure to see the decorations that it had
and its beauty. He went up a mountain and beyond
found it all flat and sown with many products of
the land and gourds so that it was wonderful
to see it; and in the middle of it a big settlement
was located. They suddenly came upon the

31v people of the town, and when they saw the Spaniards
men and women began to flee. The Indian
that he had with him of those that he brought reassured them, saying not to have fear, that they were
good people. The Admiral ordered bells and brass
rings and beads of green and yellow glass to be given
to them, with which they were very pleased. Seeing
that they had neither gold nor any other valuable
thing and that it sufficed to leave them feeling secure,
for the whole vicinity was peopled and the others had
fled from fear, the Admiral assured the sovereigns that
ten men make ten thousand flee, they are so cowardly

    1. (31r29) *Passos* are paces, probably of 5 Roman feet of 16 Roman digits each,
used (among other measures) in the *Diario* to specify short distances, e.g., the distances
of soundings from shore (34v4), the widths of river and harbor entrances (31r29),
etc. In 34v48, a thousand *passos* is said to equal one-quarter of a league. A similar, but
slightly shorter, unit, the *passada*, is also mentioned in the *Diario*, e.g., at 33v1. It is
probably the unit defined in the thirteenth-century Castilian compilation of laws, the
Siete Partidas of Alfonso X, as a pace of 5 feet, each of 15 Roman digits (see Machabey
1962, 54).
    2. (31r30) Alvar (1976) reads the canceled text as *ondo en la*.

~~acordo bolverse~~ tan cobardes y medrosos son
q̃ ni traen armas salvo vna varas y enl cabo
15 dllas vn palillo agudo tostado : acordo bolverse /.
dize q̃ las varas se las quito todas con buena
maña : resgatandoselas / de mařa q̃ todas las
dierō /. tornados adonde avian dexado las bar
cas : enbio ~~a ver vna colm~~[?] çiertos xp̃ıaños al
20 lugar por donde subierō : porq̃ le avia pareçido

              grā
q̃ avia visto vn ∧Colmenar / antes q̃ viniesen los
q̃ avia embiado : ayuntarōse mūchos yndios
y vinierō a las barcas donde ya se avia el almi͡e
recogido cō su gente toda : vno dllos se adelanto
25 en el rio junto cō la popa dla barca : y hizo vna
grāde platica q̃l almi͡e no entēdia : saluo q̄ los
otros yndios de quādo en quādo alçavā las ma
nos al çielo ——[?] y davā vna grāde boz /. pensava
el almi͡e q̃ lo aseguravan y q̃ les plazia dsu veni

                                  de
30 da : pero vido al yndio q̃ consigo traya ∧ mu
darse la cara y amarillo comō la çera y tem
blava mucho : diziendo por señas q̃ el almi͡e se
fuese ~~a los~~[?] fuera dl rio q̃ los querian matar /.
y llegose a vn xp̃ıaño q̃ tenia vna ballesta ar
35 mada y mostrola a los yndios y entendio
al almi͡e q̃ les dezia q̃ los matariā todos / por
q̃ aq̃lla ballesta tyrava lexos y matava /. tā
bien̄ tomo vna espada y la saco dla vayna mō
strandosela diziēdo lo mismo /. lo qual oydo por
40 ellos dierō todos a huyr : quedādo todavia tem
blando el d̄ho yndio de cobardia y poco coraçon / +
no quiso el almi͡e salir ~~en tr̄r̄a~~[?] dl rio : antes hizo
——[?] Remar en tr̄r̄a hazia donde ellos estavā que
——[?] erā mȳ muchos todos tyñidos de colorado
45 y dsnudos comō sus madres los pario y algu͡os
dllos cō penachos en la cabeça y otras plumas : to

a. y era hōbre d[e?]
b. buena est[a?]
c. tura y re
d. zio /.

and fearful, for they carry no arms except wooden
javelins on one end of which is a sharp little stick,
fire toasted. He decided to go back. He says that,
by a good trick, he got all the darts away from them,
trading in such a way that the Indians gave all of them.
When they returned to where they had left the launches,
he sent certain[1] Christians to the place where
they had gone up [the mountain] because it seemed
to him that he had seen a large beehive. Before
those whom he had sent came back, many Indians
collected and came to the launches where the Admiral
was already gathered with all his men. One of the
Indians advanced into the river up to the stern of the
launch and made a big speech that the Admiral did
not understand, except that the other Indians from
time to time raised their hands to the sky and gave a
great shout. The Admiral thought that they were
reassuring him and that they were pleased by his
coming; but he saw the face of the Indian he had
with him change and turn yellow as wax, and he
trembled greatly, saying by signs that the Admiral
must go away, out of the river, because the Indians
wanted to kill them. And the Indian went up to one
Christian who had a cocked crossbow and showed it
to the [other] Indians, and the Admiral understood
that he told them that the Spaniards would kill them
all, because that crossbow shot far and killed. Also,
he took a sword and drew it from the scabbard,
showing it to them and saying the same thing, which
when heard by them, put all of them to flight, the
said Indian still trembling from cowardice and faint
heart; and he was a good-sized and vigorous man.[2]
The Admiral did not want to leave the river: rather,
he had the men row to land toward the place where
the Indians were, and they were very many, all painted
red, and naked as their mothers bore them, some of
them with plumes and other feathers on their heads;

1. (31v19) Alvar (1976) reads the canceled text preceding *çiertos* as *a ver vna barca*.
It seems more likely that Las Casas has mistakenly skipped ahead at this point to tell of
the beehive (*colmenar*) mentioned in 31v21.

2. (31v41a–d) *Y era . . . rezio.* This insert is boxed in the right margin of the
manuscript.

dos con sus manojos de azagayas /. llegueme
a ellos y diles algunos bocados de pan : y demā
nõ   deles las azagayas : y davales por ellas : a vnos

Folio 32r

vn cascavelito : a otros vna sortijuela de laton
a otros vnas contezuelas . por maña q̃ todos
se apaziguarō y vinierō todos a las barcas
y davā quāto tenian porq̃ quequiera q̃ les da
5   van /. ~~ellos son gente~~ los marineros aviā
muerto vna tortuga y la cascara estava en la bar
ca en pedacos : y los grumetes davāles della
comō la uña : y los yndios les davā vn ma
nojos de azagayas /. Ellos son gente comō los
10   otros q̃ e hallado (dize el almi[e]) y dla misma creē
çia y creyan q̃ veniamos dl çielo y dlo q̃ tienē
nõ   luego lo dan por qualquiera cosa q̃ les den sin
dezir q̃s poco y creo q̃ asi harian de especeria —[?]
y de oro si lo tuviesen /. vide vna casa hermosa
15   no mȳ grāde y de dos puertas porq̃ asi son todas
y entre en ella y vide vna obra maravillosa co
m̄o camaras hechas por vna çierta maña q̃
no lo sabria dezir / y colgado al çielo della cara
coles y otras cosas : yo pense q̃ era tēplo y los
                ~~por señas~~[?]
20   llame y dixe ∧ ~~si era casa de oracion~~[?] por señas si
hazian en ella oracion. dixerō q̃ no . y subio vno
dllos arriba y me dava todo quāto alli avia y
dllo tome algo /.

martes 4º de diziēbre

25   ⸗ Hizose a la vela con poco viento y salio de aq̃l
puerto q̃ nōbro pue[r]to santo a las dos leguas
vido vn buē rio de q̃ ayer hablo : fue de
luēgo de costa y corriase toda la tr̄r̄a passado
el d̄ho cabo lessueste y guesnorueste hasta

all with their handfuls of javelins. I went up to them
and gave them mouthfuls of bread, and I asked
them for the javelins and gave them things for them:
32r   to some a small bell, to others a brass ring, to others
some small beads, so that all were pacified and
they all came to the launches and gave all that they
had for anything that was given to them. The sailors
had killed a turtle and the shell was in the launch in
pieces, and the ships' boys gave the Indians pieces of
it the size of a fingernail, and the Indians gave them
a handful of javelins. They are people like the
others that I have found (the Admiral says) and of the
same beliefs, and they believed that we came from
the heavens and they soon give what they have for
anything that is given to them, without saying that it
is too little; and I believe that they would do so with
spices and gold if they had them. I saw a handsome
house, not very large, with two doors, because all of
them are like that, and I went in and saw wonderful
work like chambers[1] made in a certain way that
I would be unable to describe; and hanging from
the ceiling of it [were] snails[2] and other things. I
thought that it was a temple and I called them and
asked by signs if they said prayers in it. They said
no. And one of them climbed up and gave me all
that there was there, and I took a bit of it.

Tuesday 4 December

He set sail with little wind and left the harbor,
which he named Puerto Santo. At two leagues
distance he saw a good river, of which he spoke
yesterday. He went along the coast reconnoitering all
the land beyond the said cape, running east-southeast
and west-northwest as far as Cabo Lindo which is

1.   (32r17) *Camaras* (chambers). Morison (1963, 110, 3 Dec., n. 5) suggests that
this word should be *cámatas* (woven mats, used as partitions), a word not in the *Diccionario* (1956), and translates the word as "rooms." Jane-Vigneras (1960) also sees
the structure as rooms, but Thacher (1903–1904) translates as "chambers." The
structure might, as Columbus seems to imply, be viewed as an altar on which *zemis*, the
Arawak Indian gods, were placed during religious ceremonies, the Indians' apparent
assertion to the contrary notwithstanding.
2.   (32r18–19) *Caracoles* (snails). These possibly were snail shells or even seashells
of unspecified variety.

30 el cabo lindo q̃sta al cabo dl mõte al leste quarta
dl sueste y ay de vno a otro çinco leguas /. dl
cabo del mõte a legua y media ay vn grā rio
algo angosto parecio q̃ tenia buena entrada y
era my hõdo y de alli a tres quartos de legua

35 vido otro grādissimo rio y deve venir de mȳ
lexos en la boca tenia bien çien passos y
en ella ningũ banco y en la boca ocho bracas
y buena entrada porq̃ lo enbio a ver y ~~sōdar~~[?]
sondar cō la barca y viene el agua dulce hasta

40 dentro en la mar / y es dlos caudalosos q̃
~~yo~~ avia hallado / y deve aver grādes poblacio
nes /. dspues dl cabo lindo ay vna grāde baya
q̃ seria buen pozo por lesnordeste y suest[e]
y sursudueste .

                                                 miercoles 5 de diziẽbre
45
/ toda esta noche anduvo a la corda sobre el cabo lindo
adonde anochecio por ver la tr̄r̄a q̃ yva al leste
y al salir dl sol vido otro cabo al leste a dos le

Folio 32v

guas y media . passado aq̃l vido q̃ la costa bolvia
al sur y tomava dl sudueste y vido luego vn

este deve ser la
punta de ^{maysi}[?]
~~quien~~[?] q̃s la po
strera d[e] cuba

cabo mȳ hermoso y alto a la d̄ha derrota : y distava
desotro siete leguas : quisiera yr alla : p[er]o por el de
seo q̃ tenia de yr a la Isla de baneque q̃ la queda
va segũ dezian los yndios q̃ llevava al nordeste
——[?] lo dexo : tanpoco pudo yr al baneque porq̃l
viento q̃ llevava era nordeste /. yendo asi ~~vido~~[?]
miro al sueste y vido tr̄r̄a y era vna Isla mūy grā

esta es la espa
ñola segun
pareçe

10 de dla qual ya tenia diz q̃ informaçion de los yndios
                           vā
a que llama∧ellos bohio poblada de gente / desta

east by south of Cabo del Monte; from one to the
other it is five leagues. A league and a half from
the Cabo del Monte there is a big river, somewhat
narrow. It appeared to have a good entrance and was
very deep, and from there, at a distance of three-
quarters of a league, he saw another extremely large
river which must come from very far [inland]; at the
mouth it had quite a hundred *passos* [width] with no
bar, and in the mouth, eight *brazas* depth and a good
entrance, because he sent the launch to see and sound
it. And the water runs sweet right out to sea. And
it is among the more copious ones that I have found;
and there should be large settlements. After Cabo
Lindo there is a large bay which would be a good
stopping place[1] for [ships coming from] the east-
northeast and southeast and south-southwest.

Wednesday 5 December

All of this night he stood off and on near Cabo Lindo
where he spent the night in order to see the land,
which went to the east, and at sunrise he saw another
cape to the east two and a half leagues away. That

32v   one passed, he saw that the coast turned south and
trended southwest and he soon saw a handsome and
high cape in the same direction; and he was distant
from that other one seven leagues. He would have
liked to go there, but because of the desire that he
had to go to the island of Baneque, which lay to the
northeast according to what his Indians said, he did
not; but he could not go to Baneque either, because
the wind was northeast. Going along thus,[2] he
looked to the southeast and saw land and it was a
very large island, of which he had already received
information, he says, from the Indians, and which
they called Bohío, inhabited by people of whom, he

---

1. (32r43) *Pozo* (stopping place). Alvar (1976), Morison (1963), and Jane-Vigneras (1960) interpret this word as *paso*, and the latter two translate it as "passage."
Thacher (1903–1904) translates the phrase *que seria buen pozo por* as "which extends
some distance to." The intended word is probably *poso*, a temporary resting or stopping place. Columbus elsewhere uses other forms of *posar: posa* (6r39), *posado* (17r30).
2. (32v8) *Yendo asi* (going along thus). Perhaps "at this juncture" or "at this
point" is what is meant.

aqui pareçe q̃
devia de aver
puesto nõbre el
almi͜e a cuva
juana

15

nõ

20

gente diz q̃ los de cuba /o juana y de todas esotras
Islas tienē grā miedo porq̃ diz q̃ comīan los hō
bres /. otras cosas le contavā los d̃hos yndios por
señas mȳ maravillosas : mas el almi͜e no

tener

diz q̃ las creya : sino q̃ devian ∧ mas astuçia y mejor
Ingenio los de aq̃lla Isla bohio p[ar]a los captivar q̃llos :
porq̃ erā mȳ flacos de coraçon /. asi que porq̃l tp̄o
era nordeste y tomava dl norte : determino de
dexar a cuba o juana q̃ hasta entonces avia tenido

porq̃ bien avria

por tr̄r̄a firme por su grādeza ~~segū avria~~ andado
en vn paraje çiento y veynte leguas : y partio al
sueste quarta del leste puesto que la tr̄r̄a q̃l avia visto
se hazia al sueste   dava este reguardo porq̃ siemp͟r

25

el viento rodea dl norte p[ar]a el nordeste y de alli
al leste y sueste /. Cargo mucho el viento y llevava
todas sus velas la mar llana y la corriente q̃ le
ayudava por mar̃a q̃ hasta la vna dspues de me

dia

dio ∧ dsde la mañana hazia de camino .8. millas por ora

30

y erā seys oras avn no cōplidas porq̃ dize q̃ alli

çerca

erā las noches ∧ de quinze oras   despues anduvo
diez millas por ora y asi andaria hasta el poner
dl sol .88. ~~leguas~~ millas q̃ son .22. leguas todo
al sueste /. y porq̃ se hazia noche mādo a la caravela

35

niña q̃ se adelantasse p[ar]a ver cō dia el pue͟rto porq̃ ~~fue~~-[?] ——[?]
era velera : y llegādo a la boca dl puerto q̃ era

y porq̃

comō la baya de Caliz ——[?] era ya de noche : en
bio a su barca q̃ sondase el pue͟rto /. la qual llevo
lūbre de candela : y antes q̃l almi͜e llegasse

40

adonde la caravela estava barloventeando y esperā
do q̃ la barca le hiziese señas p[ar]a entrar en el puer
to apagosele la lūbre a la barca /. la caravela
comō no vido lumbre corrio de largo y hizo lūbre
al almi͜e y llegado a ella cōtarō lo q̃ avia acaeçido /.

45

estādo en esto los dla barca hizierō otra lubre : la

says, those of Cuba, or Juana, and of all those other
islands have great fear, because, he says, they eat
men. Other marvelous things the said Indians told
him by signs, but the Admiral does not say that he
believes them. But [he does say that] the people
of that island of Bohío must be shrewder and
more ingenious than they in order to capture them,
because the others are very faint of heart. So,
because the weather was from the northeast and
shifting north, he decided to leave Cuba, or Juana
(which up until then he had considered to be *tierra
firme* because of its size, since he had gone along one
stretch of it quite 120 leagues). And he departed to
the southeast by east even though the land that he had
seen trended southeast. He took this precaution because the wind always went around from the north to
northeast and from there to east and southeast. The
wind blew hard and he carried all his sails. The sea
was smooth and the current helped him so that from
morning until one hour after midday he made eight
miles per hour. This was for six hours, although not
quite, because he says that there the nights were of
nearly 15 hours length.[1] Afterward he went ten
miles per hour and thus he made up to sunset about
88 miles, which are 22 leagues, all to the southeast;
and because night was approaching he ordered the
caravel *Niña* to go ahead to look at the harbor in
daylight because she was a fast sailer; and when she
reached the mouth of the harbor, which was like the
Bay of Cadiz, and because it was already night, she
sent her launch, which carried a lantern, to sound the
harbor; and before the Admiral arrived where the
caravel was tacking back and forth and waiting for the
launch to signal it to enter the harbor, the light went
out. The caravel, when it saw no light, ran out to sea
and showed a light to the Admiral, and arriving at his
ship they told what had happened. At this point the
men in the launch made another light. The caravel

1. (32v30–31) *Alli . . . quinze oras* (There the night . . . 15 hours length). In
mid-December at Columbus's latitude of about 20°N, sunrise is at about 6:30 A.M. and
sunset at about 5:25 P.M. (read from a standard sunrise-sunset diagram). Discounting
twilight, which would make the duration of night even shorter, the nights could not
have been longer than 13 hours.

caravela fue a ella y el almi^e no pudo y estuvo
toda aq̃lla noche barloventeando /.

Ӿ quādo amane[cio?] se hallo quatro leguas dl puerto

Folio 33r

pusole nōbre puerto maria y vido vn cabo
hermoso al sur quarta del sudueste al qual puso
nōbre cabo dl estrella y pareciole q̃ era la
postrera tr̄r̄a de aq̃lla Isla hazia el sur y estaria
5   ——[?] el almi^e dl xxviii millas /. pareçiale otra
tr̄r̄a como Isla ~~al leste~~ no grāde al leste y esta
ria del .40. millas /. ~~y de alli~~-[?] quedavale otro cabo
mȳ hermoso y bien hecho a quien puso nōbre
cabo del elefante al leste quarta dl sueste y dista[va?]
10   le ya .54. millas /. Quedavale otro cabo al lessueste
al q̃ puso nōbre el cabo de çinquin : estaria dl
.28. millas /. Quedavale vna gran scisura o aber
tura /o abra a la mar q̃ le pareçio ser rio al sueste
y tomava dla quarta dl leste : avria del a la abra .20
15   millas /. pareçiale q̃ entre el cabo dl elifante dl
de çinquin avia vna grādissima entrada y algu
nos dlos marineros ~~quan~~-[?] dezian q̃ era ap[ar]ta
miento de Isla aq̃lla puso por nōbre la Isla
dla tortuga /. aq̃lla Isla grāde pareçia altissima
20   tr̄r̄a no çerrada con mōtes : sino rasa como her
mosas campiñas y pareçe toda labrada /o grāde
parte d[e]lla~~s~~ y parecian las semēteras como trigo
en el mes de mayo en la cāpiña de cordova /
vierōse mūchos huegos aq̃lla noche : y de dia
25   mūchos humos como atalayas q̃ parecia estar
sobre aviso de alguna gente cō quiē tuviesen guer
ra /. toda la costa desta tr̄r̄a va al leste /. A oras
de bisperas entro en el puerto ——[?] dicho y puso
le nōbre ~~cabo~~-[?] puerto de san Nicola[s?] porq̃ era dia
de Sant nicolas por hōrra suya . y a la entrada dl se

no entiendo como
a este puerto puso
arriba pue^rto ma
ria y agora de
sā nicolas

went to it but the Admiral could not, and passed all
that night jogging off and on.

Thursday 6 December

When day came he found himself four leagues from the
33r harbor. He gave it the name Puerto María and he
saw a handsome cape south by west to which he gave
the name Cabo de la Estrella, and it appeared to him
that it was the last land of that island to the south.
It was about 28 miles from the Admiral. Other land,
like an island, not large, appeared to the east, and it
was about 40 miles from him. Another handsome
and well-formed cape which he named Cabo del
Elefante lay east by south and was 54 miles[1] distant.
Another cape lay to the east-southeast to which he
gave the name Cabo de Cinquín; he was about 28 miles
from it. A great opening to the sea, which seemed to
him to be a river, lay to the southeast, [on land]
trending southeast by east. There were between him
and the opening about 20 miles. It appeared to him
that between the Cabo del Elefante and the Cabo de
Cinquín there was a very large opening and some of
the sailors said that it was the separation of that
island, to which he gave the name Isla de la Tortuga,
from the other. That big island appeared to be very
high land not closed in by mountains, but level like
handsome and extensive farmland; and all, or a large
part of it, appeared to be cultivated, and the planted
fields looked like wheat in the month of May in the
farmlands of Cordova. They saw many fires that
night and, by day, much smoke like signals that
seemed to be warnings of some people with whom
they were at war. All the coast of this land goes to
the east. At the hour of vespers[2] they entered the
said harbor[3] and he named it Puerto de San Nicolás
in honor of Saint Nicolas, whose day it was. And
at its entrance he admired its beauty and goodness.

---

1. (33r10) *.54. millas.* This is probably an estimate from a sketch chart since 54
Diario miles (about 42 statute miles) seem too far for a direct observation.
 2. (33r28) *Bisperas* (vespers). See p. 87, n. 1.
 3. (33r28) Alvar (1976) reads the canceled text following *puerto* as *María.*

maravillo de su hermosura y bōdad / y avnq̃
tiene mūcho alabados los puertos de Cuba : p[er]o sin
duda dize el q̃ no es menos este : antes los sobre
puja y ninguᵒ le es semejante /. En boca y entra
35 da tiene legua y media de ancho y se pone la
proa al sursueste puesto q̃ por la grāde anchura
se puede poner la proa adonde quisierē /. va desta
maȓa al sursueste dos leguas : y a la entrada del
por la p[ar]te del sur : se haze com̃o vna angla y de
40 alli se sigue asi Igual hasta el cabo adonde esta
vna playa mȳ hermosa y vn campo de arboles
de mill maȓas y todos cargados de frutas q̃ creya
el almiꞔ ser de especerias y nuezes moscadas
sino q̃ no estava maduras y no se cognoscio /
45 y vn rio en medio dla playa /. El hōdo deste puer
to es maravilloso q̃ hasta llegar a la tȓȓa en longu
ra de vna   no llego la sondaresa o ploma
da al fondo con quareta braças y ay hasta esta lōgura
el hōdo de .xv. bracas y mȳ limpio /. y asi en todo el

Folio 33v

dicho puerto de cada cabo hōdo dentro a vna passada
de tȓȓa de 15. braças y limpio . y desta maȓa es
toda la costa mȳ hōdable y limpia q̃ no pareçe
vna sola baxa /. y al pie dlla tanto com̃o longura
5 de vn remo de barca de tȓȓa ~~seys~~ tiene çinco bra
ças /. y dspues dla lōgura del d̄ho puerto yen
do al sursueste (en la qual lōgura puedē barlovē
tear mill carracas : bojo vn braço dl puerto
al nordeste por la tȓȓa dentro vna grāde media
10 legua y siempre en vna misma anchura com̃o q̃
lo hizierā por vn cordel : el qual queda de ma
nera q̃stando en aq̃l braço q̃ sera de anchura de
~~35 pa~~ veynte y çinco passos no se puede ver la
boca dla entrada grāde / de maȓa q̃ queda puer
15 to çerrado : y el fondo deste braço es asi ~~com̃o~~ en
el comienço hasta la fin de onze braças y todo

And although he has had much praise for the harbors
of Cuba, without doubt, he says, this one is no less
[praiseworthy]; rather, it surpasses them and none are
like it. In the mouth and entrance it has a width of a
league and a half and you head south-southeast,
although because of the great width you can head
wherever you wish. You go in this way two leagues
to the south-southeast. And at the entrance of it,
toward the south, it forms something like a bay [?] and
from there it continues in the same way as far as the
end, where a beautiful beach is located and a field of
trees of a thousand kinds, all loaded with fruit that
the Admiral thought were spices and nutmeg except
that they were not ripe and he was not familiar with
them; and [there was] a river in the middle of the
beach. The depth of this harbor is marvelous, for
until one reaches the length of one[1]   from
land, the sounding lead with 40 *brazas*[2] [of line]
cannot reach bottom, and out to this distance
there is a depth of 15 *brazas* and the bottom is
very clean. And so within all of the said

33v   harbor from end to end there is a clean depth, at a
passada[3] from land, of 15 *brazas*. And similarly the
whole coast is very deep and clean, for there does not
seem to be a single shoal. And right up next to land
at a distance of a launch's oar, it has [a depth of] five
brazas. After going the length of the said harbor
to the south-southeast, in which length a thousand
carracks can tack back and forth, he went around
an arm of the harbor running inland to the northeast
a full half league, and it was always of the same
width, as if it were laid out by means of a cord. It is
located in such a way that when one is in that arm,
which has a width of about 25[4] *passos*, the mouth
of the main entrance cannot be seen, so that it is a
harbor closed in by land, and the bottom in this arm
from beginning to end is 11 *brazas* deep and all clean

1. (33r47) The word omitted may be *passada.* See p. 193, n. 1.
2. (33r48) *Quarenta braças* (40 brazas) may indicate the standard length of the
sounding lead line, i.e., about 108 English feet.
3. (33v1) *Passada.* See p. 193, n. 1.
4. (33v13) Alvar (1976) reads the canceled text preceding *veynte y çinco passos* as
".XXXV."

basa /o arena limpia y hasta tr̄r̄a y poner los
bordos en las yervas tiene ocho braças /. es todo
el puerto m̄y ayroso y desabahado de arboles

　　　　　　　　　　　　　　　　　　　　de
20　raso /. toda esta Isla le pareçio ∧mas peñas q̃
ningunᵃ otra q̃ aya hallado /. los arboles mas
pequeños y mūchos dllos dla naturaleza de
españa com̄o carrascas y madroños y otros y
lo mismo dlas yervas /. Es tr̄r̄a m̄y alta y
25　toda campiña /o rasa y de m̄y buenas ayres
y no se a visto tanto frio com̄o alli avn̄q no es
de contar por frio mas dixolo al respecto de
las otras tr̄r̄as /. hazia en frente de aq̃l puer
to vna hermosa vega y en medio dlla el Rio
30　susodho : y en aq̃lla comarca (dize) deve aver
grādes poblaçiones segū se vian las almadias
con q̃ navegan : tantas y tan grādes dllas com̄o vna
fusta de .15. bancos /. ~~ellos~~ todos los yndios
huyerō y huian com̄o vian los navios /. los
　　　　　　　　　　　　　—[?]
35　q̃ consigno dlas Isletas traya tenian tanta gana
[cō?] razō　~~que~~ de yr a su tr̄r̄a : q̃ pensava (dize el almiᶜ) q̃
despues q̃ se p[ar]tiese de alli los tenia de llevar
a sus casas : y q̃ ya lo tenian por sospechoso porq̃
no lleva el camino dsu casa /. por lo qual dize
40　q̃ ni les creya lo q̃ le dezian : ni los entendia
bien ni ellos a el : y diz q̃ avian el mayor
miedo ~~des~~ dl mūdo dla gente de aq̃lla Isla /. asi q̃
por querer aver lengua cō la gente de aq̃lla
　　　　fuera
Isla : le ~~sera~~-[?] neçessario detenerse algunos dias
45　en aq̃l puerto : p[er]o —[?] no lo hazia por ver mūcha
tr̄r̄a y por dudar q̃l tp̄o le duraria /. esperava en

Folio 34r
nr̄o señor q̃ los yndios q̃ traya sabrian su lēgua
y el la suya y dspues tornaria y hablara
cō aq̃lla gente y ~~q̃ antes q̃ buelva esp[er]a en su~~
plazera a su magᵈ (dize el) q̃ hallara algū buē
5　resgate de oro antes q̃ buelva /.

sand: and right up to land, where you can put the side of a ship alongside the shrubbery, it has a depth of eight *brazas*. All of the harbor is very breezy and unsheltered,[1] clear of trees. All of this island appeared to him rockier than any other that he had found, the trees smaller and many of them of the kinds found in Spain, like oak and arbutus and others, and the same with the plants. It is very high land and all level fields and of good breezes. Such cold has not been seen [elsewhere] as there, although it is not to be called cold except to say so in relation to the other lands. Facing that harbor is a handsome fertile plain and in the middle of it the river already mentioned. In that region, he says, there should be large settlements judging from the dugouts which were seen and in which they sail—so many of them and some as big as a *fusta* of 15 benches. All the Indians fled and kept on fleeing when they saw the ships. The men he brought with him from the islets had great desire to go to their own lands; for they thought, says the Admiral, that after leaving that place he would have to take them home. And now they considered it suspect that he did not take the route to their homes. Because of which, he says, he did not believe what they told him; nor did he understand them well, nor they him. And he says that they had the greatest fear in the world of the people of that island. Although he wished to speak with the people of that island, it would have been necessary for him to stop a few days in that harbor; so he did not do it in order to see much land and because of doubting that the weather would hold.

34r He hoped in Our Lord that the Indians he brought would learn his language and he theirs, and that later he would return and would speak with those people. It will please His Majesty, he says, if he were to find some good trade in gold before he returns.

---

1. (33v19) *Desabahado* (unsheltered). Alvar (1976, 2:137, n. 292), says this word is a Castilianization of the Portuguese *desabafado*, "[a place] not closed in, where wind blows freely, unsheltered." Morison (1963) translates the word as "uninhabited."

viernes .7. de diziēbre

/ al rendir dl quarto dl alva dio~~s~~ las velas y salio
de aq̃l pueʳto de Sant nicolas y navego con el
viento sudueste al nordeste dos leguas hasta
10　vn cabo q̃ haze el cheranero : y q̃davale al sueste
vn angla : y el cabo dla estrella al sudueste ~~y avia~~[?]
~~hasta alli~~
~~del cabo 24 millas hasta el~~ y dīstava dl almiᵉ
.24. millas /. de alli navego al leste luēgo de
Costa hasta el cabo çinquin q̃ seria .48. millas
15　verdad es q̃ las veynte fuerō al leste quarta del
nordeste /. y ~~esta~~ aq̃lla costa es tr̄r̄a toda
mȳ alta y mȳ grāde fondo hasta dar en tr̄r̄a
es de ~~y 30~~ veynte y treynta bracas y
fuera tanto com̄o vn tiro de lombarda no se halla
20　fondo lo qual todo lo provo el almiᵉ aq̃l por la
costa mucho a su plazeʳ con el viento sudueste /
el angla q̃ arriba dixo llega diz q̃ al puerto de
san nicolas tanto com̄o tyro de vna lombarda
q̃ si aq̃~~lla~~ espacio se atajase /o cortase quedaria he
25　cha Isla lo demas /. bojaria en el çerco 34.
millas /. toda aq̃lla tr̄r̄a era mȳ alta y no
de arboles grādes / sino com̄o carrascas y madro
ños propria diz q̃ tr̄r̄a de castilla /. antes q̃ lle
gase al d̄ho cabo çinquin cō dos leguas hallo vn
30　agrezuela com̄o la abertura de vna mōtaña
por la qual dscubrio vn valle grādissimo y vi
dolo todo sembrado com̄o cevadas y sintio q̃
devia de aver en aq̃l valle grādes poblaçiones
y a las espaldas del avia grādes mōtañas y mȳy

Friday 7 December

When the dawn watch was relieved he set sail and departed from that harbor of San Nicolás and with a
southwest wind steered to the northeast two leagues,
as far as a point which forms the careenage.   To the
southeast of him lay a promontory[?],[1] and the Cabo de
la Estrella lay to the southwest and was distant[2]
from the Admiral 24 miles.   From there he sailed east
along the coast as far as Cabo de Cinquín, which was
about 48 miles.   It is true that 20 [of these] were east
by north.   That coast is all of very high land and of
very great depth.   Until you are very close to land it
is of 20 and 30 *brazas'* depth, and at a lombard shot's
distance you do not find bottom; all of which the
Admiral found out that [day] along the coast, much
to his pleasure, with the wind southwest.   The
promontory that he spoke of above reaches, he says,
to a lombard shot from the harbor of San Nicolás,
and if that area were cut off, the rest of it would be
made an island.[3] It would be 34 miles around.[4]
All of that land was very high and not a land of big
trees, but of trees like the oaks and arbutus native, he
says, to the land of Castile.   Two leagues before he
reached the said Cabo de Cinquín, he found a small
bay,[5] like an opening in the mountain, through
which he caught sight of a very large valley, and he
saw it all planted with something like barley, and he
felt that there should be large settlements in that
valley.   Behind it there were big and very high

1.   (34r11) *Angla*, as used here, means "promontory," "point," "cape," or "head-
land," not a "bight."   Similarly, see 34r22. See Guillén Tato (1951, 29).
2.   (34r12)   In the canceled text preceding *y distava*, Alvar (1976) reads *del cabo* as
de tal (?) (Alvar's question mark).
3.   (34r24) *Si aquel espacio . . . hecha isla lo demas* (if that area . . . would be made
an island).   The text seems literally to say that if the promontory were cut off, what
would be left (*lo demas*) would become an island.   The real meaning must be that the
promontory would become an island.
4.   (34r25–26) *Bojaria . . . 34. millas* (it would be . . . miles around). Judged by
the map in Morison (1940, following p. 249), 34 miles is far too long. On the other
hand, if Navarrete is correct in thinking that the figures should be read "three or four,"
they are too small. Morison's map indicates a distance of seven or eight miles.
5.   (34r30) *Agrezuela* (small bay). Guillén Tato (1951, 23), explains the word as
the diminutive of *angra* or *angla*, "a bay." Morison (1963, 114) translates the word as
"craggy spot." Since the manuscript says that the *agrezuela* is *como la abertura de una
montaña* (like an opening of the mountain), perhaps it is the diminutive of *abra*, a
landlocked bay, with topography like that of a fjord.

35   altas / y quãdo llego al cabo de çinquin ~~a tyro~~
~~de lombarda~~ le demorava el cabo dla Isla tor

la tortuga   tuga al nordeste y avria treynta y dos millas /.
y sobre este cabo çinquin a tyro de vna lõbarda esta
vna peña en la mar q̃ sale en alto q̃ se puede

40   ver bien /. y estando el almiᵉ sobre el d̄ho cabo
le demorava el cabo del elifante al leste quarta
dl sueste y avria hasta el .70. millas y toda trra
mȳ alta / y a cabo de seys leguas ~~dlla~~ hallo vna
grande angla : y vido por la t̄r̄ra dentro mūy grãdes

45   valles y campiñas y mõtañas altissimas todo a
semejança de castilla y dende a ocho millas hallo
vn rio mȳ hõdo sino q̃ era angosto avñq̃ bien pu
diera entrar en el y vna carraca y la boca toda

Folio 34v

~~la boca~~ limpia sin banco ni baxas /. y dende
a ———[?] diez y seys millas hallo vn pueʳto

otro puerto   mȳ ancho y mȳ hondo hasta no hallar fondo
de la consola   en la entrada ni a las bordas a tres passos Sal
cion
5   uo 15. braças y va dentro vn quarto de legua /.
y puesto q̃ fuese avn mȳ tēprano comō la vna
dspues de medio dia y el viento era a popa y

çielo
rezio : p[er]o porq̃ ———[?] el ~~tp̄o~~ [?] mostrava querer
llover mūcho y avia grā çerrazon q̃ es peligrosa

10   avn p[ar]a la t̄r̄ra q̃ se sabe quāto mas en la q̃ no
se sabe : acordo de entrar en el pueʳto al qual lla
mo pu[e]ʳto dla conçepçion : y salio a t̄r̄ra ———[?]
en vn rio no mȳ grãde q̃sta al cabo dl pueʳto
q̃ viene por vnas vegas y campiñas q̃ era mara

15   villa ver su hermosura / llevo redes p[ar]a pescar
y antes q̃ llegase a t̄r̄ra salto vna liça comō las despaña
~~paña~~
~~castilla~~ propria en la barca q̃ hasta entonces no
avia visto peçe q̃ pareçiese a los de castilla /. los
marineros pescarō y matarō otras / y lenguados

20   y otros peçes comō los de castilla /. anduvo vn poco

mountains. And when he reached the Cabo de
Cinquín, the end of the island of Tortuga bore
northeast, and it was about 32 miles away. And off
this Cabo de Cinquín, at a lombard shot's distance,
there is a large rock in the sea which sticks up high so
that it can be seen very well. And the Admiral being
off the said cape, the Cabo del Elefante bore east by
south, and it was about 70 miles distant and all very
high land. And after six [more] leagues he found a
large promontory[?], and he saw inland very large
valleys and farmlands and extremely high mountains,
all very similar to Castile. Eight miles farther he
found a very deep but narrow river, although indeed
he, and [even] a carrack, could have entered

34v　　it; and the mouth was all clean, without a bar or
shoals. And 16[1] miles farther on he found a very
wide harbor and so very deep that he did not find
bottom in the entrance, and [even] at three *passos*
from shore only at 15 *brazas*, and the harbor goes
inland a quarter of a league.[2] And although it was
still very early, about one hour after midday, and the
wind was astern and strong, because there were very
dark clouds and the sky looked as if it were about to
rain heavily, and since it is dangerous even for land that
is known, and much more so for that which is not, he
decided to enter the harbor, which he named Puerto
de la Concepción. He landed in a river, not a very
large one, which is at the head of the harbor, where
it comes through some fields and farmlands, so that it
was wonderful to see its beauty. He took nets for
fishing and before he reached land a mullet[3] like
those native to Spain[4] jumped into the launch, for
until then he had not seen a fish resembling those of
Spain. The sailors fished and killed others, sole and
other fish like those of Castile. He walked about a

1. (34v2) Alvar (1976) reads the canceled number preceding *diez y seys* as "XX."
2. (34v5) The subject of the verb *va* is not clear. It may be the depth of 15
brazas that goes inland a quarter of a league, not the harbor itself.
3. (34v16) Jane-Vigneras (1960) translates the word *liça* (mullet) as "skate."
4. (34v16) *Despaña*. It looks as if this line originally ended with *las des* and line
34v17 began with *castilla*. Then Las Casas canceled *castilla* and over it wrote something
that may be *paña*. Then this word also was canceled and *paña* was added in the right
margin of line 34v16.

por aq̃lla tr̄ra q̃s toda labrada y oyo ———[?] cantar

el ruyseñor y otros paxaritos com̄o los de castilla /.

el ruyseñor
oyerō cãtar

no

vierō çinco hōbres : mas ∧ les quisierō aguardar

sino huyr /. Hallo arrajuā y otros arboles y

25   yervas com̄o los de castilla y asi es la tr̄ra y las

mōtañas /.

Sabado .8. de diziēbre

/ alli en aq̃l pue^rto les llovio mūcho cō viento norte

mȳ rezio / el pue^rto es ~~gu~~ seguro de todos los

30   vientos excepto norte puesto q̃ no le puede

haze^r daño algun^o porq̃ la resaca es grāde q̃ no

da lugar a q̃ la nao labore sobre las amarras

ni el agua dl rio /. dspues de media noche se

torno el viento al nordeste y dspues al leste : dlos

35   quales vientos es aq̃l pue^rto bien abrigado por

La isla tortuga   la Isla dla tortuga q̃ esta frontera a .36. millas /.

Domīgo .9. de diziēbre

/ este dia llovio e hizo tp̄o de invierno com̄o en castilla

por otubre / no avia visto poblaçion sino vna

40   casa mȳ hermosa enl pue^rto de Sant Nicolas

y mejor hecha~s~ q̃ en otras p[ar]tes dlas q̃ avia visto /.

dize el almiꝛ

la isla es mȳ grāde y ∧ no sera mucho q̃ boje

dozientas leguas / a visto q̃s toda mūy labrada cre

ya q̃ devian ser las poblaçiones lexos dla mar

45   de donde veen ~q̃~ quādo llegava / y asi huyan

todos y llevavā consigo todo lo q̃ tenian y hazian

ahumadas com̄o gente de guerra /. Este puerto

tiene en la boca mil passos que es vn quarto de legua

Folio 35r

en ella ni ay banco ni baxa antes no se halla quasi fondo

hasta en tr̄ra a la orilla dla mar / y hazia dentro

en luengo va tres mill passos todo limpio y

basa q̃ qualquiera nao puede surgir en el sin

little in that land, which is all cultivated, and he
heard[1] the nightingale sing, and other little birds
like those of Castile. They saw five men, but they
did not want to wait for the Spaniards, but [wanted]
to flee. They found myrtle and other trees and plants
like those of Castile, and so are the country and the
mountains.

Saturday 8 December

There in that harbor they had heavy rain with a very
strong north wind. The harbor is secure from all
winds except the north, although it can do no harm
because the surge is [not] great[2] and does not cause
the ship to work upon her cables, nor does the water
of the river. After midnight the wind turned to the
northeast and later east, from which winds that
harbor is well sheltered by the island of Tortuga,
which is opposite at 36 miles distance.

Sunday 9 December

This day it rained and the weather was wintry, as in
Castile in October. He had seen no settlement
except one very handsome house in the Puerto de San
Nicolás, better made than in other places he had seen.
The island is very big, and the Admiral says it would
not surprise him if it were 200 leagues around. In
appearance it is all very intensively cultivated. He
thought that the settlements were probably far from
the sea, from which settlements they saw when he
arrived, and so all fled and took with them all that
they had and made smoke signals like people at war.
This harbor has at the mouth a width of 1,000 *passos*,
which is a quarter of a league. In it there is nei-
35r ther bar nor shoal; rather, one finds almost no bottom
right up to the shore. And the length of it goes
toward the interior for 3,000 *passos*, all of it clean
and sandy bottomed so that any ship whatever can

1. (34v21) Alvar (1976) reads the canceled word following *oyo* as *casta*.
2. (34v31) *La resaca es grande*. The sense of this statement seems to require that
it be translated as "the surge is *not* great." (See Morison 1963, 115 n. 1.)

5   miedo y entrar sin reguardo /. al cabo dl tiene
dos bocas de rios q̃ traen poca agua /. enfrente
del ay vnas vegas las mas hermosas dl mūdo
y quasi semejables a las tr̄r̄as de castilla antes

aqui puso el
almi͜e nōbre
a la española

estas tienē ventaja por lo qual puso nōbre
10   a la d̃ha Isla la Isla española /.

lunes .10. de diziembre

/ vento mucho el nordeste y hizole garrar las
anclas medio cable de q̃ se maravillo el
almi͜e y echolo a q̃ las anclas estavā mūcho a tr̄r̄a
15   y venia sobre ella el viento / y visto q̃ era cōtrario
p[ar]a yr donde pretēdia : Embio seys hōbres bien
adereçados de armas a tr̄r̄a q̃ fuesen dos /o tres le
guas dentro en la tr̄r̄a p[ar]a ver si pudierā aver
lengua /. fuerō y bo[l]vierō no aviendo hallado
20   gente ni casas : hallarō enpero vnas cabañas
y caminos mūy anchos y lugares donde avian
hecho lūbre mūchos / vierō las mejores tr̄r̄as
dl mūdo y hallarō arboles de almaçiga mūchos
y truxerō dlla y dixerō q̃ avia mūcha saluo q̃
25   no es agora el tpo p[ar]a cogella porq no quaja /

martes 11º. de diziēbre

/ no partio por el viento q̃ todavia era leste y nor
deste . frōtero de aq̃l pue͜rto comō esta dicho esta
la Isla dla tortuga y parece grāde Isla : y va la
30   costa dlla quasi comō la española y puede aver de la
vna a la otra a los mas diez leguas conviene a

anchor in it without fear and enter without special
care. And the head of it has two mouths of rivers
that bring little water. Facing it there are some
fields, the most beautiful in the world, and almost
comparable to the lands of Castile; rather, these have
an advantage, because of which he named the said
island the Spanish Island [i.e., Hispaniola].

Monday 10 December

The northeast wind blew hard and made him drag the
anchors a half cable's length,[1] which surprised the
Admiral; and he supposed that it was because the
anchors were much toward land and the wind blew
upon it. And seeing that the wind was contrary to the
direction in which he was trying to go, he sent six
men to land, well equipped with arms, to go two or
three leagues inland to see if they might be able to
talk [to someone]. They went and returned, having
found neither people nor houses. They did find, however, some shelters and very wide paths and places
where many fires had been made. They saw the best
lands in the world and they found many trees of
mastic, and they brought some of it and said that
there was a lot of it, except that it is not the season to gather it because it does not harden.

Tuesday 11 December

He did not depart because of the wind, which still
was east and northeast. Facing that harbor, as is said
[above], is the island of Tortuga, and it appears to be
a large island; and the coast of it runs almost like
that of Hispaniola, and there can be at most ten
leagues from one to the other; that is, from the Cabo

1. (35r13) *Medio cable* (a half cable's length). The cable, as a unit of length, is now
defined as one-tenth of a nautical mile, about 100 fathoms, or 185 meters (*Diccionario*
1956), about the length of the ancient "Olympic stadium." A cable of 120 fathoms
has also been defined (see *Oxford English Dictionary*). Although there may have been no
standard-length "cable" in Columbus's day, cable-length units appear in many descrip-
tions of ports and anchorages given in portolanos of the time (cf. uses of the terms *cavo*,
gomene, and *usto* in Kretschmer 1909).

saber dsde el cabo de çinquin a la cabeça dla tortuga +

despues la costa ~~se~~ dlla se corre al sur /. dize que

queria ver aq̃l entremedio destas dos Islas por

35 ver la isla española q̃s la mas hermosa cosa del mū

do y porq̃ segū le dezian los yndios q̃ traya por

alli se ~~yva~~ avia de yr a la ~~baneque~~ isla de baneq̃ /.

los quales le deziā q̃ era isla mȳ grāde y de

mȳ grādes mōtañas y rios y valles y dizean

40 q̃ la isla de bohio era mayor q̃ la juana a q̃ llamā

<u>Cuba</u> y q̃ no esta çercada de agua y pareçe dar a

entender ser tr̄ra firme q̃s aqui detras desta

española a q̃ ellos llamā caritaba y q̃ es cosa Infi

nita /. y quasi traē razō q̃llos sean trabajados de

45 gente astuta /. porq̃ todas estas islas biven co gran

miedo dlos de Caniba /. y asi torno a dezir como otras

           dize el

vezes dixe ∧q̃ Caniba no es otra cosa sino la gente

                   mȳ

dl grā Can q̃ deve ser aqui ∧vezino . y terna navios

a. la qual esta al
b. norte dla es
c. pañola /.

Folio 35v

~~y terna na[v?]~~ y vernā a captivarlos y comō no buel

vē creen q̃ se los comido   cada dia entendemos

mas a estos yndios y ellos a nosotros ~~avnque~~

puesto q̃ muchas vezes ayā entendido vno por

5 otro / dize el almiᵉ /. Enbio gente a tr̄ra halla

rō mūcha almaciga sin quajarse . dize que

las aguas lo devē hazer / y q̃ en ~~xio~~ xio

la cogē por março y q̃ en enero la cogerian en

——[?] aq̃stas trras por ser tan tēpladas . pescarō

10 mūchos pescados comō los de castilla / albures / sal

mones / pijotas / gallos / pampanos / lisas / cor

vinas / camarones y vierō sardinas / hallarō mū

cho lignaloe /.

de Cinquín to the head of Tortuga,[1] which is to
the north of Hispaniola. Further along, its coast[2]
runs south. He says that he wanted to see that [pas-
sage] between these two islands in order to see the
island of Hispaniola, which is the most beautiful thing
in the world; and because, as the Indians that he
brought with him told him, it was the way one had to
go to the island of Baneque. They told him that it
was a very large island with big mountains and rivers
and valleys. And they said that the island of Bohío
was larger than Juana, which they call Cuba, and that
it is not surrounded by water.[3] And they appear to
mean that here behind this Hispaniola, which they
call Caritaba, there is a landmass of exceedingly large
size. And perhaps they are right, for they may be
oppressed by cunning people, because the people of
all these islands live in great fear of those from Caniba.
And thus I say again how other times I said, he says,
that Caniba is nothing else but the people of the
Grand Khan, who must be here very close to this
place. And they have ships and come to capture the
islanders, and since they do not return the other
islanders think that they have been eaten. Each day
we understand these Indians better and they us, even
though many times they have understood one thing
for another, says the Admiral. He sent men to land
where they found much mastic, but not hardened.
He says that the rains must cause this, that in Chios it
is gathered around March and that in these Indies
they probably collect it in January, since they are so
temperate. They caught many fish like those of
Castile: dace, salmon, hake, dories, pompano,
mullets, corbina, shrimp; and they saw sardines.
They found much aloe.

35v

1. (35r32a–c) The insert following *Tortuga* is boxed in the right margin.
2. (35r33) *La costa della* (its coast). *Della* does not make clear whether it is the
coast of Tortuga or of Hispaniola that runs south, but a map shows that Columbus is
referring to Hispaniola.
3. (35r41) *Y que no esta . . . agua* (and that it is not . . . water). "It," the subject
of the clause, must refer to *tierra firma* (35r42) and not to either one of the two islands,
Bohío and Cuba (35r40–41).

miercoles .12. de diziēbre /.

15 / no partio aq̄ste dia por la misma causa del vien

to contrario dicha / puso vn grā cruz a la entrada

dl pueʳto dla parte dl hueste en vn alto mūy

vistoso en señal (dize el) q̄ .v.al. tienē la tr̄r̄a

por suya y principalmēte por señal de jesu xp̄o

20 nr̄o señor : y hōrra dla xp̄iāndad /. la qual puesta

tres marineros metierōse por el mōte a ver los

arboles y yervas : y oyerō vn grā golpe de gen

te todos dsnudos comō los de atras a los quales lla

marō e fuerō tras ellos / p[er]o —[?] dierō los yndios

25 a huyr /. y finalmēte tomarō vna muger q̄ no

el dize

pudierō mas porq̄ yo ∧les avia mādado q̄ toma

sen algunos p[ar]a ~~haz~~ honrrallos y hazelles p[er]der

~~se~~

el miedo y ~~∧oviesen alguᵃ cosa~~ se oviese alguna cosa

de provecho / comō no parece poder ser otra cosa

30 segud la fermosura dla tr̄r̄a / y asi truxerō la mu

mūy

ger ∧moça y hermosa ————[?] a la nao y hablo

con aq̄llos yndios porq̄ todos tenian vna lengua :

hyzola el almiᵉ vestir y diole cuētas de vidro y

cascaveles y sortijas de laton : y tornola enbiar

35 a tr̄r̄a mȳ honrradamēte segū su costūbre : y en

bio algunas p[er]sonas dla nao cō ella : y tres dlos

yndios q̄ llevava cōsigo porq̄ hablasen cō aq̄lla

gente /. los marineros q̄ yvan en la barca quādo

la llevavā a tr̄r̄a dixerō al almiᵉ q̄ ya no quisiera

40 salir dla nao sino quedarse con las otras muge

nō   res ~~q̄~~ yndias q̄ avia hecho ~~detener~~[?] tomar en el

puerto de mares dla isla juana de Cuba /. todos

estos yndios q̄ venian cō aq̄lla yndia diz q̄ venian

en vna Canoa ~~de alguᵃ p[ar]te~~ q̄s su caravela en q̄ na

Wednesday 12 December

He did not depart that day for the same reason, i.e.,
the contrary wind already mentioned. He placed a
large cross at the western side of the entrance to the
harbor on a conspicuous height, as a sign, he
says, that Your Highnesses claim the land as your
own, and chiefly as a sign of Jesus Christ Our
Lord and in honor of Christianity. After the
cross was set up, three sailors went into the
bush to see the trees and undergrowth, and they
heard a large band of people, all naked like
those seen previously, to whom they called, and
they chased after them. But the Indians took to
flight. Finally they captured one woman—for
they could catch no more—because, he says, I [1]
had ordered them to catch some [people] in order
to treat them courteously and make them lose
their fear, which would be something profitable
since it seems that the land cannot be otherwise
than profitable, judging by its beauty. And so
they brought the woman, who was very young and
pretty,[2] to the ship and she talked to those
Indians, because they all have one language. The
Admiral ordered her clothed and he gave her glass
beads and bells and brass finger rings and returned her to land very courteously, according to
his custom. And he sent with her some persons
from the ship and three of the Indians that he
brought with him so that they might speak with
those people. The sailors who went in the launch
when they took her to land told the Admiral that
she had not wanted to leave the ship but wished
to stay with the other Indian women whom the
Admiral had had captured[3] at the Puerto de Mares
on the island of Juana, or Cuba. All the Indians
who went with that Indian woman said that [other
natives] had come in a canoe from somewhere (a

1. (35v26) *Yo* (I). Alvar's (1976) text omits this word from the manuscript.
2. (35v31) Alvar (1976) reads the cancellation following *hermosa* as *limpia (?)* (Alvar's question mark).
3. (35v41) Alvar (1976) reads the cancellation following *avia hecho* as *de
tomar (?)* (Alvar's question mark), not *detener*.

45   vegā de alguna p[ar]te : y quādo asomarō a la entra
da dl pue^rto y vierō los navios bolvierōse atras
[y?] dexarō la canoa por alli en algū lugar y fue
rōse camino dsu poblaçiō /. ella mostrava el pa
raje dla poblacion /. traya esta muger vn peda
era
50   çito de oro en la nariz q̃ -es- señal q̃ -aya-[?] avia
en aq̃lla Isla oro /.

Folio 36r

-en aq̃lla isla oro-

Jueves .13. de diziēbre

/ bolviero los tres hōbres q̃ avia enbiado el almi^e
con la muger a tres oras dla noche : y no fuero
5   con ella hasta la poblacion porq̃ les parecio lexos
/o porq̃ tuvierō miedo /. dixero q̃ otro dia verniā
mucha gente a los navios : porq̃ ya devian destar
asegurados por las nuevas q̃ daria la muger /.
El almi^e cō deseo de saber si avia -de saber- algū[a]
10   cosa de provecho en aq̃lla tr̄r̄a : y por -tomar- aver
algu^a lengua cō aq̃lla gente por ser la tr̄r̄a tā
hermosa y fertil y tomasen gana de s[er]uir a los
reyes : determino de tornar a enbiar a la po[bl?]aciō
cōfiando en las nuevas q̃ la yndia avria dado
15   dlos xp̄īanos ser buena gēte : p[ar]a lo qual esco[gi?]o nue
ve hōbres bien adereçados de armas y aptos
p[ar]a semejāte negocio / cō los quales fue vn yn
dio dlos q̃ traya /. Estos fuerō a la poblaçion
q̃stava quatro leguas y media al sueste : la qual
20   hallarō en vn grādissimo valle : y vazia porq̃ +
dexando
-todos avian huydo con- quāto tenian la tr̄r̄a den
tro /. la poblaçion era de mil casas y de mas
de tres mill hōbres /. El yndio q̃ llevavā
los xp̄īanos corrio tras ellos dando bozes diziēdo

a. cōmo sintierō yr [a]
b. los xp̄īanos
c. todos huyerō

canoe[1] is their caravel, in which they go
from one place [to another]); and when they
appeared at the entrance to the harbor and
saw the ships they turned back, left the canoe
somewhere, and took the path to their village.
The woman showed the Spaniards the location of
the village. This woman was wearing a little
piece of gold in her nose, which was a sign that
there was gold on that island.[2]

36r   **Thursday 13 December**

The three men that the Admiral had sent with the
woman returned at the third hour of night. They
did not go with her as far as the village because
it seemed to them far and because they were afraid.
They said that the next day many people would come
to the ships because they would now be reassured by
the news that the woman would give. The Admiral,
with desire to know if there was anything of profit in
that land and to converse with that people, because the
land was so beautiful and fertile, and so that they
might become desirous of serving the sovereigns,
decided to send [men] again to that village, trusting
in the report the Indian woman would have given that
the Christians were good people. For this purpose
he chose nine men well furnished with arms and
suited to such business, and with them went one of
the Indians that he had brought. These men went to
the village, which was four and a half leagues to the
southeast, and which they found in a very great
valley. [It was] empty because,[3] when they heard
the Christians coming, all of the Indians fled inland
leaving everything that they had. The village was of a
thousand houses and of more than three thousand
inhabitants. The Indian that the Christians brought
ran after them shouting, telling them not to be afraid,

---

1. (35v44) Alvar (1976) reads the canceled text following *canoa* as *de alguna gente*. Las Casas here simply jumped ahead in his copying to line 35v45: *de alguna parte*.
2. (35v51) Alvar (1976) omits the word *oro* from the (canceled) first line of folio 36r.
3. (36r20a–c) The insert following *porque* is partially boxed in the right margin.

25 q̃ no oviesen miedo : q̃ los xp̃ıãos no erã de
Caniba mas antes erã dl çielo y q̃ davã mū

nõ   chas cosas hermosas a todos los q̃ hallavã / tan
to les imprimio lo q̃ dezia q̃ se aseguraro y vi
nierō ~~just~~-[?] juntos dllos mas de dos mill : y to

30 dos venian a los xpianos y les ponian las manos
sobre cabeça q̃ era señal de grã reverẽçia y amistad
los quales estavã todos tẽblando hasta q̃ mūcho
los aseguraro ~~y dixerō~~-[?] /. dixerō los xpianos q[ue?]
despues q̃ ya estavã sin temor : yvã todos a
                                les
35 sus casas y cada vno ∧traya dlo q̃ tenia de co
mer q̃ es pan de niamas q̃ son vnas rayzes
como ravanos grãdes q̃ naçen q̃ siembra y naçen
y plantã en todas estas tr̄r̄as / y es su vida / y hazẽ
dllas pã y cuezen y asan y tienẽ sabor proprio de

40 castañas y no ay quiẽ no crea comiẽdolas q̃ no seã
castañas /. y davãles pan y p[e?]scados y dlo q̃ tenian
y porq̃ los yndios q̃ traya en el navio tenian enten
dido q̃l almiͤ deseava tener algun papagayo : pa
rez q̃ aq̃l yndio q̃ yva cō los xp̃ıãos dixoles algo

45 desto : y asi les truxero papagayos y les davã quã[to?]
nõ   les pedian sin querer nada por ello /. Rogavãles
q̃ no se viniesen aq̃lla noche y q̃ les dariã otras mu
chas cosas q̃ tenian en la sierra /. Al tp̄o q̃ toda aq̃lla
gente estava junta cō los xpianos : vierō venir

that the Christians were not from Caniba but instead
were from the heavens and that they gave many nice
things to all those whom they found. The Indians
were so impressed by what he said that they were
reassured and there came in a body more than two
thousand. All of them came to the Christians and put
their hands on their heads,[1] which was a sign of
great reverence and friendship. All of them were
trembling, until he reassured them strongly. The
Christians said that later, when the Indians were
without fear, they all went to their houses and each
one brought them something to eat of what they had,
that is, bread made from *niamas*,[2] which are roots
like large radishes[3] which they grow and seed and
plant in all these lands. And it is their sustenance.
And they make of them bread, and they cook and
roast them, and they have a flavor just like chestnuts,
and there is no one who would not believe, eating
them, that they are not chestnuts. And they gave the
Spaniards bread and fish and of what they had, and
because the Indians that he brought in the ship[4] had
understood that the Admiral wanted to have some parrots,[5] it seems that the Indian who went with the
Christians told the natives something about this, and
so they brought parrots to them and gave as many as
they were asked for without wanting anything for
them. They begged the Spaniards not to go away[6]
that night and that they would give them many
other things that they had in the mountains. At the
time when all of those people were together with

1. (36r30–31) *Les ponian . . . cabeça*. That is, the Indians put their hands over, or
on, the heads of the Spaniards.
2. (36r36) *Niamas*. Probably a misspelling of *niames*, "cassava."
3. (36r37) *Ravanos* are radishes, not carrots, as Morison (1963) and Jane-Vigneras (1960) translate. Thacher (1903–1904) translates as "radishes." Columbus used
the current word, *zanahoria*, for carrot (e.g., at 21r18 and 38r11).
4. (36r42) *Navio*. The *Niña*.
5. (36r43) *Algun papagayo*. Although singular in form, this is probably meant to
be understood in the plural (some parrots). Note that the Indians brought *papagayos*
(36r45). See p. 99, n. 6, *alguno altillo*, for a like use of singular for plural.
6. (36r47) *No se viniesen* literally means "not come away," although here it must
mean "not go away," since it is the Indians on shore who want the Spaniards to stay.

Folio 36v

nõ

vna grā batalla /o multitud de gente con el
marido dla muger q̃ avian el almi͜e : hōrra
do y enbiado la qual trayā ~~sobre~~ cavallera
sobre sus hōbros y venian a dar graçias a los
5   xp̄ianos por la hōrra q̃l almi͜e le avia hecho y
dadivas q̃ le avia dado /. dixerō los xp̄ianos al
almi͜e q̃ era toda gēte mas hermosa y de me
jor condiçion q̃ ninguᵃ otra dlas q̃ avian hasta
alli hallado : p[er]o dize el almi͜e q̃ no sabe comõ
10   puedā ser de mejor condiçion q̃ las otras : dā
do a entender q̃ todas las q̃ avian en las otras
islas hallado era de mȳ buena cōdicion /. quāto
a la hermosura dezian los xp̄ianos q̃ no avia
comp[ar]açion / asi en los hōbres comõ en las muge
15   res : y q̃ son blancos mas q̃ los otros : y q̃ entre
los otros vierō dos mugeres moças tan blancas

nõ

comõ podian ser en ~~castilla~~ españa /. dixerō tam
bien dla hermosura dlas tr̄ras q̃ vierō : q̃ ninguᵃ
comp[ar]açiō tienē las de castilla las mejores en
20   hermosura y en bondad /. y ~~que asi lo~~ el almi͜e asi
lo via por las q̃ a visto y por las q̃ tenia p[re]sentes /.
y dizianle q̃ las q̃ via ninguᵃ comp[ar]acion tenian
cō aq̃llas de aq̃l valle : ni la campiña de cordova
llegava aq̃lla cō tanta differēçia comõ tiene el dia
25   dla noche /. dizian q̃ todas aq̃llas tr̄ras estavan
labradas : y q̃ por medio de aq̃l valle passava vn
rio mȳ ancho y grāde q̃ podia regar todas
las tr̄ras /. estavā todos los arboles Vrdes y llenos
de fruta : y las yervas todas floridas y mȳ altas
30   los caminos mȳ anchos y buenos : los ayres erā
comõ en abril en castilla : cantava el ruyseñor y
otros paxaritos comõ en el d̄ho mes en españa : q̃
dize q̃ era la mayor dulçura dl mūdo /. las no
ches cantavā algunos paxaritos suauemēte : los
35   grillos y ranas se oyan mūchas : los pescados
~~de aq̃lla maña~~ comõ en españa /. vierō mū
chos almaçigos y lignaloe y algodonales : oro

36v   the Christians, they saw a large troop or crowd of
people coming with the husband of the woman whom
the Admiral had caught and treated courteously and
sent back. She was being carried "horseback" on
their shoulders and they were coming to give thanks
to the Christians for the courtesy that the Admiral
had shone to her and the gifts that he had given her.
The Christians said to the Admiral that they were all
people more handsome and of better quality than any
of the others they had found up to that point. But
the Admiral says he does not know how they could
be of better quality than the others, it having been
made clear that all those who were found on the
other islands were of very good quality. And as to
their beauty, the Christians said that there was no
comparison, of men as well as women, and that they
are whiter than the others, and that among them they
saw two young women as white as any in Spain.
They spoke also of the beauty of the lands that they
saw; and said that the most beautiful and best lands
of Castile could not be compared with them. And
the Admiral[1] also perceived this to be true because
of the lands that he had seen and those that he now
had before him. And they told him that those that he
had seen could not be compared with those of that
valley, not even the plains of Cordova, which would
fall short of it with such a difference as night from
day. They said that all these lands were cultivated,
and that in the midst of the valley there passed a
big and wide river which could water all the lands.
The trees were all green and full of fruit, and the
undergrowth full of flowers and very high, and the
paths were very wide and good. The breezes were
like those of Castile in April. The nightingale and
other small birds sang as in the said month in Spain,
for he says that it was the greatest sweetness in the
world. At night some small birds sang softly, and
one heard many grasshoppers and frogs. The fish
[were] like those of Spain. They saw many mastic
trees and aloes and cotton fields. Gold they did not

---

1.   (36v20) Alvar (1976) reads the canceled text preceding *el almirante* as *que a
sido*.

no hallarō : y no es maravilla en tā poco tpo

nõ   no se halle /. tomo aqui el almiᵉ experiençia de

40   q̃ oras era el dia y la noche y de sol a sol ha

llo q̃ passarō veynte ampolletas q̃ son de a me

dia ora / avnq̃ dize q̃ alli puede aver defe

cto porq̃ /o no la buelvē tā presto o dexa de

passar algo /. dize tābien q̃ hallo por el quadrā

esto es impossi[b]   te q̃stava dla linea equinocial .34. grados /.
le

Folio 37r

viernes .14. de diziēbre

✗ Salio de aq̃l puerto dla conçepçion con terral y luego

desde a poco calmo y asi lo experimēto cada dia dlos

q̃ por alli estuvo /. dspu[e]s vino viento levāte : navego

5   con el al nornordeste llego a la isla dla tortuga [vi?]

do vna punta della q̃ llamo la punta pierna q̃stava al les

nordeste dla cabeça dla isla y avria .12. millas : y de

alli dscubrio otra punta q̃ llamo la punta lançada en

la misma derrota del nordeste q̃ avria diez y seys mil

10   las /. y asi dsde la cabeça dla tortuga hasta la punta ~~de~~ [?]

aguda avria .44. millas q̃ son onze leguas al les

nordeste /. en aq̃l camino avia algunos pedaços de pla

                    isla

ya grādes /. Esta ∧ ~~tr̄ra~~ dla tortuga es tr̄ra ~~alta~~ mȳ alta

p[er]o no mōtañosa y es mȳ ~~pob~~ hermosa y mūy pobla

15   da de gente comō la dla isla española : y la tr̄ra asi

toda labrada q̃ pareçia ver la campiña de cordova /.

visto q̃ el viento le era contrario y no podia yr a la

isla baneque : acordo tornarse al puerto dla conçepcion

de donde avia salido : y no pudo cobrar vn rio q̃sta

20   dla p[ar]te dl leste dl d̄ho pueʳto dos leguas /.

find; and it is not surprising that in so little time it
was not found. Here the Admiral determined by
experiment what the hours of the day were and what
those of the night. From sun to sun[1] he found
that there passed 20 sandglasses of a half hour each,
although he says that there could be some error,
either from not turning the glass quickly enough or
from the sand failing somewhat to pass through. He
says also that he found by the quadrant that he was
34 degrees from the equinoctial line.

37r   Friday 14 December

He left that Puerto de la Concepción with a land breeze
and then after a short time it became calm; and such
was his experience each day of those that he spent in
those parts. Later an east wind came; he steered with
it to the northnortheast and reached the island of
Tortuga. He saw a point on it that he called Punta
Pierna, which was to the eastnortheast of the head of
the island by about 12 miles. And from there in the
same northeast direction he made out another point
which he called Punta Lanzada, which was about 16
miles. And thus from the head of Tortuga as far as
Punta Aguda it was about 44 miles, which is 11
leagues, east-northeast. On that route there were
some large stretches of beach. This island of Tortuga
is very high but not mountainous[2] and very beautiful and heavily populated with people like those
of the island of Hispaniola; and the land likewise is all
cultivated, so that one seems to be seeing the plain of
Cordova. Since the wind was against him and he was
unable to go to the island of Baneque, he decided to
return to the Puerto de la Concepción, from which
he had departed. And he could not reach a river
which is two leagues east of the said harbor.

---

1. (36v40) *Sol a sol*. "Sun to sun" must mean "sunup to sundown," not the time
from one sunup or sundown to the next.

2. (37r13–14) *Muy alta pero no montañosa*. "Very high but not mountainous" means high but more or less flat, without peaks. See Morison (1963, 120, 14
Dec., n. 5).

Sabado .15. de diziēbre

⁄ Salio dl pueʳto dla conçepçion otra vez p[ar]a su camino
p[er]o en saliendo dl pueʳto vento leste rezio su contrario
y tomo la buelta dla tortuga hasta ella y de alli
25 dio buelta p[ar]a ver aq̃l rio q̃ ayer quisiera ver y
tomar y no pudo : y dsta buelta tanpoco lo pudo
tomar −[?] auvnq̃ surgio media legua de sotaviēto
en vna playa buē surgidero y limpio /. amarrados
sus navios / fue cō las barcas a ver el rio y en
30 tro por vn braço de mar q̃sta antes dl media le
gua y no era la boca / bolvio y hallo la boca que
                         avn vna
no tenia ~~sino media~~ braça : y venia mȳ rezio /.
Entro ~~por las~~ cō las barcas por el para llegar a las
poblaçiones q̃ los q antier avia enbiado avian visto
35 y mādo echar la sirga en tr̄ra y tirādo ~~la gente de~~
los marineros dlla subierō las barcas dos ti
ros de lobarda y no pudo andar mas por la re
ziura dla corriēte dl rio /. vido algunas casas y el
valle grāde donde estan las poblaçiōes ~~q̃~~ y dixo
40 q̃ otra cosa mas hermosa no avia visto por medio
dl qual valle viene aq̃l rio /. vido tābien gente a la
entrada dl rio . mas todos dierō a huyr /. dize mas
q̃ aq̃lla gente deve ser mȳ caçada : pues bive cō tā
to temor : porq̃ en llegādo q̃ llega a qualquiera
45 p[ar]te . luego hazē ahumadas dlas atalayas por toda
la tr̄ra y esto mas en esta isla española y en la tortuga
q̃ tābien es grāde isla : ~~mas~~ q̃ en las otras q̃ atras
valle dl paray   dexava /. puso nōbre al valle : valle del parayso . y
so   al rio guadalquiuir porq̃ diz q̃ asi viene tā grāde comō
50 guadalquivir por cordova y a las veras ~~del~~ [?] ⁄o riberas
del playa de piedras mȳ hermosas / y todo andable

He left the Puerto de la Concepción again to [follow]
his route, but when he left the harbor the wind blew
strongly east against him, and he took a course for
Tortuga until [he reached] it, and from there came
about in order to see the river that yesterday he had
wanted to see and reach but could not. But neither
could he reach it on this course, although he did
anchor half a league downwind of it at a beach, a
good and clean anchorage. His ships moored, he
went with the launches to see the river and entered an
arm of the sea which is short of it half a league and
was not the mouth. He returned and found the
mouth of the river, which did not have a [depth] of
even one *braza*; and it flowed very strongly. He
entered it with the launches to reach the villages that
the men he had sent yesterday had seen, and he
ordered a cable thrown to land. The sailors, hauling
on it, pulled the launches upriver the distance of two
lombard shots, but they could go no further because
of the strength of the current. He saw some houses
and the great valley where the villages were and he
said that he had not seen[1] anything else more
beautiful [than the way] that river comes through
the middle of the valley. He also saw people at
the entrance to the river, but all took to flight.
Moreover, he says that those people must be much
hunted since they live in so much fear and because,
just as soon as we arrive anywhere, they make smoke
signals from the lookouts throughout all the land,
and more so in this island of Hispaniola and in
Tortuga (which also is a large island) than in the
others left behind. He gave to the valley the name
Valle del Paraíso, and, to the river, Guadalquivir,
because he says that it is as big as the Guadalquivir
coming through Cordova; and on its banks there is a
beach of pretty stones. And the land is suitable for
walking.[2]

---

1. (37r40) *No avia visto* (he had not seen). A word, perhaps *como*, seems to have
been omitted after *visto*.
2. (37r51) Applying the phrase *todo andable* (suitable for walking) to the river,
Morison (1963) and Thacher (1903–1904) translate *andable* as *navigable*. But the

Folio 37v

Domīgo .16. de diziēbre

ł a la media noche cō el ventezuelo de tr̄r̄a dio las velas
por salir de aq̄l golpho : y viniendo dl bordo dla Isla
española yendo a la volina porq̄ luego a ora de terçia

5   vento leste : a medio golpho hallo vna canoa con vn yn
dio solo en ella : de que se maravillava el almi꞊ comō
se podia tener sobre el agua siendo el viento grā̄de /.
~~todo~~[?] hyzolo meter en la nao a el y a su canoa : y
halagado diole cuētas de vidro cascaveles y sortijas

10   de laton : y llevolo en la nao hasta tr̄r̄a a vna poblaçiō
q̄ estava de alli diez y seys millas junto a la mar : dō
de surgio el almi꞊ y hallo buē surgidero en la pla
ya junto a la poblaçion q̄ pareçia ser de nuevo he
cha porq̄ todas las casas erā nuevas /. El yndio

15   ~~dexarō~~ fuese luego con su canoa a tr̄r̄a : y da nue
vas dl almi꞊ y dlos xp̄īanos ser buena gente : pue
sto q̄ ya las tenian por lo passado dlas otras donde
avian ydo los seys xp̄īanos : y luego vinierō mas
de quinientos hōbres : y desde a poco vino el rey

20   dllos : todos en la playa juntos a los navios porq̄sta
vā̄ surgidos mȳ çerca de tr̄r̄a /. luego vno a vno y
mūchos a mūchos venian ~~a los navios~~ a la nao : sin
traer consigo cosa alguᵃ : puesto q̄ algunos trayan al
gunos granos de oro finissimo a las orejas /o en la na

25   riz el qual luego davan de buena gana /. mā̄do ha
zer hō̄rra a todos el almi꞊ ~~porq̄ diz q̄~~ (y dize el : por
nō   q̄ son la mejor gente dl mū̄do y mas mā̄sa y
sobre todo (dize) q̄ tengo mūcha esp[er]ança en nr̄o se
ñor q̄ vr̄as altezas los harā todos xp̄īanos y serā

30   todos suyos q̄ por suyos los tengo /. vido tābiē
q̄l d̄ho rey estava en la playa y q̄ todos le hazian
acatamiº /. Embiōle vn presente el almi꞊ el qual diz
que rescibio con mūcho estado : y q̄ seria moço de hasta
veynte y vn años : y q̄ tenia vn ayo viejo y otros

35   consejeros q̄ le consejavā y respōdian : y q̄l habla

37v   Sunday 16 December

At midnight, with the light land breeze, he set sail to
depart from that channel; and coming from the coast
of the island of Hispaniola, sailing close-hauled since
it was then, at the hour of tierce, blowing east, he
found in mid-channel a canoe with one Indian alone
in it. The Admiral marveled at how he was able to
stay afloat, the wind being great. He ordered him
and his canoe into the ship and, treating him well,
gave him glass beads, bells, and brass rings; and he
took him in the ship to land, to a village 16 miles
from there, next to the sea, where the Admiral
anchored and found a good anchorage at the beach
near the village, which appeared to be newly formed
since all the houses were new. The Indian soon went
to land with his canoe and gave news about the
Admiral and the Christians being good people,
although the Indians already had such news because
of what had happened to the others[1] where the six
Christians had gone. And more than 500 men soon
came, and a little later, their king. [They were] all on
the beach near the ships, which were anchored very
close to land. Soon, one by one and in groups, they
came to the ship, without bringing anything with
them, although a few wore small pieces of fine gold in
their ears or in their noses, and they gave it quickly
and willingly. The admiral ordered that they should
all be treated courteously because they are the best
and most gentle people in the world, and especially,
he says, because I have much hope in Our Lord that
Your Highnesses will make all of them Christians and
that they will all be your subjects, for I consider them
yours [already]. He saw also that the said king was
on the beach and that all treated him with respect.
The Admiral sent him a present that the king, he says,
received with great state; and [he says] that he was a
youth of about 21 years, and that he had an old tutor
and other counsellors who advised him and gave

---

river was not navigable, because of the current (37v38). *Andable* seems rather to refer
to a quality of the land, i.e., its easy "traversability." Jane-Vigneras (1960) translates
the word as "accessible."

  1. (37v17) *Puesto . . . otras* (although the Indians . . . others). The antecedent of
the first *las* seems to be *nuevas*, and that of *dlas otras, gente*[*s*], i.e., other Indians.

va mȳ pocas palabras /. vno dlos yndios q̃ traya
el almiᵉ hablo con el : y le dixo como venian los

satis impropor
tionabitr hec
se habent

xp̄ianos del çielo : y q̃ andava en busca de oro : y
q̃ queria yr a la Isla de baneque : y el respōdio

40 q̃ biēn era y q̃ en la d̄ha isla avia mūcho oro /.
el qual amostro al alguazil dl almiᵉ q̃ ~~stava en~~
~~trra~~ le llevo el presente : el camino q̃ avia de
llevar y q̃ en dos dias yria de alli a ella : y q̃

    de su t̄r̄ra

si ∧ ~~alli~~-[?] avian menester algo lo daria de mȳ bue

45 na volūtad /. Este rey y todos los otros andava
desnudos comō sus madres los parierō : y asi las
mugeres sin algū empacho /. y son los mas
hermosos hōbres y mugeres q̃ hasta alli ovie
ro hallado /. harto blancos : que si vestidos anduvie

Folio 38r

sen y se guardasen dl sol y dl ayre serian quasi
tā blancos comō en españa /. porq̃sta t̄r̄ra es harto
fria y la mejor q̃ lengua pueda dezir /. es
mȳ alta y sobre el mayor monte podrian arar

5 bueyes : y hecha toda a campiñas y valles /. en
toda castilla no ay t̄r̄ra q̃ se pueda cōparar a ella
en hermosura y bōdad /. toda esta isla y la de la
tortuga / ~~to~~-[?] son todas labradas comō la campiña
de cordova /. tienē sembrado en ellas ~~aye~~-[?] ajes : q̃

10 son vnos ramillos q̃ plantan / y al pie dellos
naçen vnas rayzes comō çanahorias : que sirve
por pan y rallan y amassan y hazen pan dellas /
y despues tornā a plantar el mismo ramillo en
otra parte y torna ~~ad~~ a dar quatro y cinco de aq̃llas

15 rayzes q̃ son mȳ sabrosas proprio gusto de casta
ñas /. aqui las ay las mas gordas y buenas
q̃ avia visto en ninguᵃ porq̃ tābien diz q̃ de aq̃llas

answers, and that he spoke very few words. One of
the Indians that the Admiral brought spoke with the
king and told him how the Christians came from the
heavens and that the Admiral went about in search of
gold and wanted to go to the island of Baneque; and
the king responded that it was well and that in the
said island there was much gold. He showed the
Admiral's bailiff,[1] who [had] brought the present to
him, the route that had to be followed and said that
in two days one could go from there to the island;
and [he said] that if from his land they needed
something, he would give it very willingly. This king
and all the others went about naked as their mothers
bore them; and the women did also, without any
embarrassment. And they are the most handsome
men and women that they had found up to that
point: and very white, for if they went about clothed
and protected themselves from the sun and wind they
would be almost as white as people in Spain. Because
this land[2] is quite cold and the best that tongue can
tell. It is very high, and on the biggest mountain
oxen would be able to plow, and it is all formed of
plains and valleys. In all Castile there is no land
that can be compared to it in beauty and goodness.
All of this island and that of Tortuga is all cultivated like the plain of Cordova. They have sown
yams,[3] which are some little twigs that they plant,
and at the foot of the twigs some roots like carrots
grow, which serve as bread; and they scrape and knead
and make bread of them. And later they plant the
same twig elsewhere and it again produces four or
five of those roots which are very tasty, having the
same flavor as chestnuts. Here there are the fattest
and best that he has seen anywhere, because he also

38r

1. (37v41) *Alguazil*. The bailiff was Diego de Arana, cousin of Beatriz, Columbus's mistress. Morison (1963) and Jane-Vigneras (1960) call him "Marshal." See
Morison (1963, 123 n. 4).
2. (38r2–3) *Porquesta tierra es harto fria* (because this land is quite cold). This is a
separate sentence in the manuscript, but it seems disconnected unless meant as an explanation of the pale skin of the Indians.
3. (38r9) *Ajes* (yams). Probably cassava, but the identification seems uncertain. For
literature on the subject see Alvar (1976, 2:97 n. 216) and Morison (1963, 89, 4 Nov.,
n. 6).

avia en guinea /. las de aq̃l lugar erā tan
gordas como la pierna : y aq̃lla gente todos diz q̃
20   erā gordos y valientes y no flacos como lo[s?]
otros q̃ antes avia hallado / y de mūy dulçe conver
saçion sin secta /. y los arboles de alli diz q̃ erā
tā viçiosos : q̃ las hojas dexavā de ser verdes y

nõ   erā prietas de verdura /. era cosa de maravilla
25   ver aq̃llos valles y los rios y buenas aguas :
y las tr̄r̄as p[ar]a pan : p[ar]a ganado de toda suerte . de
q̃ ellos no tienē alguna : p[ar]a guertas y p[ar]a todas
las cosas del mūdo q̃l hōbre sepa pedir /. des
pues a la tarde vino el rey a la nao : el almiᵉ le

nõ   30   hizo la hōrra q̃ devia : y le hizo dezir como era
dlos reyes de castilla : los quales erā los ma

nõ   yores principes dl mūdo /. mas ni los yndios
q̃l almiᶜ traya q̃ erā los interpretes creyan na
da : ni el rey tanpoco : sino creyan q̃ venian dl
35   çielo : y q̃ los reynos dlos reyes de castilla erā
en el çielo y no en este mūdo /. pusierōle de
[c]omer al rey dlas cosas de castilla : y el comia
vn bocado y despues davalo todo a sus conseje
ros y al ayo q̃ traya cōsigo y a los demas q̃ —[?]
40   metio consigo . Crean vr̄as al. q̃stas tr̄r̄as son
en tanta Cantidad buenas y fertiles / y en especial
estas desta isla española : q̃ no ay p[er]sona q̃ lo sepa
dezir : y nadie lo puede creer sino lo viese /.

nõ   y crean q̃sta Isla y todas las otras son asi suyas
45   como Castilla : q̃ aqui no falta saluo assiento y
mandarles hazer lo q̃ quisierē / porq̃ yo con
esta gente q̃ traygo q̃ no son mūchos : correria todas

Folio 38v

estas yslas sin afrenta . q̃ ya e visto solos tres destos
marineros desçendir en tr̄r̄a   y aver multitud
destos yndios y todos huyr sin q̃ les quisiesen
hazeʳ mal /. ellos no tienē armas y son todos
5   desnudos y de nigū ingenio en las armas y mūy
cobardes q̃ mill no aguardariā tres . y asi son

says that they exist in Guinea. Those of that place
were as big as the leg. And he says that all of
these people were plump and brave and not weak like
the others he had found before. And [they were] of
very sweet speech and without false religion. And
the trees there, he says, were so vigorous that the
leaves ceased to be green, they were so dark in fo-
liage. It was a wonderful thing to see those valleys
and rivers and good water; and the lands [good] for
bread and for livestock of all kinds—of which they
have none—and for vegetable gardens and everything
in the world that man can ask for. Later in the afternoon the king came to the ship; the Admiral gave
him the honors due, and he had him told about the
kings of Castile, who were the greatest princes in the
world. But not even the Indians whom the Admiral
brought, who were the interpreters, believed a thing,
or the king either. But they did believe that the
Spaniards came from the heavens and that the realms
of the kings of Castile were in the heavens and not
in this world. They put things to eat from Castile
before the king. And he ate a mouthful and then gave
all of it to his counsellors and to the tutor and
to the others who entered the ship with him. May
Your Highnesses believe that these lands are so
greatly good and fertile, and especially those of
this island of Hispaniola, that there is no one
who can tell it; and no one could believe it if he
had not seen it. And may you believe that this
island and all the others are as much yours as
Castile; for nothing is lacking except settlement
and ordering the Indians to do whatever Your Highnesses may wish. Because I with the people that I
bring with me, who are not many, go about in all
38v   these islands without danger; for I have already
seen three of these sailors go ashore where there
was a crowd of these Indians, and all would flee
without the Spaniards wanting to do harm. They do
not have arms and they are all naked, and of no
skill in arms, and so very cowardly that a thousand would not stand against three. And so they

nõ   algo
mas parece aqui
estenderse el al
mirate dlo q̃
devria   10

buenos p[ar]a les mãdar y les hazer trabajar
sembrar y hazer todo lo otro q̃ fuere menester : y q̃
hagã villas y se enseñen a andar vestidos y a nras
costũbres /

lunes .17. de diziẽbre

/ vento aq̃lla noche reziamẽte viento lesnordeste
no se altero mũcho la mar porq̃ lo estorva
y escuda la isla dla tortuga q̃sta frontera / y
15   haze abrigo   asi estuvo alli aq̃ste dia /. Embio
a pescar los marineros cõ redes : holgarõse
mũcho cõ los xp̃ianos los yndios : y truxerõles
                    dlos de caniba /o
ciertas flechas ~~q̃ son dlas~~   ~~de cañas~~ dlos
canibales : y son dlas espigas de cañas y enxiere[n]
20   les vno palillos tostados y agudos y son mũy largas /.
mostrarõles dos hõbres q̃ les faltavan algunos pe
daços de carne de su cuerpo : y hizierõles enten
der q̃ los canibales los avian comido a bocados : el
almiᵉ no lo creyo /. torno a embiar çiertos xp̃ia
25   ños a la poblacion : y a trueque de contezuelas
resgatarõ oro   de vidro rescatarõ algunos pedaços de oro labra
do en hoja delgada /. vierõ a vno q̃ tuvo el almiᵉ
por goVrnador de aq̃lla t̃r̃a /o vn [?] provinçia q̃ lla
mavã caçique : vn pedaço tã grãde comõ la mano
30   de aq̃lla hoja de oro y pareçia q̃ lo queria resga
tar / el qual se fue a su casa : y los otros queda
                    el hazia hazer
rõ en la plaça : y ∧ ~~hazian~~ pedaçuelos de aq̃lla
pieca : y trayendo cada vez vn pedaçuelo resgata
                              por señas
va~n~lo /. despues q̃ no ovo mas dixo ∧ ——[?] q̃l
35   avia enbiado por mas y q̃ otro dia lo traerian /
Estas cosas todas —[?] y la mañra dllos y sus costũ
bres y mãsedũbre y consejo muestra de ser gẽ
te mas despierta y entendida q̃ otros q̃ hasta
alli oviese[n?] hallado dize el almiᵉ /.   En la tar
                    alli
40   de vino ∧vna Canoa dla Isla dla tortuga con

are fit to be ordered about and made to work,
plant, and do everything else that may be needed,
and build towns and be taught our customs, and to
go about clothed.

Monday 17 December

That night an east-northeast wind blew strongly.
The sea was not much stirred up because the island
of Tortuga, which is opposite, hindered [the
wind], protected [the channel], and made shelter.
So he remained there that day. He sent the sailors
to fish with nets; the Indians sported with the
Christians and brought them certain arrows, the
kind from Caniba, or from the cannibals; and they
are [made] of spikes of cane, and they insert into
them some sharp little sticks, fire-toasted, and
they are very long. Two men showed the Spaniards
that some pieces of flesh were missing from their
bodies, and they gave the Spaniards to understand
that the cannibals had eaten them by mouthfuls.
The Admiral did not believe it. He again sent certain Christians to the village; and in exchange
for small glass beads they traded for some pieces
of gold worked into thin sheets. They saw one man
who was called cacique, whom the Admiral took for
the governor of that province. [He had][1] a piece
as big as a hand of that sheet of gold and it
seemed that he wanted to trade it. He went away to
his house and the others remained in the plaza;
and he ordered small pieces of that sheet
made, and each time, bringing a small piece,
he traded for it. Later, when he had no more,
he said by signs that he had sent for more and
that the next day they would bring it. All of
these things and their behavior and customs
and gentleness and counsel show them to be
people more alert and intelligent than others
they had found up to that point, says the Admiral. In the afternoon a canoe came there
from the island of Tortuga with quite 40 men

---

1. (38v29) We have added "he had" to the translation, because something is
needed to complete the sentence.

nõ   bien quarēta hōbres : y en llegādo a la playa
toda la gente ~~q̄stava junta~~[?] dl pueblo q̄stava Junta
se assentarō todos en señal de paz : y algunos
dla canoa y quasi todos desçendierō en tr̄r̄a /.
45   el ——[?] caçique se levanto solo y cō palabras q̄
nõ   parecian de amenazas los hizo bolver a
la canoa y les echava agua / y tomava pie
dras dla playa y las echava en el agua y

Folio 39r

despues q̄ ya todos con mūcha obediencia se
pusierō y enbarcarō en la Canoa el tomo
vna piedra y la puso en la mano a mi
alguazil p[ar]a q̄ las tyrase / al qual yo avia
5   enbiado a tr̄r̄a y al escrivano y a otros p[ar]a ver
si trayan algo q̄ aprovechase / y el alguazil
no les quiso tyrar /. ~~aqui~~[?] alli mostro mū
cho aq̄l caçique q̄ se favoreçia con el almi^e /
al almi^e
la Canoa se fue luego : y dixero ∧——[?] despues
10   de yda q̄ en la tortuga avia mas oro q̄ en la
Isla española porq̄ es mas çerca de baneque /.
dixo el almi^e q̄ no creya q̄ en aq̄lla Isla espa
minas de
ñola ni en la tortuga oviese ∧oro : sino que
lo trayan de baneque : y q̄ traen poco : porq̄
15   no tiene aq̄llos que dar por ello /. y aq̄lla
tr̄r̄a es tan gruessa q̄ no ha menester q̄ trabajē
mūcho p[ar]a sustentarse ni p[ar]a vestirse comō an
den desnudos /. y creya el almi^e q̄stava mȳ
çerca dla fuente y q̄ nr̄o señor le avia de ~~de~~[?]
20   mostrar donde nasçe el oro /. tenia nueva
q̄ de alli al baneque avia quatro jornadas q̄ ~~son~~[?]
nūca este ba   podrian ser .xxx. /o .xL. leguas q̄ en vn dia de
neque pare   buē tp̄o se podian andar /.
çio por vētu
ra erā la isla
de jamayca

in it; and when it arrived at the beach, all
the people of the village who were [there]
together sat down as a sign of peace, and some
men from the canoe, almost all of them, went
ashore. The cacique rose alone and, with
words that seemed menacing, made them return
to the canoe and he threw water on them and
took stones from the beach and threw them in
the water; and then, after all [the men from
39r   Tortuga] with great obedience got into and set
off in the canoe, the cacique took a stone and
put it in the hand of my bailiff so that he
would throw it. I had sent him and the *escri-*
vano and others to land to see if they would
bring back something of benefit. And the bailiff did not wish to throw the stone at them.
There the cacique showed strongly that he was
favorably disposed toward the Admiral.[1] The
canoe went away soon, and after it had gone
the Indians told the Admiral that on Tortuga
there was more gold than on the island of
Hispaniola, because it was closer to Baneque.
The Admiral said that he did not believe that
on either the island of Hispaniola or on Tortuga there were gold mines, but that they
brought gold from Baneque, and that they
brought little because the people of Hispaniola and Tortuga had nothing to give for it.
And that land of Baneque is so rich that there
is no need to work hard in order to sustain or
dress oneself, since they go about naked. And
the Admiral believed that he was very near the
source and that Our Lord would show him where
the gold originates. He had information that
from there to Baneque was a four-day journey,
which would be 30 or 40 leagues, so that in
one day of good weather they could go [there].

---

1. (39r8) (*Alli mostro . . . que se favoreçia* (the cacique showed . . . favorably
disposed). The meaning is not clear. Perhaps the cacique's favorable view of Columbus was shown by not throwing water and stones at Columbus's men when they landed.

25 / Estuvo en aq̃lla playa surto este dia porq̃ no
avia viento y tābien porq̃ avia dicho el ~~caqui~~-[?]
caçique q̃ avia de traer oro : no porq̃ tuviese
en mūcho el almiͤ el oro (diz q̃) que podia tra
er pues alli no avia minas sino por saber

30 mejor de donde lo trayan /.   luego en ama
neçiendo mādo ataviar la nao y la caravela
de armas y vanderas por la fiesta q̃ era este dia
~~de la~~ de sancta maria dla O o comemoraçion de
la anūçiaçion : tyrarōse mūchos tyros de

35 lombardas y el rey de aq̃lla Isla española
(dize el almiͤ) avia madrugado de su casa q̃
devia de distar çinco leguas de alli segū pudo
Juzgar y llego ~~a los navios~~ a ora de terçia
a aq̃lla poblaçion /. Donde ya estavā algunos

40 dla nao q̃l almiͤ avia enbiado p[ar]a   ver si venia
oro : los quales dixerō q̃ venian con el rey
mas de doziētos hōbres : y q̃ lo trayan en vnas

                                era
vino el rey a la nao   andas quatro hōbres y ~~es~~-[?] moço comõ arriba
                                               debaxo dl
se dixo /. oy estando el almiͤ comiendo ———[?]

45 Castillo llego ~~alli~~ a la nao con toda su gente /

Folio 39v

y dize el almiͤ a los Reyes sin duda ~~vr̄as~~
~~altezas~~-[?] pareçiera bien a vr̄as altezas su
estado y acatamiento q̃ todos le tienen
puesto q̃ todos andan desnudos /. El asi

5 comõ entro en la nao hallo q̃stava comiē
         a la mesa
do ∧debaxo del castillo de popa   y el a buen
andar se vino a sentar a par de mi : y
no me quiso dar lugar q̃ yo me salie
se a el ni me levātase dla mesa : saluo

10 q̃ yo comiese /. yo pense q̃l tenia a bien
de comer de nr̄as viandas : māde lue
go traerle cosas q̃l comiesse /. y quādo entro
debaxo dl Castillo hizo señas con la mano q̃ todos
los suyos quedasen fuera y asi lo hizie

He remained at anchor at that beach this day
because there was no wind and also because the
cacique had said that he would bring gold, not
because the Admiral thought much of the gold he
could bring, since there were no mines, but in
order to know better where they brought it from.
Then, as soon as it dawned, he ordered the ship
and the caravel decorated with arms and flags,
because of the fiesta of Santa María de la O, or
commemoration of the Annunciation, which fell on
this day. They fired many lombard shots, and
the king of that island of Hispaniola, says the
Admiral, had gotten up very early at his house,
which must have been five leagues from there,
from what I can judge, and he reached the village at the hour of tierce. Some men from the
ship were there already, the Admiral having sent
them to see if gold would arrive. They said
that more than two hundred men came with the
king and that four men brought him on a litter.
He was a youth, as was said above. Today, while
the Admiral was eating under the sterncastle,
the king arrived at the ship with all his
39v   people. And the Admiral says to the sovereigns,
without doubt his dignity and the ceremony that
all observed toward him would have seemed well
to Your Highnesses, even though everyone went
about naked. The king, when he entered the
ship, found that I was at table eating under the
sterncastle. And he came at a fast walk to sit
by me, and he did not want to give occasion for
me to go out to meet him or to rise from the table, but to eat. I thought that he would ap-
preciate some of our food; I ordered that he be
brought things so that he might eat. And when
he entered underneath the sterncastle he made
signs with his hand that all of his people
should remain outside, and they did so with the

15 rō cō la mayor priesa y acatamiᵒ dl mūdo
   y se assentarō todos en la cubierta / Saluo
   dos hōbres de vna edad madura q̃ yo
   estime por sus consejeros y ayo : q̃ vinierō
   y se assentaron a sus pies /.   y dlas viā
20 das q̃ yo le puse delante : tomava de cada vna
   tanto cōmo se toma p[ar]a hazer la salua : y
   despues luego lo demas enbiavalo a los su
   yos y todos comian della y asi hizo en el be
   ver q̃ solamēte : llegava a la boca y dspues
25 asi lo dava a los otros : y todo con vn estado
   maravilloso y mȳ pocas palabras y aq̃llas
   q̃ el dezia segū yo podia entender : erā mūy
   assentadas y de seso y aq̃llos dos le miravā
   a la boca y hablavā por el y con el y con
30 mūcho acatamiento /. Despues de comido
   vn escudero traya vn çinto q̃ es p[ro]prio cōmo
   los de castilla en la hechura : saluo q̃ es de
   otra obra q̃ el tomo y me lo dio : y dos
   pedaços de oro labrados q̃ erā mūy dlga
35 dos : q̃ creo q̃ aqui alcançan poco del : puesto
   q̃ tengo q̃stan mūy vezinos de donde na
   çe y ay mūcho /. yo vide q̃ le agrada
   vā vn arābel q̃ yo tenia sobre mi cama
   yo se lo di y vnas cuentas mūy buenas de
40 ambar q̃ yo traya al pescueço : y vnos
   Çapatos colorados : y vna almarraxa de
   agua de azahar de q̃ quedo tan conten
   to q̃ fue maravilla /. y el y su ayo y
   consejeros llevā grāde pena porq̃ no me
45 entendian ni yo a ellos /. Con todo le
   cognosci q̃ me dixo / que si me compliese algo
   de aqui : q̃ toda la isla estava a mi mādar /

Folio 40r

                    yo embie por vnas cuētas mias adonde por vn
este exçelente   señal tengo vn exçelente de oro en q̃ esta escul
era moneda   pido vrās altezas y se lo amostre : y le dixe
q̃ valia dos   otra vez cōmo ayer q̃ vrās altezas mādavan y
castellanos
5   señoreavā todo lo mejor dl mūdo : y q̃ no

greatest alacrity and respect in the world. And
all of them sat down on the deck except two men
of ripe age that I took for his counsellor and
tutor, who came and seated themselves at his
feet. And of the dishes that I put before him
he took a sample from each one and afterward
sent the rest to his people, and all ate of it;
and he did the same in drinking, for he only
brought it to his mouth and afterward likewise
gave it to the others. And all with a wonderful
dignity and very few words. And those that he
spoke, so far as I could understand, were very
judicious and intelligent and those two men
watched his mouth and spoke for him and with him
and with much respect. After eating, an Indian
squire brought a belt just like those of Castile
in form, except that it is of different workman-
ship, which he took and gave to me, and two
pieces of worked gold, which were very thin; for
I think that here they get little of it, although I believe that they are very close to the
place where it originates and that there, there
is much. I saw that he was pleased with a
coverlet that I had on my bed. I gave it to him
and some very good amber beads that I wore on my
neck, and some red shoes, and a flask of orange-
flower water, with which he was so pleased that
it was a marvel. And he and his tutor and counsellors were very troubled because they did not
understand me nor I them. Nevertheless I gathered that he told me that if something from
this place pleased me that the whole island was
at my command. I sent for some beads of mine on

40r   which, as a token, I have a gold *excelente*[1] on
which Your Highnesses are sculptured, and I
showed it to him; and again, as yesterday, I told
him how Your Highnesses commanded and ruled
over all the best part of the world, and that
there were no other princes as great. And I

---

1. (40r2) *Exçelente*. Las Casas notes that this gold coin was valued at two *castellanos*. It was worth 960 *maravedís* and weighed about 9 grams. See Jane-Vigneras
(1960, 208 n. 83).

avia tan grādes prinçipes /. y le mostre las vā
deras reales y las otras dla cruz : de q̃ el
tuvo en mūcho y q̃ grādes señores serian vr̄as
altezas /. dezia el contra sus consejeros pues
10   de tal lexos y del çielo me avian enbiado ha
sta aqui sin miedo y otras cosas mūchas se -q̃- passaro
q̃ yo no entendia /. saluo q̃ bien via q̃ todo tenia
a grāde maravilla /. despues q̃ ya fue tarde
y el se quiso yr : el almi͟c le enbio en la barca
15   mȳ honrradamēte y hizo tyrar mūchas lom
bardas : y puesto en tr̄r̄a subio en sus andas y
se fue cō sus mas de doziētos hōbres /.
y su hijo le llevavā atras en los hōbros de
vn yndio hōbre mȳ hōrrado[s?] /. a todos los
20   marineros y gente dlos navios dondequiera
que lo topava : les mādava dar de comer y hazer
mūcha hōrra /. dixo vn marinero q̃ le avia
-tomado-[?] topado en el camino y visto q̃ todas las cosas
q̃ le avia dado el almi͟c y cada vna dllas lle
25   vava dlante del Rey vn hōbre -dlos suyos mas-
-hōrrado- a lo q̃ pareçia dlos mas honrrados /.
yva su hijo atras del Rey buen rato con tāta
compañia de gente comō el /. y otro tanto vn
hermano del mismo Rey / Saluo q̃ yva el
30   hrͦ a pie : y llevabanlo de braço dos hōbres
honrrados /. este vino a la nao dspues del
—[?] Rey : al qual dio el almi͟c algunas cosas
dlos d̄hos resgates : y alli supo el almi͟c
q̃ al rey llamavā en su lengua Caçique /.
35   En este dia se resgato diz q̃ poco oro : p[er]o supo
el almi͟c de vn hōbre viejo : q̃ -ay- avia
mūchas Islas comarcanas a çient leguas y
mas segū pudo entēder : en las quales
nasce mȳ mucho oro : hasta dezirle q̃ avia
40   Isla q̃ era toda oro : y en las otras q̃ ay tāta

showed him the royal banners and the others
bearing the cross, which he esteemed greatly.
What great lords Your Highnesses[1] must be, he
said (speaking toward his counsellors), since
from so far away and from the heavens they had
sent me here without fear; and many other
things passed between them that I did not
understand, except that I saw well that they
took everything as a great wonder. Afterward,
since it was already late and the king wished
to go, the Admiral sent him in the launch very
honorably and ordered many lombards fired; and
put ashore, he climbed into his litter and went
away with his more that two hundred men. And
his son was carried behind on the shoulders of
an Indian, a much-honored man. The king ordered
his people to give the sailors and men from the
ship something to eat and to treat them with
much courtesy wherever they might meet. A sail-
or who had met the king on the road said he had
seen that all the things the Admiral had given
him were carried before him, each one by a man
who seemed, from what appeared, to be among the
most honorable. His son was going along some
distance behind the king with as many more men
as company, and a brother of the king had as
many more, except that he went on foot, and two
honorable men took him by the arms. The
latter came to the ship after the king, and
the Admiral gave him some things from the
trade goods mentioned. And there the Admiral
found out that they called the king *cacique*
in their tongue. This day he says that little
gold was traded, but the Admiral learned from
an old man that within a hundred or more
leagues, as he understood, there were many
neighboring islands on which much gold originates. He even told him that there was an
island that was all gold, and that on the others

---

1. (40r8–9) In the manuscript the phrase *vuestras altezas* (Your Highnesses) ends
the sentence on lines 40r6–9. We have repunctuated, ending that sentence with "esteemed greatly" and beginning a new sentence with "What great lords."

cantidad q̃ lo cogē y çiernen cõmo con çeda
ço . y lo funden y hazen vergas y mill
labores : figurava por señas la hechura /.

Folio 40v

Este viejo señalo al almi^e la derrota y el
paraje donde ——[?] estava /. determinose
el almi^e de yr alla : y dixo q̃ si no fuera
el d̃ho viejo tā principal p[er]sona de aq̃l rey : q̃ lo

5   ~~llevara~~ detuviera y llevara consigo : /o si
supiera la lēgua q̃ se lo rogara y creya se
gū estava bien cō ~~los xp~~ el y cō los xp͞ia
ños q̃ se fuera con el de buena gana / p[er]o
porq̃ tenia ya aq̃llas gentes ~~p[ar]a~~[?] por dlos

10   reyes de castilla : y no era razō de hazelles
agravio . acordo de dexallo /.   Puso vna
cruz mȳ poderosa en ~~mitad~~[?] medio dla
plaça de aq̃lla poblaçion : a lo qual ayuda
rō los yndios mūcho y hizierō diz q̃ ora
                    y por la muestra q̃ dan
15   çion y la adorarō ∧ ——[?] espera en nr͞o señor
el almi^e q̃ todas aq̃llas Islas an de ser
xp͞ianos /.

                                              miercoles .19. de diziēbre
    ⅄ Esta noche se hizo a la vela por salir de aq̃l
20   golpho q̃ haze alli la Isla dla tortuga cō la espa
ñola : y siendo de dia torno el viento le
vāte —[?] cō el qual todo este dia no pudo salir
de entre aq̃llas dos Islas : y a la noche no
pudo tomar vn pue^rto q̃ por alli pareçia /.

25   vido por alli ~~tres /o~~ quatro cabos de tr͞ra y vna
grāde baya y rio : y de alli vido vna an
gla mȳ grāde y tenia vna poblaçion : y
a las espaldas vn valle entre mūchas mon
tañas altissimas llenas de arboles : q̃ juz

30   go ser pinos : y sobre los dos hr͞os ay vna
montaña mȳ alta y gorda q̃ va de nor
deste al sudueste : y dl cabo de torres al
lessueste esta vna Isla pequeña a la qual pu

estos dos hr͞os
y el cabo de
torres no
lo a——[?] nōbra
do hasta agora

there is such a quantity that it is collected
and separated as with a sieve; and they melt it
and make bars and a thousand objects; he showed
their shapes by signs. This old man pointed out
40v   the route to the Admiral and the place where it
was. The Admiral decided to go there; and he
said that, if the said old man were not such an
important retainer of the king, he would detain
him and take him with him; or, if he knew the
language, he would beseech him to go, and that
he believed, since the old man thought well of
him and of the Christians, he would have gone
with him quite willingly; but because the Admiral now considered those people already [sub-
jects] of the sovereigns of Castile,[1] and there
was no reason to give them offense, he decided
to leave him. He put an impressive cross in the
middle of the town plaza. The Indians helped
greatly in doing this and, he says, they prayed
and venerated it; and because of the indications
that they give, the Admiral hopes in Our Lord
that all those islands will become Christian.

Wednesday 19 December

Tonight he set sail to leave that channel that
the island of Tortuga forms there with Hispaniola; and when day came the wind turned east, with
which wind all this day he could not get out
from between those two islands; and at night he
was unable to reach a harbor that appeared nearby. He saw in the vicinity four capes and a
large bay and [a] river, and from there he saw a
very large incurving shore [?] with a village on it
and behind it a valley among many very high
mountains full of trees, which he judged to be
pines; and over the Dos Hermanos there is a
mountain, very high and wide, that goes from
northeast to southwest; and from the Cabo de
Torres to the east-southeast there is a small

1.   (40v9–10)   *Por dlos reyes de castilla* (subjects of the sovereigns of Castile). "Subjects" has been added to complete this statement.

so nōbre Sc̄to thomas porq̄ es mañana su

—[?]

35 vigilia /. ˄todo el cerco de aq̄lla Isla tiene
cabos y puertos maravillosos : segū juzga
va el dsde la mar /. antes dla Isla dla par
te del gueste ay vn cabo q̄ entra mūcho en
la mar alto y baxo / y por eso le puso nōbre
40 cabo alto y baxo /. dl cabo de torres al leste
quarta del sueste ay .60. millas hasta vna mō
taña mas alta q̄ otra q̄ entra en la mar y
pareçe desde lexos Isla por si por vn dego
llado q̄ tiene dla p[ar]te de tr̄r̄a /. pusole nōbre
45 mōte caribata : porq̄ aq̄lla provincia se lla

Folio 41r

mava Caribata /. es mȳ hermoso y lleno
de arboles Vrdes y ———[?] claros sin nie
ve y sin ñiebla : y era entōçes por alli el
tp̄o quāto a los ayres y tēplança como por
5 março en castilla : y en q̄to a los arboles y
yervas como por mayo : las noches diz q̄
eran de quatorze oras /.

Jueves .20. de diziēbre

al poner dl sol
⫮ oy˄entro en vn puerᵗo q̄stava entre la Isla
10 de Sancto thomas y el cabo de Caribata y
surgio /. este puerto es hermosissimo y q̄ ca
brian en el quātas naos ay en xp̄ıaños /.
la entrada del pareçe dsde la mar impossi
ble a los q̄ no oviesen en el entrado : por vnas
15 restringas de peñas q̄ passan desde el mō
te hasta quasi la Isla y no puestas por
orden : sino vnas aca y otra aculla vnas
a la mar y otras a la tr̄r̄a / por lo qual es me

island to which he gave the name Santo Thomás
because tomorrow is his vigil.[1] The whole
circuit of that island has marvelous capes and
harbors, as he judged from the sea. Facing the
island on the west there is a cape, partly high,
partly low, that projects far out into the sea,
and because of this he gave it the name Cabo
Alto y Bajo. From the Cabo de Torres it is 60
miles, east by south, to a mountain, taller than
any other, that projects into the sea and appears from afar itself to be an island because
of a cut off part that it has on the land side.
He gave it the name Monte Caribata, because that

41r   province was called Caribata. It is very
beautiful and full of bright[2] green trees and
without snow or mist. And in that vicinity the
weather, because of its breezes and temperate
character, was like Castile in March, and [the
province], because of the trees and undergrowth,
like Castile in May. He says that the nights
were of 14 hours.

                                              Thursday 20 December

Today at sunset he entered a harbor which is
between the island of Santo Thomás and the
Cabo de Caribata and anchored. This harbor is
extremely beautiful and would hold all the ships
of Christendom.[3] Its entrance, from the sea,
looks impossible to those who have not entered
it, because of some reefs of big rocks that run
from the mountain almost as far as the island
and [are] not placed in any order, but [are]
some here and others there, some toward the
sea, others toward land, for which reason it is

---

1. (40v35) *Vigilia*. A vigil is the day before an ecclesiastical feast. December 20
is the vigil of St. Thomas the Apostle's feast day, December 21. Since there are no
important feasts on December 19 or 20 in the Roman calendar, Columbus had to
search ahead for a suitable saint's name.

2. (41r2) Alvar (1976) reads the canceled text as *verdes (?)* (Alvar's question mark).

3. (41r12) The manuscript word here is *Xpianos* (Christians), but the sense requires "Christendom."

nester estar dspiertos p[ar]a entrar por vnas

20 entradas q̃ tiene mỹ anchas y buenas

p[ar]a entrar sin temor y todo mỹ fondo

de siete braças / y passadas las restringas

dentro ay doze braças /. puede la nao estar

con vna cuerda qualquiera amarrada : ~~que~~[?] cō

25 tra qualesquiera vientos q̃ aya /. a la

creo q̇uiere de   entrada deste pue^rto diz q̃ avia ~~vna~~[?] vn ca
zir cañaveral

ñal q̃ queda a la p[ar]te dl gueste de vna Isleta

de arena : y en ella mūchos arboles : y ha

sta el pie dlla ay siete braças /. pero ay mc̄has

30 baxas en aq̃lla comarca : y conviene abrir

el ojo hasta entrar en el pue^rto : dspues no

ayā miedo a toda la tormēta dl mūdo /. de

aq̃l pue^rto se pareçia vn valle grādissimo y [todo?]

labrado q̃ desciende a el dl sueste : todo çerca

35 do de mōtañas ~~gr~~[?] altissimas q̃ pareçe q̃ llegā

al çielo y hermosissimas llenas de arboles

Vrdes / y sin duda q̃ ay alli mōtañas mas

altas q̃ la Isla de ~~tenefe~~ tenerife en canaria

q̃s tenida por dlas mas altas q̃ ~~per~~[?] puede hallarse /.

40 desta p[ar]te dla Isla de Stō thomas : esta otra Isleta

a vna legua : y dentro dlla otra : y en todas

ay pue^rtos maravillosos / mas cūple mirar

por la baxas : vido tābien poblaçiones y ahu

madas q̃ se hazian /.

45   viernes .21. de diziēbre

X oy fue cō las barcas dlos navios a ver aq̃l puer

Folio 41v

to   el qual vido ser tal : q̃ afirmo q̃ ninguᵒ

se le Iguala de quātos aya jamas visto /

y escusase diziēdo : q̃ a loado los passados

tanto q̃ no sabe comō lo encareçer : y q̃

5 teme q̃ sea juzgado : por manificador

          ~~va~~   mas

~~q a la~~ ᴧ[?] ~~y~~ exçessivo ᴧdlo q̃ es Vrdad /.

a esto satisfaze diziēdo : q̃l trae consigo ma

necessary to be wide awake in order to go in
without fear through some very wide and good
openings that are all very deep, of seven
brazas; and the reefs passed, there is a depth
of 12 *brazas* inside. A ship can be moored with
any sort of cable against whatever winds there
may be. At the entrance to this harbor he says
that there was a channel[1] that lies to the west
of a sandy islet which has many trees on it,
and up to the base of it there are seven *brazas*.
But there are many shoals in that region, and it
is advisable to keep your eyes open until you enter
the harbor; afterward, have no fear of all the storms
in the world. From that harbor there appears a huge
valley, all cultivated, that descends to it from the
southeast, all surrounded by extremely high
mountains that seem to reach the heavens, most
beautiful and full of green trees. And without doubt
there are mountains there taller than those on the
island of Tenerife in the Canaries, which are
considered to be among the tallest that can be found.
Off this part of the island of Santo Thomás there is
another islet a league away; and inside of it, another;
and in all of them are marvelous harbors, but one
must watch out for shoals. He also saw villages and
the smoke signals that are made.

Friday 21 December

　Today he went with the ships' launches to see the
41v　harbor, which he saw to be such, he affirmed, that
none of all those he has ever seen equals it; and he
excused himself, saying that he has lauded those of the
past so much that he does not know how to praise
this one, and that he fears he may be judged to be an
excessive magnifier of what is true. He quiets
this fear by saying that he brings with him longtime

---

1. (41r26–27) *Cañal* is probably a copying error for *canal* (a channel),
although Las Casas says in a note that he believes Columbus means *cañaveral*, a
canebrake.

rineros antiguos : y estos dizē y diran
lo mismo y todos quātos andan en la mar /
10 conviene a saber / todas las alabāças q̃ a
d̄ho dlos pue^rtos passados ser Vrdad : y ser este
mȳ mejor q̃ todas ser asimismo Vrdad /.
dize mas desta mařa : yo e andado veyn
te y tres años en la mar sin salir della
15 tp̄o q̃ se aya de contar : y vi todo el levāte
y poniente q̃ dize por yr al camino de septen
trion q̃ es inglaterra : y e andado la guinea :
mas en todas estas p[ar]tidas / no se hallara la
p[er]feciō dlos pue^rtos
20
fallados siempre lo   mejor q̃l otro q̃
yo con buē tiento mirava mi escrevir / y
torno a dezir q̃ affirmo aver bien escripto
y q̃ agora este es sobre todos /. y cabrian
25 en el todas las naos del mūdo: y çerrado
q̃ cō vna cuerda la mas vieja dla nao la
tuviese amarrada /. desde la entrada hasta
el fondo avia çinco leguas /. vido vnas
tr̄r̄as mȳ labradas avnq̃ todas son asi : y
30 mādo salir dos hōbres fuera dlas barcas q̃
fuesen [p[ar]a?] vn alto p[ar]a q̃ viesen si avia pobla
çion : porq̃ dla mar no se via ningu^a : pue
sto q̃ aq̃lla noche çerca dlas diez oras vini
erō a la nao en vna Cano[a] çiertos yndios a
nō   35 ver al almi^e y a los xp̄iaños por maravilla
y les dio dlos resgates con q̃ se holgarō
mūcho /. los dos xp̄iaños bolvierō : y dixe
                    visto
rō donde aviā ∧vna poblaçion grāde vn po
co desviada dla mar /. mādo el almi^e re
40 mar hazia la p[ar]te donde la poblaçion estava
hasta llegar çerca de tr̄r̄a : y vio vnos yn
dios q̃ venian a la orilla dla mar y pare
çia q̃ venian con temor / por lo qual mādo
detener las barcas : y q̃ les hablasen
45 los yndios q̃ traya en la nao : q̃ no les haria
mal alguno /. Entōces se allegarō mas

sailors; and these men, and all who have gone to sea,
say and will say the same thing: that is, that all
the praises he has given to past harbors are justi-
fied, and that this one is very much better.   And he
says more in this wise: I have been at sea 23 years
without leaving it for any time worth telling, and I
have seen all the east and west (which he says because of going on the route north to England), and I
have traveled to Guinea; but in all of these places
the perfection of the harbors[1] seen [here] could not

be found, always [one][2] better than the other; for I
looked over my writing carefully and I again affirm
it to be well written and say that now this one
is above all others.   There would be room in it for
all the ships in the world, and [it is] so protected
that with the oldest cable of a ship it could be held
at a mooring.   From the entrance to the farthest part
it was five leagues.   He saw some cultivated lands,
although all are such; and he ordered two men out of
the launches to go toward a high place so they could
go see if there might be a village, because from the
sea none was seen, even though that night near the
tenth hour certain Indians came to the ship in
a canoe to see the Admiral and the Christians
as something wonderful, and he gave them things
from the trade goods, with which they were very
pleased.   The two Christians returned and they
told where they had seen a big village a little
way off from the sea.   The Admiral ordered the
men to row toward the place where the village
was located until they got close to land; and
he saw some Indians who were coming to the seashore and it appeared that they were coming
fearfully, because of which he ordered the
launches to stop and the Indians that he
brought with him on the ship to tell them that
the Spaniards would do them no evil.   Then they

1. (41v19) A blank line follows the word *puertos* in the manuscript, suggesting
that Las Casas intended to add material he had to look up.
2. (41v21) A blank space appears in the manuscript between *lo* and *mejor*. We
have supplied the word "one" in the Translation.

a la mar y el almi�c mas a tr̄r̄a : y despues
q̃ dl todo p[er]dier̄o el miedo : venian tantos q̃

Folio 42r

nō

cobrian la tr̄r̄a dando mill gr̄as asi hōbres
como mugeres y niños /. los vnos corri
an de aca : y los otros de alla a nos traer
pan q̃ hazen de niames aq̃llos llaman

5   ajes q̃s mūy blanco y bueno / y nos trayā
agua en calabaças y en cantaros ~~de~~ barro
dla hechura dlos de castilla : y nos trayan quā
to en el mūdo tenian y sabian q̃l almi�c que
ria : y todo con vn Coraçon tan largo y tan

10   cōtento q̃ era maravilla /. y no se diga q̃ porq̃

                                 liberalmēte

lo q̃ davā valia poco por eso lo davā ∧(dize el
almi�c) porq̃ lo mismo hazian ~~los q̃ trayan~~
~~pedaçitos de oro~~ y tan liberalmēte los q̃
davan pedaços de oro [:?] como los q̃ davā la

15   calabaca del agua / y ~~bien se~~ [?] facil cosa es de cogno
[s?]cer (dize el almi�c) quādo se da vna cosa cō mȳ
deseoso coraçon de dar /. estas son sus palabras /.
Esta gente no tiene varas ni azagayas ni
otras ningunas armas ni los otros de toda

20   esta Isla y tengo q̃ es grādissima /. Son asi
desnudos como su madre los pario : asi mu
geres como hōbres : q̃ en las otras tr̄r̄as dla
Juana y las otras dlas otras Islas trayā
las mugeres dlante de si vnas cosas de

25   algodon cō q̃ cobijan su natura tanto como
vna ~~braguillas~~ bragueta de calças de hōbre /.
en espeçial despues q̃ passan de edad de doze
años mas aqui ni moça ni vieja /. y en los
otros lugares todos los hōbres hazian escon

                      los

30   der sus mugeres de ~~nuest~~ [?] xp̄ıāos por zelos :
mas alli no /. y ay mūy lindos cuerpos
de mugeres y ellas las primeras q̃ veni
an a dar gr̄as al çielo : y traer quāto te
nian [/?] en espeçial cosas de comer pan de

came closer to the sea and the Admiral closer
to land; and later they lost fear completely.

42r So many came that they covered the land, giving
a thousand thanks, men as well as women and
children. Some of them ran this way, others that
way, to bring us bread that they make from *niames*[1]
which they call *ajes* and which are very
white and good. And they brought us water in
gourds and in clay jugs of a form like those of
Castile; and they brought us all that they had
in the world and knew that the Admiral wanted;
and all so bigheartedly and so happily that it
was a wonder. And don't say to yourself it was
because what they were giving was worth little
that they gave liberally, says the Admiral,
because those who gave pieces of gold did the
same[2] and just as liberally as those who gave
gourds of water; and it is an easy thing to
recognize, the Admiral says, when a thing is
given with a heart very desirous of giving.
These are his words. These people do not have
darts or javelins or any other arms, nor do the
others of this whole island, and I believe that
it is of great size. They are as naked as
their mothers bore them, women as well as men;
for in the other lands of Juana and the lands
of the other islands, the women wore in front
some cotton things as big as the codpiece of a
man's drawers, with which they cover their
genitals, especially after they pass the age of
12 years; but here neither young nor old women
[wear anything]. And in the other places all
the men make their women hide from the Christians out of jealousy; but there, no. And
there are women with very pretty figures and
they [are] the first who came to give thanks to
the heavens and to bring all that they had, especially things to eat: bread made of yams, and

1. (42r4) *Niames*. See p. 133, n. 2, p. 139, n. 2, p. 223, n. 2.
2. (42r12) Alvar (1976) reads the canceled text following *lo mismo hazian* as *los que avyan*.

35 ajes y gonça avellanada : y de çinco /o seys
    mañas [de?] frutas dlas quales mādo curar el
    almi꞉ p[ar]a traer a los reyes /. no menos
    diz q̃ hazian las mugeres en las otras p[ar]tes
    antes q̃ se ascondiesen /. y el [almi꞉?] mādavā en todas
40 estar todos ~~sobre aviso~~ los suyos sobre aviso
    q̃ no enojasen a alguno en cosa ninguᵃ : y q̃
    nada les tomassen contra su volūtad /.
    y asi les pagavā todo lo q̃ dllos rescibian /

Folio 42v

nõ

    finalmēte dize el almi꞉) q̃ ~~nadie~~ no puede
    creer q̃ hōbre aya visto gente de tan buenos
    coraçones y francos p[ar]a dar y tan temerosos
    q̃ ellos se deshazian todos por dar a los xp̄īā
5   ños quāto tenian /. ~~y enseñado~~ [?] y en llegando
    los xp̄īaños luego corrian a traer lo todo /. des
    pues enbio el almi. seys xp̄īaños a la poblaçiō
    p[ar]a q̃ la viesen q̃ era : a los quales hizierō quāta hōrra
    podian y sabian y les davan quāto tenian / por
10 q̃ ningunᵃ duda les queda : sino q̃ creyā el
    almi꞉ y toda su gente aver venido del çielo /.
    lo mismo creyan los yndios q̃ consigo el
    almi꞉ traya dlas otras islas : puesto q̃ ya
    se les avia dicho lo q̃ devian de tener /.
15 despues de aver ydo los seys xp̄īaños vinie
    rō çiertas canoas cō gente a rogar al almi꞉
    de p[ar]te de vn señor q̃ fuese a su pueblo : quā
    do alli se p[ar]tiese /. Canoa es vna barca en q̃ na
    vegā y son dllas grādes y dllas pequeñas /.
20 y visto q̃ el pueblo de aq̃l señor estava en el ca
    mino ~~çerca de vn Cabo~~ sobre vna punta de tr̄r̄a
    esperādo ~~el almi꞉~~ cō mūcha gēte al almi꞉ fue
    alla /. y antes q̃ se partiese : vino a la playa
    tanta gente q̃ era espanto hōbres y mugeres

peanuts,[1] and five or six kinds of fruit which
the Admiral ordered dried in order to take it to
the sovereigns. No less, he says, than the
women in other places did before they were hid-
den. And he everywhere[2] ordered all of his men
to be careful not to annoy anyone in anything
and to take nothing from them against their
will. Thus the Spaniards paid for everything
42v   they received from them. Finally, the Admiral
says, he cannot believe that any man has seen
such good-hearted people, so open in giving and
so fearful that all of them outdo themselves in
order to give the Christians all that they have,
and when the Christians arrive they run to bring
everything. Later the Admiral sent six Christians to the village to see what sort of place
it was. The Indians honored[3] them as much as
they could and knew how to, and they gave them
all that they had since no doubt remained in
them: they believed that the Admiral and all his
people had come from the heavens. The Indians
that the Admiral brought with him from the other
islands believed the same thing, although he had
already told them what they should believe.
After the six Christians had gone, [there] came
certain canoes with people to beg the Admiral,
on behalf of a lord, to go to his town when he
left that place [where he then was]. ("Canoe"
is a boat in which they navigate, and some of
them are big, and some little.) And seeing that
the lord's town was on his route near a point of
land where the lord was awaiting the Admiral
with many people, the Admiral went there. And
before he left, so many people came to the beach
that it was astonishing: men, women, and chil-

---

1. (42r35) *Gonça avellanada*. The meaning of this phrase is uncertain. Jane-
Vigneras (1960) translates it as "chufa," a small tubercule produced by the *juncia* plant;
Morison (1963) says "nut-colored (or shriveled) quinces"; Alvar (1976, 2 : 163), referring to Las Casas's *Apologetica Historia*, identifies it as *cacahuet*, or "peanut."
2. (42r39) *En todas* (everywhere). The phrase *en todas* is written in the right margin, suggesting that it was added subsequently. It looks as if Las Casas forgot to add
the word *partes* to complete the Spanish phrase meaning "everywhere."
3. (42v8) *Honrra*. This word is written in the right margin, suggesting that it
was added at a later time.

25 y niños dando bozes q̃ no se fuesse sino q̃
se quedase cō ellos /. los mēsajeros del otro
señor q̃ avia venido a cōbidar : estavā aguar
dando cō sus Canoas . porq̃ no se fuese sin
yr a ver al señor /. y asi lo hizo ~~q̃~~ y en llegādo
30 q̃ llego el almiᶜ adonde aq̃l señor le esta
va esp[er]ando y tenian mūchas cosas de comer :
mādo assentar toda su gēte : māda q̃ llevē
lo que tenian de comer a las barcas donde estava
el almiᶜ junto a la orilla dla mar /. y comō
35 vido q̃l almiᶜ avia ~~tomado~~ resçibido lo q̃ le
avian lle~~g~~vado : todos /o los mas de los yndios
dierō a correr al pueblo q̃ ~~stav~~ devia estar çer
ca p[ar]a traerle mas comida y papagayos y
otras cosas dlo q̃ tenian con tā franco coraçon
40 q̃ era maravilla /. El almiᶜ les dio Cuentas
de vidro [y?] sortijas de laton y cascaveles : no
porq̃ ellos demādassen algo : sino porq̃ le pa
recia q̃ era razō y ~~mas~~-[?] sobre todo (dize el almiᶜ)
porq̃ los tiene ya por xp̄īanos y por dlos Reyes

Folio 43r

de Castilla mas q̃ las gentes de Castilla : y dize
q̃ otra cosa no falta saluo saber la lengua y
mādarles porq̃ todo lo q̃ se les mādare harā
sin contradi[c?]çion alguᵃ /. partiose de alli el almiᶜ
                         los yndios
5 p[ar]a los navios y ~~ellos~~ davā bozes asi hōbres
                              se
comō mugeres y niños q̃ no ——[?] fuessen
y se quedasen con ellos los xp̄īan͞os /. despues
                    tras ellos
q̃ se partian venian ∧a la nao Canoas llenas
dllos : a los quales hizo hazeʳ mūcha honrra y
10 dalles de comer y otras cosas q̃ llevarō /. avia
tābien venido antes [Y?] otro señor dla parte del
                         mȳ
gueste y avn a nado venian ∧mūcha gente :
                         grād͞e
y estava la nao mas de ∧media legua de tr͞r͞a /.
El señor q̃ dixe se avia ~~ydo~~ tornado : enbioles

dren, crying out for him not to go away but to
stay there with them. The messengers of the
other lord, who had come to invite him, were
waiting with their canoes so that he would not go
away without going to see the lord. And so he did
go, and as soon as the Admiral arrived where that
lord was awaiting him and had [for him] many things
to eat, the lord ordered all his people to sit
down, and he ordered them to bring what they had
to eat to the boats where the Admiral was, near
the seashore. And when he saw that the Admiral
had received what they had taken to him, all or
most of the Indians began to run to the town,
which must have been near, to bring him more food
and parrots and other things of those that they
had, with such open hearts that it was a marvel.
The Admiral gave them glass beads and brass rings
and bells: not because they asked for something,
but because it seemed to him that it was right;
and above all, says the Admiral, because he already considers them as Christians and as more

43r   the subjects of the sovereigns of Castile
than the Castilians. And he says that nothing is
lacking except to know the language and to give
them orders, because everything they are ordered
to do they will do without any opposition. The
Admiral left that place for the ships and the Indians cried out, men as well as women and chil-
ren, not to go away and for the Christians to
stay there with them. After they left, canoes
full of Indians came behind them to the ship:
the Admiral ordered that they be treated courteously and given things to eat and other things
that the Spaniards brought. Another lord had
also come earlier from the west, and very many
people came, even swimming, and the ship was more
than a full half league from land. The lord I
spoke of had returned to land. The Admiral sent

15   çiertas p[er]sonas p[ar]a q̃ le viesen y le pregũtasen de
      stas Islas : el los resçibio mũy bien y los llevo
      consigo a su pueblo p[ar]a dalles çiertos pedaços
      grãdes de oro : y llegaro a vn grã rio : el qual
      los yndios passarõ a nado : los xp̃ianos no pu
20   dierõ y asi se tornarõ /. en toda esta comarca
                    ñas
      ay mõtallas altissimas q̃ pareçen llegar al
      çielo q̃ la dla Isla de tenerife pareçe nada en
      comp[ar]açion dllas en altura y en hermosura
      y todas son Vrdes llenas de arboledas : q̃ es
25   vna cosa de maravilla /. Entremedias dellas
      ay vegas mỹ graçiosas : y al pie deste puer
      to al sur ay vna vega tan grãde q̃ los ojos
      no puedẽ llegar cõ la vista al cabo /. sin q̃ te[n]
      ga impedimẽto de mõtaña q̃ pareçe q̃ de
30   ve tener quinze /o veynte leguas /. por la
      qual viene vn rio y es toda poblada y labra
      da : y esta tan verde agora com̃o si fuera en casti
      lla por mayo /o por junio / puesto q̃ las no
      ches tienẽ Catorze oras y sea la tr̃ra tanto septẽ
                  ——[?] asi
35   trional /. ~~Asi~~ q̃ este puerto es mỹ bueno p[ar]a
      todos los vientos q̃ puedã ventar çerrado y hõ
nõ   do : y todo poblado de gẽte mỹ buena y mã
      sa y sin armas buenas ni malas : y puede
      qualquier navio estar sin miedo en el q̃ otros
40   navios q̃ vengã de noche a los saltear /. porq̃
      puesto q̃ la boca sea bien ancha de mas de dos
      leguas : es mỹ çerrada de dos restringas de
      piedra q̃ escasamẽte la veẽ sobre agua : saluo
      vna entrada mỹ angosta en esta restringa q̃
45   no parece sino q̃ fue hecho a mano y que de
      xarõ vna ~~puesta~~ pueʳta abierta quãto los navios

Folio 43v

      puedan entrar /. En la boca ay siete braças
      de hõdo hasta el pie de vna Isleta llana q̃ tiene
      vn playa y arboles al pie della dla p[ar]te dl
      gueste tiene la entrada y se puede llegar vna

certain persons to see him and question him about
these islands. The lord received them very well
and took them with him to his town in order to
give them certain large pieces of gold. They
reached a big river, which the Indians crossed by
swimming. The Christians could not cross[1] and
so they turned back. In all of this region
there are exceedingly high mountains that seem to
reach the heavens, for the mountain of Tenerife[2]
seems nothing in comparison with them in height
and beauty, and all of them are green and tree
covered, which is a thing of wonder. In between
the mountains there are very pretty plains, and
at the foot of this harbor, to the south, there
is a plain so large that eyes cannot see the end
of it; and without having the impediment of
mountains it appears to have an extent of 15 or
20 leagues. Through it a river comes, and it is
all inhabited and cultivated, and it is as green
now as if it were in Castile around May or June,
even though the nights are 14 hours long and the
land is so far north. Also, this harbor is very
good for all the winds that can blow, landlocked
and deep, and all populated with good and gentle
people without arms, good or bad. Any ship
whatever can stay there without fear that
other ships might come at night to attack,
because even though the mouth is quite wide,
of more than two leagues, it is very closed in
by two stone reefs which can scarcely be seen
above the water; but there is a very narrow
entrance in this reef that looks just as if it
were made by hands that left an open door big
43v   enough for ships to enter. In the mouth there
is depth of seven *brazas* as far as the foot of
a flat islet that has a beach and trees on the
edge. The way in is on the west side and a

1. (43r19–20) *No pudieron* (could not cross). We have been told that at least some
sailors could swim. Perhaps their clothing or armor would have made a crossing
difficult.
2. (43r22) *Que la de la Isla de Tenerife* (for the mountain of Tenerife). The mountain must be Teide.

5   nao sin miedo hasta ~~junto a las peñas~~ poner
    el bordo junto a la peña /. ay dlas p[ar]te del no
    rueste ay tres islas y vn grā rio a vna legua
                            es
    dl cabo deste pueᵗto /. ∧el mejor dl mūdo : puso
    le nōbre el pueᵗto dla mar de Sancto thomas
10 porq̃ ora oy su dia ~~pusole~~ dixole mar por
    su grād[e]za /.

                                    Sabado .22. de diziēbre
    ⫽ En amaneçiendo dio las velas p[ar]a yr su camino
                    Islas
    a buscar las ∧ ~~yndias~~ q̃ los yndios le dezian
15 q̃ tenian mūcho oro y de algunas q̃ tenian mas
    oro q̃ tierra /. no le hizo tp̄o y ovo de tornar
    a surgir / y enbio la barca a pescar cō la red /.

Este era guacana   El señor de aq̃lla t̄r̄ra q̃ tenia vn lugar çer
gari : el Señor   ca de alli : le enbio vna grāde Canona llena
del marien don   de gente : y en ella vn principal criado suyo
de el almiᵉ hizo   a Rogar al almiᵉ q̃ fuese cō los navios a su
la fortaleza : y de t̄r̄ra y q̃ le daria quāto tuviese /. enbiole
xo los treynta
y nueve xp̄ianos
                            traya
    cō aq̃l vn çinto q̃ en lugar de bolsa ~~tenia~~ vna
    caratula q̃ tenia dos orejas grādes de oro de mar
25 tillo : y la lengua y la nariz /. y cōmo sea
no esta gente de mūy franco coraçon q̃ quāto le
    piden dan cō la mejor volūtad dl mūdo : q̃
    les pareçe q̃ pidiendoles algo les hazen grā
    de merçed : esto dize el almiᵉ /. toparō la bar
30 ca y dierō el çinto a vn grumete : y vinie
    rō cō su canoa a bordo dla nao cō su emba
    xada /. primero q̃ los entendiese passo alguᵃ
    p[ar]te del dia : ni los yndios q̃ el traya los
    entendian bien porq̃ tienē algunas diuer
35 sidad de vocablos en nōbres dlas cosas : en
    fin acabo de entender por señas su conbi
    te /. El qual determino de partir el domīgo

ship can go without fear until it is alongside
the rocks. To the northwest there are three
islands and a large river a league from the
head of this harbor. It is the best in the
world. He gave it the name Puerto de la
Mar de Santo Thomás, because today is his
day, and he calls it a sea because of its
size.

Saturday 22 December

When it dawned he set sail to go on his route
to seek the islands that the Indians told him
had much gold, and of some that had more gold
than earth. The weather was unfavorable and
he had to anchor again. He sent the launch to
fish with a net. The lord of that region, who
had a place nearby, sent him a big canoe[1] full
of people, and in it one of his principal
retainers to beg the Admiral to come to his
land and that he would give him all that he
had. The lord sent with the retainer a belt
that in place of a purse bore a mask which had
two big ears and the tongue and nose of ham-
mered gold. And as these people are very
openhearted and give all they are asked for
with the best will in the world, it seems to
them that asking them for something does them
a great favor. The Admiral says this. They
went up next to the launch and gave the belt
to a ship's boy and came with their canoe
alongside the ship with their message. Before
he could understand them some part of the day
passed; neither could the Indians that he
brought understand them well because they have
some diversity of words for the names of
things. Finally, by signs, they understood
his invitation. The Admiral decided to leave
for that place on Sunday, although he usually

---

1. (43v19) *Canona* is an error for *canoa* (canoe), probably resulting from confusion with *caona*, Arawakan for "gold" (55v13).

p[ar]a alla / avnq̃ no solia partir de pueʳto en do
mĩgo solo por su devoçıon y no por super

esperança

40   sticion alguna : p[er]o con ∧ ~~confiança~~-[?] y dize el q̃ aq̃llos
pueblos an de ser xp̄ıãnos por la volũtad
q̃ muestran y dlos reyes de castilla : ~~qui-~~
~~so partir aq̃l dia y~~ y porq̃ los tiene ya
por suyos ~~y q̃ le an de servir~~-[?] y porq̃ le
45   sirvā con amor : les quiere y trabaja hazer todo

Folio 44r

plazer /   partiese oy enbio seys hõbres
a vna poblaçion mỹ grāde tres leguas d[e]
alli dla p[ar]te del gueste . porq̃l Señor dlla ~~ve~~-[?]
vino el dia passado al almiᶜ y dixo q̃ tenia
5   çiertos pedaços de oro /. En llegādo alla los
xp̄ıãnos tomo el señor dla mano al escrivano
dl almiᶜ q̃ era vno dllos ~~q̃ yva porq̃~~-[?]
~~los otros no~~-[?] el qual enbiava el almiᶜ p[ar]a

a los demas

q̃ no consintiese hazer ∧cosa Indevida a los yn
10   dios . porq̃ cõmo fuessen tan francos los yndios
~~los espa~~ ~~q̃ por vn cabo de agujeta~~ y los espa
ñoles tan cudiçiosos y desmedidos q̃ no les

a. y [a]vn por vn pedaço de vidr[o y]

basta q̃ por vn cabo de agujeta + y por otras cosas   b. de [escudilla]
de nonada les davan los yndios quāto que
15   riā : p[er]o avnq̃ sin dalles algo se los querriā
todo aver y tomar lo q̃l almiᶜ siempre p[ro]hibia /
~~q̃~~ y avnq̃ tãbien ~~son~~ eran mūchas cosas de poco
valor sino era el oro las q̃ davā a los xp̄ıãnos

al

p[er]o el almiᶜ mirādo ~~a su~~ franco coraçon dlos
20   yndios q̃ por seys contezuelas de vidro daria
y davan vn pedaço de oro por eso mādava
q̃ ningu^a cosa se reçibiese dllos q̃ ~~para q̃~~ no
~~con~~-[?] se les diese algo en pago /. asi q̃ tomo por

did not leave port on Sunday solely because
of his devotion and not because of any super-
stition; but with the hope,[1] he says, that
those people are destined to be Christians
because of the desire that they seem to have
and that of the sovereigns of Castile, and because the Admiral already considers the Indians as their subjects. And so that they may
serve him with love, he wants and tries to
make everything pleasant for them. [Before][2]

44r   he left today he sent six men to a very
large village three leagues from there to the
west, since the lord of the village had come
to the Admiral the day before and told him
that he had certain pieces of gold. When they
arrived the Christians took the lord by the
hand to the Admiral's *escrivano*, who was one
of those[3] whom the Admiral sent to forbid the
others to do any unjust thing to the Indians.
The Indians were so open and the Spaniards so
greedy and disorderly that it was not enough
for them that for a lace-end, and even for
bits of glass and of pottery[4] and other things
of no account, the Indians give them all they
want; but even without giving the Indians
something, the Spaniards want to have and
take everything: which the Admiral always prohibited. And also even though many things
were of little value, other things that they
gave to the Christians were of gold. But the
Admiral, seeing the openheartedness of the Indians, who for six glass beads would give and
do give a piece of gold, for that reason ordered that nothing should be received from
them without giving them something in payment.

1. (43v40) Alvar (1976) reads the canceled word as *compañía*.
2. (44r1) A space is left blank in the manuscript before *partiese*. "Before," or something of the sort, seems to be required.
3. (44r7) Alvar (1976) reads the canceled text following *vno dllos* as *porque yva porque*.
4. (44r13a–b) Bracketed letters and the entire word *escudilla* are cut off at the right margin of the manuscript facsimile. We have supplied the word and the missing letters from the Raccolta edition (Lollis, 1892–94) of the *Diario*.

la mano el Señor al escrivano y lo llevo a
25 su casa cō todo el pueblo ~~q̃ le acōpañava~~ que
                                            hizo
era mȳ grāde q̃ le acōpañava : y les ∧dar
~~dar~~ de comer : y todos los yndios les trayā
mūchas cosas de algodon labradas . y en ~~v~~ ovi
llos hilado /. despues q̃ fue tarde dioles tres
30 ansares mȳ gordas el Señor y vnos pedaçitos
de oro : y vinierō con ellos mūcho numero
de gente y les trayan todas las cosas q̃ alla
avian resgatado : y a ellos mismos por
nõ   fiavan de ~~a~~-[?] traellos a cuestas : y de hecho lo
35 hizierō por algunos rios y por algunos lu
gares lodosos /. El almiᶜ mādo dar al S[eñ]ᵒʳ.
algunas cosas : y q̄do el y todo su gente cō
grā contentamiᵒ creyendo Vrdaderamēte q̃ avian
venido dl çielo y en ver los xp̄ianos se teniā
40 por bien aventurados /. ~~llegar~~ viniero este
dia mas de çiento y veynte Canoas a los na
vios todas cargadas de gente y todos traen
algo /. espeçialmēte dsu pan y pescado y agua
en Cantarillos de barro / y simientes de mūchas
45 ~~mañas espeçias~~ simientes q̃ son buenas especias /.
echavā vn grano en vn escudilla de agua y bevenla
y dezian los yndios q̃ cōsigo traya el almiᵉ q̃ era cosa
Santissima /

Folio 44v

                                                    Domingo 23. de diziēbre
Ɨ no pudo ——[?] partir cō los navios a la tr̄r̄a
de aq̃l señor q̃ lo avia ~~conbidado y rogado~~
enbiado a rogar y cōbida[r?] por falta dl vien
5   to : p[er]o enbio con los tres mensajeros q̃ alli
esperavan las barcas con gente y al escriva
no /. entre tanto q̃ aq̃llos yvan : enbio dos
dlos yndios q̃ consigo traya : ~~a tr̄r̄a~~-[?] a las po
blaçiones q̃ estavā por alli çerca del paraje dlos
10 navios : y bolvierō con vn señor a la nao

So the lord took the hand of the *escrivano* and
led him to his [own] house with all the people
of the town, which was very large, accompany-
ing him; and he ordered them to give the Spaniards something to eat; and all the Indians
brought them many things of worked cotton and
balls of thread. Later, when it was afternoon, the lord gave them three very fat geese
and a few small pieces of gold; and a large
number of people came and carried for them
everything that they had received in trade
there; and they insisted on carrying the
Spaniards on their backs; and in fact they did
so through some rivers and muddy places. The
Admiral ordered that they give the lord some
things, and the lord and all his people, with great
contentment, truly believing that the Christians had
come from the heavens, considered themselves very
fortunate in seeing them. This day there came to
the ships more than 120 canoes, all loaded with
people, all bringing something, especially bread
and fish and water in clay jars and seeds of many
kinds that make good spices. The visitors threw a
few [of the seeds] in a bowl of water and drank it,
and the Indians that the Admiral brought with him
said that the drink [?] was a most holy thing.

44v   Sunday 23 December

For lack of wind he was unable to leave with the
ships for the land of that lord who had sent to beg
and invite him to come. But he sent the manned
launches and the *escrivano* with the three Indian
messengers who were waiting there. While
those men were traveling he sent two of the Indians
that he brought with him to the villages that were
in the vicinity of the ships' anchorage, and they
returned to the ship with a lord and with news that

tenian razon
de dezirlo

    cō nuevas q̃ en aq̃lla Isla española avia grā
    cantidad de oro : y q̃ a ella lo venian a cōprar
    de otras p[ar]tes / y dixerōle q̃ alli hallaria quā
    to quisiese /. vinierō otros q̃ confirmavā aver
15 en ella mūcho oro : y mostravāle la mar̃a
    q̃ se tenia en cogello /. todo aq̃llo entēdia
    el almi^c cō pena : p[er]o todavia teñia por çier
    to q̃ en aq̃llas p[ar]tes avia grādissima cantidad
    dello : y q̃ hallando el lugar donde se saca .
20 avia grā barato dllo y segū Imaginava q̃
    por nonada /. y torna a dezir q̃ cree
    q̃ deve aver mūcho : porq̃ en tres dias q̃
    avia q̃stava —[?] en aq̃l pue^{r}to : avia avido bue
    nos pedaços de oro y ~~cree~~-[?] no puede cre
25 er que q̃ alli lo traygā de otra tr̄r̄a /. nr̄o Señor
    q̃ tiene en las manos todas las cosas vea de
    me remediar y dar com̃o fuere su s[er]ui[ci]^o /.
    estas son palabras dl almi^c /.
    Dize q̃ aq̃lla ora cree aver venido a la nao mas
30 de mill p[er]sonas : y q̃ todas trayan algo de lo q̃
    posseen y antes q̃ lleguē a la nao con me
    dio tyro de ballesta : se levantā ~~en pie~~ en sus
    canoas en pie y tomā en las manos lo q̃ traen
    diziēdo tomad tomad /. tābien cree q̃ mas
35 de quinientos vinierō a la nao nadādo por no
    tener Canoas y estava surta çerca de vna le
    gua de tr̄r̄a /. Juzgava q̃ aviā venido çinco señores y
              señores
    hijos de ∧~~muchos~~-[?] con toda su casa ~~hijos~~-[?] muge
    res y niños a ver los xp̄ianos /. a todos mā
40 dava dar el almi^e porq̃ todo diz q̃ era bien en
    pleado / y dize : nro Señor me adereça por
    su piedad q̃ halle este oro digo su mina q̃
    hartos tengo aqui q̃ dizē q̃ la saben /. estas son

nō

    sus palabras   En la noche ~~viniero~~ llegarō

on that island of Hispaniola there was a great quantity of gold and that people came there from elsewhere to buy it and they told the Admiral that there
he would find as much as he might want. Others
came who confirmed that there was much gold on the
island, and they showed him the way they had of
collecting it. All of this the Admiral understood with
difficulty. But he still considered it certain that in
these parts there was an exceedingly great quantity of
gold and that, finding the place where it was taken
out, there would be an abundance of it and, as he
imagined, [a place] where he could get it for nothing.
And he says again that he believes that there ought to
be a lot of it, since in the three days that have passed
while he was in that harbor he has obtained good
pieces of gold, and he cannot believe that it is
brought there from another land. May Our Lord,
who has all things in His power, see to assisting me
and giving me whatever will be in His service. These
are words of the Admiral.
He says he believes more than a thousand persons to
have come to the ship at that hour, and all of them
brought something of what they possessed; and
before they reached a half crossbow shot from the
ship, they rose to their feet in their canoes and took
in their hands what they brought, saying take it,
take it. He believes also that more than five
hundred came to the ship swimming because they
had no canoes, and he was anchored nearly a
league from land. He judged that five lords
and[1] sons of lords had come with all their
households, women and children, to see the
Christians. He ordered that [something] be
given to everyone, because, he says, it was
all well spent; and, he says, may Our Lord in
His mercy guide me so that I will find this
gold, I mean the mine, since I have here so
many who say they know it. These are his
words. In the night the launches arrived and

---

1. (44v37) The phrase *cinco señores y* (five lords and) is written in the right margin, suggesting a later addition.

45 las barcas y dixerō q̃ avia grã camino hasta
donde venian : y q̃ al monte de Caribatan ha
llarō mūchas Canoas cō mỹ mūcha gente q̃
~~a ver al almiͨ~~
venian ∧ ~~de lugar donde ellos yvã a ver al a~~
a ver al almiͨ y a los xp̄iaños dl lugar donde ellos

Folio 45r

yvan / y tenia por çierto q̃ si aq̃lla fiesta de
navidad pudiera estar en aq̃l puerto vi
niera toda la gente de aq̃lla Isla q̃ ———[?]
estima ya por mayor q̃ Inglaterra / por
5 verlos /. los quales se bolvierō todos con
los xp̄iaños a la poblaçion : la qual diz que
affirmavā ser la mayor y la mas conçerta
da de Calles q̃ otra dlas passadas y halladas
hasta ~~aqui~~ alli /. la qual diz q̃ es de p[ar]te de

esta punta san   la punta Sancta al sueste quasi tres leguas [/.?]
cta no a nō   y comō las Canoas andan mūcho dl remos : fue
brado   rōse delante a hazer saber al caçique q̃llos lla
                  mavā alli /. hasta entōçes no avia podido enten
der el almiͨ si lo dizē por Rey /o por goVrnador /.
15 tanbien dizen otro nōbre por grāde q̃ llaman
Nitayno : no sabia si lo dezian por hidalgo

nitayno era   /o governador /o juez /. finalmēte el Cacique
prinçipal y se   vino a ellos : y se ayuntarō en la plaça q̃estava
ñor dspues   mỹ barrida todo el pueblo q̃ avia mas de dos
dl rey comō   hizo
grāde dl rey
no
20 mill hōbres /. Este rey ∧ —[?] mūcha honrra ~~tenia~~
a la gente dlos navios : y los populares cada vno
les traya algo de comer y de bever /. dspues
el rey dio a cada vno vnos paños de algodon
q̃ visten las mugeres y papagallos p[ar]a el almiͨ +   a. y çiertos pe
25 davā tābien los p[o]p[u]lares dlos mismos paños   b. daços de oro
y otras cosas dsus casas a los marineros por pe
queña cosa q̃ les davan /. la qual segū la re
cibian pareçia q̃ la ~~tenian y~~ estimavan por

they said that there was a big pathway as far
as the place from which they had come and
that at the mountain of Caribata they found
many canoes with a great many people who were
coming[1] to see the Admiral and the Christians
from the place to which they were going. And

45r   he believed for certain that if the Christmas
celebration could be held in that harbor all
the people of that island, which the Admiral
now judged to be larger than England, would
come to see them. All of the Indians returned
with the Christians to the village, which he
affirms to be the largest and the best arranged with streets than any other of those
passed through and found up to that time. The
town, he says, is in the direction of the
Punta Santa almost three leagues southeast,
and since the canoes go fast with oars, they
went ahead to let the cacique, as they call
him there, know. Until then the Admiral had
not been able to understand whether cacique
meant king or governor. They also use another name for an important person, whom they
call *nitayno*. He does not know if they say it
for noble, or governor, or judge. Finally the
cacique came to them and the whole town, more
than two thousand persons, gathered in the
plaza, which was very well swept. This king
was very courteous to the people from the
ships, and each of the common people brought
them something to eat and drink. Afterward
the king gave to each one some of the pieces of
cotton cloth that the women wear, and parrots for the
Admiral,[2] and certain pieces of gold. The common
people also gave the sailors some of the same
pieces of cloth, and other things from their houses,
for small things that the Spaniards gave them,
which, from the way in which they received them,

1.   (44v48)   In the canceled text of this line Alvar (1976) twice reads as *adonde*
what we have written as *a ver*.
2.   (45r24a–b)   The insert following *almirante* is boxed in the right margin of the
manuscript.

reliquias /. ya a la tarde ~~el rey los~~ [?] queriendo
30 dspedir : el rey les rogava q̃ aguardasen hasta
otro dia lo mismo todo el pueblo /. visto que de
terminavan su venida : venierō con ellos mūcho
dl camino trayēdoles a cuestas lo q̃l cacique y
los otros les avian dado hasta las barcas q̃ que
35 davā a la entrada del rio /.

lunes .24. de diziēbre

/ Antes de salido el sol levanto las anclas [con?]
el viento terral   Entre los mūchos yndios q̃
ayer avian venido a la nao q̃ les avian dado
40 señales de aver en aq̃lla Isla oro : y nōbra
do los lugares donde lo cogian : vido vno
parece q̃ mas dispuesto y ~~lleno~~ [?] afiçionado /o q̃ con
mas alegria le hablava : y halagolo rogā
dole q̃ se fuese con el a mostralle las mi
45 nas dl oro ∴ este truxo otro compañero o pariē

Folio 45v

te consigo : los quales entre los otros lugares q̃ no
bravan donde se cogia el oro dixerō ~~que~~ de çi

las minas de cibao
pango al qual ellos llamā cybao /. y alli affir
mā q̃ ay grā Cantidad de oro : y q̃l Caçique
5 trae las vanderas de oro de martillo saluo
q̃ esta mūy lexos al leste /. El almiꞓ dize aqui estas

el almirante loa mūcho los yndios
palabras a los reyes /. Crean vr̄as altezas q̃ en
el mūdo todo no puede aver mejor gente
ni mas mansa : deven tomar vr̄as altezas grā
10 de alegria porq̃ luego los harā xp̄īanos y los
avran enseñado en buenas costūbres de sus
Reynos : q̃ mas mejor gente ni tr̄r̄a puede ser
y la gente y la tr̄r̄a en tanta Cantidad q̃ yo no
se ya como lo escriva /. porq̃ yo e hablado en su
15 perlativo grado la gente y la tr̄r̄a dla juana a q̃
ellos llamā Cuba : mas ay tanta differēçia dellos
y della a esta en todo como dl dia a la noche /. ni
creo q̃ otro ninguº q̃ esto oviese visto oviese hecho
ni dixesse menos dlo q̃ yo tengo dicho y digo /.
20 q̃ es Vrdad q̃ es maravilla las cosas de aca y

seemed to be esteemed as sacred relics. Now in the afternoon, the Spaniards wishing to say goodbye, the king and the whole town begged them to stay until the next day. Seeing that they had decided to go, the Indians went with them much of the way, carrying on their backs what the cacique and the others had given them as far as the launches, which remained at the entrance to the river.

Monday 24 December

Before sunrise the Admiral raised anchor with the land breeze. Among the many Indians who had come yesterday to the ship and who had given the Span- iards indications of the existence of gold on that island and named the places where it was collected, he saw one who appeared more alert and eager, or who with more pleasure spoke to him, and the Admiral flattered him, begging him to go away with him to show him the gold mines. The Indian brought a companion or relative with him. Among the other

45v   places that they named where gold is gathered, they spoke of Cipango, which they call Cybao. And they affirm that there is great quantity of gold there and that the cacique carries banners of ham- mered gold; but that it is very far to the east. The Admiral here says these words to the sovereigns: May Your Highnesses believe that in the whole world there cannot be better or more gentle people. Your Highnesses should take much joy in that soon you will make them Christians and will have instructed them in the good customs of your realms, for neither better people nor land can there be; and the quanti- ty of people and of land [is] so large that I do not know how to write about it. Because although I have spoken in superlative degree of the people and the land of Juana, which they call Cuba, there is as much difference between the people and the land of that place and this as there is between day and night. Nor do I believe that any other man who might have seen this would have done or said less than what I have said and say. For it is true that

los pueblos grādes desta Isla española q̃ asi la
llame : y ellos le llamā bohio /. y todos de
mūy singularissimo tracto amoroso / y habla
dulçe : no com̄o los otros q̃ pareçe quādo ha
25 blan q̃ amenazan /.: y de buena estatura hō
bres y mugeres y no negros /. verdad es q̃
todos se tiñen / algunos de negros y otros de
otra color y los mas de Colorado /. he sabido q̃
lo hazē por el sol q̃ no les haga tanto mal /
30 y las casas y lugares tan hermosos y con se
ñorio en todos com̄o juez /o señor dellos : y to
dos le obedeçen q̃ es maravilla /. y todos estos
señores son de pocas palabras : y mūy lindas
costūbres : y su mādo es lo mas con hazer se
35 ñas cō la mano y luego es entēdido q̃ es
maravilla /. todas son palabras dl almiᵉ

ⱡ Quien oviere de entrar en la mar de Sancto thome
se deve meter vna buena ~~lengua~~[?] legua sobre
la boca dla entrada sobre vna I[s]leta llana q̃
40 en el medio ay q̃ le puso nōbre la amiga lle
vādo la proa en ella /. y dspues q̃ llegare a ella
con el otᵒ de vna piedra passe dla p[ar]te dl gueste
y quedele ella al leste y se llegue a ella y no
a la otra p[ar]te porq̃ viene vna restringa mȳ grā

Folio 46r

de dl gueste e avn en la mar fuera dlla ay vnas
tres baxas [:?] y esta restringa se llega a la amiga
vn tyro de lōbarda y entremedias passara y
hallara a lo mas baxo siete bracas y casgajos
5 abaxo /. y dentro hallara puerto p[ar]a todas las
naos del mūdo y q̃ esten sin amarras /. otra
restringa y baxas vienē dla p[ar]te dl leste a la d̄ha
Isla amiga y son mȳ grādes y salen en la mar
mucho y llega hasta el cabo quasi dos leguas .

things here are marvelous and so are the big towns
of this island of Hispaniola, for so I named it; and
they call it Bohío. And all the people are of singu-
larly friendly behavior; and they speak pleasantly, not
like the others who, when they speak, seem to
threaten. Men and women are of good stature and
not black. It is true that all of them paint themselves,
some with black and others with other colors, most
of them with red. I have learned that they do it
because of the sun, so it will not do them so much
harm. And the houses and villages are so pretty[1] . . .
and with rule over all of them like a judge or lord;
and all obey him so that it is a marvel. And all of
these lords are of few words and of very attractive
customs; and their commands are for the most part
carried out by hand signs so soon understood that
it is a marvel. All are the Admiral's words.

Whoever may have to enter the Sea of Santo Thomás
should put himself a good league off the mouth of
the entrance and head for a flat islet in the middle of
it, to which I gave the name La Amiga. And after you
arrive at the island, at the sight of a stone,[2] pass from
the western to the eastern side and, keeping the
island to the east, stay close to that side and not the
other, because a very large reef comes from the west,
46r and even in the sea outside the entrance there are
some three shoals; this reef approaches La Amiga to
the distance of a lombard shot and you will pass in
between and find at the shallowest part seven *brazas* and
a gravelly bottom. And inside you will find harbor
for all the ships in the world and that they can remain
there without cables. Another reef and [more] shoals
come from the east to the said island of Amiga; they
are very large and go far out to sea and reach toward
the cape almost two leagues. But it seemed that there

---

1. (45v30) Following *tan hermosos* (so pretty) there appears to be an omission
from the manuscript text.
2. (45v42) *Con el oto de una piedra* (at the sight of a stone). The *Diccionario*
(1956, under *otar* and *otear*) defines *otar* as "to notice from a high place what is below."
In the present context perhaps the meaning is "to see from the crow's nest or masthead." Others have read *oto* as *tiro* and then translate as "a stone's throw."

10   p[er]o entrellas pareçio q̃ avia entrada a tiro de dos
      lõbardas / dla amiga /. y al pie del monte ca
      ribatan dla p[ar]te dl gueste ay vn mỹ bueñ
      pueᵣto y mỹ grãde /

                                        Martes .25 de diziẽbre dia de navidad

15   ⟋ Navegãdo cõ poco viento el dia de ayer dsde la
por descuido   mar de Sc̄to thome hasta la punta Sc̄ta sobre
del marine   la qual a vna legua estuvo asi hasta passado el
ro perdio el   primer quarto q̃ serian a las once oras dla no
almiᶜ su nao   che : [a?]cordo echarse a dormir porq̃ avia dos dias

20   y vna noche q̃ no avia dormido / como fuese
      calma : el marinero q̃ ~~tenia~~ goVrnava la nao
      acordo yrse a dormir y dexo el governario [de?]
      vn moço grumete : lo q̃ mũcho siempᵣ avia
      el almiᶜ prohibido en todo el viaje : q̃ ovies[s?]e

25   viento o q̃ oviese Calma /: conviene a saber
      q̃ no ~~diesen~~[?] dexasen governar a los grume
      tes /. El almiᶜ estava seguro de bancos y
      de peñas : porq̃l Domingo quãdo enbio las bar
      cas a aq̃l rey avian passado al leste dla d̄ha

30   punta sancta bien tres leguas y media : y avia
      visto los marineros toda la Costa y los ———[?]
      baxos q̃ ay dsde la d̄ha punta Sancta al leste su
      este bien tres leguas : y vierõ por donde se podia
      passar lo q̃ todo este viaje no hizo /. quiso nr̄o S[eñ]ᵒʳ.

35   q̃ a las doze oras dla noche como avian visto a
      costar y reposar el almiᶜ y vian q̃ era Calma ~~po~~
      ~~drian~~ muerta / y la mar como en vna escudilla
      todos se acostarõ a dormir / y quedo el goVrnalle
      en la mano de aq̃l muchacho /: y las aguas q̃

40   corrian llevarõ la nao sobre vno de aq̃llos
      bancos /. los quales puesto q̃ fuesse de noche
      sonavan q̃ de vna grãde legua se ~~vierã y~~ oyerã
      y vierã : y fue sobre el tan mãsamẽte q̃ casi no se

was a passage in between, two lombard shots from La
Amiga. And at the foot of the mountain Caribata on
the western side there is a very good and very large
harbor.

Tuesday 25 December, Christmas Day

Yesterday, sailing with little wind from the Mar de
Santo Thomás toward the Punta Santa, off which at a
distance of one league they stood until the first watch
was over—which would be about the eleventh hour
of the night—the Admiral decided to go to sleep
because there had been two days and a night when he
had not slept. As there had been little wind, the sailor
who was steering the ship decided to go away to sleep
and left the tiller to a ship's boy, something the
Admiral had always strictly prohibited on the whole
voyage, whether there was wind or whether it was
calm: that is, they did not let the ship's boys steer.
The Admiral was safe from banks and rocks because
on Sunday, when he sent the launches to the king,
they had passed to the east of the said Punta Santa
quite three and a half leagues and the sailors had seen
all the coast and the[1] shoals that lie from the said
Punta Santa to the east-southeast quite three leagues;
and they saw where they could pass, which was
something he did not do in the whole voyage.[2] It
pleased Our Lord that at the twelfth hour of night
when they had seen the Admiral lie down and rest
and saw that it was dead calm and the sea as smooth
as water in a bowl, all lay down to sleep and left the
tiller in the hands of that boy; and the
currents of water carried the ship upon one of
those banks, which, even though it was at night,
could be seen, and which made a sound that from
a full league off could be heard; and the ship
went upon it so gently that it was hardly felt.

---

1.   (46r31)   Alvar (1976) reads the canceled text following *y los* as *baxos*.
2.   (46r34)   *Lo que todo este viaje no hizo* (which was something he did not do in
the whole voyage);   i.e., Columbus had not relied on information provided by the
sailors.

sentia /. El moço q̃ sintio el goVrnalle y oyo el
45   sonido dla mar dio bozes : a las quales salio el al

Folio 46v

mirā̃te : y fue tan presto q̃ avn ningu⁰ avia senti
do q̃stuviesen encallados /. luego el maestre dla
nao cuya era la guardia salio : y dixoles el
almiᵉ a el y a los otros q̃ halasen el batel q̃ tra
5   yan por popa : y tomasen vn ancla / y la
echasen por popa y el con otros mūchos saltarō
en el batel / y pensava el almiᵉ q̃ hazian lo q̃ les
avia mādado : ellos no curarō sino de huyr
a la caravela q̃ estava a barlovento media legua /.
10   la Caravela no los quiso resçibir haziendolo
virtuosamēte y por esto volvierō a la nao : p[er]o
primero fue a ella la barca dla Caravela /: quā
q̃ quiere dez[ir]   do el almiᵉ̣ vido q̃ se huyan y que era su gente
q̃ mē̃guaba [el]   y las aguas menguaban y estava ya la nao la
agua /o q̃
corria hazia   no viendo otro remedio
abaxo   15   mar de traves : ∧mā̃do cortar el mastel y alijar
dla nao todo quā̃to pudierō p[ar]a ver si podian
sacarla : y comō todavia las aguas mē̃guas
                    se
sen : no ∧pudo remediar : y tomo lado hazia la
mar traviesa puesto q̃ la mar era poca /o nada /.
20   y entonçes se abrierō los conventos y no la nao /.
El almiᵉ̣ fue a la caravela p[ar]a poner en cobro la
gente dla nao en la Caravela / y comō ventase ya
ventezillo de la tr̄r̄a /: y tanbien avn quedava
mūcho dla noche / ni suppiesen quā̃to duravan
25   los bancos : temporejo a la Corda hasta q̃ fue de
dia / y luego fue a la nao por de dentro dla re
stringa del banco /. Primero avia enbiado el ~~a~~
~~barca~~ batel a tr̄r̄a con d[ie]g⁰ de arana de cordova
alguazil dl armada / y con pero gutierrez reposte
30   ro dla casa real : a hazer saber al rey q̃ los
avia enbiado a conbidar y rogar el sabado q̃
se fuese con los navios a su puerto : el qual

The boy who felt the rudder[1] and heard the
sound of the sea cried out, at which the Ad-
46v   miral came out, and it was so quick that still
no one had sensed that they were aground. Then
the master of the ship, whose watch it was, came
out, and the Admiral told him and the others to
haul in the boat that they were pulling astern
and to take an anchor and throw it astern. And
he with many others jumped into the boat, and
the Admiral thought that they would do what he
had ordered. But they cared for nothing but to
flee to the caravel, which was upwind half a
league. The caravel, dutifully, did not want
to receive them, and for this reason they returned to the ship, but the caravel's launch got
there first. When the Admiral saw that it was
his men[2] who were fleeing, that the waters were
diminishing, and that the ship already lay
crosswise to the seas, seeing no other remedy,
he ordered the mast cut and the ship lightened
of as much as they could to see if they could
get her off; and as the waters still continued
to diminish they could not remedy matters; and
she listed toward the cross sea, although there
was little or no sea running. And then the
planking opened up, but not the ship. The Admiral went to the caravel [*Niña*] in order to put
the men from the ship in safety. And since now
a small land breeze was blowing and also because
much of the night remained, and they did not
know how far the banks extended, he jogged on
and off until it was day and then went to the
ship from inside the reef in the shoal. Previously he had sent the boat to land with Diego
de Arana of Cordova, bailiff of the fleet, and
Pero Gutiérrez, a steward of the royal household, to inform the king, who on Saturday had
sent to invite and beg him to come with the
ships to his harbor. He had his town farther

1. (46r44) *Sintio el governalle* (felt the rudder); i.e., he felt the rudder ground.
2. (46v13) Las Casas's note for this line was written in the right margin, not, as
usual, in the left margin.

tenia su ~~pueblo~~ villa adelante ~~dl dicho banco~~ [?]
obra de vna legua ~~dl dho banco~~ y media dl

d̄ho banco : el qual como lo supo dizē q̃ lloro y
enbio toda su gente dla villa cō canoas mȳ
grādes y mūchas a descargar todo lo dla nao /.
y asi se hizo y se descargo todo lo dlas Cubiertas
en mūy breve espaçio : tanto fue el grāde avia

40 miento ~~q̃~~ y diligēcia q̃ aq̃l rey dio / y el cō
su p[er]sona con hr̄os y pariētes estavā poniendo
diligençia asi en la nao como en la guarda de
lo q̃ se sacava a tr̄r̄a p[ar]a q̃ todo estuvie a mȳ buē
recaudo /. de quādo en quādo enbiava vno de

45 sus parientes al almiᵉ llorādo a lo consolar diziē
do q̃ no rescibiese pena ni enojo q̃l le daria quā
to tuviese /. Certifica el almiᵉ a los reyes que en

Folio 47r

ninguᵃ p[ar]te de Castilla tan buē recaudo en todas
las cosas se pudiera poner sin faltar vn agu
jeta /. mādolo poner todo junto con las Casas
entretanto q̃ se vaziavā algunas casas que que

5 ria dar donde se pusiese y guardase todo /. mā
do poner hōbres armados en rededor de to
do q̃ velasen toda la noche . el con todo el
pueblo lloravan : tanto [(] dize el almiᵉ) son gen
te de amor y sin codiçia y convenibles p[ar]a to

10 da cosa : q̃ certifico a vr̄as altezas q̃ en el mu

nō

do creo q̃ no ay mejor gente ni mejor tr̄r̄a /.
ellos aman a sus proximos como a si mismos :
y tienē vna habla la mas dulçe dl mūdo : y
mansa y siempre con risa /. Ellos andā des

15 nudos hōbres y mugeres como sus madres
los parierō /. mas crean vr̄as altezas q̃ entre
si tienē costūbres mūy buenas : y el Rey mūy ma
ravilloso estado de vna çierta mañana tan continē
te q̃s plazer de verlo todo : y la memoria q̃ tienē

20 y todo quierē ver y pregūtar q̃ es y p[ar]a que /.
todo esto dize asi el almiᵉ

on, about a league and a half from the said
shoal; and when he learned of it, they said that
he cried and sent all his people from the town
with many large canoes to unload everything from
the ship. And thus it was done and in a very
brief time everything from the decks was un-
loaded, so great was the care and diligence that
that king exercised. And he himself and his
brothers and relatives were as diligent [unload-
ing] the ship as in guarding what was taken to
land in order that everything would be well
cared for. From time to time he sent one of his
relatives to the Admiral, weeping, to console
him, saying that he should not be sorrowful or
annoyed because he would give him all that he
had. The Admiral assures the sovereigns that in

47r   no part of Castile could they have taken such
good care of everything, so that not a lace-end
would be missing. The king ordered it put all
together near some houses that he wished to provide, which were being emptied, where everything
might be put and kept. He placed armed men
around everything and ordered that they keep
watch all night. He and the whole town were
weeping; to such a degree, the Admiral says, are
they loving people, and without greed, and doc-
ile in everything. And I assure Your Highnesses
that I believe that in the world there are no
better people or a better land. They love their
neighbors as themselves, and they have the
sweetest speech in the world; and [they are]
gentle and are always laughing. They go about
as naked, men and women, as their mothers bore
them, but may Your Highnesses believe that among
themselves they have very good customs, and the
king [observes a] very wonderful estate in such
a dignified manner that it is a pleasure to see
everything. And the memory that they have!
They want to see everything and ask what it is
and what it is for! All of this the Admiral says.

                  rey

/ oy a salir dl sol vino el∧de aq̃lla tr̄r̄a q̃stava

en aq̃l lugar a la caravela niña donde esta

25 va el almiᵉ y quasi llorādo le dixo q̃ no tuvie

se pena q̃ el le daria quāto tenia : y q̃ avia

dado a los xp̄ıan̄os q̃stavā en tr̄r̄a dos mūy grā

des Casas y q̃ mas les daria si fuesen mene

ster : y quātas Canoas pudiesen cargar y descar

                  r

30 gar la nao y ponel̶l̶o en trra quāta gente quisiese /.

y que asi lo avia hecho ayer : sin q̃ se tomase vna

migaja de pan ni otra cosa alguna : tanto (dize el

almiᵉ) son fieles y sin cudiçia dlo ageno / a̶l̶l̶a̶

           era

y asi e̶s̶ sobre todos e̶s̶t̶e̶ aq̃l rey virtuoso /. En

35 tanto q̃ el almiᵉ estava hablando con el : vino

otra Canoa de otro lugar q̃ traya çiertos pe

daços de oro los quales queria dar por vn

Cascavel : porq̃ otra cosa tanto no deseavā com̄o

Cascaveles // Que avn no llega la Canoa a bor

40 do l̶l̶a̶m̶ quādo llamavā y mostravā los pedaços

de oro diziēdo chuq̃ chuq̃ / por Cascaveles / que

estan en puntos de se tornar locos por ellos /.

despues de aver visto esto y partiendose estas Ca

noas q̃ eran dlos otros lugares : llamarō al

45 almiᵉ y le rogarō q̃ les g̶u̶a̶r̶d̶a̶s̶e̶ mādase guar

dar vn Cascavel hasta otro dia : porq̃l traeria

Folio 47v

quatro pedacos de oro tan grandes como la mano /.

holgo el almiᵉ de o[y?]r esto [y?] despues vn marinero

         tierra

q̃ venia del̶ ∧ p̶u̶e̶b̶l̶o̶ dixo al almiᵉ q̃ era cosa de ma

ravilla las pieças de oro q̃ los xp̄ıan̄os q̃stavan

5 en tr̄r̄a resgatavan por v̶n̶a̶ a̶g̶u̶j̶e̶t̶a̶[?] nonada / por

vna agujeta davā pedaços q̃ serian mas q̶̃ de dos

castellanos : y q̃ a̶g̶o̶r̶a̶[?] entonçes no era nada : al

respeto de lo q̃ seria dende a̶d̶e̶l̶a̶n̶t̶e̶ a vn mes /. El

rey se holgo mūcho con ver al almiᵉ alegre : y en

10 tendio q̃ deseava mūcho oro : y dixole por señas

Wednesday 26 December

Today at sunrise the king of that land, who was
in that place, came to the caravel *Niña*, where
the Admiral was, and almost weeping said to him
not to be downhearted for he would give him all
that he had, and that he had given the Christians who were on land two very large houses,
and that he would give them more if there were
need, and as many canoes as could load and unload the ship and put ashore as many people as
he wished, and that he had done so yesterday
without a crumb of bread or any other thing at
all being taken; to such a degree, says the Admiral, are they faithful and without greed for
what is another's and, above all, so was that
virtuous king. While the Admiral was talking to
him, another canoe came from another place
bringing certain pieces of gold which they
wished to give for one bell, because they desired nothing else as much as bells, for the
canoe was not yet alongside when they called and
showed the pieces of gold, saying *chuq chuque*
for bells, for they are on the point of going
crazy for them. After having seen this—the
canoes from other places departing—the Indians
called to the Admiral and begged him to order
one bell kept until the next day, because they
47v   would bring four pieces of gold as large as a
hand. The Admiral rejoiced to hear this and
later a sailor who came from land told the Admiral it was a thing to marvel at, the pieces of
gold that the Christians who were ashore traded
for a trifle. For a lace-end they gave pieces
that would be more than two *castellanos*, and
that [such trade] was nothing compared to what
it would be after a month. The king rejoiced to
see the Admiral happy, and he understood that he
wanted a lot of gold; and he told him by signs

 q̃ el sabia çerca de alli adonde avia dello mȳ mū

cho en grāde sūma : y q̃stuviese de buē coraçon

que el daria quāto oro quisiese /. y dllo diz que le

dava razō y en espeçial q̃ lo avia en çipango a

15 que ellos llamavā çybao en tanto graDo q̃ ellos

no lo tienē en nada y q̃l lo traheria alli

cybao era provin
çia de la misma isla
españa donde avia
las minas mȳ ri
cas

avnq̃ tābien en aq̃lla Isla española a quien lla

mā bohio y en aq̃lla provinçia Caribata lo avia

mucho mas /. El Rey comio en la Caravela cō el al

20 mirāte : y despues salio con el en tr̄r̄a : Donde ~~le~~

hazia al almiͨ mūcha honrra : y le dio colaçion de

dos /o tres mar̃as de ajes y con camarones y ca

tenian

ça y otras viandas q̃ellos ~~tienen~~ y dsu pan q̃ llama

donde lo

van Caçabi /. ∧llevo~~lo~~ a ver vnas verduras de arbo

25 les junto a las casas : y andavā con el bien mill

~~animas~~ p[er]sonas / todos desnudos /. el Señor ya traya

camisa y guantes q̃l almiͨ le avia dado : y por los

guantes hizo mayor fiesta q̃ por cosa dlas q̃ le dio /.

En su comer ~~se mostrava bien~~ con su honestidad y her

30 mosa mar̃a de limpieza : se mostrava bien ser de li

naje /. despues de aver comido q̃ tardo buen rato

estar a la mesa : truxerō çiertas yervas con q̃ se fre

go mūcho las manos (creyo el almiͨ q̃ lo hazia p[ar]a

ablandarlas : y dierolo aguamanos /. despues ‡

a. q̃ acabarō de
b. [comer]

35 llevo ~~lo~~[?] a la playa al almiͨ y el almiͨ enbio por

vn arco turquesco y vn manojo de flechas : y

el almiͨ hizo tyrar a vn hōbre de su cōpañia q̃ sa

bia dllo : y el señor cōmo no sepa q̃ sean armas

porq̃ no las tienē ni las vsan : le pareçio grā

40 cosa /. avnq̃ diz q̃ el comienço fue sobre ————[?] ha

bla de los de Caniba q̃ellos llamā Caribes q̃ los

that he knew where, nearby, there was very much,
a great quantity of it, and to be of good heart,
that he would give him as much gold as he might
want. And, about this [gold], the Admiral says
that the king gave him a report and, in particular, [said] that there was gold in Cipango,
which they call Cybao, in such degree that they
hold it in no regard and that he would bring it
there; but also that in the island of Hispaniola, which they call Bohío, and in that province of
Caribata, there was much more of it. The king had
dinner on the caravel with the Admiral and afterward
left with him to go ashore, where they did the
Admiral much honor and gave him refreshments of
two or three kinds of yams and shrimp and game and
other foods that they had and some of their bread,
which they call cassava.[1] They took him to see some
groves of trees near the houses, and there walked with
him quite a thousand persons, all naked. The lord
was still wearing the shirt and gloves that the Admiral
had given him; and he was pleased more with the
gloves than with anything else that they gave him.
In his table manners, his urbanity, and [his]
attractive cleanliness, he quite showed himself to be
of noble lineage. After having eaten, for they spent
quite a while at table, they brought certain herbs
with which they rubbed their hands (the Admiral
thought they did it to soften them), and they gave
him water for washing his hands. After they finished
[eating],[2] the king took the Admiral to the beach,
and the Admiral sent for a Turkish bow and a handful
of arrows; and he had one of the men of his company
who was familiar with it shoot it; and to the lord,
since he did not know what weapons are, because
they do not have and do not use them, it appeared a
great thing, although he says that [at] the beginning
[there] was some talk[3] about the men of Caniba,

---

1. (47v24) *Caçabi* (cassava) can mean any one of several tropical plants with edible, starchy roots used in making bread and tapioca; also called "manioc."
2. (47v34b) The word *comer* must have been written so far in the valley between
folios that it does not appear in the facsimile. We have supplied the word from the
Raccolta edition (Lollis, 1892–94) of the *Diario*.
3. (47v40) Alvar (1976) reads the canceled text preceding *habla* as *cani*.

vienē a tomar y traen arcos y flechas sin hier
ro q̃ en todas aq̃llas tr̄r̄a no avia memoria
del y de azero ni de otro metal saluo de oro y
45   de cobre avnq̃ cobre no avia visto sino poco el al
mirāte /. El almiͨ le dixo por señas q̃ los re
yes de Castilla mādarian destruyr a los Caribes

Folio 48r

y q̃ a todos se lo[s?] mandarian traer las manos
atadas / mādo el almiͨ tyrar vna lombar
da y vna espingarda : y viendo el effecto que
su fuerça hazian y lo q̃ penetravā . quedo
5   maravillado /. y quādo su gente oyo ~~y vido~~ los
tiros cayerō todos en tr̄r̄a /. truxerō al almiͨ vna
grā Caratula q̃ tenia grādes pedaços de oro en las
orejas y en los ojos y en otras p[ar]tes : la qual le
dio con otras joyas de oro q̃l mismo rey avia
10   puesto al almiͨ en la Cabeça y al pescueço : y a
otros xp̄ianos q̃ con el estavā ~~les~~[?] dio tābien mūchas /
El almiͨ resçibio mūcho plazer y consolaçion destas
~~humanidad~~ cosas q̃ via : y se le templo el angustia
y pena q̃ avia resçibido y tenia dla p[er]dida dla nao :
15   y cognosçio q̃ nr̄o Señor avia hecho encallar alli
la nao porq̃ hiziese alli asiento /. y a esto (dize el)
vinierō tantas cosas a la mano : q̃ Vrdaderamente
no fue aq̃l desastre saluo grā ventura /. porq̃ es
çierto (dize el) q̃ si yo no encallara q̃ yo fuera
20   de largo sin surgir en este lugar /. porq̃l esta
metido aca dentro en vna grāde baya y en ella
dos /o tres restringas de baxas /. ni este viaje de
xara aqui gente : ni avnq̃ yo quisiera dexarla
no les pudiera dar ~~tal aviamēto~~ tam buē avia
25   mēto ni tantos pertrechos ni tantos mantenimi
entos ni adereços p[ar]a fortaleza /. y bien es ver
dad q̃ mūcha gente desta q̃ va aqui me avi

nō

whom they call Caribs, who come to capture them
and who carry bows and arrows without iron points,
for in all of those lands they have no knowledge of
iron or of steel or of any other metal except gold and
copper, although of copper the Admiral had seen
but little. The Admiral told him by signs that
the sovereigns of Castile would order the Caribs
destroyed, and they would order all of them to
be brought with hands tied. The Admiral ordered
a lombard and a spingard[1] to be fired, and
when the king saw the effect of their force
and what they penetrated, he was astonished.
And when his people heard the shots they all fell
to the ground. They brought the Admiral a large
mask that had large pieces of gold in the ears and
eyes and on other places. The king gave it to him
with other gold jewels that he himself had put on the
Admiral's head and neck; and to the other Christians
who were with him he also gave many things. The
Admiral received much pleasure and consolation
from these things that he saw; and the anguish and
sorrow that he had received and felt because of the
loss of the ship were tempered; and he recognized
that Our Lord had caused the ship to ground there
so that he would found a settlement there. And
for this purpose, he says, so many things came to
hand that truly it was not disaster, but great luck.
Because it is certain, he says, that if I had not
gone aground I would have passed at a distance
without anchoring at this place, because it is
located here inside a large bay, and in it [there
are] two or three reefs and shoals; nor on this
voyage would I have left people here; nor, even if
I had wished to leave them, could I have given
them such good supplies or so many tools or
so much foodstuff or equipment for a fortress.
And it is quite true that many people of
those who are here have begged me and

48r

---

1. (48r3) The *espingarda* (spingard) was a forerunner of the blunderbuss and had
a bell-mouthed bronze or iron barrel mounted on a wooden stock. It was muzzle-
loaded with balls, supported by a crutch, and fired with a slow match while being aimed
with the other hand. See, e.g., Martinez-Hidalgo (1966, 68).

an rogado y hecho rogar q̃ les quisiese dar lic[enci]ᵃ
p[ar]a quedarse /. agora tengo ordenado de ha

30 zer vna torre y fortaleza todo mȳ bien y vna

nõ grāde Cava : no porq̃ crea q̃ aya esto menester
por esta gente : porq̃ tengo por dicho / que con esta
gente q̃ yo traygo sojugaria toda esta Isla : la
qual creo q̃s mayor q̃ portugal y mas gente

35 al doblo o mas son dsnudos y sin armas y mūy
cobardes fuera de remedio /. mas es razon
q̃ se haga esta torre y se este com̄o se a destar /.
                                de
estando tan lexos ∧vr̄as altezas /. y porq̃ cognoz
can el ingenio dla gente de vr̄a altezas: y lo

40 q̃ pueden hazer porq̃ con amor y temor le obe

nõ dezcan /. y asi ternā tablas p[ar]a hazer toda la for
taleza dellas y mātenimiᵒˢ de pan y vino p[ar]a
mas de vn año y simientes p[ar]a sembrar
y la barca dla nao y vn Calafate y vn Carpin

45 tero y vn lombardero / y vn tonelero y mūchos
entrellos hōbres q̃ dsean mūcho por s[er]vi[ci]ᵒ de vr̄as
altezas y me hazer plazer de saber la mina a
donde se coge el oro /. Asi que —[?] q̃ todo es veni
do mūcho a pelo : p[ar]a q̃ se faga este comienço /. y

50 sobre todo q̃ quādo encallo la nao fue tan passo

Folio 48v

⫻ q̃ quasi no se sintio ni avia ola ni viento /. todo
                        añide
esto dize el almi͡ᵉ /. [y?] ∧alli[?] mas p[ar]a mostrar q̃
        grā ventura y
fue ∧determinada volūtad de dios q̃ la nao alli
encallase porq̃ dexase alli gente : dize q̃ si no fue

5 ra por la trayçion dl maestre y dla gente q̃ erā todos +   a. /o los mas d[e]
los [?] de palos : de no querer echar el ancla por   b. tierras
popa p[ar]a sacar la nao com̄o el almi͡ᵉ les manda
va : la nao se saluara + y asi no pudiera saber

have had others beg me to be willing to give
them license to stay. Now I have ordered them
to build a tower and a fort, all very well
constructed, and a big moat, not that I believe
it to be necessary because of these Indians,
for it is obvious that with these men that I
bring I could subdue all of this island, which
I believe is larger than Portugal and double or
more in [number of] people, since they are naked
and without arms and cowardly beyond remedy.
But it is right that this tower be made and
that it be as it should be (being so far from
Your Highnesses) in order that the Indians may
become acquainted with the skills of Your Highnesses' people and what they can do, so that
with love and fear they will obey them. And
thus they have timbers from which to build the
whole fortress, and bread and wine for more
than a year, and seeds to sow, and the ship's
launch, and a caulker, and a carpenter, and a
gunner, and a barrel maker; and many among them
[are] men who greatly desire to serve Your
Highnesses and to please me by finding out
about the mine where gold is taken. So[1]
everything has worked out opportunely for this
beginning to be made, especially since when the
ship ran aground, it was so softly that it was

48v   not felt, nor was there wave nor wind. All of
this the Admiral says. And he adds more to
show that it was great luck and the particular
will of God that the ship ran aground so that
he would leave people there. He says that if
it had not been for the treachery of the master
and of the men, all or most of whom were from
[his] region [in Spain],[2] not wanting to cast the anchor astern to get the ship off, as the Admiral
ordered them, the ship would have been saved[3]

1. (48r48) Alvar (1976) reads the canceled text following *asi que* as *para*.
2. (48v5a–b) The text of these two lines is boxed in the right margin of the manuscript.
3. (48v8) A drawn line connects the " + " following *se saluara* (would have been saved) to the right margin, indicating a note that was never written.

se la tr̄r̄a (dize el) com̃o se supo aq̃llos dias q̃ alli

10 estuvo y adelante por los q̃ alli entendia dexar .
porq̃ el yva siemp^r con inteñçion de descubrir
y no parar en parte mas de vn dia / sino era
por falta dlos vientos /. porq̃ la nao diz q̃ era
mȳ pesada y no p[ar]a el offi[ci]^o de dscubrir /. ~~y aq̃llo~~

15 ~~diz q̃~~ y llevar tal nao (diz que) causarō los de
palos q̃ no cūplierō cō el rey e la reyna lo
q̃ le avian prometido dar navios convenientes p[ar]a
aq̃lla jornada y no lo hizierō /. Concluye el almi^e
diziendo q̃ de todo lo q̃ en la nao avia no se p[er]dio vna

20 agujeta : ni tabla ni clavo / porq̃ ella quedo sana
com̃o quādo ~~salio~~ partio : saluo q̃ se corto y rajo al
go p[ar]a sacar la vasija y todas las mercaderias
y pusierōlas todas en tr̄r̄a y bien guardadas como
esta d̄ho /. y dize q̃spera en dios q̃ a la buelta q̃

            dia   via
25 el ent~~e iende~~ haze^r de Castilla : a ∧ de hallar vn
tonel de oro q̃ avrian resgatado los q̃ avia de
dexar : y q̃ avrian hallado la mina dl oro y
la espeçeria /. y aq̃llo en tanta Cantidad : q̃ los
reyes antes de tres años enprēdiesen y ade

30 reçasen p[ar]a yr a conquistar la casa Sancta : que asi
(dize el) proteste a vr̄as altezas q̃ toda la ganāçia
desta mi empresa se gastase en la Conquista de hie
rusalem y vr̄as altezas se rieron y dixeron
q̃ les plazia y que sin esto tenian aq̃lla gana /.

35 estas son palabras dl almi^e

                                      Jueves .27. de diziēbre

            el sol
✓ En saliendo∧ vino a la caravela el Rey de aq̃lla tr̄r̄a
y dixo al almi^e q̃ avia embiado por oro : y q̃ lo
queria cubrir todo de oro antes q̃ se fuesse an

40 tes le rogava q̃ no se fuese y comierō con el almi^e

and thus he would not have been able to learn
about the country, he says, as he did [during]
those days when he stayed there and [as] those
who undertook to stay will do in future, because
he always went with the intention to explore and
not to stop anywhere more than one day, if it
were not for lack of wind, because the ship, he
says, was very sluggish and not suited for the
work of exploration; and in taking such a ship,
he says, the men of Palos failed to comply with
their promise to the king and queen to provide
suitable vessels for that trip, and they did not
do it. The Admiral concludes saying that of
everything that was in the ship not even a lace-
end was lost, neither plank nor nail, because
she remained in as good condition as when she
left [Spain], except that she was cut and opened
up somewhat to get out the storage jars and all
the merchandise. And they put it all on land and
guarded it well, as has been said. And he says
that he hopes in God that on the return that he
would undertake from Castile he would find a
barrel of gold that those who were left would
have acquired by exchange; and that they would
have found the gold mine and the spicery, and
those things in such quantity that the sovereigns, before three years [are over], will undertake and prepare to go conquer the Holy Sep-
ulcher; for thus I urged Your Highnesses to
spend all the profits of this my enterprise on
the conquest of Jerusalem, and Your Highnesses
laughed and said that it would please them and
that even without this profit they had that
desire. These are the Admiral's words.

Thursday 27 December

At sunrise the king of that land came to the
caravel and told the Admiral that he had sent
for gold and that he wanted to cover everything
with gold before the Admiral went away; rather,
the king begged him not to go away. And the king

el rey e vn hr° suyo y otro su pariente mūy pri
vado : los quales dos le dixerō q̃ querian yr a
a castilla con el /. Estando en esto vinierō cõmo la Ca
ravela pinta estava en vn rio al cabo de aq̃lla Isla /

45 luego enbio el cacique alla vna Canoa + /. porq̃ ama   a. y en ell[a el]
va tanto al almi͡e q̃ era maravilla /. ya entendia el almi͡e   b. almi͡e v[n ma
co quãta priesa podia por dspacharse p[ar]a la buelta de casti   c. rinero
lla /.

Folio 49r

/ p[ar]a dar orden y priesa en el acabar de hazer la for
taleza : y en la gente q̃ en ella avia de quedar
Salio el almi͡e en tr͞ra en la barca y pareçiole q̃l

5   rey le avia visto quãdo yva en la barca . el qual
se entro presto en su casa dissimulando : y enbio
a vn su hr° q̃ resçibiese al almi͡e /. ——[?] y llevolo
a vna dlas Casas q̃ tenia dadas a la gente del almi͡e
                    era
la qual es-[?] la mayor y mejor de aq̃lla villa /. en

10 ella le tenian aparejado vn estrado de Camisas
de palma donde le hizierō asentar /. despues el hr° en
bio vn escudero suyo a dezir al rey q̃l almi͡e
estava alli cõmo q̃ el rey no sabia q̃ era venido : pue
                                        mūcha
sto q̃l almi͡e creya q̃ lo dissimulava por hazelle ∧ mas

15 honrra /. Como el escudero se lo dixo : dio el caçique
diz q̃ a correr p[ar]a el almi͡e : y pusole al pescueço vna
grã plasta de oro q̃ traya en la mano /. Estuvo alli
cō el hasta la tarde : deliberãdo lo q̃ avia de hazer

and a brother of his and another relative, a fa-
vorite, dined with the Admiral. The two told him
that they wanted to go to Castile with him. At
this point there came [certain Indians with
news[1]] that the caravel *Pinta* was at a river at
the end of that island. The cacique soon sent a
canoe there, because he was so fond of the Admiral that it was a marvel, and the Admiral sent
a sailor in it. Now the Admiral undertook with
the greatest hurry that he could manage to get
ready for the return to Castile.

49r   Friday 28 December

So as to promote order and speed in finishing the
construction of the fortress and in the people who
were to stay in it, the Admiral went ashore; and it
appeared to him that the king had seen him while he
was going in the launch, and that the king went
quickly into his house, pretending [that he had
not], and sent a man, his brother, to receive the
Admiral, and the brother [?] took him[2] to one of
the houses that the king had given to the Admiral's
men, which was the largest and best of that town. In
it they had prepared for him a dais of palm fronds
where they made him sit. Then the brother sent a
squire of his to tell the king that the Admiral was
there just as if the king did not know that he had
come, even though the Admiral believed that he
pretended this so as to do him much more honor.
When the squire told him, the cacique began to run
toward the Admiral, and he put on his neck a large
flattened piece of gold that he carried in his hand.
He remained there with him until the afternoon,
considering what should be done.

1. (48v43) The phrase "certain Indians with news," inserted after "there came"
(*vinieron*) does not appear in the manuscript. Las Casas includes it in the equivalent
passage of his *Historia* (1951, 1:284).
2. (49r7) Alvar (1976) reads the canceled text as *el a*.

Sabado .29. de diziēbre

20 / En Saliendo el Sol vino a la Caravela vn sobrino
del rey mūy moço y de buē entendimiᵒ y bue
nos hygados (com̄o dize el almiᵉ) /. y com̄o siempre
trabajase por saber adonde se cogia el oro : pregū
tava a cada vno porq̄ por señas ya entendia algo /
25 y asi aq̄l māçebo ̶q̶̶̃ le dixo q̃ a quatro jornadas
avia vna Isla al leste q̃ se llamava guarione[x?]o : y
otras q̃ se llamavā macorix / y mayonic y fuma
y Çybao y Coroay : en las quales avia Infinito
oro / los quales nōbres escrivio el almiᵉ /. y supo
30 esto q̃ ——————[?] le avia d̄ho vn h͞rᷓo del rey e riño c͞o
el segū el almiᵉ entēdio /. tābien otras vezes avia
el almiᵉ entēdido q̃ el rey trabajava porq̄ no en
tendiese donde nasçia y se cogia el oro : porq̄ no
lo fuese a resgatar /o cōprar a otra p[ar]te /. mas ̶e̶r̶a̶ es
35 tanto y en tantos lugares y en [e]sta misma Isla ̶(̶ ̶d̶i̶
̶z̶e̶ ̶e̶l̶ ̶a̶l̶m̶i̶ᵉ̶ ̶q̶̶̃ ̶)̶ española (dize el almiᵉ) q̃ es maravi
lla /. siendo ya de noche le embio el rey vna
grᷓa Caratula de oro : y enbiole a pedir vn ba
çin de aguamanos y vn jarro : creyo el almiᵉ
40 q̃ lo pedia p[ar]a mandar hazeʳ otro y asi se lo en
bio /.

[e]stas no erᷓa islas
[s]ino provinçias de
isla española

Domingo .30. de diziēbre

/ salio el almiᵉ a comer a t͞rᷓ͞a y llego a t͞p͞o q̃
avian venido çinco reyes subjectos a aq̃ste
45 q̃ se llamava guacanagari : todos con sus coro
nas representado mͮy buē estado q̃ dize el almiᵉ
a los reyes q̃ sus altezas ovierᷓa plazer de
ver la maᷓra dllos /. En llegᷓado en t͞rᷓ͞a el rey
vino a rescibir al almiᵉ y lo llevo de braços a
50 misma Casa de ayer a do tenia vn estrado y sillas

en q̃ asento al almiᵉ y luego se quito la corona

Saturday 29 December

At sunrise there came to the caravel a young nephew
of the king, of good intelligence and will (*de "buenos
hygados*," as the Admiral says). And since the Admiral
always had exerted himself to learn where gold was
collected, he questioned each person, because now,
by signs, he understood somewhat. And thus that
youth told him that at a distance of a four-day
journey there was[1] an island to the east that is called
Guarionexo, and others that are called Macorix and
Mayonic and Fuma and Cybao and Coroay, in which
there were exceedingly great quantities of gold. The
Admiral wrote down these names. And a brother of
the king learned that the youth had told him this and
reprehended him, as the Admiral understood. Other
times also the Admiral had understood that the king
strove to prevent him from knowing where the gold
originated and was gathered, so that he would not go
elsewhere to trade for or buy it. But there is so much
of it and in so many places and on this very island of
Hispaniola, the Admiral says, that it is a marvel. It
now being night, the king sent him a large mask of
gold, and asked him for a hand washbasin and a
pitcher. The Admiral believed that he asked for it
so he could order another one made, and so he sent it
to him.

Sunday 30 December

The Admiral left to dine on shore and arrived at the
time when five kings had come, all subject to the one
who is called Guacanagarí, all with their crowns
displaying their high rank (for the Admiral says
to the sovereigns that Your Highnesses would take
pleasure in seeing their behavior). The king came
to receive the Admiral as soon as he reached land
and took him by the arm to the same house as
yesterday where he had a dais and chairs in which
49v　he seated the Admiral. Next he took off the crown

---

1. (49r26)   The bracketed letters in Las Casas's note to this line are cut off in the
manuscript facsimile.

dla Cabeça y se la puso al almi^e   y el almirāte
se quito dl pesqueço un Collar de buenos ala
queques y Cuentas mūy hermosas de mūy
5   lindos colores que pareçia mūy bien en toda
parte : y se lo puso a el : y se desnudo vn Capuz
de fina grana : q̃ aq̃l dia -av- se avia vestido / y se lo
vistio : y enbio por vnos borzeguies de Color
q̃ le hizo Calçar : y le puso en el dedo vn grāde
10   anillo de plata : porq̃ avian dicho q̃ vierō vna sor
tija de plata a vn marinero y q̃ avia -n-[?] hecho mū
cho por ella /. Quedo mūy alegre y mūy con
tento / y dos de aq̃llos reyes q̃stavā con el vi
nō   nierō a donde el almi^e estava con el : y truxerō
15   al almi^e dos grādes plastas de oro cada vno la
suya /. y estando asi vino vn yndio diziēdo q̃
avia dos dias q̃ dexara la Caravela pinta
al leste en vn puerto /. tornose el almi^e a la
Caravela : y viçeynte anes capitan dlla : affirmo
ruybarbo 20   q̃ avia visto ruybarbo y q̃ lo avia en -aq̃lla trr̄a-
la Isla amiga q̃sta a la entrada dla mar de
Sancto thome q̃stava seys leguas de alli : e q̃ avia
cognosçido los ramos y rayz /. Dizen q̃l
ruybarbo echa vnos ramitos fuera de trr̄a
25   y vnos frutos q̃ pareçen moras verdes quasi :
secas y el palillo q̃sta çerca dla rayz es tan
amarillo y tan fino : com̄o la mejor color
q̃ puede ser p[ar]a pintar : y debaxo dla trr̄a
haze la rayz com̄o vna grande pera /.

30   lunes .31. de diziēbre
l aq̃ste dia se ocupo en mādar tomar agua
y leña p[ar]a la p[ar]tida a españa / por dar noticia
presto a los reyes / porq̃ enbiasē navios q̃ dscu
briesē lo q̃ quedava por dscubrir . porq̃ ya el
35   negoçio parecia tan grāde y de tanto tomo
q̃ es maravilla / dixo el almi^e /. y dize q̃ no

from his own head and put it on the Admiral's.
And the Admiral took from his own neck a collar of
fine agates and handsome beads of beautiful colors
that looked well in all its parts and put it on
the king; and he took off a cape of fine red color
that he had dressed in that day and dressed the
king in it; and he sent for some colored, high-
laced shoes and had him shod with them; and he put
on his finger a large silver ring because the
king's men had said they saw a silver ring on a
sailor and that they had done a lot to get it.
The king was very happy and content, and two of
those [other] kings who were with him came where
the Admiral was with the king and brought him two
large flattened pieces of gold, each one his own.
And at this point an Indian came, saying that two
days before he had left the caravel *Pinta* in a
harbor to the east. The Admiral returned to the
caravel [*Niña*], and Vicente Anes, its captain, affirmed that he had seen rhubarb and that there was
some on the island of Amiga, which is at the entrance to the Mar de Santo Thomás, which was six
leagues from there, and that he had recognized the
stalks and roots. They say that rhubarb[1] puts out
small stalks above ground and some fruits that
look almost like dry, green mulberries; and the
stem, which is close to the root, is as yellow and
handsome as the best possible color for painting,
and under the ground it forms a root like a big pear.

Monday 31 December

This day he was busy ordering water and wood taken
for the departure to Spain in order to give prompt
notice to the sovereigns so they would send ships
that would discover what remained to be discovered, since now the business seemed so great
and of such importance that it is a marvel, the
Admiral said. And he says that he had not wished

---

1. (49v24) *Ruybardo* (rhubarb). See Morison (1963, 141 n. 1) for the identification of this plant. It was not the plant that we call rhubarb but was mistakenly
thought to be an oriental plant used in the preparation of medicines.

quisiera p[ar]tirse hasta q̃ oviera visto toda aq̃lla
tr̄r̄a q̃ yva -hast-[?] hazia el leste y andarla toda
por la costa por saber tābien (diz q̃) el transito de

40   castilla a ella / p[ar]a traer ganados y otras cosas /.
                oviese
mas cōmo -aya- quedado con vn solo navio / no
                        a los
le pareçia razonable cosa ponerse ∧-en-[?] peligros q̃
le pudierā ocurrir descubriēdo /. y quexava
se q̃ todo aq̃l mal e inconveniente averse apar

45   tado dl la caravela pinta /.

Folio 50r

martes .1º. de enero

/ a media noche dspacho la barca q̃ fuese a la
Isleta amiga p[ar]a traer el ruybarbo /. bolvio
a bisperas cō vn serō dllo [:?] no truxerō mas

5   porq̃ no llevaro açada p[ar]a cavar / aq̃llo llevo
por muestra a los reyes / el rey de aq̃lla tr̄r̄a diz q̃
avia embiado mūchas Canoas por oro /. vino
la Canoa q̃ fue a saber dla pinta y el mari
nero y no la hallarō / dixo aq̃l marinero

10   q̃ [a?] veynte leguas de alli avian visto vn rey
q̃ traya ——[?] en la cabeça dos grādes plastas
de oro : y luego q̃ los yndios dla Canoa
le hablarō se las quito / y vido tābien mūcho
oro a otras p[er]sonas /. Creyo el almiͤ quel

15   Rey guacanagari devia de aver -hecho saber-
prohibido a todos q̃ no vendiesen oro a los
xp̄ianos : porq̃ passasse todo por su mano /.
mas el avia sabido los lugares cōmo dixo
antier donde lo -ay- avia en tanta cantidad q̃

20   no lo tenian en preçio /. tābien la especeria
q̃ comē (dize el almiͤ) es mūcha y mas vale
q̃ pimienta y manegueta /. dexava encomēda
dos a los q̃ alli queria dexar q̃ ——[?] oviesen
quāta pudiesen /.

to leave until he had seen all of the land that
goes to the east and had run along the whole coast
in order to know its distance from Castile so as
to bring livestock and other things; but since
he had been left with one single ship it did not seem
reasonable to him to expose himself to the dangers
that might happen to him exploring. And he
complained that all that evil and hindrance came
from[1] the caravel *Pinta*'s having left him.

50r   Tuesday 1 January

At midnight he dispatched the launch to go to the
islet of Amiga in order to bring the rhubarb. It
returned at vespers with a pannier of it. They did
not bring more because they did not take a spade to
dig. That [basketful] they took to the sovereigns as a
sample. The king of that land said he had sent many
canoes for gold. The canoe came that went to learn
about the *Pinta*, and the sailor, and they did not find
her. The sailor said that 20 leagues from there they
had seen a king who wore on his head two large
flattened pieces of gold, and that as soon as the
Indians of the canoe spoke to him, he took them
off. And he also saw much gold on other persons.
The Admiral believed that King Guacanagarí must
have prohibited everyone from selling gold to the
Christians so all of it should pass through his hands.
But the Admiral had learned about the places, as he
said the day before yesterday, where it existed in such
quantity that they did not value it. Also the spices
that they eat, says the Admiral, are many and are
worth more than black and Malegueta pepper.[2] He
charged those who wished to remain there to get as
much as they could.

1. (49v44) "Came from." This translates a conjectural *provenía de* not in the manuscript but necessary to complete the sense of Columbus's statement. Alvar's edition (1976) includes the phrase, and in a note Alvar says that it is an addition by modern editors.

2. (50r22) *Pimienta* is pepper, one of the spices imported to Europe from India during the Middle Ages. There appears to be some doubt whether *manegueta* is the pepper from Guinea or the fruit of the *amomo*, a plant related to ginger. See Alvar (1976, 2:185, n. 370) and Morison (1963, 142 n. 2).

25   miercoles .2. de enero

/ Salio de mañana en tr̄r̄a p[ar]a se despedir dl
rey guacanagari e partirse en el nōbre del
Señor e diole vna camisa suya /. y mostrole
la fuerca q̃ tenian y effecto q̃ haziā las lōbardas /.
30   por lo qual mādo armar vna y tyrar al costado
dla nao q̃ estava en tr̄r̄a / porq̃ vino a proposito
de platica[r] sobre los caribes con quien tienē guer
ra /. y vido hasta donde llego la lombarda y cōmo
passo ~~la nao~~ [?] el costado dla nao y fue mūy lexos
35   la piedra por la mar /. hizo hazeʳ tābien vn
escaramuça con la gente dlos navios armada
diziendo al caçique q̃ no oviese miedo a los Cari
bes avnq̃ viniesen /. todo esto diz q̃ hizo el almiᵉ
porq̃ tuviese por amigos a los xp̄ıāos q̃ —[?] dexa
40   va : y por ponerle miedo q̃ los temiese /.
llevolo el almiᵉ a comer consigo a la casa don
de estava aposentado y a los otros q̃ yvā con el /.
~~mostro~~ [?] encomēdole mūcho el almiᵉ a diego de
arana / y a p[er]o gutierrez / y a Rodrigo escobedo
45   q̃ dexava juntamēte por sus tenientes de a

Folio 50v

de aq̃lla gente q̃ alli dexava porq̃ todo fuese
bien regido y goVrnado a s[er]ui[ci]º de dios y de sus
altezas /. mostro mucho amor el caçique al
almiᵉ y grā sentimiº en su p[ar]tida mayor
5   mēte quādo lo vido yr a embarcarse /.
dixo al almiᵉ vn privado de aq̃l rey q̃ avia
mādado hazer vn estatua de oro puro tan
grāde cōmo el mismo almiᵉ y q̃ de desde
a diez dias / la avian de traer /. Enbarco
10   se el almiᵉ cō proposito de se p[ar]tir luego
mas el viento no le dio lugar /.

/ Dexo en aq̃lla Isla española q̃ los yndios diz que
llamavā bohio ~~y~~ treynta y nueve hōbres con
la fortaleza y diz q̃ mūcho amigos ~~de los~~ [?] de aq̃l
15   rey guacanagari e sobre aq̃llos por sus tenien
tes a diego de arana natural de cordova : y a
pero gutierrez repostero ~~del rey~~ de estrado del

Wednesday 2 January

In the morning he went ashore to say goodbye to
King Guacanagarí and to depart in the name of the
Lord; and the Admiral gave him one of his shirts.
And he showed the king the force of the lombards
and the effect they produced by ordering one to be
loaded and fired at the side of the ship that was
aground, because he came purposely to talk about the
Caribs, with whom the Indians were at war. And the
king saw how far the lombard reached and how the
stone passed through the side of the ship and went
very far over the sea. He also ordered a skirmish
between the armed men of the vessels [and the men
remaining behind], telling the cacique not to fear the
Caribs even if they were to come. All of this the
Admiral says he did so the cacique would consider as
friends the Christians that he was leaving and, by
making him afraid, make him fear them. The Admiral
took the cacique and the others who were with him
to the house where he was lodged to eat with him.
The Admiral greatly commended to him Diego de
Arana, Pero Gutiérrez, and Rodrigo Descobedo,
whom he left jointly as his lieutenants over the men
50v   he was leaving there so that everything would be well
managed and governed to the good service of God
and of their Highnesses. The cacique showed much
love for the Admiral and great feeling over his departure [and] even more when he saw him go to embark.
An Indian intimate with the king told the Admiral
that the king had ordered a statue made of him, of
pure gold, as large as the Admiral himself, and
that they were to bring it in ten days. The
Admiral embarked with the intention of leaving
soon, but the wind did not give him opportunity.

On that island of Hispaniola, which the Indians,
he says, called Bohío, he left 39 men with the
fort and, he says, many friends of that King
Guacanagarí and, over them, as his lieutenants,
Diego de Arana, a native of Cordova, and Pero
Gutiérrez, steward of the king's dais and a

rey criado dl despensero mayor : e a Rodrigo
descobedo natural de segovia sobrino de fray
20   Rodrigo perez con todos sus poderes q̃ de los
reyes tenia /. dexoles todas las mercaderias
q̃ los reyes ~~avian~~ mādarō comprar p[ar]a los
resgates q̃ eran mūchas : p[ar]a q̃ las trocasen
y resgatasen por oro con todo lo q̃ traya la
25   nao /. Dexoles tambien pan vizcocho p[ar]a
vn año y vino y mūcha artilleria : y la
barca dla nao p[ar]a q̃ ellos cōmo marineros q̃
erā los mas fuesen quādo viessen q̃ convenia
a dscubrir la mina dl oro : porq̃ a la buelta
30   q̃ bolviese el almiᵉ hallase mūcho oro : y lu
gar donde ~~pudiese~~ se assentasse vna villa
porq̃ aq̃l no era puerto a su volūtad /. ma
yormēte q̃l oro q̃ alli trayan venia diz que
dl leste : y quāto mas fuesen al leste tanto esta
35   van çercanos despaña /. ~~del~~ [?] dexoles tanbiē
simientes p[ar]a sembrar : y sus officiales escri
vano y alguazil : y entre aq̃llos vn carpin
tero de naos y calafate / y vn buē lombarde
ro q̃ sabe bien de ingenios y vn tonelero
40   y vn phisico / y vn sastre y todos diz q̃ hō
bres dla mar /.

Jueves .3. de enero

⚡ no partio oy porq̃ anoche diz q̃ vinieron
tres dlos yndios q̃ ——————[?] traya dlas
45   Islas q̃ se avian quedado : y dixerōle q̃ los
otros y sus mugeres vernian al salir del Sol /.
                                                 la mar .

Folio 51r

la mar tābien fue algo alterada ~~por~~ [?] y no pudo
la barca estar en tr̄r̄a determino partir maña
na mediante la gracia de dios /. dixo q̃ si el
tuviera consigo la caravela pinta   tuviera por
5   çierto de llevar vn tonel de oro porque osara

servant of the chief steward, and Rodrigo Descobedo, a native of Segovia and nephew of Fray
Rodrigo Pérez, with all of the powers that he
had received from the sovereigns. He left them
all of the goods that the sovereigns ordered
purchased for barter, which were many, in order
that they might exchange and trade for gold
everything the ship brought. He also left them
biscuit for a year, and wine, and much artillery, and the ship's launch, in order that they,
since they were sailors (which most of them
were) would go, when they saw that it was a
suitable time, to look for the gold mine so
that, when he returned, the Admiral might find
much gold, and [to look for] a place where a
town could be founded, because the harbor where
they were was not to his liking, even more so because the gold they would bring there would come
from the east; and the more they went to the
east the closer they would be to Spain. He also
left them seeds to sow and his officials, the
escrivano and the bailiff, and among them a
ship's carpenter and a caulker and a good lom-
bardier who knew about machinery, and a barrel
maker and a physician and a tailor: all, he says,
men of the sea.

Thursday 3 January

He did not depart today because last night, he
says, three of those Indians that he was bringing[1] from the islands and who had remained [on
board?] came and told him that the others and
their women would come at sunrise.[2] Also, since
51r   the sea was somewhat rough and the ship's
launch could not get to shore, he decided to
depart tomorrow, by the grace of God. He said
that if he had the caravel *Pinta* with him, he
thought he would be sure to bring a barrel of

1. (50v44) Alvar (1976) reads the canceled text preceding *traya* as *solamente* (?)
(Alvar's question mark).
2. (50v46) The phrase *la mar*, just below *salir del Sol* (sunrise) is a catchword.

seguir las costas destas Islas : lo q̃ no osa
va hazer por ser solo . porq̃ no le acaeçiese algū
Inconveniente /. y se impidiese su ——[?] buelta
a castilla y la notiçia q̃ devia dar a los reyes

10   de todas las cosas q̃ avia hallado /. y si fuera
çierto q̃ la Caravela pinta llegara a saluamēto
en españa con aq̃l martin aloso pincon : dixo
q̃ no dexara de hazer lo q̃ deseava /. pero
porq̃ no sabia del : y porq̃ ya q̃ vaya podra

15   Informar a los reyes de mētiras porq̃ no le
~~den~~-[?] māden dar la pena q̃ el mereçia como
~~a~~ quiē tanto mal avia hecho y hazia en aver
se ydo sin liçençia y estorvar los bienes que
pudierā hazerse y saberse de aq̃lla vez dize

va

20   el almi͡e : confia ∧ q̃ nr̄o Señor le daria buen tp̄o
y se podra remediar todo /.

viernes .4. de enero

/ Saliendo el Sol levanto las anclas con poco
viento cō la barca por proa el camino del

[ll]amo la villa
[d]la navidad
[y?] [l]a fortaleza —[?] y   norueste p[ar]a salir fuera dla restringa por
[e]l asiento q̃ a   otra Canal mas ancha dla q̃ entro /. la qual
[ll]i hizo porq̃ lle   y otras son mȳ buenas p[ar]a yr por dlante dla
[go] alli dia dla   villa dla navidad /. ~~que asi nōbro la fortale-~~
[n]avidad como   ~~za y pueblo q̃ alli quiso começar a hazer~~
[p]areçe por lo [de]
arriba

30   ~~porq̃ como se vido arriba alli llego~~
y por todo aq̃llo el mas baxo fondo q̃ hallo
fuerō tres braças hasta ~~ocho~~ nueve y estas
dos van de norueste al sueste segū aq̃llas
restringas erā grādes q̃ durā dsde el cabo

35   Sancto hasta el cabo de sierpe q̃ son mas de
seys leguas y fuera en la mar bien tres
y sobre el cabo sancto bien tres y sobre el cabo
Sancto a vna legua no ay mas de ocho braças
de fondo / y dentro dl d̄ho Cabo dla p[ar]te del leste

gold because then he would risk following the
coasts of these islands, something he did not
dare to do being alone, [for fear that] some
obstacle would arise and prevent his return to
Castile with the report that he should give to
the sovereigns about all the things that he
had found.   And if it were certain that the
caravel *Pinta* would arrive safely in Spain
with that Martín Alonso Pinzón, he would not
give up doing what he wanted to; but because
he does not know about Pinzón, and because now
that he may be on his way, he will be able to
inform the sovereigns with lies so they will
not order him to be given the punishment that
he would deserve as someone who had done
and was doing so much evil, having gone
off without permission and hindering the valuable things that could have been done and
learned during that time, the Admiral says.
He trusted that Our Lord would give him good
weather and that everything can be put aright.

                                                                    Friday 4 January

At sunrise he raised the anchors [and], with
little wind[1] and the ship's launch going
ahead, he took a northwest course in order to
get outside the reef through a channel wider
than that by which he entered.   It and others
are very good for arriving off the town of
Navidad, and in all of that vicinity the shallowest bottom that he found was three *brazas*,
and up to nine; and these two [channels] go
from northwest to southeast, like the reefs,
which were large and which last from the Cabo
Santo up to the Cabo de Sierpe, which is more
than six leagues, and out to sea a good three;
and off the Cabo Santo at a league's distance
there is no more than eight *brazas* depth.   And
within the said cape on the east side there

---

1.   (51r24)   The bracketed letters in Las Casas's note to this line are cut off in the
manuscript facsimile.

40 ay mūchos baxos y Canales p[ar]a entrar por ellos
y toda aq̃lla Costa se corre norueste sueste y es
toda playa y la t̄r̄ra mūy llana hasta bien qua
tro leguas la t̄r̄ra adentro /. despues ay mon
tañas mūy altas y es toda mūy poblada
45 de poblaçiones grādes y buena gente segun
se mostravan con los xp̄īāños/.   Navego asi al

Folio 51v

leste camino de vn mōte mūy alto q̃ quiere pa
reçer Isla p[er]o no lo es porq̃ tiene p[ar]ticipaçion con
t̄r̄ra mūy baxa (el qual tiene forma de vn alfaneque
mȳ hermoso al qual puso nōbre monte xp̄o /.
de
5   el qual esta justamēte al este ∧‑esta‑ el Cabo Santo y avra
diez y ocho leguas /. aq̃l dia por ser el ‑dia‑[?] viento mȳ
poco no pudo llegar al mōte xp̄o con seys le
guas /. hallo quatro isletas de arena mūy baxas
cō vna restringa q̃ salia mūcho al norueste y
10 andava mūcho al sueste /. dentro ay vn grāde
golpho q̃ va dsde el d̄ho mōte al sueste bien veyn
te leguas el qual deve ser todo de poco fondo y
mūchos bancos /. y dentro del en toda la costa mū
chos Rios no navegables avñq̃ aq̃l marine
15 ro q̃l almiᶜ enbio cō la Canoa a saber nuevas
dla pinta : dixo q̃ vido vn rio en el qual po
dian entrar naos /. surgio por alli el almiᶜ +   a. seys leguas
en diez y nueve braças dando la buelta a la   b. [del] mote c[hristo]
‑la‑ mar por a[pa]rtarse de mūchos baxos y restrin
20 ga q̃ por alli avia : donde estuvo aq̃lla noche /.
Da el almiᵉ aviso : q̃ el q̃ oviere de yr a la vil
la dla navidad q̃ cognosciere a mōte xp̄o
deve meterse en la mar dos leguas etc̃.
: p[er]o porq̃ ya se sabe la t̄r̄ra y mas por alli no
25 se pone aqui /. Concluye q̃ çipango estava
en aq̃lla Isla . y q̃ ay mūcho oro y espeçeria
y almaçiga y ruybar‑[?]bo /.

are many shoals and channels for getting
through them. And all of that coast runs
northwest-southeast and is all beach. And the
land is very flat as far as a good four
leagues inland. Beyond, there are very high
mountains and it is all settled with big villages and good people, as they showed themselves [to be] with the Christians. So he

51v   sailed east toward a very high mountain which
almost seems to be an island, since it is con-
nected to very low land, but is not. It has the
shape of a handsome Moorish tent. He named it
Monte Christo. It is due east of the Cabo Santo
and is about 18 leagues distant. That day, because of little wind, he could not get within
six leagues of Monte Christo. He found four very
low sand islets with a reef that projected far
to the northwest and ran far to the southeast.
Inside [the reef] there is a large gulf which
goes from the said mountain a good 20 leagues to
the southeast. The gulf is probably all of little depth and many shoals. And inside [the
gulf?] on all of the coast there are many innav-
igable rivers, although the sailor whom the Admiral sent with the canoe to get news of the
Pinta said that he saw a river into which ships
could enter. The Admiral anchored in that
vicinity, six leagues from Monte Christo,[1] in
19 *brazas*, taking a course out to sea so as to
stay away from the many shoals and reefs that
were around. He stayed there that night. The
Admiral gives advice that he who is to go to
the town of Navidad should identify Monte
Christo and stand out to sea two leagues, etc.
(But because this land and more thereabouts is
known already, the notice is not put down
here.) He concludes that Cipango was on that
island; and that there is much gold and
spicery and mastic and rhubarb.

---

1. (51v17a–b) This insert is boxed in the right margin. The bracketed letters in
line 51v17b are cut off in the manuscript facsimile.

Sabado 5. de enero

~~Salido el sol dio la vela~~

30   ⅃ Quãdo el sol queria salir dio la vela con el
terral / despues vento leste : y vido q̃ dla p[ar]te
del susueste dl mõte xp̄o entre el y vna Isle
ta pareçia ser buē puerto p[ar]a surgir esta
noche : y tomo el camino al lessueste y
35   despues al sursueste bien seys leguas a
çerca dl monte y hallo ————[?]-~~dhas seys~~
andadas la seys leguas diez y siete braças
de hõdo y m̃y limpio y anduvo asi tres le
guas cõ el mismo fondo /. dspues abaxo a
40   doze braças hasta el morro dl mõte : y sobre
el morro dl mõte a vna legua hallo nueve
y limpio todo arena menuda /. siguio asi el
camino hasta q̃ entro entre el mõte y la Isle
ta adonde hallo tres braças y media de fondo
45   con baxa mar m̃y singular puerto adon
de surgio /. fue cõ la barca a la Isleta ~~y~~ donde
hallo huego y rastro q̃ avian estado alli pesca
dores /. vido alli mũchas piedras pintada de
colores /o cantera de piedras tales de labores

Folio 52r

           naturales
           ~~p[ar]a~~-[?] m̃y hermosas diz q̃ p[ar]a edifiçios de igle
           sia /o de otras obras reales comõ las q̃ hallo
           en la Isleta de Sant saluador /. hall[o?] tābien
           en esta Isleta mũchos pies de almaçiga /. Este

dize Vrdad q̃   mõte xp̄o diz q̃ es m̃y hermoso y alto y anda
por mar y   ble de m̃y linda hechura : y toda la t̃r̃a çerca
por t̃r̃a pare   del es baxa mũy linda Campiña : y el queda
çe isla comõ   asi alto q̃ viendolo de lexos pareçe Isla q̃ no comu
vn mõton de   nique con alguᵃ t̃r̃a /. despues dl d̃ho mõte
trigo
10   al leste vido vn cabo a xxiiiiº millas ——[?] al qual
llamo Cabo dl bezerro desdel qual hasta el d̃ho mo
te : passa en la mar bien dos leguas vnas res
tringas de baxos avnq̃ le pareçio q̃ avia en
trellas Canales p[ar]a poder entrar p[er]o conviene
15   q̃ sea de dia / y vaya soldando cõ las barca prime
ro /. desdel d̃ho mõte al leste hazia el cabo del

Saturday 5 January

When the sun was about to rise he set sail
with the land breeze. Later it blew east, and
he saw that south-southeast of Monte Christo,
between it and an islet, there appeared to be
a good harbor for anchoring this night; and he
took a course to the east-southeast, and later
to the south-southeast, a good six leagues
closer to the mountain and found, having gone
the six leagues, a depth of 17 *brazas* and a very
clean bottom. And he went thus three [more]
leagues with the same bottom. Later, nearer the
mass of the mountain, the depth diminished to 12
brazas, and a league from it he found nine,
and a clean bottom, all fine sand. He continued
on this route until he went between the mountain and the islet, where he found a depth of
three and a half *brazas* at low tide and an excellent harbor, where he anchored. He went with
the launch to the islet, where he found fire and
signs that fishermen had been there. He saw
there many colored stones or a quarry of such
stones, the work of nature: very handsome,

52r   he says, for church buildings or for other
royal works, like those stones that he found
on the islet of San Salvador. He also found
on this islet many stalks of mastic. This
Monte Christo, he says, is very beautiful and
high and traversable and of very handsome
shape. And all the land near it is low and
very pretty cultivated fields. And it seems
high, because from afar it appears to be an
island that does not communicate with any
other land. Beyond the said mountain 24 miles
to the east he saw a cape, which he named Cabo
del Becerro, from which, as far as the said
mountain, he passed in the sea a good two
leagues of reefs and shoals, although it appeared to him that there were among them channels through which one can enter, it is advisable that it be by day and with the launch going
first, sounding. From the said mountain to the

bezerro las quatro leguas : es todo playa y tr̄r̄a mȳ
baxa y hermosa y lo otro es todo tr̄r̄a mȳ alta
y grādes mōtañas labradas y hermosas y
20 dentro dla tr̄r̄a va vna sierra de nordeste
al sueste la mas hermosa q̃ avia visto q̃ pa
reçe propria com̄o la sierra de cordova /. pare
çen tābien mȳ lexos otras mōtañas mȳ
altas hazia el sur y dl sueste : y mūy grādes
25 valles y mūy verdes y mūy hermosos y mūy
mūchos rios de agua : todo esto en tanta canti
dad apazible q̃ no creya encareçerlo la milles
sima p[ar]te /. despues vido al leste dl d̄ho mō
te vna tr̄r̄a q̃ pareçia otro mōte asi com̄o aq̃l
30 de xp̄o ~y~ en grādeza y hermosura /. y den
de a la quarta dl leste al nordeste : es tr̄r̄a no
tan alta y avria bien çien millas /o çerca /

Domīgo .6. de enero

/ Aq̃l puerto es abrigado de todos los vientos
Saluo de norte y norueste y dize q̃ poco

*no avia expe
rimētado la
yra destos dos
vientos*

reynā por aq̃lla tr̄r̄a : y avn destos se pudē
guareçer detras dla Isleta /. tiene tres hasta
quatro braças /. salido el sol dio la vela
por yr la costa delante la qual toda corria al
40 leste /. saluo q̃ es menester dar reguardo
a mūchas restringas de piedra y arena q̃
ay en la d̄ha Costa : Vrdad es q̃ dentro dllas
ay buenos puertos y buenas entradas
por sus Canales /. despues de medio dia
45 vento leste rezio : y mādo subir a vn marine
ro al topo dl mastel p[ar]a mirar los baxos :

*viero la carave
la pinta*

y vido venir la caravela pinta con leste a popa /

Folio 52v

y llego al almiᵉ y porq̃ no avia donde surgir
por ser baxo bolviose el almiᵉ al mōte xp̄ī a desandar
diez leguas atras q̃ avia andado / y la pinta con

east, toward the Cabo del Becerro, for four
leagues it is all beach and low and beautiful
land, and the other part is all very high land
and big mountains, cultivated and handsome; and
inland a mountain range goes from northeast to
southeast,[1] the most handsome he had seen, for
it looked just like the sierra of Cordova.
Also, very far off toward the south and from the
southeast, other very high mountains appeared,
and very large valleys, very green and handsome,
and a great many rivers, all of this so agreeable that he did not think he was exaggerating
by a thousandth part. Later he saw to the east
of the said mountain some land where there appeared another mountain like that of Christo
in size and beauty. And beyond, to the northeast by east, there is land not so high, and
there must have been quite a hundred miles of
it or thereabouts.

Sunday 6 January

That harbor is sheltered from all winds except
the north and northwest, and he says they prevail
but little in that land, and even from these one
can take refuge behind the islet. It has from
three to four *brazas* in depth. At sunrise he set
sail to go further along the coast, which all ran
to the east. But it is necessary to be on the
watch for the many reefs of stone and sand that
there are on this coast, although it is true that
behind the reefs there are good harbors and good
ways in through the channels. After midday the
wind blew strongly east. He ordered a sailor to
climb to the masthead to watch for shoals; and he
saw the caravel *Pinta* coming with the east wind
52v   astern. She came up to the Admiral and because
there was no place to anchor, since it was shoal,
the Admiral returned to Monte Christo, backtrack-
ing ten leagues that he had already traversed,

1. (52r21) *Sueste* (southeast) is possibly a copying error for *sudueste*, "southwest."

el /. ~~como~~ ———[?] vino martin alonso pin

5   çon a la Caravela ~~dl almiᵉ~~ niña donde yva el al
mirāte a se escusar diziendo q̄ se avia p[ar]tido dl
cōtra su volūtad dando razones p[ar]a ello / p[er]o
el almiᵉ dize q̄ erā falsas todas y q̄ con mūcha
sobervia y cudiçia se avia ap[ar]tado aq̄lla noche

10   q̄ se aparto dl /. y q̄ no sabia (dize el almiᵉ) de
donde le oviese venido las sobervias y deshonesti
dad q̄ avia vsado con el aq̄l viaje /. las quales
quiso el almiᵉ dissimular : por no dar lugar a las
malas obras de Sathanas q̄ deseava impedir aq̄l

15   viaje comō hasta entōçes avia hecho /. sino q̄ por
dicho de vn yndio dlos q̄l almiᵉ le avia encomē
dado cō otros q̄ lleva en su caravela : el qual le
avia đho q̄ en vna Isla q̄ se llamava baneque
avia mūcho oro : y comō tenia el navio

20   sotil y ligero se quiso ap[ar]tar y yr por si
dexādo al almiᵉ /. p[er]o el almiᵉ quisose de
tener y costear la Isla joana y la española
pues todo era vn camino dl leste /. despues q̄
martin alonso fue a la Isla baneque diz q̄ y

25   no hallo nada de oro : se vino a la costa dla
española : por informaçion de otros yndios q̄ le
dixerō aver en aq̄lla isla española q̄ los yndios
llamavā bohio mūcha Cantidad de oro y mūchas
minas : y por esta causa llego çerca dla villa dla na
                          quinze
30   vidad obra de ∧~~veynte~~ leguas y avia entonçes mas
de veynte dias : por lo qual pareçe q̄ fuerō Vrdad
las nuevas q̄ los yndios davan por las qua
les ——[?] enbio el rey guacanagari la Canoa y
el almiᵉ el marinero / y devia de ser yda quā

35   do la Canoa llego /. y dize aqui el almiᵉ q̄
resgato la caravela mūcho oro q̄ por vn cabo
de agujeta le davan buenos pedaços de oro del
tamaño de dos dedos y a vezes comō la mano : y

and the *Pinta* with him. Martín Alonso Pinzón
came[1] to the caravel *Niña*, in which the Admiral
was traveling, to excuse himself, saying that he
had departed from him against his will, giving
reasons for it. But the Admiral says they were
all false and that with much arrogance and greed
he had left that night when he departed from him;
and that he did not know, says the Admiral,
whence had come the arrogant behavior and dis-
honesty with which Martín Alonso treated him on
the voyage. The Admiral wished to conceal [these
thoughts] so as not to give an opening to the
evil works of Satan, who desired to impede that
voyage, as up to then he had done. But, by word
of an Indian of those whom the Admiral had
entrusted to Martín Alonso with others whom he
took on his caravel, Martín Alonso had been told
that on an island which was called Baneque there
was much gold. And since he had the [more] lively
and swifter vessel, he wished to depart and go by
himself, leaving the Admiral.   But the Admiral
wished to delay and to coast the islands of Juana
and Hispaniola since it was all on a single route
east. After Martín Alonso went to the island Baneque, he says, and found no gold at all, he came
to the coast of Hispaniola because of information
from other Indians who told him that on that island of Hispaniola, which the Indians call Bohío,
there is a large quantity of gold and many mines.
And for this reason he arrived at a place about
15 leagues from the town of Navidad, and that was
more than 20 days ago. Because of this it appears
that the news the Indians gave [of sighting the *Pinta*]
was true, and because of which [news] the king,
Guacanagarí, sent the canoe, and the Admiral, the
sailor; and that Martín Alonso must have been gone
when the canoe arrived. And the Admiral says here
that the caravel traded for much gold, since for a
lace-end they gave good pieces of gold the size of two
fingers and at times as big as a hand, and that Martín

---

1.   (52v4) Alvar (1976) reads the canceled text preceding *vino* as *commo compare-
ciese con.*

llevava —[?] el martin alõso la mitad y la otra
40 mitad se rep[ar]tia por la gente /. Añide el almi^e
~~q̃ cree~~-[?] diziẽdo a los reyes : asi que Señores p^rncipes
q̃ yo cognozco q̃ milagrosamẽte mãdo quedar
alli aq̃lla nao nr̄o Señor / porq̃s el mejor lu
gar de toda la Isla p[ar]a haze^r el assiento y
45 mas açerca dlas minas dl oro /. tãbien diz q̃
supo q̃ detras dla Isla joana dla p[ar]te del sur

dize Vrdad p[er]o es ay otra Isla grãde en q̃ ay mũy mayor Canti
tr̄r̄a firme no isla dad de oro q̃ en esta en tanto grado q̃ cogian los

Folio 53r

pedaços mayores q̃ havas y en la Isla española
y avn comõ vna se cogian los pedaços de oro ~~q̃~~ dlas minas co
grã hogaça de pã m̄o granos de trigo / llamavase diz q̃ aq̃lla
de alcala /o comõ Isla yamaye /. tãbien diz q̃ supo el almi^e
vn quartal de va q̃ alli hazia el ~~gueste~~ leste avia vna Isla a
lladolid se hallo donde no avia sino solas mugeres : y esto diz q̃
grano de oro en la de mũchas p[er]sonas lo sabia /. y q̃ aq̃lla Isla espa
española . e yo lo ñola /o la otra ysla yamaye estava çerca de tr̄r̄a
vi. y otros mũc firme diez jornadas de Canoa q̃ podia ser se
chos de libra y
de dos y de tres y senta /o setenta leguas y q̃ era la gẽte vestida alli /
de ocho libras se
hallarõ en la espa
ñola 10

lunes .7. de enero

/ Este dia hizo tomar vna agua q̃ hazia la cara
vela : calafetalla : y fuerõ los marineros en
tr̄r̄a a traer leña y diz q̃ hallarõ mũchos alma
15 çigos y lignaloe /.

martes .8. de ~~he~~ enero

/ Por el viento leste y sueste mũcho q̃ ventava no
partio este dia : por lo qual mãdo q̃ se guarne
çiese la caravela de agua y leña y de todo lo
20 nesçessario p[ar]a todo el viaje /. porq̃ avñq̃ tenia
volũtad de costear toda la costa de aq̃lla espa
ñola q̃ andãdo el camino pudiese : p[er]o porq̃ los
q̃ puso en las caravelas por capitanes q̃ eran her

Alonso took half and the other half was divided
among the men. The Admiral adds, saying to the
sovereigns: Thus, Lord Princes, I recognize that Our
Lord miraculously ordered that ship to remain there,
because it is the best place in all of the
island to make the settlement and nearer the
gold mines. Also, he says he found out that
behind the island of Juana to the south there
is another big island in which there is a much
greater quantity of gold than in this one, so
much so that they gather pieces larger than
53r   beans, and on the island of Hispaniola the
pieces of gold that are gathered from the
mines are like grains of wheat. He says that
that island is called Yamaye.[1] The Admiral
says he also learned that toward the east
there was an island where there were women
only. And this he says he knew from many
persons. And that the island of Hispaniola, or
the other island of Yamaye, was near mainland,
ten days' journey by canoe, which would be 60
or 70 leagues, and that the people there were clothed.

Monday 7 January

This day he had a leak in the caravel fixed and
caulked, and the sailors went ashore to fetch
firewood; and, he says, they found much mastic
and aloe.

Tuesday 8 January

Because of the strong east and southeast wind
that blew, he did not depart this day. Because
of this he ordered that the caravel be provided with water and firewood and with everything necessary for the whole voyage. Although he had a desire to go along all of the
coast of Hispaniola (and going on his way he
could have), those whom he put in the cara-

---

1. (53r4) *Yamaye* is probably the island of Jamaica.

manos conviene a saber martin alōso pinçon y vi
25 ceynte anes y otros q̃ les seguian con sobervia
y cudiçia   estimādo q̃ todo era ya suyo no mi
rādo la hōrra q̃l almiᵉ les avia hecho y ~~les~~
dado : no avian obedeçido ni obedeçian sus mā
damiᵒˢ antes hazian y decian mūchas cosas no
30 devidas contra el : y el martin alo[nso] lo dexo
desde .21. de noviēbre hasta seys de enero
~~ni~~-[?] sin causa ni razō sino por su desobediē
çia ~~acordo de bolverse~~ todo lo qual el almiᵉ
avia çufrido y callado por dar buē fin a su
35 viaje asi que por salir de tan mala compa
ñia cō los quales dize q̃ cumplia dissimular
avnq̃ gente desmādada y avnq̃ tenia diz q̃
consigo mūchos hōbres de bien / p[er]o no era
tp̄o de entēder en castigo : acordo bolverse y
40 no parar mas : con la mayor priesa q̃ le
fuese possible /. Entro en la barca y fue al

Este rio es yaqui mūy
poderoso y de mūcho oro
y podia ser q̃ lo hallase
entōces el almiᵉ comō
dize porq̃ entonçes estava
virgē comō dizen /. p[er]o
todavia creo q̃ mūcho
dllo devia ser magasi
ta porq̃ alli ay mūcha
y pensava quiça el almiᵉ
q̃ era oro todo lo q̃ re
lucia /

rio q̃ es alli junto hazia el sursueste del mō
te xp̄o vna grāde legua donde yvan los ma
rineros a tomar agua p[ar]a el navio : y hallo
q̃ el arena dla boca del rio el qual es mȳ grā
de y hōdo era diz q̃ toda llena de oro y en
tāto grado q̃ era maravilla puesto q̃ era mūy
menudo /. creya el almiᵉ q̃ por venir por aq̃l rio
abaxo se dsmenuzava por el camino /. puesto q̃ dize
50 q̃ en poco espacio hallo mūchos granos tan grādes

Folio 53v

comō lantejas / mas dlo menudito dize que
avia mūcha Cantidad /. y porq̃ la mar era
llena y entrava la agua salada con la dulce .
mādo subir co la barca el rio arriba vn tiro
5 de piedra . hincherō los barriles desde la bar
ca : y bolviendose a la caravela hallavan me
tidos por los aros dlos barriles pedaçitos de

vels as captains were brothers: that is to
say, Martín Alonso Pinzón and Vicente Anes,
and others who followed them with arrogance
and greed, judging that everything was already theirs and not perceiving the honor
that the Admiral had done and shown them, had
not obeyed nor were they obeying his commands: rather, they did and said unjust
things against him; and Martín Alonso left
him from 21 November until 6 January without
cause or reason, except his disobedient
nature, all of which the Admiral had suffered
in silence so as to give a good ending to his
voyage as well as to leave such bad company.
He says that he carried off his dissimulation
with these unruly people, and, although he has
with him many men who do their duty, there was
no time to concern himself with punishment. He
decided to return to Spain with the greatest
speed possible for him and to stop no more. He
got into the launch and went a good league to
the river that was there nearby, to the south-
southeast[1] of Monte Christo, where the
sailors were going to get water for the
navio;[2] and he found that the sand at the
mouth of the river, which is very large and
deep, was, he says, all full of gold to such
a degree that it was marvelous, even though
the pieces were very small. The Admiral
believed that on the way coming down that
river they got smaller, although he says that
in a small space he found many grains as big
as lentils. But of the very tiny grains he

53v   says that there was great quantity. Because
the tide was high and the saltwater mixed
with the sweet, he ordered the men to go upriver a stone's throw. They filled the barrels
from the launch, and returning to the caravel,
they found inserted among the barrel hoops

---

1. (53r42) Morison (1963) asserts that *sursueste* (south-southeast) is an error for
sursudueste, "south-southwest."
2. (53r44) *Navio*. The *Niña*.

oro y lo mismo en los aros dla pipa /. puso
~~le~~ por nōbre el almiᶜ al rio / el rio del oro /.

10   el qual de dentro passada la entrada mūy hōdo
avnq̃ la entrada es baxa y la boca mȳ ancha :
y del a la villa dla navidad diez y siete leguas /.
Entremedias ay otros mūchos rios grandes
en especial tres los quales creya q̃ devian tener

mayor es este q̃   15   mūcho mas oro q̃ aq̃l porq̃ son mas grādes : pue
todos aq̃llos /. yo   sto q̃ste es quasi tan grāde comō guadalquivir
[lo?] se   por cordova : y dllos a las minas dl oro no ay
ni quatro leguas   veynte leguas /. dize mas el almiᶜ q̃ no quiso
ay dllos a las   tomar dla d̄ha arena q̃ tenia tanto oro : pues
minas /.
                                            teniā
20   sus altezas lo ~~tiene~~ todo en casa y a la puerta
dsu villa dla navidad : sino venirse ——[?] a mas
andar : por llevalles las nuevas : y por qui
tarse dla mala compañia q̃ tenia y q̃ siempʳ
avia d̄ho q̃ era gente dsmādada /.

25   miercoles .9. de enero
Ⅰ a media noche levanto las velas cō el viē
to sueste y navego al lesnordeste / llego
a vna punta q̃ llamo punta roxa q̃ esta
justamēte al leste del monte xp̄o sesenta mi
30   llas y al abrigo dlla surgio a la tarde q̃ se
                    oras
rian tres antes q̃ anocheçiese /. no oso salir
de alli de noche porq̃ avia mūchas restringas
hasta q̃ se sepā porq̃ dspues serā p[ro]vechosas si
tienē comō deven tener Canales y tienen
35   mūcho fondo y buē surgidero seguro de todos
vientos /. Estas tr̄r̄as desde mōte xp̄o hasta

little pieces of gold and the same in the hoops
of the pipes.[1] The Admiral gave the river the
name Rio del Oro. Inside, the entrance passed,
[it is] very deep, although the entrance is
shallow and the mouth very wide; and from
the river to the town of Navidad is 17
leagues. In between there are many other
large rivers, especially three which,
because they are bigger, he believed
should have much more gold than the
Rio del Oro, even though the latter
is almost as big as the Guadalquivir at
Cordova, and from them to the gold mines
it is not 20 leagues. Moreover, the Admiral says that since their Highnesses
would have all of it at home and at the
very gates of their town of Navidad, he
did not want to take any of the sand
that had so much gold but to go at top
speed to carry the news to them and to
rid himself of the bad companions that
he had, and whom he had always said were
unruly people.

Wednesday 9 January

At midnight he raised sail with the
southeast wind and steered to the north-
northeast. He reached a point that he
called Punta Roja, which is 60 miles due
east of Monte Christo, and in its shelter
he anchored in the afternoon about three
hours before dusk. He did not dare to
leave from there at night because of
the many reefs and until they were known.
Later it might be a profitable place if
there are, as there should be, channels
[through the reefs]; for the anchorage
has great depth and is secure from all
winds. These lands between Monte Christo

1.   (53v8) *Pipa*, or "pipes," are tapering casks used for wine.

alli donde surgio : son tr̄r̄as altas y llanas y
mūy lindas Campiñas y a las espaldas mūy
hermosos mōtes q̃ van de leste a gueste

40 y son todos labrados y verdes q̃ es cosa de ma
ravilla ver su hermosura y tienē mūchas
riberas de agua /. en toda esta tr̄r̄a ay mūchas
tortugas dlas quales tomarō los mari
neros en el mōte xp̄i q̃ venian a desovar

45 en tr̄r̄a : y erā mūy grādes coм̃o vna grāde
tablachina /. el dia passado quādo el almirāte

Folio 54r

vido tres sere
nas

yva al rio del oro : dixo q̃ vido tres serena[s?]
q̃ salierō bien alto dla mar p[er]o no erā tan
hermosas coм̃o las pintan q̃ en alguᵃ maр̃a
tenian forma de hōbre en la Cara /. dixo q̃ otras

5   vezes vido algunas en guinea ——[?]   en la costa dla
manegueta /. dize q̃sta noche cō el nōbre de
nr̄o Señor partiria a su viaje : sin mas dete
nerse en cosa alguna : pues avia hallado lo

nō

q̃ buscava porq̃ no quiere mas enojo con aq̃l

10 m[art]in alōso hasta q̃ sus altezas supiesen las
nuevas dsu viaje y dlo q̃ a hecho : y despues
no çufrire (dize el) hechos de malas p[er]sonas y
contra
de poca virtud /. las quales ∧a quien les dio—[?]
aq̃lla hōrra presumē hazer su volūtad con

15 poco acatamiento /.

Jueves .10. de enero

este rio es el q̃ di
zen de martin
alōso pincon q̃sta
çinco leguas de
puerto de plata .

⫽ Partiose de donde avia surgido y al sol puesto
llego a vn rio al qual puso nōbre rio de gra
çia desta [?] dla p[ar]te del sueste tres leguas surgio
a la boca q̃s buē surgidero a la p[ar]te del leste : ——[?]
p[ar]a entrar dentro tiene vn banco q̃ no tiene si
no dos braças de agua y mȳ angosto : dentro
es buē puerto çerrado sino q̃ tiene mūcha bru

and the place where he anchored are high,
with level and handsome cultivated
fields, and back of them [are] beautiful mountains that run from east to west
and are all cultivated and green so that
it is a wonderful thing to see their
beauty; and they have many streams of
water. In all this land there are many
turtles, some of which the sailors took
on Monte Christo when they came to lay
eggs on shore; and they were very large,
like wooden shields. The day before,

54r when the Admiral was going to the Rio del Oro,
he said he saw three mermaids who came quite
high out of the water but were not as pretty
as they are depicted, for somehow in the face
they look like men. He said that other times
he saw some in Guinea on the coast of Manegueta. He says that tonight in the name of Our
Lord he would depart on his voyage without
stopping again for anything, since he had
found what he was seeking, and because he did
not want more trouble with that Martín Alonso
until their Highnesses should learn the news
of his voyage and of what he has done. And
afterward I will not suffer, he says, from
the deeds of evil persons of little virtue,
who, opposing the one who granted them such
honor, presume to do what they wish, with
little respect.

Thursday 10 January

He departed from the place where he had anchored and at sunset reached a river three
leagues to the southeast, to which he gave the
name Rio de Gracia. He anchored at the mouth,
which is a good anchorage, on the east side.
To get inside, it has a shoal that has but two
brazas of water and is very narrow; inside is
a good landlocked harbor although it has a lot

ma /. y della yva la caravela pinta donde yva
25 martin alōso muy maltratada : porq̃ diz q̃
estuvo alli resgatando diez y seys dias don
de resgatarō mūcho oro q̃ era lo q̃ dseava
martin alōso /. El qual dspues q̃ supo dlos
yndios q̃ el almiᶜ estava en la costa dla misma
30 isla española y q̃ no lo podia errar : se vino
p[ar]a el /. y diz q̃ quisiera q̃ toda la gente del
navio jurara q̃ no avian estado alli sino
seys dias /. mas diz q̃ era cosa tan publica
su maldad q̃ no podia encobrir /. el qual
35 (dize el almiᶜ) tenia hechas leyes ———[?] que
fuese p[ar]a el la mitad del oro q̃ se resgatase /o
se oviese /. y quādo ovo de p[ar]tirse de alli : to
mo quatro hōbres yndios y dos moças por
fuerça /. a los quales el almiᵉ mādo dar de
40 vestir y tornar en tr̄r̄a q̃ se fuesen a sus casas
lo qual (dize) es s[er]ui[ci]º de vr̄as altezas : porq̃ hō
bres y mugeres son todos de vr̄as altezas
nō   asi desta Isla en especial com̄o dlas otras / mas
aqui donde tiene ya asiento vr̄as altezas se deve
45 hazer honrra y favor a los pueblos pues q̃ en esta

Folio 54v

Isla ay tanto oro y buenas tr̄r̄a y especeria /

viernes 11. de enero

⫽ a media noche salio dl rio de graçia cō el
terral -al-[?] navego al leste hasta vn cabo q̃ llamo
este mote llamo   belprado quatro leguas -susueste-[?] y de alli al
de plata porq̃s   sueste esta el mōte -de- a quien puso mōte
muy alto y esta   de plata y dize q̃ ay ocho leguas /. de alli
siempʳ sobre la   dl cabo de belprado al lesta quarta dl sueste
———[?] cumbre   esta el cabo que dixo dl angel y ay diez y
vna ñiebla q̃ lo
haze blāco /o pla
teado / y al pie del
esta el puerto q̃
se dize por aq̃l mō
te de plata

of shipworm.[1] And by it the caravel *Pinta*, in
which Martín Alonso was traveling, was badly
damaged, because, he says, he stayed there
trading for 16 days and bartered for much
gold, which was what Martín Alonso wanted.
Later, after he learned from the Indians that
the Admiral was on the coast of the same
island of Hispaniola and that he could not
avoid him, he came toward him. And, he says,
Martín Alonso had wanted all the people of the
ship to swear that they had been there but six
days. But, he says, his wickedness was a
thing so public that he could not hide it.
The Admiral says that Martín Alonso had made
rules that half the gold that was gotten or
bartered for would be for him. And when he
was to leave that place he took four Indian
men and two young girls by force. The Admiral
ordered that they be given clothes and returned to land, and they went away to their
houses: which, he says, is a service to Your
Highnesses, because men and women all are
subjects of Your Highnesses, particularly
those of this island, as well as of the others. But here, where Your Highnesses already
have a settlement, the people should be hon-
54v   ored and favored, since on this island there
is so much gold and good land and spicery.

                                                         Friday 11 January

At midnight he left the Rio de Gracia with the
land breeze. He steered east four leagues, as
far as a cape that he called [Cabo del] Belprado; and from there to the southeast is the
mountain to which he gave the name Monte de
Plata and he says that it is eight leagues
distant. From there, 18 leagues east by south
from the Cabo del Belprado, is the cape that
the Admiral called Del Ángel. From this cape

1. (54r23–24) *Bruma*. *Broma* (shipworm or teredo) is probably intended here.
Bruma means "mist" or "fog." See Morison (1963, 149, 10 Jan., n. 2).

10   ocho leguas /. y deste cabo al mõte de plata ay
      vn golfo y tr̄r̄as las mejores y mas lindas
      dl mūdo todas campiñas altas y hermosas
      q̃ van mūcho la tr̄r̄a dentro / y dspues ay vna
      sierra q̃ va de leste a gueste mȳ grāde y mūy
15   hermosa y al pie del ~~mundo~~ [?] mõte ay vn
      puerto mȳ bueno y en la entrada tiene qua
      torze braças /. y este mõte es mȳ alto y her
      moso / y todo esto es poblado mūcho : y creya
      el almi͞e devia aver buenos rios y mucho
20   oro /: dl cabo dl angel al leste quarta del su
      este ay quatro leguas ~~al~~ a vna punta q̃ puso
      dl hierro y al mismo camino quatro leguas
      esta vna punta q̃ llamo la punta seca /. y
      de alli al mismo camino a seys leguas esta el
25   cabo q̃ dixo redondo : y de alli al leste esta el
      cabo françes / y en este cabo dla p[ar]te dl leste
      ay vna angla grāde mas no le pareçio a
      ver surgidero /. de alli vna legua esta el
      cabo dl bue͞ t͞p͞o : desta al sur quarta dl su
30   este ay vn cabo q̃ llamo tajado ~~cabo ay vna~~
      ~~grāde~~ vna grāde legua ~~de~~ /. deste hazia
      el sur vido otro cabo y pareçiole q̃ avriā
      ~~x5~~ quinze leguas /. oy hizo grā camino por
      el viento y las corrientes yvā con el /. no
35   oso surgir por miedo dlos baxos y asi estu
      vo a la Corda / toda la noche /.

                                                                    Sabado .12. de enero

      ╱ al quarto dl alva navego al leste cõ viento
                              hasta el dia y en este t͞p͞o
      fresco y anduvo asi ∧ ~~dos oras y en ellas~~ veyn
40   te millas y en dos oras dspues andaria veyn
      te y quatro millas /. de alli vido al sur tr̄r̄a
      y fue hazia ella y estaria dlla .48. millas
      y dize q̃ dado reguardo al navio andaria

to the Monte de Plata there is a gulf and the
best and most beautiful lands in the world:
all high and handsome fields that go far inland, and beyond there is a mountain range,
very large and very handsome, that goes from
east to west; and at the foot of the mountain
there is a very good harbor, which in the entrance has a depth of 14 *brazas*. And this
mountain is very high and handsome; and all of
this land is heavily settled. And the Admiral
believed that it should have good rivers and
much gold. From the Cabo del Ángel to the
east by south it is four leagues to a point
which he named [Punta] del Hierro, and in the
same direction four more leagues there is a
point that he called the Punta Seca. And from
there in the same direction six more leagues
is the cape that he named [Cabo] Redondo, and
from there to the east is the Cabo Francés.
And at this cape on the east side there is a
large bay,[1] but it did not appear to him to
have an anchorage. One league from there is
the Cabo del Buen Tiempo; from this, south by
east a full league, there is a cape that he
named [Cabo] Tajado; from this cape toward the
south he saw another cape and it seemed to him
that it was about 15 leagues away. Today he
made much headway because the wind and
currents were with him. He did not dare to
anchor for fear of shoals and so he jogged off
and on all night.

Saturday 12 January

At the dawn watch he steered east with a fresh
wind and thus proceeded until day, and during this
time [made] 20 miles and in two hours afterward
made 24 miles. From there he saw land to the
south and went toward it. He was about 48 miles
from it. He says that, having looked carefully

---

1.   (54v27) *Angla*. The improbability of there being a "cape" on the east side of
Cabo Frances indicates that the word *angla* here means "bay."

esta noche .28 + millas al nornordeste /

45 quãdo vido la tr̄r̄a llamo a vn cabo q̃ vido el

cabo de padre y hijo porq̃ a la punta dla p[ar]te

dl leste tiene dos farallones mayor el vno q̃l

Folio 55r

otro /. dspues al leste dos leguas vido vna grãde

abra y mȳ hermosa entre dos grãdes mota

ñas y vido q̃ era grãdissimo puerto bueno

y de mȳ buena entrada . p[er]o por ser mȳ de

5 maña y no p[er]der camino / porq̃ por la mayor

p[ar]te dl tp̄o haze por alli lestes y entonces le

lleva ~~norueste~~ [?] nornorueste : no quiso de

tenerse mas siguio su camino al leste hasta

vn cabo mȳ alto y mȳ hermoso y todo de pie

10 dra tajado a quien puso por nõbre cabo del ena

morado el qual estava al leste de aq̃l puerto

a quiē llamo puerto sacro .32. millas /. y en

llegãdo a el descubrio otro muy mas hermoso

y mas alto y redondo de peña todo asi com̄o

15 el cabo de Sant viçeynte en portugal y esta

va del ~~otro del~~ enamorado al leste .12. millas /.

despues q̃ allego a emparejarse con el del enamo

rado vido entremedias dl y de otro : vido q̃ se

hazia vna grãdissima baya q̃ tiene de anchor

20 tres leguas y en medio dlla esta vna Isle

ta pequeñuela el fondo es mūcho a la entrada

hasta tr̄r̄a /. surgio alli en doze braças : enbio

la barca en tr̄r̄a por agua y por ver si avian

lengua : p[er]o la gente toda huyo /. surgio tãbien

25 por ver si toda era aq̃lla vna tr̄r̄a cō la espa

ñola y lo q̃ dixo ser golpho sospechava no

fuese otra Isla por si /. quedava espantado de

ser tan grãde la Isla española /.

at the vessel's performance, tonight he made about 28 miles[1] to the north-northeast. When he saw land, he named a cape that he saw the Cabo de Padre y Hijo because at its eastern point it has two pinnacles, one larger than the other. Later,

55r   two leagues to the east, he saw a large and handsome opening between two big mountains and he saw that it was an extremely large and good harbor with a very good entrance. But because it was early in the morning, and so as not to lose distance, because most of the time in that region, east winds blow, and at that time he had a north-northwesterly, he did not want to stop but to continue on his route to the east as far as a very high and handsome cape all of sheared-off rock to which he gave the name [Cabo del] Enamorado, which was 32 miles to the east of that harbor, which he named Puerto Sacro. And in getting to it he discovered another cape much more handsome and higher and round, all of stone, just like the Cabo de San Vicente in Portugal; and it was 12 miles to the east of the [Cabo del] Enamorado. After he had advanced to a position even with the Enamorado, he saw, between it and the other cape, that an extremely large bay was formed, which had a width of three leagues and in the middle of it a tiny little islet. The depth is great at the entrance and all the way to shore. He anchored there in 12 *brazas*; he sent the launch ashore for water and to see if they could talk to the natives; but the people all fled. He also[2] anchored to see if all that land and Hispaniola were continuous or whether, as he suspected, what he had called a gulf might not form another island by itself. He remained astonished that the island of Hispaniola was so big.

1. (54v44) The canceled *l* in the manuscript just before *millas* indicates that Las Casas was about to write *leguas* but caught himself.
2. (55r24) The word *tambien* (also) is written in the right margin, suggesting a later addition.

Domīgo .13. de enero /.

30 / no salio deste puerto por no haze^r terral cō
que saliese : quisiera salir por yr a otro mejor
puerto po^rq̃ aq̃l era algo dscubierto : y porq̃
~~via~~ queria ver en q̃ parava la conjunçiō dla luna cō el so[l]
q̃ esperava a .17. deste mes y la opposiçion
35 dlla cō jupiter y conjunçion con mercurio
y el sol en opposito con jupiter q̃ es causa d[e] grā
des vientos /. ~~p[ar]a~~-[?]————[?] Enbio la barca a
tr̄r̄a en vna hermosa playa p[ar]a q̃ tomasen dlos
~~ay~~-[?] ajes p[ar]a comer [:?] y hallarō çiertos hōbres
40 con arcos y flechas cō los quales se pararō
a hablar y les comprarō dos arcos y mūchas
flechas y ~~hizo~~-[?] Rogarō a vno dllos q̃ fuese
a hablar al almi^e / a la caravela y vino / el
qual diz q̃ era mūy disforme en el acatadura
45 mas q̃ otros q̃ oviese visto . ——[?] tenia el rostro
todo tyznado de Carbon / puesto q̃ en todas p[ar]tes
acostūbran de se teñir de diversas colores
traya todos los cabellos mūy largos y ~~co~~-[?] encogidos

por aqui pareçe q̃ el
almi^e sabia algo de
astrologia . avnque
estos planetas pare
cen q̃ no estan biē
puestos por falta
dl mal escrivano
q̃ lo treslado .

estos devian ser los
q̃ llamavā ciguayos
[q̃ todos   ?] cabellos

Folio 55v

y atados atras : y dspues puestos en vna redezi
lla de plumas de papagayos y el asi desnu
do comō los otros /. Juzgo el almi^e q̃ devia
de ser dlos caribes q̃ comē los hōbres : y
5 q̃ aq̃l golfo q̃ ayer avia visto q̃ hazia aparta

no erā caribes
ni los ovo en
la española jamas

Sunday 13 January

He did not leave this harbor, because there was no
land breeze with which to leave; he would have
liked to leave to go to another, better, harbor because that one was somewhat exposed, and because
he wanted to see how the conjunction of the moon
with the sun[1] that he expected on the seventeenth of this month would turn out, and
[to observe] the opposition of the moon with
Jupiter and conjunction with Mercury, and
the Sun in opposition to Jupiter, which is
the cause of great winds.[2] He sent[3] the
launch ashore at a handsome beach so they
could get some yams to eat, and they found
certain men with bows and arrows with whom
they stopped to talk, and they bought from
them two bows and many arrows and they
begged[4] one of them to go to the caravel
to speak with the Admiral, and he went.
The Admiral says that he was quite ugly in
appearance, more so than others that he
had seen. He had[5] his face all stained
with charcoal, although everywhere they
are accustomed to staining themselves with
different colors. He wore all his hair[6]

55v   very long, gathered and tied behind and
then put in a small net of parrot
feathers. And he also was as naked as the
others. The Admiral judged that he must
be from the Caribs who eat men, and that
the gulf that he had seen yesterday made a

---

1. (55r33) The phrase *de la luna con el sol* (of the moon with the sun) is written
in the right margin, suggesting an addition.
2. (55r33–37) *Porque queria ver . . . grandes vientos* (because he wanted to
see . . . great winds). See Morison (1963, 152 n. 1) for an explanation of this passage.
The prediction for the seventeenth of January was apparently taken from the *Ephemer-
ides* of Regiomontanus but was somewhat garbled in being copied from the original of
the *Diario*. See also Las Casas's note to line 55r34.
3. (55r37) Alvar (1976) reads the canceled text preceding *enbio* as *pero conclu-
yendo (?)* (Alvar's question mark).
4. (55r42) Alvar (1976) reads the canceled text preceding *rogaron* as *hazer.*
5. (55r45) Alvar (1976) reads the canceled text as *el que.*
6. (55r48) The third line of Las Casas's note to line 48 is badly trimmed in the
manuscript facsimile. Alvar (1976) reads the third line of the note as *que todos traian
lo[s] cabellos* and a fourth line that does not appear at all in the facsimile as *aasi muy
largos.*

miento de t̄r̄ra y q̃ seria Isla por si /. pre
guntole por los caribes y señalole al leste
çerca de alli ——[?] la qual diz q̃ ayer vio el almi^e
antes q̃ entrase en aq̃lla baya : y dixole

10   el yndio q̃ en ella avia m̄y mucho oro : se
ñalandole la popa dla Caravela q̃ era bien
grāde y q̃ pedaços avia tan grādes /. llama
va al oro tuob y no entendia por caona

Caona llamavā al
oro en la mayor
p[ar]te dla Isla espa
ñola : p[er]o avia
otras dos o tres
lenguas

no ~~ap~~-[?] entendia
el almi^e aq̃ste
yndio /.   20

este guanin no era
Isla segū yo creo : si
no el oro baxo q̃ se
gū los yndios dla
española tenia vn olor
por q̃ lo preçia
vā mūcho y a este
llamavā guanin /.

cōmo le llamā en la primera p[ar]te dla ysla : ni
por noçay cōmo lo nōbravā en sā salvador
y en las otras Islas /. al alābre /o ~~al oro~~-[?]
a vn oro baxo llamā en la española taob /. dla Isla
de matinino dixo aq̃l yndio q̃ era toda pobla
da de mugeres sin hōbres y que en ella
ay mūy mūcho tuob q̃s oro /o alābre y q̃ es
mas al leste de Carib /. tābie dixo de la Isla
de goanin adonde ay mūcho ~~oro~~-[?] tuob /.
destas Islas dize el almi^e q̃ avia por mūchas p[er]so
nas dias avia notiçia /. Dize mas el almi^e
q̃ en las Islas passadas estavā cō grā temor de
carib ~~y q̃ en la española carib lo llamā Caniba~~ y en
algunas le llamavā Caniba : p[er]o en la española
Carib / y q̃ deve de ser gente arriscada : pues
andan por todas estas Islas y comē la gente q̃

30   puedē aver /. dize q̃ entendia algunas pala
bras : y por ellas diz q̃ saca otras cosas : y q̃ los
yndios q̃ consigo traya entēdiā mas puesto
q̃ hallava differēçia d[e] lenguas : por la grā distā
            mādo dar
çia dlas t̄r̄ras /. ~~Diole~~ al yndio de comer : y

35   diole pedaços de paño verde y colorado y
cuētezuelas de vidro aq̃llos son m̄y affiçio
nados : y tornole a embiar a t̄r̄ra : y dixole

body of land that probably was an island
by itself.　He questioned him about the
Caribs, and the Indian pointed to the east
near there, which land the Admiral says
that he saw yesterday before entering that
bay; and the Indian told him that in that
land there was a great deal of gold,
pointing to the poop of the caravel, which
was quite large, and [meaning] that there
were pieces that big.　He called gold
tuob[1] and did not understand *caona*, as
they call it in the first part of the
island, nor *noçay* as they called it in
San Salvador and in the other islands.　In
Hispaniola they call *alambre*, a base gold,
tuob.　The Indian said of the island of
Matinino that it was all populated by
women, without men, and that in it there
is much *tuob*, which is gold, or *alambre*,
and that it is farther to the east of
Carib.　He also told of the island of
Goanin where there is much *tuob*.　Of these
islands the Admiral says that some days ago
he received information from many persons.
The Admiral says further that on the islands passed they were greatly fearful of
Carib and in some they called it Caniba,
but in Hispaniola, Carib; and they must be a
daring people since they travel through all
these islands and eat the people they can
capture.　He says that he understood some
words, and through them he says he found out
other things, and that the Indians he
brought with him understood more, although
they found differences between the
languages, because of the great distance
between the lands.　He had the Indian given
something to eat, and he gave him pieces of
green and red cloth and glass beads, of
which they are very fond, and sent him

1.　(55v17)　*Tuob*.　The spelling *taob*, which also appears in the manuscript, is
possibly a variant spelling.

q̃ truxese oro si lo avia lo qual creya por algu
nas cositas suyas q̃l traya /. En llegādo la

40   barca a tr̄r̄a estavā detras los arboles bien çin
quēta y çinco ~~personas~~ hōbres desnudos cō los

los que se llama
vā çyguayos
~~en s~~ en las sier
ras y costa del
norte dla españo
la dsde quasi puer
to de plata hasta
higuay inclusive /

estos çierto erā

cabellos mȳ largos asi comō ∧mugeres los
                                    las
traen en castilla /. detras dla cabeça trayā pena
chos de plumas de papagayos y de otras

45   aves y cada vno traya su arco / desçendio
el yndio en tr̄r̄a y hizo q̃ los otros dexasē
sus arcos y flechas y vn pedaço de palo q̃

Folio 56r

este es del ~~pa~~ arbol
                ma
de pal ~~ga~~ [?] q̃s duris
simo hecho a mane
ra de vna paleta
de hierro q̃ hazen
p[ar]a freyr uuevos
q̃ pescado grāde ———[?]
~~vn~~ [?] de quatro palmos
voto por todas p[ar]tes
llamanle macana /.

la primera pelea
q̃ se ovo entre yn
dios y xp̄īāños
en la isla espa
ñola

nõ

es comō vn   mūy pesado q̃ traen en lu
gar de espada [/.?] los quales despues se lle
garo a la barca y la gente dla barca salio a
tierra y comēçarōles a comprar los arcos
y flechas y las otras armas porq̃ el almiᵉ
asi lo tenia ordenado /. vendidos dos ar
cos no quisierō dar mas / antes se apare
jaron de arremeter a los xp̄īāños y pren
d[e]llos /. fuerō corriēdo a tomar sus arcos

10   y flechas : ~~y vinie~~ donde los tenian aparta
dos : y tornarō con cuerdas en las manos
p[ar]a diz q̃ atar los xp̄īāños /. viendolos ve
nir corriēdo a ellos estando los xp̄īāños aper
cibidos porq̃ siempʳ los avisava dsto el almiᵉ . ar

15   remetierō los xp̄īāños a ellos : y dieron
a vn yndio vna grā cuchillada en las nal
gas y a otro por los pechos ~~metierō por los~~
hirierō con vna saetada lo qual visto que
podian ganar poco avnq̃ no erā los xp̄īā

20   ños sino siete y ellos çinquēta y tantos .
dierō a huyr q̃ no quedo ninguno / dexā
do vno aqui las flechas y otro alli los ar
cos /. matarā diz q̃ los xp̄īāños mūchos
dllos : si el piloto q̃ yva por capitan dellos

25   no lo estorvara /. bolvierōse luego a la cara
vela los xp̄īāños con su barca : y sabido por el
almiᵉ dixo q̃ por vna p[ar]te le avia plazido y por otra no .

ashore again and told him to bring gold if
he had it, which he believed he did, because of some little things of his that he
wore.   When the launch reached shore, behind the trees there were a good 55 naked
men with very long hair, just as women wear
it in Castile.   On the backs of their heads
they wore plumes of parrot feathers and of
other birds, and each one was carrying his
bow.   The Indian got out on shore and made
the others leave their bows and arrows and
a piece of wood that is like a very heavy

56r   that they carry in place of a
sword.   Later they came up to the launch
and the men in the launch went ashore.   The
Spaniards began to buy from them bows and
arrows and other arms, because the Admiral
had so ordered.   When two bows were sold
they did not want to give more; instead,
they prepared to attack the Christians and
capture them.   They went running to get their
bows and arrows where they had left them and
returned with cords in their hands, he says,
in order to tie up the Christians.   Seeing
them come running toward them, the Christians,
being forewarned (because the Admiral was always counseling them about this) attacked the
Indians.   And they gave one Indian a great
blow with a sword on the buttocks and another
they wounded in the chest with a crossbow
shot.   The Indians, having seen by this that
they were able to achieve little, even though
the Christians were but seven and they fifty-
odd, took to flight so that none remained, one
leaving his arrows here and others their bows
there.   He says that the Christians would have
killed many of them if the pilot who went as
captain had not prevented it.   The Christians
then returned to the caravel with their
launch; and when [the news] was made known to
the Admiral, he said that on one hand he had

porq̃ ~~los~~ ayā miedo a los xp̄iāños : porq̃ sin du
da (dize el) la gente de alli es diz q̃ de mal
30 hazer y q̃ creya q̃ erā los de Carib : y q̃ co
miesen los hōbres . y porq̃ viniendo por
alli la barca q̃ dexo a los .xxxix. hōbres en
la fortaleza y villa dla navidad : tengā
miedo de hazerles algun mal /. y q̃ si no
35 son dlos caribes al menos deven ser fron
teros y dlas mismas costūbres : y gente sin
miedo : ~~porq̃~~ [?] no comō los otros dlas otras
Islas q̃ son cobardes y sin armas fuera

querria

de razō /. todo esto dize el almi͛ y q̃ ~~quisiera~~
40 tomar algunos dllos /. diz q̃ haziā mūchas
ahumadas comō acostūbrava en aq̃lla Isla
española /.

Lunes 14. de enero

/ ~~Quizo~~ Quisiera enbiar esta noche a buscar las
45 casas de aq̃llos yndios por tomar algu

creyēdo q̃ erā caribes

nos dellos ∧ : y por el mūcho leste y nordeste
y mūcha ola q̃ hizo en la mar   p[er]o ya de dia

Folio 56v

vierō mucha gente de yndios en tr̄ra : por
lo qual mādo el almi͛ yr alla la barca
con gente bien adereçada /. los quales lue
go vinierō todos a la popa dla barca : y es

tornaron los
yndios de
paz a contra
tar

pecialmēte el yndio q̃l ~~dha~~ dia antes avia

dado

venido a la caravela y el almi͛ le avia ∧ las
cosillas de resgate /. con este diz q̃ venia vn
rey el qual avia dado al yndio dicho vnas
cuentas q̃ diese a los dla barca en señal de
10 seguro y de paz /. Este rey con tres dlos

been pleased and on the other not.[1] He was
pleased because now the Indians would fear the
Christians, since without doubt the people
there, he says, are evildoers and he believed
they were people from Carib and that they
would eat men. He was also glad because if
the launch that he had left for the 39 men in the
fortress and town of Navidad came there,
the Indians would be afraid of doing them any
harm. And if they are not Caribs, at least
they must be from the frontiers and of the same
customs and be men without fear, not like the
others of the other islands, who are cowards
and, beyond understanding, without arms. All
of this the Admiral says and [also] that he
would like to capture some of them. He says
they were making many smoke signals, as was
the custom in that island of Hispaniola.

                                                                    Monday 14 January

He would have liked to send men tonight to
look for the houses of those Indians to capture some of them, believing that they were
Caribs, and because of the heavy east and
northeast wind and the big waves that it made in the
sea [he could not do so]. But when day finally came
56v   they saw many Indians on shore, because of which
the Admiral ordered the launch to go there
with well-equipped men. The Indians soon all
came to the stern of the launch, in particular the Indian who, the day before, had come
to the caravel and to whom the Admiral had
given the trinkets from the trade goods. With
him, he says, came a king who had given some
beads to the said Indian to give to the men in
the launch as a sign of security and peace.
This king with three of his men entered the

1. (56r27) *Dixo que . . . y por otra no* (he said that . . . and on the other not). The
flow of thought would be better expressed if the negative phrase came first: "He said
that on one hand he was not pleased . . . ." The phrase *y por otra no* is boxed in the
right margin.

suyos entrarō en la barca y viniero a la
caravela /. mādoles el almiᵉ dar de comer
vizcocho y miel : y diole vn bonete colora
do y cuētas y vn pedaço de paño colorado :

15 y a los otros tābien pedaços de paño el qual
dixo q̃ traeria mañana vna caratula de oro
afirmādo q̃ alli avia mūcho / y en Carib y
en matinino /. Despues los enbio a tr̄r̄a
bien contētos /. Dize mas el almiᵉ q̃ ~~le~~ ha
                                        por la quilla
20 zian agua mūcha las caravelas ∧ y quexase mū
cho dlos calafates q̃ en palos las calafatearō
~~y dize asi~~ -[?] mūy mal y q̃ quādo vierō q̃l almiᵉ
avia entendido el defecto de su obra y los quisie
ra constreñir ~~al q̃~~ -[?] a q̃ la emēdarā huyerō /.

25 p[er]o no obstante la mūcha agua q̃ las caravelas
hazian confia en nr̄o Señor q̃ le truxo : le torna
ra por su piedad y mis[er]icordia q̃ bien sabia su

nō   alta mag[es]t[ad] quanta controversia tuvo primero antes
q̃ se pudiese expedir de Castilla : q̃ ninguº otro

30 fue en su favor sino el porq̃ el sabia su cora
çon y despues de dios sus altezas / y todo lo de

acuerdase el almiᵉ   mas le avia sido contrario sin razō alguna /.
dlas difficultades que y dize mas asi : y an se[y?]do causa q̃ la corona re
tuvo en la corte quā   al de vr̄as altezas no tenga çient cuētos
do propuso su descu
brimiº
35 de renta mas dla q̃ tiene despues q̃ yo vine

a .xx. de enero   a los servir q̃ son siete años agora a veynte dias
año de 1489 en   de henero este mismo mes y mas lo q̃ acreçē
tro en la corte el
almiᵉ a proponer   tado seria de aqui en adelante /. mas aq̃l pode
su descubrimiº /.   roso dios remediara todo /. estas son sus palabras /

40   martes –[?] .15. de enero
⟋ Dize q̃ se quiere p[ar]tir porq̃ ya no aprovecha nada
detenerse –[?] por aver passado aq̃llos desconciertos
deve dezir del escandalo dlos yndios /. dize tābiē

launch and came to the caravel. The Admiral
ordered them given biscuit and honey to eat,
and he gave the king a red cap and beads and a
piece of red cloth; and to the others also
pieces of cloth. The king said that tomorrow
he would bring a gold mask, affirming that
there was much gold there, and [also] in
Carib, and in Matinino. Later the Admiral
sent them ashore well contented. In addition,
he says that the caravels were leaking a lot
around the keel and that he had complained a
lot about the caulkers who in Palos caulked
them very poorly. [He says] that when they
saw that the Admiral had become aware of the
defect in their work and would have liked to
compel them to fix it, they fled. But notwithstanding the large amount of water that
they took in, he trusted in Our Lord, who
brought him [to the Indies], to return him [to
Spain] because of His pity and mercy, for his
High Majesty well knew how much controversy he
had at first before he was able to take ship
from Castile, and that no one else but He was
in his favor, because He knew his heart, and
after God, their Highnesses. And all the others had been against him without any reason at
all. And he says more in this wise: And
[those who opposed me] have been the cause of
the royal crown of Your Highnesses not having
an income of a hundred million more than you
have had since I came to serve you, which now
is seven years ago on January 20, this very
month, and even more [if one includes] what
would probably be added from now on. But that
powerful God will remedy everything. These
are his words.

Tuesday 15 January

He says that he wishes to depart because now
there is no benefit in staying because of those
difficulties with (he should say their shameful

ꝗ oy a sabido q̃ toda la fuerça dl oro estava en la

45   comarca dla villa dla navidad de sus altezas

y q̃ en la Isla de Carib -ay-[?] avia mūcho alābre y

en matinino puesto q̃ sera dificultoso en carib por

q̃ aꝗlla gente diz q̃ come Carne humana /. y q̃ de

[?]y matinino   alli se parecia la Isla dllos y q̃ tenia determinado

Folio 57r

de yr a ella / pues esta en el camino y a la de mati

nino q̃ diz q̃ era poblada toda de mugeres / sin

hōbres y ver la vna y la otra y tomar diz q̃

algunos dellos /. Embio el almiͨ la barca a

5   tr̄r̄a : y el Rey de aꝗlla tr̄r̄a no -vino- avia ve

nido porꝗ diz q̃ la poblaçion estava lexos mas

enbio su corona de oro com̄o avia prometido /.

y vinierō otros mūchos hōbres con algodon

y cō pan y ajes todos con sus arcos y flechas

10   despues q̃ todo lo ovierō resgatado : vinierō

diz q̃ quatro mācebos a la caravela : y pareçierō

le al almiͨ dar tan buena Cuēta de todas aꝗllas

                    estavan

islas q̃ ∧ -quedā-[?] hazia el leste en el mismo Cami

fue mȳ mal   no ꝗl almiͨ avia de llevar : q̃ determino de

hecho traerlos   traer a castilla consigo /. alli diz q̃ no tenian hier

contra su volū   ro ni otro metal q̃ se oviese visto : avnꝗ en pocos

tad   dias no se puede saber de vna tr̄r̄a mūcho : asi por la

dificultad dla lēgua q̃ no entendia el almiͨ sino

por discreçion : como porꝗllos no saben lo ꝗl

20   pretendia / en pocos dias /. los arcos de aꝗlla

gente diz q̃ erā tan grādes com̄o los de fran

çia e inglaterra : las flechas son p[ro]pias com̄o

las azagayas de las otras gentes q̃ hasta alli avia

visto q̃ son dlos pinpollos dlas cañas quādo

25   son simiente q̃ quedā mūy derechas / y de

—[?] longura de vna vara y media y de dos : y

despues ponē al cabo -vn palo- vn pedaço de palo agudo

conduct toward) the Indians. He says also that
today he has learned that the principal source
of gold is in the region of Your Highnesses'
town of Navidad, and that on the island of Carib
and in Matinino there was much copper, although
it will be difficult in Carib because those
people, he says, eat human flesh, and that from
there their island was visible and that he had

57r   decided to go to it, since it is on the way, and
to the island of Matinino which, he says, was
populated entirely by women without men, to see
both and to capture, he says, some of them. The
Admiral sent the launch ashore; and the king of
that land had not come because, he says, the
town was distant; but he sent his gold crown as
he had promised. And many other men came with
cotton and with bread and yams, all with their
bows and arrows. After they had bartered everything, four youths, he says, came to the caravel, and they seemed to the Admiral to give such
a good account of all those islands to the east,
on the same route that the Admiral was to follow, that he decided to take them to Castile
with him. There, he says, they have no iron or
other metal that has been seen, although in a
few days one cannot learn much about a country,
both because of the difficulty of the language,
which the Admiral did not understand except by
guessing, and because the Indians did not know,
in a few days, what he was trying to do. The
bows of that people, he says, were as big as
those of France and England; the arrows are very
much like the javelins of the other peoples whom
he had seen up to that time, made from cane
shoots which, when they are planted, remain
very straight for a length of one *vara*[1] and a
half or two *varas*. And afterward they put at

1. (57r26) A *vara* is the Castilian regulated measure of 3 feet of 15 digits each,
equivalent to 83.7 cm. (2.75 English feet). It was called the *Cordel de la Corte* in the
thirteenth-century compilation of Spanish law, the *Siete Partidas* (also see p. 117, n. 2,
and p. 193, n. 1).

de vn palmo y medio y ençima deste palillo al
gunos le inxierē vn diente de pescado : y al
30   gunos y los mas le ponē alli yerva : y no
tyrā comõ en otras p[ar]tes : saluo por vna çierta
mařa q̃ no puedē mūcho offender /. alli avia
mȳ mūcho algodon y mȳ fino y luengo y
ay mūchas almaçigas : y pareçiale q̃ los arcos
35   erā de texo y q̃ ay oro y cobre : tābien ay
mūcho axi q̃s su pimienta : dlla q̃ vale mas

——[?] esta gēte deve
[dezir?] por los
xp̄ianos

q̃ pimienta y toda la gente no come sin
ella q̃ la halla mūy sana : pueden se cargar
çinquēta caravelas cada año en aq̃lla españo
40   la /. Dize q̃ hallo mūcha yerva en aq̃lla baya
dla q̃ hallavā en el golpho quādo venia al descubri
miento por lo qual creya q̃ avia Islas al leste
hasta en derecho de donde las comēço a hallar / porq̃

               aq̃lla
tiene por çierto q̃ ∧ la-[?] yerva nasce en poco h̵ fondo
45   cerca de-[?] junto a tr̅r̅a /. y dize q̃ es-[?] si asi es mūy
çerca estavā estas indias de las Islas de Canaria : y

bien juzgava

por esta razo creya q̃ distavan menos de quatrocien
tas leguas /

Folio 57v

sospecho q̃ este era
el golfo de Sama
na donde salen
los rios yuna y
tamo rios podero
sos dla Isla españo
la .

𝐼 Partio antes dl dia tres oras dl golfo q̃ llamo
el golfo dlas flechas cō viento dla tr̅r̅a : dspues
con viento gueste llevādo la proa al leste
        ta
5   quart∧ dl nordeste p[ar]a yr diz q̃ a la Isla de Carib
      diz q̃
donde ————————[?] -q̃- [e]stava la gente -q̃ a quien-[?] a
quien todas aq̃llas Islas y tr̅r̅as tanto miedo

oy dexo dl
todo la Isla espa
ñola

-tienē- tenian porq̃ diz q̃ con sus canoas sin
numero andavā todas aq̃llas mares y diz q̃
10   comiā los hōbres q̃ pueden aver /. la der

the end a piece of sharp[1] wood one *palmo* and a
half long, and on top of this little stick some
insert a fish tooth; and some or most of them
put poison there. And they do not shoot as
elsewhere, but in a certain way that cannot do
much harm. There was much cotton there, very
fine and long, and there are many mastic trees;
and it appeared to him that the bows were of
yew, and that there is gold and copper. There
is also much chili, which is their pepper, of a
kind more valuable than [black] pepper, and
none of the people eat without it, for they
find it very healthful. Fifty caravels can be
loaded with it each year in Hispaniola. He
says he found much weed in that bay, of the
kind they found in mid-sea when he came [on
his voyage of] discovery, because of which he
believed that there were islands straight to
the east of the place at which he began to
find it, because he considers it certain that
the weed originates in shallow water near
land. And he says that if this is so, these
Indies are very near the Canary Islands, and
for this reason he believed that they were
less than 400 leagues distant.

57v   Wednesday 16 January

He departed three hours before daybreak from
the gulf that he called the Golfo de las
Flechas with wind from the land, and later
with a west wind, taking the ship east by
north, in order to go, he says, to the island
of Carib where[2] the people are of whom those
of all those islands and lands have so much
fear; because, he says, with their numberless
canoes they travel through all those seas and,
he says, they eat the men that they can catch.

1. (57r27) The word *agudo* (sharp) is written in the right margin, suggesting a
later addition.
2. (57v6) Alvar (1976) reads the canceled text immediately following *donde* as
diz que y . . . ganava que.

rota diz q̃ le avia mostrado vnos yndio~~s~~s de aq̃llos
quatro q̃ tomo ayer en el puerto dlas flechas /.
despues de aver andado a su pareçer .64. millas
~~dexarō señalados~~ [?] señalarōle los yndios que

15 daria la d̄ha Isla al sueste : quiso llevar aq̃l
camino y mādo tēplar las velas : y despues
de aver andado dos leguas : refresco el viento
mȳ bueno p[ar]a yr a españa : noto en la gente
q̃ ~~my~~ [?] comēço a entristeçerse por desviarse

20 del camino derecho por la mūcha agua q̃ ha
                              no
zian ambas Caravelas y ∧tenian algun reme
dio saluo el de dios : ovo de dexar el cami
no ~~dla Isla~~ q̃ creya q̃ lleva dla Isla : y bolvio

buelta a españa   al derecho de españa nordeste quarta del leste
                                              millas
25 y anduvo asi hasta el sol puesto .48. ~~leguas~~
q̃ son doze leguas /. Dixerōle los yndios
q̃ por aq̃lla via hallaria la Isla de matinino
q̃ diz q̃ era poblada de mugeres sin hōbres /
lo qual el almiᵉ mūcho quisiera por llevar diz q̃
                    çinco /o seys

30 a los reyes ∧ ~~algunas~~ dllas / p[er]o dudava q̃ los
yndios supiesen biēn la derrota : y el no se

nūca esto dspues   podia detener por el peligro dl agua q̃ cogian las
se averiguo q̃ ovi   caravelas / mas diz q̃ era çierto q̃ las avia /
ese tales mugeres
                                         a ellas /
y q̃ a çierto tp̄o dl año venian los hōbres ∧ ~~co ellas~~ [?]

35 dla d̄ha Isla de Carib q̃ diz q̃ estava dllas diez
o doze leguas : y si parian niño enbiavālo a la Isla
dlos hōbres : y si niña dexavāla consigo /. di
ze el almiᵉ q̃ aq̃llas dos Islas nō devian ~~ser~~
distar de donde avia p[ar]tido ~~xx~~ .xv. /o .xx leguas

40 y creya q̃ erā al sueste y q̃ los yndios no le
supierō señalar la derrota /. despues de p[er]der
de vista el Cabo q̃ nōbro de Sant theramo

Some Indians of the four that he took yesterday in the Puerto de las Flechas had, he says,
shown him the route. After having gone, in
his opinion, 64 miles, the Indians indicated
to him that he would strike the said island to
the southeast. He wanted to take that course
and he ordered the sails trimmed. But after
going two leagues the wind freshened, very
good for going to Spain. He noticed that the
men began to get gloomy because of deviating
from the direct route, because both caravels
were leaking badly, and they had no help except that of God. So he had to leave the
route that he believed led to the island and
returned to the one straight to Spain, northeast by east, and he went thus 48 miles, which
is 12 leagues, until sunset. The Indians told
him that on that route he would find the
island of Matinino, which, he says, was inhabited by women without men, which the Admiral would have liked [to do][1] so he could take
five or six of them to the sovereigns; but he
doubted that the Indians knew the route well,
and he was unable to delay because of the
danger from the water that the caravels were
taking in. But he says that it was certain
that there were such women, and that at a
certain time of year men came to them from the
said island of Carib, which he says was ten or
12 leagues from them; and that if they gave
birth to a boy they sent him to the men's
island and if to a girl they let her stay
with them. The Admiral says that those two
islands must not be 15 or 20 leagues from the
place from which he departed and he believed
they were to the southeast and that the Indians did not know how to show him the route.
After losing sight of the cape that he called
the Cabo de Sant Théramo on the island of His-

---

1.   (57v29) *Quisiera* (would have liked) seems to require an infinitive verb following it.   Sanz (1962) supplies *ver*, "to see."

dla Isla española q̃ le quedava al gueste diez y
seys leguas anduvo doze leguas al leste quar
ta dl nordeste / llevava mūy buē t͞p͞o /.

este cabo de Sant
theramo creo cier
to q̃ es el q̃ llamā
agora el cabo dl
engaño

Jueves 17. de enero

⎰ ayer al poner dl sol Calmole algo el vieto

       tenia

andaria 14 ampolletas q̃ ~~tiene~~-[?] cada vna media
ora /o poco menos ~~y cada vna~~ hasta el rēdir del

Folio 58r

primer quarto : y andaria quatro millas por
ora q̃ son .28. millas /. despues refresco el
viento y anduvo asi todo aq̃l quarto q̃ fuerō diez
ampolletas y dspues otras seys hasta salido el
5   sol ocho millas por ora y asi andaria por to
das ochenta y quatro millas q̃ son .21. leguas
al nordeste quarta dl leste : y hasta el sol
puesto andaria mas quarēta y quatro millas
q̃ son onze leguas al leste / aqui vino vn al
10 catraz a la caravela / y dspues otro : y vido mūcha
yerva dla q̃ esta en la mar /.

Viernes .18. de Enero

⎰ navego cō poco viento esta noche al leste quarta
dl sueste quarētas millas q̃ son .10. leguas
15 y dspues al sueste q̄rta dl leste .30. millas q̃ son
.7. leguas y media hasta salido el Sol /. despues
de salido sol navego todo el dia con poco viento
~~lesde~~-[?] lesnordeste y nordeste y con leste mas
y menos puesta la proa a vezes al norte y
20 a vezes a la quarta dl nordeste y al nornordeste
y asi cōtando lo vno y lo otro creyo q̃ andaria
sesenta millas q̃ son .15. leguas / pareçio
poca yerva en la mar : pero dize q̃ ayer

~~sabado .19. de enero~~

25 y oy pareçio la mar quajada de atunes
y creyo el almiᵉ q̃ de alli deviā de yr a las

paniola, which lay to the west of him 16
leagues, he went 12 leagues east by north,
accompanied by very good weather.

Thursday 17 January

Yesterday at sunset the wind lessened somewhat, and he went for 14 sandglasses, each
of a half hour, or a little less, until the
58r   relief of the first watch; and he made about
four miles per hour, which is 28 miles. Later
the wind freshened and he went thus all of
that watch, which was ten sandglasses, and
afterward, another six at eight miles per
hour, until sunrise, and thus he made overall
84[1] miles, which is 21 leagues, northeast by
east; and up until sunset he made about 44
miles more, which is 11 leagues, to the east.
Here a booby came to the caravel, and later
another; and he saw much weed of the kind that
is in the sea.

Friday 18 January

Tonight he steered east by south with little
wind, 40 miles, which is ten leagues, and
afterward, southeast by east 30 miles, which
is seven leagues and a half, until sunrise.
After sunrise he steered all day with little
wind from the east-northeast and northeast and
more or less east, the bow at times headed
north and at times north by east and north-
northeast; and thus, counting one thing and
another, he believed he had made about 60
miles, which is 15 leagues. Little weed
appeared in the sea, but he says that yesterday and today the sea appeared thick with
tuna and the Admiral thought they must go

1. (58r6) *Ochenta y quatro millas* (eighty-four miles). Robert Fuson has pointed
out (in personal correspondence with the editors) that to obtain this figure, the number
of sandglasses in a 4-hour watch must be corrected from 10 to 8. Otherwise, 7 hours
at 4 MPH plus 8 hours at 8 MPH equals a total mileage of 92.

almadravas del duque de Coni[l?] y de caliz /. por
vn pescado q̃ se llama rabiforcado q̃ anduvo alre
dedor dla caravela y despues se fue la via
30   dl sursueste -q̃ ya-[?] creyo el almi^e q̃ avia por alli
algunas Islas /. y al lessueste dla Isla espa
ñola dixo q̃ quedava la Isla de Carib y la
de matinino y otras mūchas /.

                                             Sabado .19. de enero

35   / anduvo esta noche çinquēta y seys millas al
norte quarta dl nordeste y .64. al nordeste
quarta dl norte /. dspues dl sol salido navego
[ad?] nordeste cō el viento lessueste con viēto fresco
y despues a la quarta dl norte : y andaria .84.
40   millas q̃ son veynte y vna leguas /. vido la
mar quajada de atunes pequeños . ovo alca
trazes / rabos de juncos / y rabiforcados /.

                                             Domīgo .20. de enero

/ Calmo el viento esta noche y a rratos ventava
45   vnos bal[ç?]os de viento y andaria por todo veyn
te millas al nordeste /. despues del sol sali
do andaria onze millas -ad-[?] al sueste : despues

Folio 58v

al nornordeste .36. millas q̃ son nueve le
guas /. vido infinitos atunes pequeños / los
ayres diz q̃ mūy suaves y dulçes comō en sevilla
                        /o
-castilla- por abril -e- mayo : y la mar dize a
5   dios sean dadas -graçias- mūchas grās siemp^r :
mȳ llana /. rabiforcados y pardelas y otras
aves mūchas pareçierō /.

                                             lunes .21. de Enero

/ ayer dspues dl sol puesto navego al norte

from there to the fisheries of the Duke of
Conil and Cadiz. Because of a fisher[1] that
is called a frigate bird that flew around the
caravel and afterward went away toward the
south-southeast, the Admiral thought there
were islands in that direction. And he said
the island of Carib, and that of Matinino,
and many others lay to the east-southeast of
the island of Hispaniola.

                                                 Saturday 19 January

Tonight he made 56 miles north by east and 64
northeast by north. After the sun rose he
steered northeast with a fresh east-southeast
wind and afterward [steered] northeast by
north and he made about 84 miles, which is 21
leagues. He saw the sea thick with small
tuna. There were boobies, tropic birds, and
frigate birds.

                                                 Sunday 20 January

The wind lessened tonight but at times it blew
up a few squalls and they made in all about 20
miles northeast. After sunrise they made
about 11 miles southeast; later 36 miles,
58v   which is nine leagues, north-northeast. He
saw very large numbers of small tuna. The
breezes, he says, are very soft and sweet, as
in Seville in April and May; and the sea, he
says, always very smooth, thanks be given to
God. Frigate birds and petrels and many other
birds appeared.

                                                 Monday 21 January

Yesterday after sunset he steered north by

---

1. (58r28) Although the manuscript reads *pescado* (fish), "fisher" is probably the
intended meaning.

10   quarta dl nordeste cō el viento leste y nor
     deste andaria .8. millas por ora hasta me
                        çinquēta y seys
     dia noche q̃ serian ∧ 56-[?] millas : dspues andu
     vo al nornordeste .8. millas por ora : y asi seri
     an en toda la noche çiento y quatro millas q̃ sō
15   .xxvi. leguas a la quarta dl norte dla p[ar]te dl
     nordeste /. dspues dl sol salido navego al nor
     nordeste cō el mismo viēto leste y a vezes a la
     quarta dl nordeste : y andaria .88. millas
     en onze oras q̃ tenia el dia q̃ son .21. leguas
20   sacada vna q̃ bolvio sobre la carave[l] perdio
     porq̃ arribo sobre la caravela pinta por habla
     lle /. hallava los ayres mas frios y pensava
     diz q̃ hallarlos mas cada dia quāto mas se llega
     se al norte : y tābien por las noches ser mas
25   grādes por el angostura dla espera /. pareçierō
     mūchos rabos de juncos y p[ar]delas y otras aves
     p[er]o no tantos peçes diz q̃ por ser el agua mas
     fria : vido mūcha yerva /.

                                                   Martes .22. de Enero

30   Ɩ ayer dspues dl Sol puesto navego al nornordeste
     con viēto leste y tomava dl sueste andava .8. mi
     llas por ora hasta passadas çinco ampolletas y tres
     de antes q̃ se comēçase la guardia q̃ erā ocho ampo
     lletas y asi avria andado 78-[?] setenta y dos millas
                        diez
35   q̃ son ∧ocho leguas /. despues anduvo a la quarta
     dl nordeste al norte seys ampolletas q̃ serian
     otras .18. millas . despues quatro ampolletas dla
     segūda guarda al nordeste seys millas por ora
     q̃ son tres leguas a[d?] nordeste /. despues hasta
40   el salir dl sol anduvo al lesnordeste onze ampo
     lletas seys leguas por ora q̃ son siete leguas /. ds
     pues al lesnordeste hasta las onze oras dl dia
     32 millas /. y asi calmo el viēto y no anduvo mas

east with an east and northeast wind.[1] He
made eight miles per hour until midnight,
which would be about 56 miles; afterward he
made eight miles per hour to the north-northeast; and thus, in the whole night it would be
about 104 miles, which is 26 leagues, north by
east. After sunrise he steered north-northeast with the same east wind, and at times
northeast by north, and made about 88 miles in the
11 hours of day, which is 21 leagues, taking out
one league that he lost because he went up close to
the *Pinta* to speak to her. He found the breezes
colder and he thought, he says, that he would find
them colder each day the farther north he got; and
the nights longer, because of the narrowing of the
sphere. There appeared many tropic birds and
petrels and other birds, but not so many fish, he
says, because of the water being colder. He saw
much weed.

Tuesday 22 January

Yesterday after sunset he steered north-northeast
with a wind a little south of east. He made eight
miles per hour until five sandglasses had passed
and three from before the watch began, which was
eight sandglasses; and thus he would have gone
about 72 miles, which is 18 leagues.[2] Afterward
he went north by east for six sandglasses, which
would be another 18 miles; afterward, for four
sandglasses of the second watch, to the northeast
at six miles per hour, which is three leagues
northeast. Later, until sunrise, he went to the
east-northeast for 11 sandglasses at six leagues
per hour, which is seven leagues. Afterward to
the east-northeast until the eleventh hour of day, 32
miles. And then the wind died down and they did

1. (58v10–11) *Viento leste y nordeste* (east and northeast wind) is possibly an error
for east by north. See Morison (1963, 157, 21 Jan., n. 1).
2. (58v34–35) *Setenta y dos millas* (seventy-two miles). Alvar (1976) reads the
canceled number in line 34 as "72," not "78." The estimate of 18 leagues made good is
more than twice that implied by the stated speed and the time period measured by
sandglasses. See Morison (1963, 158, 22 Jan., n. 1).

en aq̃l dia /. nadarō los yndios / vierō rabos
45   de juncos y mūcha yerva /.

⅄ esta noche tuvo muchos mudamiētos en los vien

Folio 59r

~~todos~~
tos : tanteado ∧ ~~y guardado lo~~-[?] todo y dados
los reguardos q̃ los marineros buenos sue
len y devē dar : dize q̃ andaria esta noche al
nordeste quarta dl norte .84. millas q̃ son
                                        va
5   .21. leguas /. Espera∧ mūchas vezes a la carave
la pinta porq̃ andava mal dla bolina porq̃ se
ayudava poco dla mezana por el mastel no
ser bueno /. y dize q̃ si el capitan dlla q̃ m[art]în
alōso pinçon tuviera tanto cuidado de pro
10   verse de vn buē mastel en las yndias donde
                            fue cudicioso
tantos y tales avia : comō ∧ ———[?] de se apartar
dl pensando de hinchir el navio de oro
el lo pusiera bueno /. pareçierō mūchos
rabos de juncos / y mūcha yerva : el çielo
15   todo turbado estos dias p[er]o no avia llovido
y la mar siempʳ mỹ llana comō en vn rio
                    seā dadas
a dios ∧ mūchas grãs /. dspues dl sol salido an
daria al nordeste franco çierta p[ar]te dl dia
.30 millas q̃ son siete leguas y media : y
20   dspues lo demas anduvo al lesnordeste otras
treynta millas q̃ son siete leguas y media /.

⅄ andaria esta noche toda consideradas mūchas
mudãças q̃ hizo el viento al nordeste .44.
25   millas q̃ fuerō onze leguas /. despues
de salido el Sol hasta puesto andaria al ~~nor~~-[?]
lesnordeste quatorze leguas /.

not go farther that day. The Indians went swimming. They saw tropic birds and much weed.

Wednesday 23 January

Tonight they had many shifts of wind: considering
59r   everything with the care that good sailors
usually and should observe, he says that he must
have made 84 miles, which is 21 leagues, northeast
by north. He waited often for the caravel *Pinta*,
because she sailed badly close-hauled, being helped
but little by the mizzen, since the mast was not
sound. And he says that if her captain, who was
Martín Alonso Pinzón, had taken as much care to
provide himself with a mast in the Indies, where
there were so many and such good ones, as he was
greedy to depart from him, intending to fill the
vessel with gold, he would have put it right.
Many tropic birds appeared, and much weed. The
sky these days was all overcast, but it had not
rained and the sea was always very smooth, as
in a river, many thanks be given to God. After
the sun rose he went northeast, sailing large,[1]
about 30 miles, which is seven leagues and a
half, for a certain part of the day, and during
the rest he made another 30 miles, which is
seven and a half leagues,[2] to the east-northeast.

Thursday 24 January

Tonight, taking into consideration the many
shifts that the wind made, he went about 44
miles, which was 11 leagues, northeast. After
sunrise and until sunset he made about 14
leagues east-northeast.

1. (59r17–18) *Andaria al nordeste franco.* "Sailing large" means sailing in a wind
other than a head wind. See Guillén Tato (1951, 69) and Colcord (1945, 207). Also
see p. 37, n. 2.
2. (59r19–21) *Siete leguas y media.* Morison (1963, 158) translates this phrase
as "six and a half leagues" instead of the correct figure, seven and a half.

_/_ navego esta noche al lesnordeste vn peda
30 ço dla noche q fuerō treze ampolletas nue
ve leguas y media / despues anduvo al
~~lesnordeste otras~~ nornordeste otras seys
millas /. Salido el sol todo el dia porq̃ calmo
el viento andaria al lesnordeste .28. millas q̃
35 son .7. leguas /. matarō los marineros vna
tonina y vn grādissimo tiburō : y diz q̃ lo aviā
no
bien menester porq̃ ∧trayen la de comer sino
pan y vino y ajes dlas yndias /.

40 _/_ Esta noche anduvo al leste quarta dl sueste .56
millas q̃ son quatorze leguas /. dspues dl
sol salido navego –[?] a las vezes al lessueste y a las
vezes al sueste andaria hasta las onze oras dl
dia ~~quatro~~ quarēta millas / dspues hizo otro bor

Folio 59v

do y dspues anduvo a la relinga y hasta la
noche anduvo hazia el norte .24. millas
q̃ son seys leguas /.

5 _/_ ayer dspues dl sol puesto anduvo al nordeste
y al norte y al norte quarta dl nordeste y ~~an~~
millas
andaria çinco ~~leguas~~ por ora y en treze oras se
rian .65. millas q̃ son .16. leguas / y media /.
dspues dl sol salido anduvo hazia el nordeste
10 .24. millas q̃ son seys leguas hasta medio dia
y de alli hasta el Sol puesto andaria tres leguas
al lesnordeste /

_/_ Esta noche toda navego al lesnordeste / andaria
15 .36. millas q̃ son .9. leguas /. dspues d[el] Sol

Friday 25 January

A portion of this night he steered to the east-
northeast and in 13 sandglasses they went nine
leagues and a half. Afterward he sailed north-
northeast another six miles. Because the wind
lessened, they made, the whole day after sunrise, about 28 miles, which is seven leagues.
The sailors killed a porpoise and a tremendous
shark, and he says that they had quite some need
of it because they were carrying nothing to eat
except bread and wine and yams from the Indies.

Saturday 26 January

Tonight they made 56 miles, which is 14 leagues,
east by south. After sunrise, he steered sometimes east-southeast and sometimes southeast,
and made about 40 miles up to the eleventh hour
of day. Afterward he tacked and then sailed

59v   close-hauled, and until night he went north 24
miles, which is six leagues.

Sunday 27 January

Yesterday after sunset he went to the northeast
and north and north by east, and he made five
miles per hour, which in 13 hours would be 65
miles, which is sixteen leagues and a half.
After sunrise and until noon he went northeast
24 miles, which is six leagues, and from then
until sunset he made about three leagues east-northeast.

Monday 28 January

This whole night he steered east-northeast. He
made about 36 miles, which is nine leagues. Af-

salido anduvo hasta el sol puesto al lesnordeste
.20. millas q̃ son çinco leguas /. —[?] los ayres
hallo tẽplados y dulçes : vido rabos de juncos
y p[ar]delas / y mũcha yerva /.

martes .29. de Enero

20

/ navego al lesnordeste y andaria en la noche con
sur y sudueste .39. millas q̃ son .9. leguas y
media /. en todo el dia andaria .8. leguas /.
los ayres mũy tẽplados como en abril en castilla
25   la mar mũy llana/. peçes q̃ llamã dorados vinie
rõ abordo /.

miercoles .30. de Enero

/ En toda esta noche andaria .7. leguas al lesnor
deste /. de dia corrio al sur quarta al sueste
30   treze leguas y media /. vido rabos de juncos
y mũcha yerva y mũchas toninas /.

Jueves .31. de Enero

/ navego esta noche al ~~nordeste~~ norte quarta del
nordeste treynta millas : y dspues al nor
35   deste treynta y çinco millas q̃ son diez y seys le
guas /. salido el sol hasta la noche anduvo al
lesnordeste .13. leguas y media /. vierõ ra
bo de junco y p[ar]delas /.

viernes .1º. de hebrero

40   / anduvo esta noche al lesnordeste .10. leguas y
media /. el dia corrio al mismo camino .29.
leguas y vn quarto /. la mar muy llana a
dios grãs /.

Sabado .2. de hebrero

45   / anduvo esta noche al lesnordeste quarẽta millas
                    10
q̃ son .~~15~~ . leguas /. de dia cõ el mismo viento a
popa —[?] corrio .7. millas por ora por mãra q̃ en

ter the sun rose and until sunset he made 20
miles, which is five leagues, east-northeast. He
found the winds temperate and agreeable. He saw
tropic birds and petrels and much weed.

Tuesday 29 January

He steered east-northeast with south and southwest
[winds], and made in the night 39 miles, which is
nine leagues and a half. In the whole day he made
about eight leagues. The breezes were very
temperate, as in Castile in April. The sea was very
smooth. Fish that they call *dorados* came alongside.

Wednesday 30 January

In all of this night he made about seven leagues east-
northeast. During the day he ran south by east
thirteen leagues and a half. He saw tropic birds and
much weed and many porpoises.

Thursday 31 January

He steered this night north by east 30 miles, and
afterward northeast 35 miles, which is 16 leagues.
From sunrise until night he made 13 leagues and a
half east-northeast. They saw a tropic bird and petrels.

Friday 1 February

Tonight he made 10 leagues and a half east-northeast.
During the day he ran 29 leagues and a quarter on
the same course. The sea very smooth, God be given
thanks.

Saturday 2 February

Tonight he made 40 miles, which is 10 leagues,[1] east-
northeast. During the day, with the same stern wind,
he ran at seven miles per hour, so that in 11 hours he

---

1. (59v46) Alvar (1976) reads the canceled number as "16" instead of "15."

onze oras anduvo 77. millas q̃ son 19. leguas y q̄rta /.

Folio 60r

la mar mỹ llana grãs a dios y los aygres my
dulçes / vierō tan quajada la mar de yerva q̃ si
no la ovierā visto temierā ser baxos / parde
las vierō /.

5   Domīgo .3. de hebrero
/ Esta noche yendo a popa cō la mar mỹ llana a dios
grãs andariā .29. leguas / pareciole la estre
lla dl norte mūy alta comō en el cabo de sant
viçeynte / no pudo tomar el altura co el astrolabio
10   ni quadrāte porq̃ la ola no le dio lugar /. el
dia navego al lesnordeste ~~q̃ era~~ [?] su camino y anda
                        y asi
ria diez millas por ora ∧en onze oras .27. leguas /.

                                                              lunes .4. de hebrero
/ esta noche navego al leste quarta dl nordeste par
15   te anduvo .12 millas por ora y p[ar]te diez . y asi
andaria .130. millas q̃ son .32. leguas y media /
tuvo el çielo my turbado y llovioso y hizo algū
frio por lo qual diz q̃ cognoscia q̃ no avia llegado
a las yslas dlos açores /. despues dl sol levata
20   do mudo el camino y fue al leste : anduvo en todo
el dia .77. millas q̃ son .19. leguas y quarta /

                                                              martes .5. de hebrero
/ esta noche navego al leste andaria toda ella .54.
millas q̃ son quatorze leguas menos media /
                        millas
25   el dia corrio .10. ∧ ~~leguas~~ por ora y asi en onze
oras fuerō .110. millas q̃ son .27. leguas y me
dia /. vierō pardelas y vnos palillos q̃ era
señal q̃stavā çerca de tr̄ra /.

made 77 miles, which is 19 leagues and a quarter.

60r   The sea very smooth, thanks to God, and the breeze
very agreeable. [When] they saw how covered the
sea was with weed, if they had not [previously] seen
it so they would have feared that there were shoals.
They saw petrels.

Sunday 3 February

Tonight, going with a stern wind, with the sea very
smooth, thanks to God, they made about 29 leagues.
The North Star appeared very high to him, as on the
Cabo de San Vicente. He tried but could not take its
altitude with the astrolabe or quadrant because the
waves did not give him opportunity. During the day
he steered on his course east-northeast and made
about 10 miles per hour, and thus in 11 hours, 27 leagues.

Monday 4 February

Tonight he steered east by north; part [of the time]
he made 12 miles per hour, and part 10. And thus
he made about 130 miles, which is 32 leagues and a
half. He had an overcast and rainy sky and it was
somewhat cold, because of which he says that he
knew that he had not reached the islands of the
Azores. After the sun rose he changed course and
went east. In the whole day he made 77 miles, which
is 19 leagues and a quarter.

Tuesday 5 February

This night he steered east and in all of it made
about 54 miles, which is 14 leagues less a half.
During the day he ran 10 miles per hour, and thus in
11 hours they went 110 miles, which is 27 leagues
and a half. They saw petrels and a few small
sticks, which was a sign that they were near land.

miercoles .6. de hebrero /

30 / navego esta noche al leste andaria onze [m?]illas
por ora en treze oras dla noche andaria .143.
millas q̃ son .35. leguas y quarta /. vierō mū
cha aves y p[ar]delas / El dia corrio .14. millas por
ora y asi anduvo aq̃l dia .154. millas q̃ son .38
35 leguas y media /. ~~y~~-[?] de mar̃a q̃ fuerō entre dia
y noche .74 leguas poco mas /o menos /. viceyn
te anes q̃ oy por la mañana le quedava la Isla de
flores al norte : y la dla madera al leste / Roldā

este devia ser pelo   dixo q̃ la Isla dl fayal /o la de sant gregorio le
to
40 quedava al nornordeste y el puerto Santo al
leste / parecio mūcha yerva /.

Jueves .7. de hebrero

/ navego esta noche al leste andaria .10. millas
por ora y asi en treze oras .130. millas q̃ son

millas

45 .32. leguas y media /. el dia ocho ~~leguas~~ por
ora : en onze oras .88. millas q̃ son ~~xxi~~-[?] 22
leguas /. en esta mañana estava el almiͤ al sur dla
Isla de flores .75. leguas y el pilo[to] p[er]o alonso yen
do al norte passava entre la terçera y la de sancta ma
50 ria . y al este passava de barlovēto dla Isla dla madera
~~co~~-[?] doze leguas dla p[ar]te dl norte /. vierō los ma[rineros]

Folio 60v

yerva de otra mar̃a dla passada dla q̃ ay mucha en las
Islas dlos acores / dspues se vido dla passada /

viernes –[?] .8 de hebrero

/ anduvo esta noche tres millas por ora al leste
5 por vn rato y dspues camino a la quarta dl sueste
anduvo toda la noche .12. leguas /. ~~al dia por[q̃?]~~
~~hasta me~~-[?] salido el sol hasta medio dia corrio

Wednesday 6 February

Tonight he steered east. He made 11 miles per hour
and in the 13 hours of night made about 143 miles,
which is 35 leagues and a quarter. They saw many
birds and petrels. [During] the day he ran 14 miles
per hour and thus that day made 154 miles, which is
38 leagues and a half. So, counting day and night,
they went 74 leagues, give or take a little.
Vicente Anes [figured] that today in the morning
the island of Flores lay to the north, and that of
Madeira, to the east. Roldán said that the island
of Fayal or that of San Gregorio lay to the north-
northeast and Puerto Santo, to the east. Much weed
appeared.

Thursday 7 February

Tonight he steered east. He made about 10 miles per
hour and thus in 13 hours, 130 miles, which is 32
leagues and a half. [During] the day [he made]
eight miles per hour, and in 11 hours, 88 miles,
which is 22[1] leagues. This morning the Admiral
[figured that he] was 75 leagues south of the island
of Flores,[2] and the pilot Pero Alonso [figured that]
going [i.e., if he went] north he would pass between
Terceira and Santa María and [if he went] east he
would pass to windward of the island of Madeira, 12
leagues off the northern part. The sailors saw weed
of another kind than that already passed, of which
60v   there is much in the islands of the Azores.
Later some of the former kind was seen.

Friday 8 February

This night for a time he made three miles per hour to
the east and later, on a course east by south, made in
the whole night 12 leagues. [From] sunrise until noon

1. (60r46) Alvar (1976) reads the canceled number as *tre(?)* (Alvar's question
mark), not *xxi* [?].
2. (60r47–48) *Al sur de la isla de Flores*, i.e., south of the latitude of Flores. See
Morison (1963, 161, 7 Feb., n. 1).

.27. millas : dspues hasta el sol puesto otras tan

      treze

tas q̃ son ∧ ~~diez~~ leguas al sursueste /.

10   Sabado .9. de hebrero

/ vn rato dsta noche andaria tres leguas al sur
sueste y dspues ~~a la quarta del~~ al sur quarta dl
sueste   dspues al nordeste hasta las diez oras
dl dia otras çinco leguas : y dspues hasta la
15 noche anduvo .9. leguas al leste /.

                                  Domingo .10. de hebrero

/ dspues dl sol puesto navego al leste ——[?] toda la
noche .130. millas q̃ son .32. leguas y media /.
el sol salido hasta la noche anduvo .9. millas por
20 ora y asi anduvo en onze oras .99. millas q̃ son
24. leguas y media y vna quarta /.

§ En la caravela dl almiᵉ carteavā /o echavan punto
viçeynte yanes y los dos pilotos Sancho ruyz ~~pe~~
y pero alonso niño y Rondan / y todos ellos
25 passavā mūcho adelante dlas Islas dlos açores
al leste por sus cartas y navegādo al norte nin
guº tomara–[?] la Isla de Sācta maria q̃s la postre
ra de todas las de los açores ~~pero~~–[?] antes serian
delante co çinco leguas e ~~yra~~–[?] fuerā en la comar
30 ca dla Isla dla madera /o en el puerto Santo /. p[er]o
el almiᵉ se hallava mȳ dsviado dsu camino hallā
dose mūcho mas atras q̃llos /. porq̃ esta noche le
quedavā la Isla de flores al norte y al leste –[?]
yva en demāda a nafe en africa y pasava a
35 barlovento dla Isla dla madera dla p[ar]te dl norte
leguas /. asi q̃llos estavan mas çerca de castilla
q̃l almiᵉ con .150. leguas /. dize q̃ mediante
la grā de dios dsq̃ vean tr̄r̄a se sabra quiē anda
va mas çierto /. dize ~~alli~~ aqui tābien : q̃ prime
40 ro anduvo 263. leguas dla Isla dl hierro a la veni
da q̃ viese la primera yerva etc̃

he ran 27 miles. Afterward, until sunset, as many
again, which is 13 leagues,[1] to the south-southeast.

Saturday 9 February

For a time this night he made about three leagues to
the south-southeast and afterward, south by east and
then to the northeast, until the tenth hour of the day
he made another five leagues: and from then until
night he made nine leagues east.

Sunday 10 February

After sunset he steered east all night 130 miles, which
is 32 leagues and a half. From sunrise until night he
made nine miles per hour and thus in 11 hours made
99 miles, which is 24 leagues and a half and a quarter.

In the Admiral's caravel Vicente Anes and the two pilots, Sancho Ruyz and Pero Alonso Niño, and
Roldán charted their position; and all of them,
according to their charts, [figured they] were passing
much to the east of the islands of the Azores and,
steering north, none would encounter the island of
Santa María, which is the last of all of the islands of
the Azores; rather, [they] would be beyond it by five
leagues, and in the neighborhood of the island of
Madeira or in that of Puerto Santo; but the Admiral
found himself much off his route, and far behind
them, because he figured that tonight the island of
Flores lay to the north and that to the east he was
going toward Nafe in Africa and would be passing to
windward of the island of Madeira,   leagues off
the northern part. So that they were nearer Castile
than the Admiral by 150 leagues. He says that when,
through God's grace, they see land, it will be known
who figured most correctly. He also says here that he
made 263 leagues from the island of Hierro on the
outbound voyage when he saw the first weed, etc.

---

1. (60v9) *Treze leguas*. The daytime run (54 miles) would seem to have been
actually thirteen and a half leagues. Alvar (1976) reads the canceled number here as
doze, not *diez*.

lunes .11. de hebrero

〤 anduvo esta noche doze millas por ora a su camino
y asi en toda ella conto .39. leguas . y en todo el dia
45 corrio .16. leguas y media /. vido mūchas aves
de donde creyo estar çerca de trr̄a /.

martes .12. de hebrero

〤 navego al leste seys millas por ora esta noche y an

Folio 61r

                              73   .18.
          daria hasta el dia .~~63~~. millas q̃ son ∧~~15~~ leguas
comēco a tener y ~~tres quartos~~ vn quarto /. aqui comēço a tener
tormēta /.   grāde mar y tormeta y si no fuera la ca
                ravela diz q̃ mȳ buena y bien adereçada
5   temiera p[er]derse /. el dia correria onze /o do
    ze leguas con mucho trabajo y peligro /.

miercoles .13. de hebrero

〤 despues del sol puesto hasta el dia tuvo grā
trabajo del viento y dla mar mȳ alta y tor
10 mēta / relampagueo hazia el nornordeste
señal de mucho tres vezes dixo ser señal de grā tempestad q̃ avia
viento   —[?] de venir de aq̃lla p[ar]te /o de su contrario /. andu
                vo a arbol seco lo mas dla noche . despues dio vna
                poca de vela y andaria .52. y dos millas q̃
15 son treze leguas /. en este dia ~~calmo~~-[?] blandeo
    vn poco el viento : pero luego crecio / y la mar
    se hizo terrible y cruzavā las olas q̃ atormē
    tavā los navios / andaria .55. millas q̃ son
    treze leguas y media /.

            20   Jueves .14. de hebrero
padeçio grā 〤 Esta noche crecio el viento y las olas eran espā
tormēta   contraria vna de otra
            tables ∧q̃ cruzavā y ~~q̃~~ enbaraçavā el navio q̃

Monday 11 February

Tonight he made 12 miles per hour on his route and
thus in all counted 39 leagues; and in the whole day
ran 16 leagues and a half. He saw many birds,
whereby he thought he was near land.

Tuesday 12 February

He steered east tonight at six miles per hour
61r   and until day made about 73[1] miles, which is
18 leagues and a quarter. Here he began to
have high seas and stormy weather, and he says
that if the caravel were not very stout and
well prepared, he would fear being lost. [Dur-
ing] the day he ran about 11 or 12 leagues
with much trouble and danger.

Wednesday 13 February

After sunset until day he had much trouble
from the wind and the very high seas and
storm. There was lightning off to the north-
northeast three times, which he said was a
sign of a great storm which was to come from
that direction or from its contrary. He went
under bare poles most of the night; afterward
he raised a bit of sail and made about 52 and
two miles, which is 13 leagues. During this
day the wind softened a little but then increased, and the sea became terrible; the
waves crossed one another and tormented the
vessels. He made about 55 miles, which is
thirteen leagues and a half.

Thursday 14 February

Tonight the wind increased and the waves were
frightful, one contrary to the other, so they
crossed and held back the vessel which could

1. (61r1) Alvar (1976) reads the canceled number beneath "73" as "53," not
"63," and he reads the canceled text following "18" as *mi*.

no podia passar adelante ni salir de entreme
dias dlas y q̃bravā en el / llevava el papahi
25 go mȳ baxo p[ar]a q̃ solamēte lo sacase algo ~~dllas~~
dlas ondas andaria asi tres oras y corre
ria .20. millas /. creçia mūcho la mar y el
viento : y viendo el peligro grāde : comēço
a correr a popa donde el viento le llevase : por
30 q̃ no avia otro remedio /. entonçes comēço
a correr tābien la Caravela pinta en q̃ yva

desapareçio
la pinta /.
martin alōso y desapareçio avnq̃ toda la
noche hizo faroles el almiᵉ y el otro le res
pōdia hasta q̃ parez q̃ no pudo mas por la
35 fuerça dla tormēta y porq̃ se hallava mūy
fuera dl camino dl almiᵉ /. anduvo el almiᵉ
esta noche al nordeste quarta dl leste .54. mi
llas q̃ son .13. leguas /. Salido el Sol fue
mayor el viento y la mar cruzādo mas ter
40 rible : llevava el papahigo solo y baxo p[ar]a q̃l
navio saliese de entre las ondas q̃ cruzavan
porq̃ no lo hundiesen /. andava el camino del
lesnordeste y dspues a la quarta hasta el nordeste
andaria seys oras asi y en ellas .7. leguas y me

echan romeros   45 dia /   el ~~mādo q̃~~ [?] ordeno q̃ se echase vn ro
y hazē voto
mero q̃ fuese a Sancta maria de guadalupe y lle
vase vn cirio de çinco libras de çera y q̃ hizie[s?]sen

Folio 61v

voto todos q̃ al q̃ cayesse la suerte cumpliese la rome
ria /. p[ar]a lo qual mando traer tantos garvanços
quātas p[er]sonas en el navio ~~avia~~[?] venian y señalar
                          vn
vno con ∧cuchillo haziendo vna cruz y metellos
5 en vn bonete ~~revueltos~~[?] bien revueltos / El prime

Cayo la suerte sobre   ro q̃ metio la mano fue el almiᵉ y saco el garvāço
el almiᵉ
dla cruz y asi cayo sobre el la suerte y dsde

otro romero
luego se tuvo por romero y devdor de yr a cōplir
el voto /. Echose otra vez la suerte p[ar]a enbiar Ro
10 mero a Santa maria de loreto q̃ esta en la marca
de ancona tīrra dl papa ——[?] q̃ es casa donde nīra

neither go forward nor get out from between
them, and the waves broke on her. She carried
her mainsail very low, just high enough to be
kept somewhat out of the waves. They went
along thus for three hours and ran about 20
miles. The seas and wind were increasing
greatly, and seeing the great danger, he
began to run before the wind wherever it would
carry him, for there was nothing else to do.
Then the caravel *Pinta*, in which Martín Alonso
was sailing, also began to run before the wind
and disappeared, although the Admiral made
signal lights all night and the other answered
until it appeared that she could do no more
because of the force of the storm and because
she was very far off the Admiral's course.
The Admiral tonight made 54 miles, which is 13
leagues, northeast by east. When the sun
rose, the wind was greater and the cross seas
more terrible. He carried only the mainsail,
and low, so the vessel would get out from
among the crossing seas so they would not sink
her. He went on a course to the east-northeast and then to the northeast by east. He
went on about six hours thus and in them made
seven leagues and a half. He ordered that
lots should be drawn for a pilgrimage to Santa
María de Guadalupe and to take a five-pound
wax candle, and that all should swear that

61v   he to whom the lot should fall would carry
out the pilgrimage. For this purpose he
ordered brought as many chick-peas as there
were persons traveling on the ship and that
one be marked with a knife, making a cross,
and that they be put in a cap and well mixed
up. The first who put in his hand was the
Admiral and he drew out the chick-pea with the
cross and so the lot fell to him and from then
on he considered himself a pilgrim obligated
to go and carry out the vow. They drew lots
again to send a pilgrim to Santa María de
Loreto, which is in the March of Ancona, papal

Señora a hecho y haze mūchos y grādes milagros
y cayo la suerte a vn marinero dl puerto de
Sancta maria q̃ se llamava pedro de villa y el al

15 mirāte le prometio de le dar dineros p[ar]a las costas .

otro romero y cayo   Otro romero acordo q̃ se enbiase a q̃ velase vna
la suerte al almiᵉ   noche en Sancta clara de moguer y hiziese dezir

                                        rō
vna missa p[ar]a lo qual se torna∧ a echar el a echar
los garvāços con el dla cruz : y cayo la suerte

otro voto   20 al mismo almiᵉ /. Despues desto el almiᵉ y toda
la gente hizierō voto de en llegādo a la primera tr̄ra
yr todos en camissa en proçession a hazer oraçion
en la [?] en vna igl[es]ia q̃ se llamase [?] fuese dla invo
caçion de nr̄a señora

hazian votos   25 Allende los votos generales /o comunes cada vno
p[ar]ticulares   hazia en espeçial su voto porq̃ ninguᵒ pensava esca
par y teniendose todos por p[er]didos segū la terri
                                  va
ble tormēta q̃ padeçian /. ayuda∧a acrecentar

                          a. con falta de lastre por averse alivanado la [
el peligro q̃ venia el navio mal lastrado + /. lo qual   b. ga siendo y[a]
                                                          c. comidos los [b
30 por cudiçia del prosp[er]o tp̄o q̃ entre las yslas tuvie   d. mētos y el a[gu
                          yo   e. y vino bevi[do
rō no prove∧ cho [?] el almirāte aviendo teniendo propo
sito de lo mādar lastrar en la Isla dlas mugeres
——[?] adonde lleva proposito de yr /. El reme
dio q̃ p[ar]a esta neçessidad tuvo fue quādo hazerlo

35 pudierō henchir las pipas q̃ tenian vazias de
agua y vino : de agua dla mar y con esto en ella
se remediarō /

pone las causas
q̃ le augmētavā
el miedo s de se   ∤ Escrive aqui el almiᵉ las causas que le ponian temor
p[er]der y las q̃ le
davā esp[er]ança de
salir a saluamē
to

territory,[1] which is a sanctuary where Our
Lady has performed and performs many and great
miracles. And the lot fell to a sailor from
the port of Santa María who was named Pedro de
Villa, and the Admiral promised to give him
money for his expenses. He decided to draw
lots for another pilgrim to go to and spend a
night at vigil in Santa Clara de Moguer and to
have a Mass said, for which they again drew
lots with the chick-peas for the one with the
cross. And the lot fell to the Admiral himself. After this the Admiral and all the men
made a vow that, as soon as they reached the
first land, all would go in their shirt-
sleeves in procession to pray in a church
dedicated to Our Lady.

In addition to the general or common vows,
each one made his own special vow, because no
one thought to escape, all regarding themselves as lost because of the terrible storm
that they were suffering. The fact that the
ship was sailing with a lack of ballast
helped to increase the danger, her cargo having been lightened by consumption of provisions and the drinking of water and wine:[2]
which [ballast], because of their greediness
during the prosperous time they had in the islands, the Admiral did not provide, intending
to order the ship ballasted on the Isla de las
Mugeres where[3] he had proposed to go. The
remedy which he had for this lack was to fill
the pipes which were empty of water and wine,
when they could, with water from the sea, and
with this water in her they were helped.

The Admiral writes here the reasons which made

1. (61v11) Alvar (1976) reads the canceled word in this line as *done*.
2. (61v29a—e) This insert is partially boxed in the right margin. The letters
bracketed here are cut off in the manuscript facsimile.
3. (61v33) Alvar (1976) reads the canceled text preceding *adonde* as *cuando*.

de q̃ alli nr̄o señor no quisiese q̃ pereciese y otras

40 q̃ le davā esp[er]ança de q̃ dios le avia de llevar en sal
vamēto p[ar]a q̃ tales nuevas como llevava a los reyes
no pereçiesen /. pareçiale q̃l dseo grāde q̃ tenia de
llevar estas nuevas tā grādes y mostrar q̃ avia
salido Vrdadero en lo q̃ avia dicho y proferidose a des

45 cubrir : le ponia grādissimo miedo de no lo conseguir
                    cada
y q̃ ~~vn~~ mosquito diz q̃ le podia ~~Impedir~~ perturbar
e impedir /. ~~cosa~~-[?] atribuyolo esto a su poca fe y des
fallecimi⁰ ~~de ella~~-[?] de confiança dla providencia diuina /
confertavale por otra p[ar]te las m[erce]des q̃ dios le avia

50 hecho en dalle tanta victoria descubriendo lo q̃ descubier

Folio 62r

to avia . y cōplidole dios todos sus deseos / avien
do passado en castilla en sus dspachos mūchas adVrsidades
y cōtrariedades /. ~~y avia xpia q̃ avia~~-[?] y q̃ como
-[?] antes oviese puesto su fin y endereçado todo

5 su negoçio a dios : y le avia oydo y dado todo
lo q̃ le avia pedido : devia creer q̃ le daria
cōplimi⁰ dlo comēçado y le llevaria en salua
mēto /. mayormēte q̃ pues le avia libra
do a la yda +   de los trabajos q̃ con los marine   a. + quādo tenia mayor

10 ros y gente q̃ llevava : los quales todos a   b. razō de temer
las angustias y   vna boz estavan determinados de se bolver
turbaciones q̃
padecio a la yda   se
dla gente q̃ con   y alçar∧contra el haziendo protestaçiones : ~~mas~~-[?] y
sigo llevava   el eterno dios le dio esfuerço y valor contra
to[—?]dos y otras cosas de mūcha maravilla q̃
                    avia
15 dios ∧~~a~~ mostrado en el y por el en aq̃l viaje : allē
de aq̃llas q̃ sus altezas sabian dlas p[er]sonas

him fear that Our Lord might wish[1] him to perish and others giving him hope that God would
take him to safety so such news as he would
carry to the sovereigns would not perish. It
seemed to him that the great desire he had to
bear such great news and to show that he had
turned out to be right in all he had said and
offered to discover made him tremendously
fearful of not succeeding, so that each
gnat, he says, could upset and hinder him.
He attributed[2] this to his small faith and
loss of confidence in Divine Providence. On
the other hand, he was comforted by the favors
that God had done for him in giving him such a
victory in discovering what he had discovered,
62r   and in God's fulfilling for him all his desires,
having passed in Castile, in his affairs,
many adversities and hindrances;[3] and
[he writes here] that, since earlier he had
entrusted his destiny and dedicated all of his
enterprise to God, Who had heard him and given
him all he had asked for, he ought to believe
that God would grant him the completion of
what he had begun and would take him to
safety. And more so since He had delivered
him on the outward voyage, when he had greater
reason to fear from his troubles with[4] the
sailors and people that he took with him, who
all, with one voice, were determined to go
back and to rise against him in protest. And
the eternal God gave him strength and resolution against all of them.[5] And there were
other very wonderful things that God had
shown in him and through him on that voyage,
beyond those that their Highnesses knew about

1. (61v39) *No quisiese.* Another example of the use of a redundant *no* after a
"negative thought," i.e., fear.
2. (61v47) Alvar (1976) reads the canceled text preceding *atribuyolo* as *dicha.*
3. (62r3) Alvar (1976) reads the canceled text following *contrariedades* as *y avia
expu que avia.*
4. (62r9) De Lollis (1892–94) inserts the word *tuvo* after *trabajos que* (troubles
with).
5. (62r14) *To[—?]dos* (all of them). In the manuscript a large inkblot separates
the two syllables of *todos.*

de su casa / ~~antes su flaqueza y congoxa no~~
~~le dexava (diz q̃) asentar su anima /.~~ asi que (di
ze) q̃ no deviera temer la d̄ha tormēta /.

20   mas su flaqueza y cōgoxa (dize el) no me dexa
             la
va asensar ∧~~mi~~-[?] anima /. Dize mas q̃ tambiē
le dava gran pena dos hijos q̃ tenia en cordova
al estudio q̃ los dexava guerfanos de padre
y madre en tierra estraña : y los reyes no sa

25   bian los s[er]v[ic]iᵒˢ q̃ les avia en aq̃l viaje hecho y
nuevas tan prosp[er]as q̃ les llevava : p[ar]a q̃ se mo
viesen a los remediar /. por esto y porq̃ su
piesen sus altezas cōmo nr̄o señor le avia
dado victoria de todo lo q̃ dseava dlas yndias

30   y suppiese q̃ ninguᵃ tormēta avia en aq̃llas
p[ar]tes ~~dlas~~ lo qual dize q̃ se puede cognosçer
por la yerva y arboles q̃stan nacidos y creci

vna Industria q̃   dos hasta dentro en la mar /. y porq̃ si se p[er]die
tuvo p[ar]a q̃ supie   se cō aq̃lla tormēta los reyes oviesen noticia
sen los reyes su
viaje si se perdiese   de su viaje : tomo vn pargamino y escrivio en
el todo lo q̃ pudo de todo lo q̃ avia hallado : rogā
do mūcho a quiē lo hallase q̃ lo llevase a los
reyes /. Este pargamino ~~metio~~ enbolvio
en vn paño ençerado atado mȳ bien : y mā

40   do traer vn grā barril de madera y pusolo
en el sin q̃ ninguᵃ p[er]sona supiese q̃ era : sino
q̃ pensarō todos q̃ era alguna devoçion y asi
lo mādo echar en la mar /. despues cō los
aguaceros y turbionadas se mūdo el viento

45   al gueste y andaria asi a popa solo cō el trique
te —[?] çinco oras cō la mar mūy desconçertada y
            leguas
andaria dos ∧y media al nordeste /. avia quitado
el papahigo dla vela mayor : por miedo q̃ alguna on

Folio 62v
da dla mar no se lo llevase del todo /.

from persons of their household, so that, he
says, he ought not to fear the storm.   But
his weakness and faint heart, he says, was
not letting his spirit give assent.[1]   He
says, too, that he was much troubled that he
would leave in a foreign land, orphaned of
father and mother, two sons that he had in
Seville, studying, and that the sovereigns
would not know of the services that he had
performed for them on that voyage or the
prosperous news that he was bringing them, and
would not be moved to help them.   Because of
this, and so that their Highnesses would learn
how Our Lord had given him victory in all he
desired from the Indies and would learn that
there were no storms in those parts, which he
says one can recognize by the herbage and
trees which germinate and grow even in the
sea.   In order that the sovereigns would get
news of his voyage in case he were lost in
the storm, he took a parchment and wrote on
it all that he could about everything that he
had found, greatly beseeching him who might
find it to take it to the sovereigns.   He
wrapped it in a well-tied, waxed cloth and
ordered a large wooden barrel brought and he
put the parchment in it without anyone
learning what it was, except that everyone
thought it was some act of devotion; and he
ordered it thrown into the sea.   Later, with
heavy rainfall and squalls, the wind changed
to west and he sailed with a stern wind for
five hours with very high seas and only the
foresail set; and he made about two leagues
and a half to the northeast.   He had taken
in the mainsail for fear that some wave from
62v   the sea would carry it away[2] completely.

1.   (62r21) *Asensar* was probably intended to be *asentar*, "to assent."   De Lollis
(1892–94) actually changes *asensar* to *asentar*. *Asensar* does not appear in the *Diccionario* (1956).
2.   (62r48–62v1) *Por miedo que no se lo llevase* (for fear that some wave would
carry it away).   This is still another example of the redundant *no*, again appearing after
miedo, "fear."

⸝ Ayer dspues dl sol puesto comēço a mostrarse
claro el çielo dla vanda del gueste y mostra
va q̃ queria de hazia alli ventar / dio la bone
ta a la vela mayor todavia la mar era altis
sima avnq̃ yva algo baxandose : anduvo al
lesnordeste quatro millas por ora y en treze oras
de noche fuerō treze leguas /. Despues
dl sol salido vierō tr̄r̄a pareciales por proa ad

*esta tr̄r̄a era la
ysla de Sāta mar
ia en los açores*

                         dezian
lesnordeste /. algunos -dias- q̃ era la Isla dla ma
dera : otros q̃ era la roca de sintra en portugal
Junto a lisboa /. Salto luego el viento por proa les
nordeste : y la mar venia mūy alta dl gueste
avria dla Caravela a la tr̄r̄a .5º. leguas /. El
almiᵉ por su navegaçion se hallava estar cō las
Islas -y creya q̃ aq̃lla- dlos açores : y creya
q̃ aq̃lla era vna dllas : los pilotos y mari
neros se hallavā ya en tr̄r̄a de Castilla /

*el almiᵉ andava
mȳ çierto en lo
q̃ aviā andado :
y los pilotos
y marineros er
ravan*

⸝ toda esta noche anduvo dādo bordos por encaval
gar la tr̄r̄a -dllo- q̃ ya se cognoscia ser Isla : a ve
zes yva al nordeste / otras ad nornordeste
hasta q̃ salio el Sol q̃ tomo la buelta del sur por
llegar a la Isla q̃ ya no vian por la grā cer
razon / y vido por popa otra Isla q̃ distaria .8º.
leguas /. dspues dl Sol salido hasta la noche
anduvo dādo bueltas por llegarse a la tr̄r̄a cō
el mūcho viento y mar q̃ llevava /. —[?] al dezir dla
Salue q̃s a boca de noche algunos vierō lūbre
de sotavento y pareçia que devia ser la Isla q̃
vierō ayer primero y toda la noche anduvo bar
lovēteando y allegandose lo mas q̃ podia p[ar]a ver si
al salir dl sol via alguᵃ dlas yslas / Esta noche
reposo el almiᵉ algo porq̃ dsde el miercoles no a

Friday 15 February

Yesterday, after sunset, the sky in the west
began to clear and it looked as if the wind
were about to blow in that direction. He set
the bonnet on the mainsail, the seas being still extremely high, although they were getting somewhat
lower. He made four miles per hour east-northeast
and in the 13 hours of night went 13 leagues. After
the sun rose they saw land, which appeared ahead to
the east-northeast. Some said it was the island of
Madeira, others that it was the Rock of Sintra in
Portugal, near Lisbon. Soon the wind made a quick
change to the east-northeast, off the bow, and very
high seas came from the west. From the caravel to
land was about five leagues. The Admiral, by his
calculations, figured that they were among the islands[1] of the Azores, and believed that the island
was one of them. The pilots and sailors figured
that they were already off Castilian territory.

Saturday 16 February

All this night they tacked back and forth to make
land, which now was recognized to be an island. At
times they went northeast, at others north-northeast, until the sun rose, when they took a course to
the south to reach the island, which now they did
not see because of the great obscurity. And they
saw astern another island which was distant about
eight leagues. After sunrise until night they
tacked back and forth in the high wind and seas that
it brought, in order to get to land. When they said
the *Salve*, which is at nightfall, some saw a light
to leeward and it seemed that it should be the island that they saw first yesterday; and all night he
went beating into the wind and getting as close as
he could to see if, when the sun rose, he would see
one of the islands. This night the Admiral rested
somewhat because, since Wednesday, he had not slept

1. (62v17) Alvar (1976) reads the canceled text following *Islas* as *y veya que aquella*.

via dormido ni podido dormir y quedava mȳ tolli
do dlas piernas por estar siemp^r dsabrigado al frio
y al agua y por el poco comer /. el sol salido na
vego al sursudueste y a la noche llego a la Isla : y por
40   la grā cerrazō no pudo cognosçer q̃ Isla era /

Lunes .18. de hebrero

/ dspues ayer dl sol puesto anduvo rodeādo la
Isla p[ar]a ver donde avia de surgir y tomar lēn
gua : surgio cō vna ancla ꝭ[?] q̃ luego perdio : tor
45   no a dar la vela y barloventeo toda la noche /
despues dl sol salido : llego otra vez dla p[ar]te dl
norte dla Isla y donde le p[ar]ecio surgio cō vn
ancla y enbio la barca en tr̄r̄a y ovierō habla

Folio 63r

tomo la Isla de
Sancta maria y
asi açerto en su
navegaçion y todos
los otros errarō /.

con la gēte dla Isla y supieron como era la Isla
de Sancta maria vna dlas dlos açores : y en
señarōles el puerto donde avian de poner la
Caravela / y dixo la gente dla Isla q̃ jamas aviā
5   visto tanta tormēta comō la q̃ avia hecho los quin
ze dias passados / y q̃ se maravillava comō aviā
escapado /. los quales (diz q̃) dierō mūchas grãs
a dios y hizierō mūchas alegrias por las nue

pareçen fingi
das estas alegri
as q̃ hizierō los
portugueses /.

vas q̃ sabian de aver el almiç dscubierto las Yndias
10   dize el almiç q̃ aq̃lla su navegaçion avia sido mȳ
çierta y q̃ avia Carteado bien q̃ fuesen dadas mū
chas grãs a nr̄o señor avnq̃ se hazia algo delantero
~~puesto~~ pero tenia por çierto q̃stava en la comarca
dlas Islas dlos açores y q̃ aq̃lla era vna dllas /. y
15   diz q̃ fingio aver andado mas camino por desatinar
a los pilotos y marineros q̃ carteavā / por quedar
el Señor de aq̃lla derrota dlas yndias comō de
hecho queda porq̃ ningu^o de todos ellos traya su ca
mino çierto por lo qual ningu^o puede estar segu
20   ro dsu derrota p[ar]a las yndias /.

or been able to sleep and hardly had the use of his
legs because of always being exposed to the cold and
water and because of eating little. At sunrise he
steered south-southwest and at night reached the
island; and because of the great obscurity he could
not make out which island it was.

Monday 18 February

Yesterday, after sunset, he went around the island
to see where he should anchor and get information.
He anchored with one anchor which he soon lost.
He set sail again and beat to windward all night.
After sunrise he again reached the northern part of
the island and, where it seemed [suitable], anchored
with one anchor and sent the launch ashore where

63r   his men talked with the people of the island and
found out that it was Santa María, one of the islands
of the Azores; and they showed them the harbor
where they should put the caravel. And the islanders said never had they seen such a storm as the one
of the past 15 days, and that they were astonished
at how they had escaped. The islanders gave many
thanks to God and were joyful at the news that they
learned about the Admiral's having discovered the
Indies. The Admiral says that that navigation of
his had been very accurate and that he had charted
well—many thanks be given to Our Lord—even
though he thought himself somewhat farther along;
but he had considered it certain that he was in the
area of the Azores and that that island was one of
them. And he says that he pretended to have gone a
greater distance to confuse the pilots and sailors
who were charting their course so that he would
remain the master of the route to the Indies, as in
fact he does, since none of them showed on their
charts his true route, because of which no one could
be sure of his route to the Indies.

martes .19. de hebrero

ribera

/ despues dl sol puesto viniero a la∧ ~~caravela~~ tres
hōbres dla Isla y llamarō enbioles la barca en
la qual vinierō y truxerō gallinas y pan fresco

25   y era dia de Carnestolendas y truxerō otras cosas
 q̃ ~~le~~ [?] enbiava el capitan dla Isla q̃ se llamava Juā
de Castañeda diziēdole q̃ lo cognoscia mȳ biē
y q̃ por ser noche no venia a vello : p[er]o q̃ en a

mas

maneçiendo vernia y traeria ∧refresco / y traeria
30   consigo tres hōbres q̃ alla quedavā ~~se~~ dla caravela : y
q̃ no los enbiava por el grā plazer q̃ con ellos tenia
oyendo las cosas dsu viaje /. el almiᵉ mādo hazer
mūcha hōrra a los mēsajeros ——[?] y mādoles dar camas
en q̃ durmiesen aq̃lla noche porq̃ era tarde y
35   estava la poblaçion lexos /. y porq̃l jueves passado
quādo se vido en la angustia dla tormēta hizierō el
voto y votos susodhos : y el de que en la primera
tr̄r̄a donde oviese casa de nr̄a señora saliesen en cami
sa etc̃. acordo q̃ la mitad dla gente fue a cōplillo a vna

a. y el yria despues con la otra mitad

40   casita q̃ estava junto cō la mar como hermita + ~~confiando~~
~~en~~ viendo q̃ era tr̄r̄a segura y confiando en las ofertas
dl Capitan y en la paz q̃ tenia portugal con castilla :
rogo a los tres hōbres q̃ se fuesen a la poblaçion y hi
ziesen venir vn cl[er]igo p[ar]a q̃ les dixese vna missa /. los
45   quales ydos en camisa en complimiᵒ de su romeria

prēdio el portugues
y los suyos a la gē
te dl almiᵉ

y estando en su oraçion : salto contrellos todo el pueblo
a cavallo y a pie cō el capitan : y prendierōlos a todos /.

Folio 63v

Despues estando el almiᵉ sin sospecha esperādo la barca
p[ar]a salir el a cōplir su romeria cō la otra gente hasta
las onze dl dia : viendo q̃ no venian sospecho
q̃ los detenian /o q̃ la barca se avia quebrado
5   por toda la Isla esta çercada de peñas mūy altas /.
esto no podia ver el almiᵉ porq̃ la hermita estava de

Tuesday 19 February

After sunset three men of the island came to the
shore and hailed them. The Admiral sent the launch
for them, in which they came and brought chickens
and fresh bread and other things that the captain
of the island, who was named Juan de Castañeda, was
sending (and it was one of the days of Carnival) and
they brought a message from the captain, saying that
he knew of the Admiral very well and, because it was
night, he was not coming to see him, but at dawn
would come and would bring more refreshment, and
would bring with him three men from the caravel
who were staying there; and that he was not sending
them back because of the great pleasure he was having
with them, hearing things about the voyage. The
Admiral ordered the messengers treated with much
courtesy and given beds in which to sleep that night,
because it was late and the town was far off. And
because, on Thursday past, when they were in the
anguish of the storm, they [had] made the vow and
vows mentioned previously, and the vow that in the
first land where there was a sanctuary of Our Lady
they would go out in their shirt-sleeves, etc., the
Admiral decided that half of the men should go to a
small sanctuary near the sea, like a hermitage, to
fulfill the vow, and that he would go afterward with
the other half. Seeing that the land was safe and
trusting in the offerings of the captain and the peace
between Portugal and Castile, he beseeched the three
men to go off to the settlement and have a priest
come to say a Mass for them. While the Admiral's
men, having gone in shirt-sleeves in fulfillment of
their pilgrimage, were at their prayers, the whole
town, on foot and on horseback, with the captain,
fell upon them and captured them all. Later, the
Admiral, without suspicion, waiting until the
eleventh hour of day for the launch so he could leave
with the other men to carry out their pilgrimage,
seeing that they were not coming, suspected that the
islanders were detaining them or that the launch had
been damaged, for the whole island is surrounded by
very high rocks. The Admiral could not see what had

63v

      tras de vna punta /. levāto el ancla y dio la vela

      hasta en derecho dla hermita / y vido mūchos de

      Cavallo q̃ se apearō y entrarō en la ~~iglesia~~-[?] barca cō

10 armas y vinierō a la caravela p[ar]a prēder al almiͤ

      levantose el capitan en la barca y pidio seguro al

      almiͤ dixo q̃ se lo dava : p[er]o q̃ Innouaçion era

      aq̃lla q̃ no via ninguͦ dsu gente en la barca /. y

      añidio el almiͤ q̃ viniese ~~q̃~~ y entrase en la caravela

15 q̃l haria todo lo q̃l quisiese /. y pretendia el almiͤ

      con buenas palabras traello por prendello p[ar]a

      recuperar su gente : no creyendo q̃ violava la

      fe dandole seguro / pues el aviendo le ofreçido

      paz y seguridad lo avia quebrātado /. el capitan

20 com̃o diz q̃ traya mal proposito no se fio a entrar

      visto q̃ no se llegava a la caravela : rogole q̃ le dixe

      se la causa porq̃ detenia su gente y q̃ dllo pesaria

      al rey de portugal y q̃ en tr̄r̄a dlos reyes de casti

      lla reçibian los portugueses mūcha hōrra y en

25 travā y estavā seguros com̃o en lisboa / y q̃ los

      reyes –[?] avian dado c[ar]tas de recomēdaçion p[ar]a todos los

      prinçipes y señores y hōbres dl mūdo las qua

      les le mostraria si se quisiese llegar : y q̃l era

      su almiͤ ~~y vi~~ dl mar oçeano y visorey dlas yn

30 dias q̃ agora erā ~~dsus alte~~ dsus altezas : dlo

      qual mostraria las provisiones firmadas dsus

      firmas y selladas con sus sellos / las quales le

      enseño de lexos /. y q̃ los reyes estavā en mū

      cho amor y amistad cō el rey de portugal y le avian mā

35 dado q̃ hiziese toda la hōrra q̃ pudiese a los navi

      os q̃ topase de portugal / y q̃ dado q̃ no le quisie

      se darle su gente : no por eso dexaria de yr a

      castilla pues tenia harta gente p[ar]a navegar hasta

      sevilla y serian el y su gente bien castigados haziē

40 dole aq̃l agravio /. Entonçes respōdio el capitan y

happened because the hermitage was behind a point. He raised anchor and sailed as far as a place facing the hermitage. And he saw many men on horseback who dismounted and got into the launch with their arms and came to the caravel to capture the Admiral. The captain stood up in the launch and asked the Admiral for a safe conduct. He said he would give it to him, but what a strange thing was this, that he saw none of his men in the launch. And the Admiral added that the captain should come aboard the caravel and that he would do all that the captain might wish. And the Admiral tried with agreeable words to attract and capture him in order to recover his people, not believing that he would thereby violate his promise to give the captain safe conduct, since the latter, having offered him peace and security, had broken his. The captain, he says, since he was harboring an evil purpose, did not trust himself to board. When it was seen that he was not approaching the caravel, the Admiral asked him to tell why he was detaining his people and said that the king of Portugal would be offended by it, and that in the territory of the sovereigns of Castile the Portuguese were received with much courtesy and entered and were as safe as in Lisbon, and that the sovereigns had given him letters of recommendation for all the princes, lords, and men in the world, which he would show to him if he wished to come aboard; and that he was their Admiral of the Ocean Sea and Viceroy of the Indies, which now belonged to their Highnesses, concerning which he would show the provisions signed with their signatures and sealed with their seals, and which he showed the captain from afar. And that the sovereigns were on loving and friendly terms with the king of Portugal and had ordered the Admiral to show all the courtesy that he could to Portuguese ships that he might come across; and even if the captain were not willing to give him his men, he would not fail to return to Castile, since he had plenty of men to sail as far as Seville; and the captain and his men would be thoroughly punished for committing such an offense. Then the captain and the others

los demas no cognoscē~~mos~~ aca rey e reyna de
Castilla ni sus c[ar]tas ni le aviā miedo antes les
darian a saber que era portugal / quasi amena
zando /. lo qual oydo el almiᶜ ovo mūcho sentimiᵒ
   diz que
45 y ∧~~temio~~-[?] penso si avia passado algun desconçierto
 ~~diz q̃~~ entre vn reyno y otro dspues de su p[ar]tida /.
y no se pudo çufrir q̃ no les respōdiese lo q̃ era ra

Folio 64r

zon /. dspues tornose diz q̃ a levātar aq̃l capitan
desde lexos y dixo al almiᶜ q̃ se fuese cō la cara
vela al puerto : y q̃ todo lo q̃ el hazia y avia hecho
el rey su señor se lo avia embiado a mādar /. dlo
5 qual el almiᶜ tomo testigos los q̃ en la caravela
     el almiᶜ
estavan /. y torno ∧~~los~~-[?] a llamar al capitan y a todos
ellos y les dio su fe y prometio comō quien era
de no dscender ni salir dla caravela hasta q̃ lle
vase vn çiento de portugueses a castilla y despoblar
10 toda aq̃lla Isla /. y asi se bolvio a surgir en el
pueʳto donde estava primero porq̃l tp̄o y viento
era mȳ malo p[ar]a hazer otra cosa /.

              miercoles .20. de hebrero
ᴸ mādo adereçar el navio y hinchir las pipas de
15 agua dla mar por lastre porq̃ estava en mȳ
mal puerto y temio q̃ se le cortasen las amar
      hazia
ras y asi fue : por lo qual dio la vela ∧~~p[ar]a~~ la Isla
de Sant miguel + avnq̃ en ninguᵃ de las dlos açores a. ~~porq̃ tenia ot[ro]~~
ay buē puerto p[ar]a el tp̄o q̃ entonçes hazia / ~~y no~~ b. ~~remedio sin[o hu]~~
20 y no tenia otro remedio sino huyr a la mar /.   c. ~~yr a la mar~~

answered that in those parts they did not recognize
the king and queen of Castile nor their letters,
nor did they fear them: rather, they would give
them to understand that this was Portugal, almost menacingly. Having heard this, the Admiral felt greatly disturbed and says that he
wondered whether some disagreement between one
kingdom and the other had occurred since his
departure. And he could not tolerate not
being able to answer them suitably. Later, he

64r   says, the captain stood up again at a distance
and told the Admiral to go with the caravel to
the harbor, and that all that he was doing and
had done was by orders the king his lord had
sent. Of this the Admiral took as witnesses
those men who were in the caravel. And the
Admiral again called to the captain and all of
them and gave them his word and promised on
his honor not to disembark or leave the caravel until he could take a hundred Portuguese
[captive] to Castile and depopulate all that
island. And so he again anchored in the harbor where he had been earlier because the
weather and wind were very bad for doing anything else.

Wednesday 20 February

He ordered the vessel readied and the pipes
filled with seawater for ballast because he
was in a very bad harbor and he feared that
the cables would part on him, and so it happened; because of which he set sail toward
the island of San Miguel,[1] even though there
is no good harbor in any of the Azores in the
kind of weather they were having; and there
was no other remedy except to head out to sea.

---

1. (64r18a–b) The bracketed letters within the canceled insert following *Sant
miguel* are cut off in the manuscript facsimile.

Jueves -20-[?] .21. de hebrero

ayer

/ Partio∧de aq̃lla Isla de Sancta maria p[ar]a la Isla de
Sant miguel p[ar]a ver si hallara pueᵉrto p[ar]a poder çu
frir tan mal tp̄o com̃o hazia con mūcho viento y mū

25 cha mar y anduvo hasta la noche sin poder ver
tr̄r̄a vna ni otra por la gr̄a çerrazon y escuran[z?]a q̃
el viento y la mar causavan /. El almiᵉ dize q̃sta
va cō poco plazer porq̃ no tenia sino tres marine
ros dlos q̃ supiesen dla mar porq̃ los q̃ mas

passo esta noche alli estavā no sabian dla mar nada /. Estuvo a la
grā tormēta corda toda esta noche cō mȳ mūcha tormēta y grā
y peligro

en
de -ple-[?] peligro y trabajo /. y ∧lo q̃ nr̄o Señor le
hizo m[erce]d fue : q̃ la mar o las ondas dlla veni
an de sola vna p[ar]te : porq̃ si cruzarā com̃o las pas

35 sadas mūy mayor -pa- mal padeçiera /. Despues
del sol salido visto q̃ no via la Isla de Sant mi
guel : acordo tornarse a la Sācta maria : por ver
si podia cobrar su gēte y la barca y las amarras
-q̃- y anclas q̃ alla dexava /.

40 Dize q̃ estava maravillado de tan mal tp̄o com̃o avia
en aq̃llas islas y p[ar]tes : porq̃ en las yndias nave
go todo aq̃l invierno sin surgir q̃ avia siempᵉ buenos
tp̄os /. y q̃ vna sola ora no vido la mar q̃ no se
pudiese bien navegar / y en aq̃llas islas avia pa

45 deçido tan grave tormēta y lo mismo le acaecio a la
yda hasta las islas de Canaria / –[?] p[er]o passado dllas
siempᵉ hallo los ayres y la mar cō grā templança /. -par-[?]

Folio 64v

Concluyēdo dize el almiᵉ q̃ bien dixerō los sacros
theologos y los sabios philosophos q̃ el parayso
terrenal esta enl -oriente- fin de oriente porq̃
es lugar temperadissimo /. asi q̃ aq̃llas tr̄r̄as q̃

5 agora el avia descubierto es (dize el) el fin del
oriēte /.

Thursday 21 February

He departed yesterday from the island of Santa
María for the island of San Miguel to see if
he might find a harbor where he could withstand such bad weather, with much wind and
heavy seas, and he went until night without
being able to see land, either the one [is-
land] or the other, because of the great
obscurity and darkness that the wind and sea
were causing. The Admiral says he felt little
pleasure because he had but three experienced
sailors, most of those who were there knowing
nothing of the sea. He jogged off and on all
this night with much storm and great danger and
trouble. And Our Lord did him a great mercy in
that the sea, or its waves, came from a single
direction; because if they had crossed like those
of the past, he would have suffered a much greater
evil. After sunrise, seeing that he did not have
the island of San Miguel in view, he decided to
return to Santa María to see if he could recover his men and the launch and the cables and
anchors that he left there.

He says that he was astonished at such bad weather
as he was having in those islands and regions,
since in the Indies he sailed all winter without
anchoring and there was always good weather and
not for a single hour did he find the sea when it
could not be sailed easily, and [that] in those
islands he had suffered such a severe storm. The
same thing happened to him on his outward voyage,
as far as the Canary Islands; but, the islands
passed, he always found the breezes and the sea
64v   very moderate. Concluding, the Admiral says that
venerable theologians and wise philosophers have
well said that the terrestrial paradise is at the
end of the Orient because it is a most temperate
place. So that those lands that now he has discovered are, he says, the end of the Orient.

Viernes .22. de hebrero

/ ayer surgio en la Isla de Santa maria en el
lugar /o puerto donde primero avia surgido :
10 y luego vino vn hōbre a capear desde vnas pe
ñas q̃ alli estavā fronteras diziēdo q̃ no se fuesen
de alli /. luego vino ~~vna~~ la barca cō çinco mari
neros y dos cl[er]igos y vn escrivano /. pidierō
seguro : y dado por el almiᶜ subierō a la Caravela
15 y porq̃ era noche durmierō alli y el almiᶜ les
hizo la hōrra q̃ pudo /. a la mañana le requirie
rō q̃ les mostrasse poder dlos reyes de castilla
p[ar]a q̃ a ellos les constase comō con poder dellos
avia hecho aq̃l viaje /. sintio el almiᶜ q̃ aq̃llo
20 hazian por mostrar color q̃ no avian en lo he
cho errado sino q̃ tuvierō razō / porq̃ no avian
podido aver la p[er]sona dl almiᶜ la qual devierā
de ~~pretender aver pretēder prendella /.~~
pretēder coger a las manos ₊ /. y cō temor dlo q̃l
25 almiᶜ les avia dicho y amenazado lo qual tenia
proposito de hazeʳ / y creya q̃ saliera con ello /. ~~lo qual~~
~~y bien se parecio q̃ lo quer~~ finalmēte por aver
la gente q̃ lo tenian ovo de mostralles la c[ar]ta ge
neral dlos reyes p[ar]a todos los prinçipes y señores
30 de encomiēda y otras provisiones y dioles dlo q̃
tenia y fuerōse a t̄r̄ra contētos : y luego dexarō
toda la gente cō la barca : dlos quales supo q̃ si ~~lo~~
tomarā ———[?] al almiᶜ nūca lo dexarā libre / porq̃
dixo el capitan q̃ el rey su Señor se lo avia asi māda
35 do /.

a. ₊ pues vini[erō]
b. cō la bar[ca]
c. [ar]mada [sino]
d. q̃ no vier[ō q̃ el]
e. juego le[s sa]
f. liera bi[en]

Yesterday he anchored on the island of Santa María
in the place or harbor where he first had
anchored. Soon a man came and signaled with a
cape from some rocks opposite them, saying not to
go away from there. Then the launch came with
five sailors and two clerics and an *escrivano*.
They asked for safe conduct, and when it was given
by the Admiral they boarded the caravel, and because it was night they slept there and the Admiral treated them with all the courtesy that he
could. In the morning they demanded that he show
them the documents from the sovereigns of Castile
in order to prove that with their authority he had
made his voyage. The Admiral felt they were doing
so to show that they had not erred in what they
had done but that they had been right. Since they
had not been able to get hold of the person of the
Admiral, whom they must have intended to lay
hands[1] on since they came with the armed launch,
and when they saw that the game was not turning
out well for them, and with fear of what the
Admiral had told them and threatened to do,
and believing that he would succeed in it;
finally, to get back the people whom they
held, he had to show them the sovereigns'
general letter of commendation to all princes
and lords, and other royal documents; and he
produced for them what he had, and they went
away to land satisfied. And soon they re-
leased the launch and all the people, from
whom he found out that, if they had captured[2]
the Admiral, they would never have let him go
free, because the captain said that the king
his lord had so ordered.

---

1. (64v24a–f)   Bracketed letters in the insert following *manos* (hands) are cut off
in the manuscript facsimile.
2. (64v33)   Alvar (1976) reads the canceled text as *nunca*.

Sabado .23. de hebrero

ⴹ ayer comēço a querir abonãçar el tp̄o levanto
las anclas y fue a rodear la Isla p[ar]a buscar
algū buē surgidero p[ar]a tomar leña y ~~bue~~-[?] piedra
40   p[ar]a lastre : y no pudo tomar surgidero hasta
oras de ~~bisperas~~ cōpletas /.

Domīgo .24. de hebrero

ⴹ surgio ayer en la tarde p[ar]a tomar leña y
piedra y porq̃ la mar era mȳ alta no
45   pudo la barca llegar en tr̄r̄a y al rēdir dla
primera guardia de noche comēço a ventar gue
ste y ~~sueste~~ sudueste . mādo levantar las
velas por el grā peligro q̃ en aq̃llas Islas ay
en esperar el viento sur sobre el ancla y en ven
50   tādo sudueste luego vienta sur. y visto q̃ era buē

Folio 65r

partio dla isla
de Sancta mar
ia p[ar]a castilla

tp̄o p[ar]a yr a castilla dexo de tomar leña y piedra
y hizo q̃ governasen al leste y andaria hasta el
Sol salido q̃ avria seys oras y media .7. millas por
ora q̃ son .45 millas y media /. despues dl
5   Sol salido hasta ponerse anduvo .6. millas por
ora q̃ en onze oras fuer̄o .66 millas y quarēta
y çinco   y media dla noche fuer̄o .111 y media y
por consiguiente .28. leguas /.

Lunes .25. de hebrero

10   ⴹ ayer dspues dl Sol puesto navego al leste su cami
no çinco millas por ora en treze oras desta no
quarta /.
che andaria .65. millas q̃ son .16. leguas y ∧~~media~~
dspues del Sol salido hasta ponerse anduvo otras diez
y seys leguas y media / con la mar llana grãs a dios /
mūy
15   vino a la caravela vn ave ∧grande q̃ pareçia aguila /.

Saturday 23 February

Yesterday the weather began to show signs of
improvement; he raised anchor and set off to
go around the island in search of some good
anchorage for taking on firewood and stone for
ballast; and he was not able to reach an
anchorage until the hours of compline.

Sunday 24 February

He anchored yesterday in the afternoon to take
on firewood and stone, and because the seas
were very high the launch could not reach
land, and at the end of the first night watch
it began to blow west and southwest. He ordered the sails raised because of the great
danger in waiting for a south wind in those
islands while at anchor; and when it blows
southwest it next blows south. And seeing
65r   that it was good weather for going to Castile
he stopped taking on firewood and stone and
ordered that they steer east, and they made
seven miles per hour until sunrise, which was
about six and a half hours, which is 45 miles
and a half. After sunrise until sunset he
made six miles per hour which, in 11 hours,
was 66 miles; and [adding] the 45 and a half
of the night, they went 111 and a half
[miles], or 28 leagues.

Monday 25 February

Yesterday after sunset he steered on his
route to the east at five miles per hour and
in the 13 hours of this night he made about 65
miles, which is 16 leagues and a quarter. After sunrise and until sunset he made another
16 leagues and a half, with the sea smooth,
thanks to God. A very large bird that looked like
an eagle came to the caravel.

martes .26. de hebrero

Ɩ ayer dspues dl sol puesto navego a su   camino al leste .
la mar llana a dios grãs lo mas dla noche andaria
.8. millas por ora anduvo .100. millas q̃ son .25
20 leguas /. dspues dl Sol salido con poco viento dspues
tuvo aguaçeros anduvo obra de ocho leguas al les
nordeste /.

miercoles .27. de hebrero

Ɩ esta noche y dia anduvo fuera de camino por
25 los vientos contrarios y grãdes olas y mar /.
y ~~estava penado cō~~ hallavase çiento y veynte y çinco
leguas dl cabo de San viceynte : y ochenta dla Isla
dla madera : y çiento y seys dla de Santa maria /
estava mȳ penado cō tanta tormēta agora q̃stava
30 ——[?] a la pueʳta de casa /.

jueves .28 de hebrero

Ɩ anduvo dla mesma mañ̃a esta noche cō diuersos
vientos al sur y al sueste y ~~al~~[?] a la vna p[ar]te y a otra
y al nordeste y al lesnordeste y desta mañ̃a todo
35 este dia /.

.1º. de março

Viernes   ~~.29. de hebrero~~

Ɩ anduvo esta noche al leste q̄rta al nordeste doze leguas
el dia corrio al leste quarta del nordeste.23. leguas
y media /.

.2. de março

40
Sabado   ~~.29. de hebrero~~

Ɩ anduvo esta noche a su camino al leste q̄rta dl nordeste
28. leguas /. y el dia corrio .20. leguas

Tuesday 26 February

Yesterday after sunset he steered on his route to
the east, with a smooth sea, thanks to God. Most
of the night he went at about eight miles per hour
and made 100 miles, which is 25 leagues. After
sunrise, with little wind (later he had heavy
showers), he made about eight leagues to the east-
northeast.

Wednesday 27 February

This night and day he went off his route because
of the contrary winds and the big waves and sea.
And he reckoned himself 125 leagues from the Cabo
de San Vicente, and 80 from the island of Madeira;
and 106 from that of Santa María. He was very dis-
tressed with so much stormy weather now that he
was nearly home.

Thursday 28 February

This night he proceeded in the same way, with different winds, to[1] the south and southeast on the
one hand, and, on the other hand, to the northeast
and east-northeast, and this way all day.

Friday 1 March

This night he made 12 leagues east by north. During the day he ran east by north 23 leagues and a
half.

Saturday 2 March

This night he made 28 leagues on his route east by
north. And during the day he ran 20 leagues.

---

1. (65r33) Morison (1963, 172) translates *vientos al sur y al sueste* (winds to the
south and southeast) as "winds from the S and SE," although in the next line he translates *y al nordeste y al lesnordeste* as "to the NE and ENE." It is not clear whether the
compass directions given are those of the winds or of the Admiral's courses.

Domīgo .3. de março

/ despues dl sol puesto navego a su camino al leste : vino

padecio grā tor
mēta

le vna turbiada q̃ le rōpio todas las velas y vido
se en gra peligro. +⁺ echo suertes p[ar]a enbiar vn pere
grino diz q̃ a Santa maria dla çinta en guelva que

a. + mas dios los qui
b. so librar

Folio 65v

fuese en camisa y cayo la suerte al almiᵉ / hizie
ron todos tābien voto de ayunar el primer sa
bado q̃ llegasen a pan y agua / andaria sesenta
millas antes q̃ se le rōpiesen las velas . dspues andu

5   vierō a arbol seco por la grā tempestad del viento
y la mar q̃ de dos p[ar]tes los comia /. vierō seña
les de estar çerca de tr̄ra hallavanse todo çerca de
lisboa /.

lunes .4. de março

grā tormēta
y espantable

10   / anoche padecierō terrible tormēta q̃ se pensarō
perder dlas mares de dos p[ar]tes q̃ veniã y los
vientos q̃ parecia q̃ levātavan la caravela en los
ayres : y agua dl çielo -truenos-[?] y relāpagos
de mūchas p[ar]tes /. plugo a nr̄o señor de lo sostener /

15   y anduvo asi hasta la primera guardia q̃ nr̄o señor
le mostro tr̄ra viendola los marineros / y entonces
por no llegar a ella hasta cognoscella -sin q̃- por ver si
hallava algū -lugar- puerto /o lugar donde se saluar.
dio -la vela- el papahigo por no tener otro remedio

20   y andar algo avñq̃ con grā peligro haziēdose a la mar
y asi los guardo dios hasta el dia q̃ diz q̃ fue con in

cognoscio la tr̄ra q̃
era la roca junto
a lisboa

finito trabajo y espanto /. venido el dia cognosçio la tr̄ra
q̃ era la -peña- roca de sintra q̃s junto cō el rio de lis
boa /. adonde determino entrar porq̃ no podia hazer

25   otra cosa tā terrible era la tormēta q̃ hazia en la
villa de Casca q̃ es a la entrada dl rio / los dl pueblo
diz q̃ estuvierō toda aq̃lla mañana haziēdo plegarias
por ellos : y dspues q̃stuvo dentro : venia la gente
a verlos por maravilla de comō avian escapado /.

Sunday 3 March

After sunset he steered on his route to the east.
A squall struck him and tore all his sails and he
saw that he was in great danger, but God willed to
free them. They drew lots to send a pilgrim in his
shirt-sleeves, he says, to Santa María de la Cinta
65v   in Huelva, and the lot fell to the Admiral. All of
them also made a vow to fast on bread and water the
first Saturday when they reached land. He made
about 60 miles before his sails split. Later they
went under bare poles because of the great storm of
wind and sea, which from two directions was swal-
lowing them up. They saw signs of being close to
land and everyone figured that they were very near
Lisbon.

Monday 4 March

Last night they suffered such a terrible storm
they thought they were lost because of the winds
and the seas that came at them from two directions
and seemed to lift the caravel in the air. And
[they had] rain from the sky and lightning all
around. It pleased Our Lord to sustain him, and
he went on this way until the first watch when Our
Lord showed him land, the sailors sighting it.
And then, so as not to reach it until he could make
out what it was, to see if he would find some harbor or place where he would be safe, he set the
mainsail because he had no other recourse and made
way somewhat, although with great danger, heading
out to sea; and thus God watched over them until
day, which he says was with infinite trouble and
fright. When day came he recognized the land,
which was the Rock of Sintra, which is close to
the river of Lisbon where he decided to enter,
because he could not do anything else since the
storm blew so terribly in the town of Cascais,
which is at the entrance of the river. He says
that the people of the town spent all that morning
in fervent prayer for them, and after they got
inside the people came to see them and to marvel

30 y asi a ora de tercia ~~a pa~~ vino a passar a rastelo dē
tro dl rio de lisboa /. donde supo dla gente dla mar
q̃ jamas hizo invierno de tantas tormētas y q̃ se avian
p[er]dido .25. naos en flandes : y otras estavā alli q̃
avia~~n~~ quatro meses q̃ no aviā podido salir /

escrivio al rey de
portugal al almiᵉ

luego escrivio el almiᵉ al rey de portugal q̃stava
nueve leguas de alli de comō los reyes de casti
lla le avia mādado q̃ no dexase de entrar en
los pueʳtos de su alteza a pedir lo q̃ oviese me
nester por sus dineros : y q̃l rey le mādase dar
40 lugar p[ar]a yr cō la caravela a la çiudad de lisboa .
porq̃ algunos ruynes pensando q̃ traya mūcho
oro estando en pueʳto dspoblado se pusiesen a come
ter alguna ruyndad / y tābien porq̃ supiese q̃
no venia de guinea sino dlas yndias /.

45   martes .5. de março

/ oy dspues q̃l patron dla nao grāde dl rey de por
tugal   la qual estava tābien surta en rastelo / y la
mas bien artillada de artilleria y armas q̃ diz q̃
nūca nao se vido : vino el patron dlla q̃ se llama

Folio 66r

querian los por
tugueses q̃ el almiᵉ
fuese a dar cuēta
a los oficiales dl
rey de portugal 5

va bartolome diaz de lisboa con el batel armado
a la Caravela y dixo al almiᵉ q̃ entrase en el
batel p[ar]a yr a dar Cuēta a los hazedores dl rey
e al capitan dla d̄ha nao /. Respōdio el almiᵉ q̃l
era almirāte dlos reyes de Castilla y q̃ no dava el
tales cuētas a tales p[er]sonas ni saldria dlas
naos ni navios donde estuviese : si no fuesse por
fuerça de no poder ~~hazer aq~~ çufrir las armas
respondio el patron q̃ enbiase al maestre dla cara
10 vela   dixo el almiᵉ q̃ ni al maestre ni a otra p[er]sona si
no fuesse por fueʳça /. porq̃ en tanto tenia el dar
p[er]sona q̃ fuese comō yr el : y q̃esta era la costubre
dlos almirātes dlos reyes de Castilla de antes

at how they had escaped. And so at the hour of
tierce he moved to Restelo, within the river of
Lisbon, where he learned from seamen that never
had there been a winter with so many storms and
that 25 ships had been lost in Flanders; and
others had been there in the river four months
unable to get out. The Admiral soon wrote to the
king of Portugal, who was nine leagues from there,
telling how the rulers of Castile had ordered him
not to fail to enter the harbors of His Highness
to ask for what he had need of, in exchange for
money, and to ask that the king give him permission to go with the caravel to the city of Lisbon,
because some evildoers, thinking that he brought
much gold, while he was in a deserted harbor might
set themselves to commit some scoundrelly deed;
and also in order that the king would learn that
he did not come from Guinea but from the Indies.

Tuesday 5 March

Later today, when the master of the great ship
belonging to the king of Portugal, which was also
anchored at Restelo and [was] so well equipped
with artillery and arms, he says, that never
such a ship was seen—her master, who was named
66r   Bartolomé Díaz de Lisboa, came with her armed boat
to the caravel and told the Admiral to get into the
boat to report to the king's administrators and to the
captain of the said ship. The Admiral answered that
he was the Admiral of the sovereigns of Castile and
that he would not give such an account to such
persons nor would he leave the ships or vessels where
he might be, if it were not by force of his inability to
withstand arms [brought against him]. The master
answered that he should send the master of the
caravel. The Admiral said that [he would send]
neither the master nor anybody else if it were not by
force, because he considered giving up someone else
to go the same thing as going himself, and that it was
the custom of the Admirals of the sovereigns of
Castile to die before they gave up themselves or their

morir q̃ se dar ni dar gente suya /. el patro se

15   modero y dixo q̃ pues estava en aq̃lla determina
çion q̃ fuese como el quisiese . p[er]o q̃ le rogava q̃ le mā
dase mostrar las c[ar]t[a]s dlos reyes de Castilla si las
tenia /. al almiᵉ plugo de mostrarselas : y luego
se bolvio a la nao y hizo relacion al capitan q̃ se lla

20   mava alvaro damā /. el qual con mūcha orden ~~vino~~
con atables y trompetas y añafiles haziendo grā fiesta
~~a la~~ vino a la caravela : y hablo cō el almiᵉ y le ofre
çio de hazeʳ todo lo q̃l mādase /.

                                                    miercoles .6. de março

vino grā gente   ⁌ Sabido como el almiᵉ venia dlas yndias oy vino
a ver al almiᵉ   tanta gente a verlo y a ver los yndios ~~q̃ era~~ dla çiu
dad de lisboa q̃ era cosa de admiracion : y las mara
villas q̃ todos hazian : dando grās ~~a dios~~ a nr̄o Señor y
diziēdo q̃ por la grā fe q̃ los reyes de castilla tenian

30   y dseo de s[er]uir a dios q̃ su alta majestad ~~to~~ [?] los dava todo
esto /.

                                                    Jueves .7. de março

⁌ oy vino infinitissima gente a la caravela y mūchos
Cavalleros y entrellos los hazedores dl rey : y to

35   dos davā infinitissimas grās a nr̄o .S[en]ᵒʳ. por tanto ~~y~~
bien ~~y honrra~~ y acreçentamiᵒ dla xp̄iāndad q̃ nr̄o
S[en]ᵒʳ avia dado a los reyes de Castilla : el qual diz q̃ apro
piavā porq̃ sus altezas se trabajavā y exerçitavā en el
acreçentamiᵒ dla religiō de xp̄o /

40   viernes .8. de março
el almiᵉ
⁌ oy resçibio∧vna c[ar]ta dl rey de portugal con don mar
tin de noroña por la q̄l le ~~enbiava a~~ rogava q̃ se lle
gase adonde el estava pues el tp̄o no era p[ar]a partir
cō la Caravela /. y asi lo hizo : + y fue a dormir a sacāben   a. + por quitar sos
                                                               b. pecha puesta
                                                               c. q̃ no quisie
                                                               d. ra yr /.

people. The master became more temperate and
said, since he was so determined in that matter, it
would be as he wished; but he requested that he
would order the letters of the sovereigns of Castile
shown to him if he had them. The Admiral was
pleased to show them to him. And then the master
returned to the ship and made a report to the captain,
who was called Alvaro Damán. The latter, with great
ceremony, and with kettledrums, trumpets, and horns
sounding gaily, came to the caravel and talked to the
Admiral and offered to do all that he commanded.

Wednesday 6 March

Having learned that the Admiral was coming from the
Indies, today so many people came from the city of
Lisbon to see him and to see the Indians that it was
astounding; and they all marveled, giving thanks to
Our Lord and saying that it was because of the great
faith that the sovereigns of Castile had and their
desire to serve God that his High Majesty gave them
all this.

Thursday 7 March

Today there came to the caravel a huge crowd of
people and many gentlemen, and among them the
administrators of the king. And all of them gave
infinite thanks to Our Lord for so much good and
such increase of Christianity as Our Lord had given
to the sovereigns of Castile, which, the Admiral says,
is only proper because their Highnesses have labored
for and dedicated themselves to the increase of the
religion of Christ.

Friday 8 March

Today the Admiral received a letter from the king
of Portugal, brought by Don Martín de Noroña,
requesting that he come to the place where the king
was, since the weather was not suitable for leaving
with the caravel; and so he did in order to remove any

45 mando el rey a sus hazedores q̃ todo lo q̃ oviese el almi^e
    menester y su gente y la caravela se lo diese sin di
    neros y se hiziese todo como̅ el almi^c. quisiese /. ~~el al~~
    ~~mirãte no quisiera yr al~~

Sabado .9. de março

50 ⋎ oy partio de sacanbē p[ar]a yr adonde el rey estava

Folio 66v

    q̃ era el valle dl parayso nueve leguas de lisboa
    porq̃ llovio no pudo llegar hasta noche /. el
    rey le mãdo resçibir a los principales de su casa
    my̅ ho̅rradamēte : y el rey tambien le resci
5   bio co̅ mūcha honrra y le hizo mūcho favor y mā
    do sentar y hablo my̅ bien ofreciendole q̃ ~~le~~ mā
    daria hazer todo lo q̃ a los reyes de castilla y a su
    s[er]ui[ci]^o co̅pliese co̅plidamēte y mas q̃ por cosa suya
    y mostro aver mūcho plazer dl viaje aver avido
10 buē termino y se aver hecho / mas q̃ entendia
    q̃ en la capitulaçion q̃ avia entre los reyes y el
    q̃ aq̃lla conquista le p[er]teneçia /. a lo qual respo̅
    dio el almi^c q̃ no avia visto la Capitulaçion ni
    sabia otra cosa / sino q̃ los reyes le avian mā
15 dado q̃ no fuese a la mina ni en toda guinea
    y q̃ asi se avia mãdadꝋ a pregonar en todos los
    puertos dl andaluzia antes q̃ p[ar]a el viaje partie
    se /. el rey graçiosamēte respo̅dio q̃ tenia el
    por çierto q̃ no avria~n~ en esto menester terçeros /.
20 Diole por guesped al prior del clato q̃ era la
    mas prinçipal p[er]sona q̃ alli estava / dl qual el almi^e
    resçibio my̅ mūchas ho̅rras y favores /

Domingo .10. de março

    ⋎ oy dspues de missa le torno a dezir el rey si avia
25 menester algo q̃ luego se le daria : y departio
    mūcho con el almi^e sobre su viaje : y siemp^r le
                va
    mãda‸estar sentado y hazer mūcha ho̅rra /.

suspicion, although he did not want to go. And he went to sleep at Sacavém. The king ordered his administrators to give the Admiral and his people and the caravel all that they might be in need of, without payment, and to do everything as the Admiral might wish.

Saturday 9 March

66v

Today he left Sacavém to go where the king was, which was the Valle del Paraíso, nine leagues from Lisbon. Because it rained, he was unable to get there until night. The king ordered his principal retainers to receive him with much honor, and the king also received him with much honor, showed him much favor, asked him to be seated, and spoke very courteously, offering to have carried out completely all that might be of service to him and to the sovereigns of Castile, going beyond his own self-interest. And he showed that he took much pleasure from the voyage having had a good ending and having been made, but he understood from the treaty between the sovereigns and himself that that acquisition belonged to him. To which the Admiral answered that he had not seen the treaty nor did he know anything else except that the sovereigns had ordered him not to go to La Mina or anywhere in all of Guinea, and that this was ordered to be proclaimed in all the ports of Andalusia before he departed for the voyage. The king graciously answered he was sure that there would be no need for arbitrators to settle this. The king gave the Admiral as a guest to the prior of Crato, who was the most important person there, and from whom the Admiral received many courtesies and favors.

Sunday 10 March

Today after Mass the king again said if he needed something he would give it to him promptly, and he conversed at length with the Admiral about his voyage. And always he requested him to be seated and treated with much courtesy.

lunes .11. de março

⁙ oy se despidio dl rey e le dixo algunas cosas q̃

~~do~~[?]

30   dixese dsu p[ar]te a los reyes ~~pa~~ mostrā∧rle le siemp^r
mūcho amor /. partiose dspues de comer : y en
bio con el a don martin de voroña y todos aq̃llos
cavalleros ~~como vinierā y salierā con el~~[?] le vinie
rō a acōpañar y hazer honrra buē rato /. dspues
35   vino a vn monasterio de Sant antonio q̃s sobre

fue a ver a la rey   vn lugar q̃ se llama villafranco donde estava
na de portugal   la reyna y fuele a haze^r reverēçia y besarle las
manos / porq̃ le avia enbiado a dezir q̃ no se
fuese hasta q̃ la viese /. con la qual estava el duq̃
40   y el marques donde resçibio el almi^e mūcha hō

se   noche

rra /. partio∧ ~~dspues~~ dlla el almi^e [de] ∧y fue a dormir
allandra /.

martes .12. de março

⁙ oy estando p[ar]a partir de allandra p[ar]a la caravela
45   llego vn escudero dl rey q̃ le ofreçio dsu p[ar]te
q̃ si quisiese yr a castilla por tr̄r̄a : q̃ aq̃l fuese ~~p[ar]a~~
con el p[ar]a lo aposentar y mādar dar bestias
y todo lo q̃ oviese menest[e]r /. quādo el almi^e dl se
partio le mādo dar vna mula y otra a su piloto
50   q̃ llevava cōsigo y diz q̃ al piloto mādo hazer m[erce]d de veynte
espadines

Folio 67r

espadines segud supo el almi^e todo diz q̃ se dezia
q̃ lo hazia porq̃ los reyes lo supiesen /. llego
[a] la caravela en la noche /.

Monday 11 March

Today he said goodbye to the king, who told him
some things that he should say, on the king's behalf,
to the sovereigns, always showing him much affection.
He left after eating, and the king sent with him Don
Martín de Noroña and many gentlemen who came to
keep him company and to do him honor for a good
while. Later he came to a monastery of San
Antonio which is near a small town named
Villafranco, where the queen was, and he went
to do her reverence and to kiss her hands,
because she had sent to say not to go away
until he had seen her. With her were the duke
and the marquis, and the Admiral was received
with much honor. The Admiral parted[1] from
her at night and went to sleep at Alhandra.

Tuesday 12 March

Today, when he was about to depart from Alhandra for the caravel, there arrived a squire of
the king's who offered, on behalf of the latter, if the Admiral wished to go to Castile by
land, to go with him to secure lodging and to
order animals and everything he would have
need of. When the Admiral parted from him the
squire ordered a mule given to him, and
another to his pilot, whom he had with him,
and he says the squire ordered a gratuity of
twenty *espadines*[2] given to the pilot, as
67r the Admiral learned. All of this, he says,
was said and done so the sovereigns would
learn of it. He reached the caravel during
the night.

---

1. (66v41) Alvar (1976) reads the canceled text following *partiose* as *algunas*.
2. (66v50) *Veynte espadines*. An *espadim* was a Portuguese gold coin, first minted
during the reign of Afonso V, so called because of the hand gripping a sword that
formed the central part of the design of the reverse (see *Grande enciclopédia*). *Espadines*,
repeated at the foot of the page, is a catchword.

miercoles .13. de março

partiose de lisboa
p[ar]a sevilla

ʃ oy a las ocho oras cō la marea de Ingente y el
viento nornorueste levanto las anclas y dio la
vela p[ar]a yr a sevilla /

jueves .14. de março

ʃ ayer dspues dl sol puesto sig[u]io su camino al sur
10 y antes dl Sol salido se hallo sobre el cabo de Sant
viçeynte q̃ es en portugal / despues navego al leste
            yr
p[ar]a -andar-[?] a saltes y anduvo todo el dia con poco viē
to hasta agora q̃sta sobre farō /.

viernes .15. de março

15 ʃ Ayer dspues del sol puesto navego a su camino
hasta el dia cō poco viento y al salir dl sol se ha

entro en saltes
de donde avia
salido p[ar]a
su viaje .

llo sobre saltes . y a ora de mediodia cō la
marea de montante entro por la barra de Sal
tes hasta dentro dl puerto de donde -partio- avia
20 partido a tres de agosto dl ano passado y asi
              va
dize el q̃ acaba∧agora esta escriptura saluo q̃stava
de proposito de yr a barçelona por la mar / en
la qual çiudad le davā nuevas q̃ sus altezas
estavā /. y esto p[ar]a les hazer relaçion de todo su via
25 je q̃ nrō señor le avia dexado haze^r y le quiso —[?]
alumbrar en el /. porq̃ çiertamēte allende q̃l
sabia y tenia firme y fuerte -y-[?] sin escrupulo q̃ su
alta magestad haze todas las cosas buenas : y q̃
todo es bueno saluo el pecado : y q̃ no se puede aba
30 lar ni pensar cosa q̃ no sea cō su consentimi^o : esto
deste viaje cognosco (dize el almi^e) q̃ milagrosamē
te lo a mostrado asi como se puede cōprehender
por esta escriptura por mūchos milagros señalados q̃
a mostrado en el viaje y de mi q̃ a tanto tp̄o q̃stoy
35 en la corte de vr̄as altezas cō opposito y contra
sentençia de tantas p[er]sonas prinçipales de v[uest]ra casa

Wednesday 13 March

Today at the eighth hour, with a very high
tide and the wind north-northwest, he raised
anchor and set sail for Seville.

Thursday 14 March

Yesterday after sunset he continued on his
route to the south, and before sunrise found
himself off the Cabo de San Vicente, which is
in Portugal. Later he steered east in order
to go to Saltés, and he proceeded all day with
little wind until now, when he is off Faro.

Friday 15 March

Yesterday after sunset he steered on his
route until day, with little wind, and at
sunrise found himself off Saltés; and at the
hour of noon with the rising tide he crossed
the bar of Saltés and entered the harbor from
which he had departed on the third of August
of the year past, and so he says that he was
now finishing this writing except that he proposed
to go to Barcelona by sea, where, he was given
news, their Highnesses were. And this was to make
a report to them of the whole voyage which Our
Lord had let him make and in which He had willed
to enlighten him. Because certainly, beyond
knowing and holding firmly and strongly and without reservation, that His High Majesty brings
about all good things, and that everything is good
except sin, and that one cannot praise or think
anything which is not with His consent, I know,
says the Admiral, that, in the circumstances of
this voyage, He has miraculously made this manifest, as one may understand through this writing,
through the signal miracles that He has performed
during the voyage and for me, who, much of the
time that I was in Your Highnesses' court, met
with the opposition and contrary opinion of many
important persons of your household, who were all

los quales todos erā contra mi poniendo este hecho
q̃ era burla /. el qual espero en nr̄o señor q̃ sera
la mayor honrra dla xp̄ɪāndad q̃ asi ligera
40   mēte aya jamas apareçido /. estas son ~~sus~~ fi
nales palabras dl almirāte don xpual Colon / de
~~y ovo mūcha razō~~ [?] su primer viaje a las yndias y
al dscubrimiº dllas .

45   deo graçias

against me, alleging my enterprise to be ridicu-
lous.   I hope in Our Lord that it will be the
greatest honor to Christianity that, unexpectedly,
has ever come about.   These are the final words of
the Admiral Don Christóbal Colón concerning his
first voyage[1] to the Indies and their discovery.

Thanks be to God

1.   (67r42)   Alvar (1976) reads the canceled text preceding *su primer viaje* as *y tuve
mucha razon*.

BIBLIOGRAPHY

Alvar, Manuel, ed. 1976. *Diario del descubrimiento*. 2 vols. Gran Canaria: Cabildo Insular.

Arce, Joaquín, and M. Gil Esteve, eds. 1971. *Diario de a bordo de Cristóbal Colón*. Alpignano, Torino: A. Tallone.

Brooks, Van Wyck, ed. 1924. *Journal of the First Voyage to America by Christopher Columbus*. New York: Albert and Charles Boni.

Casas, Bartolomé de las. 1951. *Historia de las Indias*. 3 vols. Ed. A. Millares Carlo, with preliminary study by Lewis Hanke. Mexico: Fondo de Cultura Económica.

——, ed. *Diario of Christopher Columbus*. For various editions of Las Casas's transcription of the *Diario* see under names of individual editors and translators.

Castro, João de. 1968. *Tratado da esfera por perguntas e respostas*. In vol. 1 of *Obras completas de D. João de Castro*, pp. 15–114. Ed. Armando Cortesão and Luis de Albuquerque. Coimbra: Academia Internacional da Cultura Portuguesa.

Colcord, Joanna C. 1945. *Sea Language Comes Ashore*. New York: Cornell Maritime Press.

Diccionario de la lengua española. 1956. 18th ed. Madrid: Academia Española.

Columbus, Christopher. *Diario*. For various editions of the *Diario* see under names of individual editors and translators.

Columbus, Ferdinand. 1959. *The Life of the Admiral Christopher Columbus by his Son, Ferdinand*. Trans. Benjamin Keen. New Brunswick, N.J.: Rutgers University Press.

Dunn, Oliver. 1983a. Columbus's First Landing Place: The Evidence of the Journal. *Terrae Incognitae* 15:35–50.

——. 1983b. The *Diario*, or Journal, of Columbus's First Voyage: A New Transcription of the Las Casas Manuscript for the Period October 10 through December 6, 1492. *Terrae Incognitae* 15:173–231.

Fuson, Robert H. 1983. The *Diario de Colón*: A Legacy of Poor Transcription, Translation, and Interpretation. *Terrae Incognitae* 15:51–75.

Gamboa, Pedro Sarmiento de. See *Glosario de voces marítimas y antiguas*.

Glosario de voces marítimas y antiguas. 1950. In Pedro Sarmiento de Gamboa. *Viajes al estrecho de Magallanes (1579–1584)*, 2:391–468. Ed. Angel Rosenblat. Buenos Aires: Emece.

Grande enciclopédia portuguesa e brasileira. 1936–60. 40 vols. Lisbon and Rio de Janeiro: Editorial Enciclopédia.

Guillén Tato, Julio, ed. 1943. *El primer viaje de Cristóbal Colón*. Madrid: Instituto Histórico de Marina.

——. 1951. *La parla marinera en el diario del primer viaje de Cristóbal Colón*. Madrid: Instituto Histórico de Marina.

Jados, Stanley S. 1975. *Consulate of the Sea and Related Documents*. University: University of Alabama Press.

Jane, Cecil, trans. and ed. 1930. *The Voyages of Christopher Columbus, Being the Journals of His First and Third, and the Letters Concerning His First and Last Voyages, to Which Is Added the Account of His Second Voyages by Andrés Bernáldez*. London: Argonaut.

——, trans. and ed. 1960. *The Journal of Christopher Columbus*. Rev. and annotated by L. A. Vigneras, with appendix by R. A. Skelton. New York: Bramhall House. (Cited in text as Jane-Vigneras.)

Judge, Joseph, and James L. Stanfield. 1986. The Island of Landfall: Where Columbus Found the New World. *National Geographic* 170, no.5 (Nov.):566ff.

Kelley, James E., Jr. 1983. In the Wake of Columbus on a Portolan Chart. *Terrae Incognitae* 15:77–111.

Keniston, Hayward. 1937. *The Syntax of Castilian Prose: The Sixteenth Century*. Chicago: University of Chicago Press.

Kettell, Samuel, trans. 1827. *Personal Narrative of the First Voyage of Columbus to America*. Boston: T. B. Wait and Son.

Kretschmer, Konrad. 1909. *Die italienischen Portolane des Mittelalters, Ein Beitrag zur Geschichte der Kartographie und Nautik . . . mit einer Kartenbeilage*. Berlin: E. S. Mittler und Sohn.

Lane, Frederic C., and Reinhold Mueller. 1985. *Coins and Moneys of Account*. Vol. 1 of *Money and Banking in Medieval and Renaissance Venice*. Baltimore, Md.: Johns Hopkins University Press.

Lollis, Cesare de, ed. 1892–94. *Scritti di Cristoforo Colombo* [containing de Lollis's transcription of the *Diario*]. Pt. 1, vols. 1–2, of *Raccolta di documenti e studi pubblicati dalla R. Commissione Colombiana, pel quarto centenario dalla scoperta dell' America*. 14 vols. Rome: Ministero della pubblica istruzione.

McElroy, John W. 1941. The Ocean Navigation of Columbus on His First Voyage. *American Neptune* 1:209–40.

Machabey, Armand. 1962. *La métrologie dans les musées de province et sa contribution á l'histoire des poids et mesures en France depuis le treizième siècle*. Paris: Centre National de la Recherche Scientifique.

Mallett, Michael E. 1967. *The Florentine Galleys in the Fifteenth Century*. Oxford: Clarendon Press.

Markham, Clements R., trans. 1893. *The Journal of Christopher Columbus (During His First Voyage, 1492–93) and Documents Relating to the Voyages of John Cabot and Gaspar Corte Real*. Hakluyt Society Publications, 1st ser., no. 86. London.

Martínez-Hidalgo, José María. 1966. *Columbus's Ships*. Ed. Howard I. Chapelle. Barre, Mass.: Barre Publishers.

Medina, Pedro de. 1972. *The Navigator's Universe: The Libro de Cosmographía of 1538*. Trans. and with introduction by Ursula Lamb. Chicago: University of Chicago Press.

Milani, Virgil I. 1973. *The Written Language of Christopher Columbus*. Buffalo: State University of New York Press. [*Forum Italicum* supplement.]

Morison, Samuel E. 1940. *The Route of Columbus Along the North Coast of Haiti, and the Site of Navidad*. Transactions of the American Philosophical Society, n.s., no.31, pt.4.

———. 1942. *Admiral of the Ocean Sea: A Life of Christopher Columbus*. 2 vols. Boston: Little, Brown.

———, ed. and trans. 1963. *Journals and Other Documents on the Life and Voyages of Christopher Columbus*. New York: Heritage.

Navarrete, Martín Fernández de, ed. 1825–29. *Viages de Colón* [includes Navarrete's transcription of the *Diario*]. Vol. 1 of *Colección de los viages y descubrimientos que hicieron por mar los españoles desde fines del siglo XV, con varios documentos inéditos concernientes a la historia de la marina castellana y de los establecimientos españoles en Indias*. 3 vols. Madrid: Imprenta real.

Palacio, Diego García de. 1944. *Instrucción náutica para navegar*. Madrid: Ediciones Cultura Hispánica. [Facsimile edition of *Instrucion nauthica, para el buen uso, y regimiento de las naos, su traça, y govierno conforme à la altura de Mexico*. Mexico: Pedro Ocharte, 1587.]

———. *Nautical Instruction, 1587*. 1986. Trans. J. Bankston. Bisbee, Ariz.: The Press. 1986.

Parker, John. 1983. The Columbus Landfall Problem: A Historical Perspective. *Terrae Incognitae* 15:1–28.

Pontillo, James John. 1975. Nautical Terms in Sixteenth Century American Spanish. Ph.D. diss., State University of New York, Buffalo.

Power, Robert H. 1983. The Discovery of Columbus's Island Passage to Cuba, October 12–27, 1492. *Terrae Incognitae* 15:151–72.

Ramsey, Marathon M. 1956. *A Textbook of Modern Spanish*. Rev. Robert K. Spaulding. New York: Henry Holt.

Sanz, Carlos, ed. 1962. *Diario de Colón: Libro de la primera navegación y descubrimiento de las Indias*. 2 vols. Madrid: Gráficas Yagües.

Smith, John. 1970. *A Sea Grammar*. Ed. Kermit Goel. London: Printed by Michael Joseph.

Thacher, John B., ed. 1903–1904. *Christopher Columbus: His Life, His Work, His Remains, as Revealed by Original Printed and Manuscript Records, Together with an Essay on Peter Martyr of Anghera and Bartolomé de las Casas, the First Historians of America*. 3 vols. New York: G. P. Putnam's Sons.

Valdés, Juan de. 1946. *Diálogo de la lengua*. Ed. Clásicos castillanos. Madrid: Espasa-Calpe. (Clásicos castillanos, no.86)

Vigneras, L. A., ed. 1960. *The Journal of Christopher Columbus*. See Jane, Cecil. 1960.

Woodbridge, Hensley C. 1950. Spanish Nautical Terms of the Age of Discovery. Ph.D. diss., University of Illinois, Urbana.

CONCORDANCE

aletezas   10v36
alexā   5r11
alfambra   1r20
alfaneque   51v3
alfaneques   14r25 18v30 21v7
alfilel   16r34
algaravia   20r18ⁿ
40   algo   7r24 10r28 10v23 12v37 14r26ⁿ
     16r39 18v23 20r29 20v17 25v17 26v20
     20ᶜ 29r6 32r23 33 36r44 36v44 37v44
     38v7ⁿ 39r6 39v46 42v42 43v28 44r15
     23 43 44v30 45r22 48v21 49r24 51r1
     55r32 34ⁿ 57v47 61r25 62v7 35 63r12
     65v20 66v25
24   algodon aldogon
23   algodon   9r20 10r4 33 35 11v30 44
     13r24 27 30 14r30 16v29 19v32 20v25
     21r20 22r6 13 18 23r13 42r25 44r28
     45r23 57r8 33
    algodonales   36v37
    algu   8r7 25r8
    alguazil   37v41 39r4 6 46v29 50v37
21   algun algū
10   algun   5r14 9v1 12r2 23v16 24v42 25r7
     36r43 56r34 57v21 63v45
38   alguna algūa algu^a
22   alguna   3v29 4r14 5v32 7r2 20r36 21r13
     23v42 24v24 27v12 31r27 33r26 35v28
     45 38r27 43v34 40 47r32 54r8 56v32
     62r42 48 65v43
31   algunas   3v36 4v28 7r4 9v3 10v32 12r24
     12v37 39 41 14r30 22v19 24v11 20
     25r30 32 26v1 28v43 30v7 35v36
     37r38 40r32 43v15 44r37 47r4 54r5
     55v27 30 38 57v30ᶜ 58r31 66v29
8   alguno algunoᵒ alguᵒ
    alguno   15r8 19v39 28v42 41v46 42r41
44   algunos alguᵒˢ
43   algunos   4r4 9r12 9v7 10r8 11v24 30
     12r37 13v9 14r11 16v29 30 32 33
     24v23 26v21 24 27v7 30r38 30v1 19
     31v48 33r16 33v44 35v27 36v34 37r12
     37v23 23 38v21 26 43 39r39 44r35 35
     45v27 56r40 45 57r4 28 29 62v11 30
     65v41
    algunᵒ   34v31
11   algū   3v24 13r22 13v48 27r31 34r4
     35v47 37v47 51r7 60r17 64v39 65v18
    algūa   36r9
    alguᵒˢ   31v45
15   alguᵃ   2r31 13v19 22v11 26r24 26v11ᶜ
     29r11 35v28ᶜ 44ᶜ 36r11 37v23 43r4
     43v32 52r9 54r3 62v34
    alguᵒ   9v39 22v8
    alijar   46v15
    alivanado   61v29a
18   alla   10r14 15r10 20 33 20v39 30r2 32v4
     40v3 42r3 42v23 43v38 44r5 32 47r33ᶜ
     48v45 56v2 63r30 64r39
    allandra   66v42 44

allegado   26r17
allegandose   62v33
allegarō   41v46
allegase   18v29
allegava   29r1
allego   55r17
allende   1v38 28v11 61v25 67r26
allēde   62r15
184   alli   1v31 2r28 2v9 3r12 4r6 5v2 6r16
     9r4 5 9v9 10r12 11v1 14r45 17v22 28
     32 18r1 5 18v5 6 14 19r4 7 49 19v17
     27 44 47 20v2 41 44 21r6 42 47 21v24
     27 28 22r2 9 23v43 24r15 24v61 25r1
     7 12 42 25v9 12 26r25 27 39 27r39ⁿ
     27v4 8 12ⁿ 21b 21h 25 41 28v21 24
     29r41 30r17 21 27 30v13ⁿ 31r15 20
     32r22 34 32v25 30 33r7ᶜ 40 33v26 37
     34r12ᶜ 13 34v28 35r37 35v47 36v9 42
     37r4 8 24 37v11 43 44ᶜ 48 38r22
     38v15 39 40 39r7 21 29 37 45ᶜ 40r33
     40v20 24 25 26 41r3 37 42r31 42v18
     43r4 43v19 44r3 44v5 9 13 25 45r9 13
     45v3 47v11 16 48r15 16 48v2ᶜ 3 4 9 10
     49r13 17 49v22 50r10 23 50v1 33
     51r24ⁿ 24ⁿ 29ᶜ 30ᶜ 51v17 20 24 47 48
     52v43 53r5 10 42 42ⁿ 53v32 37 54r26
     32 37 54v5 7 24 25 28 41 55r6 22 55v8
     56r22 29 32 56v17 49 57r15 23 30 32
     58r26 30 59v11 60v39ᶜ 61v39 62v5
     64r30 64v11 12 15 65v33 36 66v21
    almaciga   21r50 35v6
8   almaçiga   21r35 40 22v46 23r22 24v20
     35r23 51v27 52r4
    almaçigas   57r34
    almaçigos   36v37 53r14
14   almadia almādia
13   almadia   11v16 21 24 26 28 37 40 12r43
     12v32 23r31 23v8 30r21 30v37
11   almadias   9v36 10v4 12v35 17v30 18r47
     19r31 20v24 23v5 24r11 31r35 33v31
    almadravas   58r27
    almarraxa   39v41
    almādia   12v13
    almejas   18v4
    almi   3r2 5v37 42v7
    almirables   27r43ⁿ
428   almirante almi almirāte almirate [?] almi^e
     almi^e
    almirante   45v7ⁿ
    almirate   8v28ⁿ 38v7ⁿ
24   almirāte   1r3 1v14 20ⁿ 5v30 7v21ᵃ 8r36
     8v9 32 9v21 11r1ⁿ 21r1ⁿ 22r39 23v15
     46r45 47v19 45 49v2 52v5 53v46
     61v14 31 66r5 48ᶜ 67r41
    almirātes   66r13
    almizque   25r42
307   almi^e
93   almi^e   2v5 6r1 7r4 8v14 30 38 18v4 5 26
     19r45 19v38 20r1 20v1 3 28 35 21r34
     36 22r21 25v40 26r45 28r36 31v23

  andada 18v15
  andadas 22v5 51v37
24 andado 5v29 6r3 6v27 11r40 17v41
   19r30 42 20v6 21v4 22v4 24r21 30
   26r5 7 29r14 32v21 41v13 17 52v3
   57v13 17 58v34 62v15[n] 63r15
  andadura 17v30
  andallas 24v18
6 andaluzia 4r10 14r8 16r6 17r26 18r26
   66v17
7 andan 6v10 9r27 23v5 39v4 41v9 45r11
   55v29
20 andar 1v4 4r41 7v24 11r19 39 12r34
   15v9 17r11 17v12 23v24 25 44 24r12
   37r37 38v9 39r23 39v7 53v22 65v20
   67r12[c]
  andare 29v18
49 andaria 4v19 5r38 7v1 27 25v22 27v46
   32v32 54v40 43 57v48 58r1 5 8 21 39
   45 47 58v11 18 59r3 17 23 26 34 43
   59v7 11 14 21 23 28 60r11 16 23 30
   31 43 60v11 48 61r14 18 26 44 62r45
   47 65r2 12 18 65v3
11 andarian 4r3 4v8 40 5r14 25 5v13 7r22
   23 8r32 17v19 41
6 andariã 3r24 4r18 7v31 8r34 17v22
   60r7
  andarla 49v38
  andas 39r43 40r16
  andassemos 14v28
18 andava 3r28 4r41 4v16 5r42[c] 19v11[n]
   23v45 26r15 17 27 28r5[c] 37v38 45
   51v10 58v31 59r6 60v38 61r42 62v15[n]
7 andavã 3r11 5r29 7v4 17v21 19r33[n]
   47v25 57v9
  andã 5r22 6v16 20r11 47r14
  andãdo 16r17 27 27r32 29r38 53r22
  anden 39r17
  anduve 14r4 17r48
  anduviero 8r5
  anduvieron 2r37
24 anduvierõ 2r16 18 33 2v2 3v8 11 15 20
   28 6r18 28 33 35 6v24 41 7r14 32 42
   7v33 8r29 17v44 19v36 30v33 65v4
  anduviesen 37v49
  anduvimos 2r11 17v16
75 anduvo 3r14 27 30 37 6r11 23 6v5 7v43
   45 17v39 18r4 28 18v16 19v2 23v47
   24r5 23 24v24 26r4 6 45 32r46 32v31
   34v20 51v38 54v39 57v25 44 58r3 28
   35 58v12 35 40 43 59r20 31 40 59v1 2
   5 9 16 36 40 45 48 60r15 20 34 60v4 6
   15 19 20 40 43 61r12 36 62v7 21 28
   32 42 64r25 65r5 13 19 21 24 32 37 41
   65v15 67r12
  anes 8v29 49v19 53r25 60r37
  angel 54v9 20
8 angla 15r11 19 33r39 34r11 22 44
   40v26 54v27
  angosta 10v31 24v45 43r44

  angostas 13v43
  angosto 32r33 34r47 54r22
  angostura 58v25
  angustia 48r13 63r36
  angustias 62r11[n]
  anillo 49v10
  anima 62r18[c] 21
  animal 25r17
  animas 47v26[c]
  ano 67r20
  anobleçierõ 1v12
  anoche 23v34 50v43 65v10
  anochecio 32r47
  anocheçe 6v13
  anocheçido 28v10
  anocheçiendo 6v18
  anocheçiese 53v31
  anocheçio 17r49
  anõbrarõ 11r17 14v34
  anõbre 16v42
  ansares 22r1 44r30
  ansi 27v26
  ante 8v43 20r17 21r1[n]
  anteçessores 1r28
64 antes 1v28 2r26 5r5 7v25 25[c] 11r28 32
   11v20 13v4 14v28 31 15r31 17r24
   17v43 19r51 19v24 42 20r5 20v30
   22v18 24r26 25v16 26v8 35 27r28
   30r7 31v21 42 32v39 33r33 34r3[c] 5 28
   34v16 35r1 8 36r26 37r30 38r21 40v37
   42r39 42v23 43r11 44v31 45r37 48v29
   39 39 53r29 53v31 55v9 56r7 56v5 28
   57v2 58v33 60v28 62r4 17[c] 63v42
   65v4 66r13 66v17 67r10
  antier 24r41 37r34 50r19
  antiguos 41v8
  antojo 21v37
  antonio 66v35
  anũçiaçion 39r34
  anzuelo 18r22
  anzuelos 18v41
  añafiles 66r21
  añide 48v2 52v40
  añidia 8r13
  añidio 63v14
16 año 1r12 17 1v21 27 2v31 35 38 13r33
   21r42 22r9 11 48r43 50v26 56v36[n]
   57r39 57v34
10 años 2r10 9r31 14r31 15v4 23v14
   37v34 41v14 42r28 48v29 56v36
  apagosele 32v42
  aparecierõ 7r1
  apareçido 67r40
  apareçio 4v16 23v27[c]
  aparejada 19r16
  aparejado 49r10
  aparejaron 56r7
  aparejo 27v2
  aparejos 18r23
  aparta 6r39

53v19
arguye 26r26
10 armada 1v10 8v4 28 41 26v19 31r27
31v34 46v29 50r36 64v24c
armadas 11v11
armado 66r1
armados 26v20 30v27 47r6
armar 50r30
22 armas 1r18 9r43 10v42 14r2 21r16
22v26 28r28 31v14 35r17 36r16 38v4
5 39r32 42r19 43r38 47v38 48r35 56r5
38 63v10 65v48 66r8
arme 1v23
aromaticas 20v20
aros 53v7 8
arrajuã 34v24
arremeter 56r8
arremetierõ 56r14
16 arriba 14r26ⁿ 18r28 19r19 20v15 22v13
23v16 26v33c 30r18 31r46 32r22
33r29ⁿ 34r22 39r43 51r24ⁿ 30c 53v4
arribado 26v28
arribo 58v21
arriscada 55v28
arrodeada 13v21
arrodearia 13v36
arrova 10r35
arrovas 22r8
arroyo 27r33
arroyos 25r30 32
artifiçios 18v41
artillada 65v48
artilleria 50v26 65v48
aryes 19r2
asan 36r39
ascondiesen 42r39
ascureçen 16r8
asegurados 19r33ⁿ 36r8
asegurar 19v20
aseguraro 36r28 33
asegurarõ 19v30
aseguravan 31v29
asegurolos 31v3
asemejar 14r15
asensar 62r21
asentar 49r11 62r18c
asento 4r19 4v9 30v43 49v1
191 asi 1v7 18 18 34 2r7 5v6 25 43 7v9 8r15
8v2 36 10r20 39 11r20 11v12 12r9 21
35 12v12 16 29 13r17 34 13v1 27 45
14r3 5 9 10 17 47 14v5 11 42 15r18 18
20 41 15v3 37 16r17 16v14 26 26 28
42 17r10 34 35 41 43 43 48 18r25
18v18 19r24 19v36 20r11 21r33 21v9
13 22r24 26 35 22v14 32 23r2 30 45
45 24r30 26r32 26v39 27r4 15 41
27v28 28r9 28v34 29r17 29v39 30v32
32r13 15 32v8 18 32 33r40 49 33v15
42 34v25 45 35r46 35v30 36r45 36v14
20 20c 37r3 10 15 49 37v46 38r44

38v6 15 39v4 14 23 25 41v29 42r1 20
21 43 42v29 43r5 20 35 35c 44r23
45v21 46r17 46v38 42 47r21 31 34
48r41 48 48v8 30 49r25 40 49v16
51r28c 46 51v38 42 52r8 29 52v41
53r35 54r43 54v35 39 55r14 55v2 42
56r6 56v22c 33 57r17 45 57v25 58r3 5
21 58v13 34 43 60r12 15 25 34 44
60v20 36 44 61r26 44 61v7 62r18 42
45 63r1ⁿ 64r10 17 64v4 34 65v15 21
30 66r44 66v16 67r20 32 39
asiento 23r27 48r16 51r24ⁿ 54r44
asimismo 16r16 41v12
asomarõ 35v45
asombrase 3v4
asombrava 5v5
assentadas 39v28
assentar 42v32
assentaron 39v19
assentarõ 21v16 17 38v43 39v16
assentasse 50v31
assiento 38r45 52v44
astrolabio 60r9
astrologia 55r34ⁿ
astuçia 32v16
astuta 35r45
atables 66r21
atadas 48r2
atado 62r39
atados 55v1
atajar 10v40
atajase 34r24
atalayas 33r25 37r45
atar 56r12
ataraçana 30r24 31r40
ataviar 39r31
atentandolos 21v23
atento 10r7
atormẽtavã 61r17
17 atras 7r5 11v21 14r44 24r20 26v37
27v18 28v11c 14 29v41 35v23 46
37r47 40r18 27 52v3 55v1 60v32
atravesava 21v42
atribuyolo 25r15 61v47
atrivuye 19r5
atunes 58r25 41 58v2
augmẽtavã 61v38ⁿ
auvnq̃ 37r27
avante 11v23 15r36
7 ave 4v5 5r27 6r36 38 6v39 20r6 65r15
avellanada 42r35
avemos 22v30
aventurados 44r40
75 aver 1r13 15 1v7 5v27 8r13 9v41 10r26
11r40 12r32 12v28 15v25 38 16v7
17r6 18v21 47 22r9 22v4 35 23r7
24r30 24v22 25r42 26r27 26v38 27r31
27v20 28r19 28v6c 29r21 29v4 6 28
30r4 30v11 13 29 32r41 32v12ⁿ 33v30
43 34r33 35r18 30 36r10 36v42 38v2

7 bancos 28v33 31r45 33v33 46r27 41 46v25 51v13

21 baneque babeque baneq̃ baveque vaneque vaneq̃ veneque

15 baneque 25v20 26 26 26v29 32v5 7 35r37ᶜ 37r18 37v39 39r11 14 21 22ⁿ 52v18 24

   baneq̃ 35r37

   barato 44v20

66 barca 8v28 11v22 37 18r17 28 48 20v10 29 24v33 25r26 26v40 27r28 29r31 37 31v25 32r6 39 32v38 41 42 45 33v5 34v17 35v38 40r14 42v18 43v17 29 46v12 28ᶜ 48r44 49r4ᶜ 5 50r2 50v27 51r2 24 51v46 52r15 53r41 53v4 5 55r23 37 55v40 56r3 3 26 32 56v2 4 9 11 57r4 62v48 63r23 63v1 4 9 11 13 64r38 64v12 24b 32 45

27 barcas 9r18 10v7 11v10 13v46 18v21 19v16 20 24v18 25v2 28v40 29r1 4 31r26 31v18 23 32r3 37r29 33 36 41r46 41v30 44 42v33 44v6 45 45r34 46r28

   barco 9v37

   barçelona 67r22

   barloventeando 19v3 23v24 32v40 47

   barloventear 18r7

   barloventeãdo 4v26 24r6

   barloventeo 62v45

   barlovento 46v9 60v35

   barlovẽteando 62v32

   barlovẽtear 33v7

   barlovẽteãdo 7r7

   barlovẽto 60r50

   barocoa 19r22ⁿ 25ⁿ 21r43ⁿ

   barra 2r10 26v40 67r18

   barrida 45r19

   barridas 14r23 18v33

   barriga 9v35

   barril 62r40

   barriles 13r5 13v49 14r3 53v5 7

   barro 16v32 42r6 44r44

   bartolome 66r1

   basa 24v26 26v42 33v17 35r4

   basan 20r11

   basta 44r13

   bastarã 29r43

   bastava 31v9

   bastimẽtos 61v29c

   batalla 36v1

   batatas 21r19ⁿ

10 batel 10v6 19 13r2 6 17r48 46v4 7 28 66r1 3

   baveque 22r48

13 baxa 19r51 19v4 25v13 31r6 9 17 33v4 35r1 51v3 45 52r7 18 53v11

   baxandose 62v7

   baxar 29r20

11 baxas 10v32 11r30 14v43 18r3 34v1 41r30 43 46r2 7 48r22 51v8

13 baxo 14v44 15r15 15v19 17v28 40v39 40 46r4 51r31 52v2 55v17 22ⁿ 61r25 40

9 baxos 19v7 29r28 46r32 51r40 51v19 52r13 46 54v35 60r3

10 baya 19v8 28v16 29r14 32r42 32v37 40v26 48r21 55r19 55v9 57r40

   bãcos 30r23

   belprado 54v5 8

   benefiçio 29v4

   benefiçios 29v21

   bermeja 12v2

   bermejas 20v37

   besandoles 21v22

   besar 1r22

   besarle 66v37

   besavã 21v11

   bestia 9v19 13v17

   bestias 13v14 22r2 66v47

   bevenla 44r46

   bever 10v22 12v15 39v23 45r22

   bevia 27r22

   bevian 19r10 21r9

   bevido 61v29e

   bezerro 52r11 17

96 bien biẽ biēn

85 bien 2v18 7r34 8v15 9v35 10r22 11v4 46 12r19 13r13 13v45 15r41 16r15 18r6 18v45 20r20 21r1ⁿ 22r31 23r14 22 24 26v19 38 28r6 30r35 30v26 32r36 32v21 33r8 33v41 34r40 47 34v35 35r16 36r16 38v41 39v2 10 40r12 40v7 41v23 42r15ᶜ 43r16 41 43v34 44r40 44v40 46r30 33 47v25 29ᶜ 30 48r26 30 48v23 49v5 50v2 39 51r36 37 42 51v11 35 52r12 32 53r38 54r2 55v11 40 56v3 19 27 57r47ⁿ 59r37 61r4 61v5 62r39 63r11 63v39 64r44 64v1 24f 27ᶜ 65v48 66r36 66v6

   bienes 51r18

8 biẽ 9r31 14r43 18v37 22v19 27v25 31r41 55r34ⁿ 63r27

   biēn 9v6 37v40 57v31

   bispera 26v44ⁿ

   bisperas 18v17 26r5 33r28 50r4 64v41ᶜ

   bivas 30v45

   bive 37r43

   biven 21v6 28r25 35r45

   bivia 20r25

   bivido 20r27

   bivir 21v19

   bivo 4r35

   blanca 4v5 6v39 7r20 10r34

   blancas 5r40 12v8 36v16

   blanco 9r39 16v27 42r5

   blancos 9r39 36v15 37v49 38r2

   blanda 25r21

   blandeo 61r15

   blãco 54v5ⁿ

   bledos 18r27

buscava   19v34 54r9

C

cabañas 35r20

12 cabeça   9v28 29v34 30v15 31v46 35r32
    36r31 37r7 10 48r10 49v2 50r11 55v43
    cabeças   18v36 48 23r35

6   cabellos   9r33 35 9v26 55r48 48ⁿ 55v42
    cable   35r13
    cables   24v28

146 cabo   2v20 6r41 8v35 9v3 11r41 43
    11v28 13r11 13v40 14v8 41 41 15r17
    18 20 29 33 44 15v14 15 36 16v42
    17r29 17v1 19r25 25ⁿ 29 29 30ᶜ 32
    19v6 11 21r45 22r14 23v20 21 30ⁿ 36
    48 49 25r2 25v24ᶜ 26v12 12 27r29 32
    27v10 38 39 41 42 44 28r12 20 22 40
    28v12 17 17 22 29 29r12 29v37 31r9
    25 27 31v14 32r29 30 30 32 42 46 48
    32v3 33r1 3 7 9 10 11 15 29ᶜ 40 33v1
    34r10 11 12ᶜ 14 29 35 36 38 40 41 43
    34v13 35r5 32 40v31ⁿ 32 38 40 40
    41r10 42v21ᶜ 43r28 43v8 44r11ᶜ 13
    46r9 48v44 51r34 35 37 37 39 51v5
    52r10 11 16 52v36 54v4 8 9 10 20 25
    26 26 29 30 30ᶜ 32 45 46 55r9 10 15
    57r27 57v42 44ⁿ 44ⁿ 60r8 65r27 67r10
    cabos   40v25 36
    cabras   13v17

6   cabrian   26v45 27v11 30v39 31r32
    41r11 41v24
    cacique   45r17 33 48v45
    caça   47v22
    caçabi   47v24
    caçada   37r43
    caçar   20v29

13 caçique cacique

10 caçique   38v29 45 39r8 27 40r34 45r12
    45v4 49r15 50r37 50v3

34 cada   1v38 2v31 38 6v17 8r33 8v34
    10v23 12v36 41 17r17 18r11 24 21r42
    22r9 23v45 28r13 33v1 35v2 36r35
    37r3 38v33 39v20 40r24 45r21 23
    49r24 49v15 55v45 57r39 57v48 49ᶜ
    58v23 61v25 46
    caer   3v37
    caido   21r36
    cala   24v44 45 27v10
    calabaca   42r15
    calabaça   12v1
    calabaças   10r3 16r41 31r48 42r6
    calafate   48r44 50v38
    calafatearō   56v21
    calafates   56v21
    calafetalla   53r13
    calar   12r34 17r12
    calçar   49v9
    calças   42r26
    caldeo   20r29
    caleta   31r34

calidad   20r2
calido   19r8
caliz   32v37 58r27
callado   53r34
callente   19r3
calles   18v31 45r8

11 calma   3r15 4v20 40 5r13 5v17 17r23
    25v16 26r37 46r21 25 36
    calmar   27v45
    calmas   3r19 6r29 34 6v6
    calmeria   12v25

8   calmo   14r45 17r42 27v39 37r3 58r44
    58v43 59r33 61r15ᶜ
    calmole   57v47

8   calor   17r24 19r4 6 26r20 21 23 25
    29v29
    cama   29v34 39v38
    camaras   32r17
    camarones   35v12 47v22
    camas   14r24 63r33
    cami   19r37

96 camino   1r2 1v5 29 2r14 3r22 24 3v27
    35 4r2 18 4v19 5r37 5v12 18 6r1 7 15
    28 33 6v5 24 33 7r14 22 31 42 7v22
    8r32 10v8 13v28 38 15v20 22 17r12
    48 17v4 14 20 42 19r3 20v44 21v42 45
    26r42 26v17 27v38 30v4 26 34 31r40
    32v29 33v39 35v48 37r12 22 37v42
    40r23 41v16 42v20 43v13 44v45 45r33
    51r24 51v1 34 43 52v23 53r22 49
    54v22 24 33 55r5 8 57r1 13 57v16 20
    22 59v41 60r11 20 60v5 31 43 61r36
    42 63r15 18 65r10 17 24 41 44 67r9
    15
    caminos   6r9 35r21 36v30

7   camisa camissa

6   camisa   18r15 47v27 50r28 63r38 45
    65v1
    camisas   49r10
    camissa   61v22

6   campana   27v44 28r41 41ᶜ 28v11 22 29
    campiña   33v25 36v23 37r16 38r8 52r7

6   campiñas   33r21 34r45 34v14 38r5
    53v38 54v12
    campo   7v39 33r41

10 can   1r26 16v19 18v6 19r37 48 50
    19v24b 23r15 28r37 35r48
    canal   51r26
    canales   51r40 52r14 44 53v34

11 canaria   1v29 2v1 7 15 17 3r3 4v35 9v33
    41r38 57r46 64r46
    canarias   2r14 2v32 4r38 22r20
    canarios   9r38 9v31
    candela   32v39
    candelas   22r49
    candelilla   8v7
    canela   20v32 39 41 21v25
    cangrejo   4r34
    cangrejos   5r41 25r40

8   caniba   28r24 35r46 47 36r26 38v18

47v41 55v26ᶜ 27

canibales   26v16 38v19 23

canima   28r24

25   canoa   30r22 30v37 31r43 35v44 47
        37v5 8 15 38v40 44 47 39r2 9 41v34
        42v18 43v31 47r36 39 48v45 50r8 12
        51v15 52v33 35 53r9

22   canoas   9v36ⁿ 17v32 18r45 47 18v2
        19v6 31 20v24 31r36 42v16 28 43r8
        44r41 44v33 36 47 45r11 46v36 47r29
        43 50r7 57v8

canona   43v19

canpana   28r20

cansar   15r23 20v22

cantar   8v12 16r6 18v49 34v21

cantarillos   44r44

cantaros   42r6

cantava   22r1 36v31

cantavā   18r12 36v34

cantādo   5r4

cantera   51v49

17   cantidad   10r38 15v8 18r13 22r6 22v46
        38r41 40r41 44v12 18 45v4 13 48v28
        50r19 52r26 52v28 47 53v2

cantos   20v23

caña   8r22 24

cañal   41r26

cañas   13r42 24v41 38v18ᶜ 19 57r24

cañaveral   41r26ⁿ

caona   55v13 14ⁿ

capear   64v10

capillo   22r11

18   capitan   5v20 8v30 13v32 16r43 49v19
        56r24 59r8 63r26 42 47 63v11 19 40
        64r1 6 64v34 66r4 19

capitanes   8v31 39 15v44 53r23

capitā   19r33

capitulaçion   66v11 13

captivado   26v21

captivar   32v17

captivarlos   35v1

captivavan   28r37

captiverio   5v10

captivos   9v12 11r5

capuz   49v6

caqui   39r26ᶜ

cara   28r35 31v31 54r4

caracoles   19r17 25r10 32r18

caras   9r33 41

caratona   18v36

caratula   43v24 48r7 49r38 56v16

caravel   58v20ᶜ

95   caravela   2r22 25 30 2v7 37 3r4 10 3v30
        4v13 5v20 21 7r18 7v3 16 8r21 25 35
        11v17 27 32 41 13v33 14v23 23 19r31
        25r44 26r28 31 27v9 28v41 32v34 40
        42 46 35v44 39r31 46v9 10 12 21 22
        47r24 47v19 48v37 43 49r20 49v17 19
        45 51r4 11 52r47 47ⁿ 52v5 17 36
        53r12 19 53v6 54r24 55r43 55v11

56r25 56v6 12 57r11 58r10 29 58v21
    59r5 60v22 61r3 31 62v15 63r4 22ᶜ 30
    63v10 14 21 64r2 5 8 64v14 65r15
    65v12 40 66r2 9 22 33 44 46 66v44
    67r3

12   caravelas   2v4 3r5 12 10v7 15v31 37
        53r23 56v20 25 57r39 57v21 33

carbon   55r46

carga   61v29a

cargadas   44r42

cargado   8r27 14v4

cargados   33r42

cargar   11r30 47r29 57r38

cargava   11v15

cargo   32v26

cargue   11r39

11   carib   55v21 26 26ᶜ 28 56r30 56v17 46
        47 57v5 35 58r32

caribata   40v45 41r1 10 47v18

caribatan   44v46 46r11

10   caribes   21r8ⁿ 47v41 47 50r32 37 55v4
        4ⁿ 7 56r35 46

caritaba   35r43

carne   21v23 38v22 56v48

carnes   3r1

carnestolendas   63r25

carpintero   24v37 48r44 50v37

carraca   24v16 25r3 34r48

carracas   33v8

carrascas   33v23 34r27

8   carta   1v40 5v21 22ⁿ 31 7r6 19r40 64v28
        66r41

6   cartas   16v18 20r40 60v26 63v26 42
        66r17

carteado   63r11

cartear   5v33

carteavā   60v22 63r16

33   casa   15v39 42 18r24 19v28 21v6 16
        22r7 23r34 29v19 30v12 15 17 18ᶜ
        32r14 20ᶜ 33v39 34v40 38v31 39r36
        44r25 44v38 46v30 48v30 49r6 50
        50r41 53v20 61v11 62r17 63r38 65r30
        66v3 67r36

casadas   14r29

44   casas   10v39 14r22 25 26ⁿ 28 16r31
        18r16 18 21 18v20 26 27 31ᶜ 40 19r10
        19v17 20r31 21r1ⁿ 21v5 7 10 46 28r27
        27ᶜ 29r9 30r40 30v3 20 29 33v38
        35v20 36r22 35 37r38 37v14 45r26
        45v30 47r3 4 28 47v25 49r8 54r40
        56r45

casca   65v26

cascara   32r6

cascavel   16v35 47r38 46

9   cascaveles   9r23 11v35 16r36 31v6 35v34
        37v9 42v41 47r39 41

cascavelito   32r1

casgajos   46r4

casi   46r43

casita   63r40

casse　17r43
castañas　21r19 36r40 41 38r15
castañeda　63r27
castellano　14r34
castellanos　40r2n 47v7
castigados　63v39
castigo　53r39
69　castilla　3r14 10r34 11r4 10 12v40 14r12
　　　15 20r39 20v42 25v38 26r16 30r8
　　　34r28 46 34v17c 18 20 22 25 38 35r8
　　　35v10 36v17c 19 31 38r6 31 35 37 45
　　　39v32 40v10 41r5 42r7 43r1 1 32
　　　43v42 47r1 47v47 48v25 43 47 49v40
　　　51r9 55v43 56v29 57r15 58v4c 59v24
　　　60v36 62r2 62v19 63r42 63v23 38 42
　　　64r9 64v17 65r1 1n 65v36 66r5 13 17
　　　29 37 66v7 46
　　castillo　8r41 8v15 39r45 39v6 13
　　cathalina　26v44n 27v12n 12n 36
　　cathay　19r49
　　catholicos　1r33 30r12
　　catorze　43r34
　　caudal　23r21
　　caudaloso　22v6
　　caudalosos　32r40
15　causa　3v13 17 4r30 22v39 26r24 33
　　　28r29 30v42 31r23 35v15 52v29 53r32
　　　55r36 56v33 63v22
　　causado　5v27
　　causarō　48v15
　　causas　61v38 38n
　　causavan　64r27
　　cava　48r31
　　cavallera　36v3
　　cavalleros　66r34 66v33
　　cavallo　9v27 63r47 63v9
　　cavallos　9r34
　　cavan　22v40
　　cavar　50r5
　　cavādo　30v31
　　cavila　20r10
　　cayerō　48r6
　　cayesse　61v1
　　cayēdo　1r32
6　cayo　61v7 7n 13 16n 19 65v1
　　cāpiña　33r23
　　cātar　34v22n
　　cera　8v8
　　cerca　3v11 57r45c
　　cerco　40v35
　　cerrazon　62v25
　　cerrazō　62v40
　　certifica　31v11 46v47
　　certifico　47r10
　　cestillo　30v16
　　cevadas　34r32
　　chan　20r10
　　cheranero　34r10
　　chicas　23r35
　　chico　29r8

chimeneas　14r26 26n
christo　51v17b
chuq　47r41
chuq̄　47r41
cibao　45v3n
ciertas　5v22 38v18
cierto　29v5 57v44n
ciē　20r18
ciguayos　55r48n
cinco　4v9 13v2 28r4 38r14
cipango　16v9 17r38
cirio　61r47
ciudad　13r17
clara　26v3 61v17
claras　12r28 24r44
clarissima　29r40
claro　23v32 26r20 28r42 62v4
claros　24r29 41r2
clato　66v20
clavo　48v20
clerigo　63r44
clerigos　64v13
11　co　8v33 18v24 21r34 35r45 48v47 53v4
　　　55r48c 57v34c 60r9 51c 60v29
　　cobardes　28r28 31v13 38v6 48r36 56r38
　　cobardia　31v41
　　cobija　13r31 22r18
　　cobijan　18r16 42r25
　　cobrar　20r41 37r19 64r38
　　cobrādo　22v36
　　cobre　47v45 45 57r35
　　cobrian　42r1
　　cobro　46v21
　　codiçia　47r9
　　coge　22r49 48r48
　　cogella　35r25
　　cogello　44v16
　　cogen　13r34
　　coger　21r22 40 27r39 64v24
　　cogerian　35v8
　　cogē　35v8 40r41
　　cogia　45v2 49r23 33
　　cogian　45r41 52v48 53r2 57v32
　　cogido　22r6
　　cognoscella　65v17
　　cognoscer　15r42 42r15
　　cognoscē　63v41
　　cognosci　9r10 12v8 39v46
　　cognoscia　60r18 62v22 63r27
　　cognosciere　51v22
　　cognoscierōla　20v42
　　cognoscimio　27r5
　　cognoscio　17r20 21r40 27r45 33r44
　　　65v22n
　　cognosciolo　4r28
　　cognosco　67r31
　　cognosçedores　22v29
　　cognosçen　9r43
　　cognosçer　6r17 16r14 62r31 62v40
　　cognosçi　16r24

confirmavã   44v14
congoxa   62r17[c]
conil   58r27
conjunçion   55r35
conjunçiõ   55r33
conquista   48v32 66v12
conquistar   48v30
conseguir   61v45
consejavã   37v35
consejeros   37v35 38r38 39v18 44 40r9
consejo   23v17 38v37
consentimi[o]   67r30
consentir   30r11
consideradas   59r23
consigno   33v35
20   consigo   23v31 29r7 31v30 34v46 37v23
    38r40 40v5 41v7 42v12 43r17 44v8
    45v1 50r41 51r4 53v38 55v32 57r15
    57v37 62r11[n] 63r30
consiguiente   65r8
consintiese   44r9
consolacion   34v3[n]
consolaçion   48r12
consolados   23v12
consolar   46v45
constase   64v18
constreñir   56v24
contar   3r27 24r36 33v27 41v15
contava   3v2 21
contavã   32v14
contãdo   3v16
contentami[o]   44r38
contento   16r37 39v42 49v12
4   contentos contẽtos
contentos   18v23
contezuelas   31v7 32r2 38v25 44r20
contẽtos   31v8 56v19 64v31
contiene   9r3
continẽte   47r18
17   conto   3v12 4r3 5v13 6r19 24 34 6v6 25
    34 7r1 15 25 33 7v2 8r2 8 60v44
10   contra   5v9 40r9 42r42 53r30 54r13
    57r14[n] 62r12 13 67r35 37
contradicçion   43r4
contramaestre   20v38 21r33
contraria   26r4 61r22
contrarias   3v22 26r41
14   contrario   5r29 6v37 14r46 22r42 25v28
    29v14 30v42 31r13 23 35v16 37r17 23
    56v32 61r12
contrarios   65r25
contratar   56v5[n]
contrellos   63r46
controversia   56v28
convenia   50v28
convenibles   47r9
convenientes   48v17
conventos   46v20
conversaçion   29r6 38r21
conversion   1v2

converteria   9r11
convertido   22v35
convertirã   22r26 29v26
8   conviene   17v35 23r10 35r31 41r30
    41v10 46r25 52r14 53r24
copañia   23r42
9   coraçon   31v41 32v18 42r9 17 42v39
    43v26 44r19 47v12 56v30
coraçones   42v3
7   corda   8v24 23v23 28v6 32r46 46v25
    54v36 64r31
cordel   33v11
cordeles   18r21
10   cordova   33r23 36v23 37r16 50 38r9
    46v28 50v16 52r22 53v17 62r22
coroay   49r28
corona   8v35 49v1 56v33 57r7
coronas   49r45
coronillas   14r26[n]
7   corre   11r35 12r18 13r12 13v27 14r41
    35r33 51r41
corredios   9v26
6   correr   28v20 30r33 42v37 49r16 61r29
    31
correria   38r47 61r5 26
corria   11r37 14v39 19v10 46v13[n] 52r39
corrian   42r2 42v6 46r40
corriase   24r2 32r28
corriente   26v7 32v27
corrientes   3v21 5v27 25v43 28v7 54v34
corriẽdo   56r9 13
corriẽte   4r20 37r38
corriẽtes   26r41
13   corrio   7v44 24r27 32v43 36r24 59v29
    41 47 60r25 33 60v7 45 65r38 42
corrupta   19r46
cortan   9r37 24v28
cortar   46v15
cortase   34r24
cortasen   64r16
cortavan   21r9
cortavã   9v1
corte   56v32[n] 36[n] 67r35
corto   48v21
cortos   9r34
corvinas   35v11
70   cosa   6r38 8r41 9v32 10r6 30 12v4 14r5
    18 15r4 9 31 16r15 16v24 38 38[c] 18r9
    25 18v27 42 20r5[c] 21r26 46 22r14 17
    22v15 23r21 25r21 27v24 29r11 28 38
    29v14 31v9 32r12 35r35 43 47 35v28
    28[c] 29 36r10 37r40 37v23 38r24 42r15
    16 41 43r2 25 44r9 22 47 45r27 47r10
    32 38 47v3 28 40 49v42 53v40 54r8 33
    61v47[c] 64r12 65v25 66r27 66v8 14
    67r30
63   cosas   9r15 21 22 9v4 10r27 10v14
    11v43 12r5 33 13r34 14r11 24 15r21
    17r39 19v44 20v25 37 22v23 23r18
    24v6 29r43 29v2 7 30r5 30v14 31r48

criar 19r16

criaturas 18v25

16 cruz 8v32 20r7 22v32 24v32 35[c] 36 38 40 25v3 30v43 35v16 40r7 40v12 61v4 7 19

cruzarā 64r34

cruzavan 61r41

cruzavā 61r17 22

cruzādo 61r39

cuãto 17v4 18v28

28 cuba colba

27 cuba 17r2 22 30 17v5 29 33 18r1 19r33 33n 33n 33n 34 19v11n 20v4n 23v21 30 30n 48 24r21 30v13n 32v3n 12 20 33r32 35r41 35v42 45v16

cubanacan 19r33n

cubierta 30r25 31r41 39v16

cubiertas 46v38

cubierto 30v16

cubrir 48v39

cuchillada 56r16

cuchillo 61v4

cudicioso 59r11

cudiçia 26r30 47r33 52v9 53r26 61v30

cudiçiosos 44r12

cuello 21r2

cuentas 9r14 39v39 42v40 49v4 56v9

6 cuentezillas cuētezillas

cuentezillas 9r23 12v7 38 16r36 16v2

cuerda 5v32 41r24 41v26

cuerdas 56r11

cuerno 18r22

cuero 16r19

cuerpo 9r41 13r30 38v22

cuerpos 9r32 9v8 11r25 42r31

cuestas 44r34 45r33

cuezen 36r39

cuēta 6v29 20v5 57r12 66r2n 3

cuētan 17r39

7 cuētas 11v34 20r33 35v33 37v9 40r1 56v14 66r6

cuētezillas 16v36

cuētezuelas 55v36

cuētos 56v34

cuidado 59r9

culebra 13v16

cumbre 54v5n

cumple 2r5 7

cumplia 53r36

cumpliese 61v1

cura 13v4

curar 42r36

curarō 46v8

curava 10v15

curo 15v3

cuva 32v12n

cuya 2r25 14r36 46v3

cuyas 4v2 21r48

cūple 41r42

cūplierō 48v16

cūplir 1v33

cybao 45v3 47v17n

çanahorias 21r18 38r11

çapatos 39v41

çeçilia 18r41

çedaço 40r41

çejas 9r35

çentissima 24v10 27v22

çeotis 10r33

çera 30v12 13 13n 31v31 61r47

50 çerca cerca

48 çerca 4r14 22[c] 24 4v43 5r21 22 10v28 12r27 12v23 13v40 14r1 16r29 16v42 20v16 43[c] 44 21v27 22v12 16 24v6c 28r40 30v2 36 32v31 37v21 39r11 19 41v33 41 42v21[c] 37 43v18 44v9 36 47v11 49v26 51v36 52r6 32 52v29 53r8 55v8 57r46 60r28 60v36 46 65v7 7

çercada 35r41 63v5

çercado 18r9 19v7 41r34

çercana 18r2

çercanos 50v35

çercar 18r45

5 çerco cerco

çerco 13v20 16r17 28r14 34r25

çerrada 8r42 33r20 43r42

çerrado 30v44 33v15 41v25 43r36 54r23

8 çerrazon cerrazon cerrazō çerrazō

çerrazon 4v17 14v3 34v9 64r26

çerrazō 17v15 30r33

çertifica 24r40 24v10

çertificadamēte 13v35

2 çertifico certifico

çertifico 29v27

3 çestillo cestillo

çestillo 12v6 30v16

çevadera 17r47

33 çielo 3v37 6r18 10v18 21 25 16v40 19v13 20r6 21v13 32 22v29 30 24v11 28r41 30v44 31v28 32r11 18 34v8 36r26 37v38 38r35 36 40r10 41r36 42r33 42v11 43r22 44r39 59r14 60r17 62v4 65v13

çien 32r36 52r32

çient 27v12 40r37 56v34

13 çiento 3r30 3v10 11r18 20v7 22v28 30v39 31r29 32v22 44r41 58v14 64r9 65r26 28

çiernen 40r41

çierra 10v28c

7 çierta 1v6 4v25 32r17 47r18 57r31 59r18 63r11

çiertamēte 67r26

10 çiertas ciertas

8 çiertas 4r36 7r9 20r43 27r40 31r19 42v16 43r15 47v32

26 çierto cierto

24 çierto 4v27 8v10 16r14[c] 15 19v11n

delgado   27r45
deliberãdo   49r18
20   della   4v44 13r9 15v18 16r30 17r4
     20r36 20v34 22r49 25r22 36 31r49
     32r7 18 33r22 37r6 39v23 41v14 43v3
     45v17 54r24
13   dellas   9v3 11r21 21 12v5 18v5 24v11
     25r29 30 29r24 29v10 38r12 43r25
     48r42
8   dello   5r15 37[c] 10v31 15v8 18v42 23r23
     44v19 47v11
19   dellos   9r39 39 10r8 13v5 34 16r15 35
     16v27 27 27 21v18 22 38r10 45v16 31
     56r24 46 57r4 64v18
13   demas   2v20 3r1 8r13 8v28[n] 39 31v11
     34r25 38r39 39v22 44r9 56v31 59v20
     63v41
    demãda   2r37 18r1 22v10 60v34
    demãdar   17v6
    demãdassen   42v42
    demãdava   12v12
    demãdeles   31v48
    demorava   34r36 41
    demudarse   31v30
    demuestra   16r16
6   den   7v14 10r28 30 12v20 32r12 51r16[c]
9   dende   22v5 28v26 26 27 28 34r46 34v1
     47v8 52r30
47   dentro   10v19 32 13v43 14r23 15r34
     16r21 18r7 23 18v32 19r14 19v44
     21v3 24v44 27r19 27v36 28r1 14
     29r17 30v16 28 31r17 31 32r40 33v1 9
     34r44 34v5 35r2 18 36r21 41r23 41
     46r5 46v26 48r21 51r39 51v10 13
     52r20 42 53v10 54r21 22 54v13 62r33
     65v28 67r19
    deo   5v39 67r45
    departio   66v25
    deprendã   9v18
    deprender   11r2
    deprendiesen   23r40
    derechas   9v34 57r25
    derecho   57r43 57v20 24 63v8
    derechura   27r44
    derredor   14v18 21v17 22
12   derrota   1v31 2v41 14v37 23v46 32v3
     37r9 40v1 57v10 31 41 63r17 20
    derrotas   1r2 14v27
    des   24v6j[c]
    desabahado   33v19
    desandar   52v2
    desaparecio   26r32[c]
    desapareçierõ   5r5
    desapareçio   61r32 32[n]
    desapegado   4r12
    desastre   48r18
    desatinar   63r15
    descanso   13v13
    descaramojos   8r27
    descargamos   14v29

    descargar   46v37 47r29
    descargo   46v38
    descendian   27v14
    desciende   41r34
    descobedo   8v40 50v19
    descobrirse   22v15
    desconciertos   56v42
    desconçertada   62r46
    desconçierto   63v45
    descreçe   25v8
8   descubierto dscubierto
    descubierto   24r8 25v7 27v25 61v50
     64v5
    descubri   14r40
    descubriendo   61v50
    descubrierõ   4v33 7v21f
    descubriese   1v16
    descubriẽdo   49v43
6   descubrimiento descubrimi[o] dscubrimi[o]
    descubrimiento   57r41
    descubrimi[o]   1v26[n] 56v32[n] 36[n]
5   descubrio dscubrio
    descubrio   24r1 55r13
13   descubrir dscubrir
6   descubrir   1v20[n] 15v5 22r38 30r7 48v11
     61v44
    descubrirã   23r16
    descudillas   16v32
    descuido   46r16[n]
    desçendia   25v48[c]
    desçendierõ   38v44
    desçendiẽtes   30v22
    desçendio   55v45
    desçendir   38v2
    desçienden   29r30
40   desde dsde
17   desde   4r38 14v39 19v18 23v46 24r10
     40[c] 37r3 37v19 40v43 41r15 41v27
     50v8 53r31 53v5 36 64r2 64v10
    desdel   52r11 16
8   deseava dseava
6   deseava   23v39 29r45 36r43 47v10 51r13
     52v14
2   deseavã dseavan
    deseavã   47r38
    desencasose   2r21
5   deseo dseo
    deseo   28v39 32v4 36r9
    deseos   62r1
    deseoso   42r17
    desfallecimi[o]   61v47
    deshazian   42v4
    deshonestidad   52v11
    desmayase   3r29
2   desmãdada dsmãdada
    desmãdada   53r37
    desmãdadas   6v10
    desmãparãdo   18v25
    desmedidos   44r12
2   desnuda dsnuda

devria   38v7[n]
dexa   25r22[c] 36v43
dexado   11v27 31v18 67r25
dexallas   18r30
dexallo   40v11
dexallos   31v9
dexan   14r26[n]
dexando   36r21
10   dexar   2v7 6r1 7v22 25v40 28v45 32v20
         48v10 27 50r23 57v22
dexara   10r36 48r22 49v17 51r13
dexarā   22r29 64v33
dexaria   63v37
dexarla   48r23
8   dexarō   11v13 24 16r31 35v47 37v15[c]
         43r45 57v14[c] 64v31
dexarōlo   30v7
dexase   23v11 48v4 65v37
dexasen   19v19 46r26
dexasē   55v46
12   dexava   5r8 24r20 24v32 37r48 50r22 39
         45 50v1 62r18[c] 20 23 64r39
dexavā   38r23
dexavāla   57v37
dexādo   31r33 52v21 56r21
dexe   15v42 16r33
12   dexo   3r2 14v5 21v40 26v7 32v7 43v18[n]
         46r22 50v12 53r30 56r32 57v8[n] 65r1
dexoles   50v21 25 35
16   dezia   5v23 39 6r5 6[c] 8[c] 7r36 38[c] 8r39
         9v14 20v36 24r6 31v36 36r28 39v27
         40r9 67r1
22   dezian   6r17 10r17 11r15 11v2 5 13r19
         18v2 12 19r33[n] 21r4 23v31 26r14
         27v6 32v6 33r17 33v40 35r36 36v13
         43v14 44r47 45r16 62v11
deziā   2v40 4r27 5v30 28v34 35r38
30   dezir   1r26 5v37 8v12 11v8 13v3 42
         14r14 42 18v45 21r1[n] 8[n] 24v26 29r26[n]
         32r13 18 35r46 38r3 30 43 41r26[n]
         41v23 44v21 46v13[n] 49r12 56v43
         57r37[n] 61v17 62v29 66v24 38
dezires   15r40
dezirle   40r39
dezirlo   44v11[n]
dēde   1v12 28v25
dētro   10v33 18v43 65v30
dha   15r1
dhas   13r21 24v6d
dho   11r43 28r12
12   di   9r12 11r13 11v33 38 12r4 8 13r14
         13v39 14r39 14v20 16r36 39v39
175   dia   1v36 36 39 39 2r18 33 2v2 11 3r8
         14 24 27 37 3v7 15 16 19 22 27 35 4r2
         4 19 4v8 12 19 21 38 43 5r13 14 33
         5v12 17 6r3 16 19 23 28 35 6v5 33
         7r15 23 32 7v2 28 29 32 8r1 7 29 8v25
         11r33 39 12v23 25 30 13v18 23 14r9
         14v7 26 31 15v27 17r24 41 44 17v22
         30 40 19v36 20v24 29 23v32 46 25r43

25v16 23 33 26r28 40 26v6 26 27v12[n]
         45 46 28v7 29r12 30r32 30v41 32v29
         35 33r24 29 34v7 38 35v2 15 36r6
         36v24 40 37r3 38v15 35 39r22 25 32
         40r35 40v21 22 43v10 33 43[c] 44r4 41
         45r31 45v17 46r14 15 46v26 47r46
         48v12 49v7 31 51r24[n] 51v6 6[c] 52r15
         44 53r12 18 53v46 54v39 56r47 56v5
         57v2 58r17 58v19 23 42 44 59r18 33
         44 59v10 23 29 41 46 60r11 21 25 33
         34 35 45 60v6[c] 7 14 44 61r1 5 8 15
         63r25 63v3 65r24 35 38 42 65v21 22
         67r12 16
diamātes   24v12
38   dias   1r17 1v20 26 2r9 3r6 4v10 5v21
         7r8 7v24 10v40 14v11 17v47 18r46
         18v7 19v43 20r34 21v25 22r29 43
         23v17[n] 29v37 33v44 37v43 44v22
         46r19 48v9 49v17 50v9 52v31 54r26
         33 55v24 56v36 57r17 20 59r15
         62v11[c] 63r6
diaz   66r1
dice   19v11[n]
31   dicha dcha dha đha
dicha   23r17 35v16
10   dichas dchas dhas đhas
53   dicho dho đho
16   dicho   9v24 19r50 26r34 33r28 33v1
         35r28 39r26 42v14 45v19 46v33[c]
         48r32 49v10 52v16 56v8 61v44 64v25
6   dichos dchos đhos
4   diego diego[o]
diego   21r37 50r43 50v16
diego[o]   46v28
diente   9v4 57r29
dierolo   47v34
dieron   56r15
12   dierō   14r35 16r31 29r7 30v33 31v18 40
         35v24 37r42 42v37 43v30 56r21 63r7
dierōle   30v6
dierōles   21v16
diese   10r6 20r40 44r23 56v9 66r46
diesen   8v42 14r18 28v43 46r26[c]
51   diez   2r34[c] 3r31 3v1 13 4v21 8r6 40
         8v19 11r38 12r9 12v38 13v50 14r31
         15r36 16r26 18r44 18v7 14 19v31
         22r9[n] 23v46 24v25 25v22 31r44 31v12
         12 32v32 34v2 35r31 37r9 37v11
         41r33 50v9 51v6 18 37 52v3 53r9
         53v12 54r26 54v9 57v35 43 58r3
         58v35 59v35 60r12 15 60v9[c] 13 65r13
diferēçia   14r13
differēçia   36v24 45v16 55v33
difficultades   56v32[n]
dificultad   57r18
dificultoso   56v47
diformes   13r35
diga   42r10
digamos   22v31
digan   22v31

7   digo   15r44 17r11 29v38 30r8 10 44v42
         45v19
    diles   31v48
    diligençia   12v28 22r25 46v42
    diligēcia   46v40
    diligēçia   2v19
    dineros   61v15 65v39 66r46
36 dio   7r18 11v23 19v22 23v32 24v6i
         31v1 34r7 37r25 37v2 39v33 40r32
         41v36 42v40 43v13 45r23 46r45 46v40
         47v21 28 48r9 11 49r15 50v11 51v29ᶜ
         30 52r38 54r13 60r10 61r13 62r13
         62v5 63v7 64r7 17 65v19 67r6
7   diole   35v33 37v9 50r28 55v34ᶜ 35
         56v13 66v20
    dioles   20r32 35 36 44r29 64v30
37 dios   4v2 32 6v35 7r26 7v36 10v13 24
         22r37 22v29 29v16ᶜ 39 48v3 24 50v2
         51r3 56v31 39 57v22 58v5 59r17
         59v43 60r1 6 60v38 61v40 49 62r1 5
         13 15 63r8 65r14 18 46a 65v21 66r28ᶜ
         30
    diran   41v8
    dirian   26v22
    dis   26r30ᶜ
    discreçion   57r19
    disforme   13r39 55r44
    disformes   13v8 14r8
    disposicion   10r23ⁿ 30v10
    disposiçion   1v1 19r18 22r34
    dispuesta   13r28 22r22
    dispuesto   45r42
    dissimulando   49r6
    dissimular   52v13 53r36
    dissimulava   49r14
    dista   31r7
    distar   26r12 39r37 57v39
    distaria   62v26
    distava   19r45 32v3 33r9 34r12
    distavan   17v24 57r47
    distavā   20v2
    distāçia   55v33
    distes   23v11ⁿ
    diuersa   27v28
8   diuersas diversas
7   diuersas   2v5 15r24 16r10 21r20 21v48
         22r5 55r47
    diuersidad   13r40 43v34
    diuersissimas   27v16
    diuersos   13v2 18r10 24r37 65r32
    diuidian   25r30
    diuidir   28v13
    diuina   61v48
    diversas   8v38
    dixole   43v10
125 diz   6r43 18r7 29 18v11 27 19r4 50
         20r28 20v43 21r42 49 21v5 37 38
         22r12 22v1 24v36 25r20 25v38 39
         26r15 19 30 26v17 28r23 31 30v34
         31r18 31ᶜ 37 32v10 12 13 16 33v41

         34r22 28 35v43 37r49 37v26ᶜ 32 38r17
         19 22 39r28 40r35 40v14 41r6 26
         42r38 44v40 45r6 9 47v13 40 48v13
         15 15ᶜ 49r16 49v39 50r6 38 50v12 14
         33 40 43 52r1 5 52v24 45 53r3 4 6 14
         37 46 54r25 31 33 55r44 55v8 31
         56r12 23 29 40 56v7 48 57r2 3 6 11 15
         21 57v5 6ᶜ 8 9 11 28 29 33 35 58v3 23
         27 59r36 60r18 61r4 61v46 62r18ᶜ
         63r7 15 63v20 45 46ᶜ 64r1 65r47
         65v21 27 48 66r37 66v50 67r1
179 dize   2r26 31 2v26 34 39 4r5 9 15 35 42
         4v4 5r27 5v5 37 6v17 7r7 11 26 7v36
         9r8 14r26ⁿ 18r8 31 38 18v45 47 19r15
         25ⁿ 47 51 19v39 20r1 12 13 16 17
         20v5 20 21 21r14 26 31 39 43 47 21v2
         22r9 15 21 22v24 23r3 23v15 17ⁿ
         24r45 24v6 8 10 19 25r39 25v8 26r10
         26 33 26v19 35 38 27v30 29r23 24 26ⁿ
         40 29v2 3 30r27 30v13 31r14 20
         31v16 32r10 32v30 33r33 33v30 36 39
         34r4 34v42 35r33 47 35v5 6 18 26
         36v9 33 42 44 37r42 37v26 28 38v39
         39r36 39v1 41v13 16 42r11 16 42v1
         43 43r1 43v29 40 44v29 41 45v6 47r8
         21 32 48r16 19 48v2 4ᶜ 9 24 31 49r22
         35ᶜ 36 46 49v36 50r21 51r19 52r5ⁿ 35
         52v8 10 35 47ⁿ 53r36 42ⁿ 49 53v1 18
         54r6 12 35 41 54v5ⁿ 7 43 55v23 24 30
         56r29 39 56v19 22ᶜ 33 41 43 57r40 45
         57v37 58r23 58v4 59r3 8 60v37 39
         62r18 20 21 31 63r10 64r27 40 64v1 5
         67r21 31
    dizean   35r39
11 dizen   13r17 16r26 16v11 13 22r48
         22v39 23v23 45r15 49v23 53r42ⁿ
         54r18ⁿ
12 dizē   2r28 9v14 15r34 18r44 20r5 22r48ᶜ
         26r43 28r25 41v8 44v43 45r14 46v35
    dizian   36v25
    dizianle   36v22
    diziembre   35r11
6   diziendo   21v40 27r42 31v32 48v19
         50r37 52v6
30 diziēbre   30v41 31r12 22 32r24 45
         32v48 34r6 34v27 37 35r26 35v14
         36r2 37r1 21 37v1 38v11 39r24 40v18
         41r8 45 43v12 44v1 45r36 46r14 47r22
         48v36 49r1 19 42 49v30
16 diziēdo   5v1 19v23 29r5 41 31v4 39
         36r24 41v3 7 44v34 46v45 47r41
         49v16 52v41 64v11 66r29
    diziēdole   63r27
398 dl
408 dla
    dlante   22r31 40r25 42r24 51r27
105 dlas   1r10 11 25 1v29 2v1 4 31 3r28
         4r38 7v21c 9r35 10r31 31 10v7 12v22
         13r21 13v9 14r16 15r24 16r10 16
         16v26 17v27 18r14 30 18v24 19r3 6

19v33 44 20v23 29 21r20 21v48 22r5
22v19 23r19 24v21 29 29 25r33 38
25v11 26v1 34 27r4 27v5 28r1 29r4
26^n 43 29v1 33v24 35 34v41 36v8 18
37r45 37v17 38r37 38v18^c 19 39v19
41r39 41v30 33 42r23 36 42v13 43v6
35 45r8 46v38 47v28 49r8 50v44
52v45 53r2 53v43 54r43 55v34 56r36
37 56v32^n 57r24 57v3 12 59r38 60v25
61r24 26 61v32 62r16 29 31^c 62v34 37
63r2 14 17 63v29 65v11 44 66r6 25

dlgados   39v34

34   dlla   1r35 3v37 5r17 13r13 17v34 18r2
18v45 21r38 21v27 23r7 28v17 29r6
31r42 33v4 29 34r43^c 35r24 30 33
37r36 41r29 41 44r3 46r1 49v19 53v30
54v42 55r20 35 57r36 59r8 64r33
65r49 66v41

33   dllas   1v1 2 4v30 9v41 12v38 17v25 29
18v22 19r21 24r45 24v14 19 21 25r16
26v8 27r5 28r14 29r11 31v15 33v32
36r39 40r24 42v19 19 43r23 52r42
57v30 35 61r25^c 62v18 63r14 64r46
67r43

13   dllo   5r15 10r13 22v2 26v20 28r17
32r23 44v20 47v13 38 50r4 53r42^n
62v22^c 63v22

37   dllos   3v39 9r13 37 40 40 41 41 42
10r17 13r36 16v33 19v39 40 20r43
22v8 28 23r42 29v15 30r38 31v24 46
32r22 33v22 36r29 37v20 38v36 42r43
43r9 44r7 22 49r48 53v15^n 17 55r42
56r24 40 56v49

27   dlo   6v37 9r40 12v36 14r18 16r14^c
19v25 20r19 21r14 21v14 25v9 27v22
28r44 32r11 36r35 41 38v7^n 41v6
42v39 45v19 47r33 53v1 54r11 62r7
63v30 64r4 64v24 30

111   dlos   1r13 27 2v20 26^c 40 5v8 8v26 9r18
38 9v31 11v18 24 13r35 14r9 19 16r6
8 16v4 18r42 18v22 49 19r21 41
19v27 37 20r2 30 39 21r8^n 44 21v19
22v7 22 27 24v19 39 25r40 25v4 37
26v23 28r24 29r6 25 30r37 30v2 27
31v4 32r40 33r17 34v34 35r46 35v36
36r15 18 37r3 37v16 36 38r31 35
38v18 18 40r20 25^c 26 33 40v9 41r46
41v11 19 36 42r7 42v44 43v42 44r19
44v8 9 45r21 25 46v35^n 47r44 48v13
50r36 50v44 52v16 53v7 54r28 54v35
55r38 55v4 56r35 56v10 21 43 57r24
57v37 60r19 60v2 25 62v17 63r2 14
63v23 64r18 29 64v17 29 32 66r5 13
13 17

dñi   1r8
do   8v5 15r29 37r6 49r50
doblo   48r35
doctores   1r29
doctos   29v40
dolençia   29v35

dolia   21r50
dolor   29v35
domestica   13r23

13   domingo   2r17 2v24 4r1 6v4 25v1 27r27
31r12 44v1 46r28 49r42 59v4 60v16
66v23

20   domīgo   2v13 3r26 5r35 7r41 10v5
15v31 17v47 20v27 22v18 25v14
34v37 37v1 43v37 38 52r33 55r29
58r43 60r5 64v42 65r43

domīngo   15v35

don   1r3 1v13 66r41 66v32 67r41

122   donde   1v4 5 23 2r22 2v5 4v2 36 5v21
7v20 10v36 37^c 12r25 12v31 13v32
14r46 15v12 17r31 18r36 18v1 11 19r9
47 19v3 8 28 21r30 21v5 23v28 36
24r32 35 24v31 41 25r5 13 25v27 30
26r18 27 43 26v28 32 27r45 28r17
28v3 9 29r25 26^n 29v6 30r42 30v13
31v20 23 43 34v45 35r16 21 37r19 39
37v17 39r20 30 39 39v36 40v2 41v38
40 42v33 43v18^n 44v19 46 48^c 49
45r41 45v2 46r33 47r5 24 47v17^n 20
24 49r11 33 49v14 50r19 33 41 50v31
51v20 46 52v1 5 11 53r6 43 53v37
54r17 24 26 44 56r10 57r43 57v2^n 6
39 59r10 60v46 61r29 61v11 62v43 47
63r3 38 64r11 64v9 65v18 31 66r7
66v36 40 67r17^n 19

dondequiera   40r20
doña   2v28
dorados   6r13 25 30 59v25
dormian   20v26
dormido   46r20 62v36

8   dormir   4v6 7v19 46r19 22 38 62v36
66v44 66v41

138   dos   1r17 2v24 3v2 4v42 5r4 6r9 30 41
6v11 7r17 43 7v13 24 8r33 8v7 20 22
31 39 10v11 40 11v35 12r29 40 12v8
13v40 41 14r4 17r46 17v8 16 18r18 47
18v21 19r24 19v26 20r24 30 20v7 16
31 34 21r11 30 21v2 16 41 22v8 23v10
17^n 29 34 37 24v34 25r45 25v5 33 34
26r22 27r32 27v18 28r13 14 15 29r3
29v37 30v27 31r32 32r15 26 48 33r38
34r9 29 37 35r6 17 34 36r29 36v16
37r20 36 37v43 38v21 39v17 28 33
40r2^n 30 40v23 30 31^n 41v30 37 43r41
42 43v24 44v7 45r19 46r9 10 19 47r27
47v6 22 48r22 48v42 49v13 15 17
50r11 51r33 51v23 52r12 35^n 38 53r2^n
54r22 38 54v39^c 40 47 55r1 2 41
55v14^n 56r6 57r26 57v17 38 58v34
60v23 61r14 62r22 47 64v13 65v6 11

doy   15r40 17r22

27   doze   1v20 5v14 7v32 8r32 12v38 14r28
14v40 18r6 21v4 22r42 25v23 30r23
31r4 9 31 41r23 42r27 46r35 51v40
55r22 57v26 36 44 60r51 60v43 61r5
65r37

        65r46

      echolo   35r14

      echose   19v26 61v9

      edad   9r31 14r31 39v17 42r27

      edifiçios   52r1

      effecto   48r3 50r29

      egipto   5v9

1,288   el

      elefante   33r9

      elifante   33r15 34r41

  80   ella   1r30 5v33 43 6r38 10r25 11r36 37
        11v1c 18 19 13r9 31 14r44 14v30 40
        15r8 13 15v20 41 16r19 16v20 17r32
        34 41 17v35 18v47 19r41 22v2 25v7
        26v8 15 31 29r19 29 35 36 36 38
        30v10 39 32r16 21 37 32v44 46 35r1
        15 35v36 48 36r5 37r24 37v6 43 38r6
        41r28 43v20 44v12 15 45v41 41 43 43
        46v12 48r21 48v20 45a 49r3 10 49v12
        40 54v42 55v10 19 57r1 38 60r23
        60v44 61v36 48c 65v17

  23   ellas   5r42 5v26 14r25 15r25 16r3 18v4
        38 22r19 23r38 24v3 15 27r36 30r9
        30v21 31r40 31v49 38r9 42r32 54v39c
        55v31 57v34 34c 61r44

   8   ello   1v11 15v10 18r25 22r25 36r46
        39r15 52v7 64v26

  89   ellos   7v38 9r26 38 42 9v4 8 12 30 35
        10r3 34 11v11 25 13r3 5 13v7 14r35
        37 15r44 16r39 16v10 38 19r37 19v35
        48 20r10 21r17 21v17 18 23 24 30 32
        33 34 22v28 23v11 28v39 29r21 29v12
        23 30v27 31v40 43 48 32r5c 9 32v11
        33v33c 41 35r43 35v3 24 36r24 38r27
        38v4 39v45 42v4 26 42 43r5c 7 8
        44r31 33 44v48c 49 45r18 32 45v3 16
        22 46v8 47r12 14 42 47v15 15 50v27
        51r40 56r13 15 20 60v24 63r18 31
        64r7 64v18 65r28

      embarcarse   50v5

      embaxada   1v32 43r31

      embiado   21v3 31v22 48v38 50r7 64r4

      embiar   38v24 55v37

      embiarme   1r37

      embie   13r2 40r1

      embio   35r16 38v15 49r37 57r4

      embiōle   37v32

      emēdarā   56v24

      empacho   37v47

      emparejarse   55r17

      empleado   26v38

      empresa   48v32

1,025   en

      enamorado   55r10 16 17

      enamorados   19r21

      enbaraçavā   61r22

      enbarcarō   39r2

      enbarcose   50v9

      enbiada   5v31

  20   enbiado embiado

  15   enbiado   1r28 5v21 19v48 21r11 36r3
        36v3 37r34 38v35 39r5 40 40r10 44v4
        46v27 31 66v38

  11   enbiar embiar

   9   enbiar   12r7 19r39 19v21 20r24 35v34
        36r13 56r44 61v9 65r46

      enbiaran   29v39

      enbiarle   19r40

      enbiase   5v31 61v16 66r9

      enbiasē   49v33

      enbiava   44r8 46v44 63r26 31 66r42c

      enbiavalo   39v22

      enbiavan   20r39

      enbiavālo   57v36

      enbidia   3r13

   7   enbie embie

      enbie   11v33 38 14r1 14v22 23r33

      enbien   12v19

  39   enbio embio

  35   enbio   18v21 19v16 20r29 21r37 26v39
        28v40 30v26 31v19 32r38 32v37 35v5
        35 40r14 42v7 43v17 19 44r1 44v5 7
        46r28 46v36 47v35 48v45 49r6 11 40
        49v8 51v15 52v33 55r22 37 56v18
        57r7 62v48 66v31

      enbiole   43r14 43v22 49r38

      enbioles   63r23

      enbolvio   62r38

      encabalgar   19v9

      encallados   46v2

      encallar   48r15

      encallara   48r19

      encallase   48v4

      encallo   48r50

      encantado   29r45

      encareçe   27v18

      encareçellas   24v9

      encareçello   27v22

      encareçer   27r44 41v4

      encareçerlo   52r27

      encareçierā   29v2

      encargare   23v1

      encavalga   26v12

      encavalgar   62v21

      encēdido   24v22

      encima   9r35 14r26n

      encobrir   54r34

      encogidos   55r48

      encomēdado   52v16

      encomēdados   50r22

      encomēdole   50r43

      encomiēda   64v30

      ençerado   62r39

      ençima   8v34 24v13 57r28

      ende   11r18 14r12 16v4

      enderecan   10r2

      endereçado   62r4

      enderredor   17v7

      enemigos   1r35

  36   enero   1r17 1v9 35v8 50r1 25 50v42

27v7 28r10 11 31v44 32v18 30 31
36r25 26 36v30 37v14 38r18 20 22 24
31 33 35 39r22[n] 39v27 34 48v5 49r26[n]
50v28 51r34 52v8 53v45 54r2 55v4[n]
41[n] 56r19 30 46 57r21 35 57v40 58v33
63v30 67r37

errado   64v21

errar   12r38 13v19 54r30

errarō   63r1[n]

erravan   62v15[n]

erravã   7r38

244   es

escandalo   56v43

escapado   63r7 65v29

escapar   61v26

escaramuça   50r36

escasamēte   43r43

escaseava   24r13

escassamēte   13r30

escasso   15v25 25v22

escobedo   50r44

escodilla   29r32

escogio   36r15

esconder   42r29

escondierō   16r31

6   escrevir   1v35 38 10r5 21r25 29r44
41v22

escripto   9r4 41v23

escriptura   67r21 33

escriva   45v14

8   escrivano   8v41 39r5 44r6 24 44v6
50v36 55r34[n] 64v13

escrive   61v38

escriviendo   13r14

7   escrivio   4v20[c] 21 6r8 49r29 62r35
65v35 35[n]

escrivire   13v20

escrivo   29v5

escrupulo   67r27

escuda   38v14

escudero   39v31 49r12 15 66v45

escudilla   44r13b 46 46r37

escudillas   10r31 14r20

esculpido   40r2

escuranza   64r26

escuro   21v38

escusar   52v6

escusase   41v3

esforçada   2r32

esforço   8r11

esfuerço   62r13

9   eso   4v15 17r19 19r8 21r1[n] 22r5 40v39
42r11 44r21 63v37

esotras   32v12

espacio   34r24 53r50

espaçio   14r4 46v39

espada   31v38 56r2

espadas   9r44

espadines   66v51 67r1

espaldas   34r34 40v28 53v38

espantable   65v10[n]

espantado   55r27

espantase   3r29

espanto   42v24 65v22

22   españa   5r31 5v3 15r26 17r18 25 22v37
23r14 18 37 30r9 31r33 33v23 36v17
32 36 38r2 47v17[n] 49v32 51r12 57v18
24 24[n]

españas   1r11

50   española   14r46[n] 21r1[n] 23v30[n] 28r26[n]
32v9[n] 35r9[n] 10 30 32b 35 43 37r15 46
37v4 38r42 39r11 12 35 40v20 44v11
45v21 47v17 49r26[n] 36 50v12 52v22
26 27 53r1 2[n] 2[n] 7 21 54r30 55r25 28
55v4[n] 14[n] 17 22[n] 26[c] 27 41[n] 56r12[n] 42
57r39 57v2[n] 8[n] 43 58r31

españoles   2v27 20r24 44r11

espātables   61r21

especeria   32r13 50r20 54v1

especerias   17r32 33r43

especial   38r41 53v14 54r43

especialmēte   56v4

especias   44r45

12   espeçeria especeria

9   espeçeria   15r27 15v7 16v15 17r14
20r35 22v44 24v3 48v28 51v26

3   espeçerias especerias
espeçerias   22r38

7   espeçial especial
espeçial   42r27 34 47v14 61v26

2   espeçialmēte especialmēte
espeçialmēte   44r43

3   espeçias especias
espeçias   21v26 44r45[c]

espera   34r3[c] 40v15 58v25

6   esperança esperãça
esperança   37v28 43v40 61v38[n] 40

5   esperando esperādo
esperando   16v22[c] 42v31

esperar   9v32 21r11 26r32 64v49

esperas   17r39

esperava   4v15 33v46 55r34 59r5

esperavan   44v6

esperãça   8r12 30r7

esperādo   32v40 42v22 63v1

espero   4v2 13 14v9 22r24 67r38

espessa   5r34

espessos   15r12 31r39

espigas   38v19

espingarda   48r3

espiritu   22r28

espuerta   22r13

185   esta   2v37 3v36 5v17 22[n] 7r34 7v34
8r38 9v20 32 33[n] 10r21 25 38 10v35
41 11r27 12r3 5 17 18 19 20 12v30 34
13r7 10 10 12 20 27 13v5 24 26 30
14r36 14v1 5 7 13 15r1 2 5 6 15v13 24
30 16r1 22[n] 16v6 22 42 43[n] 17r3 5 28
41 17v16 19r22[n] 33[n] 34[n] 46 20r1 18[n]
20v4 4[n] 21r15 22v45 23v8 23 24v6c

6 estrella 4r31 6v19 20 33r3 34r11 60r7
estrellas 6v12 21
estudio 62r23
estuve 11v9 16v22 17r43
estuvie 46v43
estuviera 26r20
estuvierē 31r15
estuvierō 5v44 17v43 65v27
estuviese 5r43 12r5[c] 66r7
estuviesen 21v24
14 estuvo 3r19 17v27 23v23 32v46 37r4
38v15 39r25 46r17 48v10 49r17 51v20
54r26 54v35 64r30
estuvose 30r32
11 etč 5r31[n] 17v16 25 19r33[n] 20r43 20v2
25v39 31r18 51v23 60v41 63r39
eterno 22r31 62r13
europa 1r15
excelentes 1r9
excelsis 5v39
excepto 34v30
exçelençia 12v42
exçelente 40r2 2[n]
exçessivo 41v6
exerçitavā 66r38
expedir 56r29
expeler 25r22
experiençia 36v39
experimentado 18r37
experimētado 52r35[n]
experimēto 37r3

F

f 8v34
faba 19r38
fabla 11r2 13r21
fablar 9v18
facil 42r15
faga 30r12 48r49
fago 15v9
falladas 15r7
fallados 41v21
fallan 9r40
fallando 15v7
fallar 12r35
fallare 16v15
fallarō 14r29 32
6 falle 11r34 12r39 43 15v19 40 20r22
fallo 16v45
falsas 52v8
falso 20v4[n]
6 falta 38r45 43r2 44v4 48v13 55r34[n]
61v29a
faltar 47r2
faltase 20r34
faltava 4r8 6r43
faltavan 38v21
falto 12v35
famosa 22v11
famoso 25r9

farallones 54v47
fare 29v18
farol 26v1
faroles 61r33
farō 67r13
fartas 20r33[c]
farto 9r29 10r26
23 fasta 9v29 41 10r15 30 32 11r40 14v9
26 41 15v8 16r21 16v6 17r13 41 44 49
17v5 45 18r5 20r4 21 23r26 29v20
favas 21r19
favor 54r45 56v30 66v5
favoreçelle 20r42
favoreçia 39r8
favores 66v22
faxones 21r19
fayal 60r39
faz 12r20
fazer 15v4 16v16
14 fe 1r29 34 1v2 6 8v43 9r11 10r40 15r40
22v23 35 61v47 63v18 64r7 66r29
fecho 1v24 22r36
fechos 13r28
felicidad 30v9
fenbras 23v10
feridas 9v7
fermosa 9v25 14r5 15r4
fermosas 15r23 15v45
fermoso 14v43 15r18 20 44
fermosos 9r32 9v30 18r9
fermosura 15r14 35v30
fernadina 12r42
8 fernādina 12r43[n] 44 12v11 16 24 13v25
14v37 17v1
fertibles 16r1
fertil 14v14 22r4 36r12
fertiles 11r23 12r31 21r17 25r28 38r41
fertilidad 24v6 29v28
fertilissima 13r32 29r26[n] 30v35
fexoes 22r5
fieles 47r33
fierro 9v2 2[c] 3 33
fiesta 39r32 45r1 47v28 66r21
figura 18v35
figurava 40r43
fijos 23v10
filado 10r4 35 20v25 22r7
filo 9r44 12v39
14 fin 1r13 2r33 7r10 9r24 24v1 26v31
29r7 30r13 33v16 43v36 53r34 62r4
64v3 5
fina 49v7
finales 67r40
6 finalmēte 3r4 27v30 35v25 42v1 45r17
64v27
finas 13v9 12
fingidas 63r8[n]
fingido 6r10
fingio 63r15
finissimo 37v24

fugio 11v21
fugir 11v5 16r31 29v16
fui 14v17 19 25 15v38 16r40
fuimos 16r28
fuma 49r27
funden 40r42
fusta 30r23 31r43ᶜ 44 33v33
fustas 31r36
fuy 13v46
fuyen 22v27

G

galera 29r35
gallinas 11v26 63r24
gallos 13v9 35v11
9   gana 10r26 13r3 16v34 23v1 33v35
    36r12 37v25 40v8 48v34
ganado 38r26
ganados 18v47 49v40
ganar 56r19
ganasen 1v17
ganasse 1v16
ganãçia 48v31
garjao 5r1
garrar 35r12
garvanços 61v2
garvãço 61v6
garvãços 61v19
garxao 3v30
gastase 48v32
gavia 17r48
gavilano 16v35
gaviota 5r3 6v39 7r20
generaçion 9v28
general 64v28
generales 61v25
195   gente gẽte
171   gente 1v26 3r30 3v4 5r29 43ⁿ 5v1 40
    6r6 7 34 6v25 7r1 16 25 8r2 9 8v27 9r5
    10 26 9v9 25 10v12 41 12r1 13r4 20
    23 28 13v5 14r2 15 15v44 16r30
    16v25 17r3 31 19v18 21r15 31 21v20
    42 22r12 14 49 22v24 24v23 25r12
    25v2 26v15 18 21 28r19 28v37 29v11
    33 30r5 37 30v21 31r27 31v1 5 24
    32r5ᶜ 9 32v11 12 33r26 33v42 43 34r3
    34v47 35r20 45 47 35v5 22 38 36r7 11
    49 36v1 37r15 35ᶜ 41 43 37v16 27
    38r19 47 38v42 39r45 40r20 28 42r18
    42v2 11 16 24 43r12 43v20 26 44r32
    37 42 44v6 47 45r3 21 45v8 12 13 15
    46v13 22 36 47r8 11 30 48r5 23 27 32
    33 34 39 48v4 5 49r3 8 50r36 50v1
    51r45 52v40 53r37 53v24 54r31 55r24
    55v28 29 56r3 29 36 56v1 3 48 57r21
    37 57v6 18 61v21 62r10 11ⁿ 63r4 39
    63v2 13 17 22 37 38 39 64v28 32
    65v28 31 66r14 25ⁿ 26 33 46
gentes 27v28 40v9 43r1 57r23
gestos 9v6

gete 7v2
24   gẽte 5r31ⁿ 5v40 6r19 24 6v29 34 7r33
    8r8 10r25 19v24 20r1 21r44b 28r23
    36r15 36v7 38v37 42v22 32 43r37
    53r10 57r37ⁿ 63r1 46ⁿ 64r38
gloria 5v39 28r11 30r15 31r48
goanin 55v22
6   golfo 12v33 54v11 55v5 57v2 2ⁿ 3
golõdrinos 7r28
golpe 35v22
9   golpho 12r40 23v35 24r1 37v3 5 40v20
    51v11 55r26 57r41
10   gomera 2v14 20 24 27 30 33 3r2 5 9 16
gomez 2r24
gomitar 6r36
gonça 42r35
gorda 40v31
gordas 38r16 19 44r30
gordos 27r45 38r20
governado 50v2
governador 1v15 38v28 45r14 17
governalle 2r36 46r38 44
governar 46r26
governario 2r21 2v8 46r22
governasen 65r2
governava 46r21
governavã 3r32
gozar 7v6
gozo 27v21
gra 19r37 49 27v21ⁿ 65r46
gracia 51r3
5   graçia gracia grã
graçia 54r18 54v3
22   graçias grãs
graçias 6v35 36v4 58v5ᶜ 67r45
graçiosamẽte 66v18
graçiosas 25r29 30r20 43r26
grade 8v23 30v43
grades 16r2 29r18
gradeza 24r36
gradissimos 25r40
7   grado 1v19 19 14r7 45v15 47v15 52v48
    53r47
7   grados 19r45 20v4 4ⁿ 26r8 14 22 36v45
grajaos 7v40
100   gran gra grã
8   gran 2v22 17r31 17v14 19v24a 28r37
    33r12 35r45 62r22
grana 49v7
granada 1r14ᶜ 16 1v20 20ⁿ
7   grande 11v17 26v14 27r17 27v11 34r44
    49v29 65r15
grandes 11v3 25r38 47v1 53v13
grandeza 9v6
grandissima 12r11
grandissimas 23v29
grandissimo 24v14
grano 44r46 53r2ⁿ
granos 37v24 53r3 50
grave 64r45

hablalle   58v21
hablan   45v24
hablando   47r35
6   hablar   20r38 26v18 28r32 28v39 55r41
       43
hablara   34r2
hablarō   50r13
hablasen   35v37 41v44
hablava   37v35 45r43
hablavā   39v29
hablãdo   5v19
6   hablo   21v34 32r27 35v31 37v37 66r22
       66v6
haga   45v29 48r37
hagā   12r7 31v12 38v9
hago   4r16 11r20
haiti   21r1n
halagado   37v9
halagolo   45r43
halasen   46v4
halla   27r38 34r19 35r1 57r38
halladas   45r8
19   hallado   2r27 20v38 21r35 22v7 28r23
       28v36 32r10 41 33v21 35r19 36v9 12
       37v49 38r21 38v39 48v27 51r10 54r8
       62r36
hallados   20r3
hallan   4r36 8r33n 8v13
hallando   44v19
hallar   17v7 34v3 48v25 57r43
8   hallara   2v10 24r19 19c 34r4 41v18 46r4
       5 64r23
hallaria   44v13 57v27
hallarlas   8r15
hallarlos   58v23
hallaro   5r16 25r18
hallaron   24v23c 30v11
29   hallarō   4r6 25 30 34 6r30 15v32 18v35
       19v17 21v41 45 25r14 17 29r10 30r39
       30v3 14 18 30 35r20 23 35v5 12 36r20
       36v38 44v46 50r9 53r2n 14 55v39
hallarse   41r39
hallase   50v30 53r42n 62r37
7   hallava   4v34 55v33 58v22 60v31 61r35
       62v16 65v18
hallavan   53v6
hallavanse   65v7
hallavase   65r26
6   hallavā   4r38 5r41 28r18 36r27 57r41
       62v19
hallãdo   25v39
hallãdose   60v31
7   halle   12v32 13r16 13v40 49 15r36
       36v39 44v42
65   hallo   3r15 8r37 18r20 21 27 18v45
       19r17 19v6 7c 20v4 5 40 21r42 22v5 6
       24r30 24v8 20 22 24 34 40 25r9 34 38
       26r8 40 26v40 28v16 35 29r33 30r18
       19 21 31r18 34 32v49 34r29 43 46
       34v2 24 36v40 44 37r31 37v5 12 39v5

51r31 51v8 36 41 44 47 52r2 3 52v25
53r2n 44 50 57r40 59v18 64r47 67r10
16
hallola   31r47
hamacas   14r25n 20v26
han   23v6
hara   11r6 29v23
harā   37v29 43r3 45v10
haria   27v21h 41v45 63v15
harian   9v15 32r13
harta   27v21i 63v38
hartava   18v45
harto   27r9 37v49 38r2
hartos   22r2 44v43
hast   49v38c
186   hasta   1v5 2r11 2v13 3r18 4v31 41 5r15
       38 5v18 44 6r16 17 6v28 7v1 8r15 29
       33 8v25 11v9 12v30 13r16 14r28 40
       14v7 15r2 17v19 21 22 39 40 41 18r35
       37 18v17 19r7 20r14 20v15 21v5
       22r35 42 23v19 20 43 46 24r7 10 16
       23 33 24v6h 25v22 26r4 11 24 45
       26v41 27r13 21 22 27v4 25 28r23
       28v7 29 36 29r13 35 29v33 32r29 39
       32v20 28 32 33r40 46 48 33v16 17
       34r9 12c 12c 14 17 42 34v3 17 35r2
       36r5 32 36v8 37r10 24 37v10 33 48
       38v38 40r10 39 40v31n 41 41r16 28 31
       41v27 41 43v2 5 44v45 45r9 13 30 34
       46r9 16 17 46v25 47r46 49r18 49v37
       50r33 51r32 35 42 51v40 43 52r11 37
       52v15 53r31 53v33 36 54r10 54v4 39
       55r8 22 55v41n 57r23 43 57v25 49
       58r4 7 16 58v11 32 39 42 59r26 43
       59v1 10 11 16 36 60v7 7c 8 13 14 19
       61r1 8 34 43 62r33 62v24 27 63v2 8
       38 64r8 25 46 64v40 65r2 5 13 65v15
       17 21 66v2 39 67r13 16 19
havas   22r5 53r1
haz   11r34 35v27c
21   haze   4r31 6r36 6v20 10v38 13v4 14v32
       15r11 17r24 20v11 12 27r11 14 33r39
       34r10 38v15 40v20 49v29 54v5n 55r6
       61v12 67r28
hazedores   66r3 34 45
hazelle   49r14
hazelles   35v27 40v10
16   hazen hazē
7   hazen   12r13 24v21 38r12 40r42 42r4
       43r28 56r1n
78   hazer hazer
59   hazer   1v40 10v37 11r6 13r6 15v33
       16r25 17r24 19v29 20r1 4 21r45 22v47
       24v38 25r7 25v4 26r23 27r46 27v2
       21b 29v9 22 30r26 27 35v7 37v25
       38r46 38v7 8 32 39v21 40r21 43v45
       44r9 45r12 45v34 46v30 48r29 40 41
       47 49r2 18 50v7 51r7 13 29c 54r14 45
       56r30 61v22 63r32 64r12 65v24 66r8c
       66v7 27 34 50 67r24

     16r23 24v35 32v43 42r9 48r20

   largos   9r36 55r48 55v42

449 las

   lasierras   27v14

   lastrado   61v29c

   lastrar   61v32

   lastre   61v29a 64r15 64v40

   latina   2v23

   latitud   2r4

6 laton   12v39 31v6 32r1 35v34 37v10

     42v41

   lavar   30r37

297 le

34 legua   16r30 18v15 20r15 22v21 27r30

     28v24 24 25 26 28 29r14 31r25 32r32

     34 33r35 33v10 34v5 48 37r27 30

     41r41 43r13 43v7 44v36 45v38 46r17

     42 46v9 34 51r38 51v41 53r43 54v28

     31

272 leguas lueguas

271 leguas

31 lengua leñgua lēgua

26 lengua   8v26 15r37 16v6 17r6 37 18v21

     20r8 22r22 23r40 23v3 29r5 21 29v11

     20 30v8 29 33v43 35r19 35v32 36r11

     38r3 40r34 43r2 43v25 45v38c 55r24

   lenguados   34v19

5 lenguas lēguas

   lenguas   22v22 23v7 55v14n 33

   lentisco   23r1

9 leña   3r1 20v14 30r30 49v32 53r14 19

     64v39 43 65r1

116 les   3r34 6r7 9r12 22 43 9v8 10 14

     10r19 27 30 11r6 11v14 12r37 13r31

     14r18 19 15r43 16v1 38 19r33n 19v29

     20r34 40 21r50 21v11 18 26 46 22r32

     22v31 23r18 43 23v1 24v5 25v38

     28r33c 34 28v43 29r2 30v5 31r42

     31v29 36 32r4 8 12 33v40 34v23 28

     35v26 36r5 28 30 35 45 45 46 47 38v3

     7 7 21 47 39r7 40r21 41v36 44 45

     42r42 43 42v9 10 14 40 43r3 43v28 28

     45 44r12 14 23 26 27 32 45r22 27 30

     34 39 45v29 46v7 47r28 45 48r11c 24

     28 48v7 34 53r25 27 27c 54r13 55r41

     62r25 26 63r44 63v42 47 64r7 64v15

     17 18 24e 25 67r24

   lesde   58r18c

29 lesnordeste   26v10 32r43 37r6 11 38v12

     53v27 58r18 58v40 42 59r20 27 29 32c

     34 59v12 14 16 21 28 37 40 45 60r11

     61r43 62v8 11 13 65r21 34

7 lessueste   32r29 33r10 40v33 51r34

     58r31 38 59r42

   lesta   54v8

127 leste   6v37 9v32 10v10 11r37 12r17

     13r11 14r41 14v1 2 23 29 38 15v16

     18v14 22v3 23v19 41 44 48 24r13 22

     25v17 20 46 26r3 6 37 42 26v13 27r8

     27v40 29r13 32r30 47 48 32v23 26

33r6 6c 9 14 27 34r13 15 41 34v34

   35r27 37r20 23 37v5 40v40 45v6 43

   46r7 29 32 49r26 49v18 38 50v34 34

   51r39 51v1 31 52r10 16 28 31 40 45

   47 52v23 53r5 17 53v29 39 54r20

   54v4 14 20 25 26 38 47 55r1 8 11 16

   55v7 21 56r46 57r13 42 57v4 24 44

   58r7 9 13 15 18 58v10 17 31 59r40

   60r14 20 23 30 38 41 43 60v4 15 17

   26 33 48 61r37 65r2 10 17 37 38 41 44

   67r11

   lestes   55r6

   lesueste   24r3 25v27

   letra   1r7 7v35 8v34 19r47

   letras   14r34

3 levantar levātar

   levantar   7v3 64v47

   levantā   44v32

7 levante levāte

   levante   14v22 15v12 17r28

10 levanto levāto

7 levanto   7v7 38v45 45r37 51r23 53v26

     64v37 67r6

   levantose   63v11

   levar   17r21

   levare   9v17

   levatado   60r19

   levate   19r7

   levātar   64r1

   levātase   39v9

   levātava   8v8

   levātavan   65v12

   levātavā   10v24

   levāte   30v25 37r4 40v21 41v15

   levāto   17v37 27v35 63v7

24 lexos   3v38 7v14 11r20 31 19v22 20r19

     21r6 26r40 26v8 31v37 32r36 34v44

     36r5 40r10 40v43 45v6 48r38 50r34

     52r8 23 57r6 63r35 63v33 64r2

   lexuelos   14r3

   ley   21r17

   leyes   54r35

   lēgua   29v19 34r1 40v6 57r18

   lēguas   29r43

   lēngua   62v43

   liberalmēte   42r11 13

   libra   53r2n

   librado   62r8

   librar   65r46b

   libraria   9r11

   libras   53r2n 61r47

   libre   64v33

   libro   2r2 9r7

   licencia   48r28

   liça   34v16

2 liçença licencia

   liçença   51r18

   ligeramēte   9v15 67r39

   ligero   22v48 29v23 52v20

7 lignaloe   16r25 21r43 23r20 24v20

26   llevava   4v10 8v32 17r45 17v29 19v22
        20v42 22v14 25v27 26v13 29r42 31v3
        32v6 8 26 35v37 40r24 52v39 57v45
        61r24 40 61v41 62r10 11ⁿ 26 62v29
        66v50
    llevavan   23v31
    llevavä   34v46 35v39 36r23 40r18
    llevä   17v32 18v43 39v44
    llevãdo   45v40 57v4
    lleve   1v29
    llevē   42v32
12   llevo   15r28 17r15 37 32v38 34v15
        37v42 43r16 44r24 47v24 35 49r49
        50r5
    llevolo   37v10 49r7 50r41
    lloravan   47r8
    llorãdo   46v45 47r25
    lloro   46v35
    llover   14v8 34v9
    llovia   17v15 30r32 44 30v43
    llovido   14v12 23r6 59r15
7   llovio   14v6 17r23 43 17v44 34v28 38
        66v2
    llovioso   60r17
    llovizneros   4v24
    llovizno   4r5
    llueve   17r23
    lluvia   17v44
358   lo
    loa   45v7ⁿ
    loado   29v32 41v3
    lobarda   18r7 37r37
    locos   47r42
    lodosos   44r36
12   lombarda lobarda lõbarda
    lombarda   34r19 23 36ᶜ 48r2 50r33
    lombardas   39r35 40r15
    lombardero   48r45 50v38
    longitud   2r4
    longo   15v25
    longura   29r37 33r46 33v4 57r26
    loreto   61v10
642   los
    lõbarda   7v9 12r29 31r21 34r38 46r3
    lõbardas   46r11 50r29
    lõbardos   17v8
6   lõgura   18r40 27r8 30v38 33r48 33v6 7
    lubre   32v45
    lucayos   8v26
58   luego   1r23 8v17 27 9r4 9v23 10r1 29
        10v11 11v38 13v50 14r45 14v28 16r40
        16v5 19v30 20v28 39 22r23 26r18
        27r18 31 28v22 29v37 32r12 32v2
        37r2 45 37v4 15 18 21 25 39r9 30
        39v11 22 42v6 45v10 35 46v2 26
        48v45 49v1 50r12 50v10 56r25 56v3
        61r16 61v8 62v13 44 64v10 12 31 50
        65v35 66r18 66v25
    lueguas   25v32
10   luengo luēgo

    luengo   27v37 35r3 57r33
    luēga   27r9 9
7   luēgo   3r29 9v37 10v8 17v24 27r12
        32r28 34r13
40   lugar   7v14 8v5 16v5 18v4 21r1 30
        21v30 23r27 24v39ᶜ 25r4 25v6 26v7bᶜ
        28 27v29 30r27 31v20 34v32 35v47
        38r18 39v8 43v18 23 44v19 48ᶜ 49
        47r24 36 48r20 50v11 30 52v13 43
        56r1 60r10 64v4 9 65v18 18ᶜ 40 66v36
12   lugares   2r1 22v40 24v23 35r21 42r29
        44r35 45r41 45v1 30 47r44 49r35
        50r18
8   lumbre lũbre
    lumbre   32v43
    luna   18v16 25v12 55r33
31   lunes   2r20 3r36 4r17 32 5v11 6v23
        7v30 11r26 16v21 18v9 21r27 22v40ᶜ
        44 23v18 25v15 27v34 31r22 35r11
        38v11 45r36 49v30 53r11 56r43 58v8
        59v13 60r13 60v42 62v41 65r9 65v9
        66v28
    luys   20r26
7   lũbre   8r41 8v1 32v39 42 43 35r22
        62v30

M

    macana   56r1ⁿ
    macho   23v10
11   madera   2v35ᶜ 36 27v21g 30r24 60r38
        50 60v30 35 62r40 62v11 65r28
    madero   17v31 30r22 30v38 31r44
    maderos   24v34 40 25v5
    madre   2v28 9r27 42r21 62r24
    madres   22r16 31v45 37v46 47r15
    madroños   27v1 33v23 34r27
    madrugado   39r36
    madura   39v17
    maduras   33r44
    maduro   23r12
    maestra   17r46
    maestre   21r37 46v2 48v5 66r9 10
    magasita   53r42ⁿ
4   magestad magᵈ majestad
    magestad   56v28 67r28
    magᵈ   34r4
    mahiçi   23v30ⁿ
    mahoma   1r36
    majestad   66r30
27   mal   2v8 3r32 19v24 30 22r15 22v25
        23r24 26r33 29v34 30v6 38v4 41v46
        45v29 49v44 51r17 55r34ⁿ 56r29 34
        56v22 57r14ⁿ 59r6 61v29ᶜ 63v20
        64r16 24 35 40
    mala   12r8 53r35 53v23
    malas   43r38 52v14 54r12
    maldad   22r31 54r34
    malo   64r12
    maltratada   54r25
    mames   21r18

      32r24 35r26 39r24 46r14 50r1 53r16
      56v40 58v29 59v20 60r22 60v47 63r21
      65r16 65v45 66v43

     martillo   22v1 43v24 45v5

28   martin   2r22 31 2v14 19 4v12 5v19 23
      37n 7r36c 8v29 13v32 16v43 20v31
      26r28 42 51r12 52v4 24 39 53r24 30
      54r10 18n 25 28 61r32 66r41 66v32

     martīn   5v34 39 7r34 37 59r8

56   mařa mara

55   mařa   1r7 1v1 2v23 39 41 6r8 8v12
      9v19 13r38 41 42 13v1 15 14r25 16r12
      17r17 18r11 13 41 18v30 36 19r22
      21v7 19 21 24r39 26r11 27v19 28
      28v41 29r35 30r44 30v18 21 31v17
      32r2 17 32v28 33r38 33v2 14 36v36c
      38v36 41v13 44v15 47r18 47v30 49r48
      54r3 57r32 59v47 60r35 60v1 65r32 34

16   mařas   8v38 13v2 11 16r10 11 16v28
      17r16 19 21r24 21v47 48 23v6 24r38
      33r42 42r36 44r45c 47v22

287 mas

8   mastel   3v9 5v41 7v8 27v8 46v15 52r46
      59r7 10

     masteles   27r46

     mastines   14r32

     matamos   16r18 22

     matar   22v26 31v33

     matarā   56r23

     matariā   31v36

     mataro   4r42

     matarō   6r25 34v19 59r35

     matava   31v37

7   matinino   55v18 56v18 47 49n 57r1
      57v27 58r33

     mato   16v44

     matose   6v38

12   mayo   1v21 11r11 14r7 17r18 25 18r27
      19r5 25r16 33r23 41r6 43r33 58v4

     mayonic   49r27

36   mayor   1v14 18 6r10 11r38 13r39 17r15
      22v6 46 46 23r2 25r3 28v36 30r41
      33v41 35r40 36v33 38r4 39v15 45r4 7
      47v28 48r34 49r9 50v18 52v47 53r40
      53v15n 54v47 55r5 55v14n 61r39
      62r9a 48 62v6 64r35 67r39

     mayores   22r33 27v1 38r31 53r1

     mayormēte   22v16 27v20 50v4 32 62r8

     maysi   32v3n

     mācebos   25r43 57r11

     māchado   17v9

     māchas   15v29 27r36

     māçebo   49r25

     māçebos   9v24 30v31

     māda   42v32

14   mādado   1v34 2v16 8r38 13v48 25v4
      26r31 35v26 46v8 50v7 63v34 64v34
      65v37 66v14 16

     mādamios   53r28

     mādando   28v43

7   mādar   12r4 38v7 39v47 49v31 61v32
      64r4 66v47

     mādara   10r37

     mādarā   29v25

     mādare   43r3

     mādarē   11r3

     mādaria   66v6

     mādarian   47v47

     mādarles   43r3

     mādarō   1v9 50v22

     mādase   47r45 65v39 66r16 23

6   mādava   12v37 43 40r21 44r21 44v39
      66v27

     mādavan   40r4

     mādavā   42r39

11   māde   10v6 11v36 39 12v14 13v33 16v1
      17r20 17v15 23r4 32 39v11

     māden   51r16

43   mādo   4r28 6r1 18r25 18v26 19v19 33
      21r28 24v38 25r44 27r39 32v34 37r35
      37v25 39r31 41v30 39 43 42r36 42v32
      44r36 45v34 46v15 47r5 48r2 50r30
      52r45 52v42 53r18 53v4 54r39 55v34
      56v2 57v16 61r45c 62r39 43 63r32
      64r14 64v47 66v3 5 49 50

     mādoles   56v12 63r33

     mādolo   47r3

7   māsa   5r43 10r26 19r15 21r15 44b
      37v27 43r37

     māsamēte   46r43

     māsas   18v39

     māsedūbre   38v37

     māsos   22v25

     mātenimios   48r42

     mātiene   6r38

     mātillos   13r28

     mātinimientos   1v25

     mc̄has   41r29

67   me   1v10 11 12 13 34 5r28 5v7 9r25 9v9
      15 10r17 10v34 11r12 15 32 11v2 15
      44 12r33 12v5 13r22 13v16 34 37 14r4
      22 37 14v5 15r22 23 15v8 22 24 30 43
      16r26 16v5 5 9 17r4 7 33 35 49 17v2
      21r25 22r36 23r24 23v11 26r34 29v7
      11 27 32r22 39v8 8 9 33 44 46 46
      40r10 44v27 41 48r27 47 62r20

67   media   1v28 3r34 3v2 4v39 5v13 6r4
      7v32 8r2 33 35 8v21 14v6 16r29 17r28
      27r30 28v24 25 29r14 32r32 32v1
      33r35 33v9 34v33 36r19 36v41 37r27
      30 32c 37v2 43r13 46r30 46v9 34 50r2
      51r44 53v26 54v3 57r26 57v48 58r16
      58v11 59r19 21 31 59v8 23 30 37 41
      60r16 24 26 35 45 60v18 21 45 61r19
      44 62r47 65r3 4 7 7 12c 14 39

     mediana   18r14

     mediante   51r3 60v37

     medicinas   15r27

39   medio   4v29 6r16 10r24 11r33 11v20
      12r40 12v23 33 13v18 23 42 14v26 31

      mis   17r46

      misericordia   56v27

16   misma   11r4 11v12 14r17 20r2 21v21 29r14 30v17 42 32r10 33v10 35v15 37r9 47v17ⁿ 49r35 50 54r29

      mismas   14r16 56r36

34   mismo   1v9 2v40 5v40 7r32 15v37 19r42 21v46 22r6 24v39c 26v23 27 27r19 27v29 31v39 33v24 38r13 40r29 41v9 42r12 42v12 45r31 48r9 50v8 51v39 53v8 54v22 24 56v37 57r13 58v17 59v41 46 61v20 64r45

      mismos   22v47 24v39 44r33 45r25 47r12

      missa   61v18 63r44 66v24

7   mitad   14r34 40v12c 52v39 40 54r36 63r39 40a

      moça   9r29 35v31 42r28

      moças   14r30 36v16 54r38

7   moço   7r18 13v16 37v33 39r43 46r23 44 49r21

      moços   14r19 27r41

      modero   66r15

      moguer   61v17

      monasterio   66v35

      moneda   14r36 40r2ⁿ

      montante   67r18

12   montaña mõtaña

      montaña   10r24 40v31

23   montañas motañas mõtañas

      montañas   11r22 40v28 51r43

42   monte mote mõte

6   monte   38r4 44v46 46r11 51v4 36 53v29

      moras   49v25

      morir   66r14

      moro   1r21

      moros   1r13

      morro   51v40 41

      mortales   22r29

      moscadas   33r43

      mosquito   61v46

      mostrado   57v11 62r15 67r32 34

      mostralle   45r44

      mostralles   64v28

7   mostrar   27v23 31r20 39r20 48v2 61v43 64v20 66r17

      mostraria   63v28 31

      mostrarõ   21v25

      mostrarõles   38v21

      mostrarse   62v3

      mostrarselas   66r18

      mostrasse   64v17

8   mostrava   6v29 19v13 28v12 34v8 35v48 47v29c 30 62v4

      mostravan   23v28 51r46

      mostravã   18v23 26v16 47r40

      mostravãle   44v15

      mostrãdole   66v30

      mostre   40r6

6   mostro   20v40 39r7 50r43c 50v3 65v16

      66v9

      mostrola   31v35

      mostrole   50r28

      mostroles   20v45

      motañas   55r2

      mote   51v17b 52r11 54v5ⁿ

      movi   10v34

      movia   26r15

      moviale   7v26c

      moviesen   62r26

      movimiº   4r31 6v21

      moysen   5v9

      mõstrandosela   31v38

10   mõtaña   12r21 15r9 27r8 12 34 28v18 31r46 34r30 40v41 43r29

19   mõtañas   18r39 19r20 24 23v29 30ⁿ 24r41 28r7 10 29r18 30 34r34 45 34v26 35r39 41r35 37 43r21 52r19 23

      mõtañosa   37r14

33   mõte   16r32 20v14 21r33 22r36 31r38 32r30 32 35v21 40v45 41r15 51v1 7 11 22 32 40 41 43 52r5 9 16 28 29 52v2 53r42 53v36 44 54v5ⁿ 6 6 10 15 17

6   mõtes   13v4 21r21 23v37 29r28 33r20 53v39

      mõtezillo   19r22 20v17

      mõton   52r5ⁿ

      mõtuosa   29r17

73   mucha mũcha

7   mucha   6v3 8r18 21v27 30r30 36r7 56v1 60v1

      muchacho   46r39

102   muchas mũchas m̃chas

15   muchas   3r35 4r33 6r40 7r26 12r32 18r24 21v47 48 23r38 24r24 25r37 29v13 30v34 35v4 36r47

140   mucho mũcho m̃cho

33   mucho   2r6 5r28 9r16 14v13 15r35 40 44 16r1 20v44 21r20 42 22r47 23v41 24v4 27 25v9 26r27 32 26v31 30v9 31v32 32v26 34r21 34v42 35r12 40r39 46r9 47v19 50v3 54v19 55v10 61r6 11ⁿ

68   muchos mũchos

11   muchos   1v25 6r25 7v39 10r17 15r5 18r23 24r29 25r19 31v44 44v38c 58v47

      mudado   24r18

      mudamiẽtos   58v47

      mudarõ   4v39

      mudasen   14v27

      mudava   25v28

      mudãças   59r24

6   mudo   16r13 17v20 26r5c 6 47r10 60r20

      mudose   7v43 25v45 47

      muerta   17r23 46r37

      muerto   32r6

6   muestra   20v42 21r35 27v19 38v37 40v15 50r6

N

nafe   60v34

nalgas   56r16

96   nao   3v9 4v22 41 6v7ᶜ 7r19 29 8r21
        9v36 10v7 11r12 11v16 33 12v12 14
        35 13r1 2 18 24 14r39 14v25 15v13
        16r26 40 17r21 46 21r10 28 21v39
        22r36 23r31 32 25r9 28v41 29r31
        34v32 35r4 35v31 36 40 37v8 10 22
        38r29 39r31 40 43ⁿ 45 39v5 40r31
        41r23 41v26 34 45 43r8 13 43v5 31
        44v10 29 31 35 45r39 46r16ⁿ 21 40
        46v3 11 14 16 20 22 26 37 42 47r30
        48r14 16 44 50 48v3 7 8 13 15 19
        50r31 34 34ᶜ 50v25 27 52v43 65v46 49
        66r4 19

18   naos   10v30 16v11 17r32 18v6 21r5
        24v29 26v45 27v1 12 28v32 31r15
        41r12 41v25 46r6 50v38 51v17 65v33
        66r7

10   nariz   9r42 10r10 10v1 12r15 14r33
        16r34 19v41 35v50 37v24 43v25

nasce   40r39 57r44

nasçe   39r20

nasçia   49r33

natura   13r31 21r10 22r18 42r25

natural   50v16 19

naturales   52r1

naturaleza   6v9 14r11 33v22

nav   35v1ᶜ

navegables   51v14

navegaçion   9r7 62v16 63r1ⁿ 10

navegan   33v32

12   navegar   1v31 41 2r6 2v16 7r34 14v19
        15v16 20 23v17 24r7 63v38 64r44

navegara   23v17ⁿ

navegare   1v39

navegarian   30v39

navegarō   3v7 27

navegā   35v44 42v18

navegādo   19v6 46r15 60v26

68   navego   3v35 4r2 18 4v8 19 38 5r24 36
        5v12 6r15 23 28 33 6v5 24 33 41 7r14
        22 31 42 7v31 43 8r5 18 31 17v18
        18v10 23v18 25v17 21 26r3 36 26v6
        26 27v37 34r8 13 37r4 51r46 53v27
        54v4 38 58r13 17 37 58v9 16 30 59r29
        42 59v14 21 33 60r11 14 23 30 43
        60v17 48 62v38 64r41 65r10 17 44
        67r11 15

navegue   12v25 14r47 17r41

navetas   17v31

11   navidad   45r2 46r14 51r24ⁿ 24ⁿ 28
        51v22 52v29 53v12 21 56r33 56v45

22   navio   5r3 5v14 35 6v7 7r16 19v8 20r14
        20v33 27v42 36r42 43r39 49v41 52v19
        53r44 54r32 54v43 59r12 61r22 41
        61v3 29 64r14

60   navios   1v23 4r40 5v28 6r31 7v12 8v33
        9r18 13v44 47 14r19 14v30 16v4 41
        17r37 18r46 19r11 19v5 31 37 20v14

25 21r29 32 22v13 23r28 24v19 25r5
        25v2 27r46 27v21c 29r11 29v38 30r36
        37 31r33 33v34 35r48 35v46 36r7
        37r29 37v20 22ᶜ 39r38ᶜ 40r20 41r46
        43r5 40 46 43v21 44r41 44v2 10 45r21
        46v32 48v17 49v33 50r36 61r18 63v35
        66r7

necessidad   25v38

necio   21v41ⁿ

7   neçessario nesçessario

6   neçessario   5r28 5v6 10v41 24r19 26v37
        33v44

neçessidad   31r8 61v34

negociaçion   30r9

negociar   23v1

negocio   36r17

negoçio   49v35 62r5

negro   45v27

negros   9r38 22r20 45v26

nesçessario   53r20

118   ni   6r39 6v10 9r38 39 43 9v31 13v3 4
        17 17 14r15 15r22 15v20 16r33 17r4
        22 18r3 19r2 3 19v24a 22r15 20 22v8
        24 26 26 24r43 44 27v12 28r8 33ᶜ
        28v33 33 42 29r8 8 11 44 29v12 12 14
        24 34 30r3 12 15 26 26 30v4 30 31r41
        41 31v9 14 33v40 40 41 34v1 4 33
        35r1 1 20 36v23 38r32 34 39r13 17
        39v9 45 42r18 18 19 28 28 43r38
        43v33 45v9 12 17 19 46v24 46 47r11
        32 47v39 44 48r22 23 25 25 26 48v1 1
        20 20 53r28 32 32ᶜ 53v15ⁿ 55v4ⁿ 14
        57r16 60r10 61r23 62v36 63v42 42
        64r8 26 66r6 7 10 10 14 66v13 15
        67r30

niamas   36r36

niames   42r4

6   nicolas   33r29 29ⁿ 30 34r8 23 34v40

niebla   24r44

nieve   24r44 41r2

nigū   38v5

ninas   23r35ᶜ

ningud   29v8

ninguna   9v18 13v15 27r9

ningunas   42r19

ningund   30r12

ninguno   56r21

ningunᵃ   33v21 42v10

ningū   17r24 32r37

27   ninguᵃ   7r27 9v16 19 10r24 11v7 12r21
        13v5 14 17 14r28 20r3 5 22v24 26r23
        29v24 30r2 36v8 18 22 38r17 41v32
        42r41 44r22 47r1 62r30 41 64r18

15   ninguᵒ   9r30 9v30 22v7 28r16 30r16
        33r34 41v1 45v18 46v1 56v29 60v26
        61v26 63r18 19 63v13

19   niña   3v30 4r42 4v34 5v41 7v4 16 8r26
        8v30 11v17 27 41 14v24 21r34 25r44
        27v9 32v35 47r24 52v5 57v37

niño   57v36 60v24

23v3

nucay 19v35

nuest 42r30c

9 nuestras nr̄as

36 nuestro nro nr̄o

8 nuestros nros nr̄os

nueva 1v40 21r14 23v40 39r20

17 nuevas 12v17 34 19v45 36r8 14 37v14
15 44v11 51v15 52v32 53v22 54r11
61v41 43 62r26 63r8 67r23

16 nueve 2r34 3r24 12r17 17v19 27r24
28r2 36r15 43v18n 50v13 51r32 51v18
41 58v1 59v30 65v36 66v1

nuevo 37v13

nuezes 20v37 25r38 33r43

numero 11r17 44r31

nūblado 14v7

nūblados 4r4

18 nūca 1r30 3v31 5v2 14r37 15v25 16r7
18r8 20 32c 34 21v41 23v43 26v7
27v13 39r22n 57v32n 64v33 65v49

ñiebla 41r3 54v5n

O

132 o 2r21 23 2v17 3v21 39 4v41 5r4 24 7r31
7v19 32 8v7 9v2c 10r11 10v11 11r4
12v38 13r9 17 13v2 50 14v13 15r30
37 15v7 16v15 23 24 17r7 17v23 28
18r47 18v38 19r13 13 25n 28c 38 49
19v8 31 20r19 20v24 21r19n 22r14
22v11 23v30n 25r5 18 25v26 26v12
27r29 27v18 28r24 43 28v9 29r3 21
29v40 30r22 24 28 30v37 31r30 32v12
20 33r12 13 21 47 33v17 25 34r24
35r17 36r6 36v1 43 43 37r50 37v24
38v18 28c 39r22 33 33 40v5 25c 42r35
42v36 43r30 33 45r14 17 17 42 45
45v31 46r25 46v13n 19 47v22 48r22
35 48v5a 49r34 51v49 52r2 32 53r2n 8
10 54r36 54v5n 55v14n 16 20 57v30 36
39 49 58v4 60r36 39 60v22 30 61r5 12
61v25 63v4 64r33 64v9 65v18

obedeçen 45v32

obedeçian 53r28

obedeçido 53r28

obedezcan 48r40

obediencia 39r1

obediençia 26r29

10 obra 6v34 7v28 23v34 27r30 32r16
39v33 46r34 52v30 56v23 65r21

obrado 22r7

obras 52r2 52v14

obstante 56v25

occeana 1v14

occeano 1v17

occidente 1v5 2r4

2 occeana occeana
ocçeana 1v30

3 ocçeano occeano oçeano
ocçeano 2r1

ochenta 4r37 58r6 65r27

31 ocho 2r10 3v3 4v41 7v29 12r20 13v50
14r31 17v23 39 19r13 22v4 25v36
27r24 29r13 38 30v26 32r37 33v18
34r46 51r32c 38 51v6 53r2n 54v7 10
58r5 58v33 35 60r45 65r21 67r5

ocupara 26v36

ocupo 49v31

ocurrir 49v43

oçeano 63v29

odoriferas 20v19 21v47

ofertas 63r41

offender 57r32

officiales 50v36

officio 48v14

oficiales 66r2n

ofreciendole 66v6

ofreçido 63v18

ofreçio 66r22 66v45

7 ojo 12r25 15v28 17v11 21r7 26v15
28r35 41r31

9 ojos 9r42 9v29 29c 15r23 20v22 25r22
27v13 43r27 48r8

ola 48v1 56r47 60r10

olas 61r17 21 65r25

olor 15r29 25r41 55v22n

olorosos 7v38

olvide 2r5

ombres 28r18c

once 46r18

onda 62r48

ondas 61r26 41 64r33

22 onze 6v6 7r22 7v32 22v18 33v16 37r11
58r9 47 58v19 40 42 59r25 43 59v48
60r12 25 30 46 60v20 61r5 63v3 65r6

opiniones 2v5

opposiçion 55r34

opposito 55r36 67r35

53 ora 1v28 3r31 3v1 6r16c 7r23 43 7v1 1
26 34 8r6 33 17v21 40 18v17 23v45
26v26 32v29 32 36v42 37v4 39r38
43v10 44v29 57v49 58r2 5 58v11 13
32 38 41 59v7 47 60r12 15 25 31 34
44 46 60v4 20 43 48 62v8 64r43 65r4
6 11 19 65v30 67r17

oracion 32r20c 21

oraçion 20r5 22v31 40v14 61v22 63r46

50 oras 2r10 3r18 21 4v21 6v17 7r43 8r33
8v20 12r10 13r2 14r4 14v28 15v36
17v19 26r4 32v30 31 33r27 36r4
36v40 41r7 41v33 43r34 46r18 35
53v31 54v39c 40 57v2 58v19 42 59r43
59v7 48 60r12 26 31 44 46 60v13 20
61r26 44 62r46 62v8 64r41 65r3 6 11
67r5

orden 14v25 41r17 49r2 66r20

ordenada 31r41

ordenado 7v10 10 48r29 56r6

ordenados 28v41

ordenarō 1v3

ordeno   61r45
ordinaria   6v41
7   orejas   11v36 12r15 21r3 22v41 37v24
       43v24 48r8
    oriente   1v3 23r19 64v3 3ᶜ
    oriēte   24v1 64v6
    orilla   35r2 41v42 42v34
153 oro   10r8 21 40 11v1 3 12r14 35 37
       13r9 17 13v32 14r33 15r35 40 42 15v7
       16v7 15 24 33 17r8 32 17v34 18v3
       19r33ⁿ 19v35 39 20v45 22r38 49
       22v38 40 23v41 25v40 26r27 32 44
       27r37 38 39 31r19 31v8 32r14 34r5
       35v50 51 36r1ᶜ 36v37 37v24 38 40
       38v26 26ⁿ 30 39r10 13 20 27 28 41
       39v34 40r2 35 39 40 42r13ᶜ 14 43r18
       43v15 16 24 44r5 18 21 31 44v12 15
       24 42 45r24b 40 45 45v2 4 5 47r37 41
       47v1 4 10 13 44 48r7 9 48 48v26 27 38
       39 49r17 23 29 33 38 49v15 50r7 12
       14 16 50v7 24 29 30 33 51r5 51v26
       52v19 25 28 36 37 45 48 53r2 2ⁿ 42ⁿ
       42ⁿ 46 53v8 9 15 17 19 54r1 27 36
       54v1 20 55v10 13 14ⁿ 16ᶜ 17 20 22ⁿ
       22ᶜ 38 56v16 44 57r7 35 59r12 65v42
    osara   51r5
    osava   51r6
6   oso   14r37 20v34 24r26 26v29 53v31
       54v35
111 otra   2v9 5r25 27 5v20 6r38 7r3 8r24
       8v35 9v28 32 10v9 11r24 36 38 11v12
       28 39 40 40ᶜ 41ᶜ 12r6 17 13r38 41
       13v17 14r6 15v2 29 39 16v8 12 24 44
       44 18r13 41 18v14 15 32 20r20 22r14
       23v7 30ⁿ 48 24v6i 25v2 35 26v12 44
       27r15 27v24 28v13 25 26 28 29v14
       30v2 18 18 31r3 43 31v9 32v45 33r5
       33v21 35r31 47 35v29 36v8 37r8 22
       40 38r14 39v33 40r4 40v42 41r17 40
       41 43r2 44v25 45r8 45v28 44 46r6
       47r32 36 38 49r34 51r26 52v39 47
       53r8 55r27 56r27 57r3 60v1 61r22
       61v9 49 62v26 46 63r40a 63v2 64r12
       26 65r33 65v25 66r10 66v14 49
113 otras   5r40 6v21 8r26 8v18 9r15 21 22
       9v4 4 10 40 10r5 10v14 11r21 13r25
       34 14r13 14v10 15r4 7 21 15v45
       16v14 23 26 19r3 6 19v32 21r24 47b
       21v26 22v5 23r16 18 38 23v36 24v12
       25r28 25v23 26r34 27r10 27v5 6 29r10
       29v1 30v14 31r44 31v46 32r19 32v14
       33v28 34v19 41 35r46 35v40 36r47
       36v10 11 37r47 37v17 38r44 40r7 11
       40 41r18 42r19 22 23 23 38 42v13 39
       43r10 44r13 44v13 45r26 47v23 48r8 9
       49r27 31 49v40 50r14 51r27 52r2 23
       54r4 43 55v14ⁿ 16 31 44 56r5 37
       57r23 31 58r4 33 58v6 26 37 59r20 32
       32ᶜ 60v8 14 61v39 62r14 62v23 63r25
       64v30 65r13 65v33

94 otro   2v33 4v22 42 5r40 8r22 8v36
       11v20 28 42 12r1 13r38 42 13v30 39
       14v33 15r9 16v1 17v9 18v17 19r22
       19v11 20r19 26 31 22v6 11 24v35 36
       25v9 27v13 29 40 41 28v24 25 25 26
       27 27 27 28 29v12 30r6 41 30v16
       32r31 35 48 33r7 10 34v3ⁿ 35v5 36r6
       38v8 35 40r28 41v21 42v26 43r11
       45r15 31 45 45v18 46v15 47r36 46
       47v44 48v41 49r40 52r18 29 54v32
       55r1 13 16ᶜ 18 31 56r17 22 56v29
       57r16 58r10 21 59r44 61r30 33 61v8ⁿ
       16 16ⁿ 61v20ⁿ 63v46 64r18aᶜ 20 65v19
83 otros   2v32 6r13 31 10v14 15 19 11v45
       13r26 13v11 14r2 12 13 15 16 21
       16v25 18r4 22 18v18 47 19r38 20r3 12
       21r7 23 29 22v7 26 23r16 44 24r14
       25r19 26v15 27r26 27v18 29r22 31v27
       32r1 2 10 33v23 34v20 22 24 36v15 16
       32 37v34 45 38r21 38v31 38 39r5
       39v25 42r3 19 29 43r39 44r8ᶜ 44v14
       45r34 45v1 24 27 46v4 6 47r44 48r11
       50r42 50v46 52v17 26 53r2ⁿ 25 53v13
       55r45 55v3 46 56r37 56v15 57r8
       62v12 63r1ⁿ
32 otubre   3v18ᶜ 6v23 32 40 7r13 21 30 41
       7v30 42 8r4 17 8v28ⁿ 9v22 10v5 11r26
       12v21 13v22 14v16 21 15v11 35 16v21
       17r1 27 17v17 26 36 47 18v9 19r27
       34v39
    otᵒ   45v42
    ove   13v30
    ovejas   13v17
    oviera   10r38 22v11 26r21 49v37
    ovierā   49r47 60r3
    oviere   12v20 13v20 31r1 45v37 51v21
    oviero   37v48
    ovierō   9r16 57r10 62v48
23 oviese   13v19 17v4 20r42 24r7 28v21
       35v28 38v39 39r13 45v18 18 46r25
       49v41 50r37 52v11 54r37 55r45 57r16
       57v32ⁿ 62r4 63r38 65v38 66r45 66v48
9   oviesen   5v26 19v23 29r5 31v4 35v28ᶜ
       36r25 41r14 50r23 62r34
    oviesse   46r24
    ovillo   11v30 44
    ovillos   9r20 10r3 33 16v29 44r28
16 ovo   2v4 5r33 5v17 19v13 24r15 26r5
       38v34 43v16 54r37 55v4ⁿ 56r12ⁿ
       57v22 58r41 63v44 64v28 67r42ᶜ
39 oy   1v5 4r5 6v26 11v9 15v12 16v22
       17r2 20 31 20r4 22r36 23r26 26r24
       26v8 28r20 23 28v36 29v33 39r44
       41r9 46 43v10 44r1 47r23 50v43
       54v33 56v44 57v8ⁿ 58r25 60r37 65v46
       66r25 33 41 50 66v24 29 44 67r5
    oyan   36v35
    oydo   31v39 62r5 63v44
    oyendo   63r32
    oyerā   46r42

oyere   27v32
oyerō   8r3 34v22ⁿ 35v22
oyo   5v37 16v7 34v21 46r44 48r5
oyos   18r32
oyr   4r8 6r43 47v2

P

pacificos   21v6ⁿ
padecia   26r26
padecierō   65v10
padecio   62r11ⁿ 65r45ⁿ
padeçian   61v28
padeçido   64r44
padeçiera   64r35
padeçio   61r21ⁿ
padre   1r31 22r28 23v9 54v46 62r23
pagamēto   13r26
pagavā   42r43
pago   44r23
paja   14r26ⁿ 29r9
pala   9v42

21   palabras   4v33 9r6 9v20 22r39 23v14
        29v3 30r17 37v36 38v45 39v26 42r17
        44v28 44 45v7 33 36 48v35 55v30
        56v39 63v16 67r41
paleta   56r1ⁿ
palillo   8r23 27 31v15 49v26 57r28
palillos   38v20 60r27
palma   18r21 18v34 30r25 49r11 56r1ⁿ

8   palmas   18r13 19r29 30 24r38 25r37
        27r25 29r26 26ⁿ
palmo   57r28
palmos   16r22 16v45 30v38 56r1ⁿ
palo   8r22 21r43 55v47 57r27ᶜ 27
palos   1v22 26ⁿ 48v6ᶜ 16 56v21
palpādolos   21v22
pampanos   35v11

23   pan pā
21   pan   12r45 12v15 24v22 30v12 31v48
        36r36 41 38r12 12 26 42r4 34 44r43
        47r32 47v23 48r42 50v25 57r9 59r38
        63r24 65v3
panizo   13r33 22r6
paño   55v35 56v14 15 62r39
paños   13r27 45r23 25
papa   61v11
papagallos   45r24
papagayo   36r43

9   papagayos   9r19 9v19 10r4 13v15 16r8
        36r45 42v38 55v2 44
papahigo   61r24 40 62r48 65v19
par   39v7 64r47ᶜ

278   para
paraje   25v41 32v22 35v48 40v2 44v9
paramētos   14r24
parar   48v12 53r40
pararō   55r40
parava   55r33
parayso   37r48 48ⁿ 64v2 66v1
pardales   7r17

12   pardelas   5r27 5v15 7r1 28 8r20 58v6 26
        59v19 38 60r3 27 33
7   parece   15r9 28r29 35r29 35v29 38v7ⁿ
        43r45 45r42
parecen   55r34ⁿ
parecera   24v61

12   parecia   8v1 23r44 23v29 25r17 27r30
        29r41 44 33r25 42v42 49v35 56v49
        65v12
pareciales   62v10
parecian   29r18 33r22 38v46
pareciero   18v48
parecierō   6v1

7   parecio   7v38 11v46 32r33 36r5 60r41
        62v47 64v27ᶜ
pareciole   27v43 33r3 60r7
pareciome   13v45

39   pareçe parece
32   pareçe   4r31 5v22 6v15 20 7v33 12r19
        15r43 16r7 19r15 23v17ⁿ 24r42
        26v14ⁿ 28r26 29v28 32v9ⁿ 12ⁿ 33r21
        33v3 35r41 40v43 41r13 35 43r22 29
        43v28 45v24 51r24ⁿ 52r5ⁿ 8 21 52v31
        55r34ⁿ
pareçelo   28r22

6   pareçen   13r22 31r19 43r21 49v25 52r22
        63r8ⁿ
pareçer   19r44 24r1 51v1 57v13

42   pareçia parecia
30   pareçia   4r12 5r17 5v25 6v39 8r23 18r33
        18v11 22r10 22v6 24v11 25r19 26r12
        28r11 28v12 19 33r19 37r16 37v13
        38v30 40r26 40v24 41r33 41v42 45r28
        49v5 42 51v33 52r29 62v31 65r15
pareçiale   33r5 15 57r34 61v42

6   pareçian parecian
pareçian   4r33 13v43 18v30
pareçido   6r3 22v18 28v10 15 31v20
pareçiera   8v9 22v12 39v2

6   pareçierō pareciero parecierō
pareçierō   6v38 58v7 25 59r13
pareçierōle   57r11
pareçiese   6r7 34v18

28   pareçio parecio
21   pareçio   5r32ᶜ 5v7 43 7r36 8v21 9r26
        9v16 19v18 21r43 23v34 26v2 30
        33r13 33v20 39r22ⁿ 46r10 47v39
        52r13 54v27 58r22 25

6   pareçiole pareciole
pareçiole   25r6 49r4 54v32
pareçiōle   27r39
parez   20v41 21v37 36r43 61r34
pargamino   62r35 38
parian   57v36
pariente   48v41
parientes   30v22 46v45
parierō   37v46 47r16
pariēte   45r45
pariētes   23v13 46v41
pario   9r27 22r16 31v45 42r21

penetravā   48r4
peninsula   10v38[n]
pensando   26r30 59r12 65v41
pensar   67r30
pensarō   1r37 15v32 62r42 65v10
8   pensava   17v35 19r48 31v28 33v36 46v7
       53r42[n] 58v22 61v26
pensavan   7v15
pensavā   5r30 21v32 23r41
pense   1v34 13v47 32r19 39v10
penso   21v36 22r41 63v45
8   peña   19r21 21r45 25r2 31r4 34r39 43v6
       55r14 65v23[c]
13   peñas   4r22 12r24 24v16 27 28 28r8
       30v45 33v20 41r15 43v5[c] 46r28 63v5
       64v10
6   pequeña   11v29 14r43 15v2 27r15 40v33
       45r26
pequeñas   9v40 11v35 42v19
6   pequeños   9v30 19v8 22v13 33v22 58r41
       58v2
pequeñuela   55r21
per   26r24 41r39[c]
pera   49v29
peraça   2v28 29
7   perder   10v1 12v29 35v27 55r5 57v41
       61v38[n] 65v11
perderse   61r5
perdia   2r31
perdiā   1r31
perdiçion   1r33
perdida   48r14
perdidas   6v10
perdido   65v33
perdidos   61v27
perdiera   22v14
perdierō   41v48
perdiese   62r33 33[n]
perdio   46r16[n] 48v19 58v20 62v44
perdizes   22r1
pereciese   61v39
pereçiesen   61v42
peregrino   65r46
perez   50v20
perfeciō   41v19
8   perlas   17v34 18v3 19r16 20v45 21r4
       22v43 25r13 14
81   pero   3v2 4r3 14 4v9 5v4 26 37[n] 6r39
       6v30 8r10 43 43 8v9 19v39 20v34
       21r29 21v28 22r41 24r29 25r14 25v42
       26r10 18 20 29 29r27 30r35 31r31
       31v30 32v4 33r32 33v45 34v8 35v24
       36v9 37r14 23 40r35 40v8 41r29
       43v40 44r15 19 44v5 17 46r10 46v11
       29 50r44 50v17 51r13 51v2 24 52r14
       52v7 21 47[n] 53r22 38 42[n] 54r2 55r4
       24 55v14[n] 27 56r47 56v25 57v30
       58v23 58v27 59r15 60r48 60v24 28[c] 30
       61r16 63r13 28 63v12 64r46 66r16
perpetuo   1v15

perro   18r20 28r35
perros   14r32 18v38 21r7 22r3
perrsona   29v33
perrsonas   29v1 30v40
11   persona   2r32 14r14 22v27 38r42 40v4
       46v41 62r41 64v22 66r10 12 66v21
19   personas   11r1[n] 16v23 18r24 22r22
       22v19 29v19 35v36 43r15 44v30
       47v26 50r14 53r7 54r12 55v23 41[c]
       61v3 62r16 66r6 67r36
perteneçia   66v12
pertrechos   48r25
perturbar   61v46
pesada   48v14
pesado   56r1
pesaria   63v22
pesava   2r25
pescado   18v43 44r43 56r1[n] 57r29 58r28
pescadores   18r19 18v43 51v47
pescados   35v10 36r41 36v35
pescar   18r23 18v41 34v15 38v16 43v17
pescarō   25r18 34v19 35v9
pescavan   25r10
6   pescueço   9r14 12r16 22v41 39v40
       48r10 49r16
pesqueço   49v3
pestilençia   29v31[c] 32
pez   27v21g
pēsarō   19v4
philosophos   64v2
phisico   50v40
pico   27v38 28r12
piden   6v22 43v27
pidiendole   5v36
pidiendoles   43v28
pidierō   64v13
pidio   63v11
28   pie   9v37 13r37 16v35 24r45 24v14 25r2
       27r7 38 27v10 28v22 30r12 31r4 9 27
       38 33v4 38r10 40r30 41r29 43r26 43v2
       3 44v32[c] 33 46r11 54v5[n] 15[n] 63r47
pieça   38v33
pieças   47v4
piedad   44v42 56v27
14   piedra   14v32 44 25r2 29v36 39r3 43r43
       45v42 50r35 52r41 53v5 55r9 64v39
       44 65r1
15   piedras   10r21 10v27 14r10 20v13 22v43
       24v3 27r36 36[n] 40 27v6 31r19 37r51
       38v47 51v48 49
pierna   37r6 38r19
7   piernas   9v34 11v4 12r15 36 21r3 22v42
       62v37
7   pies   5r2 18r15 21v12 22 22r2 39v19
       52r4
pijotas   35v11
6   piloto   5v33 6v26 56r24 60r48 66v49 50
8   pilotos   2v4 4r24 4v34 5v30 60v23
       62v15[n] 18 63r16
pimienta   20v41 21v25 50r22 57r36 37

31r10 32v32 33r37 33v17 41r9 43v5
46v21 47r2 3 6 30 57v47 63r3

ponerle 50r40

ponerse 7v11 23v42 49v42 65r5 13

ponē 57r27 30

pongo 12r42 13r32

ponia 61v45

ponian 9r14 36r30 61v38

poniendo 26v42 27r2 46v41 67r37

7 poniente 2v32 4r23 6v14 18v10 23r20
34 41v16

poniēte 4v1 14

20 popa 5v34 8r41 11v32 41 17r48 30r35
31v25 34v7 39v6 46v5 6 48v7 52r47
55v11 56v4 59v47 60r6 61r29 62r45
62v26

populares 45r21 25

poquita 23r8

648 por

porfiavan 44r33

porq 12v4 30r3 35r25

317 porque porq̄ porq̄

porque 1r9 13v6 15v31 51r5

313 porq̄

14 porq̄l 19v9 22v9 24r25 28r22 41 30v25
32v7 18 44r3 46r28 47r46 48r20 63r35
64r11

porq̄llos 57r19

porq̄s 15v26 52v43 54v5n

porq̄sta 38r2

porq̄stavā 37v20

19 portugal 2v35 3r12 10r33 23r40 48r34
55r15 62v12 63r42 63v23 34 36 43
65v35 35n 46 66r2n 41n 66v36n 67r11

portugues 20v32 63r46n

portugueses 7v21d 63r8n 63v24 64r9
66r2n

posa 6r39

posado 17r30

posseen 44v31

possession 8v44

possessiō 11v7

possible 21r25 26r13 53r41

poste 30v17

postrera 32v3n 33r4 60v27

postrero 28v35

pozo 10v34 32r43

poᵣq̄ 55r32

pplosa 22v11

prado 25r36

pratica 29r21

preciosas 10r21 22v43

preçiavā 55v22n

preçio 22r13 50r20

preçiosa 31v9

preçiosas 24v3

pregonar 66v16

preguntole 55v6

pregūtar 20r37 47r20

pregūtasen 43r15

pregūtava 49r23

pregūtavan 10v17

prendella 64v23c

prendello 63v16

prendellos 56r8

prenden 22v48

2 prender prēder

prender 22v26

prendierōlos 63r47

8 presente 1r12 17 24 12v6 19r40 20r41
37v32 42

presentes 36v21

11 presto pʳesto

11 presto 4v3 7r39 9v14 13v6 36 14r44
22v30 36v43 46v1 49r6 49v33

presumē 54r14

pretender 64v23c

pretendia 28v5 57r20 63v15

pretēder 64v23c 24

pretēdia 35r16

prēder 63v10

prēdio 63r46n

priesa 39v15 48v47 49r2 53r40

prietas 38r24

prieto 9r37 9v31 16v28

7 primer 1r1 2v29 8r31 46r18 58r1 65v2
67r42

9 primera 8v28n 9r7 55v14 56r12n 60v41
61v21 63r37 64v46 65v15

primeras 42r32

18 primero 4r41 7v5 6 8r38 8v16 20 11r14
15r22 43v32 46v12 27 52r15 56v28
60v39 61v5 62v32 64r11 64v9

principal 21v16 33 22v9 40v4 43v20

principales 66v3

principalmēte 35v19

6 principe 1r23 24v6bc 25v4c 30 41 49

principes 38r32 52v41

principio 3v37 26v29 31r17

prinçipal 45r17n 66v21

prinçipales 30v20 67r36

prinçipe 1r26 24v6f 25v6b 18 26v34c

10 prinçipes 1r10 34 39 1v33 38 22r21
29v5 40r6 63v27 64v29

prinçipio 26v24

prior 66v20

privado 48v41 50v6

19 proa 3r23 7v23 8v15 22v3 24r33 25v44
46 26v42 27r2 31r10 28 33r36 37
45v41 51r24 57v4 58r19 62v10 13

proçession 61v22

proferidose 61v44

prohibia 44r16

prohibido 46r24 50r16

prologo 1r6

prometido 7v7 8v18 48v17 57r7

prometio 61v15 64r7

prometioselas 21r36

propias 57r22

proponer 56v36n

proporcionados 24v38
9 proposito 1v40 30r14 50r31 50v10
    61v31 33 63v20 64v26 67r22
  propria 34r28 34v17 52r22
  proprio 25r19 30r27 36r39 38r15 39v31
  proprios 2r1 7v13
  propuso 56v32[n]
  proseguir 8r15 28v4
  prosperas 62r26
  prospero 61v30
  protestaciones 9r2
  protestaçiones 62r12
  proteste 48v31
  provado 29v15
  provar 29r21
  provecho 29v7 30r6 35v29 36r10
  provechos 8r12
  provechosa 17r13 14 21r26
  provechosas 53v33
  proverse 59r9
  proveydo 1r31
  proveyo 61v31
  providencia 61v48
  provincia 19r33[n] 40v45
  provinçia 20r11 38v28 47v17[n] 18
  provinçias 20v1 49r26[n]
  provisiones 63v31 64v30
  provo 34r20
  prudētes 29v1
  publica 54r33
6 pude 10r10 39 12v26 14v18 15v19 25
  pudē 52r36
15 pudiera 1v1 10v37 40 11r40 13v19 22r8
    24v37 25r3 25v32 30r35 34r47 45r2
    47r2 48r24 48v8
  pudieran 7r38 21r32
  pudierā 19v5 35r18 49v43 51r19
  pudiere 15v5 9 29v17
7 pudierō 2v10 3v10 30v33 35v26 43r19
    46v16 61v35
8 pudiese 8v6 11v22 29v9 50v31[c] 53r22
    56v29 63v35 64r44
  pudiesen 47r29 50r24
38 pudo 2v13 8r11 18r42 19v3 9 46 20v18
    22r42 23v38 24r36 25v42 27v45 30v5
    25 31r13 32v7 46 37r19 26 26 37
    39r37 40r38 40v22 24 44v2 46v18
    51r1 51v7 60r9 61r34 62r36 62v40
    63v47 64v16 40 45 66v2
17 pueblo 21v15 33 31v1 38v42 42v17 20
    37 43r17 44r25 45r19 31 46v33[c] 47r8
    47v3[c] 51r29[c] 63r46 65v26
11 pueblos 1r32 39 21v43 22r26 22v36 37
    29v22 30v28 43v41 45v21 54r45
  pueda 13v3 14r14 15r8 38r3 6
  puedan 23r28 43v1
  puedā 36v10 43r36
33 puede 11v8 12r30 32 13v42 17v10
    21r45 23r8 27r4 29v4 28 31r16 33r37
    33v13 34r39 34v30 35r4 30 36v42

    38r43 41r23 39 42v1 43r38 43v4
    44v24 45v8 12 49v28 57r17 62r31
    63r19 67r29 32
8 pueden 10r28 11r3 18r45 20r13 24r12
    48r40 57r38 57v10
  puedē 33v7 43r28 55v30 57r32
  puedo 10v2 12r38 13r8 16v7
  puerco 25r20
3 puerta pue[r]ta
  puerta 53v20
  puertas 1r21 32r15
150 puerto pue[r]to
99 puerto 1v23 24 26[n] 3r8 10v29 11r12
    13v41 18v8 10 19r19 22[n] 23 20v12
    24r17 18 28 24v6a 6a[c] 6e 8 25v3[c] 6 9
    13 41 48[c] 49 26v33 33[c] 35 44[n] 27r20
    27v12[n] 13 35 28v23 29r16 20 29v8 43[c]
    30r19 28 30v45 31r1 1 18 32r26 32v36
    41 49 33r1 28 29 29[n] 45 33v1 6 8 14
    19 28 45 34r22 34v3[n] 47 35v42 37r2
    18 41r11 46 43r26 35 45r2 46r5 46v32
    49v18 50v32 51v33 45 52r34 54r18[n]
    23 54v5[n] 16 55r3 11 12 30 32 55v41[n]
    60v30 61v13 63r3 64r3 16 19 64v9
    65v18 67r19
19 puertos pue[r]tos
10 puertos 18r33 27v30 28r3 15 44 28v32
    33r32 40v36 52r43 66v17
26 pues 2v42 5v1 7r10 8r14 9v32 12r35
    17r7 10 23r19 26v20 30r13 37r43
    39r29 40r9 52v23 53v19 54r8 45
    55v28 57r1 62r8 63v18 38 64v24a
    66r15 43
7 puesta 20v35 24v32 31r28 35v20 43r46[c]
    58r19 66r44b
  puestas 28r2[c] 41r16
63 puesto 1r5 5v26 34 6r5 7v25[c] 26 8r29
    31 39 11v8 22 44 14r26[n] 23v19 28[c]
    31r3 32v12[n] 23 33r36 34v6 30 35v4
    37v16 23 39v4 35 40r16 41v32 42v13
    43r33 41 46r41 46v19 48r10 49r13
    53r47 49 53v15 54r17 55r46 55v32
    56v47 57v25 58r8 58v9 30 59r26 59v5
    11 16 60v8 17 61r8 62r4 62v3 42
    63r13[c] 22 65r10 17 44 67r9 15
  puestos 8v36 55r34[n] 55v1
  pue[r]ta 43r46 65r30
51 pue[r]to 21r44 22r45 23r25 24r32 24v44
    25v18 30 26r9 26v40 29r32 29v43
    30r32 42 30v44 31r5 24 26 32r26
    32v35 38 33r29[n] 34r8 34v2 11 12 13
    28 29 35 40 35r28 35v17 46 37r20 22
    23 40v24 41r9 26 31 33 43v8 9 38
    44v23 46r13 57v12 60r40 64r11 23
    65v42
9 pue[r]tos 20v1 24r20 25 24v33 29r22
    41r42 41v11 19 65v38
  pujar 13r15
32 punta pūta
31 punta 14v31 18v12 14 23v33 24v34

26v11c 27r29 30v45 31r3 3c 6 7 32v3n
37r6 6 8 8 10 42v21 45r10 10n 46r16
30 32 53v28 28 54v21 23 23 46 63v7

puntas   24v12
punto   60v22
puntos   4v34 47r42
puntualmēte   lv35
puño   12vl
puro   50v7

8   puse   11r41 11v35 36 14v35 15r17
     15v14 30 39v20
pusiera   59r13
pusierō   39r2
pusierōlas   48v23
pusierōle   38r36
pusierōse   8v24
pusiese   47r5
pusiesen   65v42

33   puso   18v16 22v17 23v20 24r32 24v5 6e
     25v44 46 27v44 33r2 8 11 18 29n 35r9
     9n 35v16 37r48 39r3 40v11 33 39
     45v40 49v2 6 9 51v4 53r23 53v8 54r18
     54v6 21 55r10

8   pusole   19r29 26v33c 33r1 28 40v44
     43v8 10c 49r16
pusolo   62r40
pūta   23v30n

Q

9   q   8r42 17r2 23r15 29r7 40 30v10 37r34
     41v6c 59r30
3   qua q̄
qua   25v37
quadrada   28v18
quadrante   26r15
quadrate   26r10
quadrāte   20v3 36v44 60r10
quaja   35r25
quajada   5r17 58r25 41 60r2
quajarse   35v6
163   qual q̄l
162   qual   lv41 2v38 3r34 4r13 35 5v5 6r11
     6v20 7v18 8v4 8 11 21 10v39 11r14 41
     11v21 12r11 42 12v11 24 33 13v33
     14r34 46 14v29 34 35 15r17 15v40
     16r18 16v10 11 30 34 17vl 18r35
     18v16 19r37 19v22 46 20v12 19 21r21
     38 21v41 41n 22r32 41 23v3 38 41
     24v6g 25r20 25v20 26r44 26v14 44
     27v44 44 28r25 28v18 28 29r20 22
     31r7 31v39 32v10 38 33r2 33v7 11 39
     34r20 31 34v11 35r9 32a 35v30 36r15
     19 36v3 37r41 37v25 32 41 38v31
     39r4 40r32 40v13 22 33 41r18 41vl 43
     43r18 31 43v37 44r8 45r6 9 27 45v3
     46r17 46v32 35 48r8 34 49r5 9 50r30
     51r26 51v3 4 5 12 16 52r10 11 39
     52v17 31 53r18 33 45 53v10 54r18 28
     34 41 55r11 44 55v8 38 56r18 56v2 8
     15 57r42 57v29 60r18 61v2 18 29

62r31 63r19 24 63v31 44 64r5 17
64v22 25 26c 65v47 66r20 37 66v12 21
39 67r23 38
53   quales q̄les
52   quales   2r7 4r34 9r17 12v8 18r16 44
     18v24 19v33 20v19 21v11 27v8 14
     28r2 3 31 29vl 34r35 35r38 35v23
     36r17 32 38r31 39r41 40r38 42r36
     42v8 43r9 45r5 45vl 46r41 45 47r37
     48v42 49r28 29 52v12 32 53r36 53v14
     43 54r13 39 55r40 56r2 56v3 62r10
     63r7 45 63v27 32 64v32 67r37
qualesquier   23r28
qualesquiera   41r25
qualquier   43r39
11   qualquiera   10r6 30 14r18 15r43 16v37
     21r47a 22v31 32r12 35r4 37r44 41r24
quan   33r17c
6   quanta quāta
quanta   56v28
quareta   33r48
11   quarēta   2r19 3v3 7r17 20v7 26r22 41
     38v41 58r8 59r44 59v45 65r6
quarētas   58r14
66   quarta q̄rta
58   quarta   2r13 16 3r33 4r26 4v38 5r36
     6v19 7r35 7v44 22v3 23v20 24r14 22
     27 25v12 46 50 26r36 32r30 32v23
     33r2 9 14 34r15 41 40v41 52r31 54v8
     20 29 57v24 44 58r7 13 20 36 37 39
     58v10 15 18 35 59r4 40 59v6 29 33
     60r14 21 32 60v5 12 12c 21 61r37 43
     65r12 38
quartal   53r2n
16   quarto   22r46 24r31 25v46 26r38 28v24
     27 31r25 34r7 34v5 48 46r18 54v38
     58rl 3 59v42 61r2
quartos   32r34 61r2c
quartta   57v5
26   quasi   5r26 9r33 11r42 13r11 14v7 45
     15r3 18r35 23r12 25v50 26r37 35r1 8
     30 44 38r1 38v44 41r16 45r10 46r9
     47r25 48vl 49v25 53v16 55v41n 63v43
quato   27v31 29v4
8   quatorze catorze
7   quatorze   5r26c 5v13 41r7 54v16 59r27
     41 60r24
40   quatro   3v21 6v7 10 12r9 19r33 19v47
     22r2 9 22v5 30v31 31r32 32v49 36r19
     38r14 39r21 43 40v25 47vl 49r25
     51r42 51v8 52r17 38 53v15n 54r38
     54v5 21 22 41 56r1n 57r11 57v12 58rl
     6 8 58v14 37 59r44c 62v8 65v34
quatrocientas   57r47
quā   26v14n
63   quādo   1r4 1v20n 26n 3r2 3v32 5v8 37
     6v13 14 8v11 10v15 11r3 33 12r6 6c
     26 12v18 43 13v39 48 14vl 2 18r46
     21r50 26r39 26v28 27v31 29r32 31v27
     27 32v49 34r35 34v45 35v38 45 39v12

42r16 42v17 45v24 46r28 46v12 44 44
47r40 48r5 50 48v21 49r5 50v5 28
51v30 52v34 53v46 54r37 54v45
56v22 32[n] 57r24 41 61v34 62r9a 63r36
66v48

quãta   13r40 42v8 47r30 48v47 50r24
quãtas   10v30 41r12 47r29 61v3
29   quãto   14r36 14v18 15v8 16v45 20v2
30r9 32r4 22 34v10 36r21 45 36v12
41r4 42r7 33 42v5 9 43r46 43v22 26
44r14 44v13 46v16 24 46 47r26 47v13
50v34 58v23
quãtos   27v21b 31r32 41v2 9
quãtro   3v39

2,644   que q̃ q
135   que   1v22 3r1 4r28 5v6 6r34 7r4 7 7v11
8v18 19 23 9r15 29 9v41 10r27 30
10v9 21 33 11r3 13 34 36 11v1 5 7 8
11 18 22 37 46 12v19 41 13v3 30
14r27 30 14v5 13 42 15r43 15v7 44
16r13 16v37 17r16 19r19 19v35 20r21
20v41 23r28 30 45 23v24 24v6b 36
25v39 51 26r19 26v17 33[c] 27r10 27v6
28r23 37 29v39 30r14 30v1 31v43
32v11 18 23 33v36[c] 34v48 35r33 35v6
36r33 36v20[c] 37r31 37v6 33 49 38r11
39r13 15 28 39v46 40r21 41r24[c] 42v33
43r45 44r25 44v25 45r6 31 45v2[c]
46v13 47 47r4 20 31 39 41 47v13 13
15 48r3 32 48 48v15 30 34 49v5 50v12
33 51r18 28[c] 52v41 53r35 53v1 54r35
54v9 55r31 55v19 56r18 56v32[n] 57v14
61v38 62r18 62v31 63r37 63v43 45
65r47

quebradas   16v31
quebrado   63v4
quebrãtado   63v19
quebro   2r21[c]
7   queda   10v29 33v11 14 41r27 42v10
52r7 63r18
quedado   49v41 50v45
quedar   49r3 52v42 63r16
quedaria   34r24
quedarõ   8v23 9r16 38v31
quedarse   35v40 48r29
quedase   42v26
quedasen   21r30 39v14 43r7
17   quedava   14v36 17r49 17v2 23v49 25v18
31 26r39 29r13 32v5 46v23 49v34
55r27 57v43 58r32 60r37 40 62v36
6   quedavale q̃davale
quedavale   25v49 26r41 33r7 10 12
6   quedavã   7r5 23v36 27v18 45r34 60v33
63r30
quedavãle   25v26
quedã   23v12 28v30 57r13[c] 25
quedãdo   26v43 31r40
quedele   45r43
9   quedo q̃do
8   quedo   16r37 29r8 39v42 46r38 48r4

48v20 49v12 56r21
quedose   2v15
70   quel q̄ūel q̃l
quel   50r14
quequiera   32r4
quer   64v27[c]
querer   7v21 33v43 34v8 36r46 48v6
18   queria   11v31 45 13v28 38 16v3 25v34
28v1 35r34 37v39 38v30 42r8 47r4 37
48v39 50r23 51v30 55r33 62v5
6   querian   9v10 19r43 30v6 31v33 48v42
66r2[n]
queriã   21v30 44r14
querido   11v43
queriendo   45r29
queriẽdo   21v39
querir   64v37
querria   16r7 29v8 56r39
querrian   17r10
querriã   44r15
2   questas q̃stas
quexarse   8r13
quexase   56v20
quexavase   8r10 49v43
quiça   7v20 53r42[n]
30   quien quiẽ
20   quien   8v19 11v42 12v19[c] 13v30 26v16
27r5 27v32 30r10 31r1 32v3[n] 33r8
45v37 47v17 50r32 54r13 54v6 55r10
57v6[c] 7 64r7
quiera   28r18 28v3
10   quiere   1r26 12r26 24v26 29r26[n] 41r26[n]
43v45 46v13[n] 51v1 54r9 56v41
quierẽ   23r11 47r20
quiero   10v1 12r33 15r36 15v4
11   quiẽ   4r40 7v5 6 22v17 26v13 33r26
36r40 51r17 55r12 60v38 62r37
quilla   56v20
quinientas   22r8
quinientos   21v31 37v19 44v35
4   quinsay quisay quīsay
quintales   16r26 21r42 22r9
quintero   2r24
10   quinze   7v33 14r28 19r30 24v25 31r10
32v31 43r30 52v30 54v33 63r5
quisay   16v18 20r18[c]
quise   11v15 15r13 15v34
19   quisiera   2v6 9 17r2 26v3 29r41 30v8
32v4 35v39 37r25 48r23 49v37 54r31
55r31 56r39[c] 44 56v23 57v29 66r44[c]
48[c]
quisierã   21v30
quisiere   11r7 22v46
quisierẽ   33r37 38r46
quisierõ   22r27 34v23 56r7
11   quisiese   44v14 47r30 47v13 48r28
61v39 63v15 28 36 66r16 47 66v46
quisiesen   38v3
23   quiso   4v25 7r7 8r42 21v39[c] 22v7 25v31
26r33 28r42 31v42 39r7 39v8 40r14

43v43[c] 46r34 46v10 51r29[c] 52v13 20
53v18 55r7 57v15 65r46[a] 67r25
quisose   21v38 52v21
quitado   62r47
quitar   28r33[c] 34 66r44a
quitarse   53v22
quito   31v16 49v1 3 50r13
quizo   56r44[c]
quīsay   20r18 18[c]
q̄   31v26 35v50
q̄do   44r37
q̄l   66r42
q̄les   18r20
8   q̄rta   25v24 26r6 27v40 42 58r15 59v48
65r37 41
q̄to   41r5
q̄ūel   26r14
2,499   q̄
q̄bravā   61r24
q̄davale   34r10
q̄ellos   47v23 41
q̄esta   66r12
q̄estava   45r18
68   q̄l   1v39 3r13 6v30 8r37 8v3 6 11v44
12v9 16r7 19r36 19v13 20v29 35
21v26 22v18 24v26 25v16 31v26
32v23 39 33v46 36r43 36v5 37v31 35
38r28 33 38v34 39r40 39v10 12 41v7
21 42r8 42v35 44r16 45r33 45v4
46v46 47v16 27 48r9 49r4 12 14
49v23 50v33 51v15 52v16 53r27
54v47 55v39 56v5 22 57r14 19 60v37
61r40 61v42 63v15 15 28 64v24 65v39
46 66r4 23 67r26
6   q̄llos   15r42 32v17 35r44 45r12 60v32
36
41   q̄s   2v1 22 4v17 5r20 6v8 7r31 7v37
10r25 13v8 16r12 16v13 17r29 18r38
18v5 19r49 20r13 23r13 27r6 8 11[c]
29r32 29v20 32r13 32v3[n] 34v21 43
35r35 42 35v44 41r39 42r5 47r19
48r34 54r20 55v20 56r1[n] 57r36 60v27
62v30 65v23 66r35
q̄spera   48v24
19   q̄sta   14r42 15r35 17r14 20r16 22v24
26r34 30v13[n] 46 32r30 34v13 37r19
30 38r44 38v14 49v21 26 54r6 18[n]
67r13
q̄stan   39v36 62r32
q̄stando   2v34 33v12
q̄staria   27v41 43
q̄stas   10r19 38r40
22   q̄stava   11v32 18v12 19r48 19v47 20v4
29r45 36r19 36v45 37r6 38v42 42[c]
39r18 39v5 41r9 44v23 47r23 49v22
63r13 64r27 65r29 65v35 67r21
q̄stavan   47v4
q̄stavā   4r30 30v31 47r27 49v13 60r28
q̄ste   15r43 53v16
q̄stos   13r22

q̄stoy   20r17 67r34
q̄stuviese   47v12
q̄stuviesen   46v2
q̄stuvo   65v28

R

rabiforcado   58r28
rabiforcados   58r42 58v6
rabiforçado   6r36 7r19
rabo   3v31 4v5 6r26 59v37
7   rabos   6v7 58r42 58v26 44 59r14 59v18
30
rajo   48v21
rallan   38r12
ramada   30r24
ramalejo   12v7 16v1
ramillo   38r13
ramillos   38r10
ramito   13r38
ramitos   49v24
ramo   3v38 13r41
ramos   13r36 18v34 49v23
ranas   36v35
rasa   29r26[n] 33r20 33v25
rascon   2r24
raso   33v20
rastelo   65v30 47
rastro   51v47
10   rato   8r7 17v13 18r29 19v18 30r38
40r27 47v31 60v5 11 66v34
ratones   25r39
3   ratos rratos
ratos   7v33 8r6
ravanos   36r37
rayz   49v23 26 29
rayzes   24v21 36r36 38r11 15
razo   57r47
23   razon razō razo
6   razon   12r3 26r12 27v21[n] 44v11[n] 48r36
63v47
razonable   26v10 49v42
razones   25v33 28v5 52v7
16   razō   13v45 17r12 24r6 24v43 26v21
33v36[n] 35r44 40v10 42v43 47v14
53r32 56r39 56v32 62r9[b] 64v21
67r42[c]
real   8v31 18v31 46v30 56v33
reales   1r19 22 40r7 52r2
recalar   31r16
recaudo   16v15 21v29 46v44 47r1
recibian   45r27
recogido   31v24
recogierō   14v27
recomēdaçion   63v26
recuperar   63v17
2   reçibian recibian
reçibian   63v24
reçibiese   44r22
red   43v17
rededor   10v28 17r5 47r6

7 redes   14r24 18r21 18v40 20v25 25r18
      34v15 38v16
redezilla   55v1
redondo   14v43 54v25 55r14
redōda   2v23
redōdas   19r24
referillo   29r44
refetar   13r25
refiere   24r15
refresco   57v17 58r2 63r29
regar   36v27
regido   50v2
reguardo   32v24 35r5 52r40 54v43
reguardos   59r2
relacion   10v35 29r42 29v9 66r19
relaçion   67r24
relampagueo   61r10
relāpagos   65v13
religion   30r15
religiosas   22r23
religiō   22r35 66r39
relinga   59v1
reliquias   45r29
relucia   53r42[n]
reluzir   27r36
remar   31v43 41v39
remavan   18r48
remavā   9v42
remediar   44v27 46v18 51r21 62r27
remediara   56v39
remediarō   61v37
8 remedio   46v15 48r36 57v21 61r30
      61v33 64r18b[c] 20 65v19
remo   33v5
remos   45r11
rendir   34r7
renta   56v35
reñi   14r35
repararo   17v44
reparo   24r5
repartia   52v40
reposar   46r36
reposo   62v35
repostero   8r43 46v29 50v17
representado   49r46
requirian   9r2
requirierō   64v16
requiriese   16r38
resaca   34v31
rescatar   11v29
rescatarō   38v26
rescatavan   10r32
rescibian   42r43
rescibiese   46v46
rescibio   37v33 66v4
rescibir   49r49
resçebia   28v2
resçiban   12v20
resçibido   21v8 27v20 42v35 48r14
resçibidos   22r31

resçibiese   49r7
resçibiesen   28v43
resçibiēdo   1r32
resçibio   43r16 48r12 66r41 66v22 40
3 resçibir rescibir
resçibir   46v10 66r3
resgatado   44r33 48v26 57r10
resgatando   54r26
resgatandoselas   31v17
6 resgatar   14r38 16v29 20v25 35 38v30
      49r34
resgatarō   14r35 38v26[n] 54r27
resgatase   20v36 54r36
resgatasen   50v24
resgatavalo   38v33
resgatavan   47v5
resgate   25r8 30v7 34r5 56v7
resgates   28v44 40r33 41v36 50v23
resgato   40r35 52v36
resi   28v45[c]
resina   23r5
resistillos   29r1
respecto   33v27
respectos   22v8
respeto   47v8
respirarō   8r28
6 respondio respōdio
respondio   66r9
respōdia   5v24 61r33
respōdian   37v35
respōdieron   20v45
respōdierō   14r37
respōdiese   63v47
respōdio   37v39 63v40 66r4 66v12 18
respuesta   16v19
restinga   10v27 14v32 27r11 15
7 restringa   43r44 45v44 46r2 7 46v26
      51r25 51v9
10 restringas   28v34 41r15 22 43r42 48r22
      51r34 51v19 52r12 41 53v32
resultase   25r8
reverēçia   36r31 66v37
reves   25v11
reveses   2r27
revueltos   61v5 5[c]
95 rey   1r10 21 27 2v36 3r13 8v1 3 9r1
      10r12 15r35 37 43 15v18 16v6 23 17r6
      18v12 19r36 40 19v45 20r38 37v19 31
      45 38r29 34 37 39r35 41 43[n] 40r25 27
      29 32 34 40v4 45r14 17[n] 20 23 29[c] 30
      46r29 46v30 40 47r17 23 34 47v9 19
      48r9 48v16 37 41 49r5 12 13 21 30 32
      37 48 50r6 10 15 27 50v6 15 17[c] 18
      52v33 56v8 10 57r5 63v23 34 41 64r4
      64v34 65v35 35[n] 39 46 66r2[n] 3 34 41
      45 50 66v3 4 18 24 29 45
62 reyes   1r6 27 7v6 8v18 19r41 20r39
      21r39 21v36 22v20 24r40 24v8 25r24
      27r40 27v19 29r43 30v12 31r20 31v12
      36r13 38r31 35 39v1 40v10 42r37

sabra   60v38
sabrā   29v21
sabria   32r18
sabrian   34r1
sabrosas   38r15
sabrosos   6r42 19r2
saca   44v19 55v31
sacada   58v20
sacan   23r23
2   sacanben sacanbē sacāben
  sacanbē   66r50
  sacar   21r41 48v7 22
sacarla   46v17
sacase   61r25
sacava   5v9 46v43
sacāben   66r44
saco   8v30 31v38 61v6
sacro   55r12
sacros   64v1
saetada   56r18
sahumerios   21v44
sala   25r6
salada   4r38 19r9 53v3
salar   25r23
saldria   66r6
sale   19r26 34r39
salen   29r29 46r8 57v2ⁿ
salga   14r26ⁿ
sali   11v11 14r39 15v43
10   salia   18v13 14 19v7 12 23v41 25r31ᶜ 35
    25v27 31r40 51v9
salian   25r32
salida   1v28 27r3
40   salido   5r5 15v12 17v18 37 25v30 48
    26r3 27r28 37r19 45r37 51v29ᶜ 52r38
    58r4 16 17 37 46 58v16 59r17 26 33
    42 59v9 16 36 60v7 19 61r38 61v44
    62v10 27 38 46 64r36 65r3 5 13 20
    67r10 17ⁿ
7   saliendo   19v16 27r17ᶜ 29r3 37r23
    48v37 49r20 51r23
saliera   64v24e 26
salierā   66v33ᶜ
salieron   5v8
7   salierō   4r38 11v25 18r46ᶜ 47 29r4
    30r37 54r2
salierōse   21v20
saliese   21r46 25v16 39v8 55r31 61r41
saliesen   63r38
25   salio   1v20ⁿ 2v6 8v28 28ⁿ 19r28 20v10ᶜ
    29 25v2 26r39 32r25 34r7 34v12 37r2
    22 46r45 46v3 47v20 48v21ᶜ 49r4 43
    50r26 54v3 55r30 56r3 62v24
32   salir   1r21 2v21 7v11 15r13 19r12 23r10
    24r16 27v35 29r41 31v42 32r48 35v40
    37v3 40v19 22 41v14 30 47r23 50v46
    51r25 51v30 53r35 53v31 55r31 58v40
    61r23 61v38ⁿ 62v34 63v2 64r8 65v34
    67r16
salitar   28v45

salmones   35v10
saltar   2r36
saltarō   8v40 46v6
saltavā   28r18
saltear   43r40
saltes   2r10 67r12 17 17ⁿ 18
7   salto   2r21 18r17 28v19 29r31 34v16
    62v13 63r46
salua   39v21
9   saluador   11r20 35 12r13 22 12v9 14v34
    18v8 19r19 52r3
saluajes   18v39
saluamēto   51r11 61v38ⁿ 62r7
saluar   65v18
saluara   48v8
salue   8v11 20r5 62v30
55   saluo   6v16 9r35 9v19 26 31 35 10r37
    12r23 13r22 13v15 14r30 15r15 33
    15v26 27 43 17r12 20 23 17v8 10 12
    18r40 19r5 19v35 21v48 22r3 20
    22v25 23r1 8 15 29v35 30r12 31v26
    34v4 35r24 38r45 39v9 16 32 40r12 29
    43r2 43 45v5 47v44 48r18 48v21
    52r35 40 57r31 57v22 67r21 29
7   salvador   11v2 13 18 12v5 13r19 25v36
    55v15
salvamēto   61v40
salvo   1v4 5v8 11r2 23r22 31v14
samana   57v2ⁿ
samoet   13r16 13v31 14r43
15   san sā
11   san   11r35 11v2 13 12r13 13r19 18v8
    19r19 25v36 33r29 34r23 65r27
sana   48v20 57r38
sanas   29v30
sanches   8v3 42 21r37
sancho   60v23
40   sancta santa sācta sāta scta
24   sancta   1r29 11r42 12r16 22 41 44 13r19
    22r35 26v44ⁿ 27v36 39r33 45r10 10ⁿ
    46r30 32 48v30 60r49 61r46 61v14 17
    63r1ⁿ 2 64r22 65r1ⁿ
16   sancto santo scto
10   sancto   1r30 22r28 30v45 41r10 43v9
    45v37 49v22 51r35 37 38
sangrar   23r4 9
sangre   21r9
sano   29v37
18   sant   11r20 11v18 12r22 12v9 33r30
    34r8 34v40 52r3 55r15 57v42 44ⁿ 60r8
    39 64r18 23 36 66v35 67r10
santa   61v10 64v8 65r28 47
santissima   44r48
santo   32r26 51v5 60r40 60v30
saomete   14v35
saometo   15v1 14
sardinas   35v12
sartas   20r33
sastre   50v40
sathanas   52v14

satis   37v38n
satisfaze   41v7
sā   12v5 14v34 33r29n 55v15
7   sācta   1r34 9r11 12v10 13r10 22v35
      60v27 64r37
    sāta   1v2 27v12n 62v5n
    sc   14r25
    scisura   33r12
    sc̄ta   12v22 46r16
    sc̄to   40v34 46r16
512   se
9   sea   17r14 22v25 30r16 41v5 43r34 41
      43v25 52r15 67r30
8   sean   6v36 7r26 20r9 22v22 28r28 35r44
      47v38 58v5
    seā   36r40 59r17
    seca   54v23
    secas   12v3 28r8 49v26
    seco   21v39 61r13 65v5
7   secta   1r36 9v16 13v5 20r3 22v24 29v24
      38r22
    sectas   1r33
    seda   8v17
    sedas   9r34 9v27
    segovia   8v3 42 50v19
    segud   5v22 35v30 67r1
    segui   11r37 14v17
    seguian   53r25
    seguimos   16r21
    seguir   4v30 13v26 51r6
34   segun segū
    segun   17r3 32v19n 51r45
    segura   21r32 63r41
    seguramēte   17v10 19v38
    seguras   26v46
    seguridad   21r31 63v19
8   seguro   34v29 46r27 53v35 56v10 63r19
      63v11 18 64v14
    seguros   21r47 31v9 63v25
31   segū   4r12 9v39 10r17 13r8 15r37 16v9
      15 18r42 19r50 19v46 21v8 22v48
      23v40 28r26 32v6 21c 33v31 35r36
      35v35 39r37 39v27 40r38 40v6 36
      44v20 45r27 49r31 51r33 55v22n 22n
      61v27
    segūd   4r15
    segūda   58v38
    selladas   63v32
    sellos   63v32
    semana   7r8 24v6k 26v28
    sembrado   34r32 38r9
    sembrar   38v8 48r43 50v36
    sembravā   22r10
    semejables   35r8
    semejança   34r46
    semejante   33r34
    semejantes   16r23 16v25
    semejāte   1v24 2r3 13r20 36r17
    semejātes   22v15
    semēteras   33r22

senas   12r35
senbrada   31r47
sentado   66v27
sentar   39v7 66v6
sentarōse   21v21
sentençia   67r36
sentia   28r36 46r44
sentido   46v1
sentimio   50v4 63v44
senor   66r35 37
seña   8v33
24   señal   2v42 4v17 25 42 5r7 21 6v8 9 7v9
      18v5 19r41 20r7 21v6n 22v32 35v18
      19 50 36r31 38v43 40r2 56v9 60r28
      61r11 11n
    señala   19r18
    señalados   28r3 57v14c 67r33
    señalandole   55v10
    señalar   57v41 61v3
    señalarōle   57v14
10   señales   4r36 4v1 7r8 8r26 28 9v7 28r17
      18 45r40 65v6
    señalo   40v1
    señalole   21v35 55v7
    señarōles   63r3
34   señas   8r37 9v8 10r10 11r16 12r13
      13v30 15r38 15v33 16v9 17r3 35
      17v33 18r44 18v18 19r13 19v42 47
      20v43 21r50 21v27 22v49 23v32 31v32
      32r20c 32v15 41 38v34 39v13 40r43
      43v36 45v34 47v10 46 49r24
57   señor   1r23 5v38 8r16 9v17 12r39 12v18
      15v6 17r7 21r48 22r24 27v23 29v17
      32 34r1 35v20 37v28 39r19 40v15
      42v17 20 27 29 30 43r11 14 43v18 18n
      44r3 6 24 30 44v3 10 25 41 45r17n
      45v31 47v26 38 48r15 50r28 51r20
      52v43 54r7 56v26 61v39 62r28 63r12
      17 64r4 32 64v34 65v14 15 66r28
      67r25 38
7   señora   24v6 26v32 37 30r3 61v12 24
      63r38
    señorea   15r38
    señoreavā   40r5
12   señores srs
11   señores   1v37 9r1 23r17 29v5 40r8
      44v37 38 45v33 52v41 63v27 64v29
    señorio   28r37 45v30
    señorios   1v8 22r33c 34 22v36
    señor   44r36 46r34
    sepa   38r28 42 47v38
    sepā   53v33
    septentrion   41v16
    septētrional   43r34
94   ser   3r13 5r17 5v44 7v4 8v9 9v13 10v41
      12v4 24 14r44 16r22n 16v9 17r2 18r18
      18v43 48n 19r6 7 15 51 19v4 21r25
      43n 21v16n 23r9 23v13 25r15 38n
      25v14 26v11c 44n 28r17 26 26n 30 37
      29v2 30v19 22 32v3n 33r13 43 34v44

sirga   37r35
sirvā   43v45
sirve   38r11
sitio   29v42
situare   1v41
so   9v33
sobervia   52v9 53r25
sobervias   52v11
64   sobre   2r5 3r33 34 4v17 5v20 22n 41
   14v29 15r39 16r3 23v33 24v13 36
   26v11 27 30v45 31r2 3 6 31v1 32r46
   33r26 34r38 40 34v32 35r15 36r31
   36v3c 4 37v7 28 38r4 39v38 40v30
   41v24 42r40 40c 42v21 43 43r43
   45v38 39 46r16 40 43 47r34 47v40
   48r50 50r32 50v15 51r37 37 51v40
   54v5n 58v20c 21 61v7 7n 64v49 66v26
   35 67r10 13 17
sobreagua   31r6
sobredicho   24r1
sobrepuja   33r33
sobrino   49r20 50v19
sojugaria   48r33
sojuzgados   11r6
106   sol   1v28 2r12 4r25c 5r5 5v34 7v1 3 11
   25c 26 8r29 31 11r43 15v12 16r9
   17v18 37 45 19v16 22v17 23v19 28
   28c 47 24r16 25v16 18 26r3 7 40 26v9
   27r28 27v35 28r40 29v27 30r26 31r41
   32r48 32v33 36v40 40 38r1 41r9 45r37
   45v29 47r23 48v37 49r20 50v46 51r23
   51v29c 30 52r38 54r17 55r33 36 57v25
   47 58r5 7 16 17 37 46 58v9 16 30 40
   59r17 26 33 42 59v5 9 11 15 16 36
   60r19 60v7 8 17 19 61r8 38 62v3 10
   24 27 34 38 42 46 63r22 64r36 65r3 5
   10 13 17 20 44 67r9 10 15 16
sola   22r7 30v22 33v4 64r34 43
solamēte   22r18 39v24 61r25
solas   53r6
soldando   52r15
soldar   29r32
solenidad   21v8
solia   6v38 43v38
14   solo   9r42 9v41 12r43 13v1 14v2c 30v23
   38 37v6 38v45 43v39 49v41 51r7
   61r40 62r45
solos   9r42 38v1
somos   22r29
167   son sō so
164   son   1v30 2r12 3r31 3v1 4v32 6r5 6v16
   7v13 38 8r34 9r6 38 9v2 5 20 36 11r22
   25 12r27 31 13v3 4 7 7 12 42 14r24 25
   26n 15r5 42 15v45 16r5 15 16v14 17v7
   31 32 18r39 18v34 20v26 21r17 18
   21v7 22r14 19 39 22v15 24 42 23r19
   23v15 47 24r2 46 25r13 25v23 51
   26r1c 26v18 28r1 29r9 29v24 31 30r17
   31v13 32r5c 9 15 32v33 36r36 36v15
   41 37r11 37v27 47 38r8 10 15 40 44

   47 38v4 6 18c 19 20 39r21c 41v29
   42r17 20 42v19 43r24 44r17c 45 44v28
   43 45v33 36 46r8 47r8 33 48r35 48v35
   51r27 35 53v15 37 40 54r42 55v36
   56r35 38 56v36 39 57r22 24 25 57v26
   58r2 6 9 14 15 22 40 58v1 19 35 39 41
   59r4 19 21 35 41 59v3 8 10 15 17 22
   35 46 48 60r16 21 24 26 32 34 44 46
   60v9 18 20 61r1 15 18 38 65r4 12 19
   67r40
sonajas   12v39
sonavan   46r42
2   sondar sōdar
sondar   32r39
sondaresa   33r47
sondase   32v38
sondear   13v45
sonido   46r45
sorgi   11r43 11v9
sorgir   11r28
sortija   49v10
sortijas   31v6 35v34 37v9 42v41
sortijuela   32r1
sospecha   63v1 66r44a
sospechava   55r26
sospecho   2r23 57v2n 63v3
sospechoso   33r38
sostener   65v14
sotavento   62v31
sotaviento   23v49 28r43
sotaviēto   37r27
sotil   52v20
sotiles   13r23
soy   16r15
sō   21r19n 58v14
sōdar   32r38c
sta   27v12n
sto   28r41c
stos   19v21c
stoy   16r14c
stō   41r40
232   su
suaue   15r30
suauemēte   36v34
suauissimos   6r21
suaves   4r39 58v3
subdueste   10r16 27v38c
subierō   31v20 37r36 64v14
subierōse   5v41
6   subio   5v34 20v16 30r17 31r46 32r21
   40r16
subir   52r45 53v4
subito   31v1
subjecto   30r10
subjectos   49r44
sucediese   1v18
sudeste   6r4
sudsueste   17v18c
33   sudueste   2r13 14 16 6r2 17 7r36 7v18
   40 43 10r18 20 13v25 15v14 21 17v19

16r27 23v15 27r14 36v17 50v25 66v4
tambiē   12v42 21r39 62r21
tamo   57v2ⁿ
90   tan tā
74   tan   7r39 8r42 11r9 13r39 13v2 8 12
        14r8 15r20 23 24 29 42 15v19 24
        16r10 16v37 18r8 18v44 20v21 22r18
        26 22v26 24r40 43 26r16 27r43 43
        27v31 30r22 31v13 33v32 35v9 36v16
        38r18 39r16 39v42 40r6 42r9 9 13
        42v2 3 43r27 32 44r10 12 45v30 46r43
        46v1 47r1 18 47v1 48r38 50 49v26 27
        35 50v7 52r32 53r35 50 53v16 54r2 33
        55r28 55v12 57r12 21 60r2 62r26
        64r24 40 45
    tanbien   16v13 45r15 46v23
    tanbiē   23r12 50v35
    tanpoco   32v7 37r26 38r34
19   tanta tāta
17   tanta   5r16 14r6 15r14 20v22 33v35
        36v24 38r41 42v24 45v13 16 48v28
        50r19 52r26 61v50 63r5 65r29 66r26
15   tantas tātas
14   tantas   6v8 7r8 11r13 16 16 16r9 24r35
        39 24v6 33v32 48r17 60v8 65v32
        67r36
    tanteado   59r1
52   tanto tāto
50   tanto   1v31 2v33 3v25 4v16 5v29 9r16
        12r30 45 13r22 14r7 39 15r36 15v3
        17v11 24v9 26r12 29r36 31r7 7ᶜ 33v4
        26 34r19 23 36r27 39v21 40r28 41v4
        42r25 43r34 44v7 45v29 46v39 47r8
        32 35 38 47v15 48v46 49r35 49v35
        50v34 51r17 52v48 53v19 54v1 57v7
        59r9 66r11 35 67r34
10   tantos   1r31 14r14 41v48 48r25 25
        49r35 56r20 58v27 59r11 61v2
    taob   55v17
    tardar   28v4
13   tarde   4v22 7v15 10r16 27v39 38r29
        38v39 40r13 44r29 45r29 49r18 53v30
        63r34 64v43
    tardo   47v31
    taso   25r17
    taxo   25r18
16   tā   7v38 15r20 18v15 26r40 26v8 36r11
        36v38 43 37r49 38r2 23 38v29 40v4
        42v39 61v43 65v25
    tābie   55v21
49   tābien   1v37 2v39 6v18 7v10 26ᶜ 8r26
        9r28 10v10 11v40 20r8 21r6 22v43
        23r20 23v2 25r18 26r22 29v10 30v14
        36v44 37r41 47 38r17 39r26 41r43
        43r11 44r17 44v34 45r25 47v17 48r11
        49r31 49v39 50r13 20 35 51r1 52r3 23
        52v45 53r4 55r24 56v15 57r35 58v24
        60v39 61r31 65v2 43 47
    tābieñ   31v37
9   tābiē   8v2 20r11 21r3 22v14 23r8 24r12

30v13 37v30 56v43
tābiēn   17r20 26v12
tāta   40r27 40
tātas   12v33
tāto   37r43 53r47
tedio   10r5
tejo   27r38
temblando   31v40
temblava   31v31
teme   41v5
temer   62r9b 19
temerosa   21r15
temerosos   22v27 42v3
temia   10v27
temian   4r26
temiendo   28r33
temiera   61r5
temierā   29r4 60r3
temiese   50r40
temio   63v45ᶜ 64r16
14   temor   11r27 15v40 18r19 21r32 28r24
        34 36r34 37r44 41r21 41v43 48r40
        55v25 61v38 64v24
    temperada   14v14 23r29
    temperadas   17r25
    temperadissimo   64v4
    temperatissimos   4r6
    temperāçia   29v29
    tempestad   61r11 65v5
    templados   27v3
    templança   64r47
    templo   48r13
    temporejado   11r27
    temporejar   15v30 28v6
    temporejo   46v25
    temporizādo   8v24
    temporize   12v29
    temprano   15v32
    tenefe   41r38ᶜ
    tenellos   11r4
17   tener   1v2 20v20 26v1 16 27r39 31r19
        32v16 36r43 37v7 42v14 43r30 44v36
        53v14 34 61r2 2ⁿ 65v19
    tenerife   2v17 22 3r16 41r38 43r22
    tenga   43r28 56v34
    tengā   20r9 56r33
17   tengo   12r38 13r7 14v11 16v17 21r16
        22r20 29v41 30r7 37v28 30 39v36
        40r2 42r20 44v43 45v19 48r29 32
94   tenia teñia
93   tenia   3r13 5r2 5v22 6v26 7r9 7v10
        10r12 13 11r15 11v37 46 12v7 13r42
        17r6 18r5 19r36 41 20v2 32 35 21v39
        22r12 23v40 24v43 25r21 26r12 26v15
        28r43 28v2 29r34 37 31r29 30 45
        31v34 32r33 36 32v5 10 33v37 36r35
        36v21 37r32 37v34 39r20 39v10 38
        40r12 40v9 27 43v18 23ᶜ 24 44r4
        44v16 45r1 20ᶜ 46r21ᶜ 46v33 47r26
        48r7 14 49r8 50 50v21 52v19 53r20 37

53v19 23 54r35 55r45 55v22[n] 56r6
56v49 57v48 58v19 61v42 62r9[a] 22
63r13 31 42 63v38 64r18a[c] 20 28
64v25 31 66r11 18 66v18 67r27

teniamos 11v23

52 tenian 3r2 9r25 9v7 16 12v36 42 13r36
14r18 16r32 17v38 18v26 21v14 29
25v39 28r35 28v31 31v8 32r4 33v35
38 34v46 35v32 36r21 41 42 48 36v22
37v17 42r8 33 42v5 9 31 33 39 43v15
15 44v11[n] 45r28[c] 47v23 48v34 49r10
50r20 29 54r4 56r10 57r15 57v8 21
61v35 64v28 66r29

teniã 16v39 19r10 44r39 53v20

tenida 41r39

tenido 8r19 32v20

teniendo 10r27 61v31

teniendose 61v27

tenientes 50r45 50v15

teniẽdo 23r45

teñia 44v17

teñir 55r47

tercia 13r2 65v30

terçera 60r49

terçero 25v45 26r37

terçeros 66v19

5 terçia tercia
terçia 26v26 37v4 39r38

termino 20r34 66v10

terna 11r6 28r13 30r8 35r48 35v1[c]

ternã 23v1 48r41

6 terral 31r14 37r2 45r38 51v31 54v4
55r30

terrenal 64v3

terrible 61r17 39 61v27 65v10 25

testigos 64r5

testimonio 8v43

testimonios 9r3

texo 57r35

tẽblando 36r32

tẽga 29v12

tẽgo 1v40 9v24 17r34

tẽpladas 35v9

tẽplado 19r5

tẽplados 59v18 24

tẽplança 29r23 41r4

tẽplar 57v16

tẽplo 32r19

tẽprado 7r27

tẽprano 34v6

tẽto 26v40

theologos 64v2

theramo 57v42 44[n]

thomas 40v34 41r10 40 43v9

thome 45v37 46r16 49v22

tiburõ 59r36

51 tiempo tpo tp̃o tp̃õ
tiendas 18v31

46 tiene 10r29 13v42 19r20 21 24 33[n]
21r45 22r11 22v24 25v38 26r10 34

27r3 23 28r24 33r32 35 33v5 18 34v48
35r5 36v24 39r15 40v35 44 41r20
42r18 42v44 43v2 4 43 44v26 51v2 3
52r37 53v20[c] 54r21 21 23 44 54v16 47
55r19 56v35 57r44 57v48[c]

6 tienen 9v3 10r9 28 39v3 47v23[c] 53v34

36 tienẽ 7v21d 9v1 14r26[n] 17r17 18v37
19r12 13 21r18 19 19 22r35 23r1 12
24v13 28v6[c] 29v23 32r11 32v13 35r9
35v18 36r39 36v19 38r9 27 38v4
43r34 43v34 47r13 17 19 47v16 39
50r32 53v34 41 57v8[c]

tiente 2r6

tiento 41v22

352 tierra trra tr̄r̄a

21 tierra 2v31 3v33[c] 4v25 8r25 33[n] 37
8v11 10v4 26 12v2 15r30 18r17 18
24v34 25r1 30r4 30v35 43v16 47v3
56r4 62r24

43 tierras trras tr̄r̄as
tierras 24r37 48v5b

tiesta 25r21

tinturas 15r26

tiñen 45v27

tirãdo 37r35

tire 22r36

tiro 34r19 46r10 53v4

tiros 27r32 37r36 48r6

tizon 21v43

tocar 15v43

tocarõ 18v41

tocase 18r25 18v27

tocava 12r10 25v48

tocavã 21v11

142 toda 1v41 6v15 7v27 8r3 8v41 10r24
10v28 30 12r18 12v29 34 13r12 15
13v27 14r15 40 14v1 15r2 3 15v30
16r4 16v3 16 22 17r43 18r4 40 19r1 2
14 33[n] 51 19v2 10 18 48 20r8 22v16
23v3 23 24r2 5 24v5 25v21 26r46 26v1
26 28r6 15 23 29v20 33 36 30r8 33
30v35 31r16 47 31v10 24 32r28 46
32v47 33r21 27 33v3 20 25 34r16 26
42 48 34v21 43 36r48 36v7 37r16 45
38r5 6 7 26 38v42 39r45 39v47 40r40
41r32 42r19 42v11 32 43r20 31 44v38
45r3 46r31 46v36 47r7 9 48r33 41
48v31 49v5 37 38 51r41 42 44 51v13
52r6 39 52v44 53r21 46 53v42 54r31
54v36 55r24 25 55v18 56v44 57r2 37
58v14 59r23 59v14 28 60r23 60v6 17
44 61r32 61v20 62v21 32 45 63v5 35
64r10 31 64v32 65v27 66v15

96 todas 1r36 1v15 4v3 7v29 45 8v22 9v20
11r22 23 11v9 12r23 23 29 13r34
13v11 46 14r10 25 15r21 38 17r46
17v6 12 24 18r37 18v34 20r9 21r48
22r39 23v4 5 14 24r36 24v16 31
25v23 26v45 27r10 27v7 15 28r8 29v8
30r17 31r14 15 31v16 17 32r15 32v12

27 35r45 36r38 36v11 25 27 29 37v14 38r8 27 44 47 38v36 40r23 40v16 41r41 41v10 12 18 25 29 42r39 43r24 44r32 42 44v26 30 45v36 46r5 47r1 47v43 48v22 23 50v21 51r10 52v8 54v12 55r46 55v29 56r1ⁿ 57r12 57v7 9 58r5 60v28 65r45 67r28

9 todavia 20v7 26r38 31r13 31v40 35r27 44v17 46v17 53r42ⁿ 62v6

201 todo

168 todos 1v7 8 2v41 4r13 40 4v10 5v41 42 44 6r2 7v12 8r28 8v13 13 33 43 9r27 29 30 9v5 24 25 27 34 10r2 10v3 12 20 11r4 6 11v25 45 12r12 13r18 13v2 29 14r8 41 14v11 30 15v41 16r5 12 12 15 31 17r36 18v24 42 19r1 33ⁿ 20r8 21r29 32 21v9 17 46 22r16 23 29 22v37 23v4 12 13 26v46 28r3 28v38 29r7 29v22 32 38 30r40 30v30 31v36 40 44 46 32r2 3 33r42 33v33 34v29 46 35v23 32 42 36r20c 21c 27 29 32 34 36v28 37r42 37v20 26 29 30 31 45 38r19 38v3 4 43 44 39r1 39v3 4 13 16 23 40r19 41v9 24 42r29 40 42v4 36 43r36 44r27 42 44v39 45r5 45v22 27 31 31 32 46r38 47r34 47v26 48r1 6 48v5 49r45 50r16 50v20 40 52r34 53v15ⁿ 35 40 54r42 55r48 48ⁿ 56v4 57r9 59r1c 60v24 61v1 22 27 62r1 10 14 42 63r1ⁿ 18 47 63v26 64r6 64v29 65v2 66r28 34 66v16 32 67r37

tollido 62v36

toma 39v21

tomad 44v34 34

tomada 2v42 14r38

tomado 11v8 25v35 40r23c 42v35c

tomamos 16v40

45 tomar 1v31 2v9 14 3r12 3v11 7r39 9v10 10r36 37 11r1 11v2 44 13v49 16r33 16v45 21v44 22v19 25v42 26r46 28r27 32 28v20 30v8 35v41 36r10c 37r26 27 40v24 44r16 45v9 47v42 49v31 53r12 44 53v19 56r9 40 45 57r3 60r9 62v43 64v39 40 43 65r1

tomara 60v27

tomarā 64v33

tomarla 2v10

tomarlos 9v12

tomaro 8r22

tomarole 30v5

9 tomarō 4r24 4v44 6r30 7v39 11v32 14r3 19v27 35v25 53v43

tomase 11v7 47r31

tomasen 35v26 36r12 46v5 55r38

tomasse 19v33

tomassen 42r42

7 tomava 8v43 32v2 19 33r14 38v47 39v20 58v31

tomavan 9r44

tomavā 9r24

tomā 10r28 44v33

tomādo 11r15 21r8 27r17c

tome 13v13 24 14r47 32r23

tomē 22v22

25 tomo 3r9 22 8v44 11r1ⁿ 18r43 20v3 23v46 25r43 26v27 31v38 36v39 37r24 39r2 39v33 44r6 23 46v18 49v35 51v34 54r37 57v12 62r35 62v24 63r1ⁿ 64r5

tonel 48v26 51r5

tonelero 48r45 50v39

toneles 3v10

tonina 25r20 59r36

toninas 4r42 59v31

topado 40r23

topar 10v2 15v10 17r13

toparo 30v4

toparō 43v29

topase 63v36

topasen 20r36

topava 40r21

topo 7v8 52r46

tormeta 61r3

20 tormēta 31r16 41r32 61r2ⁿ 9 21ⁿ 35 61v28 62r19 30 34 63r5 36 64r30ⁿ 31 45 65r29 45ⁿ 65v10 10ⁿ 25

tormētas 65v32

torna 38r14 44v21

tornado 43r14

tornados 31v18

7 tornar 19v14 22r25 25v40 36r13 43v16 47r42 54r40

tornara 56v26

tornaria 21v41 34r2

tornarian 13v6 22r23

tornaron 56v5ⁿ

tornarose 30r41

tornarō 14r42 43r20 56r11 61v18

tornarse 37r18 64r37

tornasen 4r28 19r44

tornā 38r13

tornē 12r7

16 torno 2v17 24 17r45 19v21 21v41 25v43 27v45 28v20 34v34 35r46 38v24 40v21 41v23 62v44 64r6 66v24

tornola 35v34

tornole 55v37

tornose 2r36 18r28 49v18 64r1

torre 48r30 37

torres 1r19 20r27 40v31ⁿ 32 40

tortola 5r39

19 tortuga 32r6 33r19 34r36 37ⁿ 34v36 36ⁿ 35r29 32 37r5 10 13 24 46 38r8 38v14 40 39r10 13 40v20

tortugas 53v43

tostado 31v15

tostados 38v20

tpo 35r25 36v38

tp̄o 10v1 34v38

47 tp̄ō 4r9 4v31 5v8 9v17 10r39 11v42

turbaçion 2r29
turbado 59r15 60r17
turbiada 65r45
turbionadas 62r44
turquesco 47v36
tuviera 51r4 4 59r9
tuviero 4v20
7 tuvierō 6r35 6v25 7v35 8r18 36r6
 61v30 64v21
7 tuviese 12r5 39r27 41v27 43v22 46v47
 47r25 50r39
tuviesen 9r9 32r14 33r26
17 tuvo 3r22 4r4 4v27 8v10 19v41 28v5
 38v27 40r8 56v28 32[n] 58v47 60r17
 61r8 61v8 34 62r33[n] 65r21
tyñidos 31v44
tyrado 19v10
tyranos 46v35[n]
tyrar 39r7 40r15 47v37 48r2 50r30
tyrarōse 39r34
tyrase 39r4
tyrava 31v37
tyrā 57r31
9 tyro 7v8 17v8 18r7 31r21 34r23 35[c] 38
 44v32 46r3
tyros 12r29 39r34
tyznado 55r46

U

un 49v3
uña 32r8
use 12r3
uuevos 56r1[n]

V

10 v.al 1r19 25 33 9v18 10r37 10v42 14v13
 17r21 29v27 35v18
16 va 1r6 15r39 19r35 26v12 29v27 33r27
 37 34v5 35r3 29 40v31 41v6[c] 48r27
 51v11 52r20 54v14
vaca 18v49
vacas 18v47
vale 16r27 50r21 57r36
valen 12v40 15r26
valia 12r8 16r15 33 40r2[n] 42r11
valientes 38r20
valladolid 53r2[n]
13 valle 34r31 33 36r20 36v23 26 37r39 41
 48 48 48[n] 40v28 41r33 66v1
vallena 5r20
vallenas 13v14
7 valles 28r9 9 34r45 35r39 38r5 25 52r25
valor 9r15 44r18 62r13
5 van vā
van 28r27 51r33 53v39 54v13
vanda 4v27 25r27 62v4
vandera 8v31
vanderas 1r19 8v32 39r32 45v5
vaneque 26r43
vaneq̄ 24r10

vara 57r26
varada 30r23
varas 9v2 31v14 16 42r18
vasija 16v4 48v22
vasos 10r12
vaya 15r22 32 30r8 51r14 52r15
vayna 31v38
vaysi 32v3[n]
vazia 36r20
vazian 10r2
vazias 30r40 61v35
vaziavā 47r4
vā 5r10
vāda 19r46
vādera 7v8
vāderas 40r6
ve 44r3[c]
vea 15r37 15v27 44v26
vean 60v38
vee 12r28 27v31
veedor 8v4
veen 34v45
veē 43r43
vega 29r17 26 33v29 43r27
vegas 34v14 35r7 43r26
vehemete 25r41
25 vela 3r4 8v23 11r13 11v38 13r15 13v39
 14r39 14v20 15v30 17r22 47 17v32
 32r25 40v19 51v29[c] 30 52r38 61r14
 62r48 62v6 45 63v7 64r17 65v19[c] 67r7
19 velas 8v22 11r30 39 17r46 17v12 19v2[c]
 23v33 26v1 28v40 29r12 32v27 34r7
 37v2 43v13 53v26 57v16 64v48 65r45
 65v4
velase 61v16
velasen 47r7
velera 4v13 7v4 8r36 32v36
vella 31r48
vellas 31r37
velle 24v6h
vello 30v8 63r28
venderia 23r14
vendidos 56r6
vendiesen 50r16
veneque 23v40
vengā 43r40
22 venia 3r11 5r6 17 6v37 9v41 11v28 29
 12v9 26v2 35r15 37r32 39r40 47v3
 50v33 56v7 57r41 61v29 62v14 63r28
 65v28 44 66r25
veniamos 32r11
34 venian 4r23 7v21 9r18 9v9 39 10r19
 10v16 12v43 18v5 21v10 12 35v43 43
 36r30 36v4 37v22 37 38r34 39r41
 41v42 43 48 42r32 43r8 12 44v12 46
 48 53v44 57v34 61v3 63v3 64r33
 65v11
veniā 10v12
venid 10v20
venida 16v39 31v29 45r32 60v40

29   vide   1r18 21 9r28 30 9v6 19 10r8 14
        10v11 37 11r13 38 11v33 41 13r13 27
        34 13v14 17 37 14r19 27 27 15r19
        15v20 16r18 32r14 16 39v37

98   vido   4v4 8r38 41 8v5 7 13v16 16r20
        18r9 32ᶜ 18v4 15 17 19 48 19r29 19v3
        7 11 38 39ᶜ 40 23v42 24r28 35 24v23b
        25r28 41 25v19 34 27r18ᶜ 27v1 5 40
        41 28r16 20 28v22 37 29r15 31r35 38
        31v30 32r27 35 48 32v1 2 8ᶜ 9 43 33r1
        34r44 37r38 41 37v30 40v25 26 41r43
        41v1 28 42v35 45r41 46v13 48r5ᶜ
        50r13 33 50v5 51r30ᶜ 51v16 31 48
        52r10 28 47 54r1 1ⁿ 5 54v32 41 45 45
        55r1 3 18 18 58r10 40 58v2 28 59v18
        30 60v2 45 62v26 63r36 63v8 64r43
        65v49

     vidola   8v2
     vidolo   34r31
     vidolos   27r43
     vidose   2r28 65r45

19   vidro   9r14 23 10r32 11v34 12v8 38
        14r21 16r37 16v2 31 36 31v7 35v33
        37v9 38v26 42v41 44r13a 20 55v36

     vieja   7r2 41v26 42r28

7   viejo   10v18 29v35 30v5 37v34 40r36
        40v1 4

     viejos   21r1 25r45

8   viendo   25v28 39ᶜ 29r1 46v15 48r3
        61r28 63r41 63v3

     viendola   65v16
     viendolo   52r8
     viendolos   56r12

7   viene   20r20 32r39 34v14 37r41 49
        43r31 45v44

     vienē   9v11 13r18 46r7 47v42
     vienta   17r10 31r14 64v50

120   viento vieto viēto

110   viento   2r2 4v24 5r14 29 42ᶜ 5v3ᶜ 5 7r24
        7v44 11v14 12r10 13r15 13v25 37
        14r45 14v17 36 15r16 15v24 17r9 22
        44 17v13 19r7 19v9 11ⁿ 22r42 22v9
        23v43 24r12 18 25 25v45 45 47 26r3 6
        37 26v7 9 27v38 40 46 28r42 28v14 19
        30r34 30v25 42 31r13 32r25 32v8 25
        26 34r9 21 34v7 28 34 35r15 27 35v15
        37r4 17 37v7 38v12 39r26 40v21 44v4
        45r38 46r15 25 48v1 50v11 51r24
        51v6 53r17 54v34 38 57v3 4 17 58r3
        13 17 38 44 45 58v10 59v24 34 59v46
        61r9 11ⁿ 16 21 28 29 39 62r44 62v13
        29 64r11 24 27 64v49 65r20 65v5 67r6
        16

16   vientos   4v40 5r31 27r1 34v30 35 41r25
        43r36 48v13 52r34 35ⁿ 53v36 55r37
        58v47 65r25 33 65v12

     vierā   29r45 46r42ᶜ 43
     viere   27v33

33   viernes   1v27 2r8 9 3r17 18 3v26 5r12
        6r27 7r21 8v25 28ⁿ 14v21 15r1 17v26

        20r23 24v30 26v5 30v24 34r6 37r1
        41r45 49r1 51r22 54v2 58r12 59r28
        59v39 60v3 62v2 64v7 65r36 66r40
        67r14

     viero   4r41 21v46 48 52r47ⁿ

68   vieron vierō viērōn

     vieron   8v36 26v24 27v13

64   vierō   2v21 3v8 29ᶜ 37 4r21 33 4v22 24ᶜ
        43 5r18 20 27 39 5v14 6r25 36 41 6v2ᶜ
        3 39 7r3 8r20 21 26 8v27 14r34 17v23
        43 18r47 22r3 26v17 27r19ᶜ 20 28r31
        30v31 32 34 36 31v2 34v23 35r22
        35v12 46 36r49 36v16 18 36 38v27
        46r33 49v10 56v1 22 58v44 59v37
        60r2 4 27 32 51 62v10 30 32 64v24d
        65v6

     vierōse   6v10 33r24

6   viese   1v36 7v7 8v20 38r43 60v41 66v39

6   viesen   7v15 25r24 30v28 41v31 42v8
        43r15

     viessen   50v28
     vieto   57v47
     viērōn   6r12

9   viēto   17r42 23v45 25v27 53v26 58r38
        58v17 31 43 67r12

     vigilia   40v35
     vil   22r12

18   villa   1v22 23r27 29v42 30r28 46v33 36
        49r9 50v31 51r24ⁿ 28 51v21 52v29
        53v12 21 56r33 56v45 61v14 65v26

     villafranco   66v36
     villas   38v9
     vimos   13v47 14v29
     vine   1v22 12v30 13r12 56v35
     vinie   56r10ᶜ
     viniendo   28v34 37v3 56r31
     viniera   45r2
     vinierā   21v31 66v33ᶜ
     vinierē   12v19
     viniero   44r40 44v44ᶜ 56v11 63r22
     vinieron   19v36 50v43

39   vinierō   2v20 4v24 41 5r3 6r25 6v7 7r16
        9v23 36 10v21 22 13v50 16r40 16v24
        19v30 20v23 21v2 31v23 32r3 36r28
        37v18 39v18 41v33 42v15 43v30
        44r31 44v14 35 48r17 48v43 49v13
        56v4 57r8 10 59v25 63r24 63v10
        64v24a 66v33

     viniese   27r5 63v14
     viniesen   31v21 36r47 50r38

56   vino   2v36 4v21 5r6 32ᶜ 5v14 7r19
        10v18 13v34 15r29 20v30 21r33 21v32
        23r30 23v8 28v15 30v13ⁿ 37r4 37v19
        38r29 38v40 39r43ⁿ 39v7 40r31 42v23
        44r4 45r18 47r23 35 48r42 48v37
        49r20 49 49v16 50r7 31 50v26 52v4
        25 54r30 55r43 57r5ᶜ 58r9 59r38
        61v29e 36 64v10 12 65r15 65v30 49
        66r20ᶜ 22 25 25ⁿ 33 66v35

     vinole   65r44

INDEX

Abra: 149; discussed 149n.
Adelantado: 129
Administrators, of the king of Portugal: 393, 397
Admiral of the Ocean Sea: 19, 377
Africa: 361
Agriculture, signs of Indian: 89, 189, 193, 203, 209; *see also* names of specific crops
Aguda, Punta: 227
Ajes: 132, 133, 233, 255, 284, 285; discussed 233n; *see also niames*; yams
Alambre: 331
Algruta, Juan Quintero de: 133n.
Alhambra: 17
Alhandra: 399
Aloe: 107, 111, 135, 145, 155, 217, 225, 315
Altitude (of a star): 357
Alto y Bajo, Cabo: 249
Alvar, Manual: 3, 10, 11, 35n., 55n., 75n., 105n.
Anchor: 263, 273, 279, 289, 375, 383
Anchorages, character of: 83, 85, 91, 99, 103, 113, 123, 147, 155, 157, 179, 191, 249, 321
Anchoring, care needed in: 85, 103, 113, 155
Ancona, March of: 365
Andalusia: 33, 93, 105, 111, 117; ports of, 397
Angel, Cabo del: 325
Angla: 100, 209n., 325n.; discussion of, 101n.
Animals: *see* beasts; birds; cows; dogs; frogs; gnats; goats; grasshoppers; horses; *hutía*; livestock; lizards; mastiffs; mules; oxen; rats; serpents; sheep; snails; snakes; *taso*; terriers; turtles
Arabic: 129
Arawak Indians: 197n.
Arbitrators: 397
Arbutus: 171, 171n., 207, 209
Arce, Joaquín: 11
Archipelago: 145
Arena, Diego de: 233n.
Arena, Islas de: 115
Armed boat: 393
Armed launch: 63, 79, 385
Armed men: 191, 215, 221, 335, 379; guard flagship cargo, 281; skirmish of, 301

Arms: 93, 333, 393; *see also* weapons
Arroba: 73, 139; discussed, 73n.
Arrowhead, fish tooth: 341
Arrows: 287, 329, 333, 339; cannibals', 237; Indians', 339
Artillery: 303, 393
Astrolabe: 357
Astrology: 329, 329n.
Astronomy: *see* Guard stars; Jupiter; Little Dipper; Mercury; moon; North Star; planet; stars; sun
Aune: 117n.
Ayamonte: 129
Azores, islands of: 8, 27, 357, 361, 373, 375, 381; *see also* Fayal; Flores; San Gregorio; San Miguel; Santa María, island of (Azores); Terceira

Bailiff of the fleet: 233, 239, 279, 303; discussed, 233n.
Ballast: sailing without, 367; seawater as, 367, 381; stone for, 387
Baneque, island of: 143, 149, 161, 169, 199, 217, 227, 233, 313; distance from Río de Mares, 151; gold mines believed to be there, 151, 161, 239; distance from Hispaniola, 239
Banner, royal: 63, 245
Barcelona: 401
Barley: 209
Barnacles: 57, 57n.
Barocoa, Puerto de: 122, 134
Barrels: 31n., 291, 317, 371; water, 87, 93
Barrel hoops: 317
Barrel maker: 289, 303
Basa: 155
Basán (province in Cuba): 129
Basket: 85
Batatas: 132
Beach: 205
Beads: 197, 243, 297, 337; glass, 65, 81, 107, 109, 193, 219, 231, 237, 259, 265, 331; strings of, 85, 107, 129; amber, 243
Beans: varieties of, 133, 139; discussed, 133n.
Beasts, four-footed, not seen, except barkless dogs: 139
Beatriz (Columbus's mistress): 233n.

Becerro, Cabo del: 309
Beds: 93, 243, 377
Beehives: 195
Bells: 65, 81, 107, 193, 197, 219, 231, 259; sparrowhawk, 109; *see also chug chuque*
Belprado, Cabo del: 323
Belt: 243, 263
Birds: 39, 47; migrating, 35, 53, 55; singing of, 105, 117; hunting, 131; *see also* boobies; crows; doves; ducks; eagles; fishers; fowl; frigate birds; gannets; geese; gulls; nightingales; parrots; partridges; petrels; terns; tropic birds
Biscuit: 303, 337
Blanca, Castilian: 71, 71n., 85; value of, 63n.
Boat: 257, 393; *see also* ship's boat
Boatswain: 133n.
Body paint: 67, 195
Bohío: 109, 133, 149, 177, 201, 217n.; Indian name for "house," 132; Indians' description of, 217; misunderstood as Indian name for Hispaniola, 275; *see also* Bohío, inhabitants of; Hispaniola
Bohío, inhabitants of: 167, 177, 199, 201
Bonnet: 63, 81, 373
Boobies: 37, 37n., 39, 41, 45, 47, 51, 55, 345, 347
Bows: 329, 333, 339; Indian, 339; Turkish, 285
Bracelets, gold: 79, 145
Brazas: 117, 123, 155, 169, 183, 191, 199, 205, 205n., 209, 211, 229, 251, 261, 275, 305, 307, 309, 311, 321, 325, 327; discussed, 117n.
Bread: 85, 197, 223, 267, 339, 353, 377; Indian, 85; of *niamas*, 223; how made, 233; of yams, 255; called cassava, 285
Bruma: *see* shipworm
Buen Tiempo, Cabo del: 325
Buildings: church, 309; royal works, 309; *see also* Alhambra; church; forts; houses; mosque; sawmills; shed; temple; towers
Bulrush, green: 57

Cable, ship's: 169, 229, 253, 275,